CONSOLIDATED FINANCIAL REPORTING

aí atá

.w.

by
P A Taylor

P·C·P
Paul Chapman
Publishing Ltd

Dedication
To the students I teach. May we always understand that
teaching and learning take place in both directions.

Copyright © 1996, Paul Taylor

Paul Chapman Publishing Ltd
144 Liverpool Road
London
N1 1LA

British Library Cataloguing in Pubication Data
Taylor, P. A. (Paul A.)
  Consolidated financial reporting. – Rev. ed.
  1. Business records   2. Financial statements, Consolidated
  I. Title   II. Consolidated financial statements
  658.1'5'12

  ISBN 1 85396 250 3

Published in the USA and Canada by
Markus Wiener Publishers,
114 Jefferson Rd, Princeton, NJ 08540

ISBN 1–55876–139–X

Typeset by Anneset, Weston-super-Mare, Avon
Printed and bound in Great Britain

A B C D E F G H   9 8 7 6

CONTENTS

Part C: Other Issues in Group Accounting

SERIES EDITOR'S PREFACE

Accounting for groups of companies is probably the single most important area of modern financial reporting. At one time most groups comprised simply a parent company and several subsidiaries. Today the structure of groups can be much more complex, including partnerships as subsidiaries, shares in subsidiaries held by associates, and joint ventures. The complexity of group structures has been matched by sophisticated methods of financing and novel forms of consideration to secure the acquisitions. Not surprisingly, traditional accounting methods have been found wanting in dealing with these new structures and financial arrangements. There has been no shortage, however, in the supply of innovative accounting treatments for these developments. Rather, the opposite has been true with companies and their auditors devising new accounting treatments at a much faster rate than the standard setting bodies can deal with effectively.

There have been so many changes in the theory and practice of accounting for groups since *Consolidated Financial Statements* was published in 1987 that Paul Taylor has completely rewritten his book and given it a brand new title, *Consolidated Financial Reporting*. It has retained a number of the features which made the original book so popular with students and teachers. These include a balanced coverage of concepts, theories and techniques, a careful exposition of why particular methods for consolidation need to be used and how they should be applied, and a host of worked examples and exercises for students to complete for themselves.

There are also several major changes from the previous book which reflect the new developments in professional accounting requirements for groups. For example, there are new chapters on fair values and goodwill and group cash flow statements. The book also deals with the continuing controversies of group accounting such as merger accounting, foreign currency translation and segmental reporting. These are explored by reference to both alternative accounting theories and the recommendations of national and international accounting standard-setters.

A very useful feature of *Consolidated Financial Reporting* is the flexibility with which the book can be used. For university students taking an intermediate course in financial accounting emphasis can be given to the fundamental concepts and techniques of consolidation. For final year students with a good grounding in accounting theory the chapters and sections which discuss the main controversies of group accounts may be selected. Students taking professional examinations are also catered for by the book's extensive illustrations of consolidation techniques and the detailed coverage and evaluation of national and international accounting standards and exposure drafts.

Consolidated Financial Reporting is the most comprehensive, up-to-date and accessible book on group accounts to be found in the bookshops. It will surely be as successful as its predecessor in the series.

Michael Sherer
Colchester, Essex, 1995

PREFACE

My intention in starting this book was to write a second edition of an earlier book I wrote, *Consolidated Financial Statements: Concepts, Issues and Techniques* (Paul Chapman Publishing, 1987). It soon became apparent that the area had changed so radically in the last eight years that a complete rewrite was necessary, and hence this new book has been born (or rather quarried!). It has the same objectives as the previous one, 'to facilitate an understanding of the technical processes underlying consolidation and group financial reporting within the context of contemporary accounting theory and practice'.

Consolidated financial reporting is often viewed as a mere technical exercise. It is relegated to relative obscurity in many advanced accounting courses as a necessary evil, a series of hard techniques to be mastered. This is reflected in the treatment given in many texts. However, recent developments mean that it has also become one of the central, if not the most central, new conceptual areas in financial accounting, and certainly the most intellectually challenging area at the centre of the current accounting debate. Most new financial reporting standards focus largely or exclusively on group accounting matters. Most topical controversies also relate to group accounting matters.

How is this book different from other books on consolidated financial statements? Whilst aiming for technical excellence, it grounds consolidation procedures within a clearly structured technical and conceptual framework which stresses the development of intuitive understanding. Within this framework controversial areas and debates about group accounting are addressed and the evidence examined. Thus it becomes possible to see why alternatives exist and to obtain a sense of perspective on current practice and likely future developments. The area has become so apparently complex, that without a clear, grounded intuitive understanding, it is not possible to negotiate one's way through it with any confidence. The book also provides ample coverage of areas which are normally only cursorily covered in most professional texts on consolidation, such as consolidated cash flow statements, statements of total recognized gains and losses, foreign currency translation and segmental reporting.

The book is designed so that the reader can select sections related to his or her interests without having to plough through irrelevant material. Many of the sections are self-contained and those which can be omitted, if desired, without loss in continuity, are marked clearly. Thus, for example, the reader more interested in straight technical mastery can use the book in a streamlined way, and the reader more interested in discussions and debates can also choose a clearly defined alternative route through it. The author's experience is that most students find the area stimulating when technique is 'spiced' with concepts and issues. The blend of calculation and discussion has a synergistic effect – calculations illustrate conceptual controversies, and conceptual controversies illuminate the use of technique.

Each of the major financial statements is examined in turn, including the consolidated cash flow statement, and their interrelationships examined. A major strength of the book is in providing clear layouts for applying techniques, so that *why* they work and what exactly the figures *mean*, is given as much prominence as *how* to use the techniques. Great care has been taken in ensuring only step-by-step increases in difficulty in each chapter, so that the student is not suddenly lost in a yawning chasm of unexplained complexity. Care has also been taken not to obscure principles with unnecessarily complex calculations. There are a significant number of worked examples and of both technical and discussion-style exercises.

The book also covers controversial areas and debates in such areas as acquisition and merger accounting, fair values at acquisition, goodwill, foreign currency translation, and segmental reporting. These are examined from the point of view of modern accounting theory and empirical evidence, in addition to considering the professional debates. The materials are also set into an international context and international accounting standards examined. Certain advanced topics are also addressed including the translation of foreign currency cash flow statements, subsidiary share issues, and cross-holdings of shares.

The book is aimed at second and third year undergraduates at universities, professional examination candidates, and postgraduates. Materials within it have been class-tested in both undergraduate and Masters' level courses at Lancaster University, and similar material in the previous book has been widely used nationally and internationally. It is the author's experience that the material presented here has sufficient variety and depth to form a substantial core of advanced financial accounting and accounting theory courses. Students like it because it contains technique, but it is the author's view that only if theory, practice and technique are properly integrated is the richness of accounting as an academic and professional subject realized.

The first seven chapters are what many would regard as core chapters, and it is necessary to cover these approximately in order (though not to cover all the sections in each chapter). The remaining chapters can be covered in any order, except to note that material on the foreign currency translation and the cash flow statement in Chapter 11 requires prior reading of Chapter 9. There is a solutions manual available to adopters of the text which contains solutions to all the problems laid out consistently with the examples in the text. There are also laser-printed slide-masters for adopters which can be photocopied to make accompanying lecture slides. Possible usage of the text in different types of courses is suggested as follows:

Course emphasis	Coverage
Mainstream introduction	Core sections of 1–7 and a selection of the remaining chapters
Technical focus	1, technical sections of 3–12
Issue driven focus	Discussion areas of 1, 2, 3, 4, 5, 6, 11, 12
Accounting standards focus	Technical areas and institutional discussions in 1–5, 8, 9, 11, 12

Changes from the previous book: All the chapters and most areas within chapters have been newly written or rewritten to reflect the sea-change in professional accounting requirements and academic perspectives since 1987. There are new chapters on fair values and goodwill and cash flow statements. The translation of foreign currency cash flow statements is dealt with in Chapter 11, and the relationship between group accounting developments and professional bodies' conceptual frameworks is examined in the last chapter.

Chapters and sections within chapters which cover similar topics to the previous book have been extensively reorganized so that topics are more clearly delineated. For example, in the chapters on consolidation adjustments, the discussion of consolidation concepts has been moved to a separate section; the treatment of associates has been rationalized and extended. Many more worked examples and exercises have been included, and the presentation of techniques improved as a result of experience. More detailed institutional material has been segregated so it can be read or omitted without loss in continuity. Areas which users of the previous book have indicated were not widely used have been cut or curtailed to make room for more relevant material.

ACKNOWLEDGEMENTS

I would like to express my gratitude to the following people who through their comments, suggestions and encouragement assisted in the preparation of this book or in improving my understanding of the area of group accounting and consolidation: Cliff Taylor; my colleagues at Lancaster University, Pelham Gore, T.S. Ho, Roger Mace, Michael Mumford, Ken Peasnell and John O'Hanlon; also Professor Dieter Ordelheide, Barry Shippen, Elizabeth Stephenson, Marianne Lagrange of Paul Chapman Publishing, and past and present undergraduates on the ACF 301 courses and postgraduates on ACF 601 and 603 who endured the many errors and many drafts, and who provided the stimulus for the book. I am grateful to The BOC Group and Thorn EMI for permission to reproduce extracts from their accounts. I would also like to thank Moreen Cunliffe, Linda Airey, Jackie Downham, Penny Greer and Freda Widders for their administrative help which freed me to concentrate on writing the book, and various staff of standard-setting bodies, of technical departments of accounting firms, and of professional bodies who did their best to answer numerous difficult, obscure, or sometimes plain silly, technical or interpretive queries.

Obviously, any errors remaining are my own responsibility. I'm very grateful to my wife Trish for helping me keep some sense of perspective, by kind words, by patience, and sometimes by firm words spoken in kindness.

Part A:
Fundamentals of Group Accounting

1

INTRODUCTION

As a student, I was presented with a variety of bewildering group accounting techniques. I could tackle complex problems quite quickly, and was 'fairly' fine until someone asked me what I had done, what the figures meant, or changed the question slightly so that the procedures I'd learnt by rote did not quite apply – then I was lost. This book is my attempt to clarify the matter. I have tried to explain the concepts underlying consolidation and group accounting, why and how the techniques work, and how the make-up of the consolidated figures can be interpreted. I also discovered along the way that group accounting is a fascinating and highly controversial area and hope I can communicate some of this to you.

CONSOLIDATED FINANCIAL REPORTING

Consolidated financial reporting is currently the most important conceptual and technical area in financial accounting after a first accounting course. It is currently the subject area in four of the first seven financial reporting standards issued by the Accounting Standards Board (ASB), figures largely in the other three, and is the subject of all the outstanding discussion papers by the same body at the time this book was completed. In the first nine months of 1994 alone, the ASB issued no less than two standards, one exposure draft and three discussion papers relating to the area.

It is a broad area covering such apparent issues as fair values at acquisition, goodwill and merger accounting (the most controversial areas in financial reporting today), and in addition the most substantial elements of less apparent ones such as foreign currency translation, segmental reporting, related party transactions, the reporting of financial performance and cash flow statements. In many of these areas, the most problematic issues are group accounting issues. A substantial part of EC legislation, the 7th Directive on Company Law, enacted into the UK Companies Act 1989, dealt entirely with group accounting. Many, if not most, international conflicts over accounting approaches too relate to the area.

Today it is not possible to understand group accounting without a good working knowledge of the underlying conceptual perspectives, and any understanding is impoverished by a lack of an understanding of current controversies. It is equally true that any discussion of concepts or controversies must remain at a very superficial level without a reasonable mastery of consolidation technique. This book aims to marry the three aspects, and particularly aims to provide an intuitive and rigorous introduction to consolidation technique. Recognizing that each reader has different objectives, it aims to provide clear and selective routes through the material – for example for readers wishing to concentrate on technical aspects and current pronouncements, or for readers with a more discursive bent. Hopefully for both, however, something of the richness and interrelatedness of the area will become apparent as they read on.

DEVELOPMENT OF GROUP ACCOUNTING

The twentieth century has been characterized by accelerating technological advance, societal change and increasing complexity in business organization. A single multinational corporation today might be involved in mining, manufacturing and marketing a wide range of products incorporating vastly different technologies in a number of different countries. A marked trend towards conducting business through groups of companies controlled by a single parent has occurred, the parent company usually exercising control over its subsidiaries via its voting power. At first most subsidiaries were wholly owned, but by the 1920s and 1930s, majority holdings became more common.

In the UK until the late 1940s, parent company shareholders usually only received individual company accounts which were not very informative. Bircher shows that as late as 1944/5, only 32.5 per cent of his sample of large UK companies produced a consolidated balance sheet, and only 17.5 per cent produced a consolidated profit and loss account in addition (Bircher, 1988, p. 3). In parent company accounts, investments were stated at cost, and if a profit and loss account were provided at all, only dividends due from subsidiaries were shown. No information was given about the total assets and liabilities controlled by the group as a whole, nor details of the profitability of subsidiaries – as if the parent company was walled in, as shown in Figure 1.1.

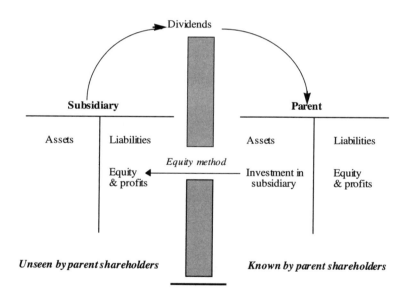

Figure 1.1 – Individual company versus group accounting

The amount of disclosure depended on the corporate form adopted. Using a divisional or departmental structure within a single legal entity would require disclosure of all the assets, liabilities and profits of the complete entity. Similar companies might carry on the same business via subsidiaries, legally separate companies controlled by the parent company. Because at that time accounts were *legal-entity*-based, these companies would disclose only the assets and liabilities of the *parent*, and only the dividends due from its investments (in subsidiaries). It was not surprising then that disclosure-shy managements usually opted for the parent–subsidiary corporate format.

The first holding company was formed in the USA in 1832, though it took until the

1890s for the first consolidated accounts to be published. US Steel set the standard in its 1900 accounts, producing consolidated accounts by aggregating the component assets and liabilities of the parent company and its subsidiaries. Effectively, the investment at cost in the parent company's own accounts was expanded into the component assets and liabilities of the subsidiaries. Further, US Steel disclosed *profits earned* by the subsidiaries rather than just dividends received – the latter being open to manipulation by management. Such consolidated accounts narrowed disclosure differences between divisional and parent-subsidiary formats. By the 1920s consolidation was generally accepted practice in the USA and there such consolidated statements were viewed as improvements on and substitutes for parent company statements.

Edwards and Webb (1984) found the earliest example of consolidated statements in the UK to be Pearson and Knowles Coal and Iron Co. Ltd in 1910, but such reporting was not widely adopted. An early and influential advocate of consolidation was Sir Gilbert Garnsey who published a book on the subject in 1923, but the publication of consolidated accounts by Dunlop Rubber in 1933 was still a newsworthy event. Edwards and Webb suggest a number of plausible explanations for this slow take-up including the inherent conservatism of the UK accounting profession, its possible lack of expertise in the area, a predisposition of UK managements towards secrecy (and the use of 'secret reserves' prior to the *Royal Mail* case) and the influence of contemporary company law which required disclosure of individual company information. Because of these company law antecedents, consolidation and group accounts have often subsequently been viewed in the UK as supplementary to parent company reports and not substitutes for them.

The state of Victoria in Australia in 1938 became the first place in the world to legally require consolidated accounts. Not until 1947 were group accounts required in the UK, *in addition to* parent company accounts. Prior to this, Edwards and Webb found evidence of experimentation in format for group accounts. Thus it was unsurprising that other formats than consolidated (aggregated) statements were acceptable under the 1947 Companies Act, e.g. separate accounts for each subsidiary, though consolidation became the norm in the UK after that date. Not until 1978 with the issue of SSAP 14, did consolidation become the format for group accounts prescribed in accounting standards. In Europe developments were even slower. Nobes and Parker (1991) comment that German companies were not obliged to consolidate until 1965, and as late as 1967 only 22 French companies published consolidated balance sheets. However, the EC 7th Directive on Consolidated Accounts was being gestated over a decade, and when it was enacted into UK company law through the Companies Act 1989 (which produced the revised Companies Act 1985!), consolidation became the only permissible form of group accounts by statute, and for the first time measurement methods for consolidated financial statements and their contents were enshrined in law.

By the 1930s majority (less than 100 per cent) interests in subsidiaries were common, and accounting for minority interests was widely discussed. Since 1947, groups have increasingly acquired substantially but not majority-owned companies, over which 'significant influence' rather than 'control' was exercisable. Accounting for such associates was only agreed in 1971 when the first UK accounting standard required the 'equity' method, midway between the cost approach, used in individual company accounts, and full consolidation. Walker (1978a) and Edwards and Webb found that such an approach had been used for subsidiaries as early as the 1920s as an alternative to consolidation, but had fallen out of favour. Particularly in the USA, a vehement debate raged in the 1960s and 1970s over the best way to account for business combinations. As stated earlier, much of the ASB's new financial reporting standards programme deals mainly with group accounting matters, including accounting for business combinations (FRS 6), fair values at acquisition under acquisition accounting (FRS 7), both highly controversial, and discussion papers, for example on goodwill, which are even more controversial.

Some argue that accounting technique has not kept pace with such environmental change, and that many of the proposals around now are merely recycled versions of debates which took place as early as the 1920s. As will be demonstrated in this book, accounting for complex corporate structures is not at all straightforward. At times aggregate information is less helpful than a detailed breakdown by segments. However, it is still true to say that consolidation has stood the test of time as the most widely used and accepted approach to accounting for complex groups.

ORGANIZATION OF COMPLEX CORPORATE STRUCTURES

Most corporations are set up as limited liability companies. Large companies deal with the problems caused by size by either organizing on a divisional basis or via subsidiaries or by some combination of the two. In the former, the divisions are subsets of a single legal entity. In the latter, a group comprises a number of separate legal entities. Non-corporate entities are usually legally constituted and accounted for as partnerships or unincorporated associations, the accounting problems of which are not examined in this book.

Divisional corporate structures

Divisionalization has legal advantages over the parent–subsidiary format. Certain legal expenses are reduced since, in a group of separate legal entities, each company is required to publish its own accounts which are to be separately audited. Only one audit is required in a divisional structure. There can be taxation advantages, and as Pahler and Mori (1994, p. 5) point out the use of a branch rather than a subsidiary can give better patent or copyright protection where legal subsidiaries might be subject to looser foreign protection laws. There are many possibilities for accounting systems in a divisionalized company. At one end of the spectrum, accounting records can be centralized at head office (often termed *departmental accounting*). Financial statements are produced for each 'department' and overheads centrally allocated, etc. At the other end of the spectrum, the division keeps its own financial records, linked to the head office records via a set of interlinking 'control' accounts (such an alternative often being termed *branch accounting*). The division produces its own financial statements which at the end of the period are combined with those of other divisions and head office by a process analogous to the consolidation of the financial statements of legally separate entities. Profits are usually transferred to head office at the end of each period.

Example 1.1 – Branch accounting

Hub Ltd has the following draft balance sheet at 1 January 1995:

Balance sheet at 1 January 1995 (£m)

Fixed assets	90	Loan	30
Stock	50	Share capital and premium	100
Cash	100	Retained profits	110
	240		240

On this date, Hub forms two divisions. Head office will administer both divisions and market bicycle hubs. The newly formed Spoke division will market bicycle spokes and rims, and will keep its own accounting records. On 2 January head office sends £50m to establish Spoke division. During the year, the following transactions take place:

Head office
(1) Stocks costing £30m were sold for £60m in cash.
(2) Depreciation of £5m was charged for the year.
(3) Administrative costs for the group were £30m.
(4) A management charge of £10m was made to Spoke division to cover its share of administration costs.

Spoke division
(5) Purchases of stocks (all for cash) totalled £30m.
(6) £20m of goods were sold for £50m in cash.
(7) Spoke sent head office a remittance covering the year's management fee.

Required

Enter the above information in 'T' accounts and prepare balance sheets for each division and for the company as a whole at 31 December 1995.

| Head office records (£m) | | Branch records (£m) | |

Cash (Head office)

Balance b/f	100	Set up cost	50
T1 Sales	60	T3 Admin	30
T7 Remittance	10		

Cash (Branch)

| Set up cost | 50 | T5 Stock purchase | 30 |
| T6 Sales | 50 | T7 Remittance | 10 |

Stock (Head office)

| Balance b/f | 50 | T1 COGS | 30 |

Stock (Branch)

| T5 Stock purch | 30 | T6 COGS | 20 |

Fixed assets

| Balance b/f | 90 | T2 Depn | 5 |

Loan

| | | Balance b/f | 30 |

Share capital & Premium

| | | Balance b/f | 100 |

Retained profits

| | | Balance b/f | 110 |

Profit and loss (Head office)

T1 COGS	30	T1 Sales	60
T2 Depn	5	T4 Mgt fee	10
T3 Admin	30	*Spoke profits*	20

Profit and loss (Branch)

T6 COGS	20	T6 Sales	50
T4 Mgt fee	10		
To H/O profits	20		

Branch account

Set up costs	50	T7 Remittance	10
T4 Mgt fee	10		
Spoke profits	20		

Head office account

T7 Remittance	10	Set up costs	50
		T4 Mgt fee	10
		To H/O profits	20

Figure 1.2 shows the bookkeeping entries for the above transactions. Balancing and closing entries have not been included.

The vital feature of *branch accounting* is the interlocking inter–divisional accounts. Consider their entries – firstly, the set up of the branch; £50m is transferred from head office. Thus the branch has a debit balance in head office's books and head office has a credit balance in the branch's books. Cash decreases at head office and increases at the branch. When a transaction involves an intra-divisional transfer it is has a *fourfold* entry, two extra components recording the intradivisional indebtedness. The management fee is treated as a contribution towards head office administration expenses. The fourfold entry affects the profit and loss accounts of both together with the interdivisional accounts. A similar fourfold entry occurs when profit is transferred to head office. Note the *payment* of the management fee (£10m) is a separate transaction from its accrual. At each stage, the interdivisional accounts should be mirror images of each other. Consider the accounts of each division and also those of the company:

Divisional and company balance sheets at 31 December 1995 (£m)

	Head office	Spoke division	Company
Fixed assets	85		85
Stock	20	10	30
Cash	90	60	150
Interlocking accounts	70	(70)	—
Loan	(30)		(30)
Share capital & premium	(100)		(100)
Retained profits	(135)		(135)

The interlocking interdivisional accounts cancel out when divisions are combined since they reflect purely *internal* indebtedness whereas the accounts of the company as a whole reflect its external relationships. *Cancellation of internal balances is central to all consolidation procedures*. Note that head office equity incorporates the branch on a *'profits earned'* basis.

Parent–subsidiary structure

Instead of divisions there are legally separate entities. Despite the statutory expenses incurred, there are advantages of this form of structure (but *not* the avoidance of disclosure as in pre-consolidation days!). Acquisitions and disposals of subsidiaries are easier to effect than divisions, since they are legally self-contained, and it is possible to buy and sell in fractional interests (e.g. 60 per cent holdings) whereas divisions are always wholly owned. A legally incorporated subsidiary may be necessary in a foreign country in order to benefit from taxation concessions. Also, in theory each company has separate limited liability, and is protected against the insolvency of the others, whereas if a division were liquidated, other divisions would be liable for its debts. In practice the use of such a device would significantly harm the creditworthiness of other group companies. However, a group's *legal* structure may only reflect the manner of its corporate acquisitions, rather than any deeper meaning.

The rest of the book focuses on accounting for groups of companies within the parent–subsidiary relationship since this is by far the most common form of organization for complex entities in the UK. However, most of the techniques discussed have counterparts in branch accounting.

Example 1.2 – Parent–subsidiary consolidation

Suppose Hub plc has the same balance sheet at 1 January 1995 as before, but on 2 January sets up a *subsidiary*, Spoke Ltd, by purchasing 50m £1 shares of Spoke for £50m in cash. Suppose also that the year's transactions were the same as previously, except that just before its year end Spoke Ltd declared a dividend of £10m.

Required
(a) Prepare individual company and consolidated balance sheets immediately after the share issue on 2 January 1995.
(b) Prepare individual company and consolidated balance sheets at 31 December 1995.

(a)   Immediately after the transaction, Spoke's balance sheet is shown, followed by Hub's:

Spoke Ltd – Balance sheet at 2 January 1995 (£m)

Cash	50	Share Capital	50

Hub – Balance sheet at 2 January 1995 (£m)

Fixed assets	90	Loan	30
Investment	50		
Stock	50	Share capital and premium	100
Cash	50	Retained profits	110
	240		240

The consolidated balance sheets at that date would be derived as follows:

Hub Spoke Group – consolidation cancellation at 2 January

	Hub	Spoke	Elimination	Consolidated
Fixed assets	90	—	—	90
Investment	50	—	(50)	—
Stock	50	—	—	50
Cash	50	50	—	100
Loan	(30)	—	—	(30)
Share capital & premium	(100)	(50)	50	(100)
Reserves	(110)	—	—	(110)

The investment has been cancelled against the equity of Spoke. In the previous example, the £50m was advanced directly to Spoke division, but now it is provided in exchange for Spoke shares. The head office account in Spoke's records in the branch accounting example is analogous to its share capital in this case. Previously Hub could remove its stake at any time since the divisional arrangement was purely for internal convenience. Now, since Spoke is a registered company, it would have to undertake the full legal process of liquidation to remove its funds (or else sell its shares). The Investment account in Hub's books is analogous to the Branch account, thus the cancellation.

(b) Transaction recording is similar to the branch case except:
   (i) The capital transaction setting up the company is segregated from trading transactions and shown as investment and share capital; trading transactions are passed through intragroup debtor and creditor accounts which function like the branch accounts of the previous section. By law, the companies are regarded as separate legal entities and each is bound not to distribute its contributed capital.
   (ii) The *profits* of the subsidiary are not automatically transferred to the parent company as in branch accounting. As with other investments, only *dividends* declared by the subsidiary are recorded in the parent's accounts.

Figure 1.3 shows the bookkeeping entries for the year assuming a parent-subsidiary relationship.

Hub Plc (£m)

Cash

Balance b/f	100	Investment	50
T1 Sales	60	T3 Admin	30
T7 Remittance	10		

Stock

| Balance b/f | 50 | T1 COGS | 30 |

Fixed assets

| Balance b/f | 90 | T2 Depn | 5 |

Loan

| | | Balance b/f | 30 |

Investment in Spoke

| Share issue | 50 | | |

Share capital & Premium

| | | Balance b/f | 100 |

Retained profits

| | | Balance b/f | 110 |

Profit and loss

T1 COGS	30	T1 Sales	60
T2 Depn	5	T4 Mgt fee	10
T3 Admin	30	Dividends	10

Debtors - Spoke Plc

| T4 Mgt fee | 10 | T7 Remittance | 10 |
| Dividends | 10 | | |

Spoke Plc (£m)

Cash

| Share issue | 50 | T5 Stock purchase | 30 |
| T6 Sales | 50 | T7 Remittance | 10 |

Stock

| T5 Stock purch | 30 | T6 COGS | 20 |

Share capital

| | | Share issue | 50 |

Profit and loss

T6 COGS	20	T6 Sales	50
T4 Mgt fee	10		
Dividends	10		

Creditors - Hub Plc

| T7 Remittance | 10 | T4 Mgt fee | 10 |
| | | Dividends | 10 |

Figure 1.3

The individual company balance sheets and the consolidation cancellation at 31 December 1995, based on the closing balances in the 'T' accounts, but after closing the profit and loss account balances to retained profits, is as follows. Note the cancellation of intercompany indebtedness.

Hub Spoke Group – consolidation cancellation at 31 December 1995

	Hub	Spoke	Elimination	Consolidated
Fixed assets	85	—	—	85
Investment	50	—	(50)	—
Stock	20	10	—	30
Intragroup debtors	10	—	(10)	—
Cash	90	60	—	150
Intragroup creditors	—	(10)	10	
Loan	(30)	—	—	(30)
Share capital & premium	(100)	(50)	50	(100)
Reserves	(125)	(10)	—	(135)

Under UK Company law, Hub plc must disclose both its own balance sheet *and* the group's consolidated balance sheet. In the divisional case only the overall company balance sheet is required, which in these examples would be analogous to the consolidated balance sheet in the group case. The consolidated profit and loss account can be derived as follows:

Hub Spoke Group – consolidated profit and loss account – year ended 31 December 1995

	Hub	Spoke	Consolidated
Sales	60	50	110
COGS	(30)	(20)	(50)
Depreciation	(5)	-	(5)
Administration expenses	(30)	—	(30)
Management fee	10	(10)	=
Net profit	5	20	25
Intragroup dividends	10	(10)	=
Retained profits	15	10	25

In branch accounting, Hub would merely disclose its company profit and loss account (which in this example is the same as its consolidated profit and loss account in the group case). Aggregate accounts under both branch and consolidation accounting are identical in this simple example. However the direct analogue of the head office account is not the parent company accounts. Head office accounts account for the subsidiary on a *profits earned* basis, whereas parent company accounts only include *dividends* receivable. The difference is the subsidiary's undistributed retained earnings of £10m. Later, it will be shown that the analogy to the head office accounts when group accounting is used is the *equity* approach – where income is recognized on a profits earned basis.

Exercises

1.1 In the Hub-Spoke example, suppose in the *divisional structure* case discussed above that the transactions from 1 January 1996 to 31 December 1996 were as follows:

Head office
(1) Stock purchases from outsiders, all for cash were £40m.
(2) Cash sales of £80m of stocks costing £30m were made to outsiders. Further non-cash sales of £20m of stocks costing £10m were made to Spoke division.
(3) Depreciation of £5m was charged for the year.
(4) Administrative costs for the company were £40m.
(5) A management charge of £12.5m was made to Spoke division.

Spoke division
(6) Purchases of stocks from outsiders totalled £40m for cash, plus £20m on credit from head office.
(7) £80m of goods were sold (including all the goods purchased from head office) whose cost was £40m.
(8) Spoke sent head office a remittance to cover its management fee, its stock purchases for the year, and an additional £10m.

Required
Prepare divisional balance sheets for both companies at 31 December 1996, and a company balance sheet.

1.2 Assume that a parent–subsidiary relationship exists and that the transactions are the same except that the dividend declared for this year is £20m.

Required

Balance off the parent's and subsidiary's 'T'accounts at 31 December 1995 in the above parent–subsidiary example and enter the above transactions for the following year in 'T' accounts. Prepare individual company balance sheets for both companies at 31 December 1996 and a consolidated balance sheet for the Hub-Spoke group at that date.

1.3 Compare the balance sheets in Exercises 1.1 and 1.2.

THE FORMAT OF GROUP ACCOUNTS

The usual format for UK group accounts is summarized in Figure 1.4, their centrepiece being the consolidated financial statements, which 'are intended to present financial information about a parent undertaking and its subsidiary undertakings as a single economic entity to show the economic resources controlled by a group, the obligations of the group, and the results the group achieves with its resources' (FRS 2, para 1). From such an overall objective is deduced the need for adjustments to reflect the change in scope of the accounts from a company to a group basis, such as the elimination of intragroup balances, transactions, and unrealized intragroup profits. In addition there are requirements for coterminous year ends and uniform accounting policies for group members, and materiality and the 'true and fair view' is to be assessed in the consolidated financial statements on the basis of 'the undertakings included in the consolidation as a whole, as far as concerns the members of the [parent] company' (Companies Act 1985, S 227 (3)).

Each of the components of the group accounting 'package' is discussed briefly below, including the consolidated financial statements, and most are examined in more detail in subsequent chapters. The purpose of this menu-like section is merely to give a flavour of the types of information provided; it can be skimmed without loss in continuity

---

Consolidated financial statements	Balance sheet, profit and loss, cash flow statement, general notes

---

Parent balance sheet	Shows investments & indebtedness

Group structure notes	Details on excluded subsidiaries
	Details of investments in (a) subsidiary undertakings (b) associated undertakings (c) others
	Details of immediate and ultimate parent

Figure 1.4 – Format of UK Group Accounts

Consolidated financial statements

The Companies Act 1985 requires parent companies to prepare consolidated (i.e. aggregated) financial statements to include the parent company and all its corporate and non-corporate subsidiary undertakings unless the group as a whole is *exempt*, or *exclusion criteria* apply to particular subsidiaries. Thus group accounts normally comprise a single set of consolidated accounts, plus further information about excluded subsidiaries.

The Act requires a consolidated balance sheet and profit and loss account, and FRS 1, *Cash Flow Statements*, requires a consolidated cash flow statement. The Companies Act also lays down usual disclosure and valuation criteria with specific provisions relating to group accounts. Only the latter are discussed here. The Act requires *uniform accounting policies* to be applied either directly or via consolidation adjustments, otherwise certain disclosures have to be made. FRS 2 requires, where practicable, that financial statements of subsidiaries should be prepared to the *same accounting date* and for the *same accounting period* as the parent. The Act offers alternatives if this is not possible of:

(1) using interim accounts of the subsidiary, to the parent's accounting date, or
(2) using the latest subsidiary accounts, provided that its year end is not more than three months earlier than its parent.

FRS 2 expresses a preference for interim accounts, and only if these are not practicable can option (2) be used, in which case adjustments of any material items over the intervening period must be made, and the name, accounting date, period and reasons for the different date must be disclosed.

In individual company accounts, investments are generally accounted for at cost. In consolidated accounts, their treatment is usually a three-tier affair as shown in Figure 1.5.

Extent of influence	Accounting approach
Passive holding presumed 0 - 19%	*Investments* at cost
Significant influence presumed 20 - 50%	*Associates* -equity approach (one line consolidation)
Controlled Usually 51 - 100%	*Subsidiaries* - full line by line consolidation

Figure 1.5 – Accounting for investments in consolidated statements

As the degree of control increases, so the accounting approach gets more comprehensive. Passively owned investments are included at cost. Investments where the parent has a participating interest and exercises significant influence over operating and financial policies are called *associates* and the Act requires them to be incorporated by an abbreviated form of consolidation called the equity approach. Investments giving control are consolidated – each item in their accounts is added line by line for the corresponding caption with other group undertakings, subject to certain adjustments.

Parent individual company accounts

Only the parent *balance sheet* is required in addition to the consolidated accounts. Section 230 exempts the parent from *publishing* its individual profit and loss account provided the profit or loss, determined in accordance with the Companies Act, is disclosed in the group account notes. FRS 1 does not require a parent individual cash flow statement. The usefulness of parent accounts is limited since group structures vary so much. In some groups, the parent comprises just investments in other group undertakings. In others it might comprise, for example, all UK operations, with a subsidiary running operations in each foreign market. The 'size' of the parent often depends purely on the path of acquisitions and on taxation considerations.

However, the parent balance sheet does contain information not disclosed by the consolidated balance sheet concerning certain items eliminated on consolidation.

1. details of the *total cost of investments* in group and other undertakings (which includes *associated undertakings*), under fixed asset investments and also if appropriate under current assets; and
2. details of *debt relationships* between the parent and the rest of the group. In addition,
3. details of *realized and unrealized* reserves of the parent – in the UK *companies* make distributions not groups.

Details of indebtedness in the parent's individual accounts

Since a group is not regarded in the UK as a legal entity with contractual rights, creditors must look to individual companies in the group for debt repayment. Hence the pattern of intragroup indebtedness between group companies, which cancels out on consolidation, is very important for them. The Balance Sheet formats of the Companies Act 1985 (Sch. 4, part 1) require in the parent company's balance sheet, disclosure of total long-term loans to group undertakings (only subsidiaries) and separately the total to undertakings in which it holds a participating interest, and within the current sections, separate headings under debtors for the total amounts owed *by* group undertakings, and *by* undertakings in which it holds a participating interest, and a similar analysis for amounts owing under creditors. However, these are totals and do not show either the debt pattern between individual group undertakings, nor the pattern of indebtedness between fellow subsidiaries.

The Profit and Loss formats (Sch. 4, part 1) indicate that, in the parent's individual company accounts, income from shares in group undertakings, income from participating interests, other income and interest from group undertakings and interest payable and similar charges to group undertakings must be separately disclosed. Note that each of these balance sheet and profit and loss disclosures are *aggregates* of (1) all subsidiaries and separately (2) of all participating interests. Nobes (1986, p. 10,) in a useful discussion of the area, questions the information content of parent company financial statements and suggests that any potentially useful information (e.g. on distributable profits) might be better provided in a note form.

Other group structure information

Excluded subsidiaries

Disclosures required include the name of the subsidiary and the reason for excluding it from the consolidation. Further disclosures are dependent on the reason for the exclusion.

Details of investments

Consolidated financial statements must disclose similar indebtedness information to the above about associates (SSAP 1), and also profit and loss information. The Companies Act requires a *list of subsidiaries*, truncated to principal subsidiaries if the list is excessive, showing for each, name, country of registration or incorporation, principal country of operation (quoted companies only), classes of shares held and proportions of nominal value of each, directly by the parent *and* indirectly by other group undertakings, and the Act requires similar information on *associated undertakings* (in which a participating influence is held and significant influence is exercised), also (excepting country of operation) for more than 10 per cent investment holdings.

FRS 2 adds a requirement that for *principal* subsidiaries, proportions of *voting rights* held by the parent and its subsidiary undertakings and an indication of the nature of its business must be disclosed. Prior to the Companies Act 1989 many of these requirements had applied merely to the parent's holdings. Note that this information does not indicate the sizes of each investment relative to each other, but merely *proportionate* holdings. An interested investor would have to look to previous years' cash flow statements for such information. Where undertakings are subsidiaries other than because the parent holds a majority of voting rights and the same proportion of equity, the reason why it is a subsidiary must be disclosed.

FRS 5 requires certain disclosures in the consolidated statements by *quasi-subsidiaries* (holdings with similar characteristics to subsidiary undertakings, but set up to fall outside the legal definition – see Chapter 2) including for *each*, summary financial statements (balance sheet, profit and loss, and cash flow statement). Within the Act there are further requirements such as details of the group's immediate and ultimate parent, where the present parent itself belongs to a larger group.

Segmental Data
Consolidation can be viewed as adding together the accounts of *legal* entities to produce a single set of accounts *as if* of a super entity (analogous to *averaging*). Segmental reporting disaggregates consolidated information into *economic* segments, in the UK by line of business and geographical location (providing indirect information about *variability*). These differ from the original company data since, for example, a single subsidiary company may operate in multiple lines of business or on the other hand, a number of subsidiaries may comprise a single geographical segment – see Chapter 12. SSAP 25, *Segmental Reporting*, issued in June 1990, requires for each segment, disclosure for example, of turnover, profit or loss, and net assets. It applies to groups headed by plc's, groups with plc's, banking and insurance companies in them, and other 'large' groups, but directors can opt out if they feel it would be prejudicial to the reporting entity, provided they disclose the fact of non-disclosure.

Related party information involving group members
Many related party matters involving relationships within groups of companies are discussed above. FRED 8, *Relating Party Disclosures*, issued in 1994, proposed a framework for disclosing details of all material related party transactions. Related parties are those where 'for all or part of the financial period: one party has direct or indirect control of the other . . ., or the ability to influence or direct the financial and operating policies of the other . . ., or the parties are subject to common control from the same source, or one is subject to control and the other to influence from the same source' (para. 2(a)).

It deems, for example, other group companies including ultimate parents, undertakings of which the current undertaking is an associate or joint venture, directors (and their immediate family) of an undertaking or its parent, to be related parties. It also outlines rebuttable presumptions of relationship, including key management (and their families) of an undertaking or its parent, or persons acting in concert to control an entity. However, there are also important group disclosure exemptions in consolidated financial statements for intra-group transactions, in the individual accounts of wholly owned subsidiaries for transactions with group members (where such subsidiaries are included in publicly available consolidated statements), and in the parent's own accounts when presented with consolidated financial statements. FRED 8's proposals are extremely controversial and many object to their extent (see for example Archer (1994b)). Space limitations preclude further discussion here.

Exercises

1.4 Assess the nature and usefulness of the additional information required by statute and accounting standards in group accounts to supplement the bare consolidated financial statements in a typical group, in providing a 'true and fair view' of a group's operations and financial position.

1.5 In what ways are consolidated financial statements more useful than parent company financial statements?

SUMMARY

The chapter has reviewed the historical development of group accounting in the UK, discussing the drawbacks of accounting for parent companies purely on a legal entity basis. Only dividends due from subsidiaries are recorded, allowing a great temptation to smooth parent company profits, and the underlying assets and liabilities under the control of the group are not disclosed. The difference between accounting for divisionalized companies (departmental and branch accounting) and group structures (consolidation accounting) was examined, and the process of consolidation as a means of achieving some comparability in disclosure was discussed. In consolidated accounts, subsidiaries' results are accounted for on a profits-earned basis, which in principle allows less scope for manipulation of results using dividend policies of subsidiaries.

The group financial reporting package in the UK normally includes a consolidated balance sheet, profit and loss account and cash flow statement, but only a balance sheet for the parent itself. The parent balance sheet discloses certain aggregate investment, debt and trading balances which are cancelled out on consolidation. Further details regarding group investment holdings, non-consolidated subsidiaries and quasi-subsidiaries is included together with segmental reporting information.

FURTHER READING

Historical development
Edwards, J.R. and Webb, K.M. (1984) The development of group accounting in the United Kingdom to 1933, *The Accounting Historians Journal*, Vol. 11, no. 1, pp. 31-61.
Walker, R.G. (1978) *Consolidated Statements: A History and Analysis*, Arno Press, New York.

Entity organizational structures
Deloitte, Haskins & Sells (1983) *Corporate Structure – Subsidiaries or Divisions?*, Deloitte, Haskins & Sells, London.
FRED 8 (1994) *Related Party Transactions*, Accounting Standards Board.

2

THE NATURE OF GROUP
FINANCIAL STATEMENTS

Modern group financial statements form a highly complex package, in some cases prepared from a data base incorporating hundreds of subsidiaries in scores of currencies. Before examining consolidation techniques, this chapter examines objectives for group financial statements, reviews the legal and institutional context for group financial statements in the UK, and discusses criteria for when they are to be prepared. They are almost always presented in consolidated form by aggregating the financial statements of the parent and its subsidiaries after adjusting for the effects of intra-group matters.

For accounting purposes the Companies Act 1985 uses the terms 'subsidiary undertaking' and 'parent undertaking'. For other legal purposes it uses the differently defined terms 'subsidiary' and 'holding company'. In this book 'subsidiary' and 'parent' are used to denote 'subsidiary undertaking' and 'parent undertaking' unless otherwise stated. The term 'group financial statements' is used in a wider sense than 'consolidated financial statements' since, in principle, it is possible to present group statements in alternative formats, e.g. consolidated statements for some subsidiaries and separate statements for others which are dissimilar, or separate statements for each subsidiary. Group financial statements also include information about economic segments, group shareholdings and indebtedness in addition to the consolidated statements.

In the UK group financial statements must take the form of consolidated statements for all subsidiaries unless the group as a whole is *exempt*, or in the case of subsidiaries which meet *exclusion* criteria. Additional disclosures for excluded subsidiaries must then be provided. Recently the world-wide trend has been towards consolidated statements as the only acceptable format for group accounts. Consolidated financial statements also include *associates* over which *significant influence* but not *control* is exercisable by the parent.

OBJECTIVES OF GROUP FINANCIAL STATEMENTS

Group accounting grew out of the limitations of individual company accounting as discussed in Chapter 1. However, internationally it has, and also can in principle, serve a variety of purposes. Walker (1978a) provides a comprehensive analysis of overlapping hypotheses in the accounting literature as to objectives and what follows draws in part on his analysis.

Traditionally, one view is that group financial statements, mere memorandum statements, are prepared for the proprietors of the parent, the primary entity, to *amplify* information in the parent's own accounts because the parent's business is carried out through alliances with other economic entities. Consolidation is one possible format for this amplification, another being for example, separate financial statements for subsidiaries. From within this perspective others attribute vastly greater importance to consolidation, since a group's legal structure as parent and subsidiaries is often a result of historical accident as to the sequence of acquisitions, or is set up for taxation or other reasons. In this case consolidated financial statements would be of primary importance and the parent's individual financial statements secondary. Some argue that the boundaries of such 'groups' should be determined only in terms of legally enforceable rights (the so-called *de jure* approach), whereas others would argue for the boundary to be defined by the ambit of direct and delegated *effective* (actual) *control* by the ultimate parent's shareholders (the *de facto* approach). Most arguing from the latter perspective would consider consolidation as the only realistic format for group accounts.

Another perspective views the group as an *economic entity* in its own right, distinct from its shareholders, who are viewed as one of the categories of financial claims on the reporting entity's resources. The focus of consolidated reports should therefore be wider than this narrow group, to include those having 'a reasonable right to information arising from the public accountability of the entity' (*ASC Corporate Report*, 1975, p. 77). For some, the boundaries of the group 'entity' are still to be defined in terms of the ambit of control of a 'parent'-headed group. Minority (non-controlling) interests are another set of claims with more limited rights and powers over only *part* of the group 'entity'.

Others within this *economic entity* perspective view the group in terms of *concentrations of economic power* over resources – termed by the FASB (FASB, 1991, p. 24) the *economic unit* concept. Options in the EC 7th Directive not taken up by the UK allow member states to require consolidation of so-called *horizontal groups*, i.e. entities which are managed on a unified basis based on contract or provisions in their memoranda or articles, or where the only link between such entities is a majority of common interlocking directors (Article 12). The group defined by the ambit of *management* control has traditionally been associated with Germany. Motivations for this latter perspective could include national economic management or the policing of abuses of economic power or even the fact that other groups, e.g. creditors, are considered the primary users of group statements in some countries. This spectrum can have consequences not only for group definition and reporting format, but also for measurement and disclosure of consolidated assets and liabilities, and in particular, for relationships between controlling and non-controlling interests. Such matters are discussed further in Chapters 4 and 6.

Walker (1978a) cites other objectives including that consolidated financial statements facilitate the assessment of firms' abilities to meet their debts (discussed in Chapter 4). Whittred (1987), using an *agency-contracting* framework, suggests that in Australia the debt assessment perspective was a major reason for the adoption of consolidation *voluntarily* prior to the existence of accounting regulation there. He observed that the period 1930–50 in Australia was one of increasing debt financing of groups. Lenders protected their interests by demanding *cross-guarantees* from other group companies, opening up access to other group companies' assets in case of default. This effectively undoes each company's limited liability and modifies it to a group level. He hypothesizes that *consolidated accounts* provide more cost-effective monitoring than individual company accounts in such circumstances, and therefore are more likely to be produced even where not required, than for similar groups without such debt. This could suggest that the scope of consolidation might be entities included within the span of debt cross-guarantees, which may be smaller than the entire controlled group. Whittred's tests, however, assumed both were coincident and claimed that his evidence supports the debt assessment/contracting hypothesis.

Bircher (1988) noted a reluctance in the UK to provide group accounts voluntarily prior to its compulsory introduction in the Companies Act 1948, even though it had been cited since the 1920s as best practice. However, he found a huge increase in the provision of consolidated accounts in 1947. As with Whittred (1987), he found that this provision coincided with a large increase (55 per cent) in debt as a percentage of total company securities issued. However, other explanations were also suggested, such as knowledge of impending legislation and the recent removal of penal taxation on excess profits after the Second World War.

There have been few studies examining the objectives of group financial statements *per se*. Figure 2.1 shows Walker's (1978a) analysis of the link between proposed objectives and the scope of consolidation. He tries to link proposals with the functional objectives for consolidation based on his historical analysis of the accounting literature of more than fifty years. The first two objectives define the scope of consolidation in terms of the parent's interests, and the third in terms of creditors' interests. The last two view the group itself as an entity, the former in terms of effective control, whereas the latter narrows this to consolidate only a homogeneous subset of economic activities. The ambit of *managerial* control is not specifically considered.

Status and supposed function	Possible scope of consolidation
Primary documents - to depict the financial position and performance of *holding* [parent] companies	Holding [parent] companies and substantially owned subsidiaries
Supplementary reports - to *amplify* the financial statements of holding [parent] companies	Substantially owned subsidiaries only, excluding the holding [parent] company, *or* A series of group statements each covering those subsidiaries engaged in a particular line of business, *or* A series of group statements each covering domestic subsidiaries, foreign subsidiaries, *or* Holding [parent] company and all 'material' subsidiaries.
Supplementary reports - to faciliate *assessments of the ability* of firms *to meet their debts*	Holding [parent] company and all 'controlled' subsidiaries, *or* All companies which have guaranteed the indebtedness of other companies plus the companies subject to those guarantees, *or* Some other combination dependant on the pattern of inter-company loans..........
Supplementary reports - to depict the position and performance of '*group* entities'	All corporations (or unincorporated associations) subject to (actually exercised) control. [NB tests of control might be based on voting power or contractual rights]
Supplementary statements - to depict the position and performance of '*economic* entities'	All 'controlled' corporations (or unincorporated associations) engaged in specified businesses or activities.

Figure 2.1 – Link between objectives and scope of consolidation. Source: Exhibit 1 in Walker (1978), Abacus. Vol 14 No 2, December 1978, page 104.

The former UK position hovered uneasily between the first and second objectives and now, in common with many other countries, is approximated by the fourth. However, as Walker points out, most proposals are compromise affairs (e.g. the exclusion of dissimilar lines of business required by the EC 7th Directive incorporates something of the fifth objective). Walker's table provides a useful framework for discussion.

Very little is known about user needs in this area or why one set of objectives should predominate over another. The ASB Discussion Draft, *Statement of Principles, Chapter 7, The Reporting Entity* (1994) merely states that the primary users are investors in the parent since they have an interest in the group as a whole, and that consolidated financial statements 'provide a frame of reference for other users' (para. 3.4). It situates general principles as to why an entity *should* produce general-purpose financial statements (which may include consolidated financial statements) in supply [the entity is a *cohesive economic unit*, i.e. having a *unified control structure*] and demand terms [there are those with a *legitimate interest*, who rely on such statements as a *major source of information* for making economic decisions], where the benefits from the statements exceed their costs (Section 2). An important issue not discussed there is whether or not the *market* will itself produce whatever it needs in a cost-effective manner to enable participants to monitor contractual arrangements in the most efficient way possible, or whether additional regulation is required. Whittred's study implicitly tends to the market provision view, and in this regard finds further evidence in this non-regulated period that, as the number of subsidiaries gets larger, groups will tend to produce consolidated accounts as a cheap, effective monitoring package. The ASB takes the latter view. Theoretical economic analysis is inconclusive as to the extent of regulation needed. More managed economies than the UK would probably travel even further down the regulation route on political as much as economic grounds.

Flint (1993) also points out that the 'true and fair view' perspective embedded in UK and now EC law dictates that consolidated financial statements are not sufficient in themselves to provide a 'true and fair view'. As discussed in Chapter 1, group financial statements also incorporate information about the legal structure of the group and about its economic segments. In addition they include information about entities over which varying degrees of influence are exercised (e.g. associates and joint ventures). The reporting of such 'strategic alliances' is discussed in later chapters.

Most countries reflect a hybrid approach to objectives. EC law reflects a compromise between differing national traditions, some of which had been clearly embedded in an amplification (parent) perspective, and others tending more towards an economic unit perspective. The EC 7th Directive clauses incorporated into UK Company Law have moved the latter more towards incorporating aspects of the entity end of a spectrum, though it contains clear aspects of a parent/amplification viewpoint with consolidated statements being viewed as primary.

In the UK, group financial statements are produced in *addition* to the parent's individual company accounts, in contrast to the USA where consolidated financial statements are often the only published statements. The Companies Act 1989 (Section 227(3)) states that '[Group] accounts shall give a true and fair view . . . so far as concerns members of the [parent] company' and in the UK, companies not groups are legal entities. Groups cannot enter into contracts or enforce them, the starting point for taxation is individual companies though some group reliefs are available, and legally, distributable profits are a company not a group matter.

The ASB Discussion Draft, *Statement of Principles Chapter 7, The Reporting Entity*, issued in 1994 (referred to hereafter as *The Reporting Entity*) reflects this perspective, stating that 'the group is sometimes referred to as the reporting entity as shorthand for the parent's reporting role with respect to its group. The group is in fact the *reported* entity' (para. 1.3, original emphasis). The group 'is an affiliation of economic interests . . . all within the control of a parent entity' (para. 1.2). Prior to the Companies Act 1989 formats other than consolidated accounts were legally permitted, though SSAP 14, *Group Accounts*, had, since 1978 by pre-empting similar options in earlier Acts, effectively required consolidation as the only treatment.

The Companies Act 1989 altered considerably the definition of a subsidiary for accounting purposes and enshrined in law rather than accounting standards the requirement for consolidation as *the* basis for group accounts. FRS 2, *Accounting for Subsidiary Undertakings*, states that '[Consolidated financial statements] are intended to present financial information about a parent undertaking and its subsidiary undertakings as a single economic entity to show the economic resources controlled by the group, the obligations of the group and the results the group achieves with its resources' (para. 1) The accounting concept that underlies this objective is that of *control*.

REQUIREMENTS FOR PREPARING CONSOLIDATED FINANCIAL STATEMENTS

The Companies Act 1985 (as amended by the Companies Act 1989) states that 'If at the *end* of a financial year a company is a *parent company* the directors shall, as well as preparing individual accounts for the year, prepare group accounts [in the form of consolidated accounts]' (S 227(1) and (2), emphases added) unless the group is *exempt*, mainly through being unlisted and 'small', or unlisted and part of a group headed by an EC-based immediate parent with the acquiescence of its minority shareholders. Further, 'all subsidiary undertakings of the parent company shall be included in the consolidation [unless they satisfy *exclusion* criteria]' (S 229 (1)). The exclusion criteria are defined mainly in terms of a lack of effective control.

UK practice also recognizes that a parent can directly or indirectly exercise differing degrees of influence over its affiliates. The key distinctions used currently distinguish between *unilateral control* of 'subsidiary undertakings' (consolidation), *significant influence* over 'associates' (equity accounting), and *joint control* over 'joint ventures (equity accounting, or as an option for *non-corporate* ventures, proportional consolidation). Other investments are treated identically to their treatment in the parent's own financial statements. In this chapter only subsidiaries are considered and other degrees of influence are examined in Chapter 4.

The Act itself only requires consolidated financial statements to be prepared by groups headed by a parent *company* (S 227(1)), though it requires *non-corporate subsidiaries* to be consolidated, since the term 'subsidiary *undertaking'* includes non-corporate bodies such as partnerships and unincorporated associations whether trading or in business for profit or not for profit (S 258/9). FRS 2, *Accounting for Subsidiary Undertakings*, requires in addition that *'all* parent undertakings that prepare consolidated financial statements intended to give a true and fair view' should comply with its requirements, unless prohibited by the statutory framework within which they report (para. 18, emphasis added). It only requires parents which *already* prepare such 'true and fair view' statements to comply with its requirements and does not therefore apply to partnerships in general, or groups controlled by common *individuals* – voluntary publication by such 'groups' is virtually non-existent in the UK. As stated earlier, 'horizontal' groups whose only connection is unified management by contract or articles/memorandum, or common management also do not have to consolidate. FRED 8, *Related Party Transactions* (1994), proposes an alternative route, through extra disclosure bringing to the attention of shareholders of groups and companies transactions which may suggest there are wider networks of control and influence than captured by say the consolidated accounts of a particular reporting entity (see Chapter 1).

This book is mainly concerned with the consolidation of the accounts of groups headed by *companies*. In practice other bodies using the technique of consolidation include friendly and industrial and provident societies, building societies, councils and local authorities, together with public sector bodies such as The Post Office and British Rail. Consolidation is recommended practice for pension schemes and charities. Banking and insurance companies are also covered by the 1985 Act, but specialized matters relating to them are also not considered here.

DEFINING A GROUP

The objectives of group/consolidated financial statements are closely intertwined with the definition of what is a group for accounting purposes, the latter predicated in the UK on the existence of a *parent*. FRS 2 states that the accounting concept that underpins its view as to the objectives of *consolidated* financial statements is that of *control*. The ASB's Discussion Draft, *The Reporting Entity*, develops this and proposes that the boundary of a group subject to a set of financial statements is set by the extent of the parent's control – the ability to direct its own economic resources and those of its subsidiaries (through its ability to direct them).

FRS 2 defines the date an undertaking becomes a subsidiary undertaking, the date of acquisition (or merger, see chapter 3) which is the date from which a new subsidiary's results can be included in the consolidated results under acquisition accounting, as 'the date on which *control* of that undertaking *passes* to its new parent undertaking' (emphases added), and the date an undertaking ceases to be a subsidiary undertaking as 'the date on which its former parent relinquishes its control' (para. 45). For public offers this is the date the offer becomes unconditional, usually through sufficient acceptances; or generally the date an unconditional offer is accepted, for private treaties; or the date of share issue if such means is used (para. 85). It may be indicated by the date the acquiring party commences its direction of operating and financial policies, or the flow of economic benefits changes, or where the consideration for transfer of control is paid (para. 85). IAS 22 also bases the normal date of acquisition on the date control passes (para. 14). APB Opinion 16 in the USA focuses more heavily on the date the consideration is given and received. It specifies and allows other acceptable dates but requires an adjustment to the consideration for the time value of money if these are chosen (para. 93).

According to the ASB's *The Reporting Entity*, control implies two *necessary* abilities:
(1) the power to *deploy* economic resources; and
(2) the ability to *benefit* or *suffer* by their deployment.

These abilities would be split for example in the case of say trustee and beneficiary and so control would not be present under such circumstances (paras 4.1/4.2).

In UK and EC law, the definition of a group is prior to the decision on which undertakings should be consolidated. Adjusting the statutory *group definition* as the parent plus its subsidiary undertakings, to determine entities to be consolidated (i.e. which satisfy the *criteria for consolidation*, examined later) is achieved by:

(a) starting with the parent and its subsidiary undertakings per the Companies Act 1985.
(b) excluding non-controlled subsidiary undertakings, and
(c) including controlled undertakings which do not meet the definition of a subsidiary undertaking (termed quasi-subsidiaries by FRS 5).

The current definition of a group in stage (a) is effected by Section 258 of the Companies Act 1985 defining a *subsidiary undertaking* as one where the parent undertaking

---

(a) holds a majority of its voting rights, or
(b) is its member and has the right to appoint a majority of its board of directors, or
(c) has the right to exercise a dominant influence via its memorandum or articles or through a control contract, or
(d) is its member and controls alone a majority of its voting rights by means of an agreement with other shareholders or members, or
(e) has a participating interest and

   (i)   actually exercises a dominant influence, or
   (ii) it and the subsidiary undertaking are managed on a unified basis, or

(f) is the parent undertaking of undertakings of which any of its subsidiary undertakings are, or are to be treated as, parent undertakings.

The development of this convoluted definition is now considered before examining the criteria for consolidation.

Group definition prior to the Companies Act 1989

The Companies Act 1985 was amended by the Companies Act 1989 enacting the EC 7th Directive on consolidated accounts into UK company law. Somewhat confusingly the Act is still called the Companies Act 1985. In what follows, the term 'Companies Act 1985' will refer to the amended Act unless stated. Where there is any possibility of confusion, 'Companies Act 1985u' refers to the unamended Act and 'Companies Act 1985a' to the amended Act.

From 1948 to 1989, the definition of a subsidiary (company) required the parent to either

(a) (i)   be a member of it and to control the composition of its board of directors, or
    (ii) hold more than half in nominal value of its *equity*, or
(b)   the company to be a subsidiary of another subsidiary (S 736 Companies Act 1985u).

This definition was criticized for not being based on any clear conceptual framework. Criterion (a) (i) was only one particular means of exercising control, whereas (a) (ii) did not necessarily imply control if all equity did not carry equal voting rights. Shaw (1976, p. 71) commented that majority ownership should have been merely an example or rebuttable presumption of circumstances of possible control. It was possible for one company to be the subsidiary of two holding companies where one held the majority of equity, and the other a minority of equity but a majority of votes. Criterion (b) recognizes 'control' through a vertical chain of 'controlled' subsidiaries.

Off-balance sheet financing
Prior to the Companies Act 1989, a surge occurred in the development and marketing of schemes enabling a parent to effectively control another enterprise without it being classed as a subsidiary and therefore consolidated. Motives were many and various including:

(1) selling goods to such vehicles (termed 'controlled non-subsidiaries' and later 'quasi-subsidiaries') and recording a profit. Under normal consolidation procedures, profit is not recognized until goods leave the *group*;
(2) keeping assets and liabilities off the consolidated balance sheet to improve gearing and to avoid breaking debt covenant restrictions;
(3) for signalling purposes: to creditors whose recourse in the event of non-payment might not be to all group assets and liabilities to show which assets and liabilities were available; to show to shareholders what the new group would look like by removing assets and liabilities of a subsidiary to be disposed of soon after the year end, though additional *pro-forma* financial statements would be a better way of doing this.

For further details see Peasnell and Yaansah (1988).

Some 'off-balance sheet financed' quasi-subsidiaries were accounted for as associates, i.e. using the equity approach instead of consolidation. As will be shown in Chapter 4, this would have a limited impact on reported consolidated profit, but would in many cases improve group gearing. In extreme cases quasi-subsidiaries were accounted for as fixed asset investments (at cost with income being recognized on a dividends basis), which would affect consolidated reported profits as well as gearing. In this case the impact of these 'vehicles' would be similar for them to the non-consolidation of subsidiaries in the 1930s discussed in Chapter 1.

Example 2.1 – Off-balance sheet schemes prior to 1989

1. Burton Group plc's 1986 annual report stated that the parent owned 50 per cent of the equity shares of Hall & Sons Ltd with the other 50 per cent owned by banks. Hall & Sons was not a subsidiary under criterion (a) (i) in the box above. However, the articles of Hall & Sons showed that there were two classes of shares with the 'A' shares having double the voting rights of the 'B' shares. The 'A' shares did not in principle have the power to appoint the majority of directors, but through the power of veto had effective control over the majority of votes at directors meetings (Peasnell and Yaansah, 1988, p. 11). Thus Hall & Co. was not a subsidiary under (a) (ii). Burton also set up finance companies, which were very highly geared, in which they held less than 50 per cent of the equity and which were accounted for using the equity approach. Burton plc has indicated that these, which were presumably set up to reduce consolidated gearing, would have to be consolidated as subsidiaries under the amended Companies Act 1985.
2. In its 1986 annual report, Storehouse plc revealed that, in addition to its 48 per cent stake in Richard Shops, it held a call option to purchase the remaining 52 per cent from a merchant bank,

Morgan Grenfell, exercisable at any time on payment of (only) £126,000. The merchant bank held a put option, exercisable on 30 January 1988, which would require Storehouse plc itself to purchase Richard Shops for £126,000. Richard Shops was accounted for under the equity method. The Storehouse group had exercised the option to increase its stake to 96 per cent by the time of the 1987 accounts. It would have been possible under the unamended Companies Act to have effective control *entirely* through the use of options without having to consolidate.

3. Burnett and Hallamshire Holdings plc arranged to purchase a bulk shipping carrier under hire purchase through a quasi-subsidiary Mincorp Shipping and Finance which it effectively controlled, though only holding a one-sixth share in its equity. The parent guaranteed the payments of the quasi-subsidiary under the hire purchase contract, but showed neither the bulk carrier as an asset, nor the liabilities under the hire purchase contract in its 1984 accounts. Also, the parent recognized profits on the sale of property to another quasi-subsidiary. A provider of finance to this latter quasi-subsidiary withdrew its support and the property ownership reverted to the parent and hence the 'profit' disappeared after the year end!

Early attempts at regulation

In the early 1980s considerable uncertainty existed over how far financial reports could or should be adjusted to record the economic substance of transactions rather than their legal form. The Argyll Foods court case (Bird, 1982) had decided that it was not permissible to restate the consolidation to include subsidiaries that were acquired subsequent to the year end, even if the motive was to show a 'true and fair view', because the directors' felt that the relevant companies were effectively controlled *prior to* the year end. A Department of Trade and Industry statement at this time expressed the view that accounting for substance over form using the 'true and fair override' could not itself pre-empt the law's definition as to which subsidiaries could be included in a consolidation.

In 1985, there was an ongoing dispute between the Institute of Chartered Accountants in England and Wales (ICAEW) in *Technical Release No. 603*, which recommended *accounting for the economic substance* of transactions rather than just their legal form, with the legal form given by note disclosures, and the Law Society, which took the opposite route – that a true and fair view should be achieved by *accounting for the legal form* and providing note disclosure to reflect the economic substance! Both interpreted the then Companies Act as supporting their position, and the Law Society questioned the legality of the accounting profession's stance. The fact that investors given sufficient additional information might be sophisticated enough to make adjustments themselves was not mentioned(!) though many note disclosures at this time were severely lacking. ED 42, *Accounting for Special Purpose Transactions* (1988), continued the debate over what were now termed 'special purpose transactions', but resolution was 'frozen' pending the passing of the Companies Bill (to become the Companies Act 1989) with its radical changes to the law on group accounts.

The Companies Act 1989 made subtle changes to the way a 'true and fair view' could be achieved, and the resulting amended Companies Act 1985 states that 'if in special circumstances compliance with any of [the amended Act's] provisions is inconsistent with the requirement to give a true and fair view, the directors shall depart from that provision to the extent necessary to give a true and fair view' (Section 226(5)) which seemed to ease the way for supporters of accounting for substance over form. ED 49, *Reflecting the Substance of Transactions in Assets and Liabilities*, was issued in May 1990. The Companies Act 1989 itself dealt a death blow to most existing off-balance sheet schemes involving quasi-subsidiaries, and its provisions now in the Companies Act 1985 are examined before the profession's attempts to mop up the residual problem.

ADOPTION OF THE EU 7TH DIRECTIVE – THE COMPANIES ACT 1989

The EU 7th Directive, contained four compulsory *de jure* criteria (Article 1) for the definition of a subsidiary, requiring consolidation where the parent undertaking has:

(a)   a majority of voting rights, or
(b)   is a member and has the right to appoint a majority of the board of directors, or
(c)   a right to exercise a dominant influence as the result of a control contract, or
(d)   is a member and as the result of an agreement with other shareholders in the subsidiary, has the right to control alone a majority of voting rights.

Article 3 states that a subsidiary of a subsidiary shall by that fact be treated as a subsidiary of the parent.

The Directive also included *optional* criteria whereby consolidation *may* be required by individual member states where a parent

(i)   holds a participating interest in a subsidiary undertaking and *either* actually exercises a dominant influence over it, *or* it and the subsidiary undertaking are managed on a unified basis by the parent undertaking (Article 1.2), or
(ii)   has appointed the majority of the board of directors, solely as a result of its voting rights (Article 1 aa), or
(iii) manages itself and the subsidiary on a unified basis pursuant to a contract or provision in its articles or memorandum (Article 12), or
(iv)   the same personnel are a majority on the boards of both companies throughout the year and up to the preparation of the accounts (Article 12).

Initially it was considered unlikely that the UK would incorporate any of these options as they introduced concepts novel at that time. However, off-balance sheet financing schemes were proliferating so fast at the time of drafting UK legislation, that option (i) was enacted into the Companies Act 1989. This radically changed the definition of 'subsidiary' for accounting purposes, and hence criteria for consolidation. It defined a 'subsidiary' for non-accounting purposes using only the four core conditions, (a)–(d) above, but for accounting purposes only, introduced the term 'subsidiary undertaking' catching many quasi-subsidiaries by utilizing some of the Directive's optional criteria above. All subsidiaries are subsidiary undertakings, but not vice versa.

Davies, Paterson and Wilson (1992, p. 144) comment that option (ii), which was not included in UK law, caters for widely dispersed shareholdings where a minority holding could exercise *de facto* control. It differs from adopted compulsory criterion (d) in that such control is achieved without explicit agreement. Options (iii) and (iv) were also not incorporated into UK law.

Option (iii) derived from the German practice of consolidating subsidiaries subject to central and unified management. Early draft versions of the Directive required groups not headed by limited companies to be consolidated, and non-EEC groups to have to consolidate all their EC activities. However, these were not acceptable to the majority of EC countries and would have caused sweeping changes to national laws. It was suggested that the Church of England might have to produce consolidated accounts(!) and the latter requirement was severely modified. The final version accommodated the wide divergences in practice in the EEC, whilst also moving the member states towards some harmonization. Consolidated accounts became compulsory only for groups headed by limited liability companies but non-incorporated subsidiaries had to be included. A very useful summary of the impact of the adoption of the EC 7th Directive into UK law is provided by Nobes (1993).

Exercises

2.1 Compare and contrast the advantages and disadvantages of *de jure* and *de facto* definitions of a group from the perspective of (a) parent company shareholders, (b) group auditors, (c) governmental regulatory agencies.

2.2 Explain how different conceptions of a 'group' can lead to different consolidation criteria.

THE CURRENT UK DEFINITION OF A SUBSIDIARY UNDERTAKING

The amended Companies Act 1985 defines a subsidiary undertaking as one where the parent undertaking:

(a) holds a majority of its voting rights, or

(b) is its member and has the right to appoint a majority of its board of directors, or

(c) has the right to exercise a dominant influence via its memorandum or articles or through a control contract, or

(d) is its member and controls alone a majority of its voting rights by means of an agreement with other shareholders or members, or

(e) has a participating interest and
   (i)   actually exercises a dominant influence, or
   (ii) it and the subsidiary undertaking are managed on a unified basis;

(f) is the parent undertaking of undertakings of which any of its subsidiary undertakings are, or are to be treated as, parent undertakings (S 258).

Criterion (e) relating to dominant influence and unified management is the radical change to previous UK practice. In order to prevent the requirements being interpreted contrary to the wishes of the Act's drafters, it also contains interpretation provisions.

Majority voting rights – (a) amends the previous Companies Act definition which required a majority stake in equity.

Membership with right to appoint a majority of directors – is similarly adjusted since Sch. 10A (2) indicates that it now means directors holding the majority of voting rights at board meetings on all, or substantially all, matters.

Control by contract or constitution – expected to have little impact in the UK. FRS 2 comments on criterion (c) control contracts, that directors (of subsidiaries) have a common law duty to act in the best interests of their company, and suggests that such contractual control of subsidiaries might be in breach of such a duty (para. 70). Such a contract, which must be *written*, must be *sanctioned* by the memorandum and articles, and be *permitted* by the law where the subsidiary undertaking is established (Sch. 10A (2)). Davis, Paterson and Wilson (1992) argue that such a provision would probably only be relevant where the parent has a German subsidiary undertaking or in a country where German style legal provisions are in force. 'Dominant interest' in this context is defined as 'a right to give directions with respect to the operating and financial policies of that other undertaking which its directors are obliged to comply with whether or not they are for [its] benefit' . . . (Sch. 10A 4(1)).

Control by agreement with other members – such agreements must be legally binding, but could, in principle, according to the DTI, include non-written agreements.

Participating interest and dominant influence or unified management – this is the most significant change to UK law, and catches most of the quasi-subsidiary schemes discussed earlier. It is examined here in some detail.

A 'participating interest' is defined as 'an interest . . . [held] on a long term basis for the purpose of securing a contribution to its activities by the exercise of control or influence arising from or related to that interest' (S 260 (1)). A holding of 20 per cent of shares is *presumed* to be a participating interest unless rebutted (S 260 (2)). However, it is important to note that smaller holdings *could* also be participating interests. Nobes (1993, p. 234) points out that the reason for requiring such an interest to be present is to prevent strong commercial relationships alone (he uses the example of Marks and Spencer and its suppliers) leading to consolidation. Options or convertibles are to be included in participating interests, even if they have not yet been exercised (S 260 (3)). However, there seems to be no provision to exclude options or convertibles which are very unlikely to be exercised or converted because adverse market conditions have rendered the option element worthless. So, for example, the old scheme of control of the board of directors without being a member, though avoiding criterion (b) above, might now be caught by this provision.

Whereas the Act defines the term 'dominant interest' in the context of the 'control contract' provision (see above), it explicitly states (Sch. 10A 4(3)) that this definition 'shall not be read as affecting the construction of the expression "actually exercises a dominant interest" ' in criterion (e), and has left its interpretation to accounting standards. Therefore FRS 2 duly defines 'the actual exercise of dominant influence' as

> the exercise of an influence that achieves the result that the operating and financial policies of the undertaking influenced are set in accordance with the wishes of the holder of the influence and for the holder's benefit whether or not those wishes are explicit. The actual exercise of dominant influence is identified by its effect in practice rather than by the way it is exercised. (para. 7b)

It indicates that a power of veto usually will only indicate such a dominant interest if it 'is held in conjunction with other rights or powers or if they relate to the day-to-day activities of that undertaking and no similar veto is held by other parties unconnected to the holder' (para. 72). Normal commercial relationships in isolation are not sufficient. Dominant influence can be evidenced by 'a rare intervention on a critical matter . . . [and] should be assumed to continue until there is evidence to the contrary' (para. 73). Each year the status should be reassessed.

The expression 'managed on a unified basis' is interpreted by FRS 2 to mean that 'the whole of the operations of the undertakings are integrated and they are managed as a single unit. Unified management does not arise solely because one undertaking manages another. The operations . . . [must be] integrated' (para. 74). This is probably the most radical new element since it clearly takes an economic entity stance on the scope of consolidation, given that a participating interest is held. It is not clear what impact this will have in the UK in practice.

Ultimate parent rule – new based on 'subsidiary undertaking,' (f) is a rather convoluted restatement of the old 'subsidiary of a subsidiary is a subsidiary' rule.

There are further explanatory provisions (in Schedule 10A) concerning, for example, rights dependent on circumstances (taken into account only if those circumstances are operative or if the circumstances are under the control of the holder), rights temporarily inoperative (which should still be taken into account), rights held on behalf of another (taken into account if a nominee, but not if in a fiduciary capacity), rights on shares held as a security (not to be considered if the rights cannot be independently exercised except to preserve the value of the security), rights by an undertaking in itself (which are to be disregarded), and last, but certainly not least, rights held by a subsidiary undertaking (which are to be treated as rights held by the parent). The wish to stamp out controlled non-subsidiaries is clearly evident!

CRITERIA FOR CONSOLIDATION – FRS 2

FRS 2 states 'the concept that underlies the presentation of consolidated financial statements for a group as a single economic entity is summarised in the definition of control' (para. 62) defined as

> 'The ability of an undertaking to direct the financial policies of another undertaking with a view to gaining economic benefits from its activities' (para. 6).

> Companies to be consolidated are the
> legally defined group – excluded subsidiaries + quasi-subsidiaries;

unless the group in aggregate meets the Act's exemption criteria in which case there are no published consolidated accounts produced. For consolidation purposes the effect of the above is to adjust the legal group definition so that all controlled undertakings are consolidated, and no non-controlled ones are. The first two terms above are derived from the Companies Act 1985a, as tied down by FRS 2. The third is the subject of FRS 5, *Accounting for the Substance of Transactions* (1994), which defines and requires the inclusion of quasi-subsidiaries. Exemptions and exclusions are now dealt with in turn.

EXEMPTION CRITERIA FOR GROUPS

A group or subgroup, headed by an unlisted parent, is exempt from preparing group accounts for two main categories of reasons, (i) its immediate parent is EEC-established and its own minority shareholders (if any) acquiesce, or (ii) it falls within the Act's size exemptions. The fine detail described below can be omitted without loss of continuity.

Intermediate parent embedded in a larger group
A(n intermediate) parent is exempt from preparing group accounts (S 228) if:
(a) the intermediate company is either

- (i)   a wholly owned subsidiary, or
- (ii) majority owned and shareholders holding either half the remaining shares or 5 per cent of its total shares have not served notice requesting preparation of group accounts – such notification to be given not more than six months into the relevant financial year, AND

(b) it is included in the audited, consolidated accounts of an EEC parent for the same date or a date earlier in the same financial year. These consolidated accounts must be filed by the exempt company with its individual accounts, together with a certified translation into English of any parts if necessary, AND
(c) it discloses in its individual company accounts that it is exempt and states the name of the parent undertaking drawing up the group accounts in (b), together with its country of incorporation or registration, or if unincorporated, its principal place of business, AND
(d) its immediate parent is established within a member state of the EC, AND
(e) none of its securities are listed on a member-state stock exchange.

Size
To be exempt under this criterion, the group must not have members which are listed or are banks, insurance companies or authorized financial services undertakings, and must fall within certain aggregate criteria for small or medium-sized groups satisfying at least two of the following: turnover, balance sheet totals or number of employees. The 'medium-sized' limits are provided in two forms: after consolidation adjustments (net) – at present, group turnover £11.2m, group assets £5.6m, or group employees of 250; or before such adjustments (gross) – the turnover and assets limits are 20 per cent larger and the employee limit the same (S 249). The latter allows exemption to be claimed without having to prepare internal draft consolidated accounts. It is permissible to satisfy some gross and others net.

EXCLUSION CRITERIA FOR SUBSIDIARY UNDERTAKINGS

It is important to understand these criteria intuitively since FRS 2 uses them to enact the concept of *control* as the basis for consolidation. They apply to individual subsidiary undertakings. There are five exclusion criteria:

(i) severe long-term restrictions hinder the parent's rights, or
(ii) the parent's interest is held exclusively with a view to resale, or
(iii) obtaining the relevant information is subject to disproportionate expense or undue delay, or
(iv) immateriality (applied to the aggregate of subsidiaries excluded for this reason), or
(v) the activities of one or more subsidiaries are too different from the others (S 229).

The last is mandatory, the first four optional, but FRS 2 *prescribes* the options to be chosen. For example, it states that disproportionate expense or undue delay cannot be used as a reason for exclusion unless the aggregate of the subsidiaries affected by this criterion is immaterial (para. 24), and severe long-term restrictions and interest held exclusively for resale are also made compulsory, operating where there is a lack of effective or desired control. We now consider (i), (ii) and (v) in turn.

Severe long-term restrictions

The Act states that these must 'substantially hinder the exercise of the rights of the parent company over the assets or management of [the subsidiary] undertaking', and the rights referred to are those 'in the absence of which [the undertaking holding them] would not be the parent undertaking' (S 229 (3)). FRS 2 provides further guidance, stating that only those restrictions identified by their effect in practice and leading to a loss of control should be considered. Disclosure rather than non-consolidation is preferred unless consolidation would be misleading.

Insolvency procedures where control passes to a receiver or liquidator is given as an example of such severe restrictions, but not necessarily those under a voluntary arrangement. Insolvency procedures abroad must be taken on their merits. Potential or minor restrictions are not sufficient. Davies, Paterson and Wilson (1992, p. 172) note that the most common use of this criterion is where there is political unrest where the subsidiary is set up.

Interest held exclusively with a view to resale

It is necessary that the subsidiary 'has not previously been included in consolidated group accounts prepared by the parent' (S 229 (3c)). FRS 2 restricts its application to either,

(a) '[where] a purchaser has been identified or is being sought, and [the interest] is reasonably expected to be disposed of within approximately one year of its date of acquisition, or

(b) [where] an interest . . . was acquired as a result of the enforcement of a security, unless the interest has become part of the continuing activities of the group or the holder acts as if it intends the interest to become so' (para. 11).

The aim of this exclusion and FRS 2's interpretation is to distinguish investments held as tradable assets from undertakings forming at some time part of the continuing operations of the group. Previously consolidated undertakings cannot be excluded. FRS 2 adds that criterion (a) is deemed to be satisfied 'if the sale is not completed within a year of acquisition . . . but if, at the date the accounts are signed, the terms of the sale have been agreed and the process of disposing of the interest is substantially complete' (para. 78d).

Activities of one or more subsidiaries too different

This mandatory exclusion is an embarrassment since, in the interval between the completion of the EC 7th Directive and its enactment into UK law, the generally accepted view as to the scope of consolidation changed radically. At the outset the UK position allowed subsidiaries to be excluded from consolidation at the directors' discretion if 'the business of the holding company and that of the subsidiary are so different that they cannot reasonably be treated as a single undertaking' (Companies Act 1985u, S 229). This was widely interpreted to allow exclusion of captive finance, banking and insurance subsidiaries. Partly at the instigation of the UK, the 7th Directive had made dissimilar activities a compulsory exclusion criterion.

With the widespread development of segmental reporting standards such as SSAP 25 and consequent improved information about the diverse business segments in a complex group, another view, that of the compulsory consolidation of all 'controlled' subsidiaries became dominant. The Financial Accounting Standards Board (FASB) in the USA had introduced a standard on segmental reporting as long ago as 1976 and led the way by issuing SFAS 94, *The Consolidation of All Majority-Owned Subsidiaries*, in 1987. In June 1987 the International Accounting Standards Committee issued IAS 27, *Consolidated Financial Statements and Accounting for Investments in Subsidiaries*, which also no longer allowed exclusion on the grounds of dissimilar activities, citing the existence of IAS 14, *Reporting Financial Information by Segment*. The UK was in an awkward situation.

By the time the Companies Act 1989 enacted the 7th Directive, its *mandatory* 'dissimilar activities' criterion was honed down by stating that it did 'not apply because some of the undertakings are industrial, some commercial and some provide services, or because they carry on industrial or commercial activities involving different products or provide different services' (Companies Act 1985a, S 229 (5)). ED 50 *Consolidated Accounts* narrowed the criterion further by limiting it to special category subsidiaries such as banking and insurance subsidiaries covered by Schedule 9 in the Companies Act. FRS 2 further narrowed the criterion, interpreting the mandatory exclusion as only applying where the activities

> are so different . . . that [the subsidiary's] inclusion would be incompatible with the obligation to give a true and fair view. It is exceptional for such circumstances to arise and it is not possible to identify any particular contrast of activities where the necessary incompatibility with the true and fair view generally occurs.   (para. 25c)

Indeed its explanatory note states that Schedule 9 special category companies do not now provide sufficient contrast to invoke the exclusion. One cannot help but conclude that the ASB has tried to overcome the UK's embarrassment, caught between EEC provisions it helped design and conflicting international requirements, by doing its best to define a null set!

Exclusion in practice

Skerratt and Tonkin (1994, p. 166) find that in a sample of 300 groups with 1992–93 year ends only fifteen had excluded subsidiaries. The most common grounds given for exclusion by these were insignificance (47 per cent), followed by lack of control/severe long-term restrictions (27 per cent), temporary control/held for resale (27 per cent). Another grounds, 'inclusion would be misleading', (7 per cent) is odd, unless it is a phrase which embraces 'too dissimilar activities' prior to FRS 2's stricter definition.

More than one parent

FRS 2 uses the exclusion criteria to achieve the effect that 'where more than one undertaking is identified as a parent of one subsidiary undertaking, *not more than one of those parents can have control* [as defined above]' (para. 62, emphasis added). Under these circumstances, either there exists *joint control*, in which case the undertaking should be accounted for not as a subsidiary undertaking, but as a *joint venture* (discussed in Chapter 4), or one of the parents may be suffering from *severe long-term restrictions*. Accounting for excluded subsidiaries is dealt with in Chapter 4.

Exercises

2.3 Explain the differences in purpose between exemption and exclusion criteria in the Companies Act 1985.
2.4 Assess in what ways the revised definition of a 'subsidiary undertaking' can be said to be an improvement over the definition of a 'subsidiary' prior to the Companies Act 1989.
2.5 Consider the following group structure (all proportions refer to voting rights):

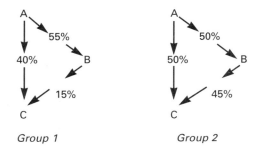

Group 1   Group 2

Required
(a) Assess whether C should be treated as a subsidiary undertaking of A in its consolidated accounts.
(b) Suppose three out of six of C's directors are members of the board of A. Would this affect your answer in (a)?
2.6 Memories plc owned a 60 per cent stake in Childtimes plc. In order to finance the growth of Childtimes, as a result of a decision by Memories plc's Board, an offer for sale of new shares in Childtimes was made. As a result of the new shares issued, Memories plc now only holds a 30 per cent stake in the enlarged company. The next largest shareholder is 5 per cent, and the remaining holdings are widely scattered. At the last three annual general meetings, Memories plc nominated candidates for all board vacancies, and all these were elected.

Required
Assess whether Childtimes is or should be a subsidiary undertaking of Memories plc.

QUASI-SUBSIDIARIES

The problems raised by the creation of quasi-subsidiaries had been apparently all but solved. Pimm (1990) suggests that undertakings could now be kept off-balance sheet only if the right to benefits was retained over a period in which control is relinquished, for example, where an investing company negotiates taking majority benefits with another partner which agrees to assume control with only minority benefits. Such a proposition and partner are only likely to exist if for commercial reasons the partner has congruent interests with the investing company. Because of the ease of adjusting transfer prices, management fees etc., it is difficult to see how such a partner could be persuaded to continue to act in a congruent way unless there were some arm-twisting ability present. If so, a dominant interest might be imputed.

Other examples cited by Pimm using the above principle include the so-called 'diamond structure', shown in Figure 2.2, where the larger share of benefits is obtained via an intermediate parent jointly controlled by the investing company and a third party, provided no other circumstances suggest the 'actual exercise of a dominant interest', for example.

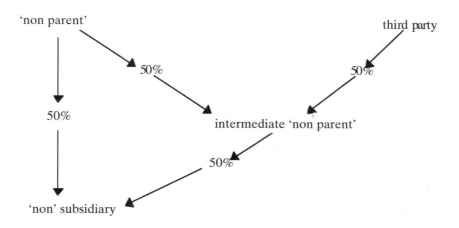

Figure 2.2 – Diamond structure

Also he suggests that where an investing company holds call options with rights to obtain a controlling stake but not exercisable until a *future* date, the Companies Act provisions discussed above would mean that the 'non' subsidiary would not be consolidated until the date in which the option could first be exercised.

It is difficult therefore to envisage straightforward schemes which can circumvent the Companies Act definitions. However, to make sure the stable door is bolted *before* the horse bolts, the ASC, and latterly the ASB, have continued to pursue off-balance sheet schemes. ED 49, *Reflecting the Substance of Transactions in Assets and Liabilities*, was issued in 1990, updating ED 42 by incorporating the effects of changes brought about by the Companies Act 1989 and providing detailed application notes. FRS 5, *Reporting the Substance of Transactions*, was issued by the ASB in April 1994, following FRED 4 of the same title in 1993. Many of its provisions relating to quasi-subsidiaries are almost identical to ED 49 and are discussed here. Its objective is stated as being 'to ensure that the substance of an entity's transactions is reported in its financial statements. The commercial effect of the entity's transactions, and any resulting assets, liabilities, gains or losses, should be faithfully represented in its financial statements' (para. 1).

FRS 5 clearly draws on the ASB's draft *Statement of Principles* (1991) in its conceptual definitions of assets and liabilities. Its main impact will probably be on schemes not involving quasi-subsidiaries since most extant quasi-subsidiary schemes have been covered by the Companies Act itself. However, there are still ingenious and devious minds around!

Definition of quasi-subsidiaries
A 'quasi-subsidiary' is defined as

> a company, trust, partnership or other vehicle that, though not fulfilling the definition of a subsidiary [undertaking], is directly or indirectly controlled by the reporting entity and gives rise to benefits for that entity that are in substance no different from those that would arise were the vehicle a subsidiary. (para. 7)

and the term 'control of another entity' as 'the ability to direct the financial and operating policies of that entity with a view to gaining economic benefit from those activities' (para. 8).

Criteria for identification of quasi-subsidiaries ('the vehicle') include (emphases added):

(i)   disposition of the *benefits* arising from its *net* assets including the *risk*s inherent in them (para. 32).
(ii) whether an entity *controls* a vehicle, i.e. has in practice the ability to direct its financial and operating policies, including ownership and other rights and also,

   (a)   the ability to prevent others from directing those policies , or
   (b)   to prevent others from enjoying the benefits arising from the vehicle's *net assets*, or
   (c)   predetermining, through contract or otherwise, that it gains the benefits arising from its *net assets*, or is exposed to the risks inherent in them (paras 32–34).

FRS 5 points out that access to the whole inflows of a quasi-subsidiary and responsibility for its whole outflows are not necessary, as for example, the limiting of liability may be one factor in its setting up and further, its liabilities have prior claim over its assets (para. 96). Concerning criterion (ii) (b) the power of veto *per se* is not sufficient unless major policy decisions are taken in accordance with the wishes of its holder. Where a third party has the ability to determine major policy issues control is absent (such as pension fund trustees). Control need not be interventionist and can be predetermined (paras 97–98).

Accounting for quasi-subsidiaries

The existence of any quasi-subsidiaries in the consolidated financial statements must be disclosed. Quasi-subsidiaries are to be accounted for *as if* they are subsidiaries. A company is penalized for using them by having to provide additional *note* disclosures in the form of *summarized financial statements* for each one, including balance sheet, profit and loss, and cash flow statement with separate headings for each material item, with comparatives. Quasi-subsidiaries of a similar nature can be combined (para. 38). If the company has no subsidiaries, *pro forma* accounts consolidating the quasi-subsidiary must be produced in addition to and having prominence with the 'parent's' individual financial statements.

Whereas ED 42 justified the inclusion of its controlled non-subsidiaries in terms of the Companies Act's 'true and fair' override, it is interesting to note that FRS 5's justification for including quasi-subsidiaries is 'to give a true and fair view ... of the group *as* legally defined and thus constitutes additional information' (para. 100, emphasis added), presumably using S 226 (4) of the Companies 1985a. This brings the debate a full circle back to the Argyll case! FRS 5 also addresses when quasi-subsidiaries can be excluded from consolidation. It concludes the Act's criterion relating to the interest being held exclusively with a view to resale, including the fact that the quasi-subsidiary has not previously been consolidated is the only valid reason for exclusion other than immateriality (para. 101). If the Act's other exclusion criteria were met, the vehicle would not meet the definition of a quasi-subsidiary.

One specific reason the setting up of a quasi-subsidiary may still be desirable is to take advantage of FRS 5's 'linked presentation' provisions. Sometimes such a quasi-subsidiary is set up to 'ring fence' group items where their financing is without recourse to the rest of the group's assets. FRS 5's 'linked presentation' in which the item and its financing are presented together, with the latter being deducted from the former, may be available in the case of a quasi-subsidiary, but not if it were a subsidiary. The former is classed by the Companies Act as 'additional information' and so there is in principle no restriction on a 'linked presentation'. In the case of a 'subsidiary' the items have legally to be treated as assets and liabilities of the group unless they are linked within the subsidiary's own financial statements (para. 102).

Clearly considerable effects are caused by the changes in definitions flowing from the enactment of the Companies Act 1989 and FRS 5. These mainly affect balance sheet ratios rather than profits as former 'associated companies' are consolidated, and spring from three areas, the new consolidation of (i) subsidiaries excluded formerly on the grounds of dissimilar activities; (ii) 'subsidiary undertakings' which were not 'subsidiaries' under the old Act; (iii) 'quasi-subsidiaries' which were not 'subsidiaries' under the old Act.

A significant amount of empirical work on the impact of (i) has been carried out in the USA and is reviewed in Chapter 4. Evidence of (ii) in the UK is at present anecdotal, for example *Company Reporting* July 1991 (p. 29) reports that the effects of LEP consolidating as a subsidiary undertaking what was previously reported as an associated company changed gearing from 100 per cent in 1989 to 189 per cent in 1990. Category (iii) is likely to be smaller because of the probable effectiveness of the definition of a 'subsidiary undertaking'.

OTHER COUNTRIES

Because of similar problems with off-balance sheet schemes using quasi-subsidiaries, many countries are moving to a control-based definition, though the definitions of control and/or benefits vary slightly. In Australia the control basis for consolidated accounts, which are the only allowable form of group accounts, has been enshrined in company law since 1991. AASB 24, *Consolidated Accounts* (which applies to corporations), and AAS 24, *Consolidated Financial Reports* (which applies to public sector and non-corporate private sector entities), were issued in 1991 and under these standards, consolidated financial statements are required for *economic* entities (i.e. groups) which are headed by a *reporting* entity (which is defined very generally as one having users dependent on general purpose financial reports for information).

The consolidated financial statements must include the parent entity and all controlled entities. Control is defined as dominance over financial and operating policies 'so as to enable that other entity to operate with it in pursuing the objectives of the controlling entity'. It is unclear to what extent unified management would fall within this definition. Many of the UK Companies Act criteria are presented as general guidance as to relationships normally constituting control. It is difficult to see how differently the Australian criteria will operate in practice.

The Canadian standard, Section 1590, issued in August 1991, defines a subsidiary in terms of both *control* and also *the right and ability to obtain future economic benefits* from the resources of the enterprise and exposure to the related risks. Such rights and benefits include dividends, interest, fees, royalties or profits on intercompany sales. Control is a question of *fact*, and is presumed when another enterprise owns an equity interest that carries the right to elect the majority of directors, and not presumed if not – however, the presumptions can be rebutted. Guidance is given concerning factors to be considered in assessing control which are very similar to the UK's provisions. One difference from the UK is that options are only taken into account where the cost of exercising them is not economically prohibitive. The Canadian standard seems very similar to FRS 2 and FRS 5 taken together.

The USA is going through a transition. ARB 51, issued in 1959, amended by SFAS 94 issued in 1987, states that 'consolidated financial statements are usually necessary . . . when one of the companies in the group directly or indirectly has a controlling financial interest in the other companies. The usual condition . . . . is ownership of a majority voting interest . . . [and such an interest] is a condition pointing towards consolidation (para. 2). Exceptions are allowed if control were likely to be temporary or if control did not rest with the majority owner. All majority owned subsidiaries (subject to the above exceptions) must be consolidated. Dissimilar activities is not a valid reason for exclusion.

A Discussion Memorandum, *Consolidation Policy and Procedures*, was issued in 1991 followed by *Preliminary Views – Consolidation Policy* in 1994. The latter proposes the requirement that

A controlling entity (parent) shall consolidate all entities that it controls (subsidiaries) unless control is temporary at the time that entity becomes a subsidiary. For the purposes of this requirement, control over an entity is power over its assets – power to use or direct the use of the individual assets of that entity to achieve the objectives of the controlling entity.

Like FRS 2 it proposes locating the ambit of consolidation within *effective* rather than *legal* control. What is interesting about the definition is its proposed application to not-for-profit as well as business enterprises. Similar to the ASB's Draft Statement of Principles, the aspect of *deployment* is present, but instead of 'benefits and risks', other objectives are also embraced. Effective control is a matter of *fact* and the way it tackles the issue is different from the UK/EC approach. It lists *rebuttable presumptions* for such control, including the existence of a large minority interest (approximately 40 per cent or more) in the absence of other significant interests (approximately 20 per cent or more), ability to control the board, and the existence of control contracts. It distinguishes these from a list of *indicators of effective control*, including the ability to control the board nomination process and solicit proxies, to fill board vacancies till the next election, and retaining a minority stake, beneficial contractual relationships, or the ability to appoint some board members *after* having held a *majority stake*. This last is an interesting advance on the UK position, though it is probable that such devices could be caught by the UK's participating interest and actual exercise of dominant influence provisions, and may be thought of as examples of influence. It is interesting that options to acquire control are a rebuttable presumption if they can be acquired cheaply and only an indicator of control if they involve a significant outlay. The UK makes no such distinction. The *Preliminary Views* document also proposes that, unlike FRS 2, management *intention* that control should be temporary at the time of acquisition is *not* sufficient – this exclusion should apply only if the parent is *obliged* to relinquish control within a certain period, or if control has been relinquished before the date of the first consolidated statements for the period control is obtained. This movement from intentions to obligations can be seen in other areas in the UK, but not in the definition of a subsidiary (see Chapter 5 on reorganization provisions at acquisition).

International Accounting Standard 27, *Consolidated Financial Statements and Accounting for Investments in Subsidiaries*, was issued in 1988. Consolidation is required for all enterprizes controlled by the parent, where control is defined as 'the power to govern the financial and operating policies of an enterprise so as to obtain benefits from its activities' (para. 6). Specific criteria resulting in control match closely the UK Companies Act definitions, as do exclusion criteria, except that, as in the USA, dissimilar activities is not a valid reason for exclusion. Thus, there is considerable convergence between the approaches to group accounts in the Anglo-Saxon countries and the Anglo-Saxon dominated International Accounting Standards Committee. There are nuances of differences in definitions, but probably these will not have a major effect in practice.

There is some demarcation between EEC countries and the rest of the world, though this is reduced according to the options adopted. The 7th Directive makes the non-consolidation of subsidiaries with too dissimilar activities compulsory, whereas other international pronouncements make their consolidation compulsory! Unless EEC countries follow the UK lead in defining this exclusion so as to make it effectively a null set, this will be a clear difference between most EEC countries and the rest of the world. Potentially too, there could be differences between EEC countries over which 7th Directive options are chosen regarding the definition of a subsidiary undertaking, but Nobes (1990, p. 85) reports that all but Italy and Luxembourg include participating interest and either dominant influence or unified management. To the extent that the criterion of unified management is invoked, this too could constitute a difference from the rest of the world, depending on how, in practice, their respective definitions of 'control' are interpreted.

Exercises

2.7 Heartbeat plc owns a 40% stake in Aorta plc. The chairman of Heartbeat is a long-time friend of the chairman of Openheart plc, which owns a 20% stake in Aorta plc, and they frequently go to lunch and play golf together. Heartbeat plc has entered into a five year contract with Aorta plc to supply it with vital components. This contract will take 45% of Aorta's projected output over the period. Heartbeat plc holds an option to renew the contract with Aorta plc on similar terms for a further three years.

Required
Assess whether Aorta plc is a subsidiary undertaking of Heartbeat plc, or its quasi-subsidiary.

2.8 Speculator plc prepares its accounts to a year end of 31 December each year, and interim accounts to 30 June. It purchased on 2nd March 19X1 10% of the ten million 'B' shares of Flab plc, which until that time was wholly owned by Smartmoney plc. On 2nd April 19X1 it purchased an option to buy 100% of the five million 'A' shares, exercisable from 30 September 19X1 to 31 March 19X2. At 31 December 19X1, the share price of Flab plc had fallen so much that Speculator plc considered it extremely unlikely that it would be worth exercising the option before it expired on 31 March 19X2. Speculator plc's financial statements were completed and published by 28 February 19X2. However, Flab plc's share price made a dramatic recovery and the option to purchase was exercised on 20 March 19X2. Each of Flab plc's 'A' and 'B' shares have the same voting power in shareholder meetings, but the 'A' shares have the right to appoint directors with double the voting power of the equivalent number of 'B' shares.

Required
Assess whether Flab plc is a subsidiary undertaking of Speculator plc for (a) the interin accounts at 30 June 19X1, (b) the annual accounts at 31 December 19X2, and (c) the interim accounts at 30 June 19X2.

2.9 Gonforaburton plc (G) arranges for its merchant bank, Moron Greenfield plc (MG) to set up Secure Ltd (S), with a share capital of £50,000, all purchased by MG for cash. S is to purchase G's credit-card accounts and to finance the purchase from the proceeds of issuing tradeable loan notes. MG signs a ten year contract with G on behalf of S, stating that S can only trade in creditcard accounts or similar debt purchased from G. The contract between G and S is such that S's net cash flows after paying a management fee and insurance premium to G, are zero. Three per cent of the accounts are expected to be uncollectable, though G in return for the insurance premium underwrites the credit card accounts. G pays MG £60,000 for setting up S.

Required
Assess whether Secure plc should be included in the consolidated accounts of Gonforaburton plc, giving reasons.

2.10 Assess how far UK pronouncements have been successful in ensuring that all controlled undertakings are consolidated, and also how far such an objective is desirable.

SUMMARY

*Differing views exist as to **objectives** of group accounts, whether they should **amplify** parent individual accounts, acting as memorandum statements, or whether the group **economic entity** is primary and group accounts the principal or only accounts. Theoretical and empirical research suggests that published group accounts may have originated in the desire of creditors to monitor debt in groups. Opinions differ over whether a group should be defined in terms of the interests of parent shareholders, control by the parent entity, or by the ambit of management control. Control by the parent seems to be gaining acceptance world-wide.*

*In the UK, it is important to distinguish between the **group**, derived from the Companies Act definition of a **subsidiary undertaking**, and the **scope of consolidation**. The latter is based on the concept of control – engineered using the Act's exclusion criteria as interpreted by FRS 2, and on the inclusion of **quasi-subsidiaries** based on FRS 5. A group as a whole can be **exempt** (within aggregate size restrictions, or as part of a larger group with minority acquiescence), or particular subsidiaries are **excluded** from the consolidation (severe long-term restrictions, or held exclusively for resale). The mandatory exclusion category of 'too different activities' is defined by FRS 2 to apply extremely rarely if at all, thus minimizing the disharmony between EEC law and international requirements. **Control** is also the basis for consolidation in many other countries, but there are subtle differences in definition, which may or may not have a significant effect in prac-*

tice. Other entities, called **associated undertakings** *over which* **significant influence** *is exercised are also included in the group accounts using the equity method.*

The UK definition of a subsidiary undertaking, derived from the EC 7th Directive, is a mixture of **de jure** *(majority voting rights, majority directors voting rights, control contract, agreement with other shareholders) and* **de facto** *elements (participating interest and either dominant influence or unified management).*

FURTHER READING

UK practice
FRS 2 (1992) *Accounting for Subsidiary Undertakings*, Accounting Standards Board.
FRS 5 (1994) *Reporting the Substance of Transactions*, Accounting Standards Board.
Discussion Draft (1994) *Statement of Principles, Chapter 7, The Reporting Entity*, Accounting Standards Board.
Chalmers, J. (1992) *Accounting Guides – Accounting for Subsidiary Undertakings*, Coopers & Lybrand/Gee, Chapters 1–5.
Davies, M., Paterson, R. and Wilson, A. (1992) *UK GAAP – Generally Accepted Accounting Practice in the United Kingdom*, Ernst & Young/Macmillan, Chapter 4, Sections 1–5, Chapter 13, Sections 1–3.1, Chapter 24.
Pimm, D. (1990) Off balance sheet vehicles survive redefinition, *Accountancy*, June, pp. 88–91.

Conceptual/Historical
Bircher, P. (1988) The adoption of consolidated accounting in Great Britain, *Accounting and Business Research*, Winter, pp. 3–13.
Discussion Memorandum (1991) *Consolidation Policy and Procedures*, Financial Accounting Standards Board, Chapters 1 and 3.
Nobes, C. (1993) Group accounting in the United Kingdom, in Gray S.J., Coenenberg A.G. and Gordon P.D. (eds.), *International Group Accounting – Issues in European Harmonisation* (2nd edn), Routledge, pp. 229–39.
Whittred, G. (1987) The derived demand for consolidated financial reporting, *Journal of Accounting and Economics*, 9, pp. 259–85.

3

BUSINESS COMBINATIONS: CHANGES IN GROUP COMPOSITION

Most business combinations involve the purchase of an equity stake in other companies, rather than their individual assets, liabilities and goodwill, for reasons similar to those set out in the 'branch versus subsidiary' discussion in Chapter 1. In the parent's individual financial statements the business combination is treated as the purchase of an investment, and only in the consolidated financial statements are the assets and liabilities of all group members aggregated. Exceptions may occur if, for example, there is some doubt about the eventual size of liabilities of the target company, e.g. if there is an outstanding lawsuit, or if ease of immediate access to particular assets such as the target's cash or near cash is required.

In the consolidated financial statements, two main alternatives are available for accounting for such changes in group composition, the *acquisition* and *merger* approaches, termed respectively the *purchase* and *pooling-of-interests* approaches in the USA, and the acquisition and uniting-of interests approaches by IAS 22. The acquisition approach views the combination as an enlargement of the existing group, the merger approach as a change in the reporting group entity itself. The latter originated in the USA in the late 1940s and many would claim it was widely abused there in the 1960s and 1970s with its potential to boost reported profits as managements chose the most favourable treatment regardless of the true substance of combinations.

In the UK, merger accounting was made legal by the Companies Act 1981 (though a few groups had used it earlier). SSAP 23, *Acquisitions and Mergers*, issued in 1985, allowed the option of merger accounting in the consolidated financial statements under reasonably easily met criteria; unlike in the USA, the expected rush to use it with its touted 'cosmetic' advantages over acquisition accounting never materialized. Indeed the reported proportion using it declined from 13 per cent between 1982 and 1987 (Higson, 1990, pp. 44–46), to 1.4 per cent between 1988 and 1993 (*Company Reporting*, July 1993, p. 6). This was mainly because of an increasing awareness of the wide range of 'creative' accounting possibilities which were available in the UK under acquisition accounting – for accounting for goodwill, and in determining of the fair values of identifiable assets and liabilities at acquisition. The ASB has tackled this by issuing FRS 7, *Fair Values in Acquisition Accounting*, and FRS 6, *Acquisitions and Mergers*, in 1994, the latter tightly defining a merger in terms of the substance of the combination rather than its legal form to prevent a rush from acquisition accounting as its 'creative' possibilities are withdrawn (see Chapter 5). Merger accounting is rarely used in continental Europe. In practice in the UK, it has a much wider application than only for mergers *per se*, since it should always be used when a new parent is set up to structure *any* business combination and in many group reconstructions.

Readers wishing to place less emphasis on merger accounting are recommended only to read the 'Overview' and the 'Accounting Techniques' sections of this chapter to understand the intuitive underpinnings for business combinations.

OVERVIEW

This book focuses only on problems of accounting for business combinations and not on their financial, strategic or legal implications (see, for example, Cooke, 1986).

Combinations can take a variety of forms:

(a) A company's assets and liabilities can be acquired directly, or control over them gained indirectly by acquiring its equity.
(b) The consideration offered can take a variety of forms, e.g. a mix of voting shares, cash, non-voting shares and loan stocks.
(c) The corporate structure may be altered, e.g. a new parent company may issue shares to obtain voting control of all the existing companies.
(d) Either or both of the parties to the transaction may be liquidated or may continue.

In the following discussion, the term 'merger' or 'acquisition' is used as an intuitive economic description of the 'reality' of a combination, as an indication whether the combination satisfies detailed accounting criteria, and as labels for the accounting approaches adopted.

Intuitive concepts

Carl Gustav Jung, the celebrated psychoanalyst, talked of 'archetypes', subconscious images or symbols which influence our everyday perceptions but underlie them. Gut notions of 'acquisition' and 'merger' can be viewed in this way. The term 'acquisition' is used to describe a combination where one company dominates the other. The parent controls and the subsidiary undertaking is the appendage. The term 'merger' is used where the combination results in a confederation of companies, each constituent preserving its own identity/autonomy in a pooling or uniting rather than a domination. When Britain joined the EC in 1971, was it a merger or an acquisition?

The ASB's *Draft Statement of Principles, Chapter 7, The Reporting Entity*, issued in June 1994, distinguishes between the situation of a group 'continuing as a reporting entity as it acquires and disposes of entities in which it has invested' and that where 'entities combine not to enlarge one of them but to create a whole new reporting entity in a combination called a merger' (para. 5.1). FRS 6 defines a merger as 'A business combination which results in the creation of a new reporting entity formed from the combining parties, in which the shareholders of the combining entities come in a partnership for the mutual sharing of the risks and benefits of the combined entity, and in which no party to the combination in substance obtains control over any other, or is otherwise seen to be dominant, whether by virtue of the proportion of its shareholders' rights in the combined entity, the influence of its directors or otherwise' (para. 2), and talks about 'combining on an equal footing' (para. c). All other business combinations other than group reconstructions are acquisitions (para. 5).

Accounting approaches

Figure 3.1 shows differences between accounting approaches, assuming at this stage in the chapter that one company invests in the equity of another. The receiver of the

Description	Acquisition accounting	Merger accounting
Investment amount in parent's records	Fair value	Nominal amount of equity consideration
Pre-combination profits of combinee	Excluded from consolidated reserves	Included in consolidated reserves
Assets and liabilities of party receiving consideration for the combination	Fair value	Original company carrying amounts
Comparative figures	Not restated	Restated

Figure 3.1 – Comparison of acquisition and merger accounting

consideration under merger accounting is termed here the 'mergee' and under acquisition accounting the 'target' or the 'acquiree'.

Merger accounting – all mergee profits contribute to group profits in the combined statements, whereas under acquisition accounting the acquiree contributes to group profits only subsequent to the combination. The spurious use of merger accounting can thus artificially boost consolidated profits by including *pre*-acquisition profits. Using a nominal value investment and not restating identifiable assets and liabilities at acquisition is also criticized.

> Pooling of interests as a device for cost suppression occurred in Union Carbide's acquisition of Visking. At the time of acquisition, the book value of Visking was $25 million. The market value was considerably higher, for Carbide gave up $97 million in stock to acquire the firm. Because pooling accounting was used, only the book value of Visking was counted. The $72 million difference between market value and recorded value disappeared from view. The potential distortion arising from such treatment can be seen in a hypothetical case. If Carbide sold Visking for $50 million in cash, the receipts would be compared to the $25 million book value, and a profit of $25 million would accrue, even though the value received was nearly $50 million less than the original purchase price paid. (*Economic Report on Mergers*, Staff Report of the Federal Trade Commission, quoted in McLean, 1972, p. 32)

Acquisition accounting – because the acquiree's assets and liabilities are restated to fair values, resulting higher write-offs of such restated assets and any gradually amortized goodwill decreases subsequent consolidated profits, giving incentives to use the merger approach. However, in the UK acquisition accounting has also been abused as will be seen in Chapters 5 and 6.

Classification criteria

Accounting bodies world-wide have tightened merger accounting criteria to prevent its abuse. Two radically different accounting approaches are available, but there is a finely graduated spectrum of ways of combining two companies. Issues arose over whether there is a real distinction between acquisition and merger, whether it is possible to draw a policeable boundary, and in any case how rare mergers are in practice. Some consider 'real world' difference dictates the accounting technique, others, mere desire to massage profits. Still others argue that real mergers are so rare that merger accounting should be abolished. A 'real world' difference is now assumed and examined in intuitive, definitional and accounting technique senses.

ACCOUNTING TECHNIQUES

In a consolidated balance sheet assets and liabilities are normally the sum of their individual company counterparts under both acquisition and merger accounting. Mechanisms for aggregating equity components are different under each approach. A company's profits for each year are characterized as its 'memory' or 'history' of performance for that year. Its equity can thus be thought of as a storehouse of past 'history', past profits, past capital inputs. Figure 3.2 shows two stages in accounting for business combinations.

Merger accounting
FRS 6 comments that

> a [genuine] merger is a true mutual sharing of the benefits and risks of the combined entity. Therefore the joint history of the enterprises . . . will be relevant to the combined group's shareholders . . . If acquisition accounting were to be used, it would focus artificially on the history of only one of the parties to the combination, which would lead to a discontinuity in information reported on the combined entity.   (para. 49).

Stage	Nature of adjustment	Purpose
1	Recognising the investment consideration in the parent's *individual company* accounts	Reflecting the combination from the *company* perspective
2	*Consolidating* the parent and subsidiary's individual company accounts	Adding their accounts together to reflect the combination in the *group / consolidated* accounts

Figure 3.2 – Two-stage recording of business combinations

As far as possible consolidated share capital, share premium and reserves are constrained to equal the sum of their individual company counterparts. Consolidated profit and loss accounts represent the sum of results for the merged companies, regardless of when during the year the merger took place.

The consolidated financial statements represent merely a change in the scope of the accounts, showing combined results as if separate streams are put side by side and nothing added, nothing taken away. Comparative figures are restated, unlike under acquisition accounting (FRS 6, para. 17). A merger is analogous to a change in the ownership rights of both groups of shareholders rather than the purchase of one entity by another. Thus new historical costs at combination are unnecessary, and assets and liabilities of the combinee are not restated to fair values at acquisition, only adjusted to achieve *uniformity in group accounting policies* (para. 16).

Acquisition accounting

The acquirer is considered to have purchased the target company, buying out its shareholders. The consolidated financial statements treat the acquisition as an enlargement of an existing group. The subsidiary contributes only *after* the combination, as if the memory banks from a used computer were wiped clean on being added to the main computer, providing storage capacity from the time they were added.

The analogy for an acquisition is the purchase of the subsidiary's assets, liabilities and goodwill as separate items rather than its equity. Its results are included only *post*-combination since, if the components had been purchased separately, they would only contribute since their purchase. Likewise, historical costs would have been determined at that date, so the identifiable assets and liabilities of the subsidiary should be *restated to fair values* at the acquisition date (FRS 6, para. 20) to reflect their 'new' historical costs *to the group*. The difference between the fair value of the purchase consideration and identifiable assets and liabilities acquired is termed goodwill. Former shareholders of the combinee do not lose out by the exclusion of *pre*-combination profits since they have been bought out.

The merger approach stresses continuity of ownership powers and rights to share in benefits and risks (i.e. a reorganization of ownership interests among continuing owners) and the acquisition approach, discontinuity (i.e. the severing of the subsidiary's former ownership rights through purchase). The fact that a parent acquires a subsidiary does *not* itself preclude merger accounting, as the merger relationship is between former ownership parties, and though the parent controls the subsidiary, the owners of the parent after the combination will, under a merger, in large measure comprise the former owners of the subsidiary acquired, and definitions of a merger focus on non-domination by one set of former owners over another in the combined entity. The term 'acquired' is used loosely in these two different senses. There is much scope for abuse of merger accounting because of difficulties in assessing intentions of parties to the combination transaction. Figure 3.3 illustrates the effects of the approaches.

Company balances

	Parent retained profits	Subsidiary retained profits
Pre-acquisition	$Parent_{pre}$	$Subsid_{pre}$
Post-acquisition	$Parent_{post}$	$Subsid_{post}$

Consolidated balances

Merger accounting   Consolidated retained profits

Pre-combination	$Parent_{pre}$	$Subsid_{pre}$
Post-combination	$Parent_{post}$	$Subsid_{post}$

Acquisition accounting   Consolidated retained profits

Pre-acquisition	$Parent_{pre}$	
Post-acquisition	$Parent_{post}$	$Subsid_{post}$

Goodwill calc

$Subsid_{pre}$

Figure 3.3 – Group retained profits under acquisition and merger accounting

Example 3.1 – Acquisition and merger accounting at the combination date

Abbreviated balance sheets for Student plc and Union plc at 30 September 1995 immediately prior to the combination were as follows:

	Student £m	Union £m
Miscellaneous assets	570	495
Miscellaneous liabilities	(70)	(45)
Share capital	(400)	(300)
Share premium	(60)	(120)
Retained earnings	(40)	(30)

The companies combined on 30 September, with Student issuing new shares and exchanging them for 100 per cent of the share capital of Union on the basis of one share in Student for every two shares in Union. The fair value of the shares issued was £3 each, and the nominal values of shares in Student were £2 per share and £1 per share in Union plc.

Required

(a) Calculate the amount of consideration offered and show Student plc's individual company balance sheet at 30 September 1995 after recording the effects of the combination.

b) Calculate consolidated balance sheets at 30 September 1995 for the Student Union group under both the acquisition and merger approaches.

c) Compare the balance sheets in part (b) under both approaches.

Stage 1: Recording the combination in the parent's individual company financial statements

Nominal amount of Union shares acquired	= 300m x £1	=	£300m
Nominal amount of Student shares issued	= 300m x $\frac{1}{2}$ x £2	=	£300m
Fair value of Student shares issued	= 300m x $\frac{1}{2}$ x £3	=	£450m
Union's carrying value of net assets acquired	= £495m – £45m	=	£450m

Student plc's individual company balance sheet after recording the investment at nominal (consistent with merger accounting) and fair value (consistent with acquisition accounting) at 30 September 1995, together with the journal entries to record the effects of the business combination are as follows.

Student's individual company balance sheet at 30 September 1995 showing combination

	Nominal value investment		Fair value investment	
	Investment entry	Updated balances	Investment entry	Updated balances
Miscellaneous assets		570		570
Investment in Union	300	300	450	450
Miscellaneous liabilities		(70)		(70)
Share capital	(300)	(700)	(300)	(700)
Share premium-like accounts		(60)	(150)	(210)
Retained profits		(40)		(40)

The combination is thus recorded in the parent's balance sheet prior to consolidation. With the fair value investment, the excess of fair value over nominal amount is here transferred to share premium/share premium-like accounts, discussed below. If the investment had been purchased for cash, 'Miscellaneous assets' would have been credited – merger accounting would not then be appropriate as Union's shareholders would have been bought out.

Consolidating the individual company balance sheets
Student plc's balance sheet after recording the investment in Union is now consolidated with Union plc's balance sheet. Fair value issues under acquisition accounting are ignored.

Merger accounting
Merger accounting stresses continuity. Technically the merger cancellation process aims as nearly as possible at *perfect additivity* of equity components, i.e. to make each at the combination date the sum of the corresponding individual company equity components at that date immediately prior to recording the combination – in this case to make the consolidated equity components at 30 September 1995 the sum of the equity components of Student *prior to* recording the investment and Union. Thus the 'history' of the mergee is preserved in the consolidated balance sheet, and the cancellation process used in merger accounting to achieve this result is shown below:

Student Union Group – merger consolidation at combination date (£m)

	Student– nominal value investment	Union	Elimination	Consolidated
Miscellaneous assets	570	495		1,065
Investment in Union	300		(300)	—
Miscellaneous liabilities	(70)	(45)		(115)
Share capital	(700)	(300)	300	(700)
Share premium-like accounts	(60)	(120)		(180)
Retained profits	(40)	(30)		(70)

Assets and liabilities are added item by item to get consolidated amounts. The elimination entry cancels the nominal value issued against the nominal value acquired, reversing the effect of the *company* combination entry. The 'consolidated share capital' of the reporting entity is £700m (the parent's), and after cancelling the investment against the share capital of the subsidiary, the combined share premium/share premium-like accounts of the group *prior to* the reclassification entry would be £180m, and this total together with the other balances can be checked against the combined sums of balances of the two companies as if the merger had never taken place. The reclassification entry is explained below.

Check – consolidated equity under perfect additivity

Equity component	Student	+	Union	=	Consolidated
Share capitals	(400)	+	(300)	=	(700)
Share premiums	(60)	+	(120)	=	(180)
Retained profits	(40)	+	(30)	=	(70)

Acquisition accounting
The acquisition accounting cancellation process aims to eliminate the subsidiary's pre-acquisition equity (share capital, share premium and retained earnings) so that it only contributes post-acquisition.

Student Union Group – acquisition consolidation at combination date (£m)

	Student–fair value investment	Union	Pre-acq equity	Elimination	Consolidated
Miscellaneous assets	570	495			1,065
Investment in Union	450			(450)	—
Miscellaneous liabilities	(70)	(45)			(115)
Share capital	(700)	(300)	300		(700)
Share premium-like accounts	(210)	(120)	120		(210)
Retained profits	(40)	(30)	30		(40)
Pre-acquisition equity			(450)	450	—

To emphasise discontinuity of ownership, the column 'Pre-acq equity' lumps all pre-acquisition equity of Union into a single figure. This is surgically removed by cancelling the investment. Consolidated equity components at acquisition are thus merely the parent's. The result is the same as if Student had purchased *directly* Union's separate assets (£495m) less liabilities (£45m) by means of a share issue instead of gaining control of them via an indirect share in its equity.

Comparing acquisition and merger balance sheets
In the following consolidated balance sheets:

1. 'Share capital' (nominal value) is the same – the externally held share capital of the group.
2. The 'share premium-like accounts' under acquisition accounting of £210m relates to *one* company, Student. Union's 'share premium' is eliminated. Under merger accounting, the total share premium-like balances are included for *both* companies (£60m and £120m). The reason why 'share premium' type balances are greater for one company than two is because the premium on the fair value investment adds £150m to Student's original 'share premium' of £60m, larger than Union's 'share premium' of £120m. See below for the reporting of 'share premium-like accounts' in published financial statements.
3. Under acquisition accounting group retained profits at acquisition is only Student's. Under merger accounting, it is the sum of the two companies.

Student Union consolidated balance sheets at 30 September 1995

	Merger accounting	Acquisition accounting	Notes
Miscellaneous assets	1,065	1,065	
Miscellaneous liabilities	(115)	(115)	
Share capital	(700)	(700)	1
Share premium-like accounts	(180)	(210)	2
Retained profits	(70)	(40)	3

Share premium-like accounts

Three labels are usually used in the UK to report 'share premium-like' accounts:

(a) share premium account;
(b) merger reserve;
(c) other (consolidated) reserves.

The distinctions are made for legal and accounting standards' reasons. When learning the basic techniques of acquisition and merger accounting they are best thought of *as if* 'share premium', and the following legal sub-classifications for reporting purposes are better assimilated later, *after* the basic principles have been grasped.

Share premium accounts – under acquisition accounting, the excess of the fair value of any equity consideration given over its nominal value is normally classified in the parent's own accounts as 'share premium'.

Merger reserve in the parent's own accounts – the merger relief provisions of S 131 of the Companies Act 1985, which allow that if at least a 90 per cent holding is acquired, the excess does not have to be classified as 'share premium', are discussed later (page 66). Here it is enough to note that, if at least a 90 per cent holding is acquired and acquisition accounting is used, the excess is often classified in the parent's own accounts as a 'merger reserve' a quasi-share premium account with fewer restrictions on its use. As will be seen later, it is commonly used for the immediate write-off of goodwill, whereas the court's permission is required to use the 'share premium' account itself. In the acquisition accounting example above, the £150m 'premium' would probably be reported as a 'merger reserve' since a 90 per cent stake was acquired. The term *merger* in 'merger reserve' has nothing to do with merger accounting – it arises only when acquisition accounting is used in the consolidated financial statements in conjunction with statutory 'merger relief' 'being available (see p. 66).

Other consolidated reserves: the subsidiary's share premium account – in the merger accounting example, the combined share premium accounts in the consolidated balance sheet after merger cancellation comprised £180m – £60m relating to the parent and £120m relating to the subsidiary. The amount labelled 'consolidated share premium' in the consolidated accounts should refer to the same shares as the amount reported as 'consolidated share capital'. This means that the reported 'share premium' is the parent's share premium, i.e. £60m is reported as consolidated share premium, corresponding to the £700m consolidated share capital of the reporting entity – the *externally* held share capital of the group. The remaining £120m here, the subsidiary's share premium remaining after merger cancellation, is reported as 'other (consolidated) reserves', and also disclosed as a movement on 'other reserves' (FRS 6, para. 41). A similar restriction applies to 'capital redemption reserves', not examined here.

Reporting of share premium-like accounts

In Example 3.1, share premium-like accounts in reported consolidated 'Capital and Reserves' under the two approaches would be:

Merger accounting capital and reserves	£m
Share capital	700
Share premium	60
Other reserves - (uncancelled subsidiary share premium)	120
Retained profits	70
	950

Since the combination was a 90 per cent take-over, the premium on the issue would probably be classified as a 'merger reserve':

Acquisition accounting capital and reserves	£m
Share capital	700
Share premium	60
Merger reserve	150
Retained profits	40
	950

Example 3.2 – simple business combination after the combination date

Post-combination results: In the year to 30 September 1996, Student plc's assets increased by £100m and Union plc's by £45m, and their liabilities by £50m and £25m respectively. Neither company made any share issues or revaluations, so the increase in net assets for each company is assumed equal to the increase in retained profits.

Incorporating the information into Student's company balance sheet at acquisition (after recording the investment in Union) and also Union's, the individual company balance sheets at 30 September 1996 are as follows and below them, using the same cancellation approaches, consolidated balance sheets under both approaches:

Individual company balance sheets at 30 September 1996 (£m)

	Student		Union
	Nominal value investment	Fair value investment	
Miscellaneous assets	670	670	540
Investment in Union	300	450	
Miscellaneous liabilities	(120)	(120)	(70)
Share capital	(700)	(700)	(300)
Share premium-like accounts	(60)	(210)	(120)
Retained profits	(90)	(90)	(50)

Student Union Group – merger consolidation at 30 September 1996 (£m)

	Student– nominal value investment	Union	Elimination	Consolidated
Miscellaneous assets	670	540		1,210
Investment in Union	300		(300)	—
Miscellaneous liabilities	(120)	(70)		(190)
Share capital	(700)	(300)	300	(700)
Share premium-like accounts	(60)	(120)		(180) *
Retained profits	(90)	(50)		(140)

* £60m would be reported as 'share premium' and £120m as 'other (consolidated) reserves'

If no combination had taken place, individual company balance sheets at 30 September 1996 would have been (assuming post-acquisition results were unaffected):

Check company balance sheets at 30 September 1996 assuming no combination

	Student	Union	Addition
Miscellaneous assets	670	540	1,210
Miscellaneous liabilities	(120)	(70)	(190)
Share capitals	(400)	(300)	(700)
Share premiums	(60)	(120)	(180)
Retained profits	(90)	(50)	(140)

Adding these 'no combination' equity components demonstrates the merger cancellation solution still results in the perfect additivity of equity components, when compared to the cancellation table balances above.

Student Union Group – acquisition consolidation at 30 September 1996 (£m)

	Student–fair value investment	Union	Pre-acq equity	Elimination	Consolidated
Miscellaneous assets	670	540			1,210
Investment in Union	450			(450)	–
Miscellaneous liabilities	(120)	(70)			(190)
Share capital	(700)	(300)	300		(700)
Share premium-like accounts	(210)	(120)	120		(210) *
Retained profits	(90)	(50)	30		(110)
Pre-acquisition equity			(450)	450	–

*Reported as £60m 'share premium' and £150m as 'merger reserve'

Pre-acquisition equity is eliminated as before. The subsidiary only contributes post-acquisition (20) to Student's (90). The relationships in Figure 3.3 earlier can now be verified:

Consolidated balances

Merger accounting   *Consolidated retained profits*   = (140)

Pre-combination

Student$_{pre}$ (40)	Union$_{pre}$ (30)
Student$_{post}$ (50)	Union$_{post}$ (20)

Post-combination

Acquisition accounting   *Consolidated retained profits*   = (110)

Pre-acquisition

Student$_{pre}$ (40)	
Student$_{post}$ (50)	Union$_{post}$ (20)

Post-acquisition

Goodwill calc

Union$_{pre}$ (30)

Exercises

3.1 Compare consolidated equity components of Student Union group at 30 September 1996 under both approaches. How is £110m consolidated retained profits under acquisition accounting constituted?

3.2 Wholla plc obtains a 100 per cent interest in the equity of Bitta plc on 31 December 1995. Summarized balance sheets before the combination was effected were as follows:

	Wholla £m	Bitta £m
Miscellaneous assets	280	230
Miscellaneous liabilities	(100)	(80)
Share capital (£1 nominal)	(60)	(50)
Share premium	(20)	(10)
Retained earnings	(100)	(90)

A one-for-one share exchange was accepted by all Bitta plc's shareholders of Bitta plc. The fair value of each share in Wholla plc was £3.

Required
(a) Calculate the amount of consideration offered, and present Wholla plc's individual company balance sheet at 31 December 1995 immediately after recording the combination/investment.
(b) Calculate consolidated balance sheets at 31 December 1995 for the Wholla Group under both acquisition and merger approaches.
(c) Compare consolidated balances in part (b) under both approaches.
3.3 Over the year to 31 December 1996, Wholla plc's assets increased by £80m and Bitta plc's by £40m, and their liabilities by £40m and £20m respectively. Neither company made any share issues or revaluations, so that the increase in net assets for each is assumed equal to the increase in its retained profits.

Required
Prepare consolidated balance sheets at 31 December 1996 under both acquisition and merger accounting approaches.
3.4 Using the financial statements prepared in either 3.2 or 3.3, explain intuitively the principles of both cancellation approaches, using your calculations to illustrate your explanation.

Example 3.3 – Changing the offer conditions

The purpose of this example is to change the offer conditions so that the nominal value issued is not equal to that acquired, and that the fair value of the investment is not equal to the pre-acquisition equity of Union. The only thing which changes from Examples 3.1 and 3.2 is that the fair value of Student's shares at combination is £3.50 per share, and 3 shares of Student are offered for every 5 in Union. To save unnecessary repetition, we focus only on the 30 September 1996 balance sheets of Example 3.2 and merely change the investment amounts to reflect the changed offer conditions.

The 30 September 1996 balance sheets from Example 3.2 assume 2 for 1 offer, so that the nominal value of the investment is £300m and fair value is £450m (i.e. share premium/merger reserve of £150m), i.e.:

Individual company balance sheets at 30 September 1996 (£m) – 2 for 1 offer

	Student		Union
	Nominal value investment	Fair value investment	
Miscellaneous assets	670	670	540
Investment in Union	300	450	
Miscellaneous liabilities	(120)	(120)	(70)
Share capital	(700)	(700)	(300)
Share premium-like accounts	(60)	(210)	(120)
Retained profits	(90)	(90)	(50)

Required
(a) Calculate the nominal and fair values offered under the revised offer conditions and recast the individual company balance sheets of Student plc at 30 September 1996 to revise the investment amounts accordingly.
(b) Prepare merger and acquisition cancellation tables to produce consolidated balances for the

Student Union Group at 30 September 1996 under both approaches.
(c) Contrast the tables with those of Example 3.2.

The nominal amount of share capital acquired is £300m (100 %). The nominal and fair values of the consideration issued under the revised offer conditions is:

Offer terms	Nominal – merger accounting	Fair value – acquisition accounting
3 for 5	$300 \times \dfrac{3}{5} \times £2 = £360m$	$300 \times \dfrac{3}{5} \times £3.50 = £630m$

Individual company journal entries to record the combination

	Dr.(£m)	Cr.(£m)
Nominal value investment		
Investment	360	
Share capital		360
Fair value investment		
Investment	630	
Share capital		360
Share premium/merger reserve		270

To adjust the Example 3.2 individual company accounts, if the effects of the investment at £300m nominal and £450m fair value are removed, the individual company accounts at 30 September 1996 would become:

	Student £m	Union £m
Miscellaneous assets	670	540
Miscellaneous liabilities	(120)	(70)
Share capital	(400)	(300)
Share premium-like accounts	(60)	(120)
Retained earnings	(90)	(50)

And adjusting these balances for the journal entries reflecting the revised offer conditions:

Individual company balance sheets at 30 September 1996 (£m) – three-for-five offer

	Student		Union
	Nominal value investment	Fair value investment	
Misc. assets	670	670	540
Investment in Union	360	630	—
Misc. liabilities	(120)	(120)	(70)
Share capital	(760)	(760)	(300)
Share premium-like accounts	(60)	(330)	(120)
Retained profits	(90)	(90)	(50)

Under merger accounting, the investment changes from the previous example's £300m to £360m, and share capital from £700m to £760m. Other balances are unchanged. Under acquisition accounting, the investment is now £630m (nominal + £270m 'premium'), and 'share premium-like accounts' £330m = £60m (original) + £270m ('premium'). The nominal amounts of shares issued by Student plc differs from the nominal amount acquired. In real-life combinations there is no reason why the total nominal amount issued should even be close to that acquired. The fair value of the consideration is agreed. Then the current market value per share determines the number of shares to be issued, and the total nominal amount of these shares is the consequence. For any company, the relationship between nominal amounts and market values is often a historical accident, nominal values usually only being used to determine the number of shares available to be issued and actually issued.

Merger accounting

Merger cancellation is affected by nominal amounts of shares issued and acquired, not fair values. Intuitively appealing but unfortunately incorrect is:

Student Union Group – *incorrect* merger consolidation at 30 September 1996 (£m)

	Student–nominal investment	Union	Elimination	Consolidated
Miscellaneous assets	670	540		1,210
Investment in Union	360		(360)	—
Miscellaneous liabilities	(120)	(70)		(190)
Share capital	(760)	(300)	360	(700)
Share premium-like accounts	(60)	(120)		(180)
Retained profits	(90)	(50)		(140)

This incorrect process enables perfect additivity of consolidated equity components. The sum of individual company balance sheets at 30 September 1996 as if no combination had taken place would have been as follows, and the equity balances as above (i.e. perfect additivity).

Check – company balance sheets at 30 September 1996 assuming no combination

	Student	Union	Addition
Miscellaneous assets	670	540	1,210
Miscellaneous liabilities	(120)	(70)	(190)
Share capitals	(400)	(300)	(700)
Share premiums	(60)	(120)	(180)
Retained profits	(90)	(50)	(140)

However, group issued share capital held by external parties is £760m (Union's being held internally). Disclosure of this overrides the 'perfect additivity' principle discussed earlier. Thus only £300m of the Investment can be cancelled against the £300m share capital of Union at combination date to remove it and no more. Group share capital is £760m as required.

Progressive cancellation of excess nominal amount under merger accounting

What of the excess nominal amount issued, in the above example, £60m? (where a mix of consideration is given, it is based on the total consideration, the nominal amount of shares issued plus the fair value of other consideration). In the 1930s some argued it should be left a debit balance in 'Capital and Reserves' as a 'negative reserve' – it is *not* goodwill since it is based on nominal amounts (SSAP 23, para. 5). This would preserve the 'perfect additivity' of the components of combined equity. Wild and Goodhead (1994, p. 301) do not see any legal barriers to such treatment. FRS 6 does not address the issue and merely comments 'the difference that arises on consolidation does not represent goodwill but is deducted from or added to reserves' (para. a).

A more common approach is to *cancel* the excess nominal amount against existing consolidated reserves including retained profits. Which reserves can be used for this? Extant company law and accounting standards again do not comment. Here the excess is cancelled progressively, firstly against reserves with most restricted uses, and so on if necessary to the least restricted, retained profits – a procedure implicitly giving priority to preserving the additivity of retained profits.

Restrictions on availability of reserves for progressive cancellation

Which reserves are available for progressive cancellation is not clear in the UK. Some argue that the subsidiary's reserves can be used for progressive cancellation since they are already removed under acquisition accounting anyway. Others argue that combined reserves can be used except where there are possible statutory restrictions – for example on the use of group revaluation reserves and the parent's share premium account (e.g. Wild and Goodhead, 1994, p. 300). The 'subsidiary's reserves' stance is generally the most conservative, except some ambiguity remains, based on the second perspective, as to whether there are statutory restrictions on using the subsidiary's revaluation reserve.

In this chapter, the conservative 'subsidiary's reserves' position is taken, purely for simplicity, and there are no revaluation reserves. The author's view is that the position that 'combined reserves not subject to legal restrictions' is tenable – there seems no general prohibition against using combined reserves for progressive cancellation. There are highly convincing arguments against using the parent's share premium account and persuasive arguments against using combined revaluation reserves, but neither set is conclusive.

A probable route many groups will take is to cancel excess nominal amount firstly against the subsidiary's share premium account, then against the combined restricted reserves which are not barred by law from being used for similar purposes (the 'merger reserve' would appear to fall into this category) and finally group retained profits. This procedure preserves as far as possible 'perfect additivity' of group retained profits. Ultimately none of this affects distributable profits since these are a parent company and not a group matter in the UK. The interpretation and function of consolidated equity raises complex issues discussed further in Chapter 12.

Arguments for both stances are now reviewed. It is suggested that they are omitted at this stage without loss in continuity, and revisited if desired after the principles of merger cancellation have been mastered. Whichever stance is adopted, remaining uncancelled reserves are added to other group reserves of the same type to obtain consolidated balances. As discussed under 'share premium-like accounts' above, any remaining subsidiary share premium would be reported as 'other (consolidated) reserves'.

Arguments on availability of reserves for progressive cancellation (optional)

Combined reserves subject to statutory restriction stance
APB Opinion No. 16 unambiguously states that combined figures should be used in the USA. Possible statutory restrictions on this stance in the UK include the fact that under the Companies Act 1985, group 'revaluation reserves' cannot be used for another related purpose, the immediate write-off of goodwill, nor can group 'share premium' without the court's approval (see Chapter 5). Thus it can be persuasively argued by analogy that reserves of this type are not available.

Another argument specifically against the use of the parent's share premium is that in particular combinations as a result of progressive cancellation, it is conceivable that some of the parent's share premium would be 'used up' and so would not appear in the consolidated balance sheet. This contravenes a long-held convention that reported consolidated share capital and premium of the group should represent balances attributable to the parent's shareholders (see arguments under 'share premium-like accounts' above). S227 of the Companies Act 1985 requires group accounts to 'give a true and fair view . . . so far as concerns members of the [parent] company', which could be interpreted to mean that the full issue details of the parent's shares should appear in the consolidated statements.

The goodwill analogy for not using combined revaluation reserves is not completely conclusive. Two relevant Companies Act 1985 requirements pull in opposite directions. Schedule 4, para. 61 allows in the preparation of consolidated accounts 'such adjustments (if any) as the directors of the holding company think necessary', but para. 62 states that 'the consolidated accounts shall, in giving the information required by paragraph 61, comply in so far as is practicable with . . . the other requirements of this Act as if they were the accounts of an actual company'. Whereas goodwill write-off has an individual company accounts counterpart (*pace* para. 61) merger cancellation does not (*pace* para. 62).

Subsidiary's reserves only
This seems the most conservative position, and the comparison with acquisition accounting is a powerful argument. However, the merger concept means that both sets of revaluation reserves in principle, belong to the combined entity. This differs from the concept of an acquisition, where the subsidiary's revaluation reserves are pre-acquisition and thus not part of the group. Does this therefore mean that, as part of group revaluation reserves, they are unavailable using the argument of the goodwill write-off analogy above? This line of argument is tricky – following it to its ultimate conclusion even the subsidiary's share premium might not be available. It could be countered by arguing that combined revaluation reserves only become group revaluation reserves *after* progressive cancellation. We are entering the realms of medieval scholastic argument here!

Other matters
If nominal value issued is less than the nominal value acquired, the 'deficit' would be credited to a consolidated capital reserve. In the USA the existence of no par value shares allows companies to define nominal amount issued as equal to that acquired, so the progressive cancellation issue does not arise. This is not possible in the UK. Davies, Paterson and Wilson (1992, p. 263) comment that if the subsidiary had made a bonus issue of their own shares before the combination to make the nominal value acquired equal to that issued, no difference would result. Reserves would then have been 'capitalized' as a consequence.

Example 3.3 continued

In this example excess nominal value debit is £60m (i.e. £360m investment less the £300m nominal share capital of Union). The equity components available for progressive cancellation are 'share premium' and 'retained profits'. The former is more restricted and is used first, and here we have no need to consider the wider question of whether to use the group's reserves or the subsidiary's. The excess is cancelled *progressively* against 'share premium', and if it were necessary (not in this case) against retained profits.

Student Union Group – merger consolidation at 30 September 1996 (£m)

	Student–nominal value investment	Union	Elimination	Consolidated
Miscellaneous assets	670	540		1,210
Investment in Union	360		(360)	—
Miscellaneous liabilities	(120)	(70)		(190)
Share capital	(760)	(300)	300	(760)
Share premium-like accounts	(60)	(120)	60	(120) *
Retained profits	(90)	(50)		(140)

*£60m reported as 'share premium' and £60m as 'other (consolidated) reserves'

Perfect additivity has been sacrificed to ensure that externally held share capital is correct. Comparing with the above incorrect 'perfectly additive' statement, share capital is 'overstated' by £60m and other reserves 'understated' by the same amount. Effectively £60m of 'other' reserves have been 'capitalized'.

Check – comparison with perfect additivity at 31 December 1996 assuming no combination

	Student – no combination	Union	Perfect additivity	Above balances	Difference
Miscellaneous assets	670	540	1,210	1,210	
Miscellaneous liabilities	(120)	(70)	(190)	(190)	
Share capital	(400)	(300)	(700)	(760)	(60)
Share premiums/share premium-like accounts	(60)	(120)	(180)	(120)	60
Retained profits	(90)	(50)	(140)	(140)	

Acquisition accounting

Acquisition accounting can be likened to radical surgery where an organ may be completely removed to prevent the growth of a tumour, merger accounting to progressive surgery where the aim is only to remove the diseased portions of the organ. The cancellation table is as follows:

Student Union Group – acquisition consolidation at 30 September 1996 (£m)

	Student– fair value investment	Union	Pre-acq equity	Elimination	Consolidated
Miscellaneous assets	670	540			1,210
Investment in Union	630			(630)	—
Miscellaneous liabilities	(120)	(70)			(190)
Share capital	(760)	(300)	300		(760)
Share premium-like accounts	(330)	(120)	120		(330) *
Retained profits	(90)	(50)	30		(110)
Pre-acquisition equity/ goodwill			(450)	630	180

*Reported as £60m 'share premium' and £270m 'merger reserve'

The only difference from the original case is that the investment has changed from £450m to £630m with consequent changes to Student's own share capital and share premium/merger reserve. Pre-acquisition equity treatment is identical. Because the investment is larger than pre-acquisition equity acquired (= net assets acquired £495m – £45m) the excess of £180m ('goodwill' or more accurately 'excess on consolidation') is shown here as a consolidated asset. SSAP 22 recommends it is written off immediately against reserves, or capitalized and amortized over its estimated useful life. Such write-off is ignored here and further discussed in Chapter 4. Variations in fair value of the consideration given affects the acquisition approach; nominal amount changes for a given fair value have no effect.

If the fair value of the investment were to be less than the fair value of the identifiable assets and liabilities acquired, the so-called 'negative goodwill' situation arises. At present this will be merely treated as a negative reserve. Its accounting treatment is discussed in Chapter 5.

Example 3.4 – Part cash offer with minority interest

The offer conditions are now changed again to show what happens when the parent offers shares and cash, but only obtains a 90 % interest in the subsidiary. In this case there will remain a 10 per cent minority (non-controlling) interest in the subsidiary. Again we focus on the 30 September 1996 balance sheets of Example 3.2 (one year after the combination) and merely change the investment amounts to reflect the changed offer conditions. These are that the fair value of Student's shares at combination is £3.50 per share, and 3 shares of Student plus 50p in cash are offered for every 5 in Union. 90 % of the shareholders in Union accept the offer.

The 30 September 1996 balance sheets from Example 3.2, which assume the nominal value of the investment is £300m and fair value is £450m (i.e. share premium/merger reserve of £150m) are shown below, i.e.:

Individual company balance sheets at 30 September 1996 (£m) – Example 3.2

	Student		Union
	Nominal value investment	Fair value investment	
Miscellaneous assets	670	670	540
Investment in Union	300	450	
Miscellaneous liabilities	(120)	(120)	(70)
Share capital	(700)	(700)	(300)
Share premium-like accounts	(60)	(210)	(120)
Retained profits	(90)	(90)	(50)

Required
(a) Calculate the nominal and fair values offered under the revised offer conditions and recast the individual company balance sheets of Student plc at 30 September 1996 to revise the investment and miscellaneous assets amounts accordingly.
(b) Prepare merger and acquisition cancellation tables to produce consolidated balances for the Student Union Group at 30 September 1996 under both approaches.

Calculating the amount of the investment

Nominal amount of Union shares acquired = 90 % $\times$ 300m $\times$ £1 = £270m

Investment	Shares	Cash	Total
Nominal	90% x 300m x $\frac{3}{5}$ x £2 = £324m	90% x 300m x $\frac{1}{5}$ x £0.50 = £27m	£351m
Fair value	90% x 300m x $\frac{3}{5}$ x £3.50 = £567m	90% x 300m x $\frac{1}{5}$ x £0.50 = £27m	£594m

Individual company journal entries to record the combination

	Dr.(£m)	Cr.(£m)
Nominal value investment		
Investment	351	
Cash		27
Share capital		324

	Dr.(£m)	Cr.(£m)
Fair value investment		
Investment	594	
Cash		27
Share capital		324
Share premium-like accounts		243

To adjust the Example 3.2 individual company accounts, if the effects of the investment at £300m nominal and £450m fair value are removed, the individual company accounts would become:

	Student £m	Union £m
Miscellaneous assets	670	540
Miscellaneous liabilities	(120)	(70)
Share capital	(400)	(300)
Share premium	(60)	(120)
Retained earnings	(90)	(50)

And adjusting these balances for the journal entries reflecting the revised offer conditions, we get:

Student plc – individual company balance sheets at 30 September 1996 (£m)

	Nominal investment	Fair value investment
Miscellaneous assets	643	643
Investment in Union	351	594
Miscellaneous liabilities	(120)	(120)
Share capital	(724)	(724)
Share premium-like accounts	(60)	(303)
Retained profits	(90)	(90)

Consolidating the balance sheets

Merger accounting approach

Student Union Group – merger consolidation at 30 September 1996 (£m)

	Student nominal inv	Union	Minority interests	Elimination	Consolidated
Miscellaneous assets	643	540			1,183
Investment in Union	351			(351)	—
Miscellaneous liabilities	(120)	(70)			(190)
Share capital	(724)	(300)	30	270	(724)
Share premium-like accounts	(60)	(120)	12	81	(87)*
Retained profits	(90)	(50)	5		(135)
Minority interests			(47)		(47)

*Reported as £60m 'share premium' and £27m 'other (consolidated) reserves'

Since Student has only acquired a 90% stake in Union, the remaining 10%, called the minority interest, is shown separately as a single figure (i.e. 10% × (300 + 120 + 50) = 47), effected by a separate column. Consolidated retained profits are Student's plus 90 per cent of Union's, i.e. 90 + 90% × 50 = 135. Progressive cancellation still applies. Parent shareholders (of Student and those of Union who accepted the offer) have a direct interest in the parent and thus a 90% indirect interest in Union. Minority (non-controlling) interests only have an interest in a part of the group (a 10% interest in Union). Minimal disclosure is usually given to the minority.

Perfect additivity of retained profits: Minority retained profit has to be included to demonstrate this, though 'consolidated retained profits' in consolidated balance sheets refers to the parent's share only.

Retained profits *as if* no combination effected	= £90m (Student) + £50m (Union)	= £140m
Total consolidated retained profits	= £135m (Majority) + £5m (Minority)	= £140m

Acquisition accounting approach

Student Union Group – acquisition consolidation at 30 September 1996 (£m)

	Student fair value inv	Union	Minority interests	Pre-acq	Elimination	Consoli-dated
Miscellaneous assets	643	540				1,183
Investment in Union	594				(594)	—
Miscellaneous liabilities	(120)	(70)				(190)
Share capital	(724)	(300)	30	270		(724)
Share premium-like accounts	(303)	(120)	12	108		(303)*
Retained profits	(90)	(50)	5	27		(108)
Minority interests			(47)			(47)
Pre-acq equity / goodwill				(405)	594	189

*Reported as £60m 'share premium' and £243 'merger reserve'

Again, a minority interest column has been introduced, identical in this simple example to merger accounting. Pre-acquisition equity is now 90 % of share capital, share premium/merger reserve and retained earnings of Union at acquisition, i.e. 90 % of £300m, £120m, and £30m respectively. The excess of the investment at £594m over the parent's share of equity at acquisition (90 % × (300 + 120 + 30) = £405m, = parent's share of net assets, 90% × (495 – 45)) is a 'goodwill' figure of £189m. When acquisition accounting adjustments are introduced in Chapters 4 and 5, minority interests under acquisition and merger accounting will differ.

Exercises

3.5 The purpose of this example is to change the offer conditions so that the nominal value issued is not equal to that acquired, and that the fair value of the investment is not equal to the pre-acquisition equity of Bitta. The only thing which changes from Exercises 3.2 and 3.3 is that Wholla offers 3 of its shares for every 2 in Bitta, when the fair value of its shares was £3 per share. The 31 December 1996 individual company balance sheets of Example 3.3 after recording the investment amounts in the earlier examples (where the nominal amount of the investment was £50m and its fair value £150m) are as follows:

Individual company balance sheets at 31 December 1996 (£m) – Example 3.3

| | Wholla | | Bitta |
	Nominal value investment	Fair value investment	
Miscellaneous assets	360	360	270
Investment in Union	50	150	
Miscellaneous liabilities	(140)	(140)	(100)
Share capital	(110)	(110)	(50)
Share premium-like accounts	(20)	(120)	(10)
Retained profits	(140)	(140)	(110)

Required
(a) Calculate the nominal and fair values offered under the revised offer conditions and recast the individual company balance sheets of Wholla plc at 31 December 1996 to revise the investment amounts accordingly.
(b) Prepare merger and acquisition cancellation tables to produce consolidated balances for the Wholla Bitta Group at 31 December 1996 under both approaches.
(c) Contrast the tables with those of Exercise 3.3.
(d) Assess the departure from 'perfect additivity' under merger accounting.

3.6 The purpose of this exercise is to show the effects where the offer is for shares and cash, and only a 90 % stake is purchased. Taking the facts of Exercise 3.3 as given and the 31 December 1996 balance sheets as in the previous example. Assume Wholla acquires a 90% interest in Bitta at 31 December 1995 by offering three shares plus 20p in cash for every two shares in Bitta. At the combination date the fair value of the shares issued is £3 per share.

Required
(a) Calculate the nominal and fair values offered under the revised offer conditions and recast the individual company balance sheets of Wholla plc at 31 December 1996 to revise the investment amounts accordingly.
(b) Prepare merger and acquisition cancellation tables to produce consolidated balances for the Wholla Bitta Group at 31 December 1996 under both approaches.

3.7 Pounce plc is always on the lookout for likely acquisition candidates. It recently acquired a 90 % interest in Quivering plc on 30 December 1994, when the latter's retained profits were £140m. The offer was 5 shares in Pounce plc (nominal amount £1, quoted price £2) plus £0.25p in cash for every 4 shares in Quivering plc (nominal amount 50p). Land included in Quivering plc's accounts was valued at the date of the combination at £40m (cost £30m) but no adjustment has been made. The combination transaction, including the cash consideration, still has not been recorded by Pounce plc , since its finance director wishes to be certain he has chosen the most favourable treatment. The balance sheets of both companies at 31 March 1995 are:

Balance sheets at 31 March 1995 (£m)

	Pounce	Quivering
Fixed assets	500	100
Other net assets	300	270
	800	370
Share capital	200	80
Share premium	250	130
Retained profits	350	160
	800	370

Required

Prepare consolidated balance sheets for the Pounce Group at 31 March 1995 under both acquisition and merger accounting principles and compare and contrast them. Ignore the write-off/amortization of goodwill subsequent to acquisition.

3.8 The following balance sheets at 30 November 1995 (in £m) are extracted from the published financial statements of Acquisator plc and Mergee plc.

	Acquisator	Mergee
Assets:		
Investment in Mergee	75	
Other assets except cash	225	150
Cash	10	5
	310	155
Liabilities and equity:		
Miscellaneous liabilities	100	60
Share capital (£1 shares)	60	20
Share premium/merger reserve	70	30
Retained profits	80	45
	310	155

Notes

1. Acquisator made an offer of two £1 ordinary shares plus 16 2/3 p in cash for each £1 ordinary share in Mergee on 28 February 1995. The offer was accepted by 90 % of the shareholders in Mergee. At the time of the combination, the market value of the shares in Acquisator was £2 per share.
2. At the date of the combination, Mergee's retained profits were £30m.

Required

Using the above financial statements to calculate relevant information, explain to the Chief Accountant of Acquisator, the main differences in consolidated balance sheet effects between merger and acquisition accounting, and assess why he might prefer one to the other.

DEFINING MERGERS AND ACQUISITIONS

The following section can be omitted without loss in continuity by those wishing only to focus on acquisition accounting.

The main issue for standard-setters has been how to 'ring fence' true mergers to prevent the spurious misuse of merger accounting. Acquisitions are defined as the business combinations that are left after defining mergers! Whilst technically merger accounting is extremely important, merger accounted combinations currently are rare. *Company Reporting* in its July 1993 issue (pp. 6-8) found only 1.4 per cent of business combinations including equity consideration used merger accounting over the five years to 1993. A subsequent tightening up of loopholes and abuses in acquisition accounting by FRS 7, *Fair Values at Acquisition* (1994) (see Chapter 5) will probably increase the frequency of merger accounting somewhat, though it will still remain rare.

Merger accounting has never been widely practised in the UK. The 1969–70 and 1970–71 Surveys of Published Accounts each refer to six merger accounted combinations, including Rowntree Mackintosh, Cadbury Schweppes and Trust House Forte. ED 3, *Accounting for Acquisitions and Mergers* (1971), never became a standard. Section 56 of the then Companies Act (1948) required a share premium to be recorded on all share issues and many interpreted this as preventing the nominal amount investment necessary for the merger accounting approach. *Shearer* v. *Bercain* (1980) appeared to confirm this.

The so-called merger relief provisions of the Companies Act 1981 removed the obligation to record a share premium where 'an issuing company has by an arrangement including the exchange of shares, secured at least a 90 per cent holding in another company' (now Companies Act 1985's. 131), thus enabling merger accounting. The Act also side-stepped a restriction prohibiting parents from distributing pre-acquisition profits. ED 31 in 1982 led to SSAP 23, *Accounting for Acquisitions and Mergers* (1985), which defined criteria under which merger accounting was an *option*. The ASB, building on ED 48 (1990), found it necessary in FRS 6, *Acquisitions and Mergers*, in 1994, to redefine merger criteria in terms of substance over form and to make merger accounting mandatory if they are met. It also tackled avoidance schemes resulting from SSAP 23.

UK merger definition

The Companies Act 1985, Sch 4A s.10 allows the *option* of merger accounting if all the following criteria are met:

(i)   that the final stake held by the parent company and its subsidiaries is at least 90 per cent in nominal value of shares with unlimited participation rights in both distributions and assets on liquidation;

(ii)   that this limit was passed by means of an equity share issue by the parent or subsidiaries;

(iii)   that in the offer mix, the fair value of the consideration given by parent or subsidiaries other than in equity shares should be less than 10 per cent in *nominal* amount of the equity shares issued;

(iv)   that the adoption of merger accounting accords with generally accepted accounting principles or practice (currently based on FRS 6's definitions and criteria below).

FRS 6's requirements are additional to these. It defines a merger as,

A business combination which results in the creation of a new reporting entity formed from the combining parties, in which the shareholders of the combining entities come together in a partnership for the mutual sharing of the risks and benefits of the combined entity, and in which no party to the combination in substance obtains control over any other, or is otherwise seen to be dominant, whether by virtue of the proportion of its shareholders' rights in the combined entity, the influence of its directors or otherwise.

(para. 2)

Any business combination not meeting this definition is an acquisition, except possibly for new parent companies or group reconstructions (para. 5), discussed later.

It sets out five criteria to make this conceptual definition operational, stressing substance over form and the need to consider all relevant information in applying the criteria (para. 56). Merger accounting must be used if all five of the criteria below and Companies Act 1985 requirements are satisfied, but acquisition accounting must be used if any are not met. FRS 6's main criteria (paras. 6–11) shown in italics, are followed by its explanation of their detailed application (paras 60–77), which can be omitted at first reading.

(i)   Portrayal of parties

No party to the combination is portrayed as either acquirer or acquired, either by its own board or management or by that of another party to the combination.

A rebuttable presumption is made that the combination is an acquisition if a premium is paid over the market value of the shares acquired. Other factors suggestive of the nature of the combination, whilst not individually conclusive (paras 60–62) are its form, plans for the combined entity's future operations (including whether closures or disposals were unequally distributed between parties), proposed corporate image (name, logo, location of headquarters and principal operations), and the content of communications of a publicly quoted party with its shareholders.

(ii) Participation in new management structure

All parties to the combination, as represented by the boards of directors or their appointees, participate in establishing the management structure for the combined entity and in selecting the management personnel, and such decisions are made on the basis of a consensus between the parties to the combination rather than purely by the exercise of voting rights.

Differing from ED 48, FRS 6 recognizes that even in a genuine merger the parties should be free to choose their management, and equal participation on the combined board is not necessary. Such management could come from a single party, but in this case genuine participation must be demonstrated. However, *consensus* decision-making in choosing, rather than voting power against the wishes of one of the parties to the merger, is necessary, and informal as well as formal management structures must be considered. Only management structure decisions made in 'the period of initial integration and restructuring at the time of the combination' need be considered, taking into account their short and long-term effects (paras 63–66).

(iii) Relative sizes

The relative sizes of the combining entities are not so disparate that one party dominates the combined entity merely by virtue of its relative size.

Such domination would be presumed if one party is substantially larger – this is inconsistent with the concept of a merger as a substantially equal partnership between the combining parties. A *rebuttable presumption* of dominance is made if, when considering the proportions of the combined equity attributable to the shareholders of the combining parties, any party is more than 50 per cent larger than each of the others. Factors such as voting or share agreements, blocking powers or other arrangements can be deemed to reduce or increase this relative size influence. If rebutted, reasons must be disclosed (paras 67–68).

(iv) Offer mix

Under the terms of the combination or related arrangements, the consideration received by equity shareholders of each party to the combination, in relation to their shareholding, comprises primarily equity shares in the combined entity; and any non-equity consideration, or equity shares carrying substantially reduced voting or distribution rights, represents an immaterial proportion of the fair value of the consideration received by the equity holders of that party. Where one of the combining entities has, within the period of two years before the combination, acquired equity shares in another of the combining entities, the consideration for this acquisition should be taken into account in determining whether this criterion has been met.

To prevent shares with unusual rights getting round the restriction in Companies Act that non-equity consideration should not exceed 10 per cent of the nominal amount of equity shares issued, FRS 6 requires that all but an immaterial portion of the fair value of the consideration should be in the form of equity shares, defining equity shares more rigorously than the Act (following FRS 4, *Capital Instruments*), excluding shares with limited rights to receive payments not calculated on underlying profits, assets or equity dividends, or with effective limitations on participation rights in any winding up surplus, or redeemable contractually, or at the option of parties other than the issuer (para. 2).

Cash, other assets, loan stock and preference shares are cited as examples of non-equity consideration (para. 69). All arrangements made in conjunction with the combination (including, e.g., vendor placings) must be taken into account unless independently made by shareholders. *Substantially* reduced voting or distribution rights indicate an acquisition, though some reduction may be compatible with a normal merger negotiating process. Where a peripheral part of one of the businesses of one of the combining parties (i.e. one disposable without material effect on the nature and focus of its operations) is excluded from the combined entity, shares or proceeds of sale distributed to its shareholders are not counted as consideration in determining offer mix (paras 69–74).

(v)   Final stake/no protected holdings

No equity shareholders of any of the combining entities retain any material interest in the future performance of only part of the combined entity.

Mutuality in sharing risks and rewards in the combined entity is deemed absent where one party's equity share depends on the post-combination performance of the entity previously controlled by it; where earnouts or similar performance-related schemes are included in the merger arrangements; or where the statutory ending stake (90 per cent) is not achieved. It is, however, permissible to allocate holdings based on the subsequently determined value of a specific asset or liability (paras 75–77).

Other anti-avoidance criteria

Boundaries: The combination transaction is to be considered as a whole, to include any related arrangements in contemplation of the combination, or as part of the process to effect it. FRS 6 also makes clear that parties to the combination include the management of each entity and the body of its shareholders as well as its business (para. 57). Financial arrangements in conjunction with the transaction are to be included.

Consideration: If convertible shares or loan stock are converted into equity as part of the combination they are to be treated as equity (para. 12). The acquisition cost/consideration includes shares issued and owned by subsidiary undertakings (Co. Act 1985 Sch 4A S 9(4)). FRS 6 applies analogously to entities without share capital (para. 59).

Time boundaries: Divested elements of larger entities are not eligible for merger accounting since they are not independent enough to be considered separate from their former owners until they have a track record of their own. An exception is if the divestment can be shown to be peripheral (see criterion (iv) above). Shareholdings acquired within the two years before the combination for non-equity consideration or for consideration with reduced equity rights must be included in assessing the criteria (para. 73).

Example 3.5 – Applying FRS 6's operational criteria

Take the facts of Example 3.4. Assume additionally that
(a) on the combined board, five directors were from Student and two from Union.
(b) on 30 November 1996 one half of the business of Union was disposed of at a consolidated accounting profit of £24m.
(c) the group's name is to be 'The Student Union Group'.

Required
Using FRS 6's criteria assess whether the combination is a merger or an acquisition for accounting purposes.

Final proportional stake
The final holding of 90 per cent satisfies Companies Act requirements that at least 90 per cent of the acquired company's equity must be held by the new parent.

Offer mix
The consideration given in the form other than in equity is £27m, i.e. 8.33 per cent (= 27 / 324), of the *nominal* value of the equity consideration. Also there is no evidence that the shares issued contain reduced voting or participation rights.

Size test rebuttable presumption
In the combined equity, the ratio of Student's former shareholders nominal to Union's is 400:324, i.e. 1.235:1, so Student is less than 50 per cent larger than Union in terms of its share of equity in

the combined entity – in this example there are not different classes of equity, so such simple comparison is possible. This is *not conclusive* – the actual criterion is 'dominance merely as a result of relative size', but here there is no presumption to rebut. Merger accounting seems supportable.

Other criteria
Is the disposal 15 months after the combination was 'entered into in contemplation of that combination' (para. 56, anti-avoidance clauses) intended, e.g. merely to magnify future disposal profits? APB Opinion 16, not binding, provides food for thought – is the disposal in the ordinary course of business or to close duplicate facilities? Disparity in management representation is not evidence against a merger provided there was *consensus participation* in setting up the joint structure and in personnel selection (board minutes of the combining companies and correspondence may give evidence). The group name does not suggest domination of one party by another.

If merger accounting is indicated under all these criteria it *must* be used. Otherwise acquisition accounting *must* be used.

Evaluation of the merger definition

A merger is more than a friendly take-over. FRS 6 considers genuine mergers are rare (para. 44). Prior to FRS 6, earlier UK definitions and attempted definitions focused on detailed criteria alone, rather than embedding such criteria within a core central definition. FRS 6's conceptual definition shows its main concern is about the relationship between the former owners of old entities in the new entity and their relative powers therein (though for certain purposes 'parties' is defined more widely than shareholders (para. 57)). It considers whether each set of separate owners has sufficient clout to claim legitimately that they have a real say in the joint control over deployment of the new reporting entity's resources, and whether they really have the ability to benefit and suffer by their deployment. It is not about a relationship between *entities*. As a result of the merger share swap, one company owned by the former shareholders may become the wholly owned subsidiary of another, but in the combined entity, one group of former owners should not dominate another. All the original shareholder groups must have stakes in the expanded parent. Where entities rather than former owners jointly control another entity, the appropriate accounting would be for a joint venture (see Chapter 4).

Detailed operational criteria

FRS 6 errs on the side of preventing spurious mergers. Earlier merger (pooling-of-interests) definitions focused purely on defining detailed criteria. In the USA, Accounting Research Bulletin No. 40 had in 1950 suggested: voting shares should be the basic medium of exchange, that previous ownership interests should continue in substantially the same proportion, relative sizes should not be too disproportionate, managements of all constituents should continue as influential, business activities of constituents should be similar or complementary, and that no substantial minority interest should exist post-combination.

Vigorous debate ensued there over whether a merger (pooling) required continuity of ownership interests, of management interests or even of existing business activities. Ownership continuity became generally accepted, complementarity of businesses was dropped, and other criteria more tightly defined. In the USA, the 1960s and 1970s were characterized by a combinations boom and by attempts to erode merger accounting criteria to enable it to be applied even more widely. Controversial research reports prepared for the Accounting Principles Board by Wyatt (1963) and Catlett and Olsen (1968) concluded no theoretical basis existed *at all* for pooling of interests accounting on the grounds that all combinations involved the acquisition of one entity by another; that the medium of consideration was irrelevant. Foster (1974) later echoed this – the idea of 'pooling as a transaction between separate groups of stockholders' is

> a flight of fantasy. One almost expects a wink when this rationale is advanced. We know that corporate officers negotiate the transaction from end to end. Indeed, we know that many corporations employ personnel for the purpose of identifying likely acquisition candidates. And potential acquisitions are reviewed by the corporation to

determine if the purchase or pooling method will look better.

Such radical conclusions were unacceptable. Instead attempts were made to fill in the cracks rather than prohibit one approach altogether. Consequently criteria became more legalistic. By the issue of the current US standard APB Opinion number 16 in 1970, the definition of a pooling had become extremely tortuous.

Even if one accepts 'continuity of ownership rights and powers' as the core concept for a merger it is difficult to discern managements' and owners' intentions regarding this. The other criteria can instead be viewed as pragmatic means for assessing such intentions. In Figure 3.4, it is proposed here that it is instructive to arrange these into three classes; *verifiable signs* of ownership continuity, *circumstantial evidence* of such continuity, and *anti-avoidance clauses* to ensure it is not just cosmetic.

Analysis of operational criteria	Examples of criteria
Verifiable signs	No acquirer identifiable
	Offer mix substantially voting equity
	Final proportional equity stake maintained
	Voting rights continue
Circumstantial evidence	Mangement structure continues
	Relative sizes not too unequal
	Substance of business continues
	Complementarity of businesses
Anti-avoidance clauses	Inclusion of prior share rights
	Offer part of a single plan
	No linked avoidance transactions
	No immediate large disposals

Figure 3.4 – Operational characteristics of 'continuity of ownership' perspective

Continuity of management, relative size, continuity of business substance, and even complementarity of businesses can in this framework be viewed not as substantive in themselves, but as providing circumstantial evidence of ownership continuity (relative to other parties) to participate in benefits and risks and to deploy economic resources. If one business is wound up, it is possible that this is decided by the *joint* owners, but this is unlikely if relative sizes are very different. From a 'continuity of ownership rights and powers' perspective these are not *necessary* conditions. They are rebuttable presumptions – managements must show why merger accounting is appropriate when they are violated.

UK precursors

The first UK attempt at defining a merger, the still-born ED 3 (1971) proposed criteria which were similar to ARB 40 issued in the USA 20 years previously. Three of its four criteria were, however, quantified – a minimum equity content in the offer mix of 90 per cent in value (with identical rights), the final stake to be at least 90 per cent of the voting and non-voting equity capital (i.e. less than 10 per cent of the minority interest remaining), and a size test (ending equity voting rights held by any one of the constituent companies not to be more than three times those of any other). The fourth required the substance of the main business of the constituent companies to continue, which differed from continuation of management and complementarity provisions of ARB 40. The offer also had to be approved by the offeror's voting shareholders. One feels that the ASSC still had not yet settled wholeheartedly on continuity of ownership rights and powers as the implicit core concept of a merger.

The first UK standard SSAP 23, *Accounting for Acquisitions and Mergers* (1985) overcompensated. In terms of Figure 3.4, it focused purely on externally verifiable signs. Its criteria for the merger accounting *option* were:

(i)   the offer to be made to all holders of equity and voting shares not already held; and
(ii) the minimum *ending stake* to be at least 90 per cent of all equity shares (each class taken separately) and 90 per cent of the votes; and
(iii) the maximum permissible *starting stake* to be 20 per cent of all equity shares (taking each class separately) and 20 per cent of the votes; and
(iv) a minimum final *offer proportion* of 90 per cent of the *fair value* given for equity capital to be in equity, and a minimum final offer proportion of 90 per cent of the fair value given for voting non-equity in equity or voting non-equity (para. 17).

SSAP 23 did not include relative size or continuing management criteria, but deliberately focused on share-for-share exchanges without significant resources leaving the combining companies (para. 3). Their shareholders only had to be in a position to continue. Such concentration on the form of the transaction spawned schemes satisfying the above criteria but enabling what many would not regard as 'true' mergers to use merger accounting, for example:

(1) *vendor rights*: although the parent's shares were offered to the subsidiary's shareholders (meeting the merger criteria), an intermediary agreed to purchase them and immediately offer them back to the *parent's* shareholders as a rights issue. However, if the parent had made the rights issue and from the proceeds offered cash, the combination would have had to be treated as an acquisition.
(2) *vendor placings*: as above except the intermediary placed the shares with outsiders.
(3) *placement of starting holdings*: the parent would 'sell' an inconvenient initial holding of more than 20 per cent to a friendly outsider just prior to the offer and buy it back just afterwards.

The narrow drawing of the group 'boundary' meant that in the first two schemes a share-for-share exchange has taken place within SSAP 23's group 'boundary' and the schemes which convert the target's shareholdings into what is in reality a cash offer take place just beyond the boundary. In the USA and in FRS 6 anti-avoidance measures implicitly take such linked transactions within a wider group 'boundary' in determining acquisitions or mergers. SSAP 23 provided a verifiable definition, but not of a merger! The enactment of the EU 7th Directive into the revised Companies Act 1985 tightened SSAP 23's minimum final offer proportion from 90 per cent of fair value to 90 per cent of the nominal value of equity issued.

Other comparisons

FRS 6 contains an interesting mix of the three categories in Figure 3.4. Comparing it with extant US (APB Opinion No 16) and international standards (IAS 22), a key change since APB Opinion 16 was issued in 1970 is FRS 6's development of the concept of substance over form. IAS 22 defines a 'uniting of interests' as one where neither party can be identified as the acquirer, derived from previous Canadian practice, but FRS 6 more explicitly focuses on portrayal of the combining parties, suggesting detection guidelines.

APB Opinion 16 contains no size test, and whereas IAS 22 makes general comments that the fair value of one enterprise must not be significantly different from another (para. 16), FRS 6 hones the criterion to that of effective domination because of disparate size and makes a rebuttable presumption of dominance where one party's share of the combined equity is more than 50 per cent larger than each of the others. Davis (1991, p. 103) comments that less than 1 per cent of his 1971–82 sample of USA combinations would have been poolings (mergers) had a similar size test been in force there.

APB Opinion 16 does not consider management continuity. Whereas IAS 22 merely comments that 'managements of the combining entities participate in the management of the combined entity' (para. 14), FRS 6 reflects that this is only circumstantial evidence, by requiring consensus in establishing management structures and selecting personnel, not overridden by voting power. How easy this will be to enforce is another matter.

IAS 22 has no quantitative restrictions on offer mix or ending stake, merely requiring that 'the substantial majority, if not all, of the voting common shares of the combining enterprises are exchanged or pooled' (para. 16). APB Opinion 16 will only allow consideration other than common voting stock to be issued to mop up fractional shares and, e.g., dissenting shareholders. It will not allow any pro-rata distribution of cash or other consideration (para. 47). FRS 6 allows pro-rata non-equity consideration only up to 10 per cent of the nominal value of equity consideration. Both APB Opinion 16 and FRS 6 agree that the final proportional (voting) equity stake must be at least 90 per cent.

Whereas IAS 22 requires that all parties maintain substantially the same voting rights as well as interests relative to each other in the combined entity as before (para. 16), both FRS 6 and its US counterpart consider how this can be achieved. All but a small portion of the fair value of the consideration should be in 'equity' shares. Its use of FRS 4's definitions prevent shares with peculiar rights being used. Whilst these 'substance over form' requirements are less specific than in APB Opinion 16, they potentially embrace a wider set of circumstances. Both IAS 22 and FRS 6 exclude preferential stakes in formerly held parts of the combined entity.

FRS 6 uses all-embracing *anti-avoidance* provisions – the combination transaction is to be considered as a whole to include any related arrangements in contemplation of the combination or as part of the process to effect it (para. 42), which precludes vendor rights and vendor placing schemes. Parties to the combinations include managements and bodies of shareholders (para. 57). Merger accounting cannot be used where one party is a non-peripheral business divested from a larger entity, until it has a track record. Unlike APB Opinion 16, FRS 6 does not quantify divestment time limits or the definition of 'peripheral'. APB Opinion 16 includes further very detailed anti-avoidance provisions requiring for example that from the date the merger is initiated until it is concluded the combining parties must not hold more than 10 per cent of the voting stock of any combining company; that the combined company must not intend or plan to dispose of a significant part of the assets of the combining companies within two years after the combination other than in the ordinary course of the business or to close duplicate facilities (para. 48). It has spawned a whole anti-avoidance industry. IAS 22 only considers anti-avoidance measures in a very general conceptual sense.

Complementarity or continuity of the substance of businesses (per ED 3) are universally dropped, probably reflecting the fact that in modern business these provide only very loose circumstantial evidence. Overall, FRS 6 seems the most successful current standard in grounding its criteria within an overall conceptual definition. It most clearly distinguishes circumstantial evidence and anti-avoidance elements (unlike SSAP 23). Only time will tell whether FRS 6's more conceptual criteria improve enforcement possibilities over specific quantified rules which some regard as arbitrary.

Alternative views

Not all authors agree on continuity of ownership control and participation in mutual benefits and risks as the core merger criterion. Parker (1966) argued the most important question was that of asset valuation. To justify the carry forward of 'old' historical costs under merger accounting, there had to be continuity in business activity. Otherwise it was incorrect to match costs to current revenues of what was in essence a different entity. He argued that day-to-day changes in ownership claims in companies are ignored for accounting purposes, the entity being regarded as independent of its owners. Thus, continuity of *ownership* was not vital.

Edey (1985) argued that the 'no significant resources leaving the group' criterion (SSAP

23) was consistent with the Companies Act 1981's intent to recognize a business need to lift the share premium requirement in share-for-share exchanges. He argues that this protects creditors and shareholders, and such protection is not diminished if significant resources do not leave the group. It implicitly treats a share swap as if it is a transaction in the secondary market. Whether business need is a sufficient basis for a merger definition is debateable.

FRED 6 (1993) had floated the idea of whether merger accounting should be abolished, whether augmented disclosures could be used rather than a different accounting approach – Willott (1993, p. 99), for example, considers that individual groups should only be able to justify departures from acquisition accounting by invoking the Companies Act 1985's general true and fair override (s. 226(5)). Even if genuine mergers do exist, abolition benefits would still include reduced policing costs of enforcing definitions and the removal of the misleading accounting effects of 'spurious' mergers. However, costs would be those of spurious uniformity. FRS 6 found little support for abolition (Appendix III, para. 27).

Exercises

3.9 Indicate whether individually each of the following circumstances, according to FRS 6's criteria, indicates a merger, an acquisition or is irrelevant.
  (a)   Overarching plc made a share for share swap and ended with a 95 per cent overall stake in Underpinned plc.
  (b)   Both businesses continue in the combined entity.
  (c)   The offer had a total fair value of shares issued of £300m (nominal amount £175m), and a total cash component of £16m.
  (d)   Both companies are in similar industries.
  (e)   The former shareholders in Overarching plc now hold 4/7 of the equity in the company after recording the combination and the former shareholders of Underpinned plc hold 3/7.
  (f)   All shares in Overarching plc have equal voting rights and rights to participate in future profits.
  (g)   A merchant bank employed by Overarching plc has agreed to buy the shares it issued to the shareholders of Underpinned plc for cash. Overarching plc has contracted with the bank to acquire these shares from the merchant bank by means of the proceeds of a rights issue to its own shareholders.
  (h)   Six months after the combination, half the business of Underpinned plc was sold off at a large profit as a result of changed market conditions.
  (i)   On the board of directors of Overarching plc after the combination, the directors' representation from the former two companies is equal to the voting rights of their respective shareholders in the new reporting entity.
3.10 In exercises 3.6 and 3.7 assess on the basis of FRS 6's quantitative criteria alone, whether each should have been accounted for as an acquisition or as a merger.
3.11 Ditto for exercise 3.8.

FURTHER ACCOUNTING MATTERS

Consolidated profit and loss

Merger accounting: the combined entity's results should include the results of all the combining entities from the beginning of the financial year in which the combination took place, and in all financial statements comparatives should be restated as if the entities had been combined in the earlier period, only adjusted to achieve uniformity of accounting policies (FRS 6, para. 16). Merger expenses are to be charged through the profit and loss account at the merger date (para. 19) on the grounds that they are akin to ongoing reorganization and restructuring costs in a continuing entity (para. 51).

Acquisition accounting: results of acquired companies are only included from their date of acquisition and comparatives are not restated (para. 20). Fair value adjustments at acquisition may affect post-acquisition expenses. Certain acquisition expenses can be 'capitalized' as a part of the 'cost' of the investment (see Chapter 5).

Example 3.6 – Consolidated profit and loss account in the year of combination

The profit and loss accounts for two companies, Teacher plc and Learner plc, for the year ended 31 December 1995 were as follows. Teacher had obtained a 100 per cent interest in Learner on 31 March 1995. Assume under acquisition accounting that goodwill at acquisition of £80m is to be capitalized and gradually amortized over a ten-year period.

	Teacher 12 months	3 months up to comb	Learner 9 months since comb	Total for year
Sales	500	100	160	260
Cost of sales	(250)	(40)	(80)	(120)
Depreciation	(60)	(4)	(12)	(16)
Other expenses	(120)	(10)	(28)	(38)
Net profit	70	46	40	86

Required

Prepare consolidated profit and loss accounts for the year ended 31 December 1995 for the Teacher Learner Group under both acquisition and merger approaches, and compare them.

Goodwill amortization is £8m p.a. (i.e. 80/10). Over the post-acquisition period of 9 months goodwill amortization under acquisition accounting will be £6m (= 8 × 9/12).

Teacher Learner Group – consolidated profit and loss account
year ended 31 December 1995

	Merger	Acquisition
Sales	760	660
Cost of sales	(370)	(330)
Depreciation	(76)	(72)
Other expenses	(158)	(148)
Goodwill amortization	—	(6)
Net profit	156	104

The merger accounting consolidated profit and loss account is the sum of the first and last columns above, two streams being merged into one. Comparative figures would be restated as if the companies had always been combined. Under acquisition accounting, Learner only contributes since acquisition, and so the first column is added to the 9 month column of Learner. Comparative figures are not restated. Goodwill amortization in the profit and loss account only occurs under acquisition accounting if the 'capitalization and gradual amortization' treatment is adopted (see Chapter 4). In more complex examples the net assets of the target company at acquisition would be restated to fair values, thus increasing post-acquisition cost of sales and depreciation over merger accounting (these aspects are ignored here).

Because only post-acquisition profits, and hence revenues and expenses of the target are included in the year of acquisition, merger accounting seems attractive for groups wishing to maximize reported profits, revenues and expenses in that year, and profits in subsequent years. Note that under both methods the subsidiary will contribute a full year's revenues and expenses in subsequent years.

New Parent Companies and Group Restructurings

FRS 6 makes clear that the accounting approach for business combinations is based on the substance of the transaction and not on its legal form.

The legal form of a business combination will normally be for one company to acquire shares in one or more others. This fact does *not* make that company an acquirer [in an accounting sense]. . . . Similarly the question of whether the combined entity should be regarded as a new reporting entity [i.e. a merger] is *not* affected by whether or not a new legal entity has been formed to acquire shares in others.

(para. 46 emphasis added)

Where a new parent company is set up to acquire the shares of the combining parties, the criterion is whether or not 'a combination of the companies other than the new parent would have been an acquisition or merger', i.e. whether one of the parties can be identified as acquirer or not (para. 14). In acquisition-type combinations, the party identified as in substance the acquirer should be merger accounted with such a company and all the others must be acquisition accounted. In merger-type combination all parties are merger accounted with the newly formed parent company (para. 14). FRS 6's provisions apply equally to any other arrangements achieving similar results (para. 15).

Merger accounting is an option for various types of group restructurings, the transfer of ownership of a subsidiary between group companies, the addition of a new parent to a group, transfer of shares in subsidiaries to a new non-group company with the same shareholders as the group's parent, and the combination into a group of two companies previously under common ownership (para. 2). The conditions are: merger accounting is not prohibited by companies legislation, the ultimate shareholders remain the same and rights relative to each other are unchanged, and no minority interest is altered by the transfer (para. 13).

Example 3.7 – Using a new parent company

Abbreviated balance sheets for Student plc and Union plc at 30 September 1996 are :

	Student £m	Union £m
Miscellaneous assets	670	540
Miscellaneous liabilities	(120)	(70)
Share capital	(400)	(300)
Share premium	(60)	(120)
Retained earnings	(90)	(50)

A new holding company, Graduate plc had been set up on 30 September 1995 to issue new shares and exchange them for 100 per cent of the share capital of both companies, one of its shares for every share in Student plc and three shares for every five in Union. The fair value of the shares issued was estimated at £3.50 each, and nominal values were £2 in Graduate plc, £2 in Student plc, and £1 in Union plc . Graduate plc has no other assets and liabilities. The retained profits of Student and Union at that date were £40m and £30m respectively.

Required
Prepare consolidated balance sheets at 30 September 1996 for the Graduate Group under the following assumptions:
(a) Graduate plc is set up by both Student plc and Union plc to effect a merger between the two companies.
(b) Graduate plc is a creation of Student plc to enable it to acquire Union plc .

Recording the combination in the parent's individual company financial statements

Case(a) – merger with Union

Number of Union shares acquired   =   £300m / £1   =   300m

Nominal amount of Graduate shares issued	=	300m × $\frac{3}{5}$ × £2	=	£360m

Number of Student shares acquired	=	400m / £2	=	200m

Nominal amount of Graduate shares issued	=	200m × $\frac{1}{1}$ × £2	=	£400m

Graduate plc is accounted for as merging with both Student plc and Union plc , so both investments are recorded at nominal amount.

Case (b) – acquisition of Union

Fair value of Graduate shares for Union	=	300m × $\frac{3}{5}$ × £3.50	=	£630m

Here Graduate plc is accounted for as merging with Student plc and acquiring Union plc, so the investment in Student is recorded at nominal amount, and Union's at fair value. The individual company and consolidated balance sheets are shown below:

Graduate's individual company balance sheet at 30 September 1995

	Nominal value investments	Nominal Student – Fair value Union
Investment in Student	400	400
Investment in Union	360	630
Share capital	(760)	(760)
Share premium-like accounts		(270)

The consolidation process assuming merger with Student plc, in the first case together with merger with Union, and secondly acquisition of Union, are shown below:

Graduate Group – merger with Union at 30 September 1996

	Graduate	Student– nominal inv	Union– nominal inv	Merger elimination Student	Merger elimination Union	Consoli- dated
Miscellaneous assets		670	540			1,210
Investment in Student	400			(400)		—
Investment in Union	360				(360)	—
Misc. liabilities		(120)	(70)			(190)
Share capital	(760)	(400)	(300)	400	300	(760)
Share premium- like accounts	—	(60)	(120)		60	(120)*
Retained profits	—	(90)	(50)			(140)

*Reported as £120m 'other (consolidated) reserves', representing subsidiary's share premium uncancelled

Graduate Group – acquisition of Union at 30 September 1996

	Graduate	Student–nominal inv	Union–fair value inv	Merger elimination Student	Pre-acq equity	Acq-uisition elim Union	Consoli-dated
Miscellaneous assets		670	540				1,210
Investment in Student	400			(400)			—
Investment in Union	630					(630)	—
Misc. liabilities		(120)	(70)				(190)
Share capital	(760)	(400)	(300)	400	300		(760)
Share premium-like accounts	(270)	(60)	(120)		120		(330) *
Retained profits	—	(90)	(50)		30		(110)
Pre-acq/ goodwill					(450)	630	180

*Reported as £270m 'merger reserve' and £60m 'other (consolidated) reserves'

The offer terms for Union were identical with Example 3.3 earlier. In the offer for Student the total nominal amount of shares issued equals the nominal amount acquired. This allows a demonstration that the above procedure results in the 'same' consolidated balance sheets as if Student plc merged with Union plc or acquired it, on the terms of Example 3.3. A very minor presentational difference is that 'consolidated merger reserves' here is £270m, and £60m, the subsidiary's share premium account is reclassified as 'other consolidated reserves', whereas the £60m in Example 3.3 was reported as 'consolidated share premium' in the earlier example, as it there related to the parent.

MERGER RELIEF AND MERGER ACCOUNTING

Whilst 'merger relief' criteria (Companies Act 1985, S 131) enabled merger accounting by allowing that a share premium need not be recorded if a 90 per cent holding in another company was acquired, this individual company accounting treatment is *not* a merger definition. Many companies satisfying S 131 will not meet FRS 6's criteria for merger accounting and then acquisition accounting *must* be used. However, if merger accounting criteria are met, the criteria for merger relief are always satisfied. FRS 4, *Capital Instruments*, issued in 1993, ensures that the investment amount recorded by the parent is consistent with the consolidation approach adopted. If merger accounting is used on consolidation, the investment can be recorded at nominal amount (FRS 4, para. 21(c)). In all other circumstances where a company issues shares to acquire a subsidiary the net proceeds (the fair value of the consideration received) must be credited to shareholders funds (para. 10). The complete S 131 criteria are intricate and are not discussed further here.

Under acquisition accounting, the excess of the fair value over nominal amount would normally be recorded as share premium. Where merger relief criteria are met, the credit is usually made to a separate reserve not share premium (FRS 6, para. 43), often termed a 'merger reserve', often used in practice for the immediate write-off of goodwill, since unlike share premium, its use does not require the court's permission (see Chapter 5).

Exercises

3.12 The profit and loss accounts for Big Cheese plc and Hard Cheddar plc, for the year ended 31 March 1996 were as follows. Big Cheese had obtained a 100 per cent interest in Hard Cheddar on 30 November 1995. Assume under acquisition accounting that goodwill at acquisition of £90m is to be capitalized and gradually amortized over a five year period

	Big Cheese 12 months	8 months up to comb	Hard Cheddar 4 months since comb	Total for year
Sales	900	500	200	700
Cost of sales	(500)	(250)	(100)	(350)
Depreciation	(100)	(60)	(30)	(90)
Other expenses	(220)	(100)	(60)	(160)
Net profit	80	90	10	100

Required

Prepare consolidated profit and loss accounts for the year ended 31 March 1996 for the Big Cheese Group under both acquisition and merger approaches, and compare them.

3.13 The individual company balance sheets of Wholla plc and Bitta plc at 31 December 1996 are:

	Wholla	Bitta
Miscellaneous assets	360	270
Miscellaneous liabilities	(140)	(100)
Share capital (£1 nominal)	(60)	(50)
Share premium	(20)	(10)
Retained earnings	(140)	(110)

On 31 December 1995, a new holding company, Mega plc, was established, which had issued new shares and exchanged them for 100 per cent of the share capital of Wholla plc and Bitta plc, making a one-for-one offer for the shares in Wholla and a three-for-two offer for the shares in Bitta. At the date of the offer, the fair value of Mega plc's shares were £3 each, and nominal value £1 each. Mega plc has no other assets and liabilities.

Required

(a) Prepare an individual company balance sheet for Mega plc at 31 December 1996 (which will be here identical to its balance sheet at 31 December 1995), and consolidated balance sheets at 31 December 1996 for the Mega Group under the following assumptions:
(b) Mega plc is set up by both Wholla plc and Bitta plc to effect a merger between them.
(c) Mega plc is a creation of Wholla plc to enable it to acquire Bitta plc.

Disclosures

FRS 6 requires the acquirer or, in mergers, the share issuer to disclose in respect of all material combinations during the year, details of the names of companies, whether acquisition or merger accounting has been used, and the effective date of the combination (para. 21).

Mergers (para. 22)

Movements on reserves — from the merger cancellation process, FRS 6 requires disclosure of both 'the difference, if any between the nominal value. . . issued plus the fair value of any other consideration given, and the nominal value . . . . received', and 'any existing balance on the [new subsidiary undertaking's] share premium account or capital redemption reserve' as movements on other reserves (para. 18) – see Chapter 8.

Profit and loss information – FRS 6 comments that users who have been tracking the combining parties separately may wish to continue to track them in the year of the merger (para. 81). Therefore for each party to the merger, other than in group reconstructions, for the pre-merger segment of the merger period and also for the prior year, information relating to the profit and loss account and statement of total recognized gains and losses should be given. The profit and loss information must include turnover, operating profit and exceptional items, split between continuing operations, discontinued operations and acquisitions (discussed in Chapter 8), taxation and minority interests, and extraordinary items. The same information should be provided for the combined merged entity in the post-combination segment of the merger period (para. 21), presumably because after the merger the two parties may not exist separately in an identifiable way.

The consideration given by the issuing company and its subsidiaries and its fair value, but only the aggregate book value of the net assets of each party to the merger at the combination date, must be disclosed – fair values of the latter are not required. The nature and amount of significant adjustments to achieve consistency of accounting policies and explanation of any other significant adjustments, together with a statement of adjustments of consolidated reserves, all as a consequence of the merger, must be disclosed. Certain of these are not required in group reconstructions (para. 82).

Acquisition accounting

All material acquisitions – FRS 6 requires similar information about the composition of the consideration and its fair value (para. 24). It requires that the post-acquisition results of the acquired company should be shown as a component of continuing operations in the profit and loss account (discussed in Chapter 8), with disclosure and explanation of material impact on any major business segment (para. 28 – discussed in Chapter 12). If this is not practicable, an indication of the contribution of the acquired entity to the turnover and operating profits of continuing operations must be given, and if even this is not possible this fact and reason must be given (para. 29).

Fuller disclosures for substantial acquisitions – these are for listed companies, where the combination is a Stock Exchange Class I or Super Class I transaction, or for all companies where the fair value of the consideration exceeds 15 per cent of the acquirer's net assets or the acquired entity's profits is more than 15 per cent of the acquirer's profits, or where such disclosure is necessary to show a true and fair view. Net profits for this purpose are those in the financial statements for the last year before acquisition, and net assets should *include* any purchased goodwill written-off directly to reserves which has not been charged to profit and loss (para. 37).

The fuller disclosures include similar details for the acquired entity's profit and loss and statement of recognized gains and losses for the current period up to the date of acquisition. For the prior period only its profit after tax and minority interests, based on the acquired entity's accounting policies prior to the acquisition (para. 36 – in the merger case this is provided for all merger parties). FRS 6 comments that 'in most cases [the acquired entity]. . . is a continuing business . . . and information . . . for the period up to the date of acquisition is relevant to the user' (para. 88).

Other disclosures relating to fair values and goodwill, including the provision of a fair value table reconciling book to fair values at acquisition, are discussed in Chapter 5.

OBJECTIVES IN ACCOUNTING FOR BUSINESS COMBINATIONS

This section examines other theoretical objectives proposed for accounting for business combinations, and whether these are mutually compatible.

The nature of the reporting entity

The ASB Discussion Draft, *Statement of Reporting Principles Chapter 7, The Reporting Entity* (1994 – hereafter 'Discussion Draft') situates the difference between acquisitions and mergers in terms of changes in the reporting entity, commenting

> In most cases, changes in membership of a group do not prevent the group from continuing as a reporting entity as it acquires and disposes of entities in which it has invested. However, in rare circumstances, entities do not combine to enlarge one of them but to create a whole new reporting entity in a combination called a merger. In a merger, entities combine on an equal footing, pooling their resources and sharing the risks and benefits, and none of them can be identified as having acquired control over the others. (para. 5.1)

The implicit definition of acquisition accounting leads to its use of fair values at acquisition, to establish group historical costs, not current costs.

In what sense then is a new reporting entity created under merger accounting – especially as 'the results of the merging entities are pooled both for the year of merger and for the comparative period to give the results of the new reporting entity on a continuous basis' (para. 5.2). The change in scope of the accounts ('new reporting entity') is characterized differently from a new entity transacting in its own right – in a merger, assets and liabilities are to be 'valued' on the basis of costs or values to previously existing entities. If it were a new entity per se, new historical costs, fair values at the combination date must be obtained for assets from all parties rather than none, and profits recognized only from formation (see Arnold *et al.* (1992), and the IASC's E22). A 'new entity' cannot have a track record, whereas the ASB envisages that a 'new reporting entity' can.

The Discussion Draft decides whether an entity should provide general purpose financial statements (a reporting entity) in terms of supply (a unified control structure of a cohesive economic unit) and demand (users with a legitimate interest relying on general purpose statements) (paras 2.2 – 2.3). In terms of the latter, FRS 6 argues that as 'a merger is a true mutual sharing of the benefits and risks of the combined enterprise . . . therefore the *joint* history of the entities that have combined will be relevant to the combined group's shareholders' (para. 49, emphasis added). Further 'merger accounting . . . treats the separate businesses as though they were continuing as before only now jointly owned and managed' (para. 49). In what sense the 'new reporting entity' was a cohesive economic unit with a unified control structure for the purposes of pre-merger comparatives is arguable. Under current cost accounting, acquisition *and* merger accounting would value assets at current cost and so valuations would be identical (see Ketz, 1984).

Distributability of profits

The acquisition approach has been characterized as freezing the distributability of the pre-combination profits of the combinee company, and the merger approach as allowing their distribution. Changes in the Companies Act 1985 remove this simple distinction. Though under merger accounting the maximum amount distributable by the parent (an individual company not a group matter) is usually greater than under acquisition accounting, the difference is more related to the amount of share 'premium' on the investment under the latter than to pre-acquisition profits.

Distributable profits (optional)

In Chapter 6 it will be shown that a parent, in determining whether distributions received from group companies are income (distributable) or capital repayments need only take an individual company rather than a group perspective. It need not consider whether the subsidiary's distribution is from its pre- or post-acquisition profits even under acquisition accounting, but only whether, consequent on the distribution, the parent's investment suffers any permanent diminution in value below its carrying amount.

A fair value carrying amount for the investment is used under acquisition accounting, but a nominal value one under merger accounting. Thus more of the subsidiary's distribution can be regarded as income by the parent under merger accounting, until permanent diminution in value of the investment below the parent's nominal carrying amount occurs. This does not depend on the pre- and post-acquisition distinction.

Predictive ability

Snavely (1975) argues the main purpose of group financial statements is to aid prediction – merger accounting is superior since comparatives are restated and the track record of group companies can be better compared pre- and post-combination. He argues it is easy to boost group profits under acquisition accounting since the subsidiary is only included from acquisition. Comparative figures will not include the assets, liabilities or results of the companies acquired, giving a misleading impression of growth in size and profit. Whittaker and Cooke (1983, p. 20) however, consider that where there are great size differences, economic changes in the running of the smaller business will make pre-/post-combination comparisons meaningless. Predictive ability is not universally accepted as the prime purpose of historical cost accounts.

To remove goodwill from the financial statements

Many are unhappy about the inclusion of purchased goodwill in financial statements because firms in a similar position which have expanded organically do not record goodwill. Thus merger accounting has been viewed as a means of keeping goodwill off the balance sheet. However, there are other ways of achieving this, such as acquisition accounting with the immediate write-off of goodwill direct to reserves, which many regard as preferable. To compare the two – merger accounting tends to show larger group retained earnings; acquisition accounting with immediate goodwill write-off tends to show larger group share premium and a smaller group retained earnings because of removal of pre-acquisition profits and goodwill write-off against reserves. See Chapter 5.

CONTEXT OF THE DEBATE

USA Evidence

Professor Abraham J. Briloff provided a number of cases showing the misuse of merger (pooling) accounting – asset stripping; high profits by comparing current revenues versus the combinee's 'old' costs, thus boosting 'tired' P/E ratios; enhancing group earnings by merging with companies near or even after the year end so that a complete year's earnings is included. His investigations implicitly assume naive investors are fooled. However, efficient markets researchers argue that capital markets are semi-strong efficient, i.e. market prices reflect all publicly available information, and that evidence shows markets can see through 'cosmetic' changes in accounting numbers. They only regard choice between accounting proposals as important if they have a direct cash flow effect, presuming that investors have enough information to judge.

Hong, Kaplan and Mandelker (1978) examined over 200 US business combinations over the period 1954–1964, hypothesizing that the New York Stock Exchange could distinguish between (cosmetic) higher earnings caused by the pooling (merger) approach and higher earnings caused by real economic events. They found no evidence that the pooling (merger) approach produces any abnormal returns around the time of the combination and concluded that investors were not 'fooled'. Davis (1990) replicated their study with greater sophistication on a later US sample (1971–82), again finding no significant abnormal returns for poolings. However like the former study, he found initially unexplained positive abnormal returns for purchase (acquisition) accounted combinations. Further analysis revealed a more complex picture – that the pooling sample differed in other respects from the purchase sample, and these different characteristics were associated with abnormal returns, thus muddying Hong et al.s earlier seemingly straightforward conclusions.

FRS 6's extra merger disclosures enable a rudimentary comparison to be made in the UK with acquisition accounting, and can be viewed as helping investors not to be fooled by differences in treatment, but they do not allow complete comparison because, e.g., disclosure of fair values of identifiable net assets acquired is not disclosed under merger accounting.

Efficient market research asserts that the market does not react to cosmetic accounting changes. Contracting cost research, the radical implications for accounting regulation of which are explored in Chapter 12, provides a more sensitive framework, showing how apparently cosmetic accounting changes can affect cash flows indirectly – higher reported earnings is not a cash flow effect per se, but by being used in other contracts may increase profit-related management compensation, or by decreasing gearing decrease the likelihood of default on gearing-based debt covenant restrictions with attendant renegotiation or even bankruptcy costs.

Earlier studies, e.g. by Gagnon (1971), had found weak supportive evidence for the 'income maximization hypothesis', a precursor of the contracting framework, that management chose between purchase (acquisition) or pooling (merger) to maximize reported income. Copeland and Wojdack (1969) found that such behaviour continued even after APB Opinion 16's new merger definitions designed to prevent opportunistic choice were implemented! However, Robinson and Shane (1990, p. 26) point out that whilst such studies (and subsequent ones by Anderson and Louderbeck (1975) and Nathan (1988)) explained the choice of pooling (merger) accounting, they gave counter-intuitive results in predicting when purchase (acquisition) accounting would be used.

Dunne (1990), in a later and more sophisticated study further examined management opportunism in choosing between purchase and pooling accounting. She hypothesized pooling-of interests (merger) accounting with its potentially income increasing properties will tend to be adopted where there are profit-based management compensation plans, where managers own low percentages of the firm's shares (so have an incentive to manipulate income to obtain personal benefits at the expense of shareholders), where gearing is high or interest cover is low for firms likely to be closer to covenant limits, but *not* by larger firms, since too-large income might attract regulatory interference. She found evidence broadly to support her hypotheses.

Robinson and Shane (1990) suggested that higher average bid premia for 1972–82 USA poolings compared to purchases showed the existence of economic benefits from structuring as a pooling (merger) rather than a purchase (acquisition). However, it might also be the case that conditions which lead to higher premia lead to the choice of pooling. Nathan and Dunne (1991) found that factors influencing the choice of accounting approach over the period 1963–85 were consistent with a contracting cost perspective.

UK evidence

UK empirical work is scarcer and more difficult to interpret. Goodwill in the USA must be capitalized and gradually amortized over 40 years, with profit and gearing effects. In the UK the picture is blurred: goodwill is usually immediately written off against reserves, bypassing profit and loss, so there is no goodwill profit effect under acquisition accounting and it is not generally included in gearing calculations in UK loan covenants. Early in the 1980s some groups which used acquisition accounting did not record goodwill, through taking advantage of the then merger relief provisions to utilize a *nominal* value investment amount. This practice was outlawed by the revised Companies Act 1985.

Higson (1990) examined 373 UK combinations and found that from 1985 to 1987, of 69 groups which qualified for the option of merger accounting under the then (SSAP 23) merger accounting criteria, only 20 did so; 44 used acquisition accounting with merger relief, and 5 used straight acquisition accounting. Of these 69 companies, the 'targets' for which merger accounting was chosen tended to be larger and more profitable relative to the acquirer. Merger accounting had a greater probability of being chosen the later into the acquirer's year the combination took place. In multivariate tests only relative profitability was significant.

Salami and Sudarsanam (1994) conclude, based on a sample of 505 take-overs over the period 1980–90, that whilst the payment method (shares or cash) influences the accounting choice (acquisition accounting, merger accounting, acquisition accounting with merger relief), the accounting method does not significantly influence the form of payment. They use a simultaneous equations estimation approach to control for other factors and to allow them to isolate more effectively the direction of causality.

Exercises

3.14 Why are identifiable assets and liabilities acquired restated to fair values under acquisition accounting, and why does the target company only contribute to the group retained profits since the combination date?

3.15 What are the main intuitive features of a merger? In what sense is a new reporting entity established?

3.16 Discuss whether or not merger accounting should be abolished, giving reasons.

3.17 What are the potential weaknesses, if any in FRS 6's merger definition? How might its definition be improved?

3.18 In terms of economic consequences, does it matter whether merger accounting is abolished or that companies use merger accounting when the substance of the take-over is an acquisition?

SUMMARY

The **acquisition** (purchase) approach records the parent's investment at **fair value**. Pre-acquisition profits of the combinee are **excluded** from group results, and its identifiable assets and liabilities are restated to **fair value** at acquisition to establish historical costs to the **group**. The **merger** (pooling of interests) approach records the investment at **nominal** amount, **includes** pre-acquisition results of all combining parties as far as possible, and only adjusts the combining parties' identifiable assets and liabilities to achieve uniform group accounting policies. Standards require that the accounting approach should depend on the substance of the combination transaction and be **independent** of the resulting corporate structure such as a new parent company or not.

The acquisition approach stresses **discontinuity** of ownership of the target company, and characterizes the acquisition of a business analogously to the purchase of its separate assets and liabilities, which therefore contribute since purchase – the **enlargement** of an existing entity. The merger approach stresses **continuity** relative to other combining parties of ownership rights to participation in benefits and risks, and of powers. It is based on the analogy of an adjustment of ownership rights of the two companies. The ASB characterizes the combination as a 'new reporting entity' in a way which is not completely consistent.

Technically, the aim in acquisition accounting is to **eliminate** pre-acquisition equity of the target (subsidiary). In merger accounting **progressive cancellation** is used. Minority interests may remain in former parties to the combination. FRS 6's provisions were contrasted with UK company law and US accounting standards, particularly its definition of a merger, and possible enforcement difficulties were examined. Finally, the **purposes** of accounting for business combinations were reviewed in a theoretical sense and then in terms of behavioural and economic consequences.

FURTHER READING

FRS 6 (1994) *Acquisitions and Mergers*, Accounting Standards Board.

ASB Draft Statement of Principles (1994) *Chapter 7 – The Reporting Entity*, Section 5, Accounting Standards Board.

IAS 22 (revised 1993) *Business Combinations*, International Accounting Standards Committee.

Higson, C. (1990) *The Choice of Accounting Method in UK Mergers and Acquisitions*, Institute of Chartered Accountants in England and Wales.

Part B:
Consolidating the Major
Financial Statements

4

CONSOLIDATED BALANCE SHEETS UNDER ACQUISITION ACCOUNTING

This is the first of five chapters to examine the consolidation of the primary financial statements, in this case the consolidated balance sheet. These chapters focus on the *acquisition* approach, used for almost all business combinations in the UK. This chapter reinforces the acquisition cancellation process using an abbreviated format and discusses the equity approach, shows how the equity approach and conventional consolidation are located as alternatives in a spectrum of possible approaches for accounting for investments, examines the current UK institutional position, briefly illustrates accounting for goodwill subsequent to acquisition, and finally, examines the usefulness of the consolidated balance sheet.

CONSOLIDATION CANCELLATION

The key element in acquisition accounting is how the parent's equity is combined with the subsidiary's. The subsidiary's pre-acquisition equity is removed (major surgery) so that the subsidiary contributes only after acquisition. Figure 4.1 shows this where a holding of less than a 100 per cent is acquired (here 80 per cent).

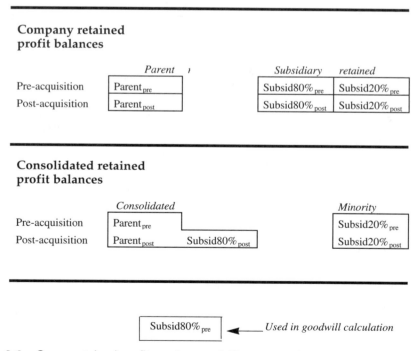

Figure 4.1 – Group retained profits under acquisition accounting

The top section shows the parent and the subsidiary companies' retained profits analysed into pre- and post-acquisition amounts. The subsidiaries are further subdivided to show majority and minority interests. The bottom section shows consolidated amounts derived from these balances, on the left consolidated retained profits (the subsidiary contributes after acquisition), on the right the minority share in the subsidiary is ongoing including pre-acquisition retained profits.

Example 4.1 – Consolidation under acquisition accounting

Largesse plc acquires 80% of the shares in Smallnesse plc on 31 March 1992 when the retained profits of the two companies were respectively £80m and £30m. The balance sheets of the two companies at 31 March 1995, were

Individual company balance sheets at 31 March 1995

	Largesse		Smallnesse	
	£m	£m	£m	£m
Fixed assets				
Tangible fixed assets		180		40
Investment in Smallnesse		80		
Investment in Minutenesse		20		.
		280		40
Net current assets				
Stocks	50		30	
Other	90		40	
		140		70
Creditors over one year		(100)		(20)
		320		90
Capital and Reserves				
Share capital		130		35
Share premium		70		15
Retained profits		120		40
		320		90

Required
Prepare a consolidated balance sheet at 31 March 1995 for the Largesse Group. The investment in Minutenesse plc is to be accounted for as a fixed asset investment.

Solution
In this example the combination (as a fixed asset investment) has already been recorded in Largesse's records at fair value consistent with acquisition accounting and in accordance with FRS 6 (80% combination).

Largesse Group – balance sheet consolidation at 31 March 1995

Description	Larg-esse	Small-nesse	Minority	Pre-acq	Elimination	Consolidated
Tangible fixed assets	180	40				220
Investment – Smallnesse	80	–			(80)	–
– Minutenesse	20					20
Stocks	50	30				80
Other current	90	40				130
Creditors over one year	(100)	(20)				(120)
Share capital	(130)	(35)	7	28		(130)
Share premium	(70)	(15)	3	12		(70)
Retained profits	(120)	(40)	8	24		(128)
Goodwill				(64)	80	16
Minority interests			(18)			(18)

The minority interest's share of retained profits is 20% of £40m, but for goodwill calculation the removal is 80% of £30m (*pre*-acquisition retained earnings). The majority's share of the subsidiary's *post*-acquisition earnings is included in consolidated retained profits, i.e. £120m + 80% × £10m = £128m.

The abbreviated cancellation table

An abbreviated format now discussed is used in the remainder of the book. Only balances which require adjustment to obtain consolidated amounts are included (thus here not tangible fixed assets, stock, other net current assets nor creditors over one year). The vertical format makes it easier to analyse balances.

Largesse Group – abbreviated balance sheet cancellation table

Description	Investment	Share capital	Share premium	Retained profits	Goodwill	Minority interests
Largesse balances	80	(130)	(70)	(120)	—	—
Smallnesse equity analysed						
(a) at acquisition				—	(64)	(16)
(b) post-acquisition				(8)	-	(2)
Investment elimination	(80)				80	
Consolidated amounts		(130)	(70)	(128)	16	(18)

Abbreviated table steps
(a) only balances requiring adjustment are included.
(b) the parent's balances are entered.
(c) the subsidiary's equity balances are analysed
  • total equity of £90m (35 + 15 + 40) between at acquisition £80m and movement post-acquisition £10m, then
  • at acquisition is split between majority/goodwill (80 per cent) and minority (20 per cent), and post-acquisition between consolidated retained earnings (80 per cent) and minority (illustrating that the minority share is ongoing).
(d) The investment is cancelled against the parent's pre-acquisition equity to determine goodwill.

Exercises

4.1 In the Largesse Group example above
  (a) interpret the change in consolidated retained profits and minority interests since acquisition.
  (b) explain the breakdown of minority interests into component parts.
  (c) discuss why under acquisition accounting the consolidated share capital and share premium are equal to the corresponding balances of the parent.
4.2 Redraft the balance sheet consolidation for Student plc and Union Ltd in Example 3.4 in Chapter 3, on page 51, into abbreviated form, checking your solution below :

Description	Investment	Share capital	Share premium	Retained profits	Goodwill	Minority interests
Student balances	594	(724)	(303)	(90)		
Union equity analysed						
a) at acquisition					(405)	(45)
b) post-acquisition				(18)		(2)
Investment elimination	(594)				594	
Consolidated amounts		(724)	(303)	(108)	189	(47)

4.3 You are presented with the following summarized company balance sheets of Bigfry plc and its subsidiary Smallfry plc at 30 November 1995.

	Bigfry £m	Bigfry £m	Smallfry £m	Smallfry £m
Fixed assets				
Land and buildings		100		40
Plant and equipment		360		100
Investment in Smallfry	72			
Investment in Tinyfry	20			
Investments		92		–
		552		140
Current assets				
Stocks	50		15	
Debtors	30		10	
Cash	5		2	
	85		27	
Current liabilities				
Trade creditors	25		18	
Other creditors	10		5	
	35		23	
		50		4
Creditors over one year		(200)		(30)
		402		114
Capital and Reserves				
Share capital		60		20
Share premium		50		30
Retained profits		292		64
		402		114

Figure 4.2 – Bigfry and Smallfry balance sheets at 30 November 1995

Notes
(a) Bigfry acquired a 60% stake in Smallfry on 31 May 1995, when the retained earnings of Smallfry were £50m.
(b) Bigfry acquired an 18% interest in Tinyfry plc on 30 November 1994. This investment should be accounted for at cost in the consolidated balance sheet.

Required
Prepare a consolidated balance sheet for the Bigfry group at 30 November 1995, using the abbreviated acquisition cancellation table.

4.4 Vampire plc purchased a 70% interest in Stake plc on 30 June 1995 for £180m. Vampire plc's retained profits at 1 January 1995 was £200m, and during the year, its net profit was £70m and dividends declared £30m. Capital and reserves of Stake plc are analysed as follows:

	£m
Share capital	50
Share premium	60
Revaluation reserve	20
Retained profits at 1 Jan 1995	80
Retained profits for year	30
	240

Required
(a) Calculate goodwill and minority interests at acquisition. Assume that Stake plc's retained profits accrue evenly throughout the year.
(b) Calculate consolidated retained profits and minority interests at 31 December 1995.

THE EQUITY APPROACH

The equity approach is used in consolidated financial statements for investments in which the investor holds a long-term interest which enables it to share in benefits and

Level of influence	Accounting treatment	Profit recognition basis
Non-significant influence (usually 0–19% owned)	Investment at cost	Dividends receivable
Significant influence but not control (usually 20–50% owned)	Equity method	Attributable profits
Joint control	Usually equity method or in defined circumstances proportional consolidation	Attributable profits
Unilateral control (includes dominant influence, usually 51–100% owned)	Conventional (full) consolidation – under the acquisition approach; rarely in a few more than 90% combinations, under the merger approach.	Total profits less deduction for minority share

Figure 4.3 – Degrees of influence and group accounting treatment

risks, and over which it is able to exercise significant influence, termed 'associates' (normally between 20 and 50 per cent ownership), and in most cases where the investor exercises joint control, termed 'joint ventures', as shown in Figure 4.3. Its relationship to the conventional consolidation approach under acquisition accounting, just discussed, is shown in the next section. Here the equity approach is contrasted with the cost approach used in the parent's own accounts for *all* investments and an example shows how to account for associates in the abbreviated cancellation table.

The cost basis for investments
In individual company accounts, investments in other entities are treated either as current assets or fixed asset investments. The historical cost basis for such assets is

if *current* – lower of cost and net realizable value;
if *long term* – cost unless there is a *permanent* decline in value in which case it is written down to *recoverable* amount (implicitly assuming temporary fluctuations will reverse themselves over the life of the asset and so should be ignored).

Normally 'cost' is the fair value at the acquisition date of any consideration given, except in the very rare case where merger accounting is used. A few investments, e.g. investment properties, are valued at current market value but are outside the scope of this text, as is the valuation of investments under current value systems. Income from such investments is normally recognized on a dividends receivable basis, and such investments remain anchored at cost, viz:

DR. Dividends receivable   **CR. Profit and loss account**

and when the cash is received

DR. Cash   **CR. Dividends receivable**

These seem unexceptionable in an individual company context. However, difficulties arose as early as the turn of the century as group structures were more widely used to conduct operations. The approach starved investors of disclosure. Controlled subsidiaries often declared increasing dividends (all that parent shareholders saw) whilst underlying profits could be fluctuating wildly.

Directors could 'prudently' build up 'secret reserves' in subsidiaries or be downright unscrupulous! Increasing pressure for better disclosure and measurement approaches for substantially owned and controlled companies was inevitable. One possibility, the increasing use of current value accounting, was nipped in the bud by conservative reactions to the Depression in the 1930s. A less radical alternative, modifying and expanding the historical cost treatment using *supplementary* group accounts, but whilst still remaining within that system's tenets, is the route that was taken.

THE EQUITY METHOD IN CONSOLIDATED FINANCIAL STATEMENTS

Cost plus attributable retained profit basis
An objective is to measure as group income, the profits of the company in which the investment is held, so that dividend based manipulations are not possible. The bookkeeping is

    DR. Investment   **CR. Profit and loss account**

with the group's share of post-acquisition profits (attributable profits) of the investee. Income is recognized in the group profit and loss account on a *profits earned* rather than a dividends declared basis. This treatment is only used in the UK in group accounts. The double entry for dividends is

    DR. Dividends receivable   **CR. Investment**

The investment is restated every period on a cost plus *attributable post-acquisition retained profit* basis, termed in this book the 'equitized' investment (adjustments are also made for other post-acquisition reserve movements of the subsidiary, e.g. revaluations, but this is beyond the scope of the present discussion). Under the cost approach, the 'income' double entry was

    DR. Dividends receivable   **CR. Profit and loss account**

Notional 'T' accounts for cost and equity approaches

A. Cost basis

Dividends receivable	Investment	Profit and loss account
	I. Cost	
II. Dividends		III. Dividends

B. Equity approach

Dividends receivable	Investment	Profit and loss account
	I. Cost	II. Profit
	II. Profit	
III. Dividends	III. Dividends	

The investment and the profit and loss account under the equity approach are both increased by attributable retained earnings compared to the cost approach. Income is thereby restated from a dividends to a profits basis.

Example 4.2 – Cost and equity approaches contrasted

Whitehall plc acquired a 40% interest in County plc on 1 April 1995 for £70m in cash. A summary of County's retained profits account for the year to 31 March 1996 is as follows:

	£m
Retained profits at 1 April 1995	60
Net profit for the year ended 31 March 1996	20
Dividends due for the year to 31 March 1996	(12)
Retained profits at 31 March 1996	68

Required

(a) Record the purchase of the investment and investment income transactions for the year to 31 March 1996 in Whitehall's own financial records.

(b) Record in 'T' accounts notional equity accounting entries for the year relating to the investment.

(c) Compare and contrast the treatments in (a) and (b).

Solution

Cost of investment acquired			=	£70m
Attributable dividends due	=	40% × 12	=	£4.8m
Attributable profits	=	40% × 20	=	£8m

A. *Cost basis (£m)*

Dividends receivable	Investment	Profit and loss account
	I. Cost 70	
II. Divs 4.8		II. Divs 4.8

B. *Equity approach (£m)*

Dividends receivable	Investment	Profit and loss account
	I. Cost 70	
	II. Cost 8	II. Profit 8
III.Divs 4.8	III.Divs 4.8	

Note – the investment under the equity approach is at *cost plus attributable retained profits since acquisition*. The latter is £3.2m = 40% × [20 – 12], so the investment is stated at £73.2m. The term used in the book for this is the 'equitized investment'. The profit and loss effect of equitizing the investment (by adding £3.2m retained earnings to the cost of £70m) is to convert it from a dividends basis to a profits basis.

Example 4.3 – the equity approach in the abbreviated cancellation table

In the Largesse–Smallnesse example earlier, Example 4.1, assume that Largesse plc acquired a 25% holding in Minutenesse plc on 31 March 1993 when the retained profits of Minutenesse plc were £14m, and that Largesse plc exercises a significant influence over it. The current balance sheet of Minutenesse is as follows

Individual company balance sheet at 31 March 1995

	Minutenesse £m	£m
Fixed assets		
Tangible fixed assets		80
Net current assets		
Stocks	25	
Other	15	
		40
Creditors over one year		(36)
		84
Capital and Reserves		
Share capital		30
Share premium		20
Retained profits		34
		84

Required

Show the incremental effects of treating Minutenesse plc as an associated company in the abbreviated balance sheet cancellation table at 31 March 1995 for the Largesse Group.

Solution

The 'Investment in Minutenesse' will be included in the cancellation table using the equity method at

$$\text{Cost} + \underset{\text{since acquisition}}{\textit{Attributable retained profit}} = 20 + 25\% (34 - 14) = £25m$$

and consolidated reserves will increase by the equitized retained profit.

Largesse Group - abbreviated balance sheet cancellation table

Description	Inv in Small-nesse	Inv in Minute-nesse	Share cap	Share prem	Ret profits	Good-will	Minority interests
Largesse balances	80	20	(130)	(70)	(120)	—	—
Smallnesse equity							
(a) at acquisition						(64)	(16)
(b) post-acquisition					(8)	—	(2)
Minutenesse post-acq retained		5			(5)		
Investment elimination	(80)					80	
Consolidated amounts	—	25	(130)	(70)	(133)	16	(18)

Later in the chapter it will be shown how to analyse the amount of £25m for the equitized investment into its underlying attributable net assets and goodwill for note disclosure purposes. The consolidated balance sheet is as follows, merely adding all other balances from the individual company financial statements of Largesse and Smallnesse (as Minutenesse is an associate).

Largesse Group – consolidated balance sheet at 30 November 1995

	£m	£m
Intangible fixed assets		16
Tangible fixed assets:		
Fixed assets (net)		220
Investment in associate		25
Net current assets:		
Stock	80	
Other	130	
		210
Creditors over one year:		
Loans		(120)
		351
Capital and reserves:		
Ordinary shares (£1)		130
Share premium		70
Retained profits		133
		333
Minority interests		18
		351

Exercises

4.5 Manipulator plc acquired a 30% interest in Gullible plc on 1 January 1995 for £40m in cash. Capital and reserves for the latter are reported as follows:

	£m
Share capital	10
Share premium	15
Retained profits at 1/1/95	25
Net profit 1/1/95 – 31/12/95	12
Dividends paid for year	(5)
	57

Required

(a) Record the purchase of the investment by Manipulator plc and investment income transactions for the year to 31 December 1995 in its own records.

(b) Record in 'T' accounts equity accounting entries for the year relating to the investment.

(c) Compare and contrast the treatments in (a) and (b).

4.6 Assume the facts are as in Exercise 4.3 except that Bigfry now has a 25% interest in Tinyfry (not 18%) and is able to exercise significant influence. When the investment was purchased, two years ago, Tinyfry's retained earnings were £31m. The balance sheet of Tinyfry plc at 30 November 1995 is

	£m	£m
Fixed assets		
Land		29
Buildings		15
Plant and equipment		40
		84
Current assets		
Stocks	25	
Debtors	12	
Cash	10	
	47	
Current liabilities	(30)	
		17
Creditors over one year		(17)
		84
Capital and reserves		
Ordinary share capital		15
Share premium		14
Retained earnings		55
		84

Required
Show the effects on the abbreviated balance sheet cancellation table at 30 November 1995 for the Bigfry–Smallfry group of including Tinyfry as an associated company under the equity approach.

GROUP MEASUREMENT AND DISCLOSURE CONCEPTS

This section examines a spectrum of alternatives for accounting for investments in other companies under the acquisition accounting 'family' of techniques. Conventional consolidation and equity accounting are both parts of the same spectrum. Each measurement and disclosure alternative characterizes the group and group ownership in different ways, some giving prominence to minority interests, others ignoring them. 'Theories' underlying accounting for investments, minorities and groups are discussed after technical alternatives have been examined. In UK group accounts, different treatments correspond approximately to differing degrees of influence as shown in Figure 4.3 earlier. In the parent's accounts, all investments including subsidiaries are recorded at cost. Merger accounting potentially contains a similar spectrum which is not discussed in this book since, as its use is limited to nearly wholly owned investments which meet merger criteria as discussed in Chapter 3, only a full consolidation equivalent is used.

In the previous section the simplest measurement alternative for overcoming defects in the cost basis, the equity approach, was discussed. Derived from it in this section are increasingly detailed disclosure alternatives. Full consolidation is one possible way of enhancing the basic information provided by the equity approach, but then consolidation has many varieties! A parent company is required to produce both an individual company balance sheet, in which investments in group companies are accounted for at cost, *and* a group one, a consolidated balance sheet which uses various techniques to enhance measurement and disclosure of these investments.

Consolidation as expansion of the equity approach
Various expansions of the equity approach are possible, analysing the total investment amount into the individual assets, liabilities and goodwill underlying it and then adding

these components individually to the corresponding components of the parent. Assume in what follows an 80 per cent take over.

At acquisition

Goodwill is the excess of investment over majority share of equity (= net assets) acquired, so

Investment at cost = Goodwill + 80% × (assets at acquisition – liabilities)   (4.1)

After acquisition

It will now be demonstrated that at any date later than acquisition the equitized investment is equal in total amount to its underlying component assets, liabilities and goodwill. In equation form, the general relationship is as follows and the a-acquisition relationship is a special case.

Investment at cost plus = Goodwill + 80% × (assets at current date – liabilities) (4.2)
attributable profit   at acquisition

Proof

Let I = investment at cost, A = assets at acquisition, ΔA = the change in assets since acquisition, G = goodwill at acquisition, ΔRE = change in retained earnings, etc. Then at acquisition,

$$I = G + 0.8 \times (A - L)$$

Assume no share issues or other capital injections. Since at acquisition the change in equity of the investee would then equal its change in its net assets

$$\Delta RE = \Delta A - \Delta L$$

$$0.8\ \Delta RE = 0.8\ (\Delta A - \Delta L)$$

Adding this to the at-acquisition equation, we get

$$I + 0.8\ \Delta RE = G + 0.8\ [(A + \Delta A) - (L + L)]$$

The left hand side is the equitized investment at the current date. The right hand is goodwill at acquisition (its treatment subsequent to acquisition is dealt with later in the chapter) plus the majority portion (80 per cent) of assets and liabilities in the current balance sheet. *Hence, the equitized investment can be analysed into component assets, liabilities and goodwill at any date.* In what follows the following equation is termed the **fundamental equation.**

$$I + 0.8\ \Delta RE = G + 0.8\ [A_{now} - L_{now}]$$

Example 4.4 – Analysing the equitized investment

Consider in Example 4.3 the 25 per cent investment in Minutenesse. Its equitized amount was £25m, i.e.

Equitized investment =   Cost   + Attributable retained profits since acquisition
            =   £20m + 25% × [34 – 14] =   £25m

According to the above fundamental equation this can be broken down into goodwill at acquisition plus attributable net assets in the current financial statements. This can be checked as:

Investment	£m
Goodwill = 20 – 25% × (30+20+14)	4
Net assets = 25% × (80+40–36)	21
	25

The figures for net assets are the subtotals for fixed assets, net current assets and loans in Minutenesse's current balance sheet. Though associates are accounted for as a single number,

£25m, in the consolidated financial statements themselves, SSAP 1, *Accounting for Associated Companies*, requires the breakdown in the above table as a note disclosure to the consolidated statements.

Revaluations

Restatements of the subsidiary's identifiable assets and liabilities at acquisition to fair values would affect the right-hand side of the equation at that date, the asset values and goodwill. If revaluations related to the period subsequent to acquisition, asset values on the right-hand side would include them and 80 per cent of the subsidiary's revaluation reserve would be included in the equitized investment (which would be cost plus attributable retained profits since acquisition plus attributable revaluation reserves since acquisition).

As shown in Figure 4.3 earlier, the equity approach is only used in group accounts for holdings over which there is *significant influence* (a rebuttable presumption if more than 20 per cent ownership). In the USA it is used in some *parent* company accounts for associates and subsidiaries. In an earlier version of SSAP 1, *Accounting for Associated Companies*, the investment was to be stated at 'cost plus attributable retained profit'. The revised version requires this amount analysed between goodwill and attributable net assets. The fundamental equation above shows the equivalence of the two analyses.

The concept of consolidation

Starting with the investment *at cost*, consolidation can be characterized as a two-stage process, *equitization* and *expansion*, as shown in Figure 4.4. The cost approach used in the parent's own accounts is before equitization and expansion. The equity approach is after equitization but before expansion (the left-hand side of the fundamental equation). Consolidation is after equitization and expansion (the right-hand side).

Stages	Steps
1) Equitisation	Investment at cost adjusted by
	DR. Investment CR. Consolidated retained profits
	with subsidiary's attributable retained profits since acquisition.
2) Expansion	Adjusted (equitised) investment in 1). is expanded (analysed) into
	components and added to corresponding components of parent.

Figure 4.4 – Consolidation as equitization and expansion

Equitizing and expanding the investment

In order to examine different consolidation concepts, Figure 4.5 shows a number of possible ways of analysing/expanding the equitized investment. Its second column shows the equitizing entry. In practice, investments giving 80 per cent ownership would normally be accounted for in the group accounts using consolidation not the equity approach, unless significant restrictions existed over the ability to control the subsidiary (see Chapter 2). For teaching reasons all the approaches are demonstrated here for an 80 per cent owned investment, including the equity approach, to allow technical comparison between them.

Each column progressively expands the 'equitized' investment, using the fundamental equation as a basis. Column 2 shows cost and attributable retained earnings since acquisition. Column 3 gives the complementary breakdown into goodwill and the majority (80 per cent) proportion of aggregate net assets at the current date. Column 4 breaks

Investment	Cost plus attrib profit	Analysed breakdown	Proportional consolidation	Parent/ conventional consolidation	Entity consolidation
			Goodwill	Goodwill	Total group goodwill
			80% Tangible fixed assets	100% Tangible fixed assets	100% Tangible fixed assets
	Investment at cost	Goodwill	80% Stocks 80% Other	100% Stocks 100% Other	100% Stocks 100% Other
Investment	*plus* attrib retained profit	80% net assets *now*			
			80% Loans	100% Loans	100% Loans
				20% Minority in net assets	20% Minority in net assets *and* goodwill

Figure 5.5 – Expansion of the basic equitize investment

down this aggregate into the majority portion (80 per cent) of each asset and each liability of the investee, the basis for proportional consolidation. Column 5 shows the parent's goodwill plus 100 per cent of each asset and liability of the subsidiary, less a deduction of 20 per cent of their aggregate, the minority interest, the basis for conventional consolidation as used in practice in the UK, expressed by the following adaptation of the fundamental equation where the last term is the minority share of the net assets/equity of the subsidiary at the current financial statement date. Note that each expansion/analysis has the same total – that of the equitized investment.

$$I + 0.8 \, \Delta RE = G + 1.0 \, [A_{now} - L_{now}] - 0.2 \, [A_{now} - L_{now}]$$

Entity consolidation – Column 6 forms the basis of entity consolidation, which is not used in the UK in practice, but forms a useful conceptual tool later for understanding existing practice. Under conventional consolidation, goodwill is computed on the majority (80 per cent) interest only. Entity consolidation computes *total* goodwill at acquisition, including minority goodwill. The bookkeeping for incorporating minority goodwill is

DR. Goodwill   **CR. Minority interest**

It can be viewed as analogous to a revaluation reserve within minority interests relating to goodwill. The valuation of such minority goodwill at acquisition is problematic, which is why the approach is not used. It would probably be worth much less than the relevant proportion of majority goodwill grossed up (i.e. 20 per cent/80 per cent of the parent's share in goodwill) because it does not give control of the subsidiary and is akin to capitalizing internally created goodwill. Such extrapolation is unacceptable to IAS 22 (para. 28). In Figure 4.5 Column 6, the entity goodwill figure is thus called total goodwill, and the minority interest includes its share in this figure

In the UK the equity approach (often termed 'one-line' consolidation) is used for associated companies, conventional consolidation for subsidiaries, and proportional consolidation is optional for unincorporated joint ventures (though new proposals by the ASB, discussed later, would require equity accounting). SSAP 1 requires for associated companies a note disclosure analysing the equitized investment between aggregate net assets and goodwill, a limited form of expansion.

The expansions illustrate a number of intuitive features of acquisition accounting.

- Different consolidation approaches as different expansions of the equitized investment.
- The intuitive analogy for acquisition accounting discussed in Chapter 3 – the purchase of the subsidiary's assets, liabilities and goodwill.
- The equity approach and all consolidation approaches at least in simple examples give the same consolidated retained profits which are only affected by the equitization step and not the expansion one.

Consolidation as a concept and as a technique

Figure 4.5 is a useful way of conceptualizing consolidation. So, consolidation under acquisition accounting could in principle be effected in two ways, both giving identical answers:

1. *The equitization/expansion approach* – Starting with *only* the parent's accounts, equitize the investment in the subsidiary and expand/analyse this into individual assets, liabilities, minority interests and goodwill, which are then added to the corresponding individual amounts of the parent.
2. *The cancellation approach* – Start with the sum of *both* the parent's and the subsidiary's balances. The subsidiary equity is reclassified using a cancellation table, and some of it is removed by cancelling against the investment to determine goodwill, some becomes part of post-acquisition profits, and some minority interests.

In the equitization/expansion approach, only post-acquisition profits are used to adjust the investment. The cancellation approach starts with the sum of the parent's and the subsidiary's total retained profits and then pre-acquisition profits are removed.

The equitization and expansion approach clearly articulates the concept of consolidation. The cancellation approach is the one almost exclusively used in the UK as a computationally efficient method for obtaining consolidated statements. In the USA where some parent companies use the equity approach for investments in individual company accounts (not allowed in the UK) the expansion approach is sometimes used to consolidate under these circumstances. There and in the UK, the cancellation approach is used where parent's accounts record investments at cost.

Example 4.5 – Consolidation as equitization and expansion

In the remainder of this chapter Tinyfry will be regarded as a *passive investment* not an associate and so will be accounted for under the *cost* approach, so that the relationship between Largesse and Smallnesse can be explored without additional complication. Consider again the Largesse Group example in Example 4.1, to illustrate the principles of equitization and expansion.

Stage 1: calculation of equitized investment in Smallnesse

Equitized investment	=	Cost	+ Attributable retained profits since acquisition	
	=	£80m +	80% × [40 – 30]	= £88m

Consolidated retained profits under the equity approach and *all* consolidation approaches is £128m (parent £120m plus subsidiary £8m).

Stage 2: expansions of the equitized amount

According to the above fundamental equation this can be broken down into goodwill at acquisition (here its subsequent write-off is ignored) plus *attributable* net assets at the current financial statement date. This can be checked as:

Investment	£m
Goodwill at acq = 80 – 80% × (35+15+30)	16
Net assets now = 80% × (40 +70–20)	72
	88

Figure 4.6 expands the equitized investment using the example data. Credits are in brackets. Check carefully the derivation of the numbers and how to distinguish between the different expansions.

Particularly work through the calculations for the equitized investment and its complement in the fundamental equation; these are used extensively in accounting for associated companies under SSAP 1 and also for accounting for disposals of subsidiaries in Chapter 7. In this simple example, minority goodwill at acquisition under the entity approach has been calculated by assuming its value is *pro-rata* with the parent's share (i.e. 20/80 × £16m), so that the whole group's goodwill would notionally be £20m and the parent's actual goodwill can be checked as 80% × £20m = £16m. Minority goodwill is likely to be worth less than the £4m difference (£20m – £16m) as unlike the parent's share it does not have control and probably does not even have significant influence.

Investment	Equilisation – cost plus attrib profit	Analysed breakdown	Proportional consolidation	Parent/ conventional consolidation	Entity consolidation
			16 Goodwill	16 Goodwill	20 Total group goodwill
			32 80% Tangible fixed assets	40 100% Tangible fixed assets	40 100% Tangible fixed assets
	80 Investment at cost	16 Goodwill	24 80% Stocks 32 80% Other	30 100% Stocks 40 100% Other	30 100% Stocks 40 100% Other
80 Investment	8 *plus* attrib retained profit	72 80% net assets *now*			
			(16) 80% Loans	(20) 100% Loans	(20) 100% Loans
				(18) 20% Minority in net assets	(18 + 4) 20% Minority in net assets *and* goodwill

Figure 4.6 – Largesse Group expansion of equitized investment

Stage 3: replacement of equitized investment by its expansion
The group balance sheets under the various approaches, shown in Figure 4.7, are obtained by adding the expansions above to the parent company balance sheet in Example 4.1. The first three columns show the equitization process and group accounts if the investment were accounted for using the equity approach ('one-line' consolidation). Group retained profits are identical for *all* consolidation approaches (until Chapter 5). The remaining columns are obtained by using the expansions in Figure 4.6, adding them to the parent's balances.
    Check – the conventional/ parent consolidated balance sheet is identical to that obtained earlier by using the cancellation table in Example 4.1.

TREATMENT OF MINORITY INTERESTS

Group accounts are based on a tiered view of accounting for investments. Here we examine alternative consolidation 'theories', proposed as alternatives for accounting for controlled, but less than wholly owned subsidiaries. The main issue addressed is that of how minority interests should be measured and disclosed in consolidated financial statements, if at all. The FASB in the USA in a Discussion Memorandum, *Consolidation Policy and Procedures* (1992), distinguishes between three consolidation concepts: economic unit, parent and proportional (termed in an earlier paper by Baxter and Spinney (1975) the entity, parent and proprietary approaches respectively).

    Proportional consolidation/proprietary – there is no minority interest; only controlling-interest proportions of the subsidiary's balances are consolidated with the parent's.

Description	Parent accounts	Equitising entry	Equity method	Proportional consolidation	Conventional /parent consolidation	Entity consolidation
Goodwill				16	16	20
Fixed assets	180		180	212	220	220
Investment in Smallnesse	80	8	88	-	-	-
Investment in Minutenesse	20		20	20	20	20
Stocks	50		50	74	80	80
Other	90		90	122	130	130
Loans	(100)		(100)	(116)	(120)	(120)
Share capital	(130)		(130)	(130)	(130)	(130)
Share premium	(70)		(70)	(70)	(70)	(70)
Retained	(120)	(8)	(128)	(128)	(128)	(128)
profits Minority interests					(18)	(22)

Figure 4.7 – Group balance sheets for the Largesse Group at 31 March 1995 under various consolidation approaches

Baxter and Spinney argue that this approach views the group through the eyes of its ultimate owners only. Since minority interests are not ultimate owners of the group, their share of net assets (equity) is disregarded. Such a 'theory' has been used to justify proportional consolidation for all subsidiaries – for example Rubin in Rosenfield and Rubin (1986) argues that it better represents the substance of the acquisition transaction, that one way to acquire say 80 per cent of another's results would be to purchase a package of 80 per cent of its separate assets and liabilities, and that this is equivalent to acquiring 80 per cent of its equity.

Parent – this views consolidation as an expansion of the parent's accounts, group equity being attributable to the parent's shareholders. The ultimate owners have a joint claim with a secondary set of owners, minority interests, to the undivided assets, and liabilities of the subsidiary, so it is meaningless to aggregate fractional assets etc. Since the minority are not important to the group as a whole, their share is condensed into a single figure. A weakness of this concept is that the status of minority interests is ill defined – is it a part of equity, or a liability or a separate class of ownership altogether? What is its nature? Rosenfield and Rubin (1986) give examples of conflicting proposals in the literature.

Economic unit – the group is a reporting entity with a variety of ownership claims. Residual equity is divided into controlling interests (parent shareholdings) and non-controlling interests. Popularized by Moonitz (1951), it regards consolidated assets, liabilities and equities as being those of a group entity. Controlling and non-controlling interests are co-owners. This perspective supports different viewpoints:

- some argue that measurement and disclosure principles for both should be the same so *minority* goodwill should be revalued at acquisition consistent with majority goodwill (whereas others argue that although it is undoubtedly an *asset* of the economic unit, it cannot be measured reliably enough to meet financial statement *recognition* criteria).
- some argue that non-controlling interests could be analysed (e.g. into share capital, share premium, goodwill revaluation reserve and consolidated retained profits) and added to the corresponding amounts for controlling interests.

Taken together these would contain both a measurement difference (goodwill) and a disclosure difference from conventional practice.

However, Rosenfield in Rosenfield and Rubin (1986), whilst supporting an entity-based report, suggests that any numerical breakdown of residual equity between classes serves no useful purpose. He argues that as a historical document showing how equity arose, or as a guide to restrictions on distributions it is inefficient; only an aggregate, equal to the excess of assets over liabilities should be reported, with matters of distributability and claims (e.g. of the minority) detailed in the notes to the accounts.

Conclusion

The different approaches are not clearly or unambiguously defined regarding the treatment of the elements of consolidated equity. One might be excused for viewing them as *rationalizations* for particular technical alternatives, rather than fundamental concepts from which consolidation procedures can be deduced.

Exercises

4.7 Using the Bigfry–Smallfry example (Exercise 4.3) – for this question treating Tinyfry plc as a *passive investment accounted for at cost*,
   (a) calculate amount of the investment in Smallfry at 30 November 1995 under the equity approach.
   (b) calculate both sides of the fundamental equation for this equitized investment.
   (c) Show numerically the different possible expansions of this figure (based on Figure 4.6).
   (d) Prepare a consolidated balance sheet under each approach (based on Figure 4.7).
   (e) Why are consolidated reserves equal under each approach?
4.8 In Exercise 4.6 calculate both sides of the fundamental equation for Tinyfry plc and show the breakdown of the equitized investment into goodwill at acquisition plus net assets at the current balance sheet date (i.e. the note disclosure required for associates by SSAP 1).

UK PRACTICE

UK practice adopts a tiered approach (brings tiers to your eyes!) to accounting for long-term investments in group accounts, based on the extent of influence or control. The term 'participating interest' is used to distinguish holdings where there is a long-term, active intent to exercise influence from more transient holdings held for speculative purposes. Given a participating interest, the level of influence determines how interests in other undertakings are accounted for in the consolidated financial statements. Two aspects of control are distinguished in *Chapter 7, The Reporting Entity* of the ASB's *Draft Statement of Principles* (1994) – the ability to *deploy* economic resources, and the ability *to benefit or suffer* by their deployment. Influence less than control contains the ability to affect but *not* control deployment through the use of that influence. Figure 4.8 gives a broad-brush schema of the relationship between influence and accounting approach. If proposals put forward in a recent ASB Discussion Paper, *Associates and Joint Ventures* (1994), were to be adopted, all case of joint control would be accounted for using the equity approach.

Associates

Definition

SSAP 1, *Accounting for Associated Companies*, was issued in 1971 and revised in 1982. Prior to 1971, company law only recognized either the cost basis or full consolidation in group accounts, and so SSAP 1 had a major impact. In it the term 'associated companies' was defined to include both companies in which a more than 20 per cent stake was held long-term with an ability to exercise significant influence, and joint ventures. Revisions in 1982 made 'significant influence' the basis, and the 20 per cent threshold (now including holdings by other subsidiaries but not associates) only a rebuttable presumption. Holdings in

Type of influence	Accounting treatment	Profit measurement basis
Fixed asset investments: Less than significant influence	Investment at cost	Dividends receivable
Associated undertakings: Significant influence	Equity approach	Attributable profits
Joint ventures: Joint control	Usually equity method, but in defined cases proportional consolidation	Attributable profits
Subsidiaries: Unilateral control (which subsumes dominant influence)	Conventional consolidation	Full profits less minority interests

Figure 4.8 – Relationship between degree of influence and accounting approach

non-corporate joint ventures and consortia were also included. Similar definitions and accounting treatments were enshrined in company law by the revised Companies Act 1985 (introducing the term 'associated undertaking' to embrace corporate and non-corporate entities, and changing slightly the relationship between associates and joint ventures).

SSAP 1 requires associated companies to be accounted for using the equity method. A more than 20 per cent ownership criterion in isolation for such companies would allow cosmetic accounting. Consider the case of the Bendix Corporation in the USA (Greene, 1980). Bendix acquired a marginally less than 20 per cent interest in ASARCO, a metals producer which allowed it under US accounting rules (APB Opinion 18) to account for its investment at cost. When conditions in the metals market improved in 1978, it increased its holding to 21 per cent which allowed it to use the equity method and to bring in for the first time ASARCO's (improved) profits which made a significant difference to Bendix's consolidated results.

ED 50 proposed to bring SSAP 1 in line with the Companies Act 1985 revisions, but never became a standard. The present situation is defined by the ASB document, *Interim Statement: Consolidated Accounts*, issued in January 1991, which minimally amends SSAP 1 to comply with the Companies Act changes, using a qualitative criterion with a quantitative backup.

An associated company is

a company not being a subsidiary of the investing group in which the interest of the investing group is for the long-term and, having regard to the disposition of the other shareholdings, the investing group or company is in a position to exercise a significant influence over the company in which the investment is made.   (para, 13)

A 'company' includes 'any enterprise which comes within the scope of statements of standard accounting practice . . . [and] can include non-corporate joint ventures and consortia' (para. 11).

Significant influence is defined as participation in financial, operating and dividend policy decisions, but not necessarily control over them. Representation on the board is indicative but not conclusive. IAS 28, *Accounting for Investments in Associates*, cites material transactions between investor and investee, interchange of management personnel, or provision of essential technical information as examples of possible indicative factors (para. 5).

Quantitative rebuttable presumptions – Paragraphs 14 and 15 state that a group holding of 20 per cent of the equity voting rights or more leads to the *positive* rebuttable presumption that the qualitative criterion is met, and less than 20 per cent leads to the *negative* rebuttable presumption that the criterion is not met. In theory such a wording should make it more difficult for a company to keep changing its treatment by marginally adjusting holdings around the 20 per cent mark, though it is difficult for auditors to discern managerial intentions. In fact the Bendix case occurred despite similar wording in the US standard!

Associated undertaking legal definition – the Companies Act 1985 defines an associated undertaking (Sch 4A, para. 20(1)) in a very similar manner: an undertaking (not a subsidiary) in which an undertaking included in the consolidation has a participating interest and exercises significant influence over its operating and financial policy. It includes partnerships and unincorporated associations. 'Participating interest' is defined in Chapter 2, one in shares held on a long-term basis for the purpose of securing a contribution to the holding undertaking's activities by the exercise of control or influence arising from or related to that interest. Specifically included are subsidiaries' holdings, options and convertibles. The positive rebuttable presumption of SSAP 1 is made but not the negative one (Section 260).

Not all authors agree that equity accounting is 'equitable', arguing that equity accounting leads to the same profits being counted in the associate's own statements and in the accounts of the parent. Others argue that since the parent does not hold a controlling share in the associate, it may not be able to get hold of the associate's reported earnings for distribution to its own shareholders. It has also been argued that the equity approach records profits of associates, but gives little indication of their debt structure for evaluating group gearing.

The ASB Discussion Paper, *Associates and Joint Ventures*, issued in June 1994, proposes interpreting the Companies Act terms 'participating interest' and 'significant interest' so that genuine influence must exist for there to be an 'associated undertaking', which then can be described as a 'strategic alliance' (para. 3.1). The term 'significant influence' would be interpreted more narrowly so that it would only apply

if [the investor's] influence arising from the rights related to the interest it holds . . . together with agreements – formal and informal – with other stake-holders or the management of that entity, result in it fulfilling three conditions . . .
(a) The investor must exercise influence over the operating and financial policies of the investee that is sufficient for it to fulfil its role as a partner in the business of that entity. This means that in the area of their mutual interest the investee will generally implement policies that are consistent with the strategy of the investor.
(b) The investor must reasonably expect to benefit, at least in the long term, from the economic benefits accumulated by the economic activities of its investee. . . Through its influence over the financial policy of the investee, particularly with respect to dividend policy and investment decisions, the investor must, therefore, have the ability to secure access in the long run to its share in [the investee's] cash flows if it is to benefit (other than by disposing of its interest) from any increases in value of its investee . . .
(c) The investor's interest must provide it with some protection from changes in the operating and financial policies of the investee that would significantly affect the benefits it expects or the risks to which it is exposed.   (para. 3.7)

It is pointed out that a current policy of non-distribution of short-run cash flows may be still consistent with access to the long-run cash flows of the investee.

This narrowing, if implemented, would mean that many current 'associates' would not be 'strategic alliances' and therefore not be 'associates' under the new proposed definitions, because 'significant influence' using this more stringent definition would not be present. The Discussion Paper proposes treating such 'ex-associates' as investments (probably fixed asset investments to be included at cost, market value or directors' valuation, the last two being preferred on the grounds of usefulness). Prior years would be restated to be consistent with the new status of the investee, and presumably in the year of change there would be much widespread impact on consolidated financial statements generally removing 'post-acquisition income' and restating to a 'cost/dividend' basis.

Accounting for associates

SSAP 1 requires the equity method to be used. The term 'equity method of accounting' also appears in Sch 4A, para. 22 of the Companies Act 1985, but neither define it. The ASB Discussion Paper, *Associates and Joint Ventures*, defines it as where the investment is initially brought in at cost, and goodwill is identified (and together with the investee's goodwill) accounted for separately. 'The initial amount for the investment is adjusted in each period by the investor's share of the results of the investee, which the investor recognizes in its profit and loss account, and any other changes in the investee's net assets. Dividends received from the investee reduce the carrying amount of the investment.' (para. 4.8). The effects of valuation adjustments and the profit and loss accounting treatment relating to the equity method are dealt with in Chapters 6 and 7 respectively.

Balance sheet disclosure

Separate note disclosure is required of attributable (proportional) net assets and goodwill underlying the equitized investment (which includes goodwill arising in the associate's own accounts plus goodwill on acquisition). This goodwill total is not added to consolidated goodwill, but is included in the notes to the consolidated balance sheet. Ma and Parker (1983, p. 121) outline the use of an Australian variation which they term the 'pure equity' approach where goodwill is severed from the 'investment' and is included in consolidated goodwill, leaving the investment reported at net asset amount, but this is different from SSAP 1's treatment.

Attributable post-acquisition reserves of the associate and movements thereon must be disclosed (part of the left-hand side of the fundamental equation). It also requires details of the associate's business, and disclosure of loans to and separately loans from associates, and greater disclosure of trading balances and a breakdown of associate assets and liabilities if 'material in the context of the financial statements of the investing group'.

This last requirement is presumably included to try to prevent Leasco-type peculiarities (Briloff, 1980). In 1979, the Reliance group in the USA sold off Leasco, a computer-leasing subsidiary, to its own shareholders. In conventional accounting terms, Leasco was now an independent company. Later, Leasco bought 3.2 per cent of Reliance's share capital. It argued that although the proportion was so small, it could use the equity approach since the two companies were under common management. Though proportionally small, Leasco's shareholding in the much larger Reliance dwarfed its other income. The additional disclosures above would in principle have required disclosure of more information about Reliance to Leasco's own shareholders (who were by now different from those of Reliance) than the minimal disclosures normally required of associates. This case illustrates how easy it is to circumvent the 20 per cent + general rule for associates. Briloff (1980) argues that common management should not have been the determining criterion as there is little evidence that Reliance's policies would be affected because of the 3.2 per cent interest of Leasco, and so Leasco did not possess significant influence.

Unlike in the UK, equity accounting is often used in the USA in the parent's company financial statements as well as in consolidated statements. The implementation of the EC 7th Directive has resulted in its adoption throughout Europe. Nobes and Parker (1991, p. 302) report that this breaks new ground for Germany, but the equity method was already in widespread use in France. In The Netherlands it is also used in the parent's own accounts for both subsidiaries and associates, but in the individual company accounts the equitized profits are taken to an unrealized reserve. In Australia, the approach has only recently been adopted for associates.

The ASB Discussion Paper, *Associates and Joint Ventures* (1994), proposes using the 'expanded' equity method for all strategic alliances, i.e. treating associates and joint ventures in the same way, augmenting the bare equity accounting amounts by extra note disclosures, many similar to current disclosures (para. 4.12). In addition, two levels of supplementary note disclosures are proposed according to whether aggregate interests in strategic alliances, i.e. associates and joint ventures, are 'material' or 'substantial' (para. 4.18).

Interests are defined as 'material' if 'omission or misstatement of information about them might reasonably be expected to influence decisions made by users of financial statements'. This might depend not only on size, but also on the nature of the potential source of risk or benefit they represent. Interests are 'substantial' where 'the investor's share exceed[s] 15 per cent of any of the following for the investor group (excluding any amounts for associates or joint ventures themselves): gross assets, gross liabilities, turnover or results (i.e. the profit or loss for the year after tax, minority interests and extraordinary items)' (para. 4.18).

The main extra disclosures proposed if interests are 'material' refer to the consolidated profit and loss account and are dealt with in Chapter 7. If interests in associates (or joint ventures) are 'substantial' it is proposed that a complete set of summarized financial statements for such 'strategic alliances' in aggregate showing the investor's share of each major balance sheet, profit and loss and cash flow heading which contains a material item, together with comparatives should be provided. Further, the consolidated statements should provide an analysis of the investor's share of aggregate borrowings per statutory headings, consistent with FRS 4, distinguishing those with recourse and those without; and also any further breakdowns necessary to understand the nature and effect of such items (see also Chapter 7). If interests in associates (or joint ventures) individually are 'material' or 'substantial', similar disclosures to the aggregate case are proposed for *each* such investee (paras 4.18–4.20).

Joint ventures

Definition

The term 'joint venture' was first used in UK pronouncements in SSAP 1 in 1971, but was not defined. It was introduced into company law by the Companies Act 1985, which whilst not providing an explicit definition, implies the criterion of joint management of the (holding) undertaking with a non-consolidated one (the venture) (Sch 4A, para. 19 (1)). ED 50 (1990) discussed the concept of a joint venture, but its draft definition was criticized for implying 'that the existence of a joint venture agreement was a necessary condition for an undertaking to be a joint venture . . . and also seem[ing] to suggest that participants had to be involved in the set up of the undertaking' (ASB *Interim Statement*, para. A9).

The ASB *Interim Statement* (1991) concluded that the Act's criterion of joint management 'could more aptly be described as joint control' (para. 32), and defines a joint venture (para. 33) as 'an undertaking by which its participants expect to achieve some common purpose or benefit. It is controlled jointly by two or more venturers. Joint control is the contractually agreed sharing of control.'

IAS 31, *Accounting for Joint Ventures* (1990) distinguishes different types of joint ventures – joint control of operations (using the assets and other resources of the parties to the venture without setting up an independent entity), of assets, and of entities.

The ASB's Discussion Paper, *Associates and Joint Ventures*, instead emphasizes a criterion of joint control of an entity with other entities, where 'none of the entities alone can control that entity but all together can' (para. 3.12). This is consistent with one venturer managing the venture provided all play an active role, at least at a strategic level, in setting the venture's financial and operating policies. Joint control by an entity requires that 'decisions on operating and financial policies *essential* to the activities, economic performance and financial position of that other entity require its consent' (para. 3.13, original emphasis). It takes issue with IAS 31's framework, and proposes distinguishing between joint activities which are a 'shared facility', where 'the joint venturers derive their benefit from product or services taken in kind rather than by receiving a share in the profits of trading', and a 'joint venture', which is a form of strategic alliance. 'Jointly controlled operations or jointly controlled assets that do not by themselves constitute a business do not amount to a joint venture' (para. 3.16). Thus, certain of IAS 31's categories of joint ventures would not be so under the ASB's proposals.

Accounting treatment

The Companies Act 1985 allows the option of proportional consolidation for unincorporated joint ventures which are not subsidiaries (Sch 4A, para. 19(1)), presumably because the venturer is deemed to hold a 'direct' stake in a proportion of the venture's assets and liabilities. This narrows the provisions of the EC 7th Directive which allows proportional consolidation for joint ventures, but not for associates. If the Companies Act option for proportional consolidation is *not* exercised for unincorporated ventures, and in addition in the case of *all* corporate joint ventures, the accounting treatment depends on whether the holding meets associated company (undertaking) or subsidiary undertaking criteria. It is likely that most joint ventures would be accounted for as associates, i.e. using the equity approach, though no discussion of the relationship between significant interest, joint management and joint control is given. Nobes and Parker (1991, p. 302) report that proportional consolidation is prescribed in France for joint ventures, but not allowed for other associated undertakings, and in The Netherlands it is a common treatment for joint ventures. If proportional consolidation is chosen in the UK, the factors on which joint management is based must be disclosed (Sch 5 S 21).

IAS 31, *Accounting for Joint Ventures* (1990), is more sophisticated with different accounting approaches required in the case of joint control of operations, assets and entities. In the case of entities, in its consolidated financial statements, it requires that the venturer should proportionally consolidate the joint venture either on a line-by-line basis or on an aggregated basis where the separate lines relating to the joint venture are reported in one place, *regardless* of whether the joint venture is incorporated or unincorporated. The equity approach is permitted but strongly discouraged (para. 42). Whilst the current UK position meets the least preferred IAS 31 requirements, clearly there is a conflict of perspective with the latter's preferred treatment, of proportional consolidation of jointly controlled *incorporated* entities, prohibited by the Companies Act 1985.

Unlike IAS 31, the ASB Discussion Paper, *Associates and Joint Ventures*, proposes that associates and joint ventures should be subsumed under 'strategic alliances'. All strategic alliances should be accounted for using the equity approach. Supplementary disclosures (identical to the Discussion Paper's proposals for associates discussed earlier) would be based *not* on the distinction between associates or joint ventures, but on whether, in aggregate, either as strategic alliances are *material* or *substantial* (i.e. material associates and joint ventures would be treated the same, as would substantial associates and joint ventures, whereas material and substantial associates would be treated differently). As with associates similar disclosures would be required for individual joint ventures which are material or substantial in their own right.

Chapter 7, The Reporting Entity of the ASB's *Draft Statement of Principles* argues against proportional consolidation for any joint ventures on the grounds that the venturer *shares* control in the *whole* venture and does not have the sole control over its proportionate share in the venture's assets and liabilities implied by proportional consolidation (para. 6.6). Indeed, 'in most cases the investor controls its *interest* in an associate or joint venture but not its share of the individual assets or liabilities'(emphasis added). Certain advantages of proportional consolidation are admitted, for example in assessing the 'size' of the group and its 'gearing', but the supplemental disclosures proposed by the Discussion

Paper are deemed to mitigate the disadvantages of the bare equity approach.

In a similar vein the Discussion Paper, *Associates and Joint Ventures*, argues that even the Companies Act option of proportional consolidation for non-corporate joint ventures should be closed, since

(a) the decision to use a corporate or non-corporate structure depends on 'tax, financing and local structural considerations; strategic alliances fulfilling the same purpose may have different structures according to where they are established';
(b) incorporation has different meanings in different legal jurisdictions; and
(c) respondents were critical of ED 50's proposal that non-corporate joint ventures should have a different accounting treatment from corporate ones (para. 2.11).

The ASB has a much narrower concept of joint venture than IAS 31. For example it proposes that 'joint activities' (which IAS 31 treats as a form of joint venture but the Discussion Paper does not) should be accounted for directly in the venturers' individual financial statements according to their share of costs, assets and liabilities, disclosing in their notes contingent liabilities potentially arising from failure of partners in the joint activities (para. 3.17).

A contracting theory perspective

Whittred and Zimmer (1994) attempt to show that in an unregulated environment the choice between proportional consolidation and one-line approaches to accounting for unincorporated joint ventures is determined by the nature of the venture's assets and the manner in which they are owned and financed. They found that in a 1984 sample of 126 Australian mining companies

(a) where lenders had recourse to the venturer's *assets* (by the co-venturers themselves borrowing to finance the venture or by the venture itself borrowing, but lenders having right of recourse to the co-venturer's assets) proportional consolidation tended to be used;
(b) where the venture borrowed but no direct recourse to the co-venturers' underlying assets was given, one-line consolidation was generally used.

This is consistent with consolidated reporting being used sensitively as a means of monitoring debt agreements, even in the absence of regulation, reducing debt contracting costs. It also suggests that this sensitivity in using the different approaches for monitoring debt contracts may be lost if the ASB's proposals are adopted, unless note disclosures are extensive and contracts are rewritten so that GAAP principles are adjusted for contract monitoring purposes. Whittred and Zimmer in the same paper extended the results to joint ventures in the Australian real-estate development sector.

Subsidiaries

Consolidation

The legal definition of a subsidiary was examined in Chapter 2. FRS 2 considers 'control' to be the basis for consolidated financial statements. The consolidation of controlled undertakings is given effect by:

Taking the parent and its subsidiary undertakings (the 'group'), then

(a) *excluding* subsidiary undertakings which satisfy the Act's exclusion criteria (are not 'controlled'), and
(b) *including* controlled undertakings which do not satisfy the definition of a subsidiary undertaking (quasi-subsidiaries) as defined in FRS 5.

Elements of an economic entity group concept are inherent here in that unified management is one criterion for a subsidiary undertaking, but only if the parent also holds a participating interest. The UK consolidation approach sits uneasily between parent and entity consolidation concepts. Aggregate minority interests (a single figure) must be placed next to Capital and Reserves (i.e. not quite a liability and not quite 'equity'), but unlike the USA include fair value adjustments and adjustments to carrying amounts on the same basis as controlling interests. However, goodwill is not attributed to the minority (FRS 2, para. 38). The US currently tends more towards the parent approach and fair value adjustments are not attributed to minority interests. These aspects will be explored in Chapters 5 and 6.

Other approaches

In Chapter 2 reasons for excluding subsidiaries from consolidation were examined. Figure 4.9 summarizes the accounting treatment for excluded subsidiaries required by FRS 2, *Accounting for Subsidiary Undertakings*.

Reasons for exclusion	Accounting treatment
Severe long-term restrictions	If still significant influence - equity approach, otherwise freeze investment at carrying amount at restriction date
Held exclusively with view to resale	Current asset - lower of cost and net realisable value
Activities too dissimilar	Equity approach with separate financial statements of such subsidiaries appended if published in their own right.

Figure 4.9 – Accounting treatment for excluded subsidiaries

As stated in Chapter 2, the 'too dissimilar activities' mandatory exclusion has been defined by FRS 2 in such a way that it is unlikely to be used in practice. It is interesting that the equity approach is required in two out of three cases (the other two statutory exclusions are not discussed here: 'disproportionate expense and delay' being deleted by FRS 2, and immateriality). This reinforces the idea that the basis for group accounting is based on the degree of influence/effective control. The severe restriction criterion is consistent with the retention of 'dominant' influence to the date of restriction, and then significant influence (equity method), or loss of significant influence thereafter (establishing the investment at a pseudo 'cost'). A good example of the 'lack of effective control' criterion was that of Trust House Forte's investment in the Savoy Hotel Group, in which it held 69 per cent of the equity, but only 42 per cent of the voting shares and where its influence on management and representation on the board of directors was consistently thwarted. Prior to 1985 this investment was accounted for at cost, but in the 1985 accounts it is measured as an associate. The Companies Act 1985 requires certain particulars where holdings in another company exceed 10 per cent of issued equity shares or of total assets.

Exercises

4.9 How is significant influence to be established in determining whether an affiliate counts as an associated company?

4.10 Should proportionate consolidation be used for joint ventures where venturers share control of incorporated entities? Contrast the stances taken by IAS 31, *Accounting for Joint Ventures* (1990), and the ASB Discussion Paper, *Associates and Joint Ventures* (1994).

4.11 Is it tenable to treat associates and joint ventures identically, based on their impact on the consolidated financial statements (material vs. substantial) rather than the form of control exercised (significant influence vs. joint control), as advocated by the ASB Discussion Paper, *Associates and Joint Ventures* (1994)?

4.12 The Resource Group has held since 1 January 1993 a 50% stake in Oilwell plc, acquired when the retained profits of the latter was £80m. The other 50% in this joint venture is held by Venturer plc. Major decisions relating to Oilwell plc require both shareholders to agree, so it is not considered to be a subsidiary of the Resource Group. The financial statements of the Resource Group excluding Oilwell plc, and of Oilwell plc itself are show below:

Balance sheets at 31 March 1995

	Resource group		Oilwell	
	£m	£m	£m	£m
Fixed assets				
Goodwill		50		—
Tangible fixed assets		1,150		250
Investment in Oilwell		200		—.
		1,400		250
Net current assets				
Stocks	500		150	
Other	600		250	
		1,100		400
Creditors over one year		(700)		(200)
		1,800		450
Capital and reserves				
Share capital	300		100	
Share premium	400		150	
Retained profits	900		200	
	1,600		450	
Minority interests	200		—	
	1,800		450	

Required

(a) Prepare a consolidated balance sheet of the Resource Group at 31 March 1995, treating Oilwell plc appropriately and giving in addition the note disclosures required by the amended SSAP 1.

(b) Explain to the finance director of Resource Group what differences it would make to the group's main ratios if Oilwell were treated as a subsidiary.

SUBSEQUENT ACCOUNTING FOR GOODWILL

Chapter 5 examines accounting for goodwill in depth. The accounting entries for the two alternative approaches permitted by SSAP 22, *Accounting for Goodwill* (1984) – its preferred treatment, immediate write-off against reserves, and its allowed alternative, gradual amortization to profit and loss account over useful economic life – are now illustrated.

Example 4.6 – Accounting for goodwill after acquisition

This example goes back to the cancellation table approach and is based on Example 4.3 (p. 81) of the Largesse Group, in which Minutenesse plc is assumed to be an associated undertaking.

1. Assume goodwill is written off immediately against share premium with court approval

Largesse Group – abbreviated balance sheet cancellation table

Description	Inv in Small-nesse	Inv in Minute-nesse	Share cap	Share prem	Ret profits	Good-will	Minority interests
Original amounts	—	25	(130)	(70)	(133)	16	(18)
Immediate write-off		(4)		20		(16)	
Consolidated amounts	—	21	(130)	(50)	(133)	—	(18)

SSAP 22 does not specify which reserves are available for immediate write-off. Revaluation reserves are prohibited, and permission of the court is necessary to use the share premium account (as in our example above). Whichever reserve is chosen, even in the case of consolidated retained profits, the write-off bypasses the profit and loss account. Minority interest is unaffected. Note that the associate's goodwill is part of its investment amount. Its immediate write-off means that the equitized investment is then stated at proportionate net asset value at the balance sheet date, viz.

Investment	£m
Net assets = 25% x (80+40–36)	21

2.   Assume goodwill is to be gradually amortized straight-line over a five year period

Largesse Group – Abbreviated balance sheet cancellation table

Description	Inv in Small-nesse	Inv in Minute-nesse	Share cap	Share prem	Ret profits	Good-will	Minority interests
Original amounts	—	25	(130)	(70)	(133)	16	(18)
Gradual amortization		(1.6)			11.2	(9.6)	
Consolidated amounts	—	23.4	(130)	(50)	(121.8)	6.4	(18)

Gradual amortization is expensed to profit and loss. The consolidated retained profits effect in the balance sheet is:

$$2 \text{ years} \quad \times \quad \frac{4}{5} \text{ (associate)} \quad + \quad 3 \text{ years} \quad \times \quad \frac{16}{5} \text{ (subsidiary)} \quad = \text{£11.2}$$

and the investment in associate is:

Investment	£m
Goodwill $= \frac{3}{5} \times [20 - 25\% \times (30+20+14)]$	2.4
Net assets = 25% x (80+40–36)	21.0
	23.4

Gradual amortization decreases consolidated profit each year compared to immediate write-off, and since consolidated equity is lower under the latter, shows higher consolidated gearing.

Exercise

4.13 Consider again the Bigfry–Smallfry example in Exercise 4.6, in which Tinyfry plc is assumed to be an associated undertaking. Smallfry was acquired six months ago and Tinyfry two years ago.

Required

Show how goodwill is accounted for subsequent to acquisition by providing extracts from the consolidation cancellation table and calculate consolidated balances at 30 November 1995 for investments, consolidated retained earnings and minority interests if consolidated goodwill is
(a) written-off immediately against consolidated retained profits, and
(b) gradually amortized over a 10 year period on a straight-line basis.

USEFULNESS OF CONSOLIDATED BALANCE SHEET

It is undoubtedly true that for most groups the consolidated balance sheet gives a better picture of the size of the 'tools' at a group's disposal than the parent company balance sheet. This alone may justify its publication. However, it is important also to understand the limitations of such consolidated statements.

The averaging problem

Consolidation can be viewed as a process of averaging – the sum of a set of items is always a constant times their arithmetic average viz.

$$\bar{x} = \sum \frac{x_i}{n} \text{ and so, } \sum x_i = n \bar{x}$$

Under some circumstances averaging is misleading. For example, the consolidation of loss-making subsidiaries without further disclosures can hide variations in performance within the group, or where businesses within a conglomerate group are highly dissimilar, e.g. a heavy engineering firm owning an equal-sized supermarket subsidiary. The former may have an extremely high current ratio because of long-term contracts in progress; the latter's may be less than unity because it collects cash from its customers much faster than it needs to settle its debts. The former may be heavily financed by long-term loans (i.e. be highly geared), the latter by retained earnings and short-term credit. 'Average' consolidated balances and ratios calculated therefrom are likely to be difficult to interpret. Conventional accounts do not report standard deviations, though segmental reporting provides a limited remedy (see Chapter 12).

Chapter 2 discusses how the criterion for mandatory exclusion of 'too dissimilar activities' in the Companies Act 1985 has been effectively redefined by FRS 2 to ensure that all subsidiaries and quasi-subsidiaries (FRS 5), no matter how dissimilar, must be consolidated. Only where severe long-term restrictions lead to an actual loss of control or where the interest is held exclusively with a view to subsequent resale are exclusions from consolidation required. Such a position has been justified, as for SFAS 94, *Consolidation of All Majority-owned Subsidiaries* (1987) in the USA, on grounds of comparability between groups, and because compulsory segmental reporting under SSAP 25, *Segmental Reporting* (1990) is claimed to provide sufficient information about group diversity.

Exclusions in the UK prior to such all-inclusive consolidation were mainly finance subsidiaries, banking and shipping subsidiaries, the latter being subject to specialized accounting regulations. Many writers suggested that since financing subsidiaries are an inseparable part of large groups, it was difficult to compare two similar groups, one which financed customers via component companies (implicitly consolidated) and the other via a specialized financing subsidiary. As Mohr (1991, p. 125) points out, the main effects of all-inclusive consolidation on previous non-consolidators is to replace equity accounting with full consolidation, increasing gearing as highly geared finance and banking subsidiaries are added to consolidated balance sheets, decreasing interest cover for similar reasons, increasing the size of consolidated revenues and assets, and probably decreasing consolidated return on assets.

In an efficient market, if there are no transaction costs, provided the market has sufficient information, the change of approach should have no effect (Conine, 1989). However, debt may need to be renegotiated as, for example, gearing-based debt covenant restrictions could be breached by the change, with possible borrowing cost increases. Some worry that consolidation could lead to information *loss* as supplemental information about non-consolidated subsidiaries is replaced by much less detailed segmental disclosures. Unlike in the USA, FRS 2 did not require continuing disclosures of non-consolidated information for a 'grace' period for comparative purposes.

There has been little systematic study of the effects of requiring all-inclusive consolidation in the UK. In the USA there is a considerable literature. Mian and Smith (1990a) argue the decision whether or not to consolidate dissimilar activities may be part of an integrated voluntary decision on the best way to report group results. They hypothesize that firms for which benefits of consolidation would exceed costs would tend to be those with more interdependent operations, those for which costs of separate disclosure are greater (e.g. preparation costs for foreign subsidiaries and competitive sensitivity of disclosures), and those for which group financial data is needed to monitor debt agreements, e.g if there are direct cross-guarantees (see Chapter 2). Such firms are more likely to consolidate. Non-consolidation would be chosen where consolidated statements are not needed for monitoring purposes by creditors or where protection of creditors tends to take place through other means – banking subsidiaries through legal liquidity regulations, property companies through securing debt on specific properties. Their empirical evidence supports their analysis.

They argue that the limiting of non-consolidation by SFAS 94 (equivalent to FRS 2) restricts management's ability to organize activities in the most efficient way possible. However, they only find weak evidence of a negative stock-price reaction (Mian and Smith, 1990b) to support this claim. They also find US firms mitigate the all-inclusive consolidation effects by, for example, retiring long-term debt adversely affected by the changes, or reorganizing or selling non-consolidated subsidiaries. Jordan, Pate and Clark (1992) found 30 US groups in 1986 which divested themselves of formerly unconsolidated subsidiaries had higher projected gearing increases under all-inclusive consolidation than a control group which did not.

Sensitivity of tiered accounting treatment to marginal ownership changes

Similar problems arise where there is a change in a holding from 'significant influence' to 'control' or vice versa. As discussed above, differential balance sheet effects of changing from reporting a single figure equitized investment to the inclusion of component balance sheet elements (consolidation) can have a dramatic effect on ratios. This could be a potential hazard for analysts comparing similar groups where one invests in 'strategic alliances' and another with slightly larger proportionate holdings invests in 'subsidiaries'. However, one could argue the differences in groups actually are substantive.

In theory SSAP 1 requires more detailed information about highly material associates' tangible and intangible assets and liabilities and results if 'the interests [and results] in the associated companies are so material in the context of the financial statements that more detailed information about them would assist in giving a true and fair view' (paras 23 and 30). However, Skerratt and Tonkin (1992, pp. 92 – 94) found in practice that only four groups out of 300 partially provide such information and only one provides both balance sheet and profit and loss account information. Rio Tinto Zinc Corporation, which has considerable holdings in associates, includes their turnover in group turnover and *then* deducts associate turnover so the net figure satisfies SSAP 1. It also gives a detailed consolidated profit and loss account and balance sheet as a supplemental disclosure using RTZ group accounting policies for the subgroup headed by a 49 per cent associate, CRA Limited (Skerratt and Tonkin, 1993).

Solvency evaluation and consolidated balance sheets

A 'group' is not a legal entity and so creditors, even of the parent, would be mistaken if they look to group accounts to evaluate their security. In principle they should look mainly to the individual accounts of subsidiaries, and creditors of the parent company mainly to its individual accounts. However, group accounts may be of help. The creditor may get a better feel of the strategic position of his company within the whole group, whether it is likely to be let slide or expanded etc. Their claims are only over the assets of the individual legal entity. However, both Whittred (1987) and Mian and Smith (1990a), point out that where such creditors have their debt rights backed up by direct cross-guarantees, consolidated financial reports may be their primary statements for monitoring purposes. Walker (1978b) shows the security of creditors often depends on the order in which companies in a group are liquidated. An appraisal of the overall financial position and strategy of the group thus may be extremely important to creditors of subsidiaries.

The Companies Act 1985 requires the parent to disclose aggregate details of its loans to subsidiaries and of its loans by subsidiaries, and of guarantees entered into on behalf of other group companies. For further details of intra-group indebtedness the investor must try to piece together an incomplete jig-saw from subsidiaries' individual accounts, but these only disclose aggregate indebtedness to and from group companies. SSAP 1 requires details of loans to and from associates, and of short-term credit if material. FRED 8, *Related Party Transactions*, proposes disclosures of certain transactions with related parties (see Chapter 1), but taken together all regulatory disclosures omit much necessary information and significant creditors need access to non-published information.

Access to the group's economic resources

The ASB Discussion Draft, *The Reporting Entity* (1994) comments that 'consolidated financial statements may overstate the degree of access the parent has to the group's economic resources that are held by its subsidiaries. . . . [in that they] do not distinguish between the activities and assets of the parent itself and those of its subsidiaries.' (para. 3.5). It cites various restrictions and potential restrictions on the parent's access to assets – the existence of minority interests' voting powers, the duty of care directors of subsidiaries owe to such subsidiaries as separate legal entities, restrictions on access to overseas assets and on their deployment and transfer, subsidiaries operating in regulated industries, or other 'commercial, financial or economic reasons impeding the parent's ability to deploy funds and resources across the group'. (paras 3.5 – 3.9). However it concludes consolidation is still the best way to reflect the economic effect of the parent's control (para. 3.10) and such limitations are offset by the additional presentation of segmental information (para. 3.11). Interestingly it suggests that showing minority interests by segment provides useful information in this regard. The ASB Statement, *Operating and Financial Review* (1993) recommends certain voluntary disclosures relating to restrictions on access to group resources (see Chapter 12).

Minority interests

Minority interests are situated between creditors and parent shareholders, having an equity interest in *part* of the group or possibly an equity interest in the whole group restricted in some way. The term 'minority interests' can be misleading in that it is possible for such interests to be extremely large in relation to the size of the parent's interests, for example in groups with vertical chains of shareholdings (see Chapter 10), or in groups where the control is primarily exercised in ways other than through majority equity ownership (see Chapter 2). The FASB Discussion Memorandum, *Consolidation Policy and Procedures* (1991) uses the terms 'controlling interests' and 'non-controlling interests' for the 'parent' and 'minority' interests. However, the term 'minority interests' is used in the Companies Act 1985. FRS 2 comments 'despite the title "Minority interests", there is in principle no upper limit to the proportion of shares in a subsidiary undertaking which may be held as a minority interest whilst the parent undertaking [qualifies as a "parent undertaking" under the statutory definition]', but still it sticks to the term 'minority interest'. In this book 'controlling' and 'non-controlling interests' are used synonymously with 'parent' and 'minority interests'.

The primary source of information for minority/non-controlling interests would be the accounts of the subsidiary or sub-group in which they hold shares, though many of their problems are analogous to those of creditors. Presumably this is why the full-blown entity approach, which portrays them as equal co-owners of the group, has attracted so little professional support. Rosenfield and Rubin (1986) provide evidence of the literature's confusion over the status of the minority, by citing authors who respectively recommend that minorities should be disclosed as liabilities, between liabilities and equity, and as a part of equity. FRS 2 (para. 37) requires aggregate minority interests to be placed next to (!) Capital and Reserves. A paucity of consolidated disclosure relating to minority interests minimizes the potential usefulness of consolidated accounts to them. The FASB Discussion Memorandum discussed above, describes them in a sense as 'a "leveraging [i.e. gearing] technique" used by the parent in the sense that the non-controlling interest finances assets controlled by the parent without making contractual debt service claims on the parent' (p. 25).

Their measurement basis depends on the consolidation concept used. Under proportional consolidation there are no minority interests; under some forms of the entity approach minority goodwill is included. Minority interests under conventional consolidation, which exclude such goodwill, were discussed earlier. Chapter 6 examines considerable international disagreements over whether minority interests should reflect any consolidation valuation adjustments. The USA has in some matters decided they shouldn't (nearer to a parent view) whereas the UK (FRS 2) has decided mainly they should (nearer to an entity view).

Their ambiguous nature is also reflected in differing proposals on how to treat *debit* balances. Prior to FRS 2, SSAP 14 and ED 50 required recognition only where, for example, there was a binding obligation to make good accumulated losses. FRS 2 requires a debit balance *always* to be recognized, and *in addition* a provision to be made to the extent that the group has a legal obligation to provide finance not recoverable in respect of the minority's share of accumulated losses (para. 37). Such a debit balance in its view does not represent a liability of the minority interest (Appendix III, para. xi).

FRS 4, *Capital Instruments* (1994) requires minority interests to be analysed between 'equity interests' and 'non-equity interests' (para. 50), distinguished by the fact that the latter has curtailed rights in that distributions and winding up surpluses are not calculated with respect to assets, profits or equity dividends, or where the shares are redeemable other than at the option of the issuer (para. 12). In addition, shares issued by subsidiaries should be classified as liabilities 'if the group taken as a whole has an obligation to transfer economic benefits in connection with the shares' (para. 49) – the example is given of guaranteed payments. Income recognition criteria for non-equity interests under FRS 4 treat them in many ways as quasi-liabilities, though they are to be positioned with other equity interests in the financial statements.

Exercises

4.14 Assess whether all-inclusive consolidation should be required for all subsidiaries, regardless of how dissimilar their activities.

4.15 Assess whether minority interests should be reported as liabilities, part of shareholders' equity or in some other way.

4.16 What potential extra information content would segmental information have over all-inclusive consolidated financial statements?

4.17 What changes in financial ratios would you expect to observe if the equity approach is used for a subsidiary instead of (a) the cost approach, (b) conventional consolidation?

4.18 What changes in current consolidation practice would be necessary to change to a full-blown entity basis for consolidation? To what extent would such changes be justified?

4.19 Should proportional consolidation be required (a) for all joint ventures, or (b) for all associated undertakings?

4.20 Are there characteristics of joint ventures which suggest they should be accounted for on a different basis than other associates or subsidiaries?

SUMMARY

*The acquisition cancellation approach removes the **parent's** share of **pre-acquisition** equity of the subsidiary. The subsidiary only contributes to consolidated results **after** acquisition. However, the minority's share is an **ongoing** one.*

*Conventional consolidation is one part of a **spectrum** of ways of accounting for investments. The **equity approach** adjusts an investment from a cost-dividends receivable basis to a cost plus attributable **retained** profits basis. The equitized investment always equals the proportionate net assets of the other company plus goodwill. Consolidation can be characterized as **equitization plus expansion**, and the different consolidation approaches correspond to different degrees of expansion, from the (minimal) equity approach to the entity approach. Conventional consolidation lies in the middle. Quasi-theoretical concepts correspond to the expansions.*

Investments with no significant influence are accounted for as trade investments at cost; where there is significant influence but not control as associated companies/undertakings (SSAP 1) using the equity approach; where there is unilateral control consolidated as subsidiaries (FRS 2) using either the acquisition or merger approach (FRS 6), according to whether merger criteria are met. There is currently some controversy over how to account for joint ventures, whether they should be treated differently from associates, or grouped together in a category 'strategic alliances' and accounted for based on their overall significance to the group. FRS 2 provides criteria of when to exclude subsidiaries from consolidation and prescribes alternative treatments.

In considering the usefulness of the consolidated balance sheet, difficulties arise over the averaging of dissimilar group components. All-inclusive consolidation may improve comparability, but may also result in a loss of information and impose debt re-negotiation costs on former non-consolidating groups. Some argue it may reduce optimal reporting alternatives. Creditors usually have claims over companies not groups, though the existence of cross-guarantees may make consolidated accounts the primary source of monitoring information. The usefulness of consolidated accounts to both creditors and minority interests is somewhat ambiguous.

FURTHER READING

The spectrum of approaches
ASC (1982) SSAP 1 – *Accounting for Associated Companies* as modified by the ASB's Interim Statement: *Consolidated Accounts* (1991).
ASB Discussion Paper (1994) *Associates and Joint Ventures*.
ASB Discussion Draft (1994) *Statement of Principles, Chapter 7, The Reporting Entity*.
ASB FRS 2 (1992) *Accounting for Subsidiary Undertakings*.
Baxter, G.C. and Spinney, J.C. (1975) A closer look at consolidated financial theory, *CA Magazine*, January, pp. 31–35.
Nobes, C. and Parker R. (1991) *Comparative International Accounting* (3rd edn), Prentice-Hall pp. 301–304.

The usefulness of consolidated financial statements
Mian, S.L. and Smith, C.W. (1990) Incentives for Unconsolidated Financial Reporting, *Journal of Accounting and Economics*, Vol. 12, pp. 141–171.
Mohr, R.M. (1991) Illustrating the economic consequences of FASB Statement No 94, Consolidation of All Majority-Owned Subsidiaries, *Journal of Accounting Education*, Vol. 9, pp. 123–136.

FAIR VALUES AND GOODWILL: ALIGNMENT ADJUSTMENTS (1)

Accounting for goodwill is probably the most controversial area in contemporary group accounting, and accounting for fair values at acquisition, necessary to compute goodwill, one of its most fraught policing problems. Fair values and goodwill are tackled within an integrating framework for alignment adjustments – measurement issues that specifically relate to consolidation itself in that cost determination, realization and matching conventions now refer to the group, not a single company. After providing an overview of alignment adjustments, this chapter focuses on adjustments relating to the acquisition transaction – fair values and goodwill. It examines why fewer than 2 per cent of UK groups recently have used merger accounting despite its apparent advantages. Chapter 6 examines alignment adjustments relating to transactions after acquisition: intra-group balances, stock 'profits' and the treatment of pre-acquisition dividends. It then examines the inter-relationships between the group concepts discussed in Chapter 4 and evaluates whether they provide a coherent framework for international practice on alignment adjustments.

AN OVERVIEW OF ALIGNMENT ISSUES

When pieces of wood are assembled to make a chair, each piece is machined so that it forms a well-fitting joint with the other pieces. If this machining is done badly, the chair will not fit together properly, though the individual pieces of wood may be fine in themselves. Similarly in group accounts, the individual accounts need to be aligned ('machined') before aggregation, so that a meaningful whole ('chair') is produced. If they are out of alignment, then the whole loses its meaning. Alignment adjustments reflect the change in scope from an individual company to a group basis and also, for example, where group companies trade with each other, the same transactions may not yet be reflected in *both* sets of records.

Figure 5.1 provides a summary of various types of alignment issues that may occur. In the process of aligning the accounts of individual undertakings prior to consolidation, for example in reconciling intra-group indebtedness, errors will be found. Then individual company adjustments will be needed prior to making other alignment adjustments. Most alignment adjustments, however, are not entered in individual company records, which reflect the impact of transactions on the company. They are made on consolidated working papers at head office, and are therefore termed here 'consolidation adjustments' – mainly relating to change in scope of the accounts. Occasionally such adjustments are 'pushed down' to be made in the subsidiary financial records, but as will be seen later this is comparatively rare.

FAIR VALUES AT ACQUISITION

The Companies Act 1985 (Sch 4) only allows the recognition of *purchased* goodwill which it defines as the difference between the fair value acquisition cost and the attributable

Type of adjustment	Summary
At acquisition transactions (Chapter 5)	
Fair values at acquisition	Restatement of subsidiary carrying values to group historical costs at acquisition
Goodwill recognition	Recognition as an asset or immediate elimination at acquisition
Post-acquisition transactions (Chapter 6)	
Intra-group transactions and balances	Elimination of amounts relating to transactions or balances not with external parties
Unrealised profit on intra-group transactions	Deferral of profits realised by individual group companies to when realised by the *group*
Dividends from subsidiary pre-acquisition profits	Restatement as a repayment of capital on a *group* basis where such dividends are legitimately treated as income by the parent *company*

Figure 5.1 – Classification of aligment problems

capital and reserves of the subsidiary *after fair value adjustments on identifiable assets and liabilities* (Sch 4A, para. 9). Attribution of fair values treats the subsidiary *as if* its individual assets, liabilities and goodwill had been purchased, establishing 'new' historical costs for the group not current values *per se*. FRS 7, *Fair Values in Acquisition Accounting* (1994), is the first UK accounting standard on the area.

Acquisition date

The subsidiary contributes only from the date 'on which control . . . passes to its new parent undertaking' (FRS 2, para. 45) – the date the offer becomes unconditional (usually because of unconditional acceptances) for public offers, or the unconditional offer is accepted for private treaties. The dates that the acquirer commences its direction of operating and financial policies of the acquired undertaking, that the flow of economic benefits changes, or that the consideration is paid are all indicative but not conclusive in determining this date (FRS 2, paras 84 and 85).

Interactions between fair values and goodwill

SSAP 22, *Accounting for Goodwill* (1984), allows two alternative treatments for purchased goodwill; it *prefers* immediate write-off direct to reserves bypassing profit and loss, but allows capitalization and gradual amortization to profit and loss over the useful economic life of the goodwill. The policy for each acquisition can be chosen independently. Permanent retention at cost is prohibited and negative goodwill must be written off immediately against reserves. Other intangible assets have not yet been dealt with by a UK standard.

Such tolerance has encouraged creative fair value treatments at acquisition in conjunction with immediate write-off of goodwill to reserves. Prior to FRS 7, there were temptations to understate assets and overstate liabilities, particularly reorganization provisions. Some claim this made acquisition accounting more attractive than merger accounting, and

(a) reduced depreciation and other post-acquisition expenses;
(b) diverted post-acquisition reorganisation expenses from post-acquisition profit and loss by utilizing inflated reorganization provisions set up at acquisition;
(c) increased post-acquisition profits by write-back of unused reorganization provisions;
(d) avoided the profit and loss 'penalty' for so doing since the resulting *increased* goodwill is written-off immediately against reserves, avoiding any profit and loss effect. Even gradual amortization results in goodwill amortization hitting profit and loss accounts much more slowly than the above expense reductions, though at least they 'hit' profit and loss.

It is impossible for outsiders to judge the accuracy of fair values at acquisition. Smith (1992, pp. 22–37) gives the example of how Coloroll acquired the John Crowther Group in 1988 for £214m in shares and cash. According to Smith, the carrying values immediately prior to acquisition in John Crowther's own records were £70m, which without fair value adjustments would have given a goodwill figure of £145m. As a result of write-downs of stocks and debtors, and the creation of provisions for redundancy and reorganization at acquisition, in total £79m, the consolidated net asset increment to the group consequent on the acquisition became a *negative* figure of £9m. Therefore the amount of goodwill immediately written off, £223m calculated as 214 + 9, or 145 + 79, ended up being £9m greater than the total acquisition cost(!) with consequent heavy reductions in post-acquisition expenses in the profit and loss account.

The downside of immediate write-off is a negative effect on consolidated equity and gearing ratios. This generated vehement debate over the nature and treatment of goodwill and spawned the practice of distinguishing and valuing brands and other intangibles on group balance sheets (achieving at one stroke the positive earnings effects of immediate write-off without its negative gearing effects!).

In 1990 the ASC abortively attempted to re-can this 'can of worms' by proposing only capitalization and gradual amortization for goodwill and other separable intangible assets (ED's 47 and 52). This was virtually laughed out of court. The 'gaping sore' was attacked on two fronts; an ASB Discussion Paper ('DP'), *Goodwill and Intangible Assets*, outlining three 'asset-based' and three 'elimination-based' alternatives for goodwill, with a wish (prayer?) to settle on one, and proposing that most other intangibles should not be capitalized; FRS 7, *Fair Values in Acquisition Accounting*, armed with theoretical rationale, has stringent valuation requirements and bans nearly all reorganization provisions at acquisition, but has raised violent opposition.

Recording fair value adjustments at acquisition

Such adjustments are *not* usually incorporated by the subsidiary in its own financial records, but made on the consolidation working papers. The technical term, if they *are* treated as revaluations in the subsidiary's own records, is 'push-down' accounting. Usually they are dealt with by consolidation adjustments at head office. In the USA it is fairly common to 'push down' fair value adjustments at acquisition. The conditions under which push-down should be allowed or required is examined by an FASB Discussion Memorandum, *New Basis Accounting* (1991).

Push-down has advantages in avoiding having to make recurring consolidation adjustments, for example, for extra depreciation. However, it is rare in the UK. Push-down of, for example, pension surpluses or contingent assets (see later) would be incompatible with accounting standards applied to the subsidiary as an ongoing concern in its own right. Imposing the parent's accounting policies may cause friction where the subsidiary is not wholly owned. However, the alternative accounting rules of the Companies Act 1985 would allow some adjustments to be pushed down in principle. Thomas and Hagler (1988) in a US context argue push-down accounting provides more relevant information where undeniably a transaction has occurred between old and new owners.

Fair value adjustment pushed-down into subsidiary's own records

The bookkeeping entries for fair value adjustments for stock, depreciable fixed assets and provisions now examined for an 80 per cent owned subsidiary. If the adjustments are pushed down, the individual company entry to reflect the increment from book value to fair value might be:

DR. Fixed asset   CR. Revaluation reserve
DR. Stock

and if the subsidiary set up a reorganization provision,

DR. Retained profits (P & L)   CR. Reorganization provision

Such a revaluation reserve and adjusted retained profits are treated as part of pre-acquisition equity, affecting consolidated goodwill, and split between parent and minority interests.

Asset not revalued in subsidiary's own records

A consolidation adjustment to effect fair value increments from book to fair value is made on the consolidation working papers. Each type of adjustment is now examined separately.

Example 5.1 – Individual fair value adjustments

Largesse acquired an 80 per cent interest in Smallnesse on 31 March 1992. Fair value adjustments for stocks, depreciable fixed assets, and provisions at that date are considered in order assuming adjustments are not pushed down. Extracts from the acquisition cancellation table (see Chapter 4) are given. In their first line the adjustment at acquisition is shown. The following lines show how it flows through in *post-acquisition* periods. The last shows net effects over the total life of the asset or provision.

Stocks

The fair value of Smallnesse plc's stocks, carrying value £35m, was estimated at £40m – increment of £5m.

Description	Consolidated retained profits	Goodwill (pre-acquisition)	Minority interests	Stock
Fair values at acquisition		(4)	(1)	5
Flow through via COGS	4		1	(5)
Net effect after stock sale	4	(4)	—	—

The *increment* from book value to fair value is apportioned between the parent stake (goodwill) and minority stake. It flows through after acquisition, increasing consolidated cost of sales and hence reducing post-acquisition retained profits. For the group shareholders (80 per cent), the pre-/post-acquisition split is important, but minority interests are ultimately unaffected because the pre-acquisition increase is offset by the post-acquisition decrease. After the stocks have left the group, it is still necessary to make the 'net' adjustment in subsequent financial statements.

Depreciable fixed assets

Smallnesse plc's depreciable fixed assets, carrying value £20m, had a fair value at acquisition of £30m. Their remaining life was 5 years with an estimated zero residual value and straight-line depreciation. Assume estimates were accurate and the fixed assets were held for their full term. Consequent extra depreciation is (£30m – £20m)/5 = £2m per annum, split pro-rata parent/minority.

Description	Consolidated retained profits	Goodwill (pre-acquisition)	Minority interests	Fixed assets
Fair values at acquisition		(8)	(2)	10
Extra depreciation – year 1	1.6		0.4	(2)
Extra depreciation – year 2	1.6		0.4	(2)
Extra depreciation – year 3	1.6		0.4	(2)
Extra depreciation – year 4	1.6		0.4	(2)
Extra depreciation – year 5	1.6		0.4	(2)
Net effect of fixed asset	8	(8)	—	—

Note the ultimate net zero effect on minority interests, whereas the increment as regards the parent shareholders is set up pre-acquisition (reducing consolidated goodwill), but the flow-through affects consolidated retained profits. *Undervaluations* of assets in conjunction with immediate goodwill write-off will *increase* post-acquisition profits through 'reduced' expenses, but immediate write-off of increased goodwill will bypass consolidated profit and loss.

Provisions at acquisition

FRS 7 effectively bans setting up reorganization and closure cost provisions as part of the fair value exercise. Nevertheless, the mechanism of such provisions is explored here to enable later comparison with international practice.

A £15m provision to cover intended closure costs at Smallnesse is to be set up by consolidation adjustment. In the two years following the acquisition actual closure expenses were respectively £6m and £4m. At the end of the two year period it was decided to write-back the unused provision. In Smallnesse's individual company accounts such expenses had passed through its profit and loss account in the years in which the expenses were incurred.

Description	Consolidated retained profits	Goodwill (pre-acquisition)	Minority interests	Reorga- nization provision
Fair values at acquisition		12	3.0	(15)
P & L expenses now set against provision – year 1	(4.8)		(1.2)	6
P & L expenses now set against provision – year 2	(3.2)		(0.8)	4
Unused provision written back – year 2	(4.0)		(1.0)	5
Net effect	(12.0)	12	—	—

As the closure expenses have passed through Smallnesse's individual company records as incurred, the setting up of the provision has not been 'pushed down', and the above entries can be considered as 'correcting' the transactions of Smallnesse to a group basis. The provision set-up at acquisition in the consolidated financial statements is split pro-rata between majority and minority. As closure items have *already* been expensed in the individual company accounts each year, the expenses are transferred each year from the profit and loss account (the company treatment) to be written off against the provision (the consolidated financial statements treatment). The effect of the provision is again neutral for the minority interest, but for the parent shareholders increases goodwill (through the reduction in pre-acquisition equity for a given investment amount) *and* also increases group post-acquisition profits, spread over the provision's usage period, compared to there being no provision. This explains why FRS 7 wishes to curtail the (ab)use of such provisions.

Example 5.2 – fair value adjustments

Largesse plc (as in Chapter 4) acquires 80 per cent of the shares in Smallnesse Ltd on 31 March 1992 when the retained profits of the two companies were respectively £80m and £30m. The balance sheets of the two companies at 31 March 1995, were

Individual company balance sheets at 31 March 1995

	Largesse £m	Largesse £m	Smallnesse £m	Smallnesse £m
Fixed assets				
Tangible fixed assets		180		40
Investment in Smallnesse		80		
Investment in Minutenesse		20		
		280		40
Net current assets				
Stocks	50		30	
Other	90		40	
		140		70

Creditors over one year	(100)	(20)
	320	90
Capital and reserves		
Share capital	130	35
Share premium	70	15
Retained profits	120	40
	320	90

Notes on Smallnesse fair value adjustments at acquisition

(a) The fair value of stocks had been estimated at £40m (carrying value at that date was £35m).

(b) Depreciable fixed assets had a fair value of £30m (carrying value £20m). The remaining life of these assets at that date was five years. These assets are still held and are depreciated on a straight line basis.

(c) A reorganisation provision of £15m for closures at Smallnesse is to be set up. In the two years following acquisition, closure expenses were £6m and £4m. It has been decided to write back the unused provision. In Smallnesse's individual company records these expenses had been treated as expenses in its profit and loss account. (The purpose of this part is to illustrate how such provisions work – such a set up would not be allowed in practice under FRS 7 in the UK – see later).

(d) None of the above adjustments has been or is intended to be recorded in the records of Smallnesse plc.

Required

Prepare an abbreviated cancellation table at 31 March 1995 for the Largesse Group. The investment in Minutenesse is to be accounted for as a fixed asset investment, and consolidated goodwill is to be immediately written off against consolidated retained profits.

Solution

Balances requiring adjustment to obtain consolidated amounts are included in Figure 5.2. A new section of the table shows *consolidation adjustments*. Three years' extra depreciation is recorded from acquisition (31 March 1992 – 31 March 1995). Consolidated goodwill of £16m is immediately written off.

Exercises

For a 60 per cent owned subsidiary give extracts from the abbreviated cancellation table showing the effects of each fair value adjustment at acquisition, its flow-through since acquisition, and its net effect over the life of the asset/provision. Each adjustment is to be recorded on the consolidation working papers.

5.1 The fair value of stocks had been estimated at £17m (carrying value £15m).

5.2 Depreciable fixed assets had a fair value of £80m (carrying value £70m). The remaining life of depreciable assets at that date was four years with a zero residual value. All these assets are still held and are depreciated on a straight line basis.

5.3 It was decided to set up a reorganization provision for the subsidiary for £10m. The amount of reorganization expenses to be written off against the provision was £6m. After two years it was decided to write-back the excess provision. In the subsidiary's individual company accounts, reorganization costs had been charged to its profit and loss account.

5.4 On May 31 1994, Blair plc acquired 75 per cent of Brown plc for £90m. At that date Brown plc's balance sheet was as follows:

	Book amount	Fair value
Fixed assets	50	40
Stocks	30	45
Other assets less liabilities	20	20
Share capital & premium	(35)	
Retained profits	(65)	

Description	Investment	Share capital	Share premium	Retained profits	Goodwill	Minority interests	Fixed assets	Reorg. provision
Largesse balances	100	(130)	(70)	(120)	-	-	180	
Smallnesse equity analysed								
a) at acquisition					(64)	(16)		
b) post-acquisition				(8)	-	(2)		
c) other balances needing adjustment							40	
Consolidation adjustments								
Stock cost adjustment				4	(4)	(2)		
Fixed asset cost adj					(8)	1.2	10	
Fixed asset extra depn				4.8			(6)	
Reorganisation provision set-up					12	3		(15)
Reorganisation expenses - 2 years				(8)		(2)		10
Reorganisation provision write-back				(4)		(1)		5
Cancellation								
Investment	(80)				80			
Goodwill write-off				16	(16)			
Consolidated amounts	20	(130)	(70)	(115.2)	-	(18.8)	224	-

Figure 5.2 – Largesse Group, expanded cancellation table with consolidation adjustments

Required

(a) Calculate goodwill and minority interests at acquisition without using a cancellation table.
(b) Show how the adjustments to fair values would be dealt with at acquisition by giving extracts from a consolidated cancellation table and also show how they would be dealt with in periods subsequent to acquisition. Assume that the stocks were sold in the year following acquisition, and the excess over book value of the fixed asset is to be depreciated to zero over a four year period straight-line.

5.5 You are presented with the following summarized company balance sheets of Bigfry plc and its subsidiary Smallfry plc at 30 November 1995 as in example 4.3, but with additional information about fair value adjustments:

Bigfry and Smallfry balance sheets at 30 November 1995

	Bigfry £m	Bigfry £m	Smallfry £m	Smallfry £m
Fixed assets				
Land and buildings		100		40
Plant and equipment		360		100
Investment in Smallfry	72			
Investment in Tinyfry	20			
Investments		92		
		552		140
Current assets				
Stocks	50		15	
Debtors	30		10	
Cash	5		2	
	85		27	
Current liabilities				
Trade creditors	25		18	
Other creditors	10		5	
	35		23	
		50		4
Creditors over one year		(200)		(30)
		402		114
Capital and reserves				
Share capital		60		20
Share premium		50		30
Retained profits		292		64
		402		114

Notes

(a) Bigfry acquired a 60 per cent stake in Smallfry on 31 May 1995, when the retained earnings of Smallfry were £50m.
(b) Bigfry acquired an 18% interest in Tinyfry plc on 30 November 1994. This investment should be accounted for at cost in the consolidated balance sheet.
(c) The fair value of stocks had been estimated at acquisition at £17m (carrying value £15m). These have now been sold.
(d) The fair value of land at acquisition was estimated at £45m (carrying value £40m) and depreciable fixed assets had a fair value of £80m (carrying £70m) at acquisition. The remaining life of the depreciable assets at that date was four years with a zero residual value. All these assets are still held and are depreciated on a straight line basis.
(e) It was decided to set up a reorganization provision at acquisition for Smallfry for £10m. The amount of reorganization expenses to be written off against the provision for the first six months was £6m. In the subsidiary's individual company accounts, reorganization costs had been charged against its profit and loss account.
(f) Goodwill at acquisition is to be gradually amortized over a three year period.
(g) Provide for depreciation and amortization adjustments over a 6 month period.

Required
Prepare a cancellation table at 30 November 1995 for the Bigfry Group. The investment in Tinyfry is to be accounted for as a fixed asset investment. Explain your treatment of each fair value adjustment. Note that FRS 7 would *not* allow the setting up of such a reorganization provision.

DETERMINING FAIR VALUES AT ACQUISITION – FRS 7

Following a Discussion Paper (1988), the ASC issued ED 53, *Fair Values in the Context of Acquisition Accounting* (1990). The ASB issued FRS 7, *Fair Values in Acquisition Accounting*, in September 1994 after a Discussion Paper and exposure draft, FRED 7, of the same title in 1993. Issues covered include:

> (a) determining the fair value of *purchase consideration* (the cost of the investment);
> (b) determining the fair values of *identifiable assets and liabilities* to be recognized in consolidated financial statements.
> Consequent on these is the need to define for (b)
>   (i) the level of detail at which the valuations should be made and the time period (the 'investigation' period) allowed to reach final valuations and to adjust initial valuations.
>   (ii) cut-off criteria for deciding which items should be included or excluded.
>
> FRS 7 introduces some innovative requirements, but most controversial is its cut-off criteria which effectively ban most reorganisation provisions at acquisition.

Purchase consideration
FRS 7 defines the cost of acquisition as, 'the amount of cash paid and the fair value of other purchase consideration given by the acquirer, together with the expenses of the acquisition' (para. 26). Only *incremental* and not allocated acquisition expenses can be included. Costs at each date are to be aggregated in multiple-stage acquisitions.

Shares and other capital instruments

FRS 7 considers that if quoted on a ready market, the acquisition date price should normally be used. It comments that market prices for a reasonable period prior to the acquisition date, during which acceptances could be made need to be considered if unusual fluctuations cause the price on a particular date to be unreliable. In unquoted or markets inactive in large transaction quantities the value of similar quoted securities, present values, the value of the cash alternative, or of securities in which there is an option to convert should be taken into account when estimating fair value. The best estimate may be to value the entity acquired if other approaches are infeasible (paras 69–70).

Ma and Hopkins (1988) argue that the acquisition date price confounds 'pure' internally generated goodwill of the target with incremental benefits which may be located in the acquirer (see later). From such a perspective some argue that the consideration should be valued to exclude any effects relating to the acquirer's plans for the target. An early ASC Discussion Paper, *Fair Values in the Context of Acquisition Accounting* (1988), had suggested valuing such instruments based on their issue price as if there had been no knowledge of the bid. However, this conceptual position has proved a minority one, and FRS 7 chooses the price at acquisition date. Its consideration of prices around the acquisition date is to ensure a 'fair' value and not a 'pre-bid' price.

Other consideration

Discounting is required for *deferred* cash consideration or for other monetary items offered using acquirer's rate on similar borrowing, taking into account its credit standing and any security given (para. 77), and market prices, estimated realizable values, independent valuations or other evidence for non-monetary consideration can be used (para. 80).

Detailed application (optional)

Acquisition and issue expenses

FRS 7 tightens the Companies Act 1985 requirement that the acquisition cost should include 'such amount (if any) in respect of fees and other expenses of the acquisition as the company may determine' (Sch 4A, para. 9) by insisting that only fees and similar *incremental* costs (such as professional fees) can be added to the purchase cost. *Allocated* costs, for example of acquisition departments or management remuneration are not allowed (para. 85). Qualifying issue costs for shares and other capital instruments, based on a similar distinction between incremental and allocated costs, are to be dealt with using the requirements of FRS 4, *Capital Instruments*, and deducted in determining the net proceeds of the issue. Debt issue expenses are subsequently accounted for analogous to an interest adjustment.

Contingent consideration

Problems arise where consideration is contingent on uncertain future events in estimating its

(a) *amount* – a 'reasonable estimate' of the fair value of the amounts expected to be payable (para. 27), or at least amounts reasonably expected to be payable (e.g. minimum amounts) if the former is too uncertain are to be used, revised as information unfolds (para. 81);

(b) *form* – estimated future share amounts should be credited to a separate caption in shareholders funds, analysed between equity and non-equity, and transferred to share capital and premium on issue. Where options exist over whether future consideration is shares or cash, a conservative position is taken – acquirer's options are to be treated as future shares, vendor's as liabilities (paras 82–3).

(c) *substance* – FRS 7 gives guidance on distinguishing acquisition payments from payments for post-acquisition expenses or services rendered (para. 84).

Merger relief

Merger relief is discussed in Chapter 3. Prior to the revision of the Companies Act 1985 a few companies took advantage of merger relief when choosing acquisition accounting to record the investment at nominal amount, and using this artificially low value to understate goodwill at acquisition. Sch 4A S 9(4) of the revised Act and FRS 4 (Chapter 3), now ensure that under acquisition accounting, even if merger relief is taken, the investment in the parent's accounts must be stated at fair value, and the excess over nominal amount credited to a separate reserve, often termed a 'merger reserve'. Consequently the acquisition cost in the consolidated accounts must include the fair value of such consideration.

Identifiable assets and liabilities

'Identifiable' is defined in FRS 7 and the Companies Act 1985 as 'capable of being disposed of or settled separately, without disposing of the business of an entity' (para. 2). FRS 7's objectives in the fair valuation process are that,

> when a business entity is acquired by another, all the assets and liabilities that *existed in the acquired entity at the date of acquisition* are recorded at fair values *reflecting their condition at that date;* and . . . all changes to the acquired assets and liabilities, and the resulting gains and losses, that *arise after control of the acquired entity. . . has passed* to the acquirer are reported as part of the post-acquisition financial performance of the acquiring group.
>
> (para 1, emphasis added)

Its controversial interpretation of the phrases in italics is discussed under 'cut-off'.

Measuring fair values – 'value to the business'

Fair value (para. 2) is 'the amount at which an asset or liability could be exchanged in an arm's length transaction between informed and willing parties, other than in forced or liquidation sale'. FRS 7's requirements are broadly consistent with the ASB's Draft Statement of Principles, *Measurement in Financial Statements* (1993), i.e. based on the *value to the business* principle, where fair value is measured as the *lower* of replacement cost (if worth replacing) or recoverable amount (if the value is impaired).

Recoverable amount is the higher of net realizable value and, where appropriate, *value in use* – 'the present value of the future cash flows obtainable as a result of an asset's continued use, including those resulting from the ultimate disposal of the asset' (para. 2). FRS 7 considers 'value in use' is applicable to fixed assets but not to stocks (paras 11, 12 and 45). *Net realizable value* in a ready market is defined as market price less realization costs and dealer's margin. However, 'value to the business' does not depend on management intentions, as it is merely a computational rule – the use of net realizable values and value in use in assessing fair values is categorically determined by their sizes in relation to each other and replacement cost, and further, FRS 7 points out that 'value in use' is based on *most profitable use* not intended use (para. 46).

Difficulties in estimating recoverable amount may necessitate considering groups of jointly used assets *as a whole* to ease the attribution of cash flows to asset groups (para. 49). The ASB's draft *Statement of Principles*, comments that the value in, or amount recoverable from, further use is mainly used in practice to decide between replacement cost or net realizable value and only in limited cases is likely to be reliable enough to be used in its own right (para. 27).

Cut-off – obligations versus intentions

The key conceptual issue in determining fair values at acquisition is how far the acquirer's intentions can be taken into account in recognizing and valuing the identifiable assets and liabilities, particularly provisions – whether the acquired company can be accounted for *as if* in what the acquirer would regard as a pruned and integrated state (providing for the costs to get it to that state) or whether it should be recorded in its *actual* state prior to pruning and integration. FRS 7 opts for the latter and deals with acquirer's plans through extra disclosures. It cites a "small majority in favour of the proposed treatment', users, analysts and institutional investors giving 'outright support', accounting firms and accountancy bodies 'substantial support' (presumably easier to audit!), and preparers giving 'strong, but not unanimous opposition' (para. 11 and Appendix III, para. 17).

Two key cut-off criteria are enunciated for recognizing and measuring identifiable assets and liabilities at acquisition:

> (a) *existence* at the date of acquisition; and
> (b) fair values *reflecting conditions* at acquisition.

A number of corollaries are drawn, relating to items which do not satisfy the criteria, and are therefore deemed *post*-acquisition (para. 7):

(i)   impairments or changes resulting from events since acquisition; and
(ii)   changes resulting from acquirer intentions or future actions; and
(iii) provisions or accruals for future operating losses or reorganization and integration costs resulting from the acquisition, regardless of whether they affect acquirer or acquiree.

Consistent with the above criteria, FRS 7's valuation requirements, discussed later, tend to use market prices based on the acquired company's access to markets, rather than the acquirer's, where those differ, in determining replacement costs etc.

However, it is expected that the *acquirer's* accounting policies will be used in determining fair values at acquisition (para. 8).

Item (i) is unexceptional. Highly controversial is its treatment of (ii) and (iii) as post-acquisition. The crux is the ASB's view that

> management intent is not a sufficient basis for recognizing changes to an entity's assets and liabilities. . . [Only] when intentions are translated into actions that commit the entity to particular courses of action, [should] the accounting . . . then reflect any obligations or changes in assets that arise from those actions. . . . [Therefore] events of a post-acquisition period that result in the recognition of additional liabilities or the impairment of existing assets of an acquired entity should be reported as [post-acquisition] events.   (Appendix III, para 14).

FRS 7 considers that, say, intended reorganizations of the acquired company by the acquirer are *discretionary*, and that the basis for recognizing 'liabilities', *obligation*, is not present – thus they are post-acquisition, and where assets are resold at a loss consequent on such reorganizations, unless they were *already* impaired at acquisition, such losses also would be post-acquisition (para. 48). Provisions for future losses are also prohibited since they do not constitute obligations. The ASB considers fair value to be a neutral concept, the result of a bargaining process and independent of the acquirer or acquiree's circumstances (Appendix III, para. 36).

Whilst prohibiting future loss provisions, ED 53, *Fair Values in the Context of Acquisition Accounting* (1990), had proposed allowing provisions for reorganization costs if 'there is a clearly defined programme of reorganisation and those costs for which provisions are to be made have been specified in reasonable detail, and there was evidence that in formulating its offer, the acquirer took account of plans or proposals for such reorganisation and associated costs' (para. 75).

In the USA, APB Opinion No 16, whilst not generally permitting reorganization provisions, will allow provisions for anticipated plant closures to be made in the *acquired* company, but not if *identical* duplicate facilities are closed by the *acquirer*. IAS 22 states 'the determination of fair values may be influenced by the intentions of the buyer', which may necessitate creation of provisions, for planned employee termination and plant relocation costs for example (para. 13). FRS 7 prohibits both. ED 53 tried to define legitimate reorganization provisions, but FRS 7 feels such a boundary cannot be effectively policed (Appendix III, para. 12c).

Other examples of applying the cut-off criteria include the determination of the net realizable value of stocks, which can be based on the acquirer's judgments, but on the circumstances of the acquired entity before acquisition. Fixed asset lives must be estimated not taking into account the acquirer's plans, but can reflect the acquirer's accounting policies on useful lives. Changes in pension rights to harmonize them across the group are also viewed as discretionary and so are post-acquisition events, whereas changes consequent on the adoption of the acquirer's accounting policies (e.g. in actuarial assumptions) can be incorporated.

If the effects of management intentions and future actions were to be provided for at acquisition, the increase in reorganization and integration provisions would reduce identifiable net assets and thus increase goodwill. The ASB, whilst recognizing that such expenditures are expected to produce future benefits, does not consider this gives sufficient justification for their effective capitalization as goodwill (para. 25). The effects of purchasing a less efficient business and reorganizing it will therefore not be incorporated at acquisition, but 'judged subsequently by the increase in profitability of the acquired business that is achieved' (Appendix III, para. 26). However, FRS 6 suggests management might wish to provide note disclosure of the total *investment* in acquiring a business (Appendix IV). The total investment comprises the cost of acquisition per the accounts, plus 'reorganization and integration expenditure announced', which under FRS 7 is not capitalized, but treated as post-acquisition expense.

FRED 7 had commented that in ongoing companies or groups reorganization expenses are expensed because any resulting internally generated goodwill is not capitalized; that if the acquired company were itself to reorganize, such pruning would be charged against profits; that if the acquirer were to close its own duplicate facilities such costs would be a consolidated profit and loss charge, whereas duplicate facilities closed down by the acquired company would not (FASB Technical Bulletin 85-5 in the USA takes this perspective).

The conceptual basis of 'obligations' rather than 'intentions' itself arises out of the more general problem of policing the validity of liabilities and so the problem has merely been abstracted one level back. Though the ASB finds itself at odds with current international practice, it believes its proposals are consistent with world-wide development of conceptual frameworks, commenting, 'the principle of accounting for obligations rather than management intentions is gaining greater acceptance internationally' (Appendix III, para. 16). It does not mind being different if it feels it is leading!

Opponents of the ASB's position argue that FRS 7 will make UK companies less willing to engage in necessary restructuring of inefficient businesses (para. 29), that its proposals are contrary to the way that acquirers assess takeover possibilities, as a single integrated decision (para. 21), and that its proposals make financial statements more difficult to understand (para. 30). In responding, FRS 7 points out *users'* enthusiasm for its proposed changes! However, Donald Main, the only Board member to dissent, supporting considerable preparer disquiet with FRS 7's conceptual position, considers that reaction to past abuses that has led to seeming user support for a considerable over-reaction by the ASB, and that more strictly defined limits on the set-up of provisions at acquisition is a better solution. It has no truck with arguments that its strictness disadvantages the competitive position of UK companies, any more than previous slackness allowed competitive advantages in bidding. It argues that accounting standards should have a neutral effect and that greater transparency in reporting will allow better economic decisions.

Example 5.3 - Reorganization provisions and FRS 7

FRS 7 effectively bans the acquirer from setting up reorganization provisions affecting pre-acquisition equity. Consider now if the reorganization provision in Example 5.1 had been set up in consequence of the acquisition, but as a post-acquisition event. The facts of the situation are repeated here.

A £15m provision to cover intended closure costs at Smallnesse is to be set up by consolidation adjustment, but now as post-acquisition event, in accordance with FRS 7. In the two years following the acquisition, actual closure expenses were respectively £6m and £4m. At the end of the two year period it was decided to write-back the unused provision. In Smallnesse's individual company accounts such expenses had passed through its profit and loss account in the years in which the expenses were incurred.

Required
Compare and contrast the treatment of reorganization provisions set up in consequence of the acquisition under FRS 7, with setting up such provisions as part of the fair value exercise at acquisition as in Exercise 5.1.

Solution

Description	Consolidated retained profits	Goodwill (pre-acquisition)	Minority interests	Reorganisation provision
Fair values at acquisition	12.0		3.0	(15)
P & L expenses now set against provision – year 1	(4.8)		(1.2)	6
P & L expenses now set against provision – year 2	(3.2)		(0.8)	4
Unused provision written back – year 2	(4.0)		(1.0)	5
Net effect	—	—	—	—

As with the setting up and use of all provisions within a single company, the effect is merely one of timing, i.e. the expenses/losses are recognized as soon as foreseen, not of amount, i.e. the effect over the life of the provision is zero for both controlling interest shareholders and for minority interests. Unlike in setting up the provision at acquisition in Example 5.1 on page 110, there is no 'transfer' of 'profits' from pre- to post-acquisition periods. If the provision had been set up say to close duplicate facilities at the parent, the treatment would have been as above, except that the set up and use would have been 100 per cent against consolidated retained profits.

Anti-avoidance measures

FRS 7 allows the set up of reorganization provisions at acquisition by the acquired company by stating that, only if the acquired company were 'already committed to [reorganization], and unable realistically to withdraw from it' can such reorganization provisions be regarded as pre-acquisition (para. 39). Because it would be comparatively easy in 'friendly' takeovers, for the acquirer to 'persuade' the acquired company to set up such provisions for future costs, FRS 7 warns that if such provisions were set up by the acquired entity shortly before the acquisition or during the course of negotiations, particular attention would need to be paid to the circumstances. Commitment is necessary for there to be an obligation and hence a liability at acquisition (para. 40).

If there were evidence of acquirer influence, control may have passed at an earlier date, and the date of acquisition would need to be reassessed accordingly. An earlier suggestion in the ASB's Discussion Paper for a *rebuttable presumption* that decisions taken within six months of the acquisition be treated as post-acquisition was dropped, but FRS 6 requires disclosure of any provisions made by the acquired entity in the twelve months to the acquisition date (para. 26).

Investigation period for fair value adjustments

FRS. 7 prefers the fair value process to be completed by the date of directors' approval of the first post-acquisition consolidated accounts. If not feasible, it is acceptable to use provisional estimates of fair values (and hence goodwill) in these accounts, and then adjust these up to the date of approval of the acquiring group's financial statements for the first full financial year after the acquisition. Subsequent to this investigation period, adjustments should be treated as normal accounting corrections in the year they occur and only if there are fundamental errors, can they be treated as prior year adjustments, per FRS 3 (paras 23-25). The fact that provisional values have been used and subsequent adjustments must be disclosed (FRS 6 – para. 27).

Applying 'value to the business' to specific assets and liabilities

FRS 7 prefers market prices at the date of acquisition to be used to determine fair values, 'where similar assets are bought and sold on a readily accessible market.' (para. 43). If unavailable, a variety of alternatives including independent valuations, and techniques such as discounting estimated future cash flows to net present values and subsequent sale prices are to be used. Depreciated replacement cost is generally required for depreciable assets rather than second-hand values because the second-hand market may be low volume and not offer similar terms to the 'new' market, e.g. in terms of technical support (para. 44).

The most striking features of the requirements are discussed before the detail. It specifies approximations to market values where there are no active markets including:

(a) *discounting* unlisted long-term receivables and payables at appropriate current market rates, post-acquisition interest charges to be calculated as a constant rate of return on new carrying amounts;

(b) *indices* for example, for plant and machinery;

(c) *current costs of reproduction* for assets of a similar type, e.g. for land under development or work-in-progress;

(d) *adjusted historical cost* – for interest, to reflect holding costs for maturing stocks where there is no intermediate market, or for attributable profits estimated on a prudent basis in the case of long-term contracts.

Accrued profit on acquired stocks

Since for stocks, production to the date of acquisition is external to the group, some argue that stocks should include profits of the acquired company to the date of acquisition (ED 53 took this line). However, the ASB considers that 'cost' is a bargained construct between independent entities. Therefore other than for commodity type stocks, FRS 7 requires fair value of stocks is its 'value to the business' to the group – the lower of replacement *cost* and net realizable value (value in use is deemed not appropriate) i.e. with *no* profit adjustment. The fair value of work-in-progress is this plus current *costs* for further processing to bring it to its current state. Although fair values for long-term contracts are to be based on cost plus attributable profit, there is no contradiction as attributable profit is calculated on a conservative basis and is likely to approximate to 'replacement' cost rather than selling value.

Assets recognized in conflict with other standards

Requirements for certain items are in conflict with analogous accounting standards relating to ongoing businesses – for example that acquired pension surpluses and deficits should be recognized as assets and liabilities, surpluses to the extent they 'are reasonably expected to be realised' (para. 19). Under SSAP 24 they are recognized gradually over an extended period. Contingent gains at acquisition are to be recognized as group assets based on reasonable estimates of the expected outcomes of the contingencies involved. SSAP 18 counsels against recognition of anticipated future contingent gains. FRS 7 gives primacy to identifying all assets and liabilities at acquisition over income smoothing, otherwise 'the reporting of post-acquisition performance is distorted by changes. . . not being recognised in the correct period.'(para. 36). For contingencies, unlike for ongoing businesses, its requirement 'represents the expectation that the amounts expended on [the acquisition of such a contingent asset] . . . will be recovered; it does not anticipate a future gain' (para. 36).

Discounting and very risky liabilities

FRS 7 requires the monetary items if quoted to be valued at market value. In other cases they are to be valued by comparison with the current terms on which similar monetary items are available or by discounting to present values. However, in the case of very risky quoted debt instruments, it balked at the full implications of using market values – that if a company from the time it issued debt to the date of acquisition were perceived to become more risky, the market value of its liabilities would go *down* (holders would expect to get less back – the discount rate would rise) which appears too much like a gain! It comments,

> in cases where a reduced pre-acquisition market value of an acquired entity's debt reflects the market's perception that it was at risk of being unable to fulfill its payment obligations, the reduction would not be recognised in the fair value allocation if the debt were expected to be repaid at its full amount.   (para. 63)

which looks suspiciously like taking an 'acquirer's' perspective!

Detailed application – optional

The following summary of FRS 7's requirements relating to specific assets and liabilities can be omitted without loss in continuity.

Tangible fixed assets (paras 9, 50–51) – Replacement cost to be based on market values if assets similar in type are bought and sold on an open market, e.g. for some property and quoted fixed asset investments. In other cases depreciated replacement cost to be used reflecting the acquired business's normal buying process and sources of supply available to it, for e.g. plant and machinery, *without there being any change in the asset's use or intended use.* Indexed historical cost can be used where replacement cost or amount recoverable from further use cannot be easily determined and even historical cost itself if prices have not changed materially.

Intangible assets (para. 10) – Replacement cost, which is normally its estimated market value.

Stocks and work-in-progress (paras 11–12, 52–57) – Stocks in markets in which acquired entity trades as both buyer and seller (e.g. commodities) at current market price. Other stocks at the lower of the *acquired entity's* replacement cost, reflecting its normal buying process and sources of supply, and net realizable value. To estimate replacement costs, market values are to be used where a ready market exists (e.g. commodities, dealing stocks, certain land and buildings held as trading stock, and certain maturing stocks readily tradable at similar completion states); if not, for most manufactured stocks, a current cost of reproduction for the acquired company (current standard costs of manufacturing for manufacturing stocks or work-in-progress where used). Interest adjusted historical costs can be used for thinly traded or non-traded maturing stocks. Long-term contracts require no further adjustment other than to reflect re-assessments of the contract outcome or change to acquirer's accounting policies. Net realizable values can be assessed using the *acquirer's* judgments, but based on circumstances of the *acquired entity* at acquisition, and careful consideration must be given if there are subsequent exceptional profits on such stocks as to whether their fair values at acquisition should be re-adjusted. Even if not, exceptional post-acquisition disclosures may be needed.

Quoted investments (para. 13) – market price adjusted for unusual price fluctuations or size of holding.

Monetary assets and liabilities (paras 14, 59–63) – Short-term monetary items usually at settlement or redemption amount. Long-term monetary items – if quoted, market price or market price of similar items, if not by discounting total amounts to be received or paid where the effect is material; using current borrowing rates reflecting the issuer's credit standing and any security given for payables, and current lending rates for receivables after making any necessary provisions. Resulting 'discounts' or 'premiums' are allocated so post-acquisition 'interest' charges reflect a constant rate on new carrying amounts. See previous discussion on very risky liabilities.

Business sold or held exclusively with a view to subsequent resale (paras 16–18, 65–69) – if an interest in a separate business is sold or expected to be sold as a single unit within one year of acquisition, it should be treated as a single asset at acquisition. Fair value is net sale proceeds adjusted for fair values of any transfers of assets and liabilities. Estimated net sale proceeds can be used where the sale has not been completed by the first post-acquisition financial statement date provided a purchaser has been identified or is being sought, and disposal must be reasonably expected within approximately a year of the date of acquisition. The term 'separate business' includes subsidiaries *or* divisions where 'the assets, liabilities and results are distinguishable, physically, operationally and for financial reporting purposes'. The interest is a current asset. Within FRS 7's investigation period any estimate must be adjusted to actual on disposal. If not sold within approximately a year, it should be consolidated normally. The intended disposal must never have been consolidated or have formed a part of the group's continuing activities. Fair value at acquisition is only to be distinguished from net sale proceeds discounted if the effect is material, if material changes occur between acquisition and disposal because of acquirer decisions or specific post-acquisition events, and the latter cannot be used if there is a reduced price in a quick sale. 'Value to the business' of intended disposals is net realizable value because they are deemed not worth replacing.

Other matters – the unusual features of pensions and other benefits (paras 19–20 and 70–73) and contingencies (paras 15 and 64) are briefly explored in the previous discussion. For these and deferred taxation (paras 21, 22 and 74, 75) the reader is referred direct to FRS 7.

Disclosures relating to fair values

The disclosure requirements relating to fair values at acquisition, together with all other disclosure requirements relating to business combinations and goodwill are collected together in FRS 6, *Acquisitions and Mergers* (1994). In relation to fair values, it requires for combinations during the year accounted for as acquisitions the disclosure of (para. 25):

(a) fair value of the consideration and amount of purchased or negative goodwill;
(b) the nature of any deferred or contingent consideration, and for the latter the range of possible outcomes and factors affecting these;
(c) a (fair value) table showing for each class of assets and liabilities of the acquired entity, original book values immediately prior to acquisition; fair value adjustments analysed into revaluations, adjustments to achieve consistent group accounting policies and other significant adjustments; and fair values. The reasons for the adjustments should be explained;
(d) in the table in (c), reorganization and restructuring provisions included in the liabilities of the *acquired* entity and related asset write-downs in the twelve months to the acquisition date should be separately identified;
(e) movements on acquisition provisions or related accruals for costs analysed between amounts used for the specific purpose created and amounts released unused;
(f) the fact that provisional values have been used and reasons. Subsequent adjustments with consequent adjustments to goodwill should be disclosed and explained;
(g) in the *post-acquisition* consolidated profit and loss account, reorganization, restructuring and integration costs relating to the acquisition should be disclosed. These costs are those which are *incremental* consequent on the acquisition, and must relate to a 'project identified and controlled by management as part of a reorganization or integration programme set up at the time of acquisition or as a direct consequence of an immediate post-acquisition review' (para. 31);
(h) any exceptional *post-acquisition* profits or losses resulting from the fair values at acquisition, per FRS 3.

The disclosures should be made separately for each material acquisition and as an aggregate disclosure where the remainder are material in total only.

FRS 6 *suggests* that for major acquisitions, managements may wish to include further *note* disclosures relating to expected reorganization, restructuring and integration costs which may occur over a number of periods, and asset write-downs, indicating the extent to which they have been charged to profit and loss. In its Appendix IV an illustrative example provides an analysis of the *'total investment'* into two main categories (the subject of more detailed illustrative disclosures, by acquisition or type of acquisition, but shown in barest outline below):

	£m
Acquisition costs	80
Details of estimated reorganisation etc. costs announced	20
Total investment	100

The first category is the amount accounted for as fair value investment, used to compute goodwill at acquisition when compared with identifiable assets and liabilities at that date. The second refers to those costs which are expected to give future benefits but under FRS 7's requirements are not allowed to be capitalized as they result from acquirer's intentions or future actions. The balance is therefore the amount management considers it invests in the acquisition. A further suggested note disclosure is a *statement of reorganization and integration costs*, further analysed in the illustrative example by FRS 7 into new acquisitions and ongoing acquisitions, but shown only in outline here:

	£m
Announced but not charged at previous year end	70
Announced in relation to acquisitions during the year	20
Adjustments to previous years' estimated	(5)
	85
Amounts charged:	
Profit and loss	(15)
Elsewhere	(10)
Announced but still to be charged at current year end	60

In essence these are the amounts that would have been measured in the financial statements themselves had FRS 7 allowed the 'pruned and integrated' perspective rather than its hard line that only obligations could be included. Other disclosures relating to business combinations, particularly with respect to *substantial acquisitions* were discussed in Chapter 3.

Transparency and neutrality in financial reporting
The ASB in FRS 7 states its proposals are consistent with the 'information set' philosophy adopted by FRS 3 (Appendix 3, para. 9). Elsewhere it argues that accounting standards should have a neutral effect, and that greater *transparency* in reporting will allow better economic decisions. The extra disclosures relating to pre-acquisition provisions of the acquired entity, the post-acquisition profit and loss disclosures relating to reorganization, restructuring and integration costs, and the optional note disclosure relating to the total investment in the subsidiary and the statement of reorganization and integration costs reflect this emphasis.

Such a perspective is consistent with the semi-strong version of the efficient markets hypothesis – that users impound 'instantaneously' publicly available information, and are able to 'see through' cosmetic accounting alternatives provided they are given enough information. What is not clear is that the changes now required by the ASB will have 'neutral' effect on the use of *measured* accounting numbers, e.g. profits or gearing ratios in management compensation contracts or debt covenant restrictions. The effect would be neutral if the contract stipulated GAAP at the date it was signed, but not if it stipulated 'rolling' GAAP. How far such considerations should constrain what the ASB views as conceptual development in accounting is a long-debated issue.

Example 5.4 – Fair value adjustments at acquisition

This example can be omitted without loss of continuity if knowledge of the more detailed fair valuation requirements relating to individual assets and liabilities is not required. Majestic plc acquired a 75% stake in Underling plc, the date of acquisition being 30 April 1995, at Majestic's own year end. Because of this, estimates needed to be made for the first set of consolidated financial statements. The two companies' balance sheets immediately prior to acquisition were:

Individual company balance sheets at 30 April 1995

	Majestic £m	Majestic £m	Underling £m	Underling £m
Fixed assets				
Land		80		20
Tangible fixed assets		200		70
		280		90
Net current assets				
Stocks	90		50	
Other	100		60	
		190		110
Creditors over one year		(120)		(40)
		350		160
Capital and reserves				
Share capital (£1 shares)		140		48
Share premium		90		32
Retained profits		120		80
		350		160

Details on fair values at acquisition

Purchase consideration
The offer, accepted by 75 per cent of the shareholders in Underling was for 2 ordinary shares of Majestic for each share in Underling (market price at the date of acquisition being £1.50 per share) and £1 cash, plus further shares to be issued representing 50 per cent of the profits after taxation for the first year post-acquisition of Underling plc (based on the market value of the Majestic's shares at 31 March 1996) with a guaranteed minimum amount of £10m under this clause.

Identifiable assets and liabilities
(a) The replacement cost of stocks had been estimated at £60m and net realizable value £54m.
(b) Fair values of land (at £16m) and depreciable fixed assets (at £92m) had only been provisionally determined and the final estimate would only be available at the end of June 1995, after the accounts had been completed.
(c) Majestic plc wished to reorganize Underling's activities, part of which involved closing facilities at Underling's main site. Estimated closure costs are £12m, and directors would like to set up a reorganization provision as the closure is likely to be spread over an eighteen month period.
(d) Creditors over one year represent a 'zero-coupon' bond (i.e. with no interest payments and just a single repayment amount of £52.34m at 31 March 1997). The market yield on such bonds when they were issued a year ago was 10 per cent per annum, the current market yield on similar bonds being 11.16 per cent per annum.
(e) None of the above adjustments has been recorded in the records of Underling plc and it has been decided to record them on the consolidation working papers.
(f) Goodwill is to be written off immediately on acquisition against consolidated retained profits.

Required
Prepare a cancellation table for the Majestic Group at acquisition showing the recording of purchase consideration and fair value adjustments. Follow FRS 7's requirements. Prepare a 'fair value' table showing the effects of the fair value adjustments on the acquired balances of Underling plc.

Solution

Purchase consideration
The number of shares acquired is 0.75 × 48m = 36m

Thus the purchase consideration would be:

		£m	
Shares	36m × 2 × £1.50	108	(share premium – £36m)
Cash	36m × £1	36	
Contingent consideration	Minimum value	10	
		154	

Note that in Figure 5.3 because the contingent consideration cannot be estimated any more accurately at the date of the first consolidated statements, the minimum amount is used, and the credit has not been made to share capital and premium, but to unissued shares, showing that it will eventually be in the form of shares. Discounting has been ignored, though is arguably appropriate here.

Fair value adjustments
The original and revalued amounts are shown below. Note that, following FRS 7, the possible reorganization provision has not been included in the at-acquisition balances, but has been set up as a post-acquisition amount.in Figure 5.3.
The adjustments *at acquisition* to satisfy part (b) of the question are as follows:

Balances	Unadjusted	Fair value adjustments	Adjusted
Land	20	(4)	16
Other fixed assets	70	22	92
Stocks	50	4	54
Other current assets	60	—	60
Creditors over one year	(40)	(2)	(42)
	160	20	180

Stocks are calculated at the lower of replacement cost (£60m) and net realizable value (£54m)

The 'loan' at present is $= \dfrac{52.34}{(1.10)^3} = $ £40m

At the market yield at the *date of acquisition*, it would be stated at
$$\dfrac{52.34}{(1.1116)^2} = \text{£42m}$$

The reorganization provision is accounted for as post-acquisition and does not therefore affect goodwill.

Exercises

5.6 Why did FRS 7 find it necessary to specify the boundary so tightly between what can be included in identifiable assets and liabilities at acquisition and what cannot? Comment on the effectiveness and relevance to users of FRS 7's resolution of the problem.

5.7 Assess the merits of the case that reorganization provisions at acquisition should be banned.

5.8 Assume that in Exercise 5.3 the facts are the same, but in accordance with FRS 7, the acquirer sets up the reorganization provision at acquisition as a *post*-acquisition event.

Required
By showing extracts from a consolidation cancellation table show the effects of setting up and using the provision. Compare and contrast the effects of this treatment on controlling and minority interests with that of setting up the provision as part of the restatement to fair values of the identifiable assets and liabilities at acquisition as in Exercise 5.3.

5.9 Identify when it may be necessary to use the 'value in use' of a depreciable fixed asset as the estimate of its fair value at acquisition. To what extent would such a fair value depend on management intentions?

5.10 Why is it necessary for FRS 7 to specify an investigation period? Explain the difference in treatment between changes in estimates of fair values at acquisition where those changes are

Description	Invest-ment	Share capital	Share premium	Unissued shares	Consol retained profits	Goodwill (pre-acq)	Minority interests	Land	Other fixed assets	Stocks	Other current assets	Reorg prov	Loans
Majestic													
Unadjusted balances		(140)	(90)		(120)			80	200	90	100		(120)
Purchase consideration	154	(72)	(36)	(10)							(36)		
Underling													
Unadjusted equity						(120)	(40)						
Unadjusted other bals								20	70	50	60		(40)
Fair value adjustments					9	(15)	(5)	(4)	22	4			(2)
Reorganisation provision							3					(12)	
Cancellation													
Investment	(154)					154 19							
Goodwill write-off					19	(19)							
Consolidated	-	(212)	(126)	(10)	(92)	-	(42)	76	292	144	124	(12)	(162)

Figure 5.3 – Expanded cancellation table for Majestic Group

determined (a) within the investigation period, and (b) after it has ended.

5.11 *Detailed valuation requirements* – Trump plc acquired a 90% stake in Outbid plc, the date of acquisition being 30 June 1995, at Trump's own year end. The two companies' balance sheets immediately prior to acquisition were:

Individual company balance sheets at 30 June 1995

	Trump £m	Trump £m	Outbid £m	Outbid £m
Fixed assets				
Land		180		90
Tangible fixed assets		400		120
		580		210
Net current assets				
Stocks	130		100	
Other	240		90	
		370		190
Creditors over one year		(320)		(100)
		630		300
Capital and Reserves				
Share capital (£1 shares)		230		120
Share premium		180		80
Retained profits		220		100
		630		300

Details on fair values at acquisition

Purchase consideration
The offer, accepted by 90 per cent of the shareholders in Outbid plc (the combination did not satisfy criteria for a merger) was for 3 ordinary shares of Trump plc (market price at the date of acquisition £1 per share), plus £1 in cash for every 2 shares in Outbid plc, plus a further £2.42 cash for every 2 shares held, payable two years after the date of acquisition. Trump plc's borrowing rate is 10 per cent p.a.

Identifiable assets and liabilities
(a) The replacement cost of stocks had been estimated at £120m with an estimated net realizable value of £110m. However, the former managing director of Outbid had commented that if Trump had continued in the same direction as Outbid's acquired business, the goods would have been saleable well above £120m.
(b) Fair values of land (at £95m) and depreciable fixed assets (at £100m) had only been provisionally determined.
(c) Trump plc wished to close some of Outbid's facilities, and estimated closure costs are £18m, payable over the next two years.
(d) Creditors over one year represent a 'zero-coupon' bond (i.e. with no interest payments and just a single repayment amount of £146.41m at 30 June 1997). The market yield on such bonds when they were issued one year ago was 13.55 per cent, the current market yield on similar bonds is 10 per cent.
(e) Damages claimed by Outbid plc in a court case pending at 30 June 1995, which it expects to win, have a fair value estimated at £12m. These have not been recognized in Outbid plc's own accounts so as not to anticipate revenues.
(f) None of the above adjustments has been recorded in the records of Underling plc and it has been decided to record them on the consolidation working papers.
(g) Goodwill is to be gradually amortized over a ten year period.

Required
Prepare an extended cancellation table for the Trump Group at acquisition showing the recording of purchase consideration and fair value adjustments. Follow FRS 7's requirements. As a part of your workings, prepare a 'fair value' table showing the effects of fair value adjustments on the acquired balances of Outbid plc.

5.12 *Detailed valuation requirements* – Hot Breath plc acquired a 65 per cent stake in Garlic plc on April 30 1995, issuing 2m shares which had a price of £2.30 per share on that date, plus a cash payment of £25m deferred for one year. Hot Breath plc supports an active acquisitions department and it devoted approximately 30 per cent of the departments's effort over 3 months to this take-over. Annual estimated costs of the Department are £2m. £1m was paid to Clineworm Butnot, the group's merchant bankers in connection with work done in connection with the acquisition. Hot Breath plc's borrowing rate of interest is approximately 12 per cent p.a.

Required

Calculate the cost of acquisition of Garlic plc based on the provisions of FRS 7. Discuss whether its proposed treatment of acquisition costs is fair.

Comparing UK and US stances on fair value adjustments

In the UK identifiable assets and liabilities are *completely* restated to fair values at acquisition and the fair valuation adjustments apportioned between controlling and minority interests. In the USA, and in the benchmark treatment recommended by IAS 22, only the controlling interest's proportion of assets and liabilities are restated to fair values and no adjustments made for the minority proportion. Because therefore the minority proportion in each asset and liability is left at the subsidiary's original carrying value, the effect in the consolidated financial statements is that each of the subsidiary's individual assets and liabilities in the USA will be measured at a *composite* amount – in the case of an 80 per cent subsidiary, 80 per cent at fair value at acquisition and 20 per cent at original subsidiary carrying amount. In the UK such assets and liabilities will be reported as 100 per cent of fair value at acquisition. So if stock with an original carrying amount of £20m had a fair value at acquisition of £30m, it would be reported in the at-acquisition consolidated financial statements in the UK at £30m, and in the USA at £28m (i.e. 80% × £30m + 20% × £20m) – which is neither a fair value nor an original cost!

In the USA therefore minority interests are based on a proportion of the *subsidiary's* carrying values of its assets and liabilities. The consequence of the UK perspective is that minority interests are calculated as a proportion of the *consolidated* book values of the subsidiary's net assets. This difference results from an extreme unwillingness in the USA to countenance any revaluations and the comparatively relaxed attitude towards them in the UK. IAS 22 permits the UK approach as an allowed alternative. The difference can be conceptualized as the distinction between whether minority interests are viewed as regards consolidation valuation adjustments, as 'insiders' (complete revaluation) or 'outsiders' (no adjustment to the subsidiary's values) to the group. In the latter case their interest is measured on the same basis as their interest in the financial statements of the company/subgroup in which they have a direct stake. This is related to the choice of consolidation concept and is explored further at the end of Chapter 6.

ACCOUNTING FOR GOODWILL

Whereas fair value determination at acquisition is a policing problem with conceptual overtones, accounting for goodwill is a conceptual problem with policing implications. One of the most problematic areas in financial reporting, it occurs at the uneasy seam between transaction based accounting and financial economics. Even with the advent of SSAP 22, *Accounting for Goodwill* (1984), a profusion of differing practices still exists and even more alternatives are proposed in the ASB's Discussion Paper, *Goodwill and Intangible Assets* (1993). This section examines the problem of accounting for purchased consolidated goodwill, and wider issues in measuring and recording goodwill and intangibles are examined only in so far as they are necessary to this aim.

Readers wishing only to focus on current and prospective UK pronouncements on goodwill and other intangibles rather than on conceptual issues and economic context can omit the sections 'Is Goodwill an Asset?', 'Recognition and Measurement Issues' and 'The Economic Context' without loss of continuity.

The nature of goodwill

Hughes (1982, p. 7) who provides a useful historical survey of the area, offers a 'working definition' of goodwill as 'the differential ability of one business, in comparison with another or an assumed average firm, to make a profit'. Colley and Volkan (1988, p. 35) measure goodwill under this perspective as 'the present value of the anticipated excess earnings, discounted over ... the estimated life or reason(s) underlying the excess returns' – potentially encompassing the valuation of both internally generated and purchased goodwill. Excess earnings are often characterized as arising from such factors as superior management, business contacts, good relations with employees, etc. However, they can only arise in imperfect markets through synergy from jointness of activities and monopoly power/barriers to entry (Arnold et al., 1992).

'Goodwill' is also commonly defined as the difference between the value of an entity as a whole and the imputed value of its component parts. Earlier writers (e.g. Gynther, 1969) saw the valuation of goodwill as part of a schema to include more relevant economic values in financial reports. However, the academic literature (e.g. Peasnell, 1977; Barton, 1974) concludes that accountants do not have comparative advantage in themselves providing valuations of companies as a whole, on feasibility as well as reliability grounds. Usually conventional accounting avoids this area by excluding proprietorial activity from financial statements. However, when one entity purchases another there is no way to avoid valuations of a firm as a whole entering the accounting equation. The transaction *as a whole* is a fact, and is dissaggregated under consolidated financial reporting *as if* separate assets and liabilities had been purchased – leading to the problem of accounting for this excess.

IS GOODWILL AN ASSET?

The reason why this is an important question from a consolidated financial statements perspective is that the answer points to whether capitalization is the appropriate possibility or immediate write-off. Figure 5.4 examines why valuation as a whole differs from the component perspective by analysing the value of the investment in a company into the imputed components proposed by various authors, termed the 'hidden assets' approach to goodwill valuation by Colley and Volkan (1988, p. 35).

Proposed layers
Tangible assets and liabilities
Separable / marketable intangible assets in practice
Conceptually distinguishable intangible assets
Residual
Amount of under- or over-payment (Arnold et al 1992)

Figure 5.4 – Decomposition of value of the company as a whole into components

The usual starting point if an investment is *purchased* is the difference between its cost and the fair value of the identifiable assets and liabilities acquired. The main accounting issue is how far the remaining difference can or should be decomposed into separately distinguished components (other intangibles, for example brand names) and how much should be treated as residual (goodwill) – the problem of *identifiability*. A similar analysis determining *internally generated* goodwill can be made in principle via the estimated value of the firm, but is not considered here.

Many argue the criterion for separately distinguishing other intangible assets for measurement or disclosure purposes should be marketability or transferability separate from the business as a whole (e.g. ED 52, *Accounting for Intangible Fixed Assets* (1990)), whereas others argue such distinguishing should be allowable even if identifiability were only of a more notional kind. A recent ASB Discussion Paper, *Goodwill and Intangible Assets* (1993), sees no case for the separate accounting for this latter class (pp. 16–20), but the debate still rages. Proposed methods for valuing identifiable but non-separable intangibles (e.g. brands) are often based on 'valuing' incremental income streams (see for example Birkin, 1991). The residual after valuing such intangibles is commonly called 'goodwill' though, for example, Arnold *et al.* (1992, p. 68) suggest it would be better to term it 'difference on consolidation'. Egginton (1990) attempts to provide *definitional* distinctions between different kinds of 'intangibles' (legal rights versus persons at large) and 'goodwill' (expectations of economic benefits carrying no legal rights).

Writers disagree over whether or not the residual 'goodwill' is an 'asset' and in what sense. The ASB's definition of an asset in its draft *Statement of Principles* (1992) is, 'rights or other access to future economic benefits controlled by an entity as a result of past transactions or events'. Archer (1994a, p. 7) considers goodwill merely to be an aggregation level issue, and comments 'a value which only emerges on aggregation, disappears on dissaggregation' and so should not be recognized in accounts. He considers 'control' implies separate transferability. Arnold *et al.* (1992), whilst recognizing that the residual is merely a synergy effect and not a separately identifiable asset, argue that 'treating it *as if it were* another such asset is the only logical, consistent and neutral way to "undo" the effect of disaggregation' (p. 36). Since the definitions of 'assets' derive from the more fundamental perspective of usefulness, some authors bypass such 'asset' definitions and argue directly from this overall perspective.

Purchased 'goodwill'

In the case of purchased goodwill, Arnold *et al.* (1992) distinguish a further category, over- or under-payment for the company as a whole, requiring different accounting treatment from the remaining 'residual', to be taken to income or expense immediately. However, other authors doubt the theoretical or practical feasibility of identifying particularly over-payments (for example, Archer, 1994; Colley and Volkan, 1988; Lee, 1993) – which management is going to admit having over-paid, and on what basis is an auditor going to challenge them?

Ma and Hopkins (1988) also point out that purchased goodwill has a different character to internally generated goodwill. The latter relates to a single company, the former includes synergy effects which may occur not in the acquired company, but in the group as a whole, e.g. access to capital markets for a larger group or ability to dominate a market. The negotiated price is based on a haggling over how much the group will pay to the acquired company's shareholders for these incremental benefits, which in the absence of the acquisition would not have accrued to the acquired company. What is capitalized in addition to the target's goodwill is *part* of the incremental benefits to the acquirer not present in the purchased company itself. They argue that purchased goodwill is thus a fairly arbitrary figure, different in kind from internally generated goodwill.

Other perspectives

The literature (e.g. Solomons, 1989) divides over whether profit should be derived from the prior determination of assets and liabilities (the 'balance sheet' approach), or whether profit measurement and 'matching' should have primacy and determine what is to be reported in the balance sheet. From the latter perspective, Grinyer, Russell and Walker (1990) argue that managers should be accountable for any costs they incur and therefore all costs including goodwill should pass through the profit and loss account as expense over the life of the investment. Grinyer and Russell (1992) cite the monitoring role of accounting reports as a justification for this viewpoint, and radically disagree with Ma and Hopkins over the 'value' interpretation of goodwill, viewing it instead more as an expenditure to be matched. From this perspective any balance sheet measurement is a cost still to be accounted for by management in the exercise of its stewardship; the write-off of purchased goodwill will reduce future 'abnormal' returns expected from the purchase by the allocated cost of acquiring these returns. The consequent normalized returns are a test of a good bargain and may still be higher than that of similar firms if the bargain is good. However, such accountability is difficult to assess because of subsequent changes in economic conditions and the arbitrariness caused by the allocation problem. These effects are difficult to separate from the effects of the original decision.

Hodgson, Okunev and Willett (1993) argue from what they term a *statistical transactions* approach to goodwill – because of imperfect markets, goodwill values are part of a probability distribution of possible values whose (population) expected value is what people refer to when they talk about the fair value of goodwill. The 'excess earnings' approach is just a way of estimating this 'average' value, and purchased goodwill a piece of sample data, one observation from the distribution of possible goodwill values. Whether or not goodwill should be included in financial statements depends on whether such observed goodwill values have as an empirical fact an expected value greater than zero (on average) or not. If so they should be explicitly reported as a synergistic effect.

RECOGNITION AND MEASUREMENT ISSUES

Even if goodwill is an asset or 'pseudo' asset, should it be recognized in financial statements, and how should it be measured? Egginton (1990) and Arnold *et al.* (1992) examine goodwill measurement under different current value systems. Such discussion is beyond the scope of this work where discussion is confined to historical costs, but historical cost can in principle include any capitalized internally generated goodwill expenditures, and is modified by occasional asset revaluations.

The criteria for recognition in the ASB's draft *Statement of Principles*, are those of *relevance* and *reliability*. Different stances can be taken over this issue, for example that though both purchased and non-purchased goodwill are relevant, reliability constraints mean that both should be written off immediately (Catlett and Olsen, 1968); another view is that both can be recognized if satisfactory tests to determine recoverable amounts can be established (Egginton, 1990; Arnold *et al.* 1992). Conventionally only purchased goodwill and purchased intangibles have been recognized in UK financial statements. However, certain companies have attempted to introduce values for internally created intangibles (e.g. brands). As shown in Figure 5.5, there are three obvious conceptual alternatives for goodwill and/or other intangibles. The debate over which is preferable hinges on the balance taken between relevance and reliability. Hughes (1982) notes that even at the turn of the century the professional literature contained arguments supporting three alternative treatments: permanent retention as an asset, capitalization and gradual amortization and immediate write-off against reserves!

Approach	Description
Level up	Recognise both purchased *and* internally generated goodwill or intangibles
Split level	Recognise only purchased goodwill or intangibles
Level down	Recognise neither purchased *nor* internally created intangibles

Figure 5.5 – Recognition of purchased and internally generated goodwill and other intangibles

Level up

Arnold *et al.* (1992) in their ASB-commissioned study, *Goodwill and Other Intangibles: Theoretical Considerations and Policy Issues*, incline towards selective levelling-up, concluding that it is permissible in principle to treat purchased *and* internally generated intangibles as assets and capitalize them provided their existence and amount can be satisfactorily justified. Their proposals are discussed as an example of what levelling up would entail, though are unlikely to be enacted. Goodwill may be treated as an asset 'as [since] ... it is expected to provide future economic benefits it possesses one essential characteristic of an asset' (p. 68). The reliability of purchased goodwill is deduced from the fact that the corresponding investment in the subsidiary is reliable enough to report in its own accounts, and the study wishes to link the accounting treatment of purchased goodwill with that of the investment. (Also, unlike research and development expenditures, one could argue that its 'recoverability' relates to the whole firm not merely a product line.)

Arnold *et al.* propose that capitalized intangibles and goodwill should be written off to profit and loss over their economic lives and that any subsequent expenditure should be capitalized as *new* internally created goodwill and written-off separately. Any purchased *and* internally created goodwill and intangibles capitalized should be subject to annual *ceiling tests* to see if their carrying value needs to be written down to a lower *recoverable amount* under the 'value to the business' concept'. The term 'ceiling test' is unfortunate since ceilings are usually looked up to rather than used to determine recoverable values and write-down amounts! Under- or over-payments relating to purchased goodwill should be written off to profit and loss immediately, having no enduring value.

The extent of levelling-up proposed is based on management discretion, influenced by cleverly balanced costs and benefits. Any *purchased* goodwill and intangibles not capitalized has to be written off through *profit and loss*. If internally generated items are included, they have to be amortized through profit and loss and are subject to extra costs of annual ceiling test reviews and extra disclosures showing the bases of valuation. The reliability question is faced head on by allowing openly that different categories of assets will have different degrees of reliability. Investors are assumed to respond appropriately if given enough information. Their suggestions could lead to selective reporting and management manipulation, though their suggested cost-benefit framework is interesting.

The report's main proposals are based on capitalizing costs. Revaluation is discussed, though the study recognizes that the Companies Act 1985 allows revaluation of intangibles but not goodwill. Whether these provisions would prevent capitalization of internally generated goodwill or just revisions in its value is uncertain. Selective revaluation of intangibles is countenanced, analogous to UK practice on land and buildings. However, only the ceiling test element of the study was brought forward into the subsequent ASB Discussion Paper, *Goodwill and Intangible Assets* (1993) discussed later.

Level down

This approach demands the immediate removal of purchased goodwill from published financial statements, and might well be advocated by those do not see it as an asset. It is the most popular option in the UK and is the preferred treatment of SSAP 22, *Accounting for Goodwill* (1984), with such immediate write-off bypassing current period profit and loss, being taken direct to reserves. Some hold this position for purchased goodwill, but a different one for other intangibles. Consistency of treatment with companies/groups which grow internally is often cited in support, but as we shall see below, consistency has many different facets. Immediate write-off also can distort gearing levels of acquisitive groups.

Some hold this view because of unreliability in the measurement of purchased goodwill (e.g. Catlett and Olsen, 1968). Knortz, quoted in McLean (1972, p. 48), seeing problems with fixing goodwill at an amount determined at an arbitrary date, that of acquisition, comments,

One may well ask whether it will make sense forty years from now [towards the end of its arbitrary write-off period], to have the earnings of the year 2010 affected by the fact that Vice President (of the USA) Agnew made a speech which affected the stock market in 1970.

Arnold *et al.* (1992) and Grinyer and Russell (1992) criticize immediate write-off direct to reserves on the grounds that under historical cost accounting it removes a level of management accountability. Such a by-passing write-off can be justified, e.g. under net realizable value accounting (Egginton, 1990) but discussion is beyond the scope of the current work.

Treat purchased and non-purchased goodwill differently

After the 'Great Crash' of 1929, the debate centred on *purchased* goodwill. Backdoor ways of incorporating non-purchased goodwill such as capitalizing advertising expenditures or early losses were frowned upon. Cooke (1985, p. 3) points out that in the USA, APB Opinion No 17's conditions for capitalizing intangible assets generally preclude capitalizing expenditures on developing, maintaining or restoring inherent (non-purchased) goodwill. SSAP 22 explicitly excludes it. In the UK there are three main proposals for *purchased* goodwill and intangibles: capitalization and gradual amortization, permanent retention at cost, and capitalization subject to regular recoverable amount (ceiling) tests.

Gradual amortization

The most commonly adopted approach world-wide is that purchased goodwill and intangibles are capitalized and gradually amortized to the profit and loss account over their economic lives (required by APB Opinion 17 (1970) in the USA, to be required from 1995 by IAS 22 (1993), and currently allowed by SSAP 22 (1984) in the UK), whereas internally generated goodwill expenditures are immediately expensed. Authors (e.g. Colley and Volkan, 1988) point out the problems of determining the economic life of goodwill (e.g. an arbitrary maximum of 40 years is used in the USA) and the arbitrary nature of depreciation patterns (e.g. Thomas, 1975), so that straight line amortization or something more conservative is often recommended.

Permanent retention at cost

This is commonly justified on the grounds that maintenance expenditure keeps up goodwill's value, and that gradual amortization results in 'double-counting' of maintenance expenditure and amortization. It is illegal in the UK and seems a crude alternative to current value accounting. Opponents argue it should not be allowed since, over time, purchased goodwill is replaced by internally generated goodwill.

Regular recoverable amount assessments

Purchased goodwill would be assessed regularly, but only written down if there has been a (permanent) diminution in value (see the ASB Discussion Paper later) – justified through consistency of treatment with the parent's investment in its own accounts.

Negative goodwill

Negative 'goodwill' arises when the investment cost is less than the fair value of identifiable assets and liabilities acquired. Suggested accounting treatments have included (De Moville and Petrie, 1989) treating the credit as:

(1) a gain, part of income – a 'bargain' purchase;
(2) transferring the credit direct to reserves – the counterpart to the immediate write-off of positive goodwill;
(3) amortizing the credit to profit and loss over some 'economic' life;
(4) reducing the fair values of the assets acquired until the credit is 'used up'.

Option 2 is required by SSAP 22, even though immediate write-off is not required for *positive* goodwill. ED 47 proposed requiring option 3, gradual amortization to profit and loss, mirroring its proposed requirement for positive goodwill. In the USA, option 4 is followed in that the credit is allocated pro-rata over non-current assets until these are reduced to zero, and then any credit left can be gradually amortized to profit and loss (the latter analogous to the US treatment for positive goodwill).

Each approach takes a different view of the credit which could arise from a number of causes – option 4 relates it to mistakes in the fair value exercise, which should not occur grossly under FRS 7; option 3 seems to relate it to expectation of future losses, amortizing the credit against the losses when they arise in future periods. However, the possibility of a genuine 'bargain purchases' exists (option 1). The problem for standard-setters is to provide criteria to distinguish between the different cases. Unscrupulous managements might claim bargain purchases, get immediate income and expected losses would only flow through later. Option 2 could only be justified on the grounds of consistency with companies which grow organically (internally generate goodwill). Pragmatically, the ASB's future treatment of negative goodwill will probably mirror its treatment of positive goodwill.

Other recognition and measurement criteria

It is interesting that the ASB does not consider that the conflict of elimination-based approaches with its draft *Statement of Principles* is conclusive in rejecting them (see examination of its Discussion Paper below). This highlights the unusual nature of purchased goodwill and the tentative nature of conceptual frameworks internationally. Accounting theory currently has no mechanism for deducing specific proposals from ultimate goals such as usefulness and commonly suggests intermediate criteria to proxy for 'usefulness'. The ASB Discussion Paper (1993) suggests the following criteria.

Consistency

Different proposed foci for consistency include:

(1) *fixed assets* – indicating gradual amortization;
(2) *balance sheet treatment of internally generated goodwill* – pointing to immediate write-off (strictly through profit and loss);
(3) *the parent's investment in its own accounts* – suggesting annual reviews of recoverable amounts and write-downs where necessary.

However, one's stance determines the critiques of other approaches. Supporters of consistency with the treatment of internally generated goodwill criticise point 1 for 'double counting' maintenance and amortization. Supporters of point 1 maintain that consistency with the parent's investment undercharges amortization – the investment cost may exceed net recoverable amount only because purchased goodwill has been replaced by internally generated goodwill. Even balance sheet consistency with internally generated goodwill can be criticized from a profit and loss perspective when the immediate write-off of goodwill bypasses profit and loss, as organically growing groups will be charging internally generated goodwill 'expenses' to profit and loss each year, whereas constant acquirers will avoid this.

Accountability

This term is used by the ASB Discussion Paper (DP) to imply the tracking of losses in value in different financial statements, namely:

(1) the consolidated balance sheet;
(2) the consolidated profit and loss account;
(3) the parent's individual accounts.

In the sense used by the DP, a rigorous annual review procedure to determine whether goodwill should be written down to its recoverable amount gives greatest accountability under all three headings as the same criteria would determine whether the parent's investment would need to be written down. Gradual amortization does not usually lead to amortization of the investment in the parent's own accounts, so this scores less highly.

Immediate write-off provides little accountability, though if a separate write-off reserve were used at least the original cost is tracked, though not subsequent changes in value.

Miscellaneous criteria

Gradual amortization scores highest under *international comparability*, though the ASB is willing to be out of step if it feels it is leading in the development of better goodwill accounting. Some argue that naïve investors have the potential to be confused into believing that immediate write-off means a loss in value rather than being merely an accounting policy choice. *Cost-benefit* constraints are suggested by the ASB to suggest why supporters of the capitalization and annual systematic review approach might accept gradual amortization as a *cheaper* alternative.

SSAP 22, *ACCOUNTING FOR GOODWILL*

Accounting for goodwill has been controversial since the turn of the century. By the 1940s there was general agreement on the cost basis although accounting treatment subsequent to acquisition remained controversial. Early UK recommendations observed that goodwill did not depreciate through use in the business and if amortized this should be disclosed separately in the profit and loss. The influential *Survey of Published Accounts* as late as 1977–8 showed that, out of 300 companies and groups surveyed, 222 stated their goodwill policy and of these, 98 kept goodwill at original cost, 81 used immediate write-off, and 43 amortized or used another write-down method. However, by 1980-81, 195 of 254 companies used immediate write-off.

The EEC 4th Directive in the late 1970s concentrated minds. In initial draft versions it allowed a maximum life for goodwill in company accounts of five years. Later drafts, whose provisions were included in the Companies Act 1981, gave member states the option to extend this period up to its economic life. Permanent retention and dangling debit were proscribed. As late as 1980 the ASC issued its first discussion paper which opted for gradual amortization. In 1982, ED 30 was issued, allowing immediate write-off or gradual amortization, the latter over a maximum period of 20 years. SSAP 22 was issued in 1984, prohibiting permanent retention, preferring immediate write-off, and tolerating gradual amortization! No maximum life was included.

In the USA an earlier debate had moved towards gradual amortization. Immediate write-off was first prohibited by (non-mandatory) ARB No. 43 in 1953 except in the cases of permanent diminution in value. It allowed both permanent retention and amortization. The ARB acquired the status of a standard when the Accounting Principles Board was set up in 1959. In 1970, APB Opinion No 17 banned permanent retention, requiring gradual amortization over a maximum period of 40 years as the only treatment, allowing immediate write-offs to the *income statement* only if diminution of value had occurred. Some argue such prohibitions fuelled the widespread adoption of pooling (merger) accounting in the USA in the 1960s and 1970s. Though the debate moved in different directions in the two countries, the tolerance of gradual amortization in SSAP 22 allows UK multinationals to meet current US requirements, though it is not the preferred UK treatment. For further excellent historical discussion of the recent development of goodwill accounting in the UK see Nobes (1992).

Calculation of goodwill

The nature of goodwill is not discussed in SSAP 22, but is to be calculated as 'the difference between the fair value of the consideration given and the aggregate of the fair values of the separable assets acquired' (para. 29). Only purchased goodwill is to be recognized, including goodwill in associates. The technical release accompanying the SSAP 22 states that when a debit balance arises under *merger* accounting, this is not goodwill under the standard because it is not based on fair values.

Subsequent accounting treatment

Following the EEC 4th Directive, SSAP 22 prohibits permanent retention and dangling debits. It is unique amongst accounting standards, expressing (for *positive* goodwill) a preference for one treatment, immediate write-off against reserves, but allowing another, gradual amortization via the profit and loss account. *Negative* goodwill should be written off immediately against reserves – not the mirror image of positive goodwill (unlike ED 30). Companies can choose afresh their treatment with each acquisition, with no requirement for consistency (again unlike ED 30 which required companies to use one approach for all future acquisitions). If immediate write-off is chosen for associated companies, then such investments are effectively stated at *net asset* value as the write-down would be a credit to the equitised investment (Chapter 4, page 100).

Where gradual amortization is used, positive goodwill should be eliminated 'in arriving at profit or loss on ordinary activities on a systematic basis over its *useful* economic life'. It should not be revalued subsequently, though it should be written down immediately if there is a permanent diminution in value. Useful economic life for which no maximum is stated (ED 30 specified a maximum of 20 years) should be estimated at acquisition. The effects of subsequent expenditures should not be used in determining this life, which may subsequently be shortened, but not increased. SSAP 22 does *not* require any correspondence between the treatment of goodwill in the consolidated accounts and the investment in the parent's own accounts.

The ASC had been squeezed – extant UK practice overwhelmingly supported immediate write-off. APB No. 17, which bound many multinationals, requires gradual amortization over a maximum 40 years. Possibly as the best it could do, the ASC argued the benefits of one treatment, but met its practical obligations through an escape clause. SSAP 22 emphasizes that immediate write-off is a matter of accounting policy not a diminution in value, stressing comparability between purchased and non-purchased goodwill. Immediate write-off against *reserves* is recommended so that current year profit is not adversely affected by a large lump sum charge since the cause was not a diminution in value. APB No 17 deduced exactly the opposite conclusion from similar data, banning discretionary write-offs and requiring amortization!

Apparently, allowing free choice at each acquisition was to encourage maximum use of immediate write-off. Companies might have been reluctant to choose this if they were bound to a single treatment in case reserves in future acquisitions might be insufficient to absorb *future* immediate write-offs. The ASC's decline in confidence since its inflation-accounting débâcle was made apparent. Critics pointed out you can adopt one treatment if you have enough profits/reserves and another if you don't.

Choice of reserves for immediate write-off

SSAP 22 does not specify which reserves can be used. The setting up of a zero-reserve against which goodwill is written off is fairly common. This is legal according to the DTI, whereas the so-called 'dangling debit' is prohibited by the Companies Act 1985, although both achieve a very similar effect. The resulting *debit* balance is apparently legal only because it is called a (negative) reserve and not goodwill! Indeed the use of a separate write-off reserve has finally achieved respectability as one of the preferred proposals in the ASB's 1993 Discussion Paper, *Goodwill and Other Intangibles*.

Most companies qualifying for *merger relief* (Chapter 3) use the *merger reserve*. Non-qualifying companies often overcome statutory restrictions on the share premium account by obtaining the court's permission, thus blurring a major distinction between acquisition and merger accounting. Two distinct treatments for combinations now shade into a spectrum of alternatives. The Companies Act 1985 outlaws the use of consolidated revaluation reserves, though it is difficult to see why the use of the share premium account makes any more sense.

Since distributability of profits is based on individual company accounts, the destination of immediate write-off does not affect this. SSAP 22 contains guidance for goodwill write-off in individual company accounts, but this does not apply to group accounts.

Considerable questions are thus raised about the usefulness of reported components of *consolidated* equity – the relative sizes of which depend on management whim and which can in aggregate because of immediate goodwill write-off be smaller than the parent's equity.

Disclosures

SSAP 22 requires the following: accounting policies followed; the amount of goodwill recognized as a result of any acquisitions during the year (with separate amounts for each acquisition if material); where the amortization approach is adopted, purchased goodwill should be disclosed in the balance sheet, also its movements, showing cost, accumulated amortization, and net book value at the beginning and end of the year, and the amount amortized, together with the period of amortization for each acquisition. The cumulative goodwill written-off for group undertakings held at the year end should also be disclosed.

Distributable profits: holding company versus group accounts

The non-mandatory Appendix of SSAP 22 deals with the write-off of goodwill in the accounts of *companies* not groups. It is a masterly example of casuistic reasoning. It tries to attain parity in *distributable* profits (i.e. *realized* reserves) between immediate write-off and gradual amortization. In the accounts of companies, immediate write-off of goodwill can be made against *unrealized* reserves because it is a decision of accounting policy not a diminution in value. Then over the goodwill's useful economic life, an amount equivalent to the amount under gradual amortization (which had that approach been adopted would have reduced realized reserves in the form of retained earnings), can be transferred from unrealized to realized reserves. This is a tortuous, but an ingenious, way to ensure parity of realized reserves between treatments. However, it does *not* apply to consolidated reserves or the write-off of consolidated goodwill.

The proper relationship between parent and group reserves is a difficult issue, for example paragraph 18 of SSAP 22 'does not require an adjustment to be made in the holding company's accounts [to the investment] in respect of any consolidation goodwill written off in the group accounts . . . except to the extent that [there is] . . . a permanent diminution in value'. Holgate (1986) suggests that write-offs of consolidated goodwill in the group accounts have no effect on distributable profits, whereas if the investment is correspondingly written down in the holding company's accounts (a form of 'push down' accounting), this could affect distributable profits of the parent company over a period. Whether group accounts should assist shareholders of the parent company in assessing *potential* distributable profits is controversial, as companies not groups make distributions.

THE LATER DEBATE

That immediate write-off improves reported profits compared with gradual amortization was well known when SSAP 22 was issued. Soon, it was widely debated whether this gives unfair competitive advantage to UK companies internationally or whether such 'improvements' are merely cosmetic so that companies bidding on the basis of profits thus inflated might overpay in acquisitions! Only later was it realized that group gearing ratios could be decimated by large immediate write-offs. Barwise *et al.* (1989, p. 21) found the ratio of goodwill to bidders' net worth rose on average from 1 per cent in 1976 and 4 per cent in 1983 to 44 per cent in the heady market conditions of 1987. Over the same 11 years the average ratio of goodwill to 'target's' net worth rose from 26 per cent to 70 per cent.

The 'Brands' debate
The service sector was particularly affected by immediate goodwill write-offs and Saatchi

and Saatchi, the acquisitive advertising agency, reported negative consolidated equity. It was argued that Nestlé was only able to acquire Rowntree-Mackintosh in 1988 because of missing intangibles in the latter's balance sheet. In the same year Grand Metropolitan Hotels capitalized certain purchased brands, and Rank Hovis MacDougall went further, capitalizing internally created brands. Both used immediate write-off for goodwill and so brand capitalization improved their reported gearing. As the measurement of brands and other intangibles was not specifically covered by legislation or accounting standards, gradual amortization was not required, unlike for capitalized goodwill. Critics suggested that some groups wanted to have their cake (no write-off to profit and loss) and eat it (re-adjust the negative gearing effect of immediate write-off).

Barwise *et al.* (1989) recommended against the use of values for brands in balance sheets (as opposed to costs) because of the lack of separability of many brands and measurement reliability problems. They questioned whether such valuations provided new market information, and analysts were also found to be sceptical. Other reasons for capitalizing brands are explored later. Power (1992) provides a good review of the debate.

ASC Exposure Drafts on Goodwill and Intangibles

In 1990 in a final act of defiance before being disbanded, the ASC in ED 47, *Accounting for Goodwill,* and ED 52, *Accounting for Intangible Fixed Assets,* proposed requiring that only purchased goodwill and separable intangibles could be capitalized and must be amortized over their useful life, with a 20 year upper limit, 40 in the case of special pleading if the justifications were disclosed. In a later Discussion Paper (1993) the ASB reported that 73 per cent of all respondents (and 93 per cent of companies) opposed ED 47's 'solution'. ED 52 was almost equally disliked. The ASB commissioned the Arnold *et al.* (1992) report, *Goodwill and Other Intangibles: Theoretical and Policy Issues,* discussed earlier, which explored ceiling tests, and proposed a selective 'levelling-up' solution, allowing intangibles to be valued separately from 'goodwill' if reliable.

ASB Discussion Paper, Goodwill and Intangible Assets (1993)

The 1993 Discussion Paper (DP) discards the levelling up alternative and is sceptical of the feasibility of identifying brands separately in most cases. It retains the concept of ceiling tests, recognizing goodwill as an 'accounting anomaly' (para. 1.3), and that each possible approach (other than 'levelling-up') 'results in inconsistencies with other aspects of financial reporting'. It presents three 'asset-based' and three 'elimination-based' alternatives, (see Figure 5.6) evaluating the advantages and disadvantages of each using the criteria discussed earlier, and wishing eventually to settle on one.

The DP analysed responses to ED 47: 93 per cent of companies and 66 per cent of Big-Six accounting firms opposed gradual amortization (overall respondents 73 per cent); 69 per cent of companies and accounting firms outside the Big-Six and 66 per cent of the Big-Six opposed immediate write-off to reserves (overall 69 per cent). Capitalization without automatic gradual amortization was more popular (33 per cent overall 'against', 52 per cent overall 'for') – 'for' comprised mainly companies (66 per cent) and Big-Six firms (50 per cent). Whether this justifies the ASB's claimed support for capitalization and annual systematic review discussed below is debatable.

Brands and other intangibles

The DP is sceptical of the current distinction between goodwill and other intangibles, noting the Companies Act 1985 defines identifiable assets and liabilities for the purposes of determining fair values as 'capable of being disposed of or discharged separately, without disposing of a business of the undertaking' (Sch 4A S9(2)). Except for costs of purchasing legal rights in order to secure benefits from internally generated intangibles, the DP proposes purchased intangible assets should be subsumed within purchased goodwill and accounted for accordingly (para. 1.7.1). Such a body blow to 'brand' supporters has met with considerable opposition. The DP's only concessions allow management to give note disclosures of the nature and estimated value of intangible benefits within the goodwill balance, and of estimation procedures, with further qualitative details in the Operating and Financial Review (para. 3.2.13). It is quite possible that the ASB will eventually ameliorate this position.

Purchased goodwill

The DP requires that only purchased goodwill should be recognized. Figure 5.6 shows the current UK position and the DP's proposed alternatives. The Board is divided between

Pronouncement	Accounting treatment
Current requirements: SSAP 22, *Accounting for Goodwill*	*Either:* I. immediate elimination against reserves, *Or* II. capitalisation and systematic amortisation to profit and loss over useful economic life.
Proposals: ASB Discussion Paper, *Goodwill and Intangible Assets*	*One from:* **Capitalisation based methods** I. Capitalisation and amortisation over a predetermined life not exceeding 20 years. (Limited) annual recoverability assessment. II. Capitalisation with (extensive) annual systematic review procedures to determine amortisation / writedown (which may be zero in some years, but never negative) III. As I. for goodwill with an estimated life of less than 20 years, with II. being used for special cases where goodwill has indeterminate life expected to be more than 20 years. **Levelling down based methods** IV. Immediate write-off against reserves V. Immediate transfer to a separate goodwill write-off reserve. VI. As V. but the balance in the separate reserve is annually assessed for recoverability. If the recoverable amount is less than the reserve balance, the deficit is to be charged to profit and loss. Board members are split between support for III. and V

Figure 5.6 – Goodwill: UK professional requirements and proposals

capitalization and elimination-based alternatives and presently supports III or V. Criteria used by the ASB have been discussed above. The main innovations are the proposals for a separate write-off reserve and for capitalization with annual systematic review.

Separate write-off reserve

This involves setting up a notional zero reserve against which goodwill can be immediately written-off. The resulting (debit) 'reserve' is placed as a deduction from shareholders' funds to obtain 'Capital and Reserves'. To overcome criticism that this is the prohibited 'dangling debit' approach, the DP comments that 'a note [can be added] explaining that the cumulative write-off reserve should strictly be regarded as part of the aggregate profit and loss account balance, which unlike other reserves may be negative as it is no more than a historical record' (para. 7.3.3). The use of such a separate reserve, which is only removed when the subsidiary is disposed of, allows immediately written-off goodwill to be tracked better than if written-off against other reserves.

Scope of annual systematic reviews

Under the three asset-based approaches, the necessity for any write-downs to recoverable amounts must be considered even if predetermined gradual amortization is adopted. The DP also suggests a new approach where the only form of amortization/write-down would be the result of annual systematic reviews. It distinguishes between limited and extensive scope annual reviews. When annual systematic review audits predetermined gradual amortization, the limited scope review is based on reasonable procedures adopted in assessing the recoverable amount of the parent's investment in its own accounts. When used as an 'amortization' approach in its own right, a more costly extensive scope approach using ceiling tests is proposed, discussed below.

Capitalization and extensive annual systematic review as the sole basis for 'amortization'

This new approach would ensure consistency of goodwill treatment with the investment's carrying amount in the parent's own accounts. Both would be compared with a recoverable amount determined by an extensive scope annual systematic review. If necessary the investment is written down, and the effect of this write-down on goodwill is termed 'amortization'. This probably will result in a zero charge in some periods. Amortization previously charged cannot be reversed nor can there be any upward revaluation of goodwill (para. 5.1.2). With these constraints, the DP argues such a procedure satisfies the Companies Act 1985 requirement for systematic amortization of capitalized goodwill over its useful life (Sch 4 s. 21). The DP also argues that if necessary the Act's 'true and fair override' could be invoked 'on the grounds of special circumstances, which . . . must obtain to make the adoption of the "capitalization and annual review" method appropriate and necessary . . . for the accounts to give a true and fair view' (DP paras 5.3.4 – 5).

In extensive scope annual reviews, the recoverable amount of goodwill is effectively the amount of goodwill that would be reported if the subsidiary had been acquired at the current financial statement date. It is determined by subtracting the current net fair value of its identifiable assets and liabilities from the current present value of the parent's investment (interest-bearing debt being excluded since it is dealt with by the discounting procedure). If the recoverable amount is lower than the carrying value of the goodwill, the latter would, under proposed rules below, be written down.

The DP proposal is that two present value estimates of the investment's value must be made:

(1) *a [best estimate] discounted cash flow (DCF) estimate* – using explicit forecasts of cash flows for up to five years, and beyond that a conservative constant growth rate (for UK businesses no higher than the average annual UK GDP growth over the last 40 years, 2.5 per cent) discounted at the weighted average cost of capital reflecting the risk of the relevant part of the business.

(2) *a [conservative] comparative estimate* – the above DCF forecasts are to be adjusted by the ratio of actual to forecast cash flows for the previous five years or since acquisition to curtail persistent management over-exuberance!

If the DCF-estimate recoverable amounts are lower than goodwill carrying values the deficit must be written off to profit and loss immediately. Comparative-estimate deficits are only to be written off after they have been in existence for the third consecutive year. Procedures for keeping track of purchased goodwill where the subsidiary's business has been scattered across other group companies are also discussed.

Separate write-off reserve with annual recoverability assessment

This provides similar information to the capitalization and annual systematic review approach above. Profit and loss charges would be the same, the only difference that the 'goodwill' carrying amount is situated within reserves. This 'sop' to opponents of asset-based approaches seems cosmetic, but positioning could affect gearing-based debt covenant restrictions.

WIDER CONTEXT

If one considers that users react mechanically to changes in accounting numbers, one would believe that the higher profits reported under immediate write-off will over-inflate share prices and affect take-over offer terms.[1] However, corresponding gearing increases would have the opposite effect. One of the DP's arguments (p. 43) that naïve investors may be fooled into believing that immediate write-off implies a loss in value, implies such investors (but not the market as a whole) could react in this way. However, under the efficient markets hypothesis it is likely one would consider the debate as merely cosmetic and of no economic consequence – it is easy to convert gradual amortization-based reported profits to equivalent immediate write-off ones. It also seems not too difficult to convert from immediate write-off to gradual amortization for international comparison as most firms use an arbitrary pre-determined life as the norm.

However, changing the treatment of goodwill or intangibles may indirectly affect cash flows through, for example, profit-based management-performance-related pay, or through costs of breaking gearing or interest-cover-based debt covenant restrictions. If such contracts had been based on GAAP frozen at the time the contract was signed, subsequent changes would not undermine existing contracts. However, many such contracts seem to be based on 'rolling' GAAP in the UK. Changes might also affect the triggering of costly Stock Market requirements. For Class 1 take-over transactions, where the target's book equity is more than 15 per cent of the acquirer's, the acquirer is required to issue a circular to its shareholders, which involves high opportunity costs for top management. It is interesting that from January 1989 the Stock Market allowed the equity figure to include the effects of brands and intangibles only if they were included in the consolidated balance sheet.

Mather and Peasnell (1991) found evidence which supported the debt covenant and the transaction cost effects (Stock Exchange Class 1 restrictions) for capitalizing brands for 13 groups which capitalized brands over the 1986–1989 period, but inconclusive support for a relationship between brand valuations and change in share prices *per se*. Grinyer *et al.* (1991) found evidence from 264 companies over the earlier period 1982–6 that management's tendency to overstate goodwill (which under immediate write-off would adversely affect consolidated equity and gearing) was reduced the higher the post-acquisition gearing of the group, supporting the debt covenant hypothesis. This tendency to overstate was also reduced the larger the target was relative to the acquirer, which they suggested was because of the increased likelihood of media attention.

It is extremely difficult to foresee if the ASB will easily be able to settle on a single approach. There is already a revolt against its proposed non-recognition of intangibles. Further, an IASC draft statement of principles on intangible assets issued in February

1994[2] proposes that 'brands, patents and other intangibles could be shown as separate items on the balance sheet . . . [and that they] should be allowed to be revalued to fair value where there is a clear secondary market in those assets.' Costs of the annual systematic review approach, which the ASB claims is most popular but some have described as academic and infeasible, could provide an indirect pragmatic justification of the internationally acceptable 'capitalization and gradual amortization' approach. The ASB might settle for annual systematic review, allowing gradual amortization with limited annual systematic review as its 'cost-effective' alternative. What seems certain is that the ASB will not be able to please anybody any of the time!

Exercises

5.13 Assess the case that purchased goodwill should not be capitalized in consolidated financial statements.

5.14 Compare and contrast the pros and cons of capitalization and gradual amortization and immediate write-off to reserves, the two alternatives allowed by SSAP 22.

5.15 'Gradual amortization of goodwill is the most satisfactory compromise which can be reached by the ASB.' Discuss.

5.16 How far is 'analogy with similar items' (consistency) a conclusive way of choosing between alternative proposals for the treatment of goodwill?

5.17 Does the choice of which reserve is used for the immediate write-off of goodwill matter? Why?

5.18 Why did the 'brands debate' arise? How effective have the various proposals by standard setting bodies for dealing with accounting for brands been in dealing with the issues involved?

5.19 Assess how far annual systematic review as the sole basis for goodwill accounting is superior to the alternatives allowed by SSAP 22.

5.20 What would be the costs and benefits of the ASB requiring a change from the currently prevalent practice of immediate write-off to reserves to an alternative that required capitalization and some form of gradual write-down through profit and loss, however determined?

Example 5.5 – Discussion Paper proposals on goodwill

The draft consolidated balance sheet of the Largesse Smallnesse Group at 31 March 1995 is as follows. Largesse acquired Smallnesse on 31 March 1992. Goodwill in this balance sheet has not been adjusted since acquisition and is stated at cost:

Consolidated balance sheets at 31 March 1995 – Largesse Smallnesse Group

	£m	£m
Fixed assets		
Goodwill at cost		16
Tangible fixed assets		220
Investment in Minutenesse		20
		256
Net current assets		
Stocks	80	
Other	130	
		210
Creditors over one year		(120)
		346
Capital and reserves		
Share capital		130
Share premium		70
Retained profits		128
		328
Minority interest		18
		346

Required

Show the consolidated balance sheet at 31 March 1995 for the Largesse group under the following assumptions about goodwill. Also assess the amount of any profit and loss charge for goodwill amortization over the year to that date, based on the ASB Discussion Paper's proposals discussed above:

(a) Goodwill is written off immediately against consolidated retained profits.
(b) Goodwill is written off immediately against a separate goodwill write-off reserve.
(c) Goodwill is to be gradually amortized over a period of ten years.
(d) Goodwill is written off using the annual systematic review approach. The recoverable amounts for goodwill assessed by this approach were:

Year	£m
1992	16
1993	14
1994	18
1995	12

Solution

Largesse Group – balance sheet under goodwill assumptions at 31 March 1995

Description	W/off vs retained profits	W/off vs separate reserve	Gradual amortiz-ation	Annual systematic review
Intangible fixed assets	—	—	11.2	12
Tangible fixed assets	220	220	220	220
Investment –Minutenesse	20	20	20	20
Stocks	80	80	80	80
Other current assets	130	130	130	130
Creditors over one year	(120)	(120)	(120)	(120)
Share capital	(130)	(130)	(130)	(130)
Share premium	(70)	(70)	(70)	(70)
Retained profits	(112)	(128)	(123.2)	(124)
Goodwill write-off reserve		16		
Minority interests	(18)	(18)	(18)	(18)

Note
Under gradual amortization, goodwill write-off $= \frac{3}{10} \times 16 = £4.8m$, and there would be no write-down to recoverable amount as the book value £11.2m is less than recoverable amount of £12m.

Consolidated profit and loss charges for goodwill – year ended 31 March 1995

Approach	£m
Immediate write-off vs retained earnings	—
Immediate write-off vs separate reserve	—
Gradual amortization	1.6
Annual systematic review	2

Note
The first three approaches are currently practised by UK companies under SSAP 22, the third being very rare. If the annual systematic review approach proposed by the ASB Discussion Paper were adopted as the *sole* method of amortization, the carrying value of the goodwill would be: 1992 – £16m, 1993 – £14m, 1994 – £14m, 1995 – £12m since the annual systematic review can only be used to write goodwill *down* and not to reverse previous year's charges or to write it up. Therefore the profit and loss charge for the year ended 31 March 1995 would be £14m–£12m = £2m as above.

Exercises

5.21 *Goodwill* – Bigfry acquired Smallfry on 31 May 1995. The consolidated balance sheet for the Bigfry Group is as follows. Goodwill is stated at cost and has not been adjusted since acquisition:

Bigfry Group balance sheet – 30 November 1995

	£m	Bigfry £m
Fixed assets		
Goodwill		12
Land and buildings		140
Plant and equipment		460
Investment in Tinyfry		20
		632
Current assets		
Stocks	65	
Debtors	40	
Cash	7	
	112	
Current liabilities		
Trade creditors	43	
Other creditors	15	
	58	
		54
Creditors over one year		
		(230)
		456
Capital and reserves		
Share capital		60
Share premium		50
Retained profits		300.4
		410.4
Minority interests		45.6
		456.0

Required

Show the consolidated balance sheet at 30 November 1995 for the Bigfry Group under the following assumptions about goodwill. Also assess the amount of any profit and loss charge for goodwill amortization over the year to that date:

(a) Goodwill is written off immediately against consolidated share premium with permission of the court.
(b) Goodwill is written off immediately against a separate goodwill write-off reserve set up for the purpose.
(c) Goodwill is gradually amortized over a period of twenty years (use a half a year for this); the recoverable amount at 30 November 1995 for this part is £12m.
(d) Goodwill is written off using the annual systematic review approach. The recoverable amounts for goodwill assessed by this approach for this part were:

Year	£m
At acquisition	12
1995	11

5.22 *Review problem* – Maximiser plc acquired a 70 per cent stake in Sitting Target plc at 31 May 1993 when the latter's retained profits were £40m. At 31 May 1994 the abbreviated balance sheets of both companies were respectively:

	Maximiser (£m)	Sitting Target (£m)
Net assets		
Investment in Sitting Target	130	—
Other tangible fixed assets	920	80
Other	400	50
	1,450	130
Capital and reserves		
Share capital	200	20
Share premium	400	40
Revaluation reserve	350	10
Retained profits	500	60
	1,450	130

Notes
(i)   The fair value of plant and machinery of Sitting Target at acquisition (included in 'other tangible fixed assets') had been conservatively estimated by the directors at £45m (£40m carrying value in Sitting Target's own records), with a remaining life of 10 years, to be depreciated straight line. The valuers completed their at-acquisition valuation by 30 August 1993 (finally agreed figure £50m), too late to include in the accounts for that year. Maximiser's directors decided to stick their estimate of fair value in all subsequent accounts, as 'the other valuation was too late to change things'. Land with a book value of £20m had been estimated to have a fair value of £25m at 31 May 1993. Sitting Target's stock of £30m was estimated to have a fair value of £40m at acquisition, but Maximiser's directors decided that, as the main product line of Sitting Target was to be discontinued, such stocks had a net realizable value to the Maximiser Group at that date of no more than the carrying value in Sitting Target's books. None of these revalued amounts have been pushed down into the subsidiary's records.

(ii) Maximiser plc had been keen to optimize post-acquisition income. At the date of acquisition, there was some possibility of a reorganization after acquisition (the parent and subsidiary had certain duplicate manufacturing facilities) so the directors required that a provision of £20m be set up to cover generously estimated costs in Sitting Target. In the year to 31 May 1994, expenses of £10m were incurred in closing duplicate facilities located at Sitting Target which the directors wish to be written off against the reorganization provision. No further expenses are foreseen so the unused provision is to be written back to profit and loss in the year ending 31 May 1994. The company accountant had not known how to treat the actual closure expenses of £10m of the companies (above) and so had charged these in the respective company profit and loss accounts, and these charges are included in the above figures.

(iii) Goodwill at acquisition is to be immediately written off against the consolidated share premium account as permission of the court has been obtained, and the directors wish for £30m of the acquisition costs to be reclassified as brands. These are to be permanently retained at original costs in future financial statements as 'we'll spend plenty to maintain the brands in pristine condition'.

Required
(a) Prepare an acquisition cancellation table for the Maximiser Group at 31 May 1994, assuming the wishes of the directors of Maximiser plc were *exactly* followed.
(b) Explain possible motivations the directors of Maximiser may have had for their proposed treatments of goodwill, brands, asset revaluations and provisions.
(c) Discuss how FRS 7's requirements would have affected the accounting in part (a) if it had been in force when the financial statements at 31 May 1994 had been prepared.

SUMMARY

Alignment adjustments are mainly adjustments to reflect the change in scope of the financial statements from an individual company to a group basis. They can be recorded in the acquired entity's records ('push-down') or more usually by consolidation adjustments on the consolidation working papers.

Fair values at acquisition are used to establish **group** costs **as if** the identifiable assets, liabilities and goodwill had been separately purchased. The key controversy in valuing the former is in defining the cut-off boundary between pre- and post-acquisition events. FRS 7 allows the acquirer's accounting policies to be reflected in fair values, but not the effects of the acquirer's intentions or future actions, virtually banning reorganization and other provisions at acquisition.

Goodwill arises because of the desire to disaggregate a transaction to purchase a stake in a subsidiary as a whole into components. Non-purchased goodwill is excluded from financial statements. Purchased goodwill can in principle be dealt with in a number of ways. SSAP 22 prefers immediate write-off against reserves, and tolerates gradual amortization to the profit and loss account, the only treatment allowed in the USA and to be required by IAS 22 from 1995. Annual systematic reviews instead of pre-determined gradual amortization have been proposed, and present professional pronouncements propose limiting severely the reporting of brands and other intangibles in published financial statements. The relationship between parent company and group reserves is unresolved.

NOTES

1. See for example Hodgkinson, R. (1989) Ruling out the unfair advantage, *Accountancy Age*, July, p. 20.
2. Anon (1994) ASB hit by intangibles alternative, *Accountancy Age*, 10 February, p. 3.

FURTHER READING

Accounting for Fair Values at Acquisition
FRS 7 (1994) *Fair Values at Acquisition* Accounting Standards Board.
Smith, T. (1992) *Accounting For Growth*, Chapter 4, Century Business.
Thomas, P. B. and Hagler J. L. (1988) Push-down accounting: a descriptive assessment, *Accounting Horizons*, September pp. 26–31.

Accounting for Goodwill and other Intangibles
ASC (1984) SSAP 22 – *Accounting for Goodwill*.
Discussion Paper (1993) *Goodwill and Intangible Fixed Assets*.
Arnold, J., Egginton, D., Kirkham, L., Macve, R. and Peasnell, K. (1992) *Goodwill and Other Intangibles: Theoretical Considerations and Policy Issues*, Institute of Chartered Accountants in England and Wales.
Grinyer J.R., Russell A. and Walker M. (1990) The Rationale for Accounting for Goodwill, *British Accounting Review*, September, pp. 223–235.
Nobes, C. (1992) A political history of goodwill in the UK: an illustration of cyclical standard setting, *Abacus*, Vol. 28, no. 2, pp. 142–161.
Power, M. (1992) The politics of brand accounting in the United Kingdom, *The European Accounting Review*, Vol 1., no. 1, pp. 39–68.

6

INTRA-GROUP TRANSACTIONS AND DISTRIBUTIONS: ALIGNMENT ADJUSTMENTS (2)

This chapter focuses on alignment adjustments relating to *post*-acquisition events: intra-group balances, accounting for unrealized profits on intra-group transactions, and the treatment of intra-group dividends, as outlined in Figure 5.1. After a comprehensive example integrating all the different types of adjustments, the usefulness of different consolidation concepts in providing a coherent framework for alignment adjustments is evaluated.

INTRA-GROUP BALANCES

The Companies Act 1985 requires that if material, 'debts and claims between undertakings included in the consolidation, and income and expenditure relating to transactions between such undertakings, shall be eliminated in preparing the group accounts' (Sch 4A, para. 6(1)). When group companies trade, debit (debtor) balances in one set of records should equal credit (creditor) balances in the other. On consolidation, these balances – internal to the group hence 'intra-group' – should cancel. In practice, especially where the number of transactions is large, perfect agreement is rare and a major task in large audits is reconciliation of such intercompany balances prior to consolidation. Much faxing and headscratching is needed before agreement.

Lack of agreement is usually because of

(1) *Mistakes* in recording by either company.
(2) *Timing differences* caused by goods or cash in transit between companies at the period end, recorded by the originating company but not yet by the receiving

Mistakes are corrected in *individual* company financial statements. Timing differences are usually corrected at head office by *consolidation adjustments* so that balances will cancel. The convention here is that items in transit are usually treated as if they are at the *originating* company, *as if* the intra-group transaction had not taken place prior to the year end. This usually makes consolidation adjustments simpler than if the goods are treated as if at the receiving company, though the latter assumption is logically as valid. Dividends declared by the subsidiary but not yet recorded by the parent company can be handled in a similar way.

Different year ends (optional)
If a subsidiary's year end is different from the parent's, changes in the intervening period which materially affect the view given by the consolidated financial statements must be included through consolidation adjustments. Remaining immaterial differences in inter-company balances would be disclosed under appropriate balance sheet or profit and loss headings. FRS 2 (paras 42 and 43) only tolerates different year ends if it is not practicable either to have the same year end, or for the subsidiary to produce interim accounts to the parent's year end for consolidation purposes.

Example 6.1 – Intra-group balances

Acid plc and Alkali plc, two companies in the Corrosive Chemicals Group, trade regularly with each other. At the group year end of 30 November 1995, Alkali is a £20m debtor in Acid's records. In Alkali's records, Acid is a £4m creditor. The group auditors, Delight, Hassle and Soles, contacting both companies find the following reconciling items:

	£m
Stock dispatched by Acid on 28 November not received by Alkali until 2 December (cost £8m)	10
Cash sent by Alkali on 29 November, not received by Acid until 1 December	8
Goods received by Alkali on 15 November still in stock, recorded in error at £5m instead of £3m	5

Required

Correct both balances for any individual company adjustments, and by using consolidation adjustments calculate the aligned consolidated balances.

Solution

The first two reconciling items are *timing differences*. They are treated correctly from the point of view of the individual companies, but are out of alignment for group purposes – the goods and cash are shown as being at neither company at the year end (which is true), but they do belong to the group! They are usually dealt with by *consolidation adjustments* and the goods or cash are treated *as if* at the originating company. The third is an error by Alkali and so will be corrected at the *individual company* level. The reconciliation below can be more easily derived if it is noted that all debit balances and adjustments are positive figures and all credit balances and adjustments are negative figures.

Alkali plc – debtor in Acid plc's records	£m
Unadjusted company balance	20
Goods in transit (sales by Acid)	(10)[1]
Aligned consolidation debtor	10

Acid plc – creditor in Alkali plc's records	£m
Unadjusted company balance	(4)
Purchases recording error	2[2]
Corrected company balance	(2)
Cash in transit	(8)[3]
Aligned consolidation creditor	(10)

Notes

1. **Consolidation adjustment**

	DR		CR
Acid stocks	8	Acid debtors	10
Acid P & L	2		

Reversing sale back to originating company.

2. **Mistake – individual company adjustment**

	DR		CR
Alkali creditors	2	Alkali stocks	2

Alkali's stocks are reduced.

3 **Consolidation adjustment**

	DR		CR
Alkali cash	8	Alkali creditors	8

Cash reversed to originating company.

Exercise

6.1 What is the difference between an individual company adjustment and a consolidation adjustment in aligning intra-group balances?

6.2 Yeltsin plc and Clinton plc are both part of the Worldwide Group. At the group's 31 December year end Yeltsin plc is shown as a £14m creditor in the draft accounts of Clinton plc. In Yeltsin plc's draft accounts, Clinton plc is shown as a £65m debtor. As group accountant, you find the following reasons for the differences:

	£m
On 30 December Clinton returned stock (cost to Yeltsin of £3m) not received by Yeltsin plc until the new year.	5
Cash sent by Clinton plc on 29 December not received by Yeltsin plc until 2 January	16
Goods received by Clinton on 15 December incorrectly recorded at £5m	15
Goods dispatched by Yeltsin plc on 28 December (cost of £17m) not received by Clinton plc until 4 January	20

Required

(a) Assess which of the above correspond to individual company adjustments and which to consolidation adjustments.
(b) Correct the individual balances and calculate the aligned consolidated intra-group balances.

UNREALIZED PROFITS ON INTRA-GROUP TRANSACTIONS

Adjustments are necessary here because of a change in the scope of the accounts from an individual company to a group basis. Profits realized by the company, may not yet be realized by the group, and so are eliminated (*deferred*) until realization by the *group* has been effected. Such balances are adjusted to group cost. The Companies Act 1985 (Sch 4A para. 6(2)) states that 'Where profits and losses resulting from transactions between undertakings included in the consolidation are included in the book value of assets, they shall be eliminated in preparing the group accounts.'

Operating transactions

Suppose one group company sells raw material goods to another and the second processes and resells finished goods outside the group. Provided both transactions take place in the same period, no adjustment is necessary as profits are realized by both the originating company and by the group. However, if the intra-group transaction is completed, but not the second transaction, the goods will still be part of the stocks of the second company, and will include the originating company's profit margin.

Group profit should be realized only when the goods leave the *group*. A consolidation adjustment is needed to eliminate *unrealized group* profits on such operating transfers not yet resold across group boundaries – restating such goods at *group* cost. This *defers* the recognition of the originating company's profits for consolidated financial statement purposes from the period the goods left the originating company to the period when the goods leave the group. Each year's group profits therefore will be increased by the effects of previous periods' intra-group profits on goods transferred across group boundaries in this period (deferred from previous periods, realized by the group this period), and decreased by this period's intra-group profits on goods which will be sold across group boundaries in future periods.

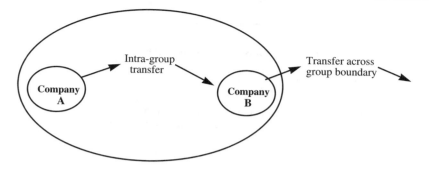

Figure 6.1 – Intra-group transfers

Example 6.2 – Intra-group stocks and financial statements

Assume that Thatcher plc acquired a 100% interest in Cabinet plc, its sole subsidiary, on 1 July 1991. In the year to 30 June 1992, Cabinet plc started selling raw materials to Thatcher plc for incorporation in its products, and adjustments were made at the end of each year to eliminate (unrealized) profits on intra-group stocks held by Thatcher plc at the year end. Assume also that intra-group stocks held at any year end are always sold in the following year. Other alignment adjustments are to be ignored.

Figure 6.2 illustrates the effects of the stock profit *deferrals* for each year subsequent to acquisition, and the adjustment necessary to the aggregate profits of the group for each year. Each 'slice' (segregated by the dotted horizontal lines) represents consolidated retained earnings for a particular year.

Profits on Cabinet's 1993 intra-group sales where the goods are still held by Thatcher at 30 June 1993 are realized by the group in the year to 30 June 1994 when the goods resold across group boundaries, and so on. Aggregate retained earnings for year ended 30 June 1994 would be increased by the stock profit deferral from 1993 and decreased by the stock profit deferral for 1994. *Balance sheet* consolidated retained earnings comprises the total area in the diagram, the *total* of all the separate slices. If the slices are added together, the stock profits for 1992 to 1994 *cancel* as they are excluded one year and included the following. The only stock profit adjustment remaining in *balance sheet* consolidated retained profits is the one for the current year (to 30 June 1995), so:

Balance sheet consolidated retained profits at 30 June 1995

= Parent only profit prior to 1991 + aggregate profits parent and subsidiary 1992 to 1995 – stock profit 95

> **Summary**
>
> *Consolidated profit and loss* is adjusted for profits in *opening* and *closing* intra-group stocks.
>
> *Consolidated balance sheet* is adjusted only for profits in closing intra-group stocks.

The consolidated balance sheet consolidation adjustment is

DR	**CR**
Consolidated retained profit	Consolidated stocks

with the amount of (unrealized) profits on intra-group closing stocks still held.

Example 6.3 – Intra-group stock calculations

Ballcock plc has a 100% stake in Looseat plc. Looseat sells washers to Ballcock (at a mark up of $33\frac{1}{3}\%$) which are incorporated into their high quality toilet seats. During the year ended 31 March 1995, total sales of washers by Looseat to Ballcock were £100m. Stocks of such washers held by Ballcock at the start of the year were £10m, and at 31 March 1995, £12m.

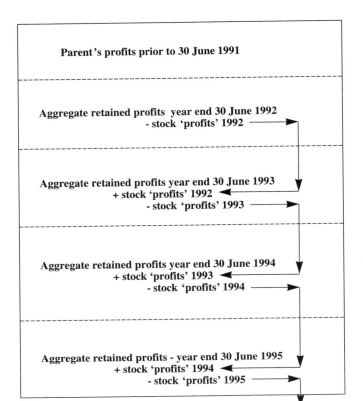

Figure 6.2 – Effects of stock profits deferral on consolidated retained profits

Required
Calculate the amount of intra-group stock profits in the opening and closing intra-group stocks and explain how they would be dealt with in both the consolidated profit and loss account and consolidated balance sheet.

Solution
Cost to Ballcock is Looseat's selling price, which is 133 1/3% of original cost:

$$\text{Opening stock profit} \quad = \quad \frac{33\ 1/3 \ \times \ 10}{133\ 1/3} \quad = \quad £2.5\text{m}$$

$$\text{Closing stock profit} \quad = \quad \frac{33\ 1/3 \ \times \ 12}{133\ 1/3} \quad = \quad £3\text{m}$$

So *group* cost of opening stock is £7.5m, and of closing stock £9m.

Consolidated profit and loss
The net effect of profit deferral on intra-group transfers will be a debit of £0.5m (debit of £3m closing less a credit of £2.5m opening).

Consolidated balance sheet
A credit (decrease) of £3m in consolidated stocks, and a debit (decrease) of £3m in consolidated retained profits.

Exercises

6.3 Why do profits on intra-group stocks held at the group reporting date need to be eliminated?

6.4 When should profit on intra-group sales be recognized in consolidated financial statements?

6.5 Ryker plc, a 100% owned subsidiary of Luc-Picard plc, sold £50m of goods to its parent during the year at a mark-up on cost of 20%. At the start of the year, Luc-Picard plc held £12m of such goods in stock and at the group year end £24m.

Required

Calculate the amount of intra-group stock profits in the opening and closing intra-group stocks and explain how they would be dealt with in both the consolidated profit and loss account and consolidated balance sheet.

Intra-group profits and minority interests

In the 100 per cent owned subsidiary case, the intra-group stock adjustment reduces stocks and consolidated retained profits. For subsidiaries less than wholly owned a proportion of any intra-group stocks relates to sales by or to the minority interests in the group. The key question is whether for group profit realization/elimination purposes this minority interest should be regarded as inside or outside the group. If they are regarded as insiders, adjustments for unrealized intra-group profits affects their stake in the transaction ('complete' adjustment); if outsiders, the minority stake in intra-group transactions is 'realized' and only the parent stake should be adjusted ('proportional' adjustment). The former when used in conventional consolidation is termed the 'parent extension' approach, and the latter the 'pure parent' approach.

In the UK, minority interests are for this purpose treated as insiders (*parent extension* approach). Hence say all the intra-group stocks at the end of the period are deemed to relate to sales within the group. *Complete* stock profits on these stocks should be eliminated, and the question arises of how to apportion such elimination between controlling and minority interests. Under the other alternative (*pure parent*), the proportion of intra-group stocks resulting from sales to or by minority interests would be regarded as realized; only the proportion of the unrealized profits relating to controlling interests would be eliminated. The amended Companies Act 1985 (Sch 4A, para. 6(2)) allows either treatment.

However, *FRS 2* narrows the options by requiring *complete elimination* (minority as insiders) 'set against the interests held by the group and the minority interests in respective proportion to their holdings in the undertaking whose financial statements recorded the eliminated profits and losses' (para. 39).

Thus,, profits on intra-group stocks sold by a subsidiary to the parent (*upstream* sales) would be eliminated *pro-rata* between controlling interests and minority interests in that subsidiary, and profits on intra-group stocks sold by the parent to a subsidiary (*downstream* sales) would be eliminated *all* against consolidated retained profits, reflecting that there is no minority stake in the parent.

Example 6.4 – Intra-group stocks and minority interests

Consider the consolidated balance sheet effects in the example of Ballcock plc and Looseat plc above, except that now, Ballcock plc holds a 75% stake in Looseat plc. Closing intra-group stocks were £12m at a mark-up on cost of 33$\frac{1}{3}$%, where firstly (a) the intra-group sales were from Looseat to Ballcock, then secondly (b) the intra-group sales were from Ballcock to Looseat.

Solution

FRS 2 requires full elimination so, as in the previous example, the closing stock profit to be eliminated is £3m (since minority interests are regarded as *inside* the group for this purpose), according to the ownership of the *originating* company (since this is the one that has recorded the profit on the intercompany sale).

(a) *Upstream sale* – where the sale is from Looseat to Ballcock, the profit on sale will have been recorded in Ballcock's post-acquisition retained earnings which will have been split between consolidated retained profits (75%) and minority interests (25%) in the cancellation table. Thus the elimination will be in these proportions.

b) *Downstream sale* – where the sale is from Ballcock to Looseat, the profits will have been part of the parent's retained profits and so will all be taken to consolidated profits, and hence must be eliminated 100% against consolidated profits.

Elimination entries are shown in the following cancellation table extract (debits are positive, credits are negative):

Description	Consolidated retained profits (75%)	Goodwill (pre-acquisition)	Minority interests	Stock
If upstream	2.25		0.75	(3)
If downstream	3.0			(3)

Comparison with US and international standards

Prior to the amendment to the Companies Act 1985 in 1989, the most common UK practice was for the complete elimination of stock profits, but 100 per cent against consolidated retained profits – the majority being deemed to bear the whole effect of intra-group transfers regardless of the direction of the transfer. This is no longer allowed by FRS 2. In the USA, either complete elimination of 100 per cent against only consolidated retained profits *or* a complete elimination apportioned between controlling and minority interests is practised, but is not necessarily linked to the direction of the transfer. IAS 27, *Consolidated Financial Statements and Accounting for Investments in Subsidiaries* (1985) requires full elimination of unrealized stock profits (para. 30), but does not specify how such elimination should be apportioned between controlling and minority interests. The relationship between alignment adjustments and consolidation concepts is explored later.

Exercise

6.6 Under what circumstances are minority interests affected by the elimination of unrealized intra-group stock profits?

6.7 Why should the direction of intra-group sales determine how unrealized intra-group stock profits is apportioned between controlling and minority interests?

6.8 Ryker plc, a 60% owned subsidiary of Luc-Picard plc, sold £50m of goods to its parent during the year at a mark-up on cost of 20%. At the end of the year, Luc-Picard plc held £24m of such goods in stock.

Required

Calculate the consolidated *balance sheet* intra-group profit elimination entries and show the cancellation table effects where

(a) the intra-group sales were from Ryker to Luc-Picard, and if

(b) the intra-group sales had been from Luc-Picard to Ryker.

Capital transactions

Group companies may also trade in items which become say depreciable fixed assets to the receiving company. Profits on the transfer of such fixed assets are deferred and realized as the assets are *depreciated*, in product or period costs. This can be distinguished from the fair value exercise at acquisition in that the initiating transaction and the reversals through *lower* depreciation are both post-acquisition. Whereas fair values at acquisition are often an uplift to cost, removal of intra-group profits is a *downward* shift, both to book values and depreciation.

Example 6.5 – Intra-group fixed asset transactions

Vanguard manufactures vans, and in the year ended 31 December 1993 sold one to Grocer, its 75% subsidiary, for £20,000 at a mark up on cost of 25%. Grocer estimated the van had a five-year life with no scrap value, straight-line depreciation to be used. Fixed assets are not depreciated in the year of addition.

Required

Show the consolidation adjustment for the elimination of intra-group profits on the sale of the fixed asset, and how the deferred profit is 'realized' in subsequent consolidated financial statements.

Solution

The amount of Vanguard's profit incorporated in the cost to Grocer is

$$\frac{25}{125} \times £20,000 = £4,000$$

so the cost to the group of the van is £16,000 and the annual depreciation reduction is

$$\frac{4,000}{5} = £800 \text{ p.a.}$$

Similar principles apply as to unrealized intra-group stock profits on apportionment between parent and minority interests. This is a downstream sale, so the profit is eliminated 100% against consolidated retained profits (based on ownership proportions of the selling company). The following extract from the cancellation table shows the deferral of intra-group profits on the sale of the van, and its subsequent realization (decreasing subsequent depreciation charges and increasing subsequent consolidated profits) as the van is depreciated.

Description	Consolidated retained profits	Goodwill	Minority interests	Fixed assets
Fixed asset profit elimination				
– y/e Dec 1993	4,000			(4,000)
Reduced depreciation – y/e Dec 1994	(800)			800
Reduced depreciation – y/e Dec 1995	(800)			800
Reduced depreciation – y/e Dec 1996	(800)			800
Reduced depreciation – y/e Dec 1997	(800)			800
Reduced depreciation – y/e Dec 1998	(800)			800
Net effect over asset life	—	—	—	—

The first entry reverses the intra-group profits recognized by Vanguard in its own records and ensures that the van, which is still held by the group, appears at *group* cost. The other entries, made each year for five years as consolidation adjustments reduces depreciation on the van from cost to Vanguard (i.e. £20,000/5 = £4,000 per year) to cost to the group (i.e. £16,000/5 = £3,200 per year).

Exercises

6.9 Why are intra-group profits on the sale of fixed assets eliminated? How are such eliminated profits treated in subsequent accounting periods?

6.10 Warped plc purchased a weaving machine for £18,000 (whose cost of manufacture was £14,000) from its 80% owned subsidiary Weft plc, which Weft used to manufacture tablecloths. This machine has a life of 10 years with no scrap value, and is to be depreciated on a straight-line basis. A full year's depreciation is to be provided in the year of addition.

Required

Calculate and explain any adjustments necessitated in the consolidated financial statements by the above transaction, and show extracts from the consolidation cancellation table over the life of the asset.

6.11 Thesis plc sells specialized machinery to its 90% owned subsidiary Antithesis plc for £300,000 on 1 February 1992 (cost of manufacture to Thesis £210,000). The machinery has an expected life of six years with a zero scrap value and is to be depreciated on the straight-line basis. On 30 January 1995 the machine is sold by Antithesis plc for £100,000. The Thesis Group's year end is 31 January.

Required
(a) Calculate the cost of the fixed asset, annual depreciation charge and gain or loss on sale as would be reported in Antithesis plc's own financial statements;
(b) perform similar calculations, but this time for the consolidated accounts;
(c) calculate consolidation adjustments for the years 31 January 1993 to 31 January 1995 to effect the adjustment from (a) to (b), showing how adjustments are split between controlling and minority interests.

INTRA-GROUP DIVIDENDS

Generally the treatment of dividends is as for other intra-group balances. Journal entries for the declaration of a dividend of say £5m by a 100 per cent owned subsidiary to its parent would be

	DR		CR
Subsidiary			
Profit and loss	5	Dividends payable	5
Parent			
Dividends receivable	5	Profit and loss	5

Income effects would net to zero on consolidation and dividends payable by the subsidiary would cancel dividends receivable by the parent. When paid, the reduction in cash by the subsidiary would exactly equal cash received by the parent. The net consolidation effect of what is merely a transfer of resources within the group is thus nil. If the £5m dividend declared is from say an 80 per cent owned subsidiary, individual company journal entries would be

	DR		CR
Subsidiary			
Profit and loss	5	Dividends payable	5
Parent			
Dividends receivable (80%)	4	Profit and loss (80%)	4

In consolidated terms, on cancellation of intra-group balances, the net effect relates to *minority* dividends of £1m, credited to minority dividends payable in the current assets section in the consolidated balance sheet.

Dividends from pre-acquisition profits

Either at acquisition or at a later date, it is feasible that a subsidiary could distribute dividends in excess of its post-acquisition retained profits or for such dividends to be otherwise connected to pre-acquisition profits. As far as *consolidated* accounts are concerned, any declaration out of subsidiary profits earned prior to acquisition is in effect a repayment of capital and must be treated consistently by both companies. However, current Companies Act 1985 regulations relating to the recognition of investment income by *individual* companies ignore the group position. Therefore the parent may in many circumstances legitimately recognize as income in its *own* accounts dividends which must be treated as effective repayments of capital in the consolidated accounts. A *consolidation adjustment* is required to adjust from an individual company basis to a group basis.

Assume again a £5m dividend declared by a 100 per cent owned subsidiary, but from its pre-acquisition profits, and that the dividend can legitimately be recognized as income by the parent in its individual company accounts. The company journal entries would be as above. The following extracts from the consolidation cancellation table show the consolidated financial statement effects of the dividend recording of the subsidiary – its debit to profit and loss is a reduction in pre-acquisition profits, and by the parent – its credit to its own profit and loss account is included in consolidated retained profits as all the parent's own profits are so included.

Consolidated effect if parent treats pre-acquisition dividend as its income

Description	Consolidated retained profits	Goodwill (pre-acq) equity)	Dividends receivable	Dividends (payable)
Subsidiary's treatment		5		(5)
Parent's treatment	(5)	—	5	—
Net effect of individual company entries	(5)	5	5	(5)
Intra-group bal cancellation	—	—	(5)	5
Consolidation effect if no dividend adjustment	(5)	5		
Pre-acq dividend alignment adjustment	5	(5)		
Consolidation effects after adjustment	—	—	—	—

If there is no pre-acquisition dividend consolidation adjustment, what is in reality just a cash transfer between the group companies *increases* consolidated goodwill (by decreasing the pre-acquisition equity) by £5m, and *increases* consolidated retained profits. Imagine the income generating possibilities of such mere cash transfers! The transfer should have no consolidated effect and so in *all* subsequent balance sheets a consolidation adjustment is required, treating the dividend for consolidation alignment purposes *only*, as if a repayment of original consideration given and hence a reduction in goodwill/investment. The consolidation adjustment would be

	DR		CR
Consolidated retained profits	5	Consolidated goodwill	5

Reducing consolidated profits and goodwill to their values before the transfer

Occasionally no consolidation adjustment is necessary. In principle, with all dividends the parent has to decide whether they can be regarded as income or whether, consequent on the dividend, any write-down to the investment is necessary because of a permanent diminution in its value below its carrying amount – the standard valuation basis for fixed assets. A starting point for such an assessment would be a comparison between the *ex-dividend* value of the investment and its carrying amount. Such an *individual company* write-down is usually unlikely because dividend payments are not normally that large, and any decline may be viewed as temporary as investment values usually recover over time. Indeed, Davis, Paterson and Wilson (1992, p. 217) consider such legal provisions have been used to support a view which allows an acquiring company to 'distribute immediately all the pre-acquisition profits shown in the subsidiary's balance sheet provided that it could foresee that the subsidiary would earn an equivalent amount of profits in the future', though they question whether such a view is good accounting.

However, to continue the discussion – to the extent that the parent has written down the investment consequent on the receipt of a dividend from 'pre-acquisition' profits – no further consolidation adjustment is necessary as the treatment adopted is consistent with the *consolidated* financial statement treatment. Adjustment would only be necessary to the extent that such dividend income exceeds the write-down, the net amount treated as income by the parent. Arcane!

If a £5m dividend from pre-acquisition profits was made by an 80 per cent subsidiary, the amount treated as income by the parent would be 80% × £5m = £4m and, since only 80 per cent of the pre-acquisition equity is used to determine consolidated goodwill, this is the amount which needs to be subject to consolidation adjustment, viz.

	DR		**CR**
Consolidated retained profits	4	Consolidated goodwill	4

Reducing consolidated profits and goodwill to their values before the transfer

Summary

If a subsidiary declares dividends out of *pre-acquisition* profits, a consolidation adjustment is necessary only to the extent the parent treats such a dividend as its *income*. The adjustment is

	DR		**CR**
Consolidated retained profits		Consolidated goodwill	

Reducing consolidated profits and goodwill to their values before the transfer

---

Example 6.6 – Dividends from pre-acquisition profits

The following are extracts from the company balance sheets of Striver plc and Settled plc at 31 December 1995 in £m. Striver owns a 100% stake in Settled plc. Settled's retained profits at acquisition were £25m. Settled's balance sheet retained profits figure of £60m is before adjusting for its dividends declared for the year.

	Striver	*Settled*
Investment in Settled	100	
Share capital	250	20
Share premium	150	30
Retained profits	75	60

Required
(a) Assuming Striver declares a dividend of £10m for the year ended 31 December 1995, prepare a consolidation cancellation table prior to the dividend declaration. Then in the table show the consolidated effects of the dividend transaction.
(b) Assuming Striver declares a dividend of £45m for the year ended 31 December 1995 (i.e. £10m from pre-acquisition profits) calculate the total amount of income that can be legitimately recognized in Striver's individual company accounts in respect of the dividend, assuming no permanent diminution in the value of the investment as a result of the dividend. Show in the consolidated cancellation table the consolidated effects of the dividend transaction, and any consolidation adjustments necessary.

Solution
(a) Consolidated effect of normal intra-group dividend
Note – after intra-group balances are cancelled, consolidated balances are unchanged as a result of the dividend:

Description	Invest-ment	Share capital & premium	Consol retained profits	Goodwill (pre-acq equity)	Dividends receivable	Dividends (payable)
Striver's balances	100	(400)	(75)			
Settled's balances:						
Pre-acquisition			(35)			
Post-acquisition				(75)		
Investment						
cancellation	(100)			100		
Consolidated						
pre-dividend	—	(400)	(110)	25		
Dividend treatment:						
Settled			10			(10)
Striver			(10)		10	
Net effect	—	(400)	(110)	25	10	(10)
Intra-group bal						
cancellation					(10)	10
Consolidated						
post-dividend	—	(400)	(110)	25	—	—

(b) Effects of dividend from pre-acquisition profit
The parent can include all £45m in its own income as there is no write-down of the investment necessary. In consolidated terms the amount of the pre-acquisition dividend is £10m, since retained post-acquisition profits are £35m. This is a reduction in pre-acquisition equity in the following table. The unadjusted effect of the dividend is to increase consolidated retained profits and consolidated goodwill by £10m from the pre-dividend position.

Debiting consolidated retained profits and crediting goodwill by £10m, the amount of the pre-acquisition dividend treated as income by the parent, restores consolidated balances to their pre-dividend position. The cash transfer has no effect on consolidated income.

Consolidated effect if parent treats pre-acquisition dividend as income

Description	Invest- ment	Share capital & premium	Consol retained profits	Goodwill (pre-acq equity)	Dividends receivable	Dividends (payable)
Consolidated balances pre-dividend (as above)	—	(400)	(110)	25		
Dividend treatment:						
Settled			35	10		(45)
Striver			(45)		45	
Net effect	—	(400)	(120)	35	45	(45)
Intra-group bal cancellation					(45)	45
Consolidation effect without pre-acq dividend — adjustment	—	(400)	(120)	35	—	–
Pre-acq dividend alignment adjustment			10	(10)		
Consolidation effects after adjustments	—	(400)	(110)	25	—	—

Exercises

6.12 When a parent company receives a dividend from its subsidiary, what criterion should it use in deciding whether to treat all such dividend as income, or whether any other adjustments are necessary in its individual company financial statements?

6.13 If a subsidiary declares and pays a dividend out of pre-acquisition profits and this is treated as income by its parent, will this increase or decrease (a) pre-acquisition equity and (b) consolidated goodwill, if no further adjustment is made?

6.14 Consider the following balance sheets of Demarkation plc and Openplan plc on 31 March 1995 in £m prior to the declaration of a dividend by Openplan plc at that date. Demarkation acquired a 100 per cent interest at 31 March 1993 when the retained earnings of Openplan plc were £100m. Openplan's retained profits figure below is before adjusting for dividends declared for the year.

	Demarkation	Openplan
Assets less liabilities	400	175
Investment in Openplan plc	200	—
Share capital	(100)	(20)
Share premium	(150)	(30)
Retained earnings	(350)	(125)

Required

(a) Assuming Openplan declares a dividend of £15m for the year ended 31 March 1995, prepare a consolidation cancellation table prior to the dividend declaration. Then show the consolidated effects of the dividend transaction.

(b) Assuming Openplan declares a dividend of £38m for the year ended 31 March 1995 (i.e. £13m from pre-acquisition profits), calculate the total amount of income that can be recognized in the parent's accounts relating to the dividend, assuming no write-down of the investment is necessary as a result. Show in the consolidated cancellation table the consolidated effects of the dividend transaction, and any consolidation adjustments necessary.

ILLUSTRATION OF ALIGNMENT PROBLEMS

The following comprehensive example draws together the technical discussions in this chapter and the previous one and illustrates how various types of alignment problems are dealt with under conventional consolidation as required by FRS 2, *Accounting for Subsidiary Undertakings*.

Example 6.7 – Review of alignment adjustments

The balance sheets of Kelly plc and Sipowicz plc at 31 March 1995 are as follows:

Kelly plc and Sipowicz plc individual company balance sheets at 31 March 1995 (£m)

	Kelly £m	Kelly £m	Sipowicz £m	Sipowicz £m
Tangible fixed assets				
– cost	400		153	
– accumulated depreciation	(200)		(50)	
		200		103
Investment in Sipowicz		162		—
Loan to Sipowicz		16		
Current assets				
Stock	190		42	
Dividends receivable	8		—	
Debtors	110		40	
Cash	70		25	
	378		107	
Creditors within one year				
Creditors	78		35	
Dividends payable	32		10	
	110		45	
		268		62
Creditors over one year				
Loan from Kelly		—		(10)
		646		155
Capital and reserves				
Ordinary shares (£1)		180		80
Share premium		104		15
Revaluation reserves		70		25
Retained profits		292		35
		646		155

Other information

1. Kelly plc purchased an 80% interest in Sipowicz plc on 31 March 1993 when the latter's retained earnings were £25m (after the dividend in note 2).
2. In its financial statements at 31 March 1993, Sipowicz had declared a final dividend of £5m which was paid on 30 April 1993. Kelly plc had decided it was entitled to include its share of this dividend in investment income for the year ended 31 March 1993.
3. Sipowicz plc had made a loan repayment to Kelly plc which had not been received by March 31.
4. At acquisition the fixed assets and stocks of Sipowicz plc were assessed to have a fair value of £115m and £30m respectively (costs respectively £100m and £20m). The stocks were sold in the following year, but the fixed assets are still held and are to be depreciated over 10 years straight-line from the date of acquisition.

Details	Investment	Share cap	Share prem	Reval-uation reserves	Consol reserves	Good-will	Mino-rity interests	Intra-group Loans	group Dividends	Fixed assets	Stocks	Debtors	Cash	Cred-itors
Kelly balances	162	(180)	(104)	(70)	(292)			16	(32) pble 8 rble	200	190	110	70	(78)
Sipowicz - at acq equity						(116)	(29)							
Sipowicz post-acq equity					(8)		(2)							
Sipowicz other balances								(10)	(10)	103	42	40	25	(35)
Consolidation adjustments														
Pre-acq dividend					4	(4)								
Cash in transit								(6)					6	
Stock at acquisition					8	(8)								
Fixed asset revaluation						(12)	(3)			15				
Extra depreciation					2.4		0.6			(3)				
Intra-group stock profits					1.6		0.4				(2)			
Intra-group balances												(5)		5
Cancellation of investment	(162)					162		-	-					
Subtotal	-	(180)	(104)	(70)	(284)	22	(33)	-	Parent (32) Mino (2)	315	230	145	101	(108)
Goodwill amortized					8.8	(8.8)								
Consolidated amounts	-	(180)	(104)	(70)	(275.2)	13.2	(33)	-	Parent (32) Mino (2)	315	230	145	101	(108)

Figure 6.3 – Consolidated balance sheet cancellation table for New York Group

5. Since acquisition, Sipowicz plc had regularly sold items for resale to Kelly plc at a mark up on cost of 20%. At 31 March, Kelly's stocks of such items totaled £12m. Kelly is shown as a debtor of £5m in Sipowicz's records and a corresponding amount is shown in Kelly's records.
6. Sipowicz plc's revaluation reserve had existed at acquisition.
7. Consolidated goodwill is to be amortized over 5 years straight line.

Required

(a) Prepare a consolidated balance sheet for the New York Group at 31 March 1995 using an extended cancellation table.
(b) Calculate the components comprising minority interests in the consolidated balance sheet in part (a).
(c) Explain how the calculations in part (a) would be affected if intra-group sales of stocks were instead from Kelly plc to Sipowicz plc.

Solution

(a) The extended cancellation table

Figure 6.3 shows the balance sheet cancellation table with alignment adjustments. As in the previous chapter the left section corresponds roughly to the cancellation table in Chapter 4 dealing with consolidated equity; the right section to other balances to be aligned (adjusted) before aggregation. Balances that do not add immediately to the corresponding consolidated balance appear in the table.

Kelly's balances are recorded first, then Sipowicz's and finally consolidation adjustments. It is helpful to leave space between rows and for an extra column for any overlooked adjustments. Sipowicz's equity is split pre- and post-acquisition, and then its other balances are entered. Consider how 'Other Information' is used to determine alignment adjustments. Be careful, adjustments cannot always be made in the order given. Here adjustment 2 (pre-acquisition dividend) revises equity at acquisition before determining goodwill (adjustment 1).

Treatment of alignment adjustments
1. Amount of dividend out of pre-acquisition profits of £4m (80% × £5m) recorded as income by Kelly and therefore requires a consolidation adjustment. In periods subsequent to payment the only adjustment required is to DR Consolidated retained profits and CR Consolidated goodwill with the parent's share (see page 156).
2. Only the revaluation reserve of the parent is shown in consolidated reserves as both the subsidiary's revaluation reserves and the fair value adjustments at acquisition are used to determine goodwill.
3. Cash in transit is reversed to the originating company.
4. See Chapter 5 page 109 for the treatment of fair values of stocks at acquisition. The subsidiary's fixed assets are completely restated to fair values at acquisition (parent extension per FRS 2); minority interests thus include a revaluation reserve (20% – see later). On the fair value adjustment of £15m, two year's extra depreciation is

$$£15m \times \frac{1}{10} \times 2 = £3m, \text{ split between controlling interests and minority.}$$

5. Under parent extension approach, intra-group stock profits are *completely* eliminated per the ownership proportions of the *originating* company, here Sipowicz plc.

$$£12m \times \frac{20}{120} = £2m, \text{ split between controlling interests and minority.}$$

The intercompany *trading* balances are adjusted in debtors and creditors respectively.
6. The amortization of goodwill cannot be correctly calculated until all of the consolidation adjustments at acquisition have been entered.
Calculated as £22m × $\frac{1}{5}$ × 2 = £8.8m, the group choosing the gradual amortization option (SSAP 22).
7. Consolidated dividends payable includes the parent's and the minority's share in the subsidiary. The controlling interest share is cancelled as an intra-group balance.

With practice, if speed is required, adjustments to consolidated balances can be made in memorandum form on the face of the balance sheets in the question and only the left hand section of the cancellation table need be used. However, the extended table is recommended as an aid in understanding the *whole* process, and also in complex examples so that entries are not omitted. The consolidated balance sheet of the New York Group at 31 March 1995 is shown in the first two columns of Figure 6.4.

	£m	£m	£m	£m
		Consolidated		**Sipowicz as excluded subsidiary**
Intangible fixed assets		13.2		
Tangible fixed assets:				
- cost	568		400	
- accumulated depreciation	(253)		(200)	
		315		200
Investment in excluded subsidiary				146.8
Loan to excluded subsidiary				16
Current assets:				
Stock	230		188.4	
Dividends receivable			8	
Debtors	145		110	
Cash	101		70.0	
	476		376.4	
Creditors within one year:				
Creditors	108		78	
Dividends payable	34		32	
	142		110	
		334		266.4
Creditors over one year:				
Loans		-		-
		662.2		629.2
Capital and Reserves:				
Ordinary shares (£ 1)		180		180
Share premium		104		104
Revaluation reserves		70		70
Retained profits		275.2		275.2
		629.2		
Minority interests		33.0		-
		662.2		629.2

Figure 6.4 – New York Group balance sheet at 31 March 1995

(b) Calculation of minority interests
The minority interest single figure balance of £33m (deduced from its column in Figure 6.3) is analysed below:

Components	£	£
Share capital (20%)		16
Share premium (20%)		3
Revaluation reserves (20%):		
per subsidiary's accounts	5	
per fair value exercise	3	
		8
Retained profits (20%):		
per subsidiary's accounts	7	
extra depreciation	(0.6)	
stock profits (*upstream*)	(0.4)	
		6
Per consolidated balance sheet		33

Note
1. There is no need to split pre- and post-acquisition figures as the minority interest is ongoing.
2. The fact that alignment adjustments affect the minority interests means that the *parent extension* approach (see Chapter 5, pp. 169) is being used (per FRS 7 and FRS 2).
3. The elimination of unrealized intra-group stock profits affects minority interests here because the originating company is Sipowicz (*upstream* sale). If the sale had been downstream, there would have been no adjustment to minority interests as elimination would have been 100% against consolidated retained profits.

4. In consolidated dividends payable in 'creditors under one year' is an amount of £2m (20% × £10m) relating to minority interests.

(c) Downstream sales from Kelly plc to Sipowicz plc

Suppose the sales of intra-group stocks had been *downstream*. The calculations would change as follows:

Consolidated retained profits	=	275.2	– 2.0	+ 1.6	=	£274.8m
Minority interests	=	33.0		+ 0.4	=	£33.4m

Reflecting that stock profits must be eliminated 100 per cent against Kelly plc's retained profits rather than according to the ownership proportions of Sipowicz plc, the second basis is removed and the first inserted.

DIRECT CALCULATIONS

This section is designed to sharpen understanding of the consolidation process, taking it beyond a mechanical level. Though it is *optional*, it is highly recommended. The New York Group example is revisited without the enforced structure of the cancellation table. Attempt the following before looking at the solutions. It is very unlikely that you will get them right first time. Understanding comes from comparing imperfect attempts with the solutions below. Direct calculations provide an intuitive way of checking cancellation table figures.

Example 6.8 – Direct calculation of consolidated balances

In the above New York Group example, *ignore* the effects of alignment adjustments. Using the original data on page 158 only, attempt to calculate directly the following consolidated balances at 31 March 1995 unless another date is specified:
(a) fixed assets;
(b) stocks;
(c) goodwill at acquisition (31 March 1993);
(d) net book amount of current balance sheet goodwill (31 March 1995);
(e) share capital;
(f) minority interests;
(g) retained profits.

Solution

Fixed assets	=	200 + 103	=	£303m
Stocks	=	190 + 42	=	£232m

Under the parent approach including 100% of the subsidiary's assets

Goodwill at acquisition	=	investment – 80% × equity at acquisition	
	=	162 – 80% × (80 + 15 + 25 + 25) =	£46m
Current goodwill	=	46 – ($\frac{2}{5}$ × 46)	= £27.6m

Based on straight line depreciation over five years

Share capital   = £180m

Only the parent's share capital; the subsidiary's is either cancelled or included in minority interests

Minority interests   = 20% × (80 + 15 + 25 + 35)   = £31m

Based on current balance sheet equity as minority share is ongoing

Retained profits   = 292 + 80% (35 – 25) – 18.4 = £281.6m

Includes attributable postacquisition retained profits of the subsidiary, less goodwill write-off

Example 6.9 – Direct calculation with adjustments

In the above New York Group example, now *including* the effects of alignment adjustments and using the original data on page 158, attempt to recalculate *directly* the above consolidated balances using the above figures as a starting point.

Solution

Fixed assets = 200 + 103 + 15 − 3 = £315m
Stocks = 190 + 42 − 2 = £230m

The parent extension approach includes 100% of fair value adjustments, extra depreciation and stock profit adjustments

---

Goodwill at acquisition = Investment − 80% × Fair value equity at acquisition
= (162 − 4) − 80 % x (80 + 15 + 25 + 25 + 10 + 15) = £22m

Current goodwill = 22 − $\frac{(2 \times 22)}{5}$ = £13.2m

This is complex to calculate – fair value adjustments are included in pre-acquisition equity, and the investment adjusted for pre-acquisition dividends – you are doing fine if you only get most of the equity correct.

Share capital = £180m

Only the parent's share capital as before

Minority interests = 20% × (80 + 15 + 25 + 35 + 15 − 3 − 2) = £33m

Includes fair value and extra depreciation adjustments as well as stock adjustment as intra-group sales are upstream (parent extension approach). The effects of the fair value adjustment (£10m) on stock at acquisition has been ignored as it has a zero net effect. Since it has subsequently been sold, the effect would have been + 20% × £10m at acquisition and − 20% × £10m when 'revalued' stock flowed through into cost of goods sold.

Retained profits = 292 + 80% [(35 − 25) − 5 − 10 − 3 − 2] − 8.8 = £275.2m

Again rather tricky. In order: removal of pre-acquisition dividend treated as income by the parent, then flow through effects of fair value adjustments on stocks at acquisition (on sale) and fixed assets (as depreciated), then stock profits (80% eliminated, upstream) and finally two years' parent goodwill write-off (which differs from the first example because inclusion of alignment adjustments affects the calculation of goodwill at acquisition).

Exercises

6.15 Proud plc is the holding company of Humble Ltd. It acquired a 90% interest on 30 June 1993 when the retained profits of Humble were £50m. The The acquisition transaction must be accounted for using acquisition accounting. The following draft balance sheets are available for the year ended 30 June 1995:

	Proud £m	£m	Humble £m	£m
Tangible fixed assets:				
– cost	220		150	
– accumulated depreciation	(100)		(60)	
		120		90
Investment in Humble		120		
Current assets:				
Stock	80		40	
Dividends receivable	9		—	
Debtors	86		30	
Cash	20		40	
	195		110	
Creditors within one year:				
Creditors	50		60	
Dividends payable	20		10	
	70		70	
		125		40
		365		130

Capital and Reserves:

Ordinary shares (£1)	70	15
Share premium	80	25
Revaluation reserves	20	10
Retained profits	<u>195</u>	<u>80</u>
	<u>365</u>	<u>130</u>

Additional information:

(i) Proud sold certain goods to Humble for £6m at a mark up of 25% on cost, but these were not received by Humble until after the group year end. Also, when reconciling its bank statements, Proud found a cash payment of £22m from Humble received on 29 June was wrongly recorded in its records as £20m.

(ii) At acquisition, certain of Humble's fixed assets had a fair value of £50m (carrying amount £40m). These are still held by Humble and to be depreciated straight-line over 10 years. No entry has been made to record a revaluation in Humble's records. No other assets were revalued.

(iii) Proud's consolidated retained profits includes an amount from Humble of £4m in respect of Humble's year ended 30 June 1993.

(iv) Humble has in stock at 30 June 1995 £16m of goods purchased from Proud (at a mark-up on cost of 25%).

(v) In its own balance sheet Proud plc has a trade debtor from Humble plc of £38m, and Humble plc has Proud plc as a trade creditor of £30m.

(vi) Goodwill is written off on the straight line basis over 10 years.

Required

(a) Prepare a consolidated balance sheet for the Proud Group at 30 June 1995 using an extended cancellation table.

(b) Calculate the components comprising the minority interests balance in the balance sheet in part (a).

(c) Explain how the calculations in part a) would be affected if intra-group sales of stocks were instead from Humble plc to Proud plc.

6.16 In the Proud Group exercise (question 6.15 above), *ignoring* the effects of alignment adjustments and using the original data above, attempt to calculate *directly* the following consolidated balances:

(a) fixed assets;
(b) stocks;
(c) goodwill at acquisition;
(d) current balance sheet goodwill;
(e) share capital;
(f) minority interests;
(g) retained profits.

6.17 In the Proud Group exercise in question 6.15, now *including* the effects of alignment adjustments attempt to recalculate *directly* the consolidated balances using the figures from question 6.16 as a starting point.

6.18 Vampire plc purchased a 70% interest in Stake plc on 30 June 1995 for £190m. Vampire plc's retained profits at 1 January 1995 were £200m, and during the year, its net profit was £70m and dividends declared £30m. Capital and Reserves of Stake plc are analysed as follows:

	£m
Share capital	50
Share premium	60
Revaluation reserve	20
Retained profits at 1 Jan 1995	80
Retained profits for year to 31 Dec 1995	30
	<u>240</u>

Notes

(i) At acquisition the fair value of Stake's land (still held) was estimated at £30m (cost £20m). No adjustment for this has been made in its own records and land is not depreciated.

(ii) Stake plc since acquisition has started selling goods to Vampire plc at a mark-up on cost of 50%. At 31 December 1995 the amount of such stocks held by Vampire plc was £9m.

(iii) Goodwill is to be depreciated straight-line over four years (allow for six months depreciation).

Required

(a) Ignoring the effects of notes (i) and (ii), *directly* calculate (i.e. without cancellation table) good will, consolidated retained profits and minority interests at acquisition. Assume that Vampire's and Stake plc's retained profits accrue evenly throughout the year.

(b) Ignoring the effects of notes (i) and (ii), *directly* calculate consolidated goodwill, consolidated retained profits and minority interests at 31 December 1995.

(c) Now including the effects of notes (i) to (iv), i.e. with alignment information, *directly* recalculate parts (a) and (b) and comment on your results.

ALIGNMENT PROBLEMS AND EQUITY ACCOUNTING

This section can be omitted without loss of continuity.

Equity accounting is used in a number of different situations.

(a) *Associates* – the ASB Discussion Paper, *Associates and Joint Ventures*, following ED 50 earlier, proposes *proportional elimination* of unrealized 'intra-group' profits on transactions with associates. This reflects the close conceptual link of equity accounting and proportional consolidation (see Chapter 4), but is not the subject of any current UK standard.

(b) *Subsidiary exclusion on grounds of severe long-term restrictions* – as discussed in Chapter 4, if significant influence is still retained, the equity approach is used and FRS 2 requires the excluded subsidiary to be treated as an associate, and comments that 'it is important to consider whether it is prudent to record any profits arising from transactions with subsidiary undertakings excluded on these grounds' (para. 83). If even significant influence is not retained, then the investment is to be 'frozen' at its equitized amount the date the restrictions came into force. In this case profits or losses on transactions with such undertakings, or where 'subsidiaries' are excluded on the grounds of being held exclusively with a view to resale, need not be eliminated (para. 83).

(c) *Subsidiary exclusion on grounds of dissimilar activities* – FRS 2 requires the basis for the elimination of unrealized intra-group profits to be same as if the subsidiary were to be included in the consolidation (para. 39) i.e. *full elimination* must be practised – the reason for exclusion is *not* loss of control.

The extra disclosures required in the latter two cases are discussed in Chapters 2 and 4.

Example 6.10 – Alignment adjustments and the equity approach

Consider the New York example above, but show how alignment adjustments must be treated in the following cases where equity accounting is used for Sipowicz:

(a) though Kelly plc holds an 80% stake in equity and voting rights, it can only exercise significant influence because of other contractual arrangements in place;

(b) Sipowicz plc is a subsidiary excluded because severe long-term restrictions substantially affect Kelly plc's ability to control Sipowicz plc, though Kelly plc can still exercise significant influence;

(c) Sipowicz plc is an excluded subsidiary on the grounds of dissimilar activities (see Chapter 2).

Required

Calculate the amount for the equitized investment under each scenario and its breakdown into net assets and goodwill (required by SSAP 1 for associates). Outline any extra disclosures required by FRS 2 in parts (b) and (c).

(d) Explain how your calculations would be different in each case if instead intra-group sales of stocks were from Kelly plc to Sipowicz plc.

Solution

(a) Sipowicz as an associate

As a technical exercise, restatement of Sipowicz plc to the equity approach is enlightening as it shows directly how consolidation adjustments incrementally affect: (a) the investment, (b) the subsidiary's contribution to consolidated retained profits, (c) goodwill and (d) the subsidiary's net assets.

Without alignment adjustments

The fundamental equation of Chapter 4, p. 85 is used, i.e.

$$I + 0.8 \, \Delta \, RE = G + 0.8 \, [\, A_{now} - L_{now} \,]$$

The equitized investment is equal to goodwill at *acquisition,* plus the parent's share of the subsidiary's net assets at the *current* balance sheet date. The top half of Figure 6.5 shows the resulting calculations for the current example *ignoring* the effects of any alignment adjustments; the bottom part, with alignment adjustments, is discussed below:

Post-acquisition profit	=	80% × (35 – 25)	=	£8m
Goodwill at acquisition	=	162 – 80% × (80+15+25+25)	=	£46m
80% of net assets now	=	80% × (103 + 62 – 10)	=	£124m

Without alignment adjustments

Cost plus attributable retained profit		Goodwill plus proportionate assets	
Investment at cost	162	**Goodwill at acquisition**	46
80% post-acq profit	8	**80% net assets now**	124
	$\overline{170}$		$\overline{170}$

With alignment adjustments

Cost plus attributable retained profit		Goodwill plus proportionate assets	
Investment at cost	162	**Goodwill at acquisition**	46
1. Pre acq dividend	(4)	1. Pre-acq dividend	(4)
		2. Stock fair value at acq	(8)
		3. Fixed asset fair value at acq	(12)
		6. Goodwill amortisation	(8.8)
	$\overline{158}$		$\overline{13.2}$
80% post-acq profit	8	**80% net assets now**	124
2. Stock fair value at acq	(8)	3. Fixed asset fair value at acq	12
4. Extra depreciation	(2.4)	4. Extra depreciation	(2.4)
5. Intra-group stock profits	(1.6)		$\overline{133.6}$
6. Goodwill amortisation	(8.8)		
	$\overline{(12.8)}$	5. Intra-group stock profits	$\overline{(1.6)}$
	$\overline{145.2}$		$\overline{145.2}$

Figure 6.5 – Incremental effects of using equity approach

With alignment adjustments – incremental overall effects
As discussed earlier, the most authoritative pronouncements, the ASB Discussion Paper *Associates and Joint Ventures,* and ED 50, both propose requiring *proportionate elimination,* and this is used here. The bottom half of Figure 6.5 shows the *incremental* effect on the company accounts of Kelly plc of accounting for Sipowicz under the equity approach. Consider how alignment adjustments affect the four components in the top half of the figure. Each adjustment affects the four subsections in such a way that for each the total left-hand side effect equals the total right-hand side effect.

1. Since equity accounting is basically a *group* accounting procedure, the pre-acquisition dividend is treated as a capital repayment (though not in the individual accounts of Kelly plc).
2. Stock fair value increases fair values of assets at acquisition (i.e. reduces goodwill) but reduces

post-acquisition profits as the increased cost flows through subsequently on sale.
3. Fair valuation of fixed assets at acquisition increases consolidated assets now over the subsidiary's carrying amounts, and at-acquisition equity (reducing goodwill).
4. Extra depreciation reduces the excess of consolidated over the subsidiary's carrying amounts, also consolidated post-acquisition profits.
5. Intra-group stock profits reduce consolidated stocks over company carrying amounts (and consolidated profits).
6. Goodwill amortization reduces goodwill and post-acquisition consolidated profits.

Financial statements treatment
In this example there are no other subsidiaries. SSAP 1 states that if there are only associates, information about associates should *supplement* the individual company accounts (one form of supplementation being pro-forma accounts as shown in the last two columns of Figure 6.4).
The unrealized stock profit made by Sipowicz must be eliminated. In the last two columns of Figure 6.4 and in Figure 6.5:

(1) under the equity approach proportional elimination is used
i.e. elimination = 80% × 2 = £1.6m;
(2) the stock written down to group cost is situated at Kelly plc, and so the elimination entry must be against *Kelly's* stock and not the equitized investment (which includes *Sipowicz's* stock)

	DR		**CR**
Group retained profits	1.6	*Kelly* stock	1.6

Hence equitized investment	=	13.2 + 133.6	= £146.8m
and group stock	=	190 − 1.6	= £188.4m

(3). All the other balances are as for the individual company balance sheet except group retained profits, which is on an equity accounting basis. There is no separate goodwill balance as this is included in the equitized investment figure.

SSAP 1 disclosures
SSAP 1 requires (a) a breakdown of the investment into the net book amount of goodwill and share of net assets; (b) the aggregate share of associates' post-acquisition accumulated reserves; and in both, if deemed material, consolidation adjustments should be made (as in the example above) to include 'matters such as unrealized profits on stocks transferred'. Consider now how such disclosures would be provided. The parent's contribution to consolidated retained profits is adjusted for dividends from pre-acquisition profits.

(a) *Investment in Associate* £m
    Goodwill 13.2
    Net assets <u>133.6</u>
    <u>146.8</u>

(b) *Consolidated retained profits* £m
    Parent 288.0
    Associate <u>(12.8)</u> Removing pre-acquisition dividends for group pur-
    <u>275.2</u> poses) (Includes 80% stock profit elimination)

Note
Consolidated retained profits are the same here as under conventional consolidation in Example 6.7. How can this be, when full elimination is practised for subsidiaries and proportional elimination for associates? The reason is that the sales in Example 6.7 were all upstream, and so full elimination was made according to the ownership proportions of the originating company, Sipowicz, which is 80% owned. Therefore the full elimination had been allocated 80% against consolidated retained earnings and 20% against minority interests. The effect on consolidated retained earnings *itself* is thus the same as if only 80% had been eliminated.

(b) Exclusion because of severe long-term restrictions, significant interest retained
Although control has been lost, significant influence is retained. FRS 2 requires the equity method (para. 27). The Companies Act 1985 also requires reasons for exclusion and details of balances and transactions with the rest of the group (Sch 5, para. 15), but these are not illustrated further here. Where the 'associate' is an excluded subsidiary, supplemental financial statements *must* be provided in addition to Kelly's parent company accounts. Otherwise the calculations are as in (a) above.

(c) Sipowicz excluded on the grounds of dissimilar activities

As stated above, FRS 2 requires in this case the *full elimination* of unrealized intra-group profits. In this case separate financial statements for Sipowicz are required under FRS 2 and the Companies Act 1985 to be appended to 'group' accounts in which Sipowicz is accounted for under the equity approach (see Chapter 4). The calculations would also be as in part (a) because the sales are upstream.

(d) Downstream sales from Kelly plc to Sipowicz plc

In parts (a) and (b), proportional elimination of unrealized intra-group profits is used, so

		£m	
Group stocks	=	190	(stock adjustment is now against subsidiary stocks)
Investment in excluded subsidiary	=	146.8 – 1.6	
	=	145.2	
Consolidated retained profits	=	275.2	(now including adjustment on subsidiary stocks)

Note disclosures required by SSAP 1 would be:

(a) *Investment in associate/excluded subsidiary*

	£m
Goodwill	13.2
(Elimination of £1.6m)	
Net assets	132.0
	145.2

(b) *Consolidated retained profits*

	£m	
Parent	286.4	(No stock profit elimination because downstream)
(Removing pre-acquistion div & stock profits)		
Associate/excluded subsidiary	(11.2)	
	275.2	

Note – now consolidated retained profits are *not* the same as in the equivalent part (c) of Example 6.7. Because the sale was downstream, under the full elimination approach the unrealized profit would have been eliminated 100% against consolidated retained profits, whereas under proportional elimination only 80% is eliminated. This is one example of how consolidated retained profits are no longer necessarily identical under the different consolidation approaches once valuation adjustments are taken into account.

In part (c), 100% of the stock profit adjustment (£2m) would be charged against the investment and consolidated retained profits instead of £1.6m. as when Sipowicz is treated as an associate. Since the basis for elimination is identical to the conventional consolidation basis (i.e. full elimination), it is not surprising that consolidated retained profits would be identical to that in the equivalent part (c) of Example 6.7 whether the sales are upstream or downstream. Since this reason for exclusion is unlikely to be used in practice (see Chapter 2), no further calculations are illustrated here.

Exercise

6.19 Consider the Proud Humble exercise (6.15), but show how alignment adjustments must be treated in the following cases where equity accounting is used for Humble:

   (a) though Proud plc holds a 90% stake in equity and voting rights, it can only exercise significant influence because of other contractual arrangements in place.

   (b) Humble plc is a subsidiary excluded because severe long-term restrictions substantially affect Proud plc's ability to control it, though Proud plc can still exercise significant influence.

   (c) Humble plc is an excluded subsidiary on the grounds of dissimilar activities (see Chapter 2).

Required

Calculate the amount for the equitized investment under each scenario, and its breakdown into net assets and goodwill (required by SSAP 1 in the case of associates). Outline any extra disclosures required by FRS 2 in parts (b) and (c).

   (d) Explain how your calculations would be different in each case if intra-group sales of stocks were instead from Humble plc to Proud plc.

CONSOLIDATION CONCEPTS AS A FRAMEWORK FOR ALIGNMENT ADJUSTMENTS

This section can be omitted without loss in continuity by those merely wishing to focus on current UK requirements.

In Chapter 4, three main consolidation concepts were identified – proportional, parent and entity. The analysis of consolidation concepts is now extended to include the valuation-type consolidation adjustments discussed in Chapters 5 and 6, and the practical usefulness of such extended consolidation concepts in providing a framework for alignment adjustments in parent–subsidiary relationships is examined. The key contrasts are in the measurement of minority interests.

Valuation-type adjustments and consolidation concepts

There are two dimensions on which consolidation concepts differ, affecting the measurement and disclosure of minority interests:

> (1) the fraction of the subsidiary's assets, liabilities and goodwill to be included in the consolidation; and
>
> (2) whether minority interests are considered outsiders or insiders for consolidation valuation adjustment purposes.

Though the key approach for understanding current practice is the parent approach, it is easier to understand these two effects by first examining the proportional and entity approaches. Under the proportional/proprietary approach minority interests are ignored (as having a 'nil' value) as complete 'outsiders' to the group. Only the parent's proportion of assets, liabilities and goodwill are included in the consolidation. This proportion is adjusted to group costs ('proportional adjustment') via, for example, proportional fair value adjustments at acquisition and proportional adjustments for extra depreciation and unrealized intra-group profits on stocks.

Under the entity/economic unit approach minority interests are conceptualized as insiders to the group. So all the identifiable assets and liabilities of majority owned subsidiaries (including the minority share) are included in the balance sheet together with minority goodwill. These total amounts are adjusted to/included at group costs ('complete adjustment') via fair value adjustments at acquisition and adjustments for unrealized profits on intra-group transactions. The effects of these 'complete' adjustments are apportioned as appropriate between controlling and minority interests. Thus minority interests are included and measured at their proportion of consolidated (adjusted) carrying values.

Unfortunately the parent approach, upon which most current practice for accounting for subsidiaries is based internationally, is not well-specified in this regard. It includes the total identifiable assets and liabilities of the subsidiary (and hence minority interests) but only parent goodwill. However, there are two variants as to how to perform consolidation valuation-type adjustments on such identifiable assets and liabilities. Each variant treats minority interests differently:

(1) *The pure parent approach* – as regards valuation adjustments minority interests are regarded as outsiders. Therefore, for example, on intra-group stocks, the proportion of the profits arising from sales to and from such minority interests is regarded as *realized* because they are treated as outsiders. Only the parent's proportion of such profits needs to be taken into account in adjusting such stocks to group costs. Analogously, only the parent's proportion of fair value adjustments at acquisition is recognized. Consequently minority interests are measured based on the carrying values of assets in the subsidiary's own accounts.

(2) *The parent extension approach* – as regards valuation adjustments minority interests are now regarded as insiders. The minority share of profits on intra-group transactions is now regarded as unrealized because they are insiders. Thus their proportionate stake in intra-group stocks must be adjusted to group cost. This leads to complete adjustment of profits and restatement to original group cost. Similar complete adjustment

must be made for fair value adjustments at acquisition, apportioned between controlling and minority interests. Under this approach minority interests are measured based on consolidated (adjusted) carrying values of assets.

In the first variant the parent approach leans towards proportional consolidation valuation adjustment concepts (termed the pure parent approach) and in the second towards the entity approach (termed the parent extension approach (Baxter and Spinney, 1985)). Figure 6.6 summarizes the approaches. Thus proportional and pure parent approaches regard minority interests as outsiders, parent extension and entity as insiders.

Subsidiary's asset / liability inclusion basis	Alignment / valuation adjustment basis	Consolidation approach
Proportional	Proportional	Proportional
Parent ⟶	Proportional	Pure parent
	Complete	Parent extension
Entity	Complete	Entity

Figure 6.6 – Consolidation approaches and consolidation adjustments

Example 6.11 – Parent consolidation concept variants

Parental plc owns a 75% stake in Childish plc. At the current year end Parental plc has, based on its cost, £20m of intra-group stocks purchased from Childish plc (original cost to the latter, £16m). At the acquisition of Childish plc some years ago, land with carrying value of £40m was estimated to have a fair value at acquisition of £48m. This land is still held and no entries have been made by the subsidiary to record fair values.

Required

Prepare journal entries to show under both the parent extension and pure parent approaches, consolidation adjustments to record the fair value at acquisition for the land, and to eliminate the unrealized intra-group profits on the stocks. Calculate the carrying value of the land and intra-group stocks per the consolidated accounts under each approach.

Solution

Parent extension – minority as insiders (UK basis per FRS 7 and FRS 2)

Fair values at acquisition	DR	CR	Unrealized intra-group profits	DR	CR
Land (100%)	£8m		Stocks (100%)		£4m
Goodwill/pre-acquisition equity (75%)		£6m	Consolidated retained profits (75%)	£3m	
Minority interests (25%)		£2m	Minority interests (25%)	£1m	

The land would be completely restated to its fair value at acquisition (£48m). The £8m 'revaluation' adjustment would be part of the subsidiary's equity at acquisition and so would be apportioned as above. There would be complete elimination of unrealized intra-group stock profits according to the ownership proportions of the originating company (i.e. Childish plc as it recorded the original (upstream) profit of £4m = 20 – 16). As minority interests are regarded as insiders, their share of the profit, 25% × £4m = £1m is regarded as unrealized, and therefore minority interests are based on their share of consolidated (i.e group) costs. Such complete elimination reduces intra-group stocks to a group original cost of £16m.

Pure parent – minority as outsiders

Fair values at acquisition	DR	CR	Unrealized intra-group profits	DR	CR
Land (75%)	£6m		Stocks (75%)		£3m
Goodwill/pre-acquisition equity (75%)		£6m	Consolidated retained profits (75%)	£3m	

As far as the land is concerned, as minority interests are regarded as outsiders, their 25 per cent stake in the land would not be restated and would be based on the subsidiary's carrying values. Only a proportional restatement to fair values would be made of £8m × 75% and land would be stated at £46m. There would also be only proportional elimination of unrealized intra-group stock profits. As minority interests are regarded as outsiders, their share of the profit (25% × £4m = £1m) on sales by them is regarded as realized. Only the parent's proportion is regarded as unrealized. Minority interests remain at their share of the subsidiary's cost and intra-group stocks would be stated at £17m (20 – 3).

The UK tends towards the parent extension (complete adjustment) approach – FRS 7 requires complete restatement to fair values at acquisition (see Chapter 5) and FRS 2 requires complete elimination of unrealized intra-group profits apportioned between consolidated reserves and minority interests according to the ownership proportions of the originating company. Minority interests are thus based on the consolidated carrying values of the subsidiary's identifiable net assets. Figure 6.7 summarizes the effects of the different consolidation concepts – note particularly the parent extension approach.

The basis of measurement of the subsidiary's assets, liabilities and goodwill in the consolidated financial statements differs between consolidation concepts. Under the proportional approach the proportional group cost of each is disclosed. Under the entity approach their total group cost is included including imputed minority goodwill. Under the parent extension approach the total group cost of identifiable assets and liabilities is included but only the parent's purchased goodwill. In the above example the total group cost of land (£48m) and of intra-group stocks (£16m) would be reported.

The oddball is the pure parent approach. All the subsidiary's identifiable assets and liabilities are included but only the parent's proportion of valuation adjustments.

Consolidation concept	Inclusion of subsidiary assets, liabilities & goodwill	Proportion of valuation adjustments accounted for	Minority interests measurement & disclosure
Proportional	Parent's *proportion* of subsidiary's assets, liabilities and goodwill	Parent stake only	Nil
Pure parent	All subsidiary's assets & liabilities. Parent goodwill	Parent proportion only - individual assets part at group cost and part at subsidiary costs	Based on the *subsidiary's* carrying values of identifiable assets & liabilities
Parent extension	All subsidiary's assets & liabilities. Parent goodwill	Complete - assets completely restated to *group* costs	Based on the *consolidated* carrying values of subsidiary's identifiable assets and liabilities
Entity	All subsidiary's assets, liabilities *and* majority *and* minority goodwill	Complete - assets completely restated to *group* costs	Based on the *consolidated* carrying values of subsidiary's identifiable assets and liabilities and minority goodwill

Figure 6.7 – Effects of different consolidation concepts

Identifiable assets and liabilities are therefore included at amounts which are neither original group nor subsidiary costs. In the example above land is reported at £46m (75% × 48 + 25% × 40) and intra-group stocks at £17m (75% × 16 + 25% × 20), 75 per cent at group cost and 25 per cent at subsidiary cost, as there was only a proportional adjustment for fair value adjustments and unrealized intra-group stock profits.

Associates

Though current accounting standards in the UK do not specify the valuation adjustment basis where the equity approach is used, the ASB Discussion Paper, *Associates and Joint Ventures*, stipulates 'the part relating to the investor's or venturer's share should be eliminated' (para. 5.4). This proposed requirement for proportional adjustment is consistent with proportional consolidation being the closest relative to equity accounting. This is evidenced by the note disclosure under SSAP 1, requiring the breakdown of the equitized investment into proportional net assets and goodwill.

International Practice

The entity approach is not used. No country currently imputes minority goodwill at acquisition. The UK (FRS 7) uses the parent extension/complete adjustment approach for fair values at acquisition, whereas the USA follows the pure parent/proportional adjustment in this regard. IAS 22 also prefers proportional adjustment as its benchmark treatment for fair values at acquisition, though complete adjustment is an allowed alternative.

FRS 2 also follows the parent extension/complete adjustment approach on the elimination of unrealized intra-group profits. ARB 51 (1961) in the USA requires 100 per cent elimination but allows the option of apportioning it entirely against controlling interests or between controlling and minority interests. It does not specify when each should be used. IAS 27 (1988) also requires 100 per cent elimination, but does not specify how such eliminated profits should be apportioned. Thus, both ARB 51 in the USA and IAS 27 internationally would therefore allow the parent extension approach for unrealized intra-group profits, but also permit any other apportionment methods based on complete elimination.

No country treats minority interests as insiders in the treatment of piecemeal acquisitions and disposals of investments in group companies. The group records profits or losses on such sales. FRS 2 requires this – see Crichton (1991) for supporting arguments. If minority interests were instead to be viewed as insiders, the FASB Discussion Memorandum, *Consolidation Policy and Procedures* (1991), comments that where a parent retains overall control of a subsidiary, transactions which vary the strength of that control (e.g. by the parent reducing its stake from 80 per cent to 60 per cent) would be viewed as transactions between group shareholders, and thus no gain or loss reported. See Chapter 10.

Usefulness of the consolidation concepts

Consolidation concepts are different stances on the treatment of the relationship between controlling and minority (non-controlling) interests. They are conceptually distinct from, but related to, the span of consolidation i.e. which entities to include in the consolidation (see Chapters 2 and 4). These two issues overlap in practice. Supporters of a narrow ownership based span of consolidation might see consolidation as an amplification of the parent shareholders' investments. This would probably lead towards the proprietary/proportional end of the consolidation concepts spectrum. Supporters of a full-blown unified management/economic unit based span of consolidation would probably support an entity consolidation concept. Controlling and minority interests would merely be financial claims on the group entity with different rights, as indeed would liabilities.

Otherwise the relationship between consolidation concept and span of consolidation is ambiguous. The 'control' based span of consolidation used in the UK (see Chapter 2) is founded in the ownership of the ultimate entity by parent shareholders (ultimately a 'proprietary' perspective). Only then are all subordinate entities under the control of this ownership nexus consolidated. Thus individual shareholders controlling a number of groups through their private shareholdings do not have to publish mega-consolidations of such holdings. Groups under common management do not have to consolidate if there is not an over-arching common ownership of the ultimate entity, though it only needs to be a 'participating' interest (Chapter 2). Any focus on a group 'entity' in the UK is thus embedded within this overarching proprietorial interest in the parent.

Over time, a control-based span of consolidation has developed in the UK, with the EU 7th Directive flowing through into FRS 2, leading to a parallel movement towards the entity end of the consolidation concepts spectrum – compare the UK treatment of fair value adjustments at acquisition with the US position and FRS 2's banning of proportional elimination of unrealized intra-group profits. However, because of the above over-arching proprietorial focus, there has not been a complete embracing of the entity consolidation concept. Profits are recognized on piecemeal disposals of investments where control is retained. Baxter and Spinney's (1975) term 'parent extension' more accurately describes UK practice than 'entity' or 'economic unit'. The US Discussion Memorandum, *Consolidation Policy and Procedures* (1991), groups together proportional consolidation and pure parent concepts under its 'parent view' of the group, and the 'parent extension' and 'entity' concepts as different forms of its 'economic unit' perspective. The current author believes they are mistaken in doing this for the reasons outlined above.

Contracting cost factors

Contractual relationships between management and shareholders such as profit-based performance-related pay may also provide good reasons why international consolidation practices do not follow exactly any consolidation concept. In such circumstances parent shareholders will be keen to prevent performance payments based on consolidated gains untested by the market, but keen to reward performance based on market-tested transactions. If unrealized profits on intra-group transactions were not eliminated, management compensation could be boosted by generating 'fictitious' profits at their whim by merely shifting stocks around the group. Further, even if proportional elimination were used, management could generate 'profits' on 'sales' to minority interests. On the other hand parent shareholders would be also interested in monitoring management's success in generating profits or losses on sales of investments in group companies to third parties. Even in the absence of accounting standards, parent shareholders are likely to encourage such dealing by including such gains and losses in assessing profit-based management compensation. Hence information on gains or losses on piecemeal disposals of investments in subsidiaries even where control was retained would be demanded.

Qualitative characteristics of financial information

Reliability arguments rather than consolidation concepts seem to drive the US position. The UK has traditionally had a fairly relaxed attitude to revaluation of assets. This is evidenced by the 'alternative accounting rules' in the Companies Act 1985. The USA has always viewed any departure from historical cost in the main accounts with suspicion. Whilst the purchase of the parent's proportion of net assets at acquisition could be regarded as a transaction, the fair valuation of the minority portion looked suspiciously like a revaluation as minority interests were not directly involved in the transaction. Inclusion of minority goodwill would cross an even higher pain threshold. Whereas the minority share of fixed assets could be argued to have a simple pro-rata relationship with the majority portion (and hence be fairly reliable) such pro-rata relationships are unlikely to hold true for minority goodwill, 'control' having a value in its own right. Imputing minority goodwill would then be very similar to capitalizing internally generated goodwill.

The elimination of unrealized profits on intra-group transactions is different because it is a conservative accounting procedure – a reduction in cost. The pure parent/proportional elimination approach might not be conservative enough! It is consistent to require only proportional fair value adjustments at acquisition (mainly upward), but complete elimination of unrealized intra-group profits (mainly downwards).

Other rationales: the separate legal entities approach

Eggington (1965) criticizes consolidation concept approaches for missing an important dimension – that the group is composed of distinct and separate legal entities. He argues that the main reason for eliminating profits on uncompleted intra-group transfers is to prevent overstatement of profits not verifiable from external transactions; transfer of legal rights has occurred and the company that is 'at risk' if the ultimate profit margin is not realized is the purchasing company, not the originating company. Under this viewpoint, ownership rights of the *buying* company should determine eliminations, since legally profit is legitimately recognized by the selling company, and cash may already have passed – direction of sale is important, but 'weights' are of the purchasing company. This approach, which looks further behind the corporate 'veil' in enforcing shareholders' rights, has undesirable consequences in certain circumstances (Egginton, 1965) and is not explored further here.

Conclusions

Should accounting for subsidiaries be more tightly defined by a particular consolidation concept? The parent concept is incompletely specified and needs features of proportional consolidation (minority outside) or entity consolidation (minority inside) grafted on to make it operational. Consolidation 'concepts' are better viewed as labels for different technical properties, useful for classification purposes, but are not sufficient for arbitrating say between UK and US practice. Other criteria such as reliability and contracting implications seem to have greater explanatory power. The nature, status, measurement and disclosure of minority interests is a fundamental conceptual problem which still needs to be tackled by conceptual frameworks internationally (see Chapter 12).

Exercises

6.20 How do minority interests differ in amount between the pure parent approach and the parent extension approach? What is the conceptual reason for such a difference?

6.21 To what extent should the fact that the UK is closer in adopting the parent extension approach for alignment adjustments than the USA and the IASC's benchmark treatments lead to the conclusion that it is leading international practice?

6.22 Primary Products plc, a 65% subsidiary of Valued Added plc, sells goods to its parent. At the end of the year, the latter has £50m of such goods in stock sold by Primary Products at a markup on cost of 25%.

   Required
   (a) Calculate the amount of Primary Product plc's profits contained in the £50m of stocks.
   (b) Show how unrealized intra-group stock profits would be eliminated under the pure parent and parent extension approaches to consolidation.
   (c) Explain the rationales for the treatments in part (b).

6.23 Critically evaluate different proposals for the accounting treatment of the elimination of unrealized intra-group stock profits in consolidated financial statements.

Review exercises

6.24 *Review problem*: Threadbare plc purchased a 60% stake in Stitched Up plc on 31 January 1994 for £190m when the retained profits of the latter company were £90m. However, other rights possessed by the a third party mean that Stitched Up plc is to be treated as an associated company of Threadbare as only significant influence can be exercised. Abbreviated balance sheets of both companies are as follows:

Balance sheets at 31 January 1996

	Threadbare		Stitched Up	
	£m	£m	£m	£m
Fixed assets (net)		600		200
Investment in Stitched Up plc		190		—
Investment in other group companies		200		—
		990		200
Current assets:				
Stock	300		150	
Other	200		80	
	500		230	
Creditors due within one year	(145)		(50)	
Net current assets		355		180
Creditors due over one year		(80)		(20)
		1,265		360
Capital and reserves:				
Shares		300		150
Retained profits		965		210
		1,265		360

Notes

(i) At 31 January 1994, certain of Stitched Up's fixed assets were estimated to have a fair value of £40m (carrying amount at that date £20m). The excess on revaluation is to be depreciated on a straight line basis over a five-year period. All these assets are still held. The revaluation has not been recorded by Stitched Up.

(ii) Stitched Up buys thread from Threadbare plc, at a mark up on cost of 33 1/3%. At 31 January 1995, Stitched Up plc had £15m of such items in stock and at 31 January 1996, £20m.

(iii) Goodwill is written off over a ten-year period on a straight-line basis.

Required

(a) Prepare a consolidated balance sheet for the Threadbare Group at 31 January 1996 in which Stitched Up plc is treated as a subsidiary.

(b) Calculate the amount at which the 'Investment in Stitched Up plc' would appear in the group balance sheet for the Threadbare Group at 31 January 1996, assuming it is treated as an *associated* company and that alignment adjustments are made, and prepare a group balance sheet on this basis.

(c) Compare and contrast the group balance sheets in parts (a) and (b)

(d) Prepare a breakdown of the investment amount in part (b) into
  (i) Cost plus attributable retained profits AND
  (ii) Net assets and goodwill.

6.25 *Review problem*: Tubthumper plc acquired a 100% interest in the 'A' shares of Tub plc for £50m on 28 February 1993 (payable £35m immediately and £15m on 30 March 1994) when the retained profits of Tub plc were £15m. 'A' and 'B' shares carry equal voting rights at shareholder meetings, but holders of 'A' shares can appoint twice as many directors as holders of 'B' shares. By a ten-year contract signed between the two companies at the date of acquisition, Tub plc is required to sell 75% of its output to Tubthumper plc at prices agreeable to the latter's board of directors, but is free to sell the remaining 25% at open market prices. The balance sheets of both companies at 31 March 1994 are as follows:

	Tubthumper		Tub	
	£m	£m	£m	£m
Fixed assets				
Tangible fixed assets (net)	135		70	
Investment in Tub	35		—	
		170		70
Current assets	90		30	
Less: current liabilities	(40)		(15)	
Net current assets		50		15
		220		85

Capital and reserves (£1 shares)		
Ordinary shares	50	
'A' ordinary shares		10
'B' ordinary shares		20
Share premium	60	15
Revaluation reserve	20	5
Retained profits	90	35
	220	85

Notes

(i) At acquisition land of both companies, still included in fixed assets, was revalued by the group:

	Original	Fair value
Tubthumper	15	35
Tub	10	20

Because it was difficult to gain access to Tub plc's records immediately after the acquisition, the fair value for Tub was only provisionally estimated for the 31 March 1993 consolidated accounts. The valuation of Tub's land at acquisition was only completed in May 1993, the final valuation being £24m.

(ii) Stocks held by Tubthumper included in current assets above at 31 March 1994 include £33m purchased from Tub plc at a mark-up on cost of 10%.

(iii) At the time of the acquisition, the directors of Tubthumper plc decided to set up a reorganization provision of £13m to cover the closure of duplicate facilities of the two companies, this provision being set up in the consolidated financial statements only. The surplus facilities, which were closed in late 1993, were those situated at Tub plc. The costs of £6m of closing these facilities are to be written off against the provision and as no further costs are expected, the directors have therefore asked that any surplus provision be written back.

(iv) Goodwill at acquisition is immediately written off against consolidated retained profits.

(v) Share premium and other reserves should be assumed to be split pro-rata between 'A' and 'B' shares according to their nominal amounts.

Required

(a) Assess whether Tub plc is a subsidiary undertaking of Tubthumper plc.

(b) Whatever your answer to (a), treat Tub plc as a subsidiary undertaking for this part, prepare a cancellation table and calculate consolidated retained profits and minority interests based on the above information and the director's wishes. Show clearly how you have dealt with each item.

(c) Explain how the FRS 7 would have influenced accounting for the above acquisition if its proposals had been embodied in a Financial Reporting Standard at the date of acquisition, and assess for the board of Tubthumper plc the plausibility of any arguments used to support its proposals. Concentrate on fundamental principles rather than specific methods.

SUMMARY

Intra-group (intercompany) **balances** *are first corrected for errors by individual company adjustments and then aligned for timing differences by consolidation adjustments.* **Unrealized profits on intra-group transactions** *are eliminated by consolidation adjustment and group profit recognition is deferred until group realization criteria are met. FRS 2 requires* **complete** *elimination of such profits, apportioned according to the ownership proportions of the* **originat-**ing *company.* **Dividends from a subsidiary's pre-acquisition profits which are included in parent company income** *must be aligned by consolidation adjustment so that for consolidation purposes such dividends are treated* **as if** *a repayment of investment.*

The **different consolidation concepts** *provide some guidance for treatment of alignment adjustments for subsidiaries. However, the parent approach, used internationally, is only partially defined. The UK mainly follows the parent extension concept in which minority interests are* *conceptualized as insiders to the group for valuation adjustment purposes. Internationally, practice is not uniformly consistent with any one consolidation concept, and it may be that the concepts, whilst providing useful classification properties, do not adequately reflect deeper underlying criteria such as reliability and contracting cost issues.*

FURTHER READING

ASC (1982) SSAP 1 – *Accounting for Associated Companies* as modified by the ASB's Interim Statement: *Consolidated Accounts* (1991).

ASB (1992) FRS 2, *Accounting for Subsidiary Undertakings.*

ASB (1994) Discussion Paper, *Associates and Joint Ventures* .

Baxter, G.C. and Spinney, J.C. (1975) A closer look at consolidated financial theory, *CA Magazine*, January, pp. 31–35.

Crichton, J. (1990) Consolidation – a deceptive simplicity, *Accountancy*, February, pp. 26–27.

Crichton, J. (1990) Consolidation – minority calculations, *Accountancy*, June, pp. 30–31.

Financial Accounting Standards Board (1991), *Consolidation Policy and Procedures*, Chapter 2.

CONSOLIDATED PROFIT AND LOSS REPORTING FINANCIAL PERFORMANCE (1)

Measuring, presenting and interpreting consolidated financial performance is a many faceted area, which includes the classification and disclosure of relevant components of profit and other gains, and the reporting of other changes in shareholder equity. This chapter examines techniques for compiling a consolidated profit and loss account for ongoing activities of subsidiaries and associates under *acquisition* accounting. It also uses the different consolidation concepts to provide an intuitive understanding of the format of the conventional consolidated profit and loss account, and examines the links between the consolidated profit and loss account and balance sheet. Chapter 8 examines published consolidated profit and loss accounts under FRS 3, *Reporting Financial Performance*, including the acquisition and disposal of subsidiaries, together with the other financial statements required by the standard. In this chapter and in Chapter 8, revenues (credits) are shown as positive and expenses (debits) negative, so that profit and loss accounts and worksheets are consistent with the convention that revenues, and profits (credits) are positive.

Chapter 3 showed that, in the year of a combination, the subsidiary's revenues and expenses were included only after combination under acquisition accounting, whereas under merger accounting they were included for the whole year. A simple acquisition accounting consolidated profit and loss account is now discussed:

Example 7.1– 100 per cent owned subsidiary

Largesse has held a 100% interest in Smallnesse for a number of years. Consider the following profit and loss accounts:

Profit and loss accounts for the year ended 31 March 1995

	Largesse £m	Smallnesse £m
Sales	376.0	192.5
Cost of goods sold	(228.0)	(150.0)
Gross profit	148.0	42.5
Distribution costs	(70.0)	(14.0)
Administrative expenses	(30.0)	(6.0)
Dividends receivable	12.0	—
Profit before tax	60.0	22.5
Corporation tax	(20.0)	(7.5)
Profit after tax	40.0	15.0
Dividends	(20.0)	(8.0)
Profit retained	20.0	7.0

Further information :

(1) Smallnesse sold £50m of goods to Largesse during the year but none were in stock at the year end.

(2) Largesse acquired its interest for £100m at 31 March 1991, when the share capital, share premium and retained profits of Smallnesse were £35m, £15m and £30m respectively. Consolidated goodwill is to be written off over 10 years.

(3) Dividends receivable include £4m from Minutenesse plc, in which Largesse holds a 10% investment, acquired some years ago for £35m. Largesse is not in a position to exercise a significant influence over Minutenesse.

Solution

Description	Largesse	Smallnesse	Adjustments	Consolidated
Sales	376.0	192.5	(50.0)	518.5
COGS	(228.0)	(150.0)	50.0	(328.0)
Distribution costs	(70.0)	(14.0)		(84.0)
Admin expenses	(30.0)	(6.0)		(36.0)
Goodwill			(2.0)	(2.0)
Dividends receivable	12.0		(8.0)	4.0
Corporation tax	(20.0)	(7.5)		(27.5)
Profit after tax	40.0	15.0	(10.0)	45.0
Dividends	(20.0)	(8.0)	8.0	(20.0)
Retained for year	20.0	7.0	(2.0)	25.0

Figure 7.1 – Cancellation table for 100% subsidiary

When consolidating profit and loss accounts, there are two important areas:

(a) *Avoidance of double counting* by removing intra-group items. £50m of goods have been sold within the group and resold externally in the year. The internal transfer effects must be removed, here intra-group sales, expenses and dividends. This type of adjustment cancels to zero. The £4m dividend receivable left in the consolidated profit and loss account is £4m from a trade investment (a lack of 'significant influence').

(b) *Making alignment adjustments* to reflect the change in scope of the accounts to a group basis, here the amortization of goodwill (though if immediate write-off had been adopted, it would have bypassed the profit and loss account), and in later examples intra-group stock 'profits'. This type of adjustment does not add to zero since its double entry falls *outside* profit and loss (here goodwill is credited).

Exercise

7.1 Overbearing plc is the parent of Inadequate Ltd, acquiring a 100% interest on 1 July 1992 for £250m when the share capital, share premium and the aggregate retained profits of Inadequate were respectively, £50m, £70m, and £80m. Consolidated goodwill is to be written off over a 5 year period. Consider the following:

Profit and loss accounts for the year ended 30 June 1995

	Overbearing (£'000)	Inadequate (£'000)
Sales	835	460
Cost of sales	(300)	(250)
Gross profit	535	210
Distribution costs	(250)	(50)
Administration expenses	(150)	(70)
Dividends receivable	40	—
Profit before tax	175	90
Corporation tax	(45)	(25)
Profit after tax	130	65
Dividends – interim	(30)	(10)
– final	(50)	(20)
Profit retained	50	35

Further information

(i) Inadequate sold Overbearing £40,000 of goods during the year. Intra-group stocks were zero at the start and end of the year.

(ii) Overbearing has held a 15% stake in Grovel plc for a number of years, which it purchased for £20,000, without being able to exercise 'significant influence'.

Required

Prepare a consolidated profit and loss account for the Overbearing Group for the year ended 30 June 1995.

MINORITY INTERESTS – CONSOLIDATION CONCEPTS

Most people struggle with understanding the treatment of minority interests in consolidated profit and loss accounts. For subsidiaries, minority interests are calculated based on the subsidiary's profit *after* tax, and minority dividends are *not* accounted for in the profit and loss account itself. This section, a digression, examines intuitively *why* minority interests are treated in this way, using the consolidation concepts which were discussed in the context of consolidated balance sheets in Chapter 4. Unlike in Chapter 4, the objective here, however, is specific – to illustrate the structure and 'shape' of consolidated profit and loss accounts when conventional consolidation (subsidiaries) and equity accounting (associates) is used. Because the particular emphasis is to understand mainstream UK practice, the subsection entitled 'Other consolidation concepts' (i.e. proportional and entity approaches) can be omitted without loss in continuity, unless one has a specific desire to explore consolidation concepts *per se*. Proportional consolidation is rarely used in the UK except as a statutory option for non-corporate joint ventures.

The last part of this section, entitled 'The cancellation table and conventional consolidation', continues the earlier cancellation table/worksheet approach to 'doing' consolidated profit and loss accounts, and it is this method that is the basis for the remainder of the chapter.

Example 7.2 – Consolidation concepts

The facts are modified from Example 7.1. Largesse now holds an ongoing 80% interest in Smallnesse and the investment, acquired at 31 March 1991, when the share capital, share premium and retained profits of Smallnesse were £35m, £15m and £30m respectively, is correspondingly reduced pro rata to £80m. Dividends payable by Smallnesse are increased to £10m, reducing its retained earnings to £5m. Intra-group sales, and investment holdings in Minutenesse are as before:

Profit and Loss Accounts for the year ended 31 March 1995 (£m)

	Largesse	Smallnesse
Sales	376.0	192.5
Cost of goods sold	(228.0)	(150.0)
Gross profit	148.0	42.5
Distribution costs	(70.0)	(14.0)
Administration expenses	(30.0)	(6.0)
Dividends receivable	12.0	—
Profit before tax	60.0	22.5
Corporation tax	(20.0)	(7.5)
Profit after tax	40.0	15.0
Dividends payable	(20.0)	(10.0)
Profit retained	20.0	5.0

Required

Prepare consolidated profit and loss accounts for the Largesse Smallnesse Group for the year ended 31 March 1995 under the equity approach and proportional, parent/conventional and entity consolidation concepts.

Solution
Goodwill now becomes £80 – 80% × (35+15+30) = £16m, 80% of its former amount, amortized at £1.6m per annum. This amortization is included in the calculations below.

Equity approach
Under the equity approach, the affiliate's contribution to group profit and loss would be:
Equitized profit for the year   = (80% × Profit after tax) – goodwill amortization

$$= (80\% \times 15m) - 1.6m \qquad\qquad = £10.4m$$

So, *group* profit after tax   = £32m (parent) + £10.4m (Smallnesse)   = £42.4m

The parent's profit is measured prior to intra-group dividends receivable (£40m – £8m = £32m), consistent with the affiliate's equitized profit being calculated before the deduction of dividends. Figure 7.2 progressively expands the £10.4m equitized profit under the different consolidation concepts. The incremental sales etc. of the subsidiary are after eliminating intra-group sales (i.e. 192.5 – 50.0 = £142.5m).

Conventional practice – associates and subsidiaries

The equity approach is used for *associates*. SSAP 1 requires that the equitized profit figure of £10.4m is analysed into profit before taxation (£16.4m) and separately taxation (£6m). When the analysed figures are added to the parent's profit and loss account figures, the group profit and loss account is as shown in Figure 7.3. It can be seen that associates' revenues and expenses are *not* included in the consolidated profit and loss account (analogous to the fact that their individual assets and liabilities are not included in a consolidated balance sheet). Only their profit before taxation and taxation are included. The international standard IAS 28 (para. 30), and APB Opinion 18 in the USA (para. 19c) both require equity accounting for associates, but do not require SSAP 1's further analysis of equitized profit after tax into profit before tax and taxation. Dividends receivable in the group profit and loss account (£4m) relate to Minutenesse, which is a trade investment.

Conventional consolidation is used for *subsidiaries* and *quasi-subsidiaries*. The equitized (80 per cent) profit after tax figure (£10.4m) is analysed under conventional consolidation to show 100 per cent of the subsidiary's individual revenues and expenses, less a single figure (20 per cent) deduction for minority interests in profit after tax. This results in the same *net* contribution of the subsidiary to the group profits as the original equitized (80 per cent) profit after tax. Goodwill amortization under conventional consolidation is based on the parent's share only (the parent approach). The consolidated profit and loss account under conventional consolidation is shown in the third column of Figure 7.3, and has a two-tier structure discussed below. In consolidated profit and loss accounts under conventional consolidation, minority interests are calculated as follows:

| Minority interests = Minority ownership proportion × Subsidiary profit *after* taxation |

In this example the share is 20% of £15m = £13m. This is equal to the aggregate of the minority's share in the subsidiary's individual revenues and expenses, i.e.

20% × [142.5 (sales after elim) – 100 (COGS) – 14 (Distn) – 6 (Admin) – 7.5 (tax)]

The two-tier conventional profit and loss account

Analogous to Chapter 4, profit and loss consolidation can be viewed as *equitization and expansion*. Consolidated profit and loss accounts under proportional and entity approaches deal with the subsidiary on homogeneous 80 per cent and 100 per cent bases respectively. Conventional consolidation is a two-tier hybrid. Revenues and expenses are reported on a 100 per cent basis to profit after tax. Then minority interests in profit *after* tax are removed as a single lump sum. The remainder is on an 80 per cent basis, focusing on to profits attributable to *parent* shareholders.

Equity approach	SSAP 1 approach	Proportional consolidation		Conventional consolidation		Entity consolidation	
		80% Sales	114.0	Sales	142.5	Sales	142.5
		80% COGS	(80.0)	COGS	(100.0)	COGS	(100.0)
		80% Distn.	(11.2)	Distribution	(14.0)	Distribution	(14.0)
		80% Admin	(4.8)	Admin.	(6.0)	Admin.	(6.0)
		Goodwill	(1.6)	Goodwill	(1.6)	Goodwill	(2.0)
	Profit before tax 16.4	*Prop. profit before tax*	16.4	*Parent profit before tax*	20.9	*Entity profit before tax*	20.5
	80% tax (6.0)	80% tax	(6.0)	100% tax	(7.5)	100% tax	(7.5)
				Minority	(3.0)	Minority dividend	(2.0)
						Minority retained	(0.6)
Profit after tax 10.4							

Figure 7.2 – Alternative expansions/treatments of equitized profit

Details	Equity / SSAP1	Proportional	Conventional	Entity
Sales	376.0	490.0	518.5	518.5
Cost of goods sold	(228.0)	(308.0)	(328.0)	(328.0)
Distribution costs	(70.0)	(81.2)	(84.0)	(84.0)
Admin expenses	(30.0)	(34.8)	(36.0)	(36.0)
Goodwill		(1.6)	(1.6)	(2.0)
Dividends rec	4.0	4.0	4.0	4.0
Associate profit before tax	16.4			
Profit before tax	68.4	68.4	72.9	72.5
Corporation tax	(20.0)	(26.0)	(27.5)	(27.5)
Assoc. corp'n tax	(6.0)			
Profit after tax	42.4	42.4	45.4	45.0
Minority interest			(3.0)	
Attributable or Entity profit	42.4	42.4	42.4	*Entity* 45.0
Divs - Largesse	(20.0)	(20.0)	(20.0)	(20.0)
Divs - minority				(2.0)
Retained profits	22.4	22.4	22.4	23.0[*]

* Entity retained profits = £23m = £22.4m (majority share) + £0.6m (minority share)

Figure 7.3 – Consolidated profit and loss accounts under different approaches

Other consolidation concepts

This section can be omitted without loss in continuity. The *proportional* approach, currently optionally used in the UK only for interests in unincorporated joint ventures, expands equitized profit into its proportional (80 per cent) components. The *entity* approach, not used in the UK, includes minority goodwill amortized. Making the assumption that minority goodwill is valued pro-rata with controlling interests' goodwill, we get:

$$\text{Total goodwill write-off} \quad = \quad 100/80 \times £1.6m = £2m$$

and the minority share of this is £0.4m (= £2m – £1.6m), and *entity* minority interest in profit includes their goodwill write-off, i.e. £3.0 – £0.4 (goodwill amortization) = £2.6m. Its disclosures give minority interests greater analysis than conventional consolidation, showing separately minority dividend (i.e. 20% × 10m) and retained earnings (£0.6m), rather than the single figure of the parent approach.

Profit before tax differs under the different approaches. Under the proportional approach and the equity approach, the profit contributed by the subsidiary to the group is 80 per cent of its profit before tax less the parent's goodwill write-off. Under the entity approach it contributes 100 per cent of its profit before tax, less an amortization of the total (i.e. 100 per cent) group goodwill. *Conventional* consolidation is a hybrid, being 100 per cent of its profit before tax less only the parent's (i.e. 80 per cent of group) goodwill. Consolidated profit and loss accounts under each approach are obtained by adding the expansions to the parent's corresponding figures as shown in Figure 7.3.

The Cancellation Table and Conventional Consolidation

The cancellation table for the conventional profit and loss account first used on page 180, is shown in Figure 7.4, now updated for facts of the 80 per cent holding in Smallnesse. Note particularly the change in the dividend payable and in the goodwill figure consequent on the changes in the facts of the case.

A separate column has been added to show the entries relating to minority interests. From the last column it can be seen that, as discussed earlier, their charge in the profit and loss account is based on profit *after* tax (£3m). Also, as discussed earlier, dividends payable in the final column (£20m) only relate to the parent, reflecting the *two-tier* structure of the conventional profit and loss account. In the consolidated *balance sheet*, minority interests is a *credit* balance, increased by their profit and loss interest in profits after tax (i.e. the amount due to them) and decreased by any dividends due to them (i.e. the

Description	Largesse	Smallnesse	Adjustments	Minority interests	Consolidated
Sales	376.0	192.5	(50.0)		518.5
COGS	(228.0)	(150.0)	50.0		(328.0)
Distribution costs	(70.0)	(14.0)			(84.0)
Admin expenses	(30.0)	(6.0)			(36.0)
Goodwill			(1.6)		(1.6)
Dividends receivable	12.0		(8.0)		4.0
Corporation tax	(20.0)	(7.5)			(27.5)
Profit after tax	40.0	15.0	(9.6)		45.4
Minority interests				(3.0)	(3.0)
Dividends	(20.0)	(10.0)	8.0	2.0	(20.0)
Retained for year	20.0	5.0	(1.6)	(1.0)	22.4

Figure 7.4 – Cancellation table showing effects of minority interests

amount paid off). *Check that the final column in Figure 7.4 is identical to the conventional consolidation column in Figure 7.3.*

In the same way as there are two routes to get to the consolidated balance sheet – starting with the parent's profit and loss account, and equitizing and expanding the investment, or starting with both balance sheets and cancelling out redundant elements – the approach adopted in Figure 7.3 and the above cancellation table are the analogous approaches for consolidated profit and loss accounts. Here the expansion approach is only used to explore the nature of the conventional profit and loss account. In future sections only the cancellation table approach is used.

Exercises

7.2 Overbearing plc is the parent of Inadequate Ltd, and acquired a 60% stake in Inadequate on 1 July 1992 for £150m, when the share capital, share premium and the aggregate retained profits of Inadequate were respectively, £50m, £70m, and £80m. Consolidated goodwill is to be written off over a five-year period. Consider the following:

Profit and loss accounts for the year ended 30 June 1995 (£m)

	Overbearing	Inadequate
Sales	835	460
Cost of sales	(300)	(250)
Gross profit	535	210
Distribution costs	(250)	(50)
Administration expenses	(150)	(70)
Dividends receivable	40	
Profit before tax	175	90
Corporation tax	(45)	(25)
Profit after tax	130	65
Dividends – interim	(30)	(20)
– final	(50)	(30)
Profit retained	50	15

Further information

(i) Overbearing sold to Inadequate £40m of goods during the year. Intra-group stocks were zero at the start and end of the year.

(ii) Overbearing has held a 15% stake in Grovel plc for a number of years, which it purchased for £20m, without being able to exercise 'significant influence'.

Required

(a) Calculate the equitized profit after tax for the year relating to Inadequate plc.

(b) Produce a table expanding this figure according to the various consolidation concepts.

(c) Prepare consolidated profit and loss accounts under the various consolidation concepts and contrast the treatment of minority interests under these different approaches.

(d) Prepare a consolidated profit and loss cancellation table as in Figure 7.4 under the conventional consolidation approach.

7.3 Meglo plc acquired a 55% stake in Minnow plc on 31 December 1992 when the latter's retained profits were £10m. The Profit and Loss Accounts for both companies for the year ended 31 December 1995 are as follows. Meglo plc has trade investments other than its investment in Minnow. Goodwill at acquisition of £55m is to be written off over a 10-year period.

Profit and loss accounts – year ended 31 December 1995 (£m)

	Meglo		Minnow	
Sales		400		175
Cost of sales		(150)		(85)
Gross profit		250		90
Distribution costs	(45)		(15)	
Administrative costs	(100)		(25)	
Dividends receivable	28			
		(117)		(40)
Operating profit		133		50
Interest payable		(20)		(10)
Profit before tax		113		40
Taxation		(25)		(8)
Profit after tax		88		32
Dividends payable		(55)		(20)
Retained profit for the year		33		12
Retained profits brought forward		78		35
Retained profits carried forward		111		47

Required
(a) Prepare a table showing the subsidiary's contribution to the consolidated profit and loss account under the equity approach and proportional, conventional and entity consolidation concepts.
(b) Prepare consolidated profit and loss accounts for the Meglo Minnow Group for the year ended 31 December 1995 under the equity approach and proportional, parent/conventional and entity consolidation concepts.

7.4 The company profit and loss accounts in £m for Dredge plc and its 75% subsidiary Barge plc for the year ended 31 December 1995 are as follows. Goodwill at acquisition of £16m is to be amortized over an eight-year period on a straight-line basis.

Profit and loss accounts for the year ended 31 December 1995

	Dredge	Barge
Sales	200	145
Cost of sales	(100)	(80)
Gross profit	100	65
Distribution costs	(30)	(20)
Administration expenses	(20)	(15)
Dividends receivable	9	=
Profit before tax	59	30
Corporation Tax	(18)	(10)
Profit after tax	41	20
Dividends – interim	(5)	(4)
– final	(15)	(8)
Profit retained	21	8

Required
Calculate for the year ended 31 December 1995 in the consolidated profit and loss account under conventional consolidation:
(a) consolidated cost of sales;
(b) consolidated profit after tax;
(c) minority interest charge;
(d) consolidated dividends.

ALIGNMENT ADJUSTMENTS

For the purposes of later sections, Example 7.2 is used with the following additional information relating to alignment adjustments:

1. Smallnesse sold to Largesse £50m of goods during the year. The opening stock of such goods held by Largesse was £10m, and the closing stock, £15m. The mark-up on cost of these goods was 25%. These intragroup stocks are included in the *total* opening and closing stocks held by both companies (e.g. Largesse's externally purchased closing stocks are £50 – £15 = £35m) as follows :

Total stocks	Largesse	Smallnesse
Opening stock	40	25
Closing stock	50	30

Purchases for the year, derived using the above figures and the COGS figures in Example 7.2 were, for Largesse £238m, and Smallnesse £155m.

2. At acquisition, certain of Smallnesse's fixed assets, depreciated straight line over a 4 year period, and used for distribution were revalued upwards by £10m for consolidation purposes.

Unrealized intragroup profit calculation

Unrealized group profits in opening and closing intra-group stocks are:

$$\text{Opening stock} \quad = \quad £10m \times \frac{25}{125} \quad = \quad £2m$$

$$\text{Closing stock} \quad = \quad £15m \times \frac{25}{125} \quad = \quad £3m$$

Opening intragroup stock profits are deferred from last year to this year and closing ones from this year to next (see Chapter 6, Figure 6.2). The top part of Figure 7.5 shows consolidated sales, cost of sales and gross profit using the above data. The shaded area shows the calculation of the cost of goods sold.

Profit & loss	Largesse	Smallness	Transfers	Intra-group Profit	Dividends	Minority interests	Goodwill write off	Extra depreciation	Consolidated
Sales	376.0	192.5	(50.0)						518.5
Opening stock	(40.0)	(25.0)		2.0					(63.0)
Purchases	(238.0)	(155.0)	50.0						(343.0)
Closing stock	50.0	30.0		(3.0)					77.0
Cost of sales	(228.0)	(150.0)	50.0	(1.0)					(329.0)
Distribution costs	(70.0)	(14.0)						(2.5)	(86.5)
Admin costs	(30.0)	(6.0)							(36.0)
Goodwill							(0.8)		(0.8)
Divs received	12.0				(8.0)				4.0
Corporation tax	(20.0)	(7.5)							(27.5)
Minority interests						(2.3)			(2.3)
Dividends	(20.0)	(10.0)			8.0	2.0			(20.0)
Retained profit	20.0	5.0	–	(1.0)	–	(0.3)	(0.8)	(2.5)	20.4

Figure 7.5 – Consolidated profit and loss worksheet: Largesse-Smallnesse Group

Intragroup sales of one company, which are the purchases of the other, are eliminated to prevent double counting. Opening stock has been adjusted to group cost by a consolidation adjustment. This 'reduced' cost flows into this period's consolidated profit. Consolidated cost of sales is lower than the sum of Largesse's and Smallnesse's cost of sales to the extent of this adjustment. Closing stock is also adjusted to group cost, *increasing* consolidated cost of sales. Since cost of sales is a deduction in determining profit, consolidated profit is therefore *increased* by opening stock profits, deferred from last year to this year, and *decreased* by closing stock profits, deferred from this year to next year. The net consolidation adjustment to cost of sales is an increase (credit) of £1m, the subtotal of the 'profit elimination' column.

Fixed asset revaluation and extra depreciation

Subsidiary equity at acquisition is increased by £10m, the increase in fixed assets, the controlling interests' share of which is $80\% \times £10 = £8m$ and hence goodwill falls from the

£16m in Example 7.2 to £8m. This is amortized at £8/10 = £0.8m per annum. The depreciation charge is increased by £2.5m (i.e. £10m/4), included in distribution expenses.

THE CONSOLIDATED PROFIT AND LOSS ACCOUNT WORKSHEET

Figure 7.5 above gives the worksheet including alignment adjustments, which forms the basis for consolidating profit and loss accounts in this book.

Adjustment columns – there is a column for each adjustment and each column total shows the destination, whether debit (positive) or credit (negative), of the other side of the double entry to the profit and loss account. For example, the intra-group profit column total shows that the balance sheet provision for intra-group stock profits (which is deducted from stocks) is to be increased (credited) by £1m for the year, to bring the balance sheet provision to £3m. The net change in minority interests in the balance sheet is an increase (credit) of £0.3m, their share of profits of £2.3m less dividends received of £2m. Consolidated goodwill is credited with £0.8m. Accumulated depreciation is increased by £2.5m. These consolidation adjustments are made in the consolidated working papers.

Minority interests – following FRS 2, *Accounting for Subsidiary Undertakings*, discussed in Chapter 6, intra-group stock profits are to be eliminated in full (100 per cent) against stock in the consolidated balance sheet. The credit is to be made 80 per cent against consolidated retained profits and 20 per cent against minority interests (upstream sale). The net 80% retained profits elimination is achieved in the consolidated profit and loss account by a two-stage process: 100% stock profit elimination in the part before profit *after tax*, then reduced by 20 per cent in the single figure minority interest deduction, leaving a net 80 per cent in the bottom part, to be taken to the balance sheet retained profits caption. Extra depreciation has a similar two-tier treatment.

So the adjustments for unrealized intra-group stock profits in the shaded area of Figure 7.5 totalling (£1m) (i.e. 2–3), are based on 100 per cent elimination, as is the (£2.5m) extra depreciation adjustment just below it. The following equations show that the minority share in profit after tax (now £2.3m, not as earlier £3m) bears 20 per cent of these adjustments, so leaving 80 per cent to be borne by controlling interests. Thus

$$
\begin{aligned}
\text{Minority interests} \quad &= 20\% \times \text{Net profit after tax} & -\,20\% \times \text{Stock adj} & \quad -\,20\% \times \text{Extra depn} \\
&= 20\% \times 15 & -\,20\% \times 1 & \quad -\,20\% \times 2.5 \\
&= \quad 3 \text{ (above)} & -\,0.2 \text{ (stocks)} & \quad -\,0.5 \text{ (depn)} \\
&= £2.3\text{m}
\end{aligned}
$$

Intra-group adjustments revisited
The *net* effect on consolidated retained profits is therefore:

Stocks   £1 (in gross profit) – £0.2 (in minority) = £0.8m (in retained profit)
Extra depn £2.5(in gross profit) –£0.5 (in minority)   = £2.0m (in retained profits)

Exercise

7.5 The facts are as in Question 7.2, except for the following additions:
   (a) Overbearing sold to Inadequate £40m of goods during the year. Opening stocks of such goods held by Inadequate were £12m, and closing stocks £14m. The mark up on cost of such goods was 33 1/3%.
   (b) At acquisition, certain buildings used by central administration were revalued from £60m to £80m. The remaining life of these at that time was estimated at 20 years. Straight line depreciation is used.

Required
Prepare a consolidated profit and loss account worksheet for the year ended 30 June 1995, including the effects of the above adjustments.

7.6 The facts are as in question 7.3, except for the following additions:
(a) At acquisition, Minnow's administrative premises were revalued from £65m to £95m, and their remaining life was estimated at 30 years with a zero salvage value.
(b) At 31 December 1993 Meglo plc sold Minnow plc a fleet of vans used for distribution purposes for £20m (cost to Meglo £14m). Minnow estimates the life of the fleet at 3 years with residual value of £5m.
(c) During the year Minnow plc sold Meglo plc £30m of chemical products at a continuing mark-up on cost of 20%. At 31 December 1994, Meglo plc had £9m of these products in stock, and at 31 December 1995, £12m.
(d) Goodwill at acquisition of £55m is to be written off over a 10-year period.

Required

Prepare a consolidated profit and loss account worksheet for the year ended 31 December 1995, including the effects of the above adjustments.

7.7 The facts are as in Exercise 7.4, and in addition:
(a) Barge plc sold Dredge plc £50m of goods during the year. At 31 December 1994, Dredge had £10m of such goods in stock, and at 31 December 1995, £14m. The mark-up on cost on such goods was 33 1/3%.
(b) When Barge was acquired, its head office premises were revalued from £40m to £80m. The premises are to be amortized on the straight line basis over 40 years.

Required

Calculate for the year ended 31 December 1995 in the consolidated profit and loss account:
(a) consolidated cost of sales;
(b) consolidated profit after tax;
(c) minority interest charge;
(d) consolidated dividends.

LINK WITH CONSOLIDATED BALANCE SHEET

This section shows how the retained profit figure in the consolidated profit and loss account links with the retained profits figures in the opening and closing consolidated balance sheets, how to calculate these linking figures and how to incorporate them into the profit and loss worksheet. The consolidated profit and loss example in this chapter is therefore linked with the Largesse-Smallnesse balance sheet example on Chapter 4 page 76, modified to include alignment adjustments:

Example 7.3 – Links between retained profits figures

Largesse plc acquired 80% of the shares in Smallnesse Ltd for £80m on 31 March 1992 when the retained profits of the two companies were respectively £80m and £30m. It also acquired a 10% stake in Minutenesse on 31 March 1993, held as a trade investment. Their draft financial statements at 31 March 1995, were:

Draft balance sheets at 31 March 1995

	Largesse £m	Smallnesse £m
Fixed assetes	180	40
Investments	100	—
Stocks	50	30
Other assets	90	60
Liabilities	(100)	(20)
Share capital	(130)	(35)
Share premium	(70)	(15)
Retained earnings	(120)	(40)

Profit and loss accounts for the year ended 31 March 1995

	Largesse £m	Smallnesse £m
Sales	376	192.5
Cost of goods sold	(228)	(150)
Gross Profit	148	42.5
Distribution costs	(70)	(14)
Administration expenses	(30)	(6)
Dividends receivable	12	—
Profit before tax	60	22.5
Corporation tax	(20)	(7.5)
Profit after tax	40	15
Dividends payable	(20)	(10)
Profit retained	20	5

Further information

(1) Smallnesse sold to Largesse £50m of goods during the year. The opening amount of such intra-group stocks held by Largesse was £10m and closing, £15m. The mark-up on cost on such goods was 25%. These intra-group stocks are included in the *total* opening and closing stocks below (i.e. the externally purchased closing stock of Largesse is £50m – £15m = £35m) held by both companies:

	Largesse	Smallnesse
Opening stock	40	25
Closing stock	50	30

Total purchases for the year were for Largesse £238m, and Smallnesse £155m.

(2) At acquisition, fixed assets of Smallnesse, depreciated straight-line over a 4 year period, used in distribution were revalued upwards by £10m for consolidation purposes.

The consolidated balance sheet

Figure 7.6 shows the balance sheet cancellation table. Only the *closing* deferral of stock profits affects the consolidated balance sheet.

Deducing opening and closing consolidated retained profits

To calculate opening retained profits, we need the subsidiary's contribution to group retained profits *since acquisition* to add to the parent's figure. To pave the way for the 80% ownership case, consider first the 100% case:

i) Smallnesse (100% owned):

Retained profits at acquisition   = £30m
Retained profits at start of year   = £40m(closing) – £5m (retained for year)   = £35m
So the subsidiary's contribution from acquisition to the start of the year is £5m.

Retained profits at the end of the year   = £40m
So the subsidiary's contribution from acquisition to the end of the year is £10m.

ii) Smallnesse (80% owned):

The subsidiary's contribution from acquisition to the start of the year is 80% × (35 – 30) = £4m and from acquisition to the end of the year, 80% × (40 – 30) = £8m.

And hence consolidated retained earnings (CRE) would be:

Opening CRE	= parent opening + subsidiary contribution to start of year	
	= 100 + 80% × 5	= £104m
Closing CRE	= parent closing + subsidiary contribution to end of year	
	= 120 + 80% × 10	= £128m
	= 104 (consol opening) + 20 (parent for year) + 80% × 5 (subsid for year)	

Details	Investment	Share capital	Share premium	Retained earnings	Goodwill	Minority interests	Stock	Fixed assets
Largesse	80	(130)	(70)	(120)	-	-	50	250
Smallnesse:								
- at acquisition					(64)	(16)		
- since acquisition				(8)		(2)		
Elimination	(80)				80			
Subtotal	-	(130)	(70)	(128)	16	(18)	50	250
Smallnesse:								
Other balances							30	60
Consolidation adj :								
fixed asset reval					(8)	(2)		10
extra depn (3yrs)				6		1.5		(7.5)
goodwill w/o (3 yrs)				2.4	(2.4)			
closing stock profits				2.4		0.6	(3)	
Consol amounts	-	(130)	(70)	(117.2)	5.6	(17.9)	77	312.5

Figure 7.6 balance sheet acquisition table with alignment adjustements

Analysis of Smallnesse retained earnings

A systematic way of obtaining the above results is via a diagrammatic analysis of the subsidiary's retained profits as shown in Figure 7.7, divided as above into three time periods, pre-acquisition, from acquisition to the start of the current year, and finally the current year itself. For each of these periods, change in retained profits is apportioned between majority and minority. The minority interest is ongoing so pre-acquisition and prior year are combined (6 + 1 = £7m). Largesse's 80 per cent portion of Smallnesse's pre-acquisition retained profits (£24m) is used in determining consolidated goodwill.

Date	Retained Earnings	Majority Share (80%)	Minority Share (20%)	Time Period
31 March 1991	30	80% x 30 = 24	20% x 30 = 6	Pre-acquistion
31 March 1994	35	80% x 5 = 4	20% x 5 = 1	Prior year since acq
31 March 1995	40	80% x 5 = 4	20% x 5 = 4	Current year P & L

Figure 7.7 – Analysis of Smallnesse's retained profits with alignment adjustments

Deducing opening and closing retained profits with alignment adjustments

Alignment adjustments, which are apportioned between majority and minority, are placed respectively on the left and right hand sides of the diagram for the three periods. Figure 7.8 summarizes the subsidiary's contribution to retained profits in both consolidated balance sheets and profit and loss accounts.

Alignment adjustments

(i) *Goodwill* – Two years' goodwill was written off prior to 31 March 1994, and one year more in the year to 31 March 1995. Since the minority share of goodwill is not recognized under conventional consolidation, its write-off is made only against the majority stake.

(ii) *Stock* – In upstream sales as in this example, 'profit' eliminations are made according to the ownership proportions of the *originating* company, per FRS 2. Hence the adjustments (£2m at 31 March 1994, and £3m at 31 March 1995) are split 80/20. Extra depreciation is also split 80/20.

Contribution to current year's consolidated retained profits

This is obtained by adding majority share of profit (£4m) *plus* all alignment adjustments in the bottom right hand corner (viz. +1.6 – 0.8 – 2.4 – 2.0 = – £3.6m) making £0.4m.

Stock alignment adjustments

(i) *Profit and loss* – retained profits is affected by the reversal of the previous period's stock adjustment, 1.6, and the deferral of this year's, (2.4), i.e. 1.6 – 2.4 = (0.8).

(ii) *Closing balance sheet* – affected by the addition of all the stock alignment adjustments, i.e. (1.6) + 1.6 – 2.4 = (2.4). This shows that *only* the *closing* adjustment (2.4) is necessary in the balance sheet as discussed in Chapter 6.

Date	Retained earnings	Goodwill	Majority share (80%) Stock	Depreciation	Retained profits Majority	Minority	Minority share (20%) Stock	Depreciation	Time period
					24				Pre-acq
31 Mar 1991	30					7			
		(1.6)	(1.6)	(4.0)	4		(0.4)	(1.0)	Prior year
31 Mar 1994	35								
					1.6				0.4
		(0.8)	(2..4)	(2..0)	4	1	(0.6)	(0.5)	Current year
31 Mar 1995	40								

Figure 7.8 – Smallnesse's retained profits with alignment adjustments

Calculating opening and closing consolidated retained profit figures for the cancellation table

Subsidiary contributions to consolidated amounts (£m)
Opening retained profits (middle left)   = 4 + (1.6) + (1.6) + (4.0) = (£3.2m)
                                                  G/Will   Stock   Depn
Consol retained profits for current year (above)   = 4 + (0.8) + 1.6 + (2.4) + (2.0) = £0.4m
                                                          G/Will   Stock   Depn

Thus, consolidated closing retained profits   =   (3.2) + 0.4   = (£2.8m)

Consolidated amounts (£m)

Opening retained profits = Parent + Subsidiary   =   100   – 3.2   = £96.8m
Retained profits for year   =   20   + 0.4   = £20.4m
Closing retained profits   =   120   – 2.8   = £117.2m

Minority interests (£m)

In opening retained profits (top right)   = 7 + (0.4) + (1.0)   = £5.6m
                                                         Stock   Depn
In current year retained profits (bottom right) = 1 + 0.4 +   (0.6) + (0.5)   = £0.3m
                                                         Stock   Depn
In closing retained profits (top & bottom right) =   5.6 + 0.3   = £5.9m

COMPLETE PROFIT AND LOSS WORKSHEET

The complete worksheet, Figure 7.9, includes consolidated retained profits brought forward (top line), and carried forward (bottom line). Note the highlighted figures above are included in the table – the opening, current year and closing figures in the consolidated retained profits column, and the corresponding figures for minority interests in the 'minority interests' column.

Reconciling retained profits brought forward with the diagrammatic analysis
The top line of Figure 7.9, opening retained profits, is a grossed up version of the diagrammatic analysis of consolidated retained profits in Figure 7.8. Under the diagram-

Profit and loss	Largesse	Smallnesse	Intra Transfers	Profit	group Dividends	Minority interests	Pre-acq profits	Goodwill writeoff	Extra depreciation	Consolida-ted
Ret profit b/f	100.0	35.0		(2.0)		(5.6)	(24.0)	(1.6)	(5.0)	96.8
Sales	376.0	192.5	(50.0)							518.5
Opening stock	(40.0)	(25.0)		2.0						(63.0)
Purchases	(238.0)	(155.0)	50.0							(343.0)
Closing stock	50.0	30.0		(3.0)						77.0
Cost of sales	(228.0)	(150.0)	50.0	(1.0)						(329.0)
Distribution costs	(70.0)	(14.0)							(2.5)	(86.5)
Admin costs	(30.0)	(6.0)								(36.0)
Goodwill								(0.8)		(0.8)
Divs receivable	12.0				(8.0)					4.0
Corporation tax	(20.0)	(7.5)								(27.5)
Minority interests						(2.3)				(2.3)
Dividends	(20.0)	(10.0)			8.0	2.0				(20.0)
Retained profit yr	20.0	5.0		(1.0)		(0.3)		(0.8)	(2.5)	20.4
Retained profit c/f	120.0	40.0	-	(3.0)	-	(5.9)	(24.0)	(2.4)	(7.5)	117.2

Figure 7.9 – Consolidated profit and loss

matic approach, the subsidiary's contribution is based on the parent's proportion of the subsidiary's retained profits since acquisition. The worksheet starts with the whole of the subsidiary's retained profits, removing pre-acquisition and minority retained profits to determine the consolidated figure. These two approaches can be reconciled easily by analysing the minority figure, £5.6m and reallocating its components:

The top line in (£m) is:

Largesse Smallnesse   Stock pr. Goodwill   Minority   Pre acq.   Depn   Consol

100   + 35   –   2   – 1.6   –   5.6   –   24   –   5   = £96.8m

where the £5.6m minority interest comprises £7m – £0.4m (net stock adj) – £1m (extra depreciation). If the minority interests figure of £7m and the pre-acquisition profits figure of £24m is netted off against Smallnesse's total retained profits of £35m, and also the unrealized stock profits element and extra depreciation elements are combined with the other similar items, we get the net version used in the diagrammatic analysis, viz.

Largesse Smallnesse (net)   Stock pr.(net)   Goodwill   Depn (net)   Consol
100 + (35 – 24– 7) –   (2 – 0.4)   –   1.6   –   (5 – 1)   =   £96.8m, i.e.
100 +   4   –   1.6   –   1.6   –   4   =   £96.8m

The diagrammatic analysis can be used

i. to check the worksheet top line for opening retained profits
ii. to help calculate many of its adjustments (e.g. pre-acquisition profits of £24m and minority interests of £5.6m).

However, in the worksheet, the unrealized stock profit and extra depreciation figures are 100 per cent figures, not *majority* figures as in the diagrammatic analysis. Similar relationships can be deduced for the profit for the year (subtotal) and for closing retained profits (bottom line).

Other aspects of the worksheet – completing the double entry
The bottom line of the complete worksheet gives total entries made in the consolidated balance sheet:

(£3m)   credit to consolidated stocks
(£2.4m)   written off (credit) consolidated goodwill to date
(£5.9m)   the retained profits element in minority interests
(£24m)   the retained profits eliminated to obtain goodwill

The £5.9m retained earnings credit to minority interests is not the whole of the balance sheet figure which also includes its stake in the subsidiary's share capital, share premium *and* retained earnings:

Minority at 31 March 1995   =   20% × (s cap + s prem + rev res) + 20% × ret profits
                            =   20% × (35 + 15 + 10)   +   5.9 = £17.9m

Similarly the goodwill figure is obtained by subtracting the total pre-acquisition equity, not just the pre-acquisition retained profits, from the investment:

Goodwill at acq =   Inv − 80% × (s cap + s prem + rev res) − 80% × Ret profits at acq
                =   80 − 80% × (35 + 15 + 10) − 24 (above)   = £8m

Goodwill now   =   £8m − £2.4m (above)   = £5.6m

and these figures tie up with the balance sheet cancellation table in Figure 7.6.

Checking minority interests in the consolidated profit and loss account

In the consolidated profit and loss account, the minority interests deduction is in profits *after* tax, as shown in Example 7.2, i.e.

20% × (15 (profit after tax) − 1 (stock profit increase) − 2.5 (extra depreciation))= £2.3m

The diagrammatic analysis can be used to check this computation.

Minority interest in *retained* profits for the year (bottom right) = 1 + 0.4 − 0.6 − 0.5 = £0.3m
Add back minority interest in subsidiary dividends   = 20% × £10m   = £2.0m
Equals minority interest in profit after tax   = £2.3m

In more intricate examples direct calculation is complex and can be checked by a separate diagrammatic analysis of retained profits for each subsidiary.

ABBREVIATING THE CANCELLATION PROCESS

One can dispense with the diagrammatic analysis of reserves, and calculate directly using the cancellation worksheet when one is familiar with and proficient in handling the above relationships. A further shortcut is condensing the analysis columns into two, debit and credit, an approach taken by many accounting texts – fine for examination purposes *after* one understands the cancellation relationships, but not very helpful at the outset. Further, such abbreviation is prone to error in complex examples, where the fuller layout provides a more systematic treatment. The reader is advised to become familiar with the full approach before abridging it.

Exercises

7.8 The Overbearing-Inadequate example is repeated with additional data to show the link between financial statements, which are as follows:

Profit and loss accounts for the year ended 30 June 1995 (£m)

	Overbearing	Inadequate
Sales	835	460
Cost of sales	(300)	(250)
Distribution costs	(250)	(50)
Administration expenses	(150)	(70)
Dividends receivable	40	—
Profit before tax	175	90
Corporation tax	(45)	(25)
Profit after tax	130	65
Dividends – interim	(30)	(20)
– final	(50)	(30)
Profit retained for year	50	15
Retained profit b/f	150	140
Retained profit c/f	200	155

Balance Sheets at 30 June 1995 (£m)

	Overbearing	inadequate
Fixed assets	300	200
Investments	170	—
Stocks	220	180
Other assets	100	170
Liabilities	(320)	(275)
Share capital	(100)	(50)
Share premium	(170)	(70)
Retained profits	(200)	(155)

Further information

(i)   Overbearing acquired a 60% interest in Inadequate on 1 July 1992 for £150m when the share capital, share premium and retained earnings of Inadequate were respectively, £50m, £70m and £80m.

(ii) Overbearing sold to Inadequate £40m of goods during the year. Opening stocks of such intra-group transfers held by Inadequate amounted to £12m, and closing stocks to £14m. The mark-up on cost of such goods was 33 1/3%. The total purchases of both companies were £320m and £270m respectively.

(iii) At acquisition, certain buildings of Inadequate, used by central administration were revalued from £60m to £80m. The remaining life of those buildings at that time was estimated at 20 years (depreciated straight line).

(iv) Overbearing has held a 15% stake in Grovel plc for a number of years, which it purchased for £20m. It is not in a position to exercise significant influence.

(v)   Consolidated goodwill is amortized straight-line over a 5 year period.

Required

(a) Prepare a balance sheet cancellation table at 30 June 1995.

(b) (i)   Analyse diagrammatically Inadequate's retained profits at that date.
    (ii) Incorporate alignment adjustments into the diagram.
    (iii) Calculate consolidated retained profits and minority interests at 30 June 1995.

(c) Prepare a profit and loss account worksheet for the year ended 30 June 1995, linking the closing retained profits with the balance sheet cancellation table in part (a). (The solution to Exercise 7.5 can be adapted by adding a top line (retained profits brought forward) and bottom line (carried forward)).

(d) Discuss the relationships between figures in the profit and loss worksheet and the balance sheet cancellation table.

7.9 The Meglo-Minnow example is repeated with additional data to show the link between financial statements, which are as follows. Meglo plc acquired a 55% stake in Minnow plc on 31 December 1992 for £128m when the latter's share capital, share premium and retained profits were £30m, £90m and £10m. The profit and loss accounts for both companies for the year ended 31 December 1995 are as follows. Meglo plc has trade investments other than its investment in Minnow.

Profit and loss accounts – year ended 31 December 1995 (£m)

		Meglo		Minnow
Sales		400		175
Cost of sales		(150)		(85)
Gross profit		250		90
Distribution costs	(45)		(15)	
Administrative costs	(100)		(35)	
Dividends receivable	28		10	
		(117)		(40)
Operating profit		133		50
Interest payable		(20)		(10)
Profit before tax		113		40
Taxation		(25)		(8)
Profit after tax		88		32
Dividends payable		(55)		(20)
Retained profit for the year		33		12
Retained profits brought forward		78		35
Retained profits carried forward		111		47

Balance sheets at 31 December 1995 (£m)

	Meglo	Minnow
Fixed assets	400	110
Investments	208	—
Stocks	90	40
Other assets	100	57
Liabilities	(120)	(40)
Share capital	(200)	(30)
Share premium	(367)	(90)
Retained profits	(111)	(47)

Further information
(a) At acquisition, Minnow's administrative premises were revalued from £65m to £95m, and their remaining life was estimated at 30 years with a zero salvage value.
(b) At 31 December 1993 Meglo plc sold Minnow plc a fleet of vans used for distribution purposes for £20m (cost to Meglo £14m). Minnow estimates the life of the fleet at 3 years with residual value of £5m.
(c) During the year Minnow plc sold Meglo plc £30m of chemical products at a continuing mark-up on cost of 20%. At 31 December 1994   , Meglo plc had £9m of these products in stock, and at 31 December 1995, £12m.
(d) Goodwill at acquisition is to be written off over a 10 year period.
(e) None of these adjustments have been 'pushed-down' into the records of Minnow plc.

Required
(a) Prepare a balance sheet cancellation table at 31 December 1995.
(b) (i)   Analyse diagrammatically Minnow's retained profits at that date.
    (ii) Incorporate alignment adjustments into the diagram.
    (iii) Calculate consolidated retained profits and minority interests at 31 December 1995.
(c) Prepare a profit and loss account worksheet for the year ended 31 December 1995, linking the retained profits carried forward with the balance sheet cancellation table in part (a). (The solution to Exercise 7.6 can be adapted by adding a top line (retained profits brought forward) and bottom line (carried forward)).
(d) Discuss the relationships between figures in the profit and loss worksheet and the balance sheet cancellation table.

ASSOCIATES AND THE WORKSHEET

Associates are accounted for in the consolidated profit and loss account on a profits rather than a dividends basis. Therefore an associate is incorporated into the consolidation worksheet by removing dividends from associate, and replacing them by the proportionate share of profits before tax, and separately its proportionate share of tax. Its revenues and expenses are *not* included in the consolidated figures (see Figure 7.3) but SSAP 1 requires them to be a note disclosure if 'the results of one or more associated companies are so material [from a group perspective] that more detailed information . . . would assist in giving a true and fair view' (para. 23). SSAP 1 also requires the group's aggregate share of associates' extraordinary items to be included with the group's and separately disclosed if extraordinary from a *group* perspective. This corresponds to similar international requirements in IAS 28 and APB Opinion 18, but the requirement is likely to be redundant in the UK because of the effective emasculation of extraordinary items as a class (see Chapter 8).

Example 7.4 – Treatment of associates

In Example 7.3, suppose that instead of acquiring a 10% stake in Minutenesse plc, Largesse had acquired a 40% stake for £35m a number of years ago, when the equity of Minuteness plc comprised: share capital £10m, share premium £15m and retained profits of £15m. The group writes off all goodwill over 10 years on a straight-line basis. Largesse is in a position to exercise significant influence over Minutenesse. Extracts from Minutenesse plc's profit and loss account for the year ended 31 March 1995 are as follows:

	£m
Profit before tax	25
Corporation tax	(8)
Profit after tax	17
Dividends	(10)
Retained profits	7

Required

Show how Minutenesse plc will be dealt with in the consolidated profit and loss account for the Largesse Group for the year ended 31 March 1995, and prepare a consolidated profit and loss account at that date.

Solution

Because Largesse plc can exercise significant influence, Minutenesse plc is an associate and the *equity* approach is used:

Attributable profit before tax	= 40% × Minutenesse profit before tax − Goodwill write-off
	= 40% × 25 − 1/10 × 19
	= £8.1m

(where goodwill at acquisition = 35 − 40% x (10 + 15 + 15) = £19m), and
Associate's taxation = 40% × 8 = £3.2m

In Figure 7.9, we adjust the final column by removing the dividends receivable by Largesse of £4m (= 40% × £10m), and replacing them by the above two entries to get:

Largesse Group – Consolidated profit and loss account for the year ended 31 March 1995

	£m	£m
Sales		518.5
Cost of sales		(329.0)
Gross profit		189.5
Distribution costs	86.5	
Administration expenses	36.0	
Goodwill write-off	0.8	
		(123.3)
Associated undertakings		8.1
Profit before tax		74.3
Corporation tax group	27.5	
associates	3.2	
		(30.7)
Profit after tax		43.6
Minority interests		(2.3)
Profit for the financial year		41.3
Dividends		(20.0)
Profit retained for the year		21.3

The revenues and expenses of Minutenesse are *not* added to the group's (see the equity approach in Figure 7.3). Reconciling the above retained profits figure for the year with the final column of Figure 7.9:

20.4 (per Figure 7.9) − 4 (dividends) + 8.1 (assoc profit before tax) − 3.2 (assoc tax) = £21.3m

Associated company goodwill amortized appears in the consolidated profit and loss as part of the aggregate figure for associated company profit or loss before taxation and not with any separately labelled consolidated goodwill amortization (analogous to the fact that other associate revenues and expenses do not appear separately).

Exercise

7.10 In Exercise 7.5, now assume that Overbearing owns a 40% stake in Grovel plc. Extracts from Grovel's profit and loss account for the year ended 30 June 1995 are:

	£m
Profit before tax	55
Corporation tax	(15)
Profit after tax	40
Dividends	(25)
Retained profits	15

(i)   The stake was acquired for £20m a number of years ago, when Grovel's equity was: share capital £5m, share premium £5m and retained profits of £20m. Overbearing is deemed in a position to exercise significant influence over Grovel.

(ii) The group writes off all goodwill over 5 years on a straight-line basis.

Required

Prepare a consolidated profit and loss account for the year ending 30 June 1995 (ignoring brought forward and carried forward balances) for the Overbearing Group, and show how Grovel plc is to be treated.

7.11   In exercise 7.6, now assume that Meglo owns a 50% stake in Roe plc. Extracts from Grovel's profit and loss account for the year ended 31 December 1995 are:

	£m
Profit before tax	81
Corporation tax	(27)
Profit after tax	54
Dividends	(34)
Retained profit	20

(i)   The stake was acquired for £65m three years ago, when Roe's equity was: share capital £25m, share premium £35m and retained profits of £60m. Overbearing is deemed in a position to exercise significant interest over Roe.

(ii) The group writes off all goodwill over 5 years on a straight-line basis.

Required

Prepare a consolidated profit and loss account for the year ending 31 December 1995 (ignoring brought forward and carried forward balances) for the Meglo Group, and show how Roe plc is to be treated.

SUMMARY

*Two areas are important: the **elimination** of intragroup flows (e.g. sales, purchases, dividends), and making **alignment adjustments** to reflect the change in scope of the accounts to a group basis. There is a **spectrum** of approaches for the treatment of minority interests in the consolidated profit and loss account. Conventional consolidation (the parent approach) results in a **two-tier** profit and loss account. Above profit after taxation, 100 per cent of revenues and expenses are shown (except goodwill which is based on the controlling interests' stake only). The minority share in **profits after tax** is removed and below this, the statement deals with the controlling interests' share only.*

Alignment adjustments follow the same logic as in Chapters 5 and 6. Unrealized stock profit adjustments for the previous period are realized by the group in this period, and for this period *deferred until future periods. The minority calculation is affected by certain alignment adjustments (e.g. where unrealized intra-group stock profits are split pro rata in **upstream** sales). Calculations to effect the link between balance sheet and profit and loss account are systematically set out by a **diagrammatic** analysis of the subsidiary's retained profits and alignment adjustments.*

8

REPORTING FINANCIAL PERFORMANCE (2)

This chapter examines the reporting of *published* consolidated performance statements. Prior to FRS 3, *Reporting Financial Performance*, issued in October 1992, such reporting focused very narrowly on profit before extraordinary items, used for the then calculation of earnings per share. The debate then centred on which items should be included in this measure, and on the ancillary issue of which items could bypass the profit and loss account altogether by being taken direct to reserves – the subject of four exposure drafts (ED 5, 7, 16 and 36), one standard and its revision (SSAP 6), by the ASC. The ASB has introduced through FRS 3 a radically different approach which introduces a variety of performance statements, redefines extraordinary items and earnings per share, and introduces a range of new disclosures. First the published consolidated profit and loss account is considered, including the acquisition and disposal of subsidiaries during the reporting period. Then group accounting aspects of the other statements and reconciliations required by FRS 3 are examined, followed by an analysis of the standard.

PUBLISHED CONSOLIDATED PROFIT AND LOSS ACCOUNTS

Companies Act 1985 profit and loss account formats

The Companies Act 1985 in Schedule 4 Part 1 requires the choice of one from four possible profit and loss account formats. Formats 1 and 2 are in vertical form, whereas 3 and 4, which segregate income from charges, are rarely used in the UK. The choice between Formats 1 and 2 is significant, in that 1 analyses expenses by *function* (e.g. cost of sales, distribution costs, administrative expenses), whereas 2 analyses expenses by *type* (e.g. cost of raw materials used, depreciation, staff costs etc.). In this chapter, the examples comply with Format 1.

Goodwill and extra depreciation

Under Format 1, items like depreciation, goodwill etc., are apportioned over the relevant functional headings (e.g. manufacturing depreciation will be classified as cost of goods sold, etc.). The Act does not specify how goodwill write-off is to be classified. Most companies using Format 1 do not disclose where goodwill is included if gradual amortization is chosen, though under this option SSAP 22 requires an analysis of movements on the goodwill account, including the amount amortized in the year, but not the disclosure of which expense heading this amount is included under. Using the Act's flexibility to allow increased disclosure, goodwill amortized is given a separate heading in the examples here, since it is difficult to justify classification under another functional heading.

It is assumed here that fixed assets restated to fair values at acquisition are related to distribution. If instead they were to relate to manufacturing, part of the extra depreciation charge would relate to cost of sales and part to closing stocks if absorption costing is used. The charge for cost of goods sold would therefore include extra depreciation as follows:

> *last year's absorbed in opening stocks + extra charge for year – this year's in closing stocks.*

In practice, the accounting policies of companies in this area are rarely disclosed. Either companies make such an adjustment or decide it is immaterial where intragroup stock levels remain approximately constant. However, it may not be immaterial if a new subsidiary is acquired during the year, the fair value adjustment was large, stock levels change substantially, or the absorption basis or rates change substantially. This problem arises under all formats.

Minority interests

Schedule 4A Section 17 of the amended Companies Act 1985 requires that minority interests be measured *after* taxation but *before* extraordinary items and disclosed between the headings 'profit or loss on ordinary activities after taxation' and 'extraordinary items'. Minority interests in extraordinary items should further be disclosed as part of the breakdown of the extraordinary items figure, measured net of tax.

Associated undertakings

SSAP 1 requires the separate disclosure of the parent's share of: (a) profit before tax, (b) taxation, (c) extraordinary items, and (d) net profit retained by associated companies. If additional information is to be given (e.g. turnover, depreciation etc.) it should be done by means of a note, not in the statements themselves – consistent with the equity approach.

The measurement and disclosure of income prior to FRS 3
This section can be omitted without loss of continuity by those wishing only to focus on current UK requirements. The consolidated profit and loss account is only one caption under 'Capital and Reserves', and what should be included in it is dependent on the wider issue of deciding the optimal way of disclosing changes in shareholder funds, discussed here only in so far as is necessary to appreciate group accounting features. For example, possibilities range from separate statements for each class of reserves, profit and loss being one such statement, to a single aggregated statement for all changes. Another issue relates to the classification of movements within such statement(s).

Historically there have been two main schools:

(i)   the *all inclusive* or *comprehensive* income approach (the former term used by ARB 43 published in 1953, the latter by the FASB in SFAC 6), colloquially known in the USA as the *clean surplus* approach. Income or surplus is defined as 'the change in equity of a business enterprise during a period from transactions and other events and circumstances from non-owner sources' (i.e. everything apart from share issues and dividends).

(ii) the *current operating performance* (or *profit from ordinary activities*) approach, which focuses on the income from the 'normal' operations of an enterprise. Other reserve movements, whilst disclosed, are assumed of lesser importance. It is driven by the search for a reliable performance measure, and its imperative is to segregate items not relating to ordinary activities from those which do.

In practice the two schools are not necessarily mutually exclusive, and the FASB in the USA, for example, distinguishes between 'earnings' and 'comprehensive income', allowing a comprehensive income statement to disclose earnings (on ordinary activities) as an intermediate total.

Until recently, the UK has (in three exposure drafts ED 5, ED 7 and ED 36 and a revised standard, SSAP 6) fallen between the two 'pure' approaches. The current year consolidated profit and loss account had implicitly focused on providing a main profit measure (on ordinary activities) mandated by SSAP 3 for calculating *earnings per share* (EPS), and hence the *price-earnings ratio* (PE ratio), but was extended to include 'extraordinary items'. The term 'above the line' was coined to include all items used in calculating EPS, and 'below the line' for the rest. SSAP 6 had strictly ring-fenced items which could bypass current year profit and loss as 'prior year adjustments' and 'reserve movements'.

SSAP 6, issued in 1974 defined four classifications:

(a)   *Exceptional* items – deriving from ordinary activities ('above the line'), needing separate disclosure because of their size and incidence.

(b)   *Extraordinary* items – 'deriving from events or transactions outside ordinary activities and thus not expected to recur frequently or regularly' and material – 'below the line', net of tax.

(c)   *Prior year adjustments* – not the normal recurring corrections or adjustments of prior year accounting estimates, but tightly defined to include *only* material adjustments arising from changes in accounting policies or the correction of fundamental errors. These were disclosed as a restatement of retained profits brought forward and comparatives, and therefore did not have to appear on the face of the profit and loss account.

(d)   *Reserve movements* – only specified items were allowed to bypass the profit and loss account including fixed asset revaluations, and in the context of group accounting, immediate goodwill write-off (SSAP 22) and foreign currency translation gains or losses under the closing rate approach (SSAP 20), discussed in Chapter 11.

Categories (c) and (d) proved relatively uncontroversial. Prior year adjustments were severely restricted presumably to prevent window-dressing. The most controversial area was the distinction between 'exceptional' and 'extraordinary', which straddled the boundary of the then widely used performance measure, profit *after* tax and minority interests, *before* extraordinary items, and in this context the most frequently disputed items related to group matters.

Prior to FRS 3, Skeratt and Tonkin (1992, p. 276) reported that out of 300 companies examined, 54 per cent reported profits or losses on sales of fixed assets, investments, businesses or subsidiaries as extraordinary, and 45 per cent as exceptional. For discontinuance, reorganization and redundancy expenses, the figures were 55 per cent extraordinary and 28 per cent exceptional. More than half the companies had extraordinary items relating to the two areas!

Policing has been a nightmare, and various surveys revealed the then tendency for large negative items to be accounted for 'below the line' and large positive items above it! *Accountancy* (March 1993, p. 1) commented that only 5 per cent of US listed companies report extraordinary items in a comparable period.

The newly formed ASB's Urgent Issues Task Force issued UITF Abstract 2, *Restructuring Costs*, in October 1991, to prevent what it saw as an abuse of the extraordinary items category, noting that the treatment of restructuring and reorganizations had been subject to 'varying and selective interpretations'. Even fundamental restructuring costs could now only be treated as extraordinary if the event or transaction giving rise to such costs was itself extraordinary. Tonkin and Skerratt (1993, pp. 24–5) noted that the incidence of extraordinary restructuring costs then decreased. The ASB also issued a discussion draft and an exposure draft on the reporting of financial performance (FRED 1) in 1991.

FRS 3 AND THE CONSOLIDATED PROFIT AND LOSS ACCOUNT

The subsequent standard, FRS 3, *Reporting Financial Performance*, instituted radical changes including the redefinition of exceptional and extraordinary items, new reporting requirements for acquired and discontinued operations, additional statements, including one – the statement of total gains and losses – which functions like a comprehensive income statement, and the deliberate de-emphasis of a single performance measure by redefining earnings per share. In this section we only consider FRS 3's impact on the consolidated profit and loss account. FRS 3 applies to all financial statements intended to give a true and fair view of an entity's financial position and profit or loss (or income and expenditure), unless not permitted by the entity's statutory reporting framework (para.

12). Three major areas in the profit and loss account are examined in the order they would be encountered in reading down it – the determination of operating profit; between operating profit and profit before interest; then 'below the line', extraordinary items.

Analysis down to operating profit – acquisitions, continuing and discontinued operations

FRS 3 took matters considerably further than UITF Abstract 2 by requiring much greater disclosure of continuing and discontinued activities 'above the line' as now discussed. FRS 3 requires separate disclosure of continuing operations, acquisitions (as a separate component of such operations) and discontinued operations. Each statutory heading between turnover and operating profit must be so analysed either on the face of the profit and loss account or as a note. At least turnover and operating profit must be analysed on the *face* of the main profit and loss account.

Interest and tax are not required to be analysed into the three areas, since for many groups financing is on a group-wide basis, but if they are the basis must be disclosed (para. 14). FRS 3 contains the somewhat enigmatic statement that 'for non-financial reporting entities operating profit is normally before income from shares in group undertakings, although in certain cases income from associated undertakings or from other participating interests may be considered to be part of operating profit' (para. 39) without giving any guidance on what such circumstances might be. This is not helped by the fact that FRS 3 does not define operating profit.

Though 'acquisitions' and 'discontinued operations' do not necessarily refer to subsidiaries or even group accounting, in practice they usually do, and are therefore illustrated here in a group accounting context through the technique of acquiring and disposing of subsidiaries.

Acquisitions

Traditionally there were two alternative approaches to including the results of subsidiaries acquired during the year:

(i)   *Post*-acquisition revenues and expenses of the subsidiary are added to those of the parent.
(ii) The subsidiary's revenues and expenses for the *whole* year are added to the parent's, and *pre*-acquisition profits of the subsidiary are removed at the profits after tax stage.

FRS 3 indicates that it wishes the first approach to be used, i.e. *as if* the subsidiary had been purchased as a set of assets, liabilities and goodwill at the acquisition date. In the US the second approach is used. The term 'acquisitions' is helpfully defined as 'operations of the reporting entity that are acquired in the period'! They are not limited to acquisitions of subsidiaries, but in this case FRS 2 defines the date of acquisition as the date control passes (see Chapter 5).

Discontinued operations

The term 'discontinued operations' refers to material sales or terminations of operations or activities whose assets, liabilities and results are clearly distinguishable physically, operationally and for reporting purposes, representing a material reduction in the reporting entity's operating facilities resulting either from:

(i)   its withdrawal from a particular market, whether class of business or geographical, or
(ii) a material reduction in turnover in the reporting entity's continuing markets (para. 4).

Further, the sale or termination, a 'termination' being defined as a permanent cessation of activities, must be completed prior to a qualifying date:

(a) in the period, or

(b) before the *earlier* of three months into the next period and the date of approval of financial statements (para. 4).

Somewhat controversially, reorganization or restructuring costs relating to continuing operations should be accounted for under continuing operations, even though they are consequent on a sale or termination (para. 17). Income and costs associated with a sale or termination not completed by the above qualifying date must be included in continuing operations, though FRS 3 states that it may be appropriate in a note to the accounts to show the results of operations which are in the process of discontinuing, but not discontinued (para. 41). The standard requires hard evidence of sales, a binding agreement, and for terminations, a detailed formal plan which the reporting entity cannot realistically withdraw.

Discontinued operations could include, for example, disposals of a division or the material contraction of a particular category of business operations at one extreme, to disposals of a large, multi-company business segment or even all foreign operations at the other. It is not necessarily tied to the disposal of subsidiaries, and further, not all disposals of subsidiaries will meet the criteria for discontinued operations – e.g. if they are not material. The example given by FRS 3 of a sale 'which has a material effect on the nature and focus of the reporting entity's operations and represent a material reduction in its operating facilities [etc.]' are either a hotel chain in the lower end of the market which sold its existing chain and bought instead luxury hotels, whilst still remaining in business to manage hotels, or a similar chain which sold all its US hotels, and bought European ones instead (para. 42). Further examples in this area are provided by Wild and Goodhead (1993a, pp. 92–92). In this chapter the focus is on the disposal of a single subsidiary, which we assume qualifies as a discontinued operation. FRS 2 defines the date of disposal of a subsidiary as the date control is relinquished.

The US has since 1973 required separate disclosure of discontinued operations on the face of the income statement, and the revised IAS 8 (1993) *Net Profit for the Period, Fundamental Errors and Changes in Accounting Policies,* requires note disclosures about discontinued operations, but not analysis on the face of the profit and loss account.

Comparative figures

FRS 3 requires restatement of last period's comparatives to reflect this period's status of the operations concerned. Therefore last period's continuing operations, as restated, will correspond to the same operations as this period's continuing operations. This has the following consequences:

(a) any operations corresponding to this period's discontinued operations (which would have been part of last period's continuing operations) must be reclassified for comparative purposes as discontinued in last period's comparatives.
(b) last period's discontinued operations will still be classed as discontinued.
(c) last period's acquisitions will be subsumed in the continuing operations category for last period but not be separately disclosed in the comparative figures.

Therefore to compare the effects on operating profits of last year's acquisitions with this year's it will be necessary to refer to the previous year's financial statements.

In principle it is possible to see that for forecasting purposes a consistent definition of continuing operations may be helpful. However, there are problems even with last year's restated comparatives since last year's acquisitions will only be included for the part of last year they were owned. This year (as part of continuing operations other than acquisitions) they will be held for the whole year, so comparing last year's continuing operations with this year's continuing operations is still not comparing like with like. Some readjustment for last year's acquisitions will need to be made for the period they were not held if one wishes to make a comparison. If they were substantial acquisitions (see Chapter 5), FRS 6 requires this information to be disclosed, but on the basis of the acquired entity's accounting policies (para. 36, see also Chapter 5). Therefore, if material, some attempt would have to be made to compute the effects of fair value adjustments at acquisition on subsequent profit measurement. Another cruder approach would be to try to adjust the 'acquisitions' part of last year's FRS 3 profit and loss account on some kind of pro rata basis for the whole year, but this would be difficult if there were a number of acquisitions taking place at different times.

However, it is still a moot point whether such simplistic projections are of value if the group has been reorganized or economic conditions have radically changed. As if to illustrate the point, FRS 3 states that, if it is not practicable to determine the post-acquisition results of an acquisition (e.g. because its activities have been reorganized and integrated with the other companies in the group) a (qualitative) indication of its contribution to the turnover and operating profits of the continuing operations must be given, or if even this is not possible, that fact and the reason must be given (para. 16).

This is not the only place where the ASB 'violates' the principle that last year's reported figures are this year's comparatives in that, as discussed in Chapter 3, comparatives under merger accounting are restated for the previous year as if the parties had always been combined. Chopping (1993, p. 7) comments that restatement of comparatives in principle has no limit and that the ASB should clarify what its impact should be on say 5 year summaries. However, as a general rule it seems reasonable that usefulness can override mere convention.

Exceptional items

Under FRS 3 exceptional items are

> Material items which derive from events or transactions that fall within the ordinary activities of the reporting entity and which individually or, if of a similar type, in aggregate, need to be disclosed by virtue of their size or incidence if the financial statements are to give a true and fair view   (para. 5).

FRS 3 requires most exceptional items to be reported under the statutory profit and loss headings to which they relate. However, certain exceptional items and provisions in respect of such items are to be separately disclosed on the face of the profit and loss account between 'operating profit' and 'profit before interest'. These should also be analysed between acquisitions, other continuing items and discontinued operations.

Separately disclosed exceptional items and related provisions
Separately disclosed exceptional items shown on the face of the profit and loss account between 'operating profit' and 'profit before interest' include

(a)   profits or losses on sales or terminations of operations; and
(b)   costs of fundamental reorganizations and restructurings having a material effect on the nature and focus of the reporting entity's operations;
(c)   profits or losses on fixed asset disposals.

Headings for (a) and (c) must be disclosed if they contain material items even if the *net* balance is immaterial, when note disclosures must analyse elements of such netting. Tax and minority interests effects must be disclosed in the notes in aggregate unless they differ for the categories when further disclosures must be given (para. 20).

The main items which concern us in this book are (a) and (b). Though both can in principle occur in individual company accounts, in practice they will be mainly group accounting matters and this aspect is discussed here.

The timing of reported profits in each category will be affected by the use of provisions and in accordance with its policy of 'transparency', the ASB requires in FRS 3 not only the reporting of the profit effect of the setting up of provisions, but also in the period they are used, the costs set against them and the amount previously provided must be disclosed on the face of the profit and loss account (para. 18). We now consider in turn (a) and b).

Profits or losses and provisions relating to discontinued operations

General principles – if the discontinued operation involves the disposal of a subsidiary, and this satisfies FRS 3's criteria described above, FRS 2 requires that:

(a) the date of disposal is the date that control is relinquished, and
(b) consolidated financial statements in the disposal period should include the subsidiary's results up to the disposal date, and any gain or loss to the extent it has not already been provided for.

Such gain or loss is to be determined by comparing the disposal proceeds with the *consolidated* carrying values of the attributable net assets of the subsidiary at the disposal date, plus any related goodwill not previously written off to consolidated profit and loss. It is helpful to remember that in Chapter 4 consolidation was characterized as equitization and expansion. When a subsidiary is disposed of, this notional expansion is reversed and the 'book' value on disposal is obtained by *contracting* the subsidiary's balances (assets, liabilities, *goodwill* and minority) back into its *equitized* amount at the date of disposal which is then matched with the sales proceeds.

Provisions – the problem faced by the ASB in framing its requirements for sale and termination provisions is that of preventing the manipulation of profit from one period to the next, since all provisions in principle merely alter timing. In the name of prudence the recognition of 'losses' or 'costs' can be accelerated legitimately. However, they can also be brought into periods where profits are too high as a cushion, or overestimated and the excess released in future 'sparse' periods. Accordingly FRS 3 sees two movements; the first to limit management's discretion in when provisions can be set up, moving from a prior basis of management *intention* more towards an *obligations* ('demonstrable commitment') basis; the second to limit the range of costs etc. that can be provided for ('direct costs'). Such a dual pincer movement has already been seen in Chapter 5 when FRS 7, *Fair Values at Acquisition,* was discussed. FRS 3's requirements are now discussed in more detail.

FRS 3 allows provisions relating to terminations or sales to be set up only to the extent that obligations have already been *incurred.* They are limited to direct costs and operating losses up to the termination or sale date to the extent they are not expected to be covered by profits to that date or by disposal profits (para. 18). They should only be set up from the date of *demonstrable commitment* to the discontinuance, indicated by, for example, a binding sales agreement or a detailed formal plan which the reporting entity cannot realistically withdraw. Prior to FRS 3 provisions tended to be made earlier (see for example Wild and Goodhead, 1994, p. 90). Further, if the sale or termination is not completed by the current period's qualifying date, such provisions must be included in 'continuing operations' for this period. However, when they are used up, they are reported under the relevant category, e.g. 'discontinued operations', in *that* period, even though they might have been set up under 'continuing operations' originally (para. 18).

The treatment of goodwill --FRS 2, *Accounting for Subsidiary Undertakings*, requires that the consolidated profit or loss on disposal is determined by comparing the disposal proceeds with the consolidated 'book value', i.e. the consolidated carrying values of the attributable net assets of the subsidiary at the disposal date, plus any related goodwill *not* previously written off to consolidated profit and loss (para. 47). This seemingly innocuous requirement actually requires the *writing-back* of any goodwill immediately written-off to reserves so that it is included in the 'book value' and hence used in the determination of consolidated profit or loss on disposal. Some explanation of this requirement is necessary.

Many groups adopting the policy of the immediate write-off of goodwill to reserves, had previously calculated a 'book value' for the subsidiary at disposal excluding all goodwill, thus reporting higher profits than companies which amortize goodwill which included it at written down value as a part of the 'book value' of the subsidiary at the date of disposal. This was problematical since SSAP 22 states that immediate write-off is a policy decision rather than a valuation one. Though a revision of SSAP 22 in 1989 required the disclosure of goodwill related to disposals and how it was treated in assessing disposal profits or losses, this did not prevent their overstatement. In December 1991, the ASB's urgent issues task force issued UITF Abstract 3, *Treatment of Goodwill on Disposal of a Business.* This requires the profit or loss on the sale of businesses to be adjusted by writing *back* any goodwill written off on acquisition, to the extent that it has not previously been charged in the profit and loss account, and also its disclosure. FRS 2, issued in 1992, included these requirements.

This would seem to disadvantage companies with an immediate write-off policy as it requires the *original amount* of goodwill to be brought back, whereas under gradual amortisation, the amortized net book amount of goodwill is used in calculating the disposal 'book value'. However, over the 'life' of the subsidiary, profits will be higher under immediate write-off because immediately written off goodwill bypasses current year profit and loss, but at disposal they will be lower by the amounts of the 'missing' annual goodwill charges to the profit and loss compared with the gradual amortization approach.

Company Reporting (February 1993, p. 2) provides evidence of considerable resistance to the then UITF requirement with a number of groups reporting the goodwill write-back to profit and loss on disposal separately from the disposal gain or loss. In the August 1993 issue (p. 1) another practice had developed of writing down the immediately written off goodwill by charging profit and loss, for 'permanent diminution in value'. This meant that there were two charges, for the write-down and then for the disposal profit based on the written-down value of the goodwill. Such a procedure allows more comparability with profits or losses determined by groups using gradual amortization, but it begs the question of what immediate write-off means – how can you write-off to profit and loss account something that has already been written-off against reserves?

Costs of and provisions for fundamental reorganizations and restructurings

FRS 3's requirement in this area must be seen in conjunction with the ASB's stance on the setting up of reorganization and restructuring provisions at the acquisition of a subsidiary. As discussed in Chapter 5, FRS 7 effectively prohibits them, a major reason being that they are not obligations and that management intentions are not a sufficient basis for recognizing them. Therefore what had previously been pre-acquisition provisions, if set up now must be post-acquisition ones. In FRS 7 the ASB states that its proposals are consistent with the 'information set' philosophy of FRS 3. It argues that its increased disclosure requirements relating to the setting up of provisions and their use (discussed above) allow greater transparency in reporting.

However, FRS 3 does not contain any requirements which prevent the setting up of post-acquisition reorganization and restructuring provisions or ones in ongoing enterprises based on management intentions rather than when 'demonstrably committed'. This seems to be inconsistent with the ASB's philosophy elsewhere.

Extraordinary items
Unlike exceptional items, which are either reported under the statutory headings to which they relate 'above' operating profit, or in the three specified cases discussed above, reported between operating profit and profit before interest, extraordinary items are to be reported after profit after tax *and* minority interests. At first glance, the definitions in FRS 3 seem almost the same as those previously in SSAP 6: as stated above, exceptional items are

> Material items which derive from events or transactions that fall within the ordinary activities of the reporting entity and which individually or, if of a similar type, in aggregate, need to be disclosed by virtue of their size or incidence if the financial statements are to give a true and fair view.   (para. 5)

and extraordinary items,

> Material items possessing a high degree of abnormality which arise from events or transactions which fall outside the ordinary activities of the reporting entity and which are not expected to recur. They do not include exceptional items nor do they include prior period items merely because they relate to a prior period.   (para. 6)

However, similarities are deceptive and the class of extraordinary items has been effectively abolished by FRS 3. This has been achieved in a number of ways:

(i) Redefining ordinary activities
These now have much wider scope than previously understood, and are defined as,

> Any activities which are undertaken by a reporting entity as part of its business and such related activities in which the reporting activity engages in furtherance of, or incidental to, or arising from, these activities. Ordinary activities include the effects on the reporting entity of any event in the various environments in which it operates, including the political, regulatory, economic and geographical environments, irrespective of the frequency or unusual nature of the events.   (para 2)

This excludes whole areas previously classified as 'extraordinary', for example expropriations of foreign assets and currency devaluations. In addition, the analysis above operating profit of ordinary activities between continuing and discontinued items, prescribes the treatment and disclosure at a stroke of what was one of the main problem areas.

(ii) The separate disclosure of specified exceptional items
As stated above FRS 3 requires exceptional sale and termination profits and losses, reorganization and restructuring costs, and fixed asset disposal profits and losses to be disclosed separately on the face of the profit and loss account, including provisions in respect of each, and disclosing taxation and minority interest components – see above. This too deals with many items formerly classified as extraordinary.

Critics were concerned that FRS 3's preceding exposure draft's (FRED 1) proposal to collect all exceptional items together on the face of the profit and loss account would give them too much prominence and might create a new class of 'pseudo'-extraordinary items (see, for example, Davies, Paterson and Wilson, 1992). The ASB responded in FRS 3 by requiring all exceptional items apart from the three specific ones discussed above to be included under the statutory format headings to which they relate, attributed to continuing or discontinued activities as appropriate (para. 19).

(iii) The frequency of extraordinary items
Where SSAP 6 required extraordinary items 'not [to be] expected to recur frequently or regularly', FRS 3 is more blunt, 'not expected to *recur*'. So periodic flood damage, for example, would not be extraordinary, if it were periodic. Earthquake damage in California? It depends on the timescale. This now makes the UK definition closer to the US one in APB 30, where the event or transaction 'would not reasonably be expected to occur again in the foreseeable future'. The standard also lists items not to be regarded as extraordinary, including gains or losses from the abandonment of property, plant and equipment, unless the precipitating event is extraordinary.

IAS 8, *Unusual and Prior Period Items and Changes in Accounting Policies*, revised in 1993 tends more towards the pre-FRS 3 definition of 'extraordinary', and includes the phrase 'not expected to recur frequently or regularly'. Its definition of 'ordinary' whilst in many respects similar to FRS 3's does not contain the latter's clause which makes it clear that ordinary activities include the effects of any event in the political, regulatory, economic and geographical environments, irrespective of the frequency or unusual nature of the events.

Earnings per share
This, measured in pence, must be disclosed, and is defined in FRS 3 as

> based on the profit (or in the case of the group the consolidated profit) of the period after tax, minority interests and extraordinary items and after deducting preference dividends and other appropriations in respect of preference shares, divided by the number of equity shares in issue and ranking for dividend in respect of the period.   (para. 25).

Calculations of earnings per share on other bases may be disclosed, but the basis required by FRS 3 must be at least as prominent as any additional versions, and reasons for calculating such versions must be given. In such cases the level of profit used for additional versions must be reconciled to that used for the FRS 3 measure   (para. 25).

In keeping with its stated objective of de-emphasizing a single performance measure, FRS 3 requires that earnings per share must now be calculated *after* extraordinary items. This will make it much more volatile than previously, when SSAP 3 required its calculation after exceptional but before extraordinary items. This plus the allowing of the reporting of other measures, could take some pressure off a single performance measure, but it is interesting that the Institute of Investment Management and Research (IIMR), the professional body for investment analysts, has found it necessary to issue an Exposure Draft specifying the method of calculation of a 'headline' earnings figure from the FRS 3 proposals. Old habits die hard. Chopping (1993, p. 18) is concerned that whatever 'profit' definition becomes used as the accepted measure of performance (for example, a pre-exceptional-items or IIMR measure could be as readily manipulated) will then just recalibrate the debate of what is to be included or excluded from that measure and the abolition of extraordinary items will not prevent this.

Early experience with FRS 3

Holgate (1993) carried out a survey 111 groups with year ends from September 1992 to March 1993, from the *Financial Times* top 100 'companies' by market capitalization or by turnover and found 62 per cent were early adopters of FRS 3. He found that 'acquisitions' and 'discontinued activities' were often relatively small. In particular

(a)   34 companies reported discontinued operations, and for these the average turnover of such operations was only 2.2 per cent of their total turnover, and average operating profit/loss for such operations was only 0.9 per cent of their total turnover (with maxima of 11 per cent and 8.4 per cent respectively).

(b)   23 companies reported acquisitions. Of these the average turnover of acquisitions was 4.8 per cent of their total turnover (maximum 21.5 per cent).

(c)   there were no extraordinary items reported. The major cause (50 per cent) of exceptional items related to reorganization costs.

Based on these results Holgate recommends that the ASB formulates materiality guidelines for the separate reporting of such categories.

Exercises

8.1 Management of a group you are advising are intending to sell certain operations within the group and are fairly certain they will find a buyer before the year end. They wish to set up a provision to cover costs of preparing the company for sale and for operating losses to the date of sale. Advise them on whether they will be able to report the intended sale as discontinued activities or how it should be reported in the current year's financial statements – the year end is 2 months away. Advise them also what items they can include in their disposal provision.

8.2 In what ways does the definition of 'extraordinary items' differ from that of 'exceptional items'? Why does the distinction matter less since FRS 3 was issued?

8.3 In what ways has the Accounting Standards Board moved to prevent the abuse of provisions in consolidated financial statements?

8.4 How far are the reported figures under FRS 3 useful for forecasting purposes? Does it matter that this year's comparatives do not correspond to last year's reported figures in every respect?

Prior period adjustments and reserve movements

These are defined similarly to SSAP 6. By implication, *reserve movements* (which are allowed to bypass the consolidated profit and loss account), are items which are 'specifically permitted or required to be taken directly to reserves by this, or other accounting standards or, in the absence of a relevant accounting standard, by law'. In practice these are mainly fixed asset revaluations, certain foreign currency gains and losses (see Chapter

10), and immediately written-off goodwill (see Chapter 5).

Technical aspects

In order to illustrate FRS 3's basic principles relating to acquisitions and disposals, the examples that follow consider a group which acquires a subsidiary (Smallnesse) half-way through the year, and disposes of a long-time subsidiary (Minutenesse) three-quarters of the way through the year.

Readers wishing to understand the general principles of FRS 3 without working through detailed calculations can study the section 'Published Profit and Loss Accounts under FRS 3' and the general discussions only.

The first example examines the consolidation of the acquisition (Smallnesse) with the parent (Largesse); the second the consolidation of the subsidiary disposed of (Minutenesse) with Largesse & Smallnesse. The first example gives the data for both.

Example 8.1 – Acquisitions during the year

Consider the draft profit and loss accounts for companies in the Largesse Group:

Profit and loss accounts for the year ended 31 March 1996 (£m)

	Largesse	Smallnesse	Minutenesse
Sales	376.0	194.5	100.0
Cost of goods sold	(228.0)	(150.0)	(60.0)
Gross profit	148.0	44.5	40.0
Distribution costs	(85.0)	(14.0)	(10.0)
Administration expenses	(27.0)	(6.0)	(5.0)
Minutenesse disposal gain	23.0	—	—
Dividends receivable	6.0	—	—
Interest payable	(5.0)	(2.0)	(1.0)
Profit before tax	60.0	22.5	24.0
Corporation tax	(20.0)	(7.5)	(8.0)
Profit for the financial year	40.0	15.0	16.0
Dividends payable – interim	(7.0)	(4.0)	(2.0)
– final	(13.0)	(6.0)	(8.0)
Profit retained	20.0	5.0	6.0

Further information

(i)   Largesse acquired an 80% interest in Smallnesse for £80m at 30 September 1995. At 31 March 1995, the share capital, share premium and retained profits of Smallnesse were £35m, £15m and £35m respectively. No share issues were made by Smallnesse during the year.

(ii) Largesse sold its 60% interest in Minutenesse on 31 December 1995 for £58m. The interest had been acquired at 31 March 1992 for £35m, when the share capital, share premium and retained profits of Minutenesse were £10m, £10m and £15m respectively. No share issues had been made by Minutenesse since that date, and retained profits at 31 March 1995 (the start of the year) were £29m.

(iii) Goodwill is to be written off over 10 years using the straight-line basis.

(iv) Smallnesse sold £25m of goods to Largesse during the second half of the year but none of these goods were held at the end of the year.

(v)   Dividends receivable are the final dividend from Smallnesse and the interim dividend from Minutenesse.

(vi) Included in Largesse's distribution expenses are losses of £10m on the disposal of properties held for distribution purposes, and in its administrative expenses is £2m relating to restructuring expenses of one of its divisions. A provision was set up last year of £5m, but the actual restructuring expenses were £7m.

(Vii) Ignore fair value adjustments at acquisition.

(viii) Assume that revenues and expenses (except the dividend) occur at an even rate throughout the year.

Required

Consolidate the profit and loss accounts for Largesse and Smallnesse for the year ended 31 March 1996. Treat Minutenesse as a fixed asset investment for now.

Solution

Figure 8.1 shows the effects of consolidating Largesse with Smallnesse where its revenues and expenses are only included from the date of acquisition – all items are one-half of full-year amounts except the dividend. Ideally, interim accounts would be prepared to the acquisition date, but here for simplicity, we apportion profit and loss items on a time basis. For dividends, we assume the interim dividend was paid to the *previous* shareholders of Smallnesse, and only the final one to Largesse.

Description	Largesse	Smallnesse (6 months)	Intra-group transfers	Intra-group dividends	Goodwill writeoff (6 months)	Minority interests	Consolidated
Sales	376.0	97.25	(25.0)				448.25
Cost of sales	(228.0)	(75.0)	25.0				(278.0)
Distribution costs	(85.0)	(7.0)					(92.0)
Admin expenses	(27.0)	(3.0)					(30.0)
Disposal gain	23.0						23.0
Dividends rec'd	6.0			(4.8)			1.2
Interest	(5.0)	(1.0)					(6.0)
Goodwill					(0.46)		(0.46)
Corporation tax	(20.0)	(3.75)					(23.75)
Mino interest						(1.5)	(1.5)
Divs interim	(7.0)						(7.0)
Divs final	(13.0)	(6.0)		4.8		1.2	(13.0)
Retained profits	20.0	1.5			(0.46)	(0.3)	20.74

Figure 8.1 – Acquisition of Smallnesse half-way through the year

Dividends receivable – £4.8m is from Smallnesse, 80% x £6 (final), and £1.2m is from Minutenesse, 60% x £2m (interim). The former is removed by cancellation, but not the latter as in this part of the question it is as if from a trade investment. (One could make the case that of the £4.8m, only £4m [i.e. 80% x 6/12 x (4.0 + 6.0)] relates to the post-acquisition period, and £0.8m to the pre-acquisition period. If so, an assessment needs to be made (based on the discussions in Chapter 6 relating to dividends from pre-acquisition profits) as to whether the £0.8m needs to be adjusted against consolidated goodwill at acquisition and balance sheet retained profits, reducing both. Following from this, the current year amortization of Smallnesse's goodwill would be reduced accordingly in the profit and loss cancellation worksheet, Figure 8.1, by £0.04m [i.e. 1/2 x 1/10 x 0.8m]. This has been ignored here on materiality grounds. How far such adjustments are made and how material they are in practice is not disclosed by companies.)

Goodwill amortization – Consider the following:

Equity at acquisition   = Opening + pro rata profit after tax – divs prior to acq
             = (35 + 15 + 35) + 6/12 x £15   –   4.0
             = £88.5m

Goodwill at acquisition	= £80.0 – 80% x £88.5	= £9.2m
6 months amortization	= 1/2 x 1/10 x £9.2	= £0.46m.

| *Minority in profit after tax* | = 20% x 15 x 1/2 year | = £1.5m |

Exercise

8.5 Consider the following profit and loss accounts for the Overbearing group:

Profit and loss accounts for the year ended 30 June 1995 (£'000)

	Overbearing	Inadequate	Grovel
Sales	835	460	100
Cost of sales	(300)	(250)	(60)
Gross profit	535	210	40
Distribution costs	(250)	(50)	(8)
Administration expenses	(141)	(64)	(5)
Dividends receivable	22	—	—
Profit on sale of Grovel plc	19	—	—
Interest payable	(10)	(6)	(2)
Profit before tax	175	90	25
Corporation tax	(45)	(25)	(9)
Profit after tax	130	65	16
Dividends – interim	(30)	(20)	(5)
– final	(50)	(30)	(5)
Profit retained for year	50	15	6

Further information

(i)   Overbearing acquired a 60% interest in Inadequate on 31 December 1994 for £150,000. At 30 June 1994 the share capital, share premium and retained earnings of Inadequate were respectively, £50,000, £70,000 and £80,000.

(ii) Overbearing sold to Inadequate £30,000 of goods during its six months of ownership. None were in stock at the year end.

(iii) Overbearing sold its 80% interest in Grovel on 31 March 1995, for £47,000, which had been acquired for £28,000 on 1 July 1992 when the share capital, share premium and retained earnings were £5,000, £5,000 and £16,000 respectively. At 30 June 1994, Grovel's retained profits were £30,000. No share issues were made by Grovel since its acquisition.

(iv) Consolidated goodwill is amortized straight-line over a 5 year period.

(v)   Assume all revenues and expenses except dividends occurred at a constant rate throughout the year. Overbearing plc was entitled to receive only the final dividend of Inadequate plc, and only the interim dividend of Grovel plc.

Required

Prepare a consolidated profit and loss account worksheet to consolidate Overbearing and Inadequate for the year ended 30 June 1995. Treat Grovel for this part as a trade investment.

Example 8.2 – Disposals during the year

Consider now the consolidation of Minuteness with the Largesse-Smallnesse consolidation per the last column of Figure 8.1. Since Minutenesse was disposed of on 31 December 1995, we must consolidate its results up to the date of disposal, for the first 9 months of the year, so since we are not given interim accounts, in this simple example, revenues and expenses are apportioned as 9/12 of the full year's figures, except for dividends. It is assumed that the interim dividend was paid to Largesse, but the final one to third-party shareholders. In Figure 8.2, the first column represents the consolidated figures from Figure 8.1.

Goodwill – consider the following:

Goodwill at acquisition	= 35 – 60% x (10+10+15)	= £14m
9 month *goodwill write-off*	= 9/12 x 1/10 x 14	= £1.05m

Description	Largesse & Smallnesse	Minuteness - 9/12 of year	Subsidiary disposal	Goodwill writeoff 9/12 of year	Minority interest 9/12 of year	Intra-group dividend	Consolidated
Sales	448.25	75.0					523.25
Cost of sales	(278.0)	(45.0)					(323.0)
Distribution costs	(92.0)	(7.5)					(99.5)
Admin expenses	(30.0)	(3.75)					(33.75)
Dividends rec'ble	1.2					(1.2)	-
Interest p'ble	(6.0)	(0.75)					(6.75)
Goodwill	(0.46)			(1.05)			(1.51)
Profit on disposal	23.0		(9.15)				13.85
Corporation tax	(23.75)	(6.0)					(29.75)
Minority interest	(1.5)				(4.8)		(6.3)
Dividends interim	(7.0)	(2.0)			0.8	1.2	(7.0)
Dividends final	(13.0)	-					(13.0)
Retained profit	20.74	10.0	(9.15)	(1.05)	(4.0)*	-	16.54

Figure 8.2 – Consolidated profit and loss worksheet - disposal of 80% subsidiary

Minority interests in profit after tax	= 40% x 9/12 x 16	= £4.8m
Parent's profit on disposal	= Proceeds – investment at cost	
	= £58 – £35	= £23m

Consolidated profit on disposal:
We need the consolidated 'book value' of the subsidiary, i.e. its attributable consolidated net assets including goodwill at disposal date. Using the consolidation identity in Chapter 4, p. 87, this is equal to the amount of the *equitized investment* on that date, i.e. the equitized investment is equal to goodwill plus the subsidiary's net assets at the date of disposal less the minority stake at that date, viz.:

$$I + 0.6 \, \Delta RE = \quad G + 1.0 \, [\, A_{now} - L_{now} \,] - 0.4 \, [\, A_{now} - L_{now} \,]$$

The equitized investment must include the effects of alignment adjustments (Chapter 6), here only consolidated goodwill amortization. So in order to determine its amount we need:

Retained profits at acquisition   =   £15m
Retained profits at disposal = 29 (opening) + 9/12 x 16 (9 months profits) – 2 (interim dividend)
                        = £39m
Retained profits since acq   = 39 – 15   =   £24m, and
Goodwill amortisation since acq   = 3.75 years x 1/10 x 14   =   £5.25m

$$I + 0.6 \, \Delta RE- = 35 + 60\% \times (39 - 15) - 3.75 \times 1/10 \times 14 \qquad = \qquad £44.15m$$

Consolidated profit on disposal   =   58 –   44.15   =   £13.85m
This is less than the *parent's* profit on disposal by the amount of the attributable retained profits since acquisition: (i.e. £23m (parent) – £13.85m (consolidated) = £9.15m = £44.15m – £35m).

The corresponding consolidated profit and loss account is shown below in publishable format.

Published consolidated profit and loss accounts under FRS 3
FRS 3 illustrates two different presentation formats, multicolumnar and vertical. The multicolumnar one is illustrated here:

Consolidated profit and loss account – Largesse Group
for year ended 31 March 1996 (£m)

	Continued operations Acquistions	Ongoing	Discontinued operations	Total
Sales	72.25	376.00	75.00	523.25
COGS	(50.00)	(228.00)	(45.00)	(323.0)
Gross profit	22.25	148.00	30.00	200.25
Distribution costs	(7.0)	(75.00)*	(7.50)	(89.50)*
Admin expenses	(3.0)	(25.00)**	(3.75)	(31.75)**
Goodwill	(0.46)	—	(1.05)	(1.51)
Operating profit	11.79	48.00	17.70	77.49
Restructuring costs in continuing ops		(7.00)**		(7.00)
Less 1995 provision		5.00 **		5.00
Property sales losses – continuing ops		(10.00)*		(10.00)
Disposal profit on discontinued activities	—	—	13.85	13.85
Profit on ordinary activities before interest	11.79	36.00	31.55	79.34
Interest payable				(6.75)
Profit on ordinary activities before tax				72.59
Corporation tax				(29.75)
Profit on ordinary activities after tax				42.84
Minority interests				(6.3)
Profit for the financial year				36.54
Dividends				(20.00)
Retained profit for the financial year				16.54

*Note:*The items (*) and (**) included in distribution costs and administration expenses are required to be disclosed separately under FRS 3.

Effects of disposals on the balance sheet cancellation table

Only subsidiaries at the year-end are included in the closing consolidated balance sheet, and hence in its balance sheet cancellation table, Minutenesse will be omitted. The disposal of Minutenesse requires no further adjustments in this cancellation table. This can be shown as follows: the total effects of Minutenesse on consolidated retained profit from the date of its acquisition to its disposal come from two sources, retained profits contributed to the group whilst it was a member, and the profit on disposal itself, as shown below:

Contribution to consolidated   = Attrib retained earnings since acq −
   retained profits   consolidated goodwill amortized over period   (1),
                                 = 60% × (39 − 15) − 3.75 × 1/10 × 14 = £9.15m

Consolidated gain on disposal   = Proceeds − equitized investment
                                   = 58 − 44.15   = £13.85m

Adding (1) and (2), we get:

Total consolidated contribution   =   9.15 + 13.85   = £23m
                                 =   *Parent* gain on disposal   = £58m − £35m

Thus the total impact of the subsidiary on the consolidated accounts equals the gain on its disposal calculated on the parent's historical cost, which will be automatically brought in to the balance sheet cancellation table from the parent's own accounts.

Exercises

8.6 Prepare a consolidated profit and loss account worksheet to consolidate Overbearing, Inadequate and Grovel, using the final column of your worksheet in Exercise 8.5 as the first column in your worksheet.

8.7 Prepare a consolidated profit and loss account for the Overbearing Group for the year ended 30 June 1995 to satisfy the requirements of FRS 3.

8.8 Consider the following profit and loss accounts for members of the Meglo Group:

Profit and loss accounts – year ended 31 December 1995 (£m)

	Meglo	Minnow	Roe
Sales	420	185	294
Cost of sales	(150)	(85)	(140)
Gross profit	270	100	154
Distribution costs	(45)	(15)	(20)
Administrative costs	(120)	(35)	(50)
Profit on sale of Roe	10	—	—
Dividends receivable	18	—	—
Operating profit	133	50	84
Interest payable	(20)	(10)	(12)
Profit before tax	113	40	72
Taxation	(25)	(8)	(17)
Profit after tax	88	32	55
Dividends payable – interim	(20)	(5)	(10)
– final	(35)	(15)	(15)
Retained profit for the year	33	12	30

Notes

(a) Meglo plc acquired a 55% stake in Minnow plc on 30 March 1995 for £100m. At 31 December 1994 the share capital, share premium and retained earnings of Minnow were respectively, £20m, £30m and £46m.

(b) Meglo sold a 70% interest in Roe on 30 June 1995 for £86m which had been acquired for £76m on 1 July 1992 when its share capital, share premium and retained earnings had been £10m, £15m and £55m respectively. At 30 June 1995, Roe's balance sheet retained profits were £90m. No share issues were made by Roe since its acquisition.

(c) Roe sold to Meglo £20m of goods during the year at an approximately even rate. None were in stock at the year end.

(d) Assume revenues and expenses occurred at an even rate throughout the year except for dividends. The interim dividends of Minnow were paid to shareholders on its share register at 30 April 1995. Interim dividends of Roe were paid to shareholders on its share register on 15 June 1995.

(e) Goodwill at acquisition is gradually amortised over a 5 year period.

Required
Using a cancellation table prepare a consolidated profit and loss account for the Meglo group for the year ended 31 December 1995 complying with FRS 3's requirements. Assume that the disposal of Roe constitutes a 'discontinued activity' under the standard for this purpose.

OTHER PERFORMANCE STATEMENTS

FRS 3 requires three other statements to be reported in addition to the consolidated profit and loss account,

(i)   a statement of total recognized gains and losses,
(ii)   a reconciliation of movements in shareholders funds, and
(iii)   A note of historical cost profits and losses.

The first two statements taken together with consolidated profit and loss account can be viewed as a *tiered* system, consolidated profit and loss having the narrowest focus, widening through the statement of total recognized gains and losses (which includes 'profit for the financial year' and other gains and losses which bypass profit and loss), to the movements on shareholder funds, which includes elements of the statement of total recognized gains and losses, and in addition, transactions with owners, such as share issues and dividends, and for reasons explored later, immediate goodwill write-offs to reserves for the period. Consider each statement in turn:

The Statement of Total Recognized Gains or Losses
This is treated by FRS 3 as another *primary* financial statement. In Chapter 3 of the ASB's Statement of Principles, *The Elements of Financial Statements*, the terms 'gains' and 'losses' are used to describe all changes in equity apart from transactions with owners, unlike in the USA, where the corresponding SFAC 6 splits the former into 'revenues' and 'gains', and the latter into 'expenses' and 'losses'. Davies, Paterson and Wilson (1992, p. 81) comment that the words chosen by the ASB are counterintuitive – in everyday language they are used to apply to net figures.

Given these definitions, it is not surprising that the statement is analogous to a form of *comprehensive income statement*, including the consolidated profit and loss account as a subset. FRS 3 intends that the two statements 'are intended to present all the entity's gains and losses recognized during the period (para. 37)'. Only items specifically allowed by accounting standard or law to bypass the profit and loss account, excluding transactions with owners and immediately written off goodwill, can be given separate disclosure in this statement (para. 37). SSAP 22 notes that the immediate write-off of goodwill is a matter of *policy* not valuation, and so FRS 3 decides that it is not to be treated as a recognized loss (para. 27). However, goodwill does seem to meet the definition of a loss in the Statement of Principles as described above! An example of a consolidated statement of total recognized gains and losses is shown below, in which it is assumed that the Largesse Group has a foreign subsidiary. (The numbers do not relate to the earlier example in the chapter, and relevant notes to the accounts are not shown.)

Largesse Group – Statement of total recognized gains and losses for year ended 31 March 1995

	£m
Profit for the financial year	36.54
Unrealized surplus on property revaluations	20.50
Currency translation gains	
on foreign currency net investments	(4.50)
Total gains or losses recognized for the year	52.54
Prior year adjustment	(5.25)
Total gains or losses recognized	
since the last annual report	47.29

The treatment of gains and losses on the translation of foreign currency financial statements of subsidiaries, is dealt with in Chapter 11. Prior year adjustments (the definition of which is unchanged since SSAP 6, including only changes in accounting policy or the correction of fundamental errors) pass through this statement, even though comparatives are readjusted. More controversial is the decision in FRS 3 that gains or losses which pass through this statement, e.g. unrealized gains on revaluations, will *not* subsequently be reported in the consolidated profit and loss account when the asset is sold, and the gain on disposal will be computed on the revalued amount.

Intercompany transfers and revaluations

Revaluations at acquisition will not pass through this statement, as they are the establishment of 'new' historical costs to the group. Alignment adjustment issues arise on the consolidation of statements of total recognized gains and losses if there have been revaluations, as shown below:

Example 8.3 – Statements of total recognized gains and losses

Consider the following individual company statements of total recognized gains and losses for the year ended 31 March 1996:

Statements of total recognized gains and losses for year ended 31 March 1996 (£m)

	Largesse	Smallnesse	Minutenesse
Profit for the financial year	40.0	15.0	16.0
Unrealised property revaluation surplus	10.0	10.0	—
Total recognized gains and losses	50.0	25.0	16.0

Further information
(i)   Largesse has a 100% stake in Smallnesse, acquired on 30 September 1995. On 1 October 1995, land held by Smallnesse was revalued from £15m to £25m to reflect the fair value at acquisition, and this revaluation was incorporated in Smallnesse's own financial records. No other fair value adjustments were made. Goodwill at acquisition (after incorporating the results of this revaluation) was £9.2m.
(ii) Largesse has held a 60% stake in Minutenesse for a number of years. Goodwill at acquisition was £5m.
(iii) Minutenesse sells land to Largesse for £20m on 2 July 1995, which originally cost £15m in 1993. For the 31 March 1996 financial statements, Largesse has had all the group's land revalued, and this particular plot was revalued at £22m.
(iv) Assume that all goodwill is to be written off on the straight-line basis over a ten year period, that profit for the financial year can be apportioned on a time basis where necessary, and that there were no other intra-group transactions during the year. There were no prior year adjustments for any of the companies.

(v) Dividends due to Largesse for the period from Smallnesse and Minutenesse were £6m.
(vi) Opening shareholders funds are £220m.

Required
Based on the above information, prepare a consolidated statement of total recognized gains and losses for the Largesse Group for the year ended 31 March 1996.

Solution
Figure 8.3 shows the adjustments that need to be made in constructing a consolidated statement of recognized gains and losses for the Largesse Group:

Revaluation at acquisition
Since Smallnesse was acquired half-way through the year, profit for the financial year is apportioned on a time basis, but because the revaluation was carried out on 1 October, it is included at this stage and not apportioned. The £10m revaluation at acquisition, as far as the group was concerned, is the establishment of 'new' historical costs, and so is not a revaluation as far as the group is concerned (being used in the calculation of the goodwill figure of £9.2m).

Sale and revaluation of land
The individual company and consolidated treatments of the sale and subsequent revaluation of land are now examined:

Individual company treatment

Smallnesse	Profit £5m	Profit and loss account
Largesse	Revaluation gain £2m	Total gains/losses statement

Consolidated accounts treatment

Consol Revaluation gain £7m	Total gains/losses statement

Normally profits on intra-group transfers are eliminated on consolidation. However, in this case the value has been fixed by an external revaluation. For group purposes the whole revaluation gain of £7m is unrealized. Consolidated profit on sale of fixed assets will be adjusted downwards by £5m and revaluation gains in the statement of total recognized gains and losses upwards by the same amount.

Minority interests
Remember that minority interest is in company profit *after* tax, making necessary alignment adjustments:

$$= 40\% \times (16.00 - 5.00 \text{ (profit elimination))}$$
$$= £4.4m$$

Goodwill
Note that, if the policy of *immediate write-off against reserves* had been chosen, goodwill write-off would not have been recorded in this statement, but taken direct to the movement in shareholders' funds statement, but because *gradual amortization* has been chosen, it is incorporated in the profit figure. Consider now the calculations:

For Smallnesse	= 1/2 yr × 1/10 × £9.2m	= £0.46m
For Minutenesse	= 1/10 × £5m	= £0.50m

The consolidated statement is the final column of the worksheet.

Reconciliation of movements in shareholders' funds
FRS 3 views this as a note disclosure (para. 28), but allows it to be presented as a primary statement, in which case it must be presented separately from the statement of total recognized gains and losses (para. 59). Its consolidation aspect is that consolidated goodwill immediately written off is one of its movements, for reasons discussed above. A specimen statement is given below. FRS 3's illustrative example shows in addition, reserve movements as required by the Companies Act 1985 (Sch 4, para. 46) – note in Chapter 3 that if merger accounting is used, any uncancelled share premium of the subsidiary must be shown as a movement on 'their reserves' (FRS 6, para. 41). Reserve movements are not discussed further here.

Description	Largesse	Smallnesse	Minutenesse	Revaluation at acquisition	Intra-group sale	Minority interest	Goodwill	Consolidated
Profit for the financial year	40.0	7.5	16.0	–	(5.0) (6.0) div receivable*	(4.4)	Sm (0.46) Mi (0.50)	47.14
Unrealised revaluation surplus	10.0	10.0	–	(10)	5.0	–	–	15.00
Total recognised gains and losses	50.0	17.5	16.0	(10.0)	(6.0)*	(4.4)	(0.96)	62.14

* - Largesse's profit for the financial year has to be restated to before intra-group dividends receivable (40 - 6) to be consistent with Smallnesse's and Minutenesse's profits for the financial year (which are before intra-group dividends payable).

Figure 8.3 – Largesse Group – Statement of total gains and losses worksheet

Largesse Group – Reconciliation of movements in shareholders' funds for year ended 31 March 1996

	£m
Profit for the financial year	47.14
Dividends	(20.00)
	27.14
Other recognized gains or losses	15.00 [1]
New share capital subscribed	80.00 [2]
Goodwill immediately written off	—
Net additions to shareholders' funds	122.14
Opening shareholders' funds	220.00
Closing shareholders' funds	342.14

Notes

1. = 62.14 (total recognized gains/losses for the year) minus 47.14 (profit for the financial year, disclosed separately)
2. To acquire Smallnesse during the year, all for shares.

Note of historical profits and losses

This again is a note disclosure, not a primary financial statement, and is merely shown below for completeness:

Largesse Group _ Note of historical cost profits and losses for year ended 31 March 1996

	£m
Reported profit on ordinary activities before tax	72.59
Realization of property revaluation gains of previous years	50.00
Difference between historical cost depreciation charge and actual calculated on revalued amounts	20.00
Historical cost profit on ordinary activities before tax	142.59
Historical cost profit retained after tax, minority interests, extraordinary items and dividends	86.54*

*   = 16.54 + (50.00 + 20.00) adjustments above.

FRS 3 cites two common justifications for this statement: that it provides more comparable data in a world of *ad hoc* valuations, and that some users wish such a statement. Presumably too, it allows comparisons with US companies, where revaluations are not permitted to the same extent as in the UK. When such statements are consolidated, intragroup stock and other profits must be eliminated. Fair value adjustments at acquisition will need to be included as they are 'new' *historical costs* for the group, and not technically revaluations from its point of view. However, to the extent that such adjustments have been 'pushed down' into the subsidiary's own records, they will have been removed from its own statements (as from a company basis they are revaluations) and will need to be reinstated on consolidation.

Exercises

8.9 In what ways does the type of information produced by the 'Statement of total recognized gains and losses,' and the 'Reconciliation of movements in shareholders' funds' differ from that included in the 'Consolidated profit and loss account'? List group accounting items that will appear in such statements.

8.10 Consider the following information for individual companies in the Hangover Group for the year ended 31 December 1995:

Extracts from profit and loss accounts (£m)

	Hangover	Damocles	Putupon
Profit after tax	45.0	20.0	20.0
Dividends – interim	(8.0)	(4.0)	—
– final	(10.0)	(8.0)	—
Retained profit for the year	27.0	8.0	20.0

Extracts from movements on reserves

	Hangover	Damocles	Putupon
(a) *Retained profits*			
Balance b/f	120.0	60.0	32.0
Retained for the year	27.0	8.0	20.0
Balance c/f	147.0	68.0	52.0

	Hangover	Damocles	Putupon
(b) *Revaluation reserves*			
Opening balance	20.0	15.0	16.0
Revaluations of properties	12.0	—	8.0
Closing balance	32.0	15.0	24.0

	Hangover	Damocles	Putupon
(c) *Share capital & share premium*			
Opening balance	80.0	75.0	26.0
Share issues	25.0	—	—
Closing balance	105.0	75.0	26.0

Further information

(i) Hangover plc acquired a 70% stake in Damocles five years ago, when its retained profits were £20m. Goodwill at acquisition was £10m.

(ii) Hangover acquired a 60% stake in Putupon plc on 31 March 1995, for £63m. Its land was revalued from £26m to £34m at acquisition, and the revaluation was included in Putupon's own records. Land is not depreciated.

(iii) All consolidated goodwill is to be immediately written off against consolidated retained profits.

Required

Prepare a 'statement of total recognized gains and losses', and a 'reconciliation of movements in shareholders funds' for the Hangover Group for the year ended 31 December 1995.

EVALUATING FRS 3

Assessing financial performance has become more complex, and some might say more confusing. However, the proposals in FRS 3 get closer to the underlying complexities of measuring the performance of large groups, by requiring the disclosure of an 'information set' of financial statistics, enabling and requiring users to disentangle the situation. Efficient markets research suggests that markets are constituted by sophisticated users who would not be likely to be overloaded by more information. Less sophisticated users, under this view, would be well advised to recognize their limitations and to employ the services of financial analysts. In addition to FRS 3's statements, users also need to consider, for example, consolidated cash flow statements (discussed in Chapter 9), and segmental information (examined in Chapter 12). Further issues include:

(a) Boundary problems

A number of respondents have criticized FRS 3 for its inflexibility, e.g. over the reporting of discontinued operations. For example, the CBI considers that discontinued operations should be classified as such when the *decision* is made, not according to when a binding sale agreement is made, or the activities are completely terminated. Presumably however, the ASB was worried about the ease of expressing intention, and the difficulty of policing it.

Davies, Paterson and Wilson (1992, p. 1106) consider that too much prominence is given to the disclosure of discontinued activities, which 'might encourage preparers of accounts to try to boost continuing results at the expense of discontinued operations'. They consider that such discontinuations should be given in the segmental information provided by the group, as the disclosure in the profit and loss account gives greater disclosure to discontinued 'segments' than to ongoing ones.

(b) Status problems

A major area of concern is that unrealized gains once reported in the 'statement of total recognized gains and losses', will not be reported in the consolidated profit and loss account as realized gains, i.e. that profits on disposals will be calculated on revalued book amounts. The CBI in *Accountancy*, June 1992, p. 34, argues that this will materially affect the results of companies depending on the policies they adopt concerning revaluation, and gives the example that when prices fall, groups might retain assets longer than is economically viable in order to record downward revaluations, rather than losses on disposal in the profit and loss account.

However, users will probably learn to interpret the new statements. Indeed the statement of total gains and losses would gain in relevance if the ASB moves in an evolutionary way towards current values. For example, the statement of total gains and losses would be the home of 'holding' type gains, and the profit and loss 'operating' type profit figures under a current cost system. If the ASB's assessment of the lack of usefulness of historical cost is accurate (ASB, 1993a), the 'statement of total recognized gains and losses' might increase in importance, whilst the note on historical cost profits decline in use (except in providing comparisons with the USA where revaluations are almost non-existent).

(c) The economic context of change

Supporters of the efficient markets hypothesis might claim that it is not so important *where* significant items are disclosed, provided that they are sufficiently well described. Indeed Chopping (1993, p. 23) comments that the information in the 'statement of total recognized gains and losses' could be gleaned already from elsewhere in the financial statements, and suggests that it 'does not really add anything of substance', However, the fuss that the removal of extraordinary items has provoked from both preparers and some analysts, suggests that either they do not believe in the hypothesis, or that the new rules may affect cash flows indirectly where there is a cash flow impact determined by the fact that contracts are enforced on the basis of reported profits, e.g. debt covenant restrictions and performance related pay etc., and changes in the definition of 'headline profit' or its effective abolition may have an economic impact. Management may also be concerned that they are not able to manage their performance measure because of uncertainty amongst analysts, who felt safer when there is an agreed (if spurious) measure as a starting point. The incremental preparation costs of the new statements are also relatively unknown.

(d) Forecasting future flows

FRS 3's preferred treatment of only recording revenues and expenses from the date of acquisition, rather than for the whole year with a removal of pre-acquisition amounts (see page 203) makes extrapolation of results more difficult. Davies, Paterson and Wilson (1992, p. 1,108) comment that if a group with a December 31 year end acquires a subsidiary on January 2, the whole year's results are included under the acquisitions category of continuing operations, whereas if it had been acquired two days earlier, all the subsidiary's results will be reported in the non-acquisition section of current year's operations. However, as discussed earlier, in many cases simple extrapolation is likely to be over simplistic.

Exercises
8.11 To what extent has the effective removal of the extraordinary items category, and the decision to define earnings per share as based on profits after extraordinary items, reduced the usefulness of published consolidated profit and loss accounts to users?

8.12 What totally new information does FRS 3 require in published consolidated financial statements not available before it?

8.13 'There is also the question of the relative costs and benefits of compliance with [FRS 3]. Even if we accept that FRS 3 represents an improvement in financial reporting there is little doubt that many companies will incur considerable costs in complying. We need to be sure that the benefits of the Standard outweigh the related costs.' (Chopping 1993, p. 4.) Discuss.

SUMMARY

Prior to FRS 3, unusual items were classified as **exceptional, extraodinary, prior period** *or* **reserve movements** *– exceptional items were included in the earnings per share performance measure, and hence in price-earnings ratios, but extraordinary items were not, resulting in abuse in classification.*

FRS 3 introduced new disclosure analyses for **continuing** *and* **discontinued** *operations (and* **acquisitions** *within continuing operations). This analysis, the redefinition of ordinary activities, the requirement for the disclosure of profits or losses on the* **sale or termination of an operation***, and the* **disposal of fixed assets***, and* **fundamental reorganization or restructuring costs***, together with details of related provisions, has effectively abolished the category of extraordinary items. Also FRS 3 redefined primary earnings per share* **after** *extraordinary items.*

Further new statements required by FRS 3 include a new primary statement: the **statement of total recognized gains and losses***, and note disclosures of* **reconciliation of movements on shareholders' funds***, and the* **note of historical costs and losses***. Some question whether the benefits of such statements outweigh the costs of preparation. Efficient markets and contracting cost perspectives give different insights on this issue.*

Accounting techniques were explored for dealing with the acquisition and disposal of subsidiaries during the year, and for consolidating statements of total recognized gains and losses. When subsidiaries are acquired during the year, revenues and expenses are **included from the date of acquisition***, when disposed of, up* **to the date of disposal or termination***. Consolidated profits or losses are determined by matching the subsidiary's 'carrying value' of attributable net assets and goodwill, obtained by 'contracting' its balances into a single* **equitized** *amount at the date of disposal, with the proceeds.*

FURTHER READING

This is mainly technical. However, readings from the previous two chapters also apply:

FRS 3 (1992), *Reporting Financial Performance*, Accounting Standards Board.
Davies, M., Paterson, R. and Wilson, A., *UK GAAP*, Ernst and Young/Macmillan, Chapter 19.
Hodgson, E. (1992), *Reporting Financial Performance*, Coopers and Lybrand/Gee.
Smith T (1992), *Accounting for Growth*, Century Business, Chapters 5 and 7.
Chopping, D. (1993) The Comparability of Financial Statements: A Review of FRS 3, in Tonkin and Skerrat (eds.) (1993), *Financial Reporting 1993-4*, Institute of Chartered Accountants in England and Wales, pp. 3–30.

9

CONSOLIDATED CASH FLOW STATEMENTS

This is the last primary financial statement to be discussed. It was introduced by FRS 1, *Cash Flow Statements*, in 1991. Chapter 6 of the ASB's *Statement of Principles, The Objective of Financial Statements* considers that cash flow information is helpful in conjunction with the other primary statements in assessing risk, liquidity, financial viability, financial adaptability and particularly the way in which profits are converted to cash. This chapter focuses on the consolidated cash flow statement and some knowledge of the preparation and formats of individual company cash flow statements is presumed. Different approaches to preparation are appropriate in different circumstances. These are illustrated and their circumstances of use examined. The cash flow matrix approach outlined here is also a very useful and systematic way of preparing individual company cash flow statements. FRS 1 is then analysed together with related theoretical issues and empirical evidence.

BASIC CONCEPTS

FRS 1, *Cash Flow Statements*, requires analysis of an entity's cash inflows and outflows for the period under five main headings: 'operating activities', 'returns on investments and servicing of finance', 'taxation', 'investing activities' and 'financing', in that order. It prescribes items to be included under each heading, and requires any exceptional cash flows under each heading to be separately disclosed. SFAS 95 in the USA and the revised international standard IAS 7 require only three headings: 'operating', 'investing' and 'financing'. However, no unequivocal rationale has been found for allocating dividends, interest and taxation over these headings. FRS 1 gave up the attempt and instead groups dividends and interest under a 'returns on investments and servicing of finance' heading, and gives 'taxation' its own heading.

Presentation of net cash flow from operating activities
Two alternative methods of calculating 'net cash flows from operating activities' are widely canvassed: the *direct* approach, which discloses the individual operating receipts and payments underlying it, and the *indirect* approach, which reconciles operating profit to it in total. This reconciliation (note 1 above) reconciles something which is not a cash flow, i.e. operating profit, via reconciling items which are themselves not cash flows, i.e. depreciation add-backs, stock, operating debtor and creditor changes, to a total that is, i.e. net cash flow from operating activities.

In order to give an intuitive rationalization for the indirect approach, it can be helpful to consider the reconciliation as taking place in three stages:

(1) Operating profit is viewed as if *potential total net cash flow*.
(2) Adjusting for depreciation and any relevant gains or losses on fixed assets removes non-operating activity elements from potential total cash flow, leaving *potential net*

Example 9.1 – Cash flow statement for an individual company

The following illustrates an individual company cash flow statement under the 'gross' format alternative of FRS 1, together with some of the notes required by the standard:

Marx and Sparks plc – cash flow statement –year ended 30 June 1995

	£m	£m
Operating activities		
Cash received from customers	524	
Cash payments to suppliers	(369)	
Cash paid to and on behalf of employees	(82)	
Net cash inflow from operating activities		33
Returns on investments and servicing of finance		
Interest paid	(2)	
Dividends paid	(5)	
Net cash outflow from returns on investment and servicing of finance		*(7)*
Taxation		
Corporation tax paid	(10)	
Tax paid		(10)
Investing activities		
Payments for fixed assets	(41)	
Sale proceeds for fixed assets	24	
Net cash outflow from investing activities		(17)
Net cash outflow before financing		(1)
Financing		
Issue of ordinary share capital	5	
Issue of loans	14	
Repayment of loans	(10)	
Net cash inflow from financing activities		9
Increase in cash and cash equivalents		8

Note

1. **Reconciliation of operating profit to net cash inflow from operating activities:**

		£m
Operating profit		38
Depreciation charges	5	
Loss on fixed asset sale		2
Increase in (operating) debtors	(19)	
Increase in (operating) credit	5	
Decrease in stocks		2
Net cash inflow from operating activities		33

2. **Analysis of changes in cash and cash equivalents during the year**

		£m
Balance at 1 July 1994	12	
Net cash inflow		8
Balance at 30 June 1995		20

cash flow from operating activities. The items removed are investing-type flows, relating to fixed assets – see below).

(3) Adjusting for changes in accrual-type balances (stocks, operating debtors and operating creditors) can be viewed as if a decision was being made on how much potential cash flow from operating activities (the result of step 2) to tie up in working capital. Increases in stocks and operating debtors are as if tying up potential cash (i.e. negative reconciling items), whereas increases in operating creditors, rather like interest free loans, are as if releasing potential cash (i.e. positive). What is left after these

imputed 'decisions' is *actual net cash flow from operating activities*, as required. The opposite effect is true for decreases.

The above 'explanation' is no more than a useful device for seeing what should be added on and subtracted, and to give a 'feel' for the reconciliation process. There is actually no such sequential decision process. Note that the term 'operating' in 'operating activities' has a slightly different connotation from that in 'operating profit' as used in the profit and loss account. The former excludes all fixed asset elements, which are included under 'investing activities'. The latter includes matched effects for fixed assets, e.g. depreciation, and certain gains or losses on disposals. The term 'operating' is not addressed satisfactorily anywhere in any conceptual sense.

FRS 1's net and gross bases

FRS 1 requires the indirect approach, i.e. the reconciliation of 'operating profit' to 'net cash flow from operating activities' (note 1), to be given as a note disclosure in all cash flow statements, not on the face of the statement. In addition, companies are given the *option* whether to disclose the individual operating receipts and payments of the direct approach on the face of the statement. If they take the option, FRS 1 terms this the 'gross' basis. If they do not, it is termed the 'net' basis. The terms refer to the *treatment* on the *face of the statement*. The example above is a gross basis cash flow statement. If it were on the net basis, the shaded area would be omitted and only a single figure subtotal, 'net cash flows from operating activities' would be shown. The *gross* basis thus includes both *direct* and *indirect* approaches to calculating 'net cash flow from operating activities', the *net* basis only the *indirect* approach. *Company Reporting* (April 1994, p. 3) found that 98 per cent of 500 companies publishing financial statements in the previous 12 months had produced FRS 1 cash flow statements, but of these, only 5 per cent used the gross basis.

Preparation approaches

If the gross basis option were chosen, the statement would probably be prepared by setting up the accounting system to collect cash flow statement information at source. This is not quite the same as analysing receipts and payments, since under FRS 1, the cash flow statement is based on cash and cash equivalents, the latter being

> short-term, highly liquid investments which are readily convertible into known amounts of cash without notice and which were within three months of maturity when acquired; less advances from banks repayable within three months from the date of the advance. Cash equivalents include investments and advances denominated in foreign currency provided that they fulfil the above criteria (para. 3).

If the net basis were chosen (the default option) it would usually be prepared by being derived from other financial statements, A technique for doing this is the cash flow matrix illustrated later. The matrix could also be used in principle for gross basis cash flow statements, but space constraints preclude a discussion of this rarely used alternative.

Exercises

9.1 Under which of the five cash flow statement headings would the following items be classified: interest payments, loan repayments, dividends received, advance corporation tax, proceeds from sale of land, reorganization payments.

9.2 What is the difference between direct and indirect approaches to 'net cash flow from operating activities'?

9.3 How does the FRS 1's net basis for cash flow statements differ from its gross basis?

9.4 What is the relationship between net and gross bases for cash flow statements, and direct and indirect approaches to calculating 'net cash flow from operating activities'?

CONSOLIDATED CASH FLOW STATEMENTS

Consolidated cash flow statements can be prepared in two ways:

> (a) **Aggregation**: Individual company cash flow statements are added and consolidation adjustments made to reflect the change in scope of the accounts to a group basis.
> (b) **Deduction**: Consolidated cash flow statements are deduced from the other consolidated financial statements.

Either method can be used in principle for preparing gross or net basis cash flow statements. In practice, the link between preparation method and format is usually as shown in Figure 9.1.

Basis chosen Preparation method	Gross basis	Net basis
Aggregate company cash flow statements	Yes	Yes for some groups with foreign subsidiaries (see Chapter 11).
Deduce statements from consolidated balance sheets, profit and loss account and notes.	Rare	**Yes for groups with domestic subsidiaries.**

Figure 9.1 – Methods for preparing consolidated cash flow statements

The aggregation approach would usually be preferred where a group chooses to prepare cash flow statements under FRS 1's gross basis. Consolidation adjustments are not complicated, mainly the elimination of intra-group cash flows. The deduction approach would be the preferred approach for domestic groups who chose the net basis. These two approaches, shaded in Figure 9.1, are illustrated in this chapter. Some groups with foreign subsidiaries, whether they choose the net or gross basis, may find it necessary to use the aggregation approach (see Chapter 11). The deduction approach is probably the more commonly used approach in practice. The aggregation approach can be covered or omitted as desired without loss in continuity.

The aggregation consolidation approach

This basically straightforward approach is illustrated here for the gross basis, since all the calculations for the net basis are contained within it. A group wishing to use the aggregation approach for this purpose will need each of its subsidiaries to report to head office their cash flows analysed over the five categories, plus details of intra-group cash transactions. Careful checking at the parent is necessary to ensure the final figures are consistent with the other consolidated financial statements and that intra-group eliminations have been made consistently in all the types of consolidated financial statements.

Example 9.2 – Aggregating cash flow statements

Cash flow statements for Outpouring plc, its 80% owned subsidiary Incontinent plc, and its 25% owned equity accounted associate Swamped plc are as follows:

Cash flow statements for the year ended 31 December 1995

	Outpouring £m	£m	Incontinent £m	£m	Swamped £m	£m
Operating activities						
Receipts from customers	600		355		100	
Payments to suppliers	(300)		(255)		(40)	
Payments to employees	(150)		(60)		(30)	
Net cash inflow from operating activities		150		40		30
Returns on inv & servicing of financing						
Interest paid	(10)		(5)		(4)	
Interest received	7		—		—	
Dividends received – subsidiary	8		—		—	
– associate	3		—		—	
Dividends paid	(16)		(10)		(12)	
Net cash outflow on inv & serv. of financing		(8)		(15)		(16)
Investing activities						
Payments for fixed assets	(165)		(35)		(10)	
Sales proceeds from fixed assets	40		10		3	
Net cash outflow on investing activities		(125)		(25)		(7)
Financing activities						
Loan issues	20		17		—	
Loan repayments	(16)		(10)		—	
Net cash inflow from financing activities		4		7		—
Increase in cash and cash equivalents		21		7		7

Note – Reconciliation of operating profit to cash inflow from operating activities

	Outpouring £m	Incontinent £m	Swamped £m
Operating profit	154	34	28
Depreciation	30	13	10
Gain on fixed asset disposal	—	(4)	(2)
Increase in (operating) debtors	(28)	(8)	(3)
Increase in stocks	(12)	(10)	(4)
Increase in (operating) creditors	6	15	1
Cash inflow from operating activities	150	40	30

Further information

(i) Intra-group cash flows were as follows:

	£m
On intra-group trading between Outpouring and Incontinent	100
Fixed asset sales from Incontinent to Outpouring	(10)
Loans from Outpouring to Incontinent	12
Loan payments from Incontinent to Outpouring, split:	
capital	(5)
interest	(4)

(ii) Outpouring sells goods to Incontinent plc at a mark-up of 25% on cost. Stocks of such goods held by Incontinent plc and related debtors and creditors were as follows. There is no intra-group trading with Swamped plc.

	Opening	Closing
Incontinent stocks (DR)	15	20
Outpouring operating debtors (DR)	16	18
Incontinent operating creditors (CR)	(16)	(18)

(iii) The gain on fixed asset sale of £4m by Incontinent plc all related to the sale to Outpouring.

Required
Prepare a consolidated cash flow statement for the Outpouring Group for the year ended 31 December 1995 in gross format using the aggregation approach.

Solution
The approach involves eliminating the intra-group cash flows as shown in Figure 9.2. Swamped plc is an associate, and only *dividends received* from it are shown in the consolidated cash flow statement. Therefore no amendment to the parent's cash flow statement is needed to reflect the associate's impact on the consolidated statement. Note that after the elimination of intra-group dividends with Outpouring, the cash flow remaining relating to minority interests is minority dividends paid.

Reconciliation of operating profit to cash flow from operations
Though consolidation adjustments, e.g. fair values at acquisition, extra depreciation and unrealized intra-group profits, do *not* affect cash and so are not reflected in the above *direct* format cash flow statement, they *do* affect the indirect format reconciliation at the bottom of Figure 9.2. This is because 'operating profit', 'depreciation', 'increase in stocks', etc., must be based on *consolidated* figures and so are not the simple aggregation of the subsidiary's balances. The aggregated balances are therefore adjusted for relevant alignment adjustments. The 'consolidated operating profit' figure and 'consolidated depreciation', etc., can be checked with the other consolidated financial statements. However, in more complex examples there is not always a simple correspondence to the change in consolidated balances so the procedures below are necessary.

Reconciling items

(i) Increase in stocks
The aggregate stock increase of parent and subsidiary (not associate) of £22m (i.e. 12 + 10) is expressed at company cost and has to be adjusted to reflect the *consolidated* stock increase. Unrealized intra-group profits in opening and closing stocks must therefore be determined, i.e.

			£m
Opening	$25/125 \times 15$	=	3
Closing	$25/125 \times 20$	=	(4)
Net decrease		=	(1)

Closing stocks are adjusted downwards by more than opening stocks, so the increase in consolidated stocks will be £21m (i.e. 22 – 1). Operating profits are also adjusted downwards by £1m reflecting the adjustment.

(ii) Increase in debtors
Aggregate debtors have increased by £36m (i.e. 28 + 8). Intra-group debtors have increased by £2m (i.e. 18 - 16) , therefore *third-party* (consolidated) debtors have increased by £34m (36 – 2).

(iii) Intra-group fixed asset transfers

	£m
Cost to Incontinent	10
Cost to group	(6)
Net difference	4

All the gains on fixed asset disposals are intra-group and none are on transactions to *third-parties*.

Consolidated cash flow statement – Outpouring Group – year ended 31 December 1995

	£m	£m
Operating activities		
Receipts from customers	855	
Payments to suppliers	(455)	
Payments to employees	(210)	
Net cash inflow from operating activities		190

Description	Outpouring	Incontinent	Adjustments	Consolidated
Receipts from customers	600	355	(100)	855
Payments to customers	(300)	(255)	100	(455)
Payments to employees	(150)	(60)		(210)
Net cash inflow from operating activities	150	40	-	190
Interest paid	(10)	(5)	4	(11)
Interest received	7	-	(4)	3
Dividends received - subsidiary	8	-	(8)	-
- associate	3			3
Dividends paid - parent	(16)	-	-	(16)
- subsidiary		(10)	8	(2) minority dividend
Fixed asset payments	(165)	(35)	10	(190)
Fixed asset sale proceeds	40	10	(10)	40
Loans issued	20	17	(12) (5)	20
Loans repaid	(16)	(10)	5 12	(9)
Increase in cash & cash equivalents	21	7	-	28

Indirect format reconciliation	Outpouring	Incontinent	Adjustments		Consolidated
Operating profit	154	34	Intra-group stocks adjustment	(1)	183
			Intra-group fixed asset gain	(4)	
Depreciation	30	13	-		43
Gain on fixed asset disposal	-	(4)	Intra-group fixed asset gain	4	-
Increase in operating debtors	(28)	(8)	Intra-group debtors adjustment	2	(34)
Increase in stocks	(12)	(10)	Intra group stock adjustment	1	(21)
Increase in operating creditors	6	15	Intra-group creditor adjustment	(2)	19
Net cash inflow from operating activities	150	40	-		190

Figure 9.2 – Outpouring Group – Consolidated cashflow statements by direct aggregation

Returns on inv & servicing of financing

Interest paid	(11)	
Interest received	3	
Dividends received – associate	3	
Dividends paid – parent	(16)	
– minority interests	(2)	
Net cash outflow on inv & serv. of financing		(23)

Investing activities

Payments for fixed assets	(190)	
Sales proceeds from fixed assets	40	
Net cash outflow on investing activities		(150)

Financing Activities

Loan issues	20	
Loan repayments	(9)	
Net cash inflow from financing activities		11
Increase in cash and cash equivalents		28

Note – Reconciliation of consolidated operating profit to net cash inflow from operating activities:

	£m
Operating profit	183
Depreciation charges	43
Increase in (operating) debtors	(34)
Increase in (operating) creditors	19
Decrease in stocks	(21)
Net cash inflow from operating activities	190

Other notes required by FRS 1 are dealt with in later sections. Note that the only cash flows relating to associates and minority interests in the above example are dividends.

Exercises

9.5 What cash flows would normally appear in consolidated cash flow statements relating to minority interests and associates?

9.6 Cash flow statements for Hangover plc and its 60% owned subsidiary Damocles plc are as follows:

Cash flow statements for the year ended 30 June 1995

	Hangover		Damocles	
	£m	£m	£m	£m
Operating activities				
Receipts from customers	405		245	
Payments to suppliers	(195)		(58)	
Payments to employees	(100)		(120)	
Net cash inflow from operating activities		110	67	
Returns on inv & servicing of financing				
Interest paid	(6)		(3)	
Interest received	9		—	
Dividends received	9		—	
Dividends paid	(23)		(15)	
Net cash outflow on inv & serv. of financing		(11)		(18)
Investing activities				
Payments for fixed assets	(98)		(40)	
Sales proceeds from fixed assets	—		15	
Net cash outflow on investing activities		(98)		(25)

Financing Activities		
Loan issues	30	10
Loan repayments	(10)	(30)
Net cash inflow from financing activities	20	(20)
Increase/decrease in cash and cash equivalents	21	4

Note – Reconciliation of operating profit to cash inflow from operating activities

	Hangover £m	Damocles £m
Operating profit	100	64
Depreciation	15	10
Loss on fixed asset disposal	6	2
Decrease in (operating) debtors	8	12
Increase in stocks	(18)	(11)
Decrease in (operating) creditors	(1)	(10)
Net cash inflow from operating activities	110	67

Further information

(i) Intra-group cash flows were as follows:

	£m
On intra-group trading	78
Fixed asset sales from Damocles to Hangover	(15)
Loans from Hangover to Damocles	15
Loan payments from Damocles to Hangover, split:	
capital	(6)
interest	(3)

(ii) Damocles sells goods to Hangover plc at a mark-up of 20% on cost. Stocks of such goods held by Hangover plc and related debtors and creditors were as follows:

	Opening	Closing
Hangover stocks	24	18
Damocles debtors	20	10
Hangover creditors	(20)	(10)

(iii) The loss on fixed asset sale of £2m by Damocles plc all related to the sale to Hangover.

Required
Prepare a consolidated cash flow statement for the Hangover Group for the year ended 31 March 1995 using the aggregation approach.

The deduction consolidation approach

As stated above, the net basis is the most commonly used basis for cash flow statements. Below the deduction consolidation approach based on a cash flow matrix preparation technique is used below to deduce the consolidated cash flow statement from the other consolidated primary financial statements. The approach has advantages for some groups compared with the aggregation approach. Whilst being technically slightly more tricky, it is often computationally more efficient. This is because only a smaller number of (previously prepared) consolidated financial statements are used – i.e. opening and closing balance sheets, profit and loss account, statement of total recognized gains and losses, and reconciliation of movements in shareholders' funds. Under the aggregation approach the number of individual company financial statements used is equal to the number of subsidiaries. The deduction approach also does not usually require further intra-group eliminations, since the statements from which the cash flow statement is derived have already had intra-group items adjusted. The matrix approach also ensures consistency since it *forces* a common database. For our purposes it also provides a useful overview of the consolidation process. However, it can lead to a mistaken view that the consolidated cash flow statement is a secondary statement, since it is prepared after the other consolidated statements, and using their data. But, in principle, *any* of the primary statements can be deduced from the set of the others.

The Cash Flow Matrix

The matrix layout used to prepare the cash flow statement has the following basic structure:

1. *Opening balance sheet balances* .
2. Reconstruction of double entries for profit and loss and statement of total recognized gains and losses
3 Investing/financing transactions from notes to accounts
4. Amounts deduced by differencing .
5. *Closing balance sheet balances* .

Each column is effectively a 'T' account, but in a vertical format. *Debits* are *positive* (+) and *credits* are *negative* (−). Consider for example, dividends payable:

T Account

Dividends payable

Divs paid	5	Balance b/f	5
		Divs payable	6
Balance c/f	6		
	11		11
		Balance b/f	6

Matrix column

Description	Divs payable
Opening balance	(5)
Dividends payable	(6)
Dividends paid	5
Closing balance	(6)

The rule 'debits equal credits' translates as 'each set of entries adds to zero across the matrix'. The opening and closing balance sheets are top and bottom lines respectively, and a summarized profit and loss account/retained profits 'account' is the right-hand column. *The cash flow statement is an analysis of the left-hand column, and is the end product of the matrix.*

Steps in constructing the matrix are shown in Figure 9.3. They reconstruct in summarized form the accounting entries linking opening and closing consolidated balance sheets:

(1) starting by reconstructing profit and loss/statement of total recognized gains and losses entries,
(2) then reconstructing in as detailed form as possible entries from other notes to the accounts,
(3) and finally reconstructing in net form any entries remaining − differencing.

Steps	Description
Matrix headings	Determine headings from balance sheet captions or notes to the accounts. Decide which balances to include in cash and cash equivalents. Combine headings where separate analysis is unnecessary to determine cash flows: e.g. fixed asset cost and accumulated depreciation, share capital and premium, current and long-term portions of long-term loans. Where necessary under each of the five categories (i.e. 'operations', 'returns on investments and servicing of finance', 'taxation', 'investing', and 'financing'), there should be a heading for 'debtor' and one for 'creditor' type balances, since cash flows must be determined for each category.
Top and bottom lines	Fill in opening and closing balance sheet amounts.
Top section	*Profit and loss items above operating profit* - start by treating 'operating profit' *as if* it were 'potential' *total* cash flow, a debit (positive) in the cash column, and a credit (negative) in the retained profits column. *Non-operating items:* transfer out of the cash column, profit and loss items which relate to *non-operating activities,* completing the double entry to the appropriate asset or liability column, e.g. depreciation is transferred out by debiting (positive) the cash column, and crediting (negative) the fixed assets column. This step leaves 'potential' *operating* cash flow. *Adjust for accruals:* 'potential' operating cash flow is adjusted to actual operating cash flow. Increases in stock / *operating* debtors are a negative (credit) figure in the cash column, completed to stocks and *operating* debtors columns. *Operating* creditor increases are positive (debit) to the cash column, completed to *operating* creditors. Decreases are the opposite. *Profit and loss items below operating profit* - Enter them (e.g. exceptional fixed asset gains and losses, interest, tax & dividends) in the right-hand (retained profits) column and reconstruct their double entries to their appropriate columns (eg. dividends to dividends payable). Exceptional gains or losses on fixed asset disposals must be reconstructed to the fixed asset column. Enter other items in the *statement of total recognised gains and losses* and *note of movements in shareholder funds* not covered by the profit and loss account entries above, e.g. revaluations and share issues, to revaluation reserves, share capital & premium columns etc. Reconstruct their double entries to appropriate columns.
Middle section	Enter double entries for any 'investing' and 'financing' transactions gleaned from *notes to the accounts.* This includes acquisition and disposals of subsidiari *Sub total each column of the matrix*
Bottom section	Where the subtotal for any column is different from the closing balance (the bottom line), deduce any remaining cash flows by *differencing.*

Figure 9.3 – Steps in constructing indirect (net) approach matrix.

The matrix approach to preparing cash flow statements is illustrated with an individual company example, followed by the preparation of a consolidated cash flow statement.

Example 9.3 – The cash flow matrix, for an individual company

Consider the following financial statements for Marx and Sparks plc:

Balance sheets at 30 June (£m)

	£m	1995 £m	£m	1994 £m
Fixed assets – cost [2]		75		60
– accumulated depreciation		(25)		(30)
		50		30
Current assets				
Stocks	35		37	
Operating Debtors	62		43	
Cash	20		12	
	117		92	
Creditors due within a year				
Operating creditors	37		32	
Corporation tax	12		10	
Interest payable	3		2	
Dividends payable	6		5	
	58		49	
Net current assets		59		43
Creditors over one year				
Loans [3]		(27)		(23)
		82		50
Capital and reserves				
Share capital		7		5
Share premium		18		15
Revaluation reserve [1]		10		—
Retained profits		47		30
		82		50

Profit and loss account for year ended 30 June 1995

	£m	£m
Sales		543
Cost of sales		(377)
Gross profit		166
Depreciation	5	
Loss on fixed asset sale	2	
Other operating expenses	121	
		(128)
Operating profit		38
Interest payable		(3)
Profit on ordinary activities before tax		35
Tax		(12)
Profit on ordinary activities after tax		23
Dividends proposed		(6)
Profit retained for the year		17

Description	Cash	Operating Debtors	Stock	Fixed assets	Operating Creditors	Tax payable	Interest payable	Dividends payable	Loans	Share cap & prem	Reval reserve	Retained profits
Opening balances	12	43	37	30	(32)	(10)	(2)	(5)	(23)	(20)	-	(30)
Operating profit	38											(38)
Remove non-operating items												
Depreciation	5			(5)								
Loss on fixed asset sale	2			(2)								
Adjust for accruals												
Increase in operating debtors	(19)	19										
Decrease in stocks	2		(2)									
Increase in operating creditors	5				(5)							
[Net cash inflow from operations	33	19	(2)	(7)	(5)							(38)
Interest payable							(3)					3
Tax						(12)						12
Dividends								(6)				6
Fixed asset revaluation (*St of recognised gains and losses*)				10							(10)	
Notes:												
Fixed assets payment	(41)			41								
Loans issued	14								(14)			
Subtotal	18	62	35	74	(37)	(22)	(5)	(11)	(37)	(20)	(10)	(47)
Other flows - differencing:												
Fixed asset sale proceeds	24			(24)								
Tax paid	(10)					10						
Interest paid	(2)						2					
Dividends paid	(5)							5				
Loans repaid	(10)								10			
Shares issued	5									(5)		
Closing balances	20	62	35	50	(37)	(12)	(3)	(6)	(27)	(25)	(10)	(47)

Figure 9.4 – Cash flow matrix – table example for a single company

Extracts from the accounts

1. Extract from 'Statement of total recognized gains and losses'
   Revaluation of land   £10m

2. *Fixed asset movements (NBV)*   *£m*
   Opening NBV   30
   Purchases   41
   Depreciation for year   (5)
   Revaluations (Note 1)   10
   Disposals at NBV   (26)
   Closing NBV   50

Fixed asset purchases and sales were all for cash (i.e. there were no investing debtors or creditors)

3. Loans issued during the year were £14m.

Required

Prepare a cash flow matrix and a net basis cash flow statement for the year ended 30 June 1995 for Marx and Sparks plc.

Solution

Cash flow statements are manageable provided you take it one step at a time. Follow the steps in Figure 9.3 carefully in conjunction with the explanations below. The cash flow matrix is shown in Figure 9.4. The area in the matrix referring to the reconciliation of 'operating profit' to 'net cash inflow from operating activities' is shaded.

Matrix headings

When considering potential debtors and creditors for the five headings, note there are no investing debtors and creditors in this simpler example. Tax 'creditor' has its own heading. Dividends and interest payable are 'returns creditors'. They are given separate columns because there is enough space! Fixed assets and shares only have one heading each since more are not necessary to deduce cash flows. Now check each of the headings in Figure 9.4.

Top section – profit and loss account above operating profit

This is the basis of the reconciliation of 'operating profit' to 'net cash flow from operating activities'. Operating profit is treated initially as 'potential total cash inflow' and is entered as a positive entry (DR) in the cash column and a negative (CR) in the profit and loss/retained profits column.

Adjustment for items not relating to operating activities: removal of such 'investing type' items as depreciation and loss on fixed asset disposals (they were deductions in determining operating profit so they are added back) adjusts 'potential total cash flow' (operating profit) to 'potential cash net flow from operating activities'. Loss on fixed asset sale is taken to the fixed asset column for reasons to be discussed below.

Adjustment for accruals: the adjustments for accruals in the cash column convert 'potential cash flow from operating activities' to actual 'net cash inflow from operating activities'. Increases in operating debtors can be viewed as tying up potential cash in working capital and are thus negative (credit) figures in the cash column, completed to stocks and operating debtors columns. Operating creditor increases and stock decreases can be viewed as releasing cash so each are a positive figure (debit) to the cash column. The line in italics in the matrix, 'Cash inflow from ops' is a subtotal of the shaded matrix lines.

Top section – profit and loss account below operating profit

Operating profit has been entered above as a single figure in the profit and loss/retained profits column. Each item below operating profit is entered in the retained profits (right-hand) column, and its double entry is completed to the appropriate column/account. From the extract from the 'Statement of total recognized gains and losses' the revaluation entry is reconstructed.

Middle section – notes to the accounts

Usually the notes relevant to cash flow statement preparation relate to fixed asset movements and changes in borrowings. Putting loan issues in this section means that the gross amount of loan repayments can be deduced below.

Bottom section – differencing

The matrix must now be subtotalled in each column. In carrying out the differencing between the subtotal and the closing balance sheet in the bottom line, columns should be tackled left to right. Usually the difference on taxation is tax paid, on dividends and interest, the respective amounts paid.

Fixed assets: Disposals of fixed assets in notes to published accounts are measured at net book amounts (as in note 2 to the accounts above). The instruction in the top section of the matrix above to reconstruct gains on disposals of fixed assets direct to the fixed asset account is merely a handy device to ensure the difference on the fixed asset column is fixed asset disposal revenues, to enable the determination of cash flows. In this example the net book amount removed from the fixed asset account on disposal of fixed assets (brackets indicate a negative/credit figure) is (£26m). This is analysed in the fixed asset column into loss on sale (£2m), and disposal revenues of (£24m). In this example, fixed asset purchases and sales are assumed to be for cash.

Cash flow statement
The cash flow statement is taken from the first column of the matrix. It is the same cash flow statement used to introduce this chapter in Example 9.1, except that the individual operating receipts and payments (shaded in grey on that page) have not been deduced since we are only considering here the net basis. The reconciliation note to the cash flow statement is the shaded area in the cash column.

EXERCISE

9.7 Consider the following financial statements for Hardup plc

Balance sheets at 31 December (£m)

	£m	1995 £m	£m	1994 £m
Fixed assets – net [2]		146		120
Current assets				
Stocks	120		90	
Operating debtors	150		60	
Cash	9		80	
	279		230	
Creditors due within a year				
Operating creditors	70		60	
Corporation tax	80		60	
Interest payable	3		4	
Dividends payable	37		56	
	190		180	
Net current assets		89		50
Creditors over one year				
Loans[3]		(30)		(40)
		205		130
Capital and reserves				
Share capital		50		40
Share premium		55		40
Revaluation reserve [1]		30		–
Retained profits		70		50
		205		130

Profit and loss account for year ended 31 December 1995

	£m	£m
Sales		1,000
Cost of sales		(600)
Gross profit		400
Depreciation	36	
Gain on sale of fixed asset	(5)	
General expenses	229	
		(260)
Operating profit		140
Interest payable		(3)
Profit on ordinary activities before tax		137
Tax		(80)
Profit on ordinary activities after tax		57
Dividends proposed		(37)
Profit retained for the year		20

Extracts from the accounts
1. Extract from 'Statement of total recognized gains and losses'
   Revaluation of land   £30m
2. Fixed asset movements (at net book value, i.e. cost less accumulated depreciation)

	£m
Opening NBV	120
Purchases	50
Depreciation for year	(36)
Revaluations (Note 1)	30
Disposals at NBV	(18)
Closing NBV	146

Fixed asset purchases and sales were all for cash (i.e. there were no investing debtors or creditors)

3. Loans issued during the year were £10m.

Required
By first preparing a cash flow matrix, prepare a net basis cash flow statement for the year ended 31 December 1995 for Hardup plc.

Consolidated cash flow statements

The following example applies the above technique to a more realistic situation involving consolidated financial statements. It appears at first sight to be rather complex. Consolidated cash flow statements involve detective work, but are not conceptually very difficult, involving a series of systematic steps and mainly a basic familiarity with first course double entry principles. Once you have worked through one example, you will find they all have very similar structure – what you need to look for is fairly constant, so the second problem is very much easier. The differences between this and the first example to look out for are:

(1) There are now cash equivalents as well as cash.
(2) There are investing creditors and the current portion of long-term loans is included in current liabilities.
(3) Group accounting aspects include an investment in an associate, minority interests, a reorganization provision, and the acquisition of a subsidiary.

Example 9.4 – Deduction of consolidated cash flows from other primary consolidated statements

The accountant of the Fundsflow Group produces the following draft accounts. The analysis of continuing and discontinued operations in the profit and loss account, required by FRS 3, is not needed here and so is not included.

Balance sheets at 31 December

	Note	£m	1995 £m	£m	1994 £m
Fixed assets					
Intangible assets	1		72.0		80.0
Tangible assets	2		175.5		164.0
Invs in assoc undertakings	3		36.0		35.0
			283.5		279.0
Current assets					
Stocks		189.0		193.0	
Debtors	4	134.5		116.0	
Deposits due within a year	5	66.0		50.0	
Cash		21.5		20.0	
		411.0		379.0	
Creditors due within one year					
Bank borrowings	6	(10.0)		(8.0)	
Current portion of long-term loan	6	(12.0)		(9.5)	
Other creditors and accruals	7	(157.0)		(149.5)	
		(179.0)		(167.0)	
Net current assets			232.0		212.0
Creditors over one year					
Bank borrowings	6		(111.0)		(123.0)
Provisions for liabilities and charges	8		(6.0)		(10.0)
			398.5		358.0
Capital and reserves					
Share capital (£1 ordinary)	9		49.0		40.0
Share premium	9		115.0		106.0
Revaluation reserve			40.0		30.0
Retained profits			165.5		157.0
			369.5		333.0
Minority interests			29.0		25.0
			398.5		358.0

Consolidated profit and loss account – year ended 31 December 1995

	Note	£m
Sales		778.5
Cost of sales		(496.0)
Gross profit		282.5
Net operating expenses	10	(228.0)
Operating profit		54.5
Loss on fixed asset disposal		(3.5)
Profit on ordinary activities before interest		51.0
Income from investment in associate		10.0
Interest payable		(9.0)
Profit on ordinary activities before tax		52.0
Taxation – associated undertaking		(5.0)
Taxation – group		(17.0)
Profit on ordinary activities after tax		30.0
Minority interests		(7.5)
Profit for the financial year		22.5
Dividends – interim		(6.0)
Dividends – final		(8.0)
Retained profit for the financial year		8.5

Statement of total recognized gains and losses – year ended 31 December 1995

	£m
Profit for the financial year	22.5
Revaluation gains on properties	10.0
Total recognized gains for the year	32.5

Notes to the accounts

1. Intangible assets:

	1995	1994
	£m	£m
Cost	102	100
Amortization to date	(30)	(20)
Net book amount	72	80

2. Tangible assets (net book amounts):

	£m
Opening amount	164.0
Additions – purchases	32.0
Additions – subsidiary acquisition	7.0
Revaluation of properties	10.0
Disposals	(19.5)
Depreciation for year	(18.0)
Net book amount at 31 December 1995	175.5

3. Investments in associates:

	1995	1994
	£m	£m
Goodwill	8	10
Net assets	28	25
	36	35

4. Debtors:

	1995	1994
	£m	£m
Operating debtors	134.5	116.0

5. Deposits less than one year:
All deposits are readily convertible into known amounts of cash and were less than three months to maturity when acquired.

6. Borrowings:

	1995	1994
Due within one year	£m	£m
Bank overdrafts	10.0	8.0
Current portion of long-term loans	12.0	9.5
	22.0	17.5
Due in more than one year		
Bank borrowings	111.0	123.0

No new long-term borrowings were made during the year.

7. Other creditors and accruals:

	1995	1994
	£m	£m
Operating creditors	93	86
Investing creditors	25	20
Taxation payable	27	28.5
Dividends payable	8	10
Interest payable	4	5.0
	157	149.5

8. Provisions:

	1995	1994
	£m	£m
Reorganization provision	6.0	10.0

The provision was set up last year for closure expenses.

9. Share issues:

	£m
Opening	146
Acquisition of subsidiary	8
Purchase of fixed assets	10
Closing	164

10. Net operating expenses:

	£m
Depreciation	18
Goodwill amortization	10
Other operating costs	200
	228

11. Acquisition of subsidiary:
An 80% interest in Subservient plc was acquired at 30 June 1995 for £10m. Its balances then were as follows. At acquisition, the fair value of its fixed assets were £7m.

	£m
Fixed assets	5
Stocks (raw materials)	4
Operating debtors	3
Cash	1
	13
Operating creditors	3
Taxation	2
Share capital & premium	3
Retained profits	5
	13

Required
Prepare a cash flow matrix for the Fundsflow Group and a cash flow statement under the net basis for the year ended 31 December 1995.

Solution
Follow the steps in Figure 9.3 carefully in conjunction with the explanations below, one step at a time. The consolidated cash flow matrix is shown in Figure 9.5. Areas shaded are those matters particularly referring to group accounting and also the reconciliation of 'operating profit' to 'net cash inflow from operating activities'.

Matrix headings
Cash and cash equivalents: now there are cash equivalents as well as cash. FRS 1's definition of 'cash equivalents' is repeated here for convenience:

> short-term, highly liquid investments which are readily convertible into known amounts of cash without notice and which were within three months of maturity when acquired; less advances

Description	Cash equiv	Op debtors	Stock	Fixed assets	Good-will	Inv in assoc	Op creds	Inv creds	Tax creds	Return creds	Loans	Reorg prov	Mino interest	S cap & prem	Reval res	Retained profits
Opening balances	62.0	116.0	193.0	164.0	80.0	35.0	(86.0)	(20.0)	(28.5)	(15.0)	(132.5)	(10.0)	(25.0)	(146.0)	(30.0)	(157.0)
Operating profit	54.5															(54.5)
Depreciation	18.0			(18.0)												
Goodwill amortise	10.0				(10.0)											
Stock decrease	8.0		(8.0)													
Op debtors increase	(15.5)	15.5														
Op creditors increase	4.0						(4.0)									
[Net cash inflow from operating activities	79.0	15.5	(8.0)	(18.0)	(10.0)		(4.0)									(54.5)
Loss on fixed asset				(3.5)												3.5
Associate profits						10.0										(10.0)
Interest charge										(9.0)						9.0
Taxation charge						(5.0)			(17.0)							22.0
Minority interest													(7.5)			7.5
Dividends paid & prop										(14.0)						14.0
F Asset revaluations (st of recognised G&L)				10.0											(10.0)	
Notes:																
Fixed asset purchases				32.0				(22.0)						(10.0)		
Subsidiary:																
consideration	(2.0)													(8.0)		
net assets acquired	1.0	3.0	4.0	7.0	2.0		(3.0)		(2.0)				(2.0)			
Subtotal	140.0	134.5	189.0	191.5	72.0	40.0	(93.0)	(42.0)	(47.5)	(38.0)	(132.5)	(10.0)	(34.5)	(164.0)	(40.0)	(165.5)
Fixed asset receipts	16.0			(16.0)												
Assoc div received	4.0					(4.0)										
Fixed asset payments	(17.0)							17.0								
Tax paid	(20.5)								20.5							
Dividends paid	(16.0)									16.0						
Interest paid	(10.0)									10.0						
Loans repaid	(9.5)										9.5					
Reorganis cost paid	(4.0)											4.0				
Mino dividends paid	(5.5)												5.5			
Closing balances	77.5	134.5	189.0	175.5	72.0	36.0	(93.0)	(25.0)	(27.0)	(12.0)	(123.0)	(6.0)	(29.0)	(164.0)	(40.0)	(165.5)

Figure 9.5 – Consolidated cash flow matrix Funds Flow Group.

from banks repayable within three months from the date of the advance. Cash equivalents include investments and advances denominated in foreign currency provided that they fulfil the above criteria.

(para. 3)

As deposits (note 5) have an *original* maturity of less than three months, they and the bank overdraft are included in cash equivalents. The current portion of long-term bank loan is not included in cash equivalents since its original maturity is greater than three months. So 'cash and cash equivalents' are:

	Cash	plus	Deposits	less	Overdraft	equals	Total
Opening	20.0	+	50.0	–	8.0	=	62.0
Closing	21.5	+	66.0	–	10.0	=	77.5

Considering debtors and creditors for the five headings, note separate headings are needed for investing and operating creditors – there are no investing debtors in this example. Tax 'creditor' has its own heading. Under 'returns creditors', dividends and interest payable are combined into a single heading purely to enable the matrix to be fitted to a page. 'Borrowings' in creditors under one year and over one year are combined into one heading for 'loans payable'. Now check each of the headings in Figure 9.4.

'Combined' creditors	Closing	Opening
Returns creditors		
Interest payable	4	5
Dividends payable	8	10
	12	15
Loans (financing creditors):		
Current portion of long-term loans	12	9.5
Long-term loans	111	123
	123	132.5

Top section – profit and loss account above operating profit
This is the basis of the reconciliation of 'operating profit' to 'net cash flow from operating activities'. Operating profit is treated initially as 'potential total cash inflow'.

Adjustment for items not relating to operating activities: removal of 'investing type' items now includes goodwill amortization in adjusting 'potential total cash flow' to 'potential cash net flow from operating activities'. Profit on fixed asset sale is taken to the fixed asset column as before.

Adjustment for accruals: these convert 'potential cash flow from operating activities' to actual 'net cash flow from operating activities' and are added on or deducted according to whether they are deemed to 'release' or 'tie up' potential cash. The matrix line 'net cash inflow from operating activities' is a subtotal of the shaded matrix lines. In consolidated cash flow statements, these adjustments for accruals must *exclude any balances arising from subsidiaries acquired or disposed of.* These are dealt with in the middle section of the matrix (i.e. reconstruction from notes to the accounts). The simplest way to obtain these amounts is to start with the total balance sheet increase/decrease in operating debtors, operating creditors and stocks. Then remove the part of the increase or decrease relating to balances from subsidiaries acquired or disposed of here (note 11). For example, the overall consolidated stock decrease for the year from the consolidated balance sheets is £4m (£193m – £189m). Within this overall decrease is £4m stock acquired with the subsidiary (note 11). Therefore ongoing activities must have a stock decrease of £8m, and it is this £8m which is used in the reconciliation of 'operating profit' to 'net cash flow from operating activities'.

Top section – profit and loss account below operating profit
Operating profit has been entered above as a single figure in the profit and loss/retained profits column. The double entry for each item below operating profit is completed as before. The group accounting items of interest are income from associates, which is completed to the 'investment in associates' column, and the minority interest profit and loss charge, completed to the 'minority interests' column. From the statement of total recognized gains and losses the fixed asset revaluation entry is reconstructed.

Middle section – notes to the accounts
Relevant notes relate to fixed asset movements, changes in borrowings, and acquisitions or disposals of the subsidiaries, notes 2, 6 and 11 above. From these notes it can be deduced that there was an issue of shares to finance directly the purchase of fixed assets – a non-cash transaction. The

rest of the fixed asset purchases, unlike the earlier example are presumed to be on credit, and reconstructed to investing creditors. Crucial from a group accounting perspective, the effect of the acquisition of the subsidiary on the matrix and in the cash flow statement is now considered in detail.

Acquisition of subsidiary

In the matrix this is dealt with over two lines, the first shows the consideration given, the second, the subsidiary's balances acquired measured on a consolidated basis – the assets, liabilities, goodwill and minority interests underlying the investment. The consideration of £10m from note 13, is made up of shares £8m (note 9) and therefore £2m cash. This total of £10m must now be analysed into the underlying assets, liabilities, goodwill and minority interests. Note 13 gives the individual company balances of the subsidiary. The table below shows how to convert these to corresponding balances expressed on a consolidated basis.

Consolidated financial statement effects of the acquisition transaction

| Description | Raw data | | Consolidation adjustments | | | Consolidated statement effects of acquisition | |
	Inv recording	Orig subsid balances	Fair value adjustment	Reclassify equity	Elimin-ation	Consid-eration	Consol-idated
Cash	(2.0)	1.0				(2.0)	1.0
Operating debtors		3.0					3.0
Stocks (materials)		4.0					4.0
Fixed assets		5.0	2.0				7.0
Investment	10.0				(10.0)		
Trade creditors		(3.0)					(3.0)
Taxation		(2.0)					(2.0)
Share cap & prem	(8.0)	(3.0)		3.0		(8.0)	
Revaluation reserve			(2.0)	2.0			—
Retained profits		(5.0)		5.0			—
Goodwill				(8.0)	10.0		2.0
Minority interest				(2.0)			(2.0)

The last two columns are the consolidated financial statement effects of the purchase, the end product, and will become the relevant lines of the cash flow matrix. The first two columns show the acquisition transaction in the *parent's* individual accounts and the subsidiary's individual company balances at acquisition. The next three columns enter the fair value adjustments for fixed assets at acquisition, analyse the subsidiary's equity at that date between pre-acquisition equity/goodwill and minority interests, and cancel the investment, £10m, against pre-acquisition equity (£8m) to determine goodwill. The effect of the last two columns is as if the *group* had issued shares and paid cash to acquire the subsidiary's individual assets, liabilities, goodwill and minority interests.

Only the cash element of the consideration given and acquired will affect the cash column of the matrix, and therefore appear in the consolidated cash flow statement. FRS 1 requires that in the consolidated cash flow statement, the cash flow relating to the purchase of a subsidiary (to be disclosed under '*investing*' activities) should be *net of the subsidiary's cash acquired.* Here the net cash outflow will be:

| Net cash outflow | = | *Cash* consideration | – | *Cash* acquired |
| | = | £2m | – £1m = | £1m |

Bottom section – differencing

The matrix must now be subtotalled in each column. In differencing, columns should be tackled left to right. In nearly all examples the difference on associates is dividends received, on taxation – tax paid, on returns – dividends and interest paid, and on minority interest – minority dividends paid.

Fixed assets: as in the individual company example, reconstructing the gain/loss on fixed assets to the fixed asset column ensures the difference on the column is fixed asset disposal revenues. As there are no investing debtors here (Note 4) we assume this was a cash sale. The net book amount removed from the fixed asset account (£19.5m) is analysed in the fixed asset column into loss on sale (£3.5m), and disposal revenues of (£16m).

Investing debtors and creditors: the investing creditor column contains fixed asset purchases of (£22m), and the differencing entry is fixed asset payments of £17m, completed to the cash column. If there were an investing debtor column it would contain fixed asset disposal revenues and the differencing entry would be fixed asset receipts.

Pay particular attention to the following items which arise from a consolidated cash flow perspective.

1. Investment in associates – dividends received.
2. Reorganization provision – reorganization payments.
3. Minority interests – minority dividend paid.

A sub-analysis of the combined column 'returns payable' is necessary to determine separately (parent) dividends paid and taxation paid.

Analysis of returns on investments & servicing of finance creditors

Returns payable	Opening	Subsid acq	Charge	Payment	Closing
Interest	(5)	—	(9)	**10**	(4)
Dividends	(10)	—	(14)	**16**	(8)
Total	(15)	—	(23)	**26**	(12)

The published cash flow statement in net format

This is taken from the first column of the cash flow matrix and is shown below with some of the other notes required by FRS 1 to accompany the statement – the effects of major non-cash transactions (found usually by analysing 'fixed asset' and 'loan' columns) including acquisitions and disposals of subsidiaries, an analysis of opening and closing cash and cash equivalents and changes, and an analysis of changes in financing:

Fundsflow Group – Consolidated cash flow statement
for the year ended 31 December 1995

	£m	£m
Net cash inflow from operating activities (Note 1)		79.0
Returns on investments and servicing of finance		
Interest paid	(10.0)	
Dividends paid – parent	(16.0)	
Dividends paid – minority interests	(5.5)	
Dividends received from associate	4.0	
Net cash outflow from returns on investments and servicing of finance		(27.5)
Taxation		
Corporation tax paid	(20.5)	
Tax paid		(20.5)
Investing activities		
Payments for fixed assets (note 2)	(17.0)	
Sale proceeds for fixed assets	16.0	
Acquisition of subsidiary (note 3)	(1.0)	
Reorganization payments	(4.0)	
Net cash outflow from investing activities		(6.0)
Net cash outflow before financing		25.0
Financing		
Issue of ordinary share capital (note 2)	—	
Repayment of loans	(9.5)	
Net cash outflow from financing activities		(9.5)
Increase in cash and cash equivalents		15.5

Note

1. Reconciliation of operating profit to cash inflow from operating activities:

	£m
Operating profit	54.5
Depreciation charges	18.0
Increase in (operating) debtors	(15.5)
Increase in (operating) creditors	4.0
Decrease in stocks	8.0
Goodwill amortized	10.0
Net cash inflow from operating activities	79.0

2. Major non-cash transactions

(a) The group purchased £10m of fixed assets and issued in consideration £10m of ordinary shares.

(b) *Acquisition of subsidiary* – part of the consideration for acquiring Subservient plc was a share issue. Further details of the acquisition is set out below:

	£m
Net assets acquired	
Tangible fixed assets	7.0
Stocks	4.0
Debtors	3.0
Cash	1.0
Creditors	(3.0)
Taxation	(2.0)
Minority interest	(2.0)
	8.0
Goodwill	2.0
	0.0
Satisfied by	
Shares allotted	8.0
Cash	2.0
	10.0

3. Analysis of changes in cash and cash equivalents during the year

	Cash at bank and in hand	Deposits less than 3 months original maturity	Bank overdrafts	Total
Opening balances	20.0	50.0	(8.0)	62.0
Net increase in cash and cash equivalents				15.5
Closing balances	21.5	66.0	(10.0)	77.5

4. Analysis of changes in financing during the year

	Share capital & premium £m	Loans £m
Balances at 1 January 1995	146.0	132.5
Cash inflows/(outflows) from financing	—	(9.5)
Changes through non-cash transactions (Note 2)	18.0	—
Balances at 31 December 1995	164.0	123.0

In addition to the information in note 2b, FRS 1 requires in the year of acquisition or disposal, that material effects on amounts reported under each of the standard headings reflecting the cash flows of any subsidiary acquired or disposed of during the period, should be given as a cash flow statement note disclosure (para. 42). This information is not included here. Note particularly associates and minority interests on a dividends received and paid (cash) basis respectively, the treatment of the subsidiary acquisition on the face of the statement, and that the amount relating to reorganizations is based on payments. In a gross format statement, in addition, underlying receipts and payments relating to operating activities would have been disclosed on the face of the statement.

Other matters

The effect of including items such as the deposits as cash equivalents is that their inflows and outflows are not disclosed in the cash flow statement. If say the deposits had been *originally* repayable in nine months rather than three months, they would have been disclosed in the 'financing activities' section of the cash flow statement, and their gross inflows and outflows disclosed. FRS 1 criteria refer to the *original* maturity so that apparent (but not real) inflows and outflows would not be generated when say a one year deposit reaches three months to repayment. Under such circumstances no cash passes.

The example here is of a trading group. In manufacturing groups, the add-back for depreciation would be the amount of depreciation *incurred* for the year (i.e. the amount in the fixed asset note to the accounts) if the stock increase/decrease is stated on an absorption costing basis (i.e. the stock includes manufacturing depreciation absorbed). For a demonstration of this and further discussion, see Nurnberg (1989).

Example 9.5 – Disposal of subsidiary

This example can be omitted without loss in continuity. Sceptre plc, which has a year end of 31 December 1995, disposes of an 80% subsidiary Orb plc on 30 September 1995 for £14m in cash. It requires Orb plc to prepare interim accounts at that date, and these are as follows:

	£m		£m
Fixed assets	5	Operating creditors	3
Stocks (raw materials)	4	Taxation	2
Operating debtors	3	Share capital & premium	3
Cash	_1_	Retained profits	_5_
	13		13

The *consolidated* carrying values of all the assets and liabilities at that date is as above except for fixed assets which have a consolidated carrying value of £7m. In the consolidated profit and loss account for the year ended 31 December 1995, the gain on disposal is stated at £5m, and at 30 September 1995 the carrying amount of goodwill relating to Orb plc is £1m.

Required
Show how the Sceptre Group would deal with the disposal in its consolidated cash flow matrix for the year ended 31 December 1995.

Solution
The balances to be *removed* in the matrix are the *consolidated* carrying values, hence fixed assets must be restated to £7m. The net book amount of consolidated goodwill at disposal will also form part of these carrying values to be removed. Minority interests at disposal (20%) are based on the consolidated equity of Orb plc at the disposal date, i.e. the company equity of £8m (share capital and premium of £3m and retained profits of £5m) plus the fixed asset adjustment of £2m, viz.

Minority interest = 20% [3 + 5 + 2] = £2m.

The matrix columns to be affected will be shown here in *journal entry* form, a debit representing a positive entry in a column and a credit, a negative entry. The clearest way to enter the disposal transaction into the matrix is to put the proceeds and gain or loss on disposal on one matrix line, and the *consolidated* carrying values of the assets and liabilities removed (*assets removed are negative* entries) on another – the demarcation between the two matrix lines is indicated below by the dotted line. The amount reported in the cash flow statement itself would be £13m (14–1) and the rest of the information below as a note disclosure.

Columns affected (DR = plus, CR = minus)	DR.	CR.
Retained profits		5
Cash (proceeds)	14	
Cash (subsidiary's balance removed)		1
Operating debtors		3
Stocks		4
Fixed assets (consolidated value)		7
Operating creditors	3	
Taxation	2	
Goodwill		1
Minority interests	2	

Exercises

9.8 What factors would determine a management decision over whether to use the aggregation approach or the deduction approach to consolidating cash flow statements?

9.9 What cash flows would appear on the face of a cash flow statement, relating to (a) acquisition of subsidiaries, and (b) disposal of subsidiaries?

9.10 Which of the following would be included in 'cash equivalents'?
(a) demand deposits repayable in two months with an original maturity date of 4 months.
(b) short-term borrowing facilities from a supplier with a 2 month original repayment date.
(c) bank overdraft which is treated by the company as a 'revolving credit' facility.
(d) portion of a 5 year loan which is repayable within one month.

9.11 The accountant of the Gruppe Group produces the following draft accounts. They exclude the analysis of continuing and discontinued operations in the profit and loss account required by FRS 3.

Balance sheets at 31 December

	Note	1995 £m	1995 £m	1994 £m	1994 £m
Fixed assets					
Intangible assets	1		18		12
Tangible assets	2		101		46
Invs in assoc undertakings	3		_5_		_10_
			124		68
Current assets					
Stocks		29		22	
Debtors	4	25		16	
Deposits due within a year	5	15		17	
Cash		_18_		14	
		87		69	
Creditors due within one year					
Bank borrowings	6	(10)		-	
Other liabilities	6&7	_(51)_		_(45)_	
		(61)		(45)	
Net current assets			26		24
Creditors over one year					
Borrowings	6		(32)		(14)
Provisions for liabilities and charges	8		_(6)_		_–_
			112		78
Capital and Reserves:					
Share capital (£1 ordinary)	9		19		11

Share premium	9	24	7
Revaluation reserve		18	15
Retained profits		27	23
		88	56
Minority interests		24	22
		112	78

Consolidated profit and loss account – year ended 31 December 1995

	Note	£m
Sales		106
Cost of sales		(49)
Gross profit		57
Net operating expenses	10	(27)
Operating profit		30
Gain on fixed asset disposal		3
Loss on sale of associated undertaking		(2)
Restructuring provision		(6)
Profit on ordinary activities before interest		25
Income from associate		4
Interest payable		(4)
Profit on ordinary activities before tax		25
Taxation – associated undertaking		(1)
Taxation – group		(10)
Profit on ordinary activities after tax		14
Minority interests		(4)
Profit for the financial year		10
Dividends – interim		(2)
Dividends – final		(4)
Retained profit for the financial year		4

Statement of total recognized gains and losses – year ended 31 December 1995

	£m
Profit for the financial year	10
Revaluation gains on properties	3
Total recognized gains for the year	13

Notes to the accounts

1. Intangible assets:

	1995 £m	1994 £m
Cost	28	20
Amortization to date	(10)	(8)
Net book amount	18	12

2. Tangible assets (net book amounts):

	£m
Opening amount	46
Additions – purchases	64
Additions – subsidiary acquisition	8
Revaluation of properties	3
Disposals	(5)
Depreciation for year	(15)
Net book amount at 31 December 1995	101

3. Investments in associated undertakings:

	1995 £m	1994 £m
Goodwill	1	4
Net assets	4	6
	5	10

The net book amount of the associate disposed of during the year was £6m.

4. Debtors:

	1995 £m	1994 £m
Operating debtors	25	16

5. Deposits less than one year:

All deposits are readily convertible into known amounts of cash and were three months to maturity when acquired.

6. Borrowings:

	1995 £m	1994 £m
Due within one year		
Bank overdrafts	10	—
Current portion of long-term loans	5	8
	15	8
Due in more than one year		
Borrowings	32	14

£26m of new long-term borrowings were made during the year.

7. Other liabilities:	1995	1994
	£m	£m
Operating creditors	25	20
Investing creditors	2	3
Tax	11	10
Current portion of long-term loans	5	8
Dividends payable	4	3
Interest payable	4	1
	51	45

8. Provisions:	1995	1994
	£m	£m
Reorganization provision	6	—

The provision was set up this year for closures.

9. Share issues:	1995
	£m
Opening	18
Acquisition of subsidiary	14
Purchase of fixed assets	11
Closing	43

10. Net operating expenses:	£m
Depreciation	15
Goodwill amortization	2
Other operating costs	10
	27

11. Acquisition of subsidiary:

A 75% interest in Appendage plc was acquired at 30 June 1995 for £14m in shares and £6m in cash. At that date its balances were:

	£m		£m
Fixed assets	8	Trade creditors	5
Stocks (all materials)	9	Taxation	2
Operating debtors	4	Share capital & premium	10
Cash	2	Retained profits	6
	23		23

Required

Prepare a cash flow matrix for the Gruppe Group and produce a cash flow statement on the net basis for the year ended 31 December 1995 together with supporting notes required by FRS 1.

9.12   The accountant of the Wind-down Group produces the following draft accounts. They exclude the analysis of continuing and discontinued operations in the profit and loss account required by FRS 3.

Balance sheets at 30 April

	1995 Note	1995 £m	£m	1994 £m	1994 £m
Fixed assets					
Intangible assets	1		8		16
Tangible assets	2		70		95
Invs in assoc undertakings	3		15		12
			93		123
Current assets					
Stocks		28		40	
Debtors	4	24		20	
Cash		10		22	
		62		82	
Creditors due within one year					
Bank borrowings	6	(10)		(8)	
Other liabilities	6&7	(40)		(35)	
		(50)		(43)	
Net current assets			12		39
Creditors over one year					
Borrowings	6		(25)		(70)
Provisions for liabilities and charges	8		(4)		(16)
			76		76
Capital and reserves					
Share capital (£1 ordinary)	9		10		10
Share premium	9		15		15
Revaluation reserve			12		15
Retained profits			29		27
			66		67
Minority interests			10		9

Consolidated profit and loss account – year ended 30 April 1995

	Note	£m
Sales		348
Cost of sales		(210)
Gross profit		138
Net operating expenses	10	(109)
Income from associate		7
Operating profit/(loss)		36
Gain on fixed asset disposal		4
Loss on sale of subsidiary		(9)
Restructuring costs		
Use of restructuring provision		—
Profit on ordinary activities before interest		31
Interest payable		(7)
Profit on ordinary activities before tax		24
Taxation – associated undertaking		(2)
Taxation – group		(6)
		(16)
Profit on ordinary activities after tax		16
Minority interests		(6)
Profit for the financial year		10
Dividends – interim		(8)
Dividends – final		(—)
Retained profit for the financial year		2

Statement of total recognized gains and losses – year ended 30 April 1995

	£m
Profit for the financial year	10
Revaluation write-downs on properties	(3)
Total recognized gains for the year	7

Notes to the accounts

1. Intangible assets:

	1995 £m	1994 £m
Cost	14	24
Amortization to date	(6)	(8)
Net book amount	8	16

2. Tangible assets (net book amounts):

	£m
Opening amount	95
Additions – purchases	5
Revaluation of properties	(3)
Disposals	(5)
Disposals – sale of subsidiary	(7)
Depreciation for year	(15)
Net book amount at 30 April 1995	70

3. Investments in associated undertakings:

	1995 £m	1994 £m
Goodwill	3	4
Net assets	12	8
	15	12

No associates were acquired or disposed of during the year.

4. Debtors:

	1995 £m	1994 £m
Operating debtors	24	20

5. Deposits less than one year:

All deposits are readily convertible into known amounts of cash and were three months to maturity when acquired.

6. Borrowings:

	1995 £m	1994 £m
Due within one year		
Bank overdrafts	10	—
Current portion of long-term loans	9	2
	19	2
Due in more than one year		
Borrowings	25	70

£10m of new long-term borrowings were made during the year.

7. Other creditors:

	1995 £m	1994 £m
Operating creditors	14	10
Investing creditors	2	3
Tax	5	6
Current portion of long-term loans	9	2
Dividends payable	4	3
Interest payable	6	11
	40	35

8. Provisions:

	1995 £m	1994 £m
Reorganization provision	4	16

The provision was set up last year for closures starting this year.

9. Share issues:

	1995
	Nil

10. Net operating costs:

	£m
Depreciation	10
Goodwill amortization	2
Other operating costs	97
	109

11. Disposal of subsidiary:

A 60% interest in Slough plc was sold at 31 December 1994 for £3m cash. Wind-down plc requires Slough plc to prepare interim accounts at that date, and these are as follows:

	£m		£m
Fixed assets	6	Operating creditors	4
Stocks	3	Taxation	2
Operating debtors	4	Share capital & premium	3
Cash	1	Retained profits	5
	14		14

The consolidated book value of all the assets and liabilities is as above except for fixed assets which have a consolidated book value at that date of £8m. At 31 December 1994, the carrying amount of goodwill relating to Slough plc is £6m.

Required

Prepare a cash flow matrix for the Wind-down Group and produce a cash flow statement on the net basis for the year ended 30 April 1995 together with supporting notes required by FRS 1.

9.13 The following extracts are taken from the draft accounts and notes for the Glitterati Group for the year ended 31 March 1996 (in £m):

i. **Consolidated profit and loss account**

	£m
Gain on disposal of fixed assets	3

ii. **Movements on fixed assets**

	£m
Opening balance	150
Purchases	35
Acquisition of Tinsel plc	35
Disposals	(15)
Depreciation for the year	(20)
Closing balance	185

iii. **Share capital and premium (combined)**

	£m
Opening balance	70
Purchase of fixed assets	35
Acquisition of Tinsel plc	10
Other share issues for cash	20
Closing balance	135

iv. **Consolidated debtors**

	1996 £m	1995 £m
Operating debtors	30	25
Dividends receivable from associate	15	10
Investing debtors	7	5
	52	40

v. **Acquisition of Tinsel plc**

An 80% stake in Tinsel plc was acquired at 31 December 1995 for £38m in shares and cash. At that date Tinsel's balance sheet was as follows:

	£m
Fixed assets (net)	35
Share capital and premium	(12)
Retained profits	(23)

vi. **Investment in associate**

	£m
Opening balance	45
Attributable profits	25
Dividends due	(15)
	55

vii. **Creditors**

	1996 £m	1995 £m
Operating creditors	18	23
Investing creditors	16	14
	34	37

Required

Calculate the relevant cash flows as they would appear in a net format cash flow statement for the year ended 31 March 1996 relating to

(a) fixed assets.
(b) acquisition of subsidiary.
(c) cash flows relating to associates.

In addition draft the note required by FRS 1 relating to non-cash transactions, which should include the acquisition of Tinsel plc.

FRS 1, *CASH FLOW STATEMENTS*

FRS 1, issued in September 1991, significantly altered the form of the 'third' primary statement. The changes from its predecessor SSAP 10, *Statements of Source and Application of Funds* (1976) reflected radical international developments in the way this statement was to be formulated and presented. The previous style of statement was reflected in the title of the then US standard, APB 19, *Reporting Changes in Financial Position*, and internationally, IAS 7, *Statements of Changes in Financial Position*. Such statements embraced the 'all financial resources rationale' for a third primary statement – that its essential purpose is to show *all* 'significant' balance sheet changes (see for example, McKinnon, Martin and Partington, 1983). So the purchase of fixed assets directly for shares, which has no effect on cash, would have been reported as an increase in shares (source) *and* fixed assets (application). The approach was criticized for being ambiguous as to precisely which flows to include or exclude (Robb, 1985). SSAP 10 adopted features of this approach. It presented 'funds' flows in a plus (sources) and minus (applications) format rather than by analysing them by category as FRS 1 does. It was much less prescriptive in defining treatments.

SSAP 10 combined the 'all financial resources' approach with a 'working capital' funds concept. Fixed asset purchases were shown rather than fixed asset payments, and 'funds from operating activities' were measured on an accrual accounting basis rather than a receipts and payments one. Receipts and payments usually do not affect working capital taken as an aggregate. Their double entry causes an increase in one component of working capital (e.g. cash) *and* a decrease in another (e.g. debtors). FRS 1 criticizes working capital 'funds' statements for omitting information useful in assessing liquidity. Creditor payments or an increase in debtors through non-payment will both worsen liquidity, but not affect working capital as a whole. See Taylor (1987, pp. 164–199) for a comprehensive analysis of SSAP 10 and its defects.

By 1987 the USA had issued SFAS 95, *Statement of Cash Flows*. In 1991 the ASB issued FRS 1, *Cash Flow Statements*. By 1992 an international transformation of perspective was complete when a revised IAS 7 entitled, not surprisingly, *Cash Flow Statements*, was issued. However, in certain respects the FRS 1 took its own direction. It expanded the three headings of SFAS 95 and revised IAS 7 to five. Instead of allowing the option of direct or indirect approaches on the face of the statement, it made the indirect format the baseline, but required its reconciliation as a note disclosure *not* on the face of the cash flow statement. The direct approach became an option in its 'gross' approach. *Company Reporting* (April 1994, p. 3) found that 98 per cent of 500 companies publishing financial statements in the previous twelve months had produced FRS 1 cash flow statements, but of these, only 5 per cent disclosed the direct approach.

Scope
FRS 1 applies to all financial statements intended to give a true and fair view of financial position and profit or loss except for

(a) companies (and implicitly groups) satisfying the *small companies* criteria of the Companies Act which are not public companies, banking or insurance companies or authorized persons under the Financial Services Act 1986, or members of a group containing one of these.
(b) *wholly owned subsidiaries* of parents established under the law of an EC member state, provided the parent produces consolidated financial statements including the subsidiary, containing a consolidated cash flow statement enabling users to derive the subtotals under the five standard categories.
(c) certain *special category entities* governed by other legislation.

FRS 1's exemptions are in harmony with many other EC-based requirements such as for abbreviated accounts. Category (b) is consistent with the practice within groups of adopting a group basis for treasury management but it prevents analysts from determining cash flow profiles for entities within a group.

Disclosures

Many of these have been dealt with earlier. They are summarized for convenience:

(a) the statement must be analysed under five headings 'operating activities', 'returns on investments and servicing of finance', 'taxation', 'investing activities' and 'financing' in the order given. A total must be given for 'net cash inflow or outflow before financing'. FRS 1 gives prescribed classifications of items under each heading and allows further subdivision or segmental analysis. If a cash flow is of a non-standard type it should be classified most appropriately. In 'extremely rare circumstances' where such classification would not give 'a fair representation of the activities of the reporting entity . . . informed judgement should be used to devise an appropriate alternative treatment' (para. 13).

(b) disclosures of non-cash transactions and the acquisition and disposal of subsidiaries must be given (paras 40 and 43).

(c) movements in cash and cash equivalents and the items shown in the financing section should be reconciled to the related items in opening and closing balance sheets, disclosing separately for each class, movements relating to cash flows, foreign currency exchange differences (see Chapter 11) and other movements (para. 44).

(d) cash flows which relate to items classified as exceptional in the profit and loss account are to be classified under the appropriate standard heading with sufficient explanation to allow a user to understand their effect on the reporting entity's cash flows. Cash flows relating to items classified as extraordinary in the profit and loss account are to be disclosed separately under the appropriate standard heading, or given their own heading where this is necessary, with sufficient explanation. However, extraordinary items have been effectively abolished by FRS 3

Group accounting requirements

Foreign currency translation and the cash flow statement is dealt with in Chapter 11. FRS 1's consolidated cash flow statement provisions are summarized here:

Intra-group cash flows should be eliminated. Dividends paid to minorities should be included under the 'returns' heading (para. 38).

Equity accounted entities should only be included to the extent of actual cash flows between the entity and the group, e.g. dividends from associates and loans to them. Acquisitions and disposals of investments in such entities should be separately disclosed (paras 26 and 39).

Joint ventures and non-consolidated subsidiaries: Davies, Paterson and Wilson (1992, p. 1235) are concerned that different accounting treatments will be available for very similar entities, e.g. proportionately consolidated non-corporate joint ventures could be included on a line-by-line basis under the five headings, whereas equity accounted corporate joint ventures, will only disclose cash flows to and from the entity (as for associates). Only cash flows to and from non-consolidated subsidiaries should be included.

Acquisition and disposal of subsidiaries: in the period of acquisition or disposal if practicable, a note disclosure must be given of the subsidiary's contribution to group cash flow under each of the five categories if material (paras 40–43).

Acquisition and merger accounting: cash flows of the subsidiary must be included for the same periods as the profit and loss account shows the results of the undertaking (para. 41). Under acquisition accounting this would be from the date of acquisition. Under merger accounting cash flows for the whole year would be included in the year of combination, and comparatives restated. On disposals cash flows would be included up to the date of disposal. Using the matrix approach will ensure this. Dividend receipts from pre-acquisition profits under acquisition accounting should probably be shown under 'investing' activities. For consolidated accounting purposes they are akin to repayment of the investment (see Chapter 6).

Optional disclosures: FRS 1's illustrative Example 2 separately discloses 'cash outflow in respect of discontinued activities and reorganisation costs'. This is not required by FRS 1, though a number of groups, e.g. Inchcape and BOC, do so. It is possible that any revision of FRS 1 could follow FRS 3 (see Chapter 8) and require a similar analysis to the profit and loss account.

Non-cash transactions

The cash element of any transaction must be disclosed in the cash flow statement itself, but FRS 1 requires note disclosure of any material non-cash transactions if necessary to understand them (para. 43). It gives the example of vendor placings. Such a treatment is different from SSAP 10 which had included certain non-cash transactions in its statement, following the 'all financial resources' rationale. What is material? SFAS 95 in the USA limits their reporting to *investing* and *financing* activities, whereas FRS 1 has no such limitation. Purchases of goods is an *operating* non-cash transaction, and is indeed material, but it seems unlikely that FRS 1 envisages it being reported.

FRS 1 requires the cash flow relating to the purchase or disposal of a subsidiary to be shown *net* of the cash and cash equivalent balance of the subsidiary acquired or disposed of. Non-cash elements must be shown as a note (para. 40).

Another problem is how to report subsequent cash effects of non-cash transactions, particularly relating to 'investing' non-cash transactions. The key issue is whether the non-cash transaction is the *primary* transaction and the subsequent cash effect a separate 'financing' transaction, or whether the subsequent cash flow is sufficiently related to be classified itself as an 'investing activity'. There is a whole spectrum from normal fixed asset credit purchases to finance leases, instalment purchases or loan financed purchases. In a group accounting context, for example, it seems clear-cut that deferred consideration for an acquisition, where the amount is fixed, is a 'financing' transaction. Where consideration is contingent on post-acquisition profit levels the late payment is *not* purely a financing matter, but a resolution of the amount of the investment (Chapter 5). FRS 1 gives little specific guidance beyond requiring the capital element of finance lease rental payments to be shown as a 'financing' cash flow. SFAS 95 in the USA only allows advance payments, down payments or amounts paid at or near to the time of purchase to be 'investing' cash flows.

There is no easy resolution. One possibility could be that if a transaction is reported as a non-cash transaction, any subsequently related cash flows should be regarded as financing cash flows. For example, instalment purchases and finance lease transactions are non-cash transactions since the holder enjoys substantially the rights of ownership. Under SSAP 21, finance lease payments are treated *as if* loan repayments. However, more certain is that the ASB should give *equal* prominence to non-cash transactions, and adjacent to the cash flow statement, rather than their being relegated to note disclosure. This would draw users' attention to the fact that the cash flow statement is not sufficient *per se* to understand the 'investing' transactions of the entity.

Critics of FRS 1

Cash equivalents

The maximum original maturity date of three months has proved controversial. Many groups operate with longer treasury management horizons. BTR and Dunhill Holdings both intimate a twelve months horizon is used. Tweedie (Holmes and Sugden, 1993, p. 120), justifies the ASB's position 'firstly to make sure it wasn't fiddleable, and secondly [for] international harmonisation' and states that, although 'some group treasurers would like a year, some of the banks would like a month'.

Olusegun Wallace and Collier (1991) show that cash equivalents are differently defined in different national jurisdictions. FRS 1 defines cash and cash equivalents *net* of 'advances from *banks* repayable within three months from the date of the advance' (para. 3). SFAS 95 and IAS 7 define them *gross* of any such advances. However, as Davies, Paterson and Wilson (1992, p. 1215) point out, overdrafts as understood in the UK are not a normal feature of US banking practice. A similar three months original maturity date is normally used. Unlike FRS 1, SFAS 95 allows entities to nominate which of the qualifying investments it wishes to classify as cash equivalents. Canada and New Zealand define cash equivalents net of *all* (not just bank) short-term borrowings.

Commercial paper (company short-term borrowing) just 'misses' the definition of cash equivalents (Dealy, 1994). FRS 1's definition only allows the deduction of advances by *banks*. The consequence for 'just missing' is great since 'gross' inflows and outflows for the non-qualifying borrowing have to be disclosed. In the USA 'just missing' is less crucial as SFAS 95 allows the netting off of inflows and outflows of quick turnover, short maturity items where amounts are large. Such inflows and outflows can misleadingly dominate the statement.

Reorganization provisions

FRS 1 does not provide guidance here. Two main positions have been advanced for dealing with cash flows relating to such provisions: (a) analyse components separately (e.g. redundancy payments as 'operating', fixed asset disposal proceeds as 'investing'), or (b) classify overall cash flows under one heading (e.g. all cash flows relating to particular divestment are classified as 'investing'). Davies, Paterson and Wilson (1992, pp. 1246–7) favour splitting by type. However, equally convincing arguments exist for treating them as 'investing' activities. Dealy (1994) comments that FRS 1 does not deal with cash flows relating to 'pre-acquisition' provisions (extremely rare under FRS 7) and therefore FRS 1's 'true and fair' paragraph becomes operative. 'Where a cash flow is not specified [under the contents of the five headings] . . . then it should be shown under the most appropriate standard heading' (para. 14). Dealy suggests they be classified as 'investment activities'. This is consistent with a consolidated treatment of dividends from the subsidiary's pre-acquisition profits as an adjustment to the investment (Chapter 6).

Other presentation formats

Some groups emphasize 'free cash flow'. *Company Reporting* (April 1994) reports that Thorn EMI defines it as 'cash flows from operating activities [adjusted] for purchases and sales of tangible fixed assets, dividends from associates or paid to minorities, net of interest and taxation'. It seems to be an attempt at a measure of the cash generation of the entity after 'maintenance' cash expenditure, before purchases and disposals of subsidiaries. However, it does not completely distinguish between replacement and expansion expenditure (Lawson, 1985). Some fixed asset purchases might maintain the business and others expand it. *Company Reporting* also reports a number of groups netting cash and borrowings as the focus of their statement.

USEFULNESS OF CONSOLIDATED CASH FLOW STATEMENTS

General theoretical justifications for cash flow statements and their ability to improve the assessment of solvency and financial adaptability are not explored here – see for example Heath (1977), Lee (1984) and FRS 1 itself.

Comparison with SSAP 10
FRS 1 asserts that a cash flow statement is superior to a working capital based funds statement. It argues that cash flow monitoring is more widely used and the concept more widely understood. It criticizes SSAP 10 for merely reorganizing existing published data and not providing new information. Such 'funds' statements were widely viewed merely as *supplementary* statements. The necessity of analysing debtors, creditors etc. to determine cash flows under each of FRS 1's five headings means that its cash flow statement incorporates otherwise unpublished information. Gross format statements require even more underlying analysis in preparation. Under SSAP 10, *all* debtors and creditors etc. were often used in an undifferentiated way to determine 'funds from operations' which could therefore have been deduced from the other financial statements.

The fact that FRS 1 argues that historical cash flows can provide more relevant direct input into a 'business valuation model' (NPV) is less convincing, since, for example SFAC No 1, *Objectives of Financial Reporting*, in the USA, states that such a model 'leads primarily to an interest in earnings rather than information directly about its cash flows' (para. 43). The ASB's *Statement of Principles* rightly takes the middle ground. 'Although each statement provides information that is different from the others, none is likely to serve only a single purpose or provide all the information necessary for particular needs of users.'

Direct (gross) versus indirect (net) formats

The ASB decides it cannot unambiguously support the direct format over the indirect commenting

> knowledge of the specific sources of [operating] cash receipts and the purposes for which [operating] cash payments were made in past periods *may* be useful in assessing future cash flows. However, the Board does not believe at present that in all cases that the benefits to users of this information outweigh the costs to the reporting entity of providing it.
>
> (para. 70, emphasis added)

It cites the principal benefit of the indirect method as highlighting the differences between 'operating profit' and 'net cash flow from operating activities', which 'many users . . . believe is essential to give an indication of the quality of an entity's earnings' (para. 71). Since the Board allows the breakdown of 'net cash flows from operating activities' into component cash flows only as an optional extra, it is unlikely the extra information will be widely produced as preparers will compare costs and benefits to themselves rather than to users. The Board has achieved baseline comparability but seems to have followed the line of (preparer) least resistance here.

Heath (1977) criticizes the reconciliation approach because he feels it is only an early analysts' tool developed at a time when sufficient disclosure was not given. It causes the 'third' statement to be widely viewed as derivative. Further there is the potential for naive users to interpret the depreciation add-back as a 'source' of funds, and for the mistaken view that the funds/cash flow statement shows where an entity's profit 'went'. He comments that profits are not a physical thing like cash, but the *change* in net assets. Presumably to minimize such misinterpretation, FRS 1 requires that the reconciliation *not* be shown on the face of the statement, but as a note. However, early evidence indicates that some companies are presenting it on the face of the statement.

Problems of averaging

Similar problems in interpreting consolidated cash flow statements arise to those discussed in Chapter 4 relating to balance sheets. Consolidation in conglomerate groups may mask a wide variety of cash flow profiles, or the non-remittability of cash. For example, in a supermarket, cash from operations may predominate, whereas in capital intensive firms, investing and financing flows may do so. The non-mandatory recommendations in the ASB Statement, *Operating and Financial Review* (1993), address some of these issues. They include the call for commentary on 'any restrictions on the ability to transfer funds from one part of the group to meet the obligations of another part of the group, where these represent, or might forseeably come to represent, a significant restraint on the group' (para. 34). Exchange controls are given as an example. Another area to be covered is where segmental cash flows are out of line with segmental profits (para. 31). The revised IAS 7 has similar provisions on restricted balances.

Similar caveats on the usefulness of consolidated cash flow statements for creditors and minority interests apply, though they are likely to be more useful in practice since most groups' treasury management programmes are carried out on a group-wide basis.

Empirical evidence

Empirical evidence on the usefulness of consolidated cash flow reporting is extensive, but mainly US based. A useful review is provided by Neill *et al.* (1991). Researchers have tried to establish whether consolidated cash flow information has additional information content over accounting income and working capital based funds statements.

Market reaction

US-based evidence is contradictory. Empirical studies by Rayburn (1986), Bowen, Burgstahler and Daley (1987) and Wilson (1987) concluded that cash flow from operations has incremental information content over earnings. However, Bernard and Stober (1989), replicating and expanding the Wilson study over a longer period, found *no* incremental information content of cash flow data, even after allowing for changes in market conditions or industry specific factors. Livnat and Zarowin (1990) examined market reaction to operating, investing and financing cash flow components separately. They found 'operating' and 'financing' cash flow components generated significant market reactions, but not 'investing' components. However, *none* of the individual components possessed significant *incremental* information content over earnings. Charitou and Ketz (1991) found a cross-sectional association between cashflow components and security prices.

Analysts' forecasts

Moses (1991) examined whether cash flow data had incremental information content over earnings in predicting revisions in analysts' published earnings forecasts in the 1982–3 period. He found that 'cash flow from operations' and 'cash flow after investment' both contained additional information content over earnings in this regard. Somewhat surprisingly, he found that 'working capital from operations' had even higher incremental information content.

Financial failure prediction

Apart from isolated examples of case study analysis (e.g. Kochanek and Norgaard, 1988), the main focus of bankruptcy prediction studies has been the use of statistical modelling to examine whether cash flow data improves the prediction of corporate failure over traditional accrual accounting ratios. Early studies such as Casey and Bartczak (1985) and Gentry *et al.* (1985a) found a lack of incremental predictive power except for dividend cash flow. More sophisticated follow up studies, e.g. Gentry *et al.* (1985b, 1987) found that investing cash flows had only marginal descriptive power. Gombola *et al.* (1987) confirm that the lack of predictive and explanatory power is consistent over different time periods. Bahnson and Bartley (1991), in an unpublished paper, reported in Neill *et al.* (1991), experiment with different definitions of failure and found that the usefulness of cash flow information is affected by these. The major problem with such studies is the lack of a theoretical framework. Their results are inconclusive.

Other studies

Klammer and Reed (1990) conducted a 'laboratory' style experiment, finding that bank analysts reached a greater consensus as to the size of loans to be granted to a fictitious company when the direct approach cash flow information was given than when indirect approach information was given. It is difficult to assess how far such a result can be extrapolated to real-life situations in general. Other studies examine the ability of cash flow to predict future cash flows. But, for example, both Bowen *et al.* (1987) and Greenberg *et al.* (1986) fail to show that cash flow is a better predictor of future cash flows than net income is – see Neill *et al.* (1991).

Exercises

9.14 Assess whether cash flow statements are more useful to analysts than statements of sources and applications of funds.

9.15 'Net format cash flow statements are merely a reorganization of the data in the other financial statements and notes to the accounts. They are therefore of minimal use.' Discuss.

9.16 What are the main practical and conceptual difficulties in applying FRS 1?

SUMMARY

*FRS 1 requires the preparation of consolidated cash flow statements, analysed under five headings, 'operating activities', 'returns from investing and servicing of finance', 'taxation', 'investing activities' and 'financing'. 'Cash equivalents' must have an **original** maturity of less than three months, but at the time of writing does not include **non**-bank borrowings. FRS 1 allows two presentation alternatives. The **net** format presents 'net cash flow from operating activities' as a single figure on the face of the statement, with a reconciliation of 'operating profit' to 'net cash flow from operating activities' shown as a **note**. The **gross** format discloses **in addition** individual operating receipts and payments on the face of the statement. The gross format therefore includes **both** direct and indirect approach information about 'net cash flow from operating activities'. Significant non-cash transactions must be given note disclosure.*

Cash flow reporting for groups must be consistent with the consolidation treatment adopted. If full consolidation is adopted, cash flows should be included on a line-by-line basis (proportionately for proportionate consolidation) and intra-group cash flows eliminated. Equity accounted entities are to be included on the basis of cash flows to and from the group, and similarly for minority interests.

*When a subsidiary is acquired or disposed of, the cash impact should be reported **net** of the subsidiary's cash balances. The non-cash impact should be disclosed as a note. In the year of acquisition or disposal, the subsidiary's cash flows in the consolidated cash flow statement should be measured consistently with the subsidiary's treatment in the other primary statements. Under acquisition accounting they should be included only from the date of acquisition. If merger accounting is used cash flows for the whole year should be included, and comparatives restated. For disposals cash flows should be included up to the date of disposal. A note disclosure is required of any material cash flow impact of any subsidiaries acquired or disposed of during the year under FRS 1's five headings.*

Reaction to the change from SSAP 10 to FRS 1 has been favourable. Criticisms include the fact that the direct approach is only optional, that the definition of cash and cash equivalents is inconsistent with firms' treasury management policies, and that the subsequent treatment of non-cash transactions is not specified. There is also lack of guidance on certain group accounting matters e.g. dividends from pre-acquisition profits and cash flows relating to reorganization provisions at acquisition. Also there are no mandatory requirements to disclose limitations on remitting funds within a group. US-based empirical evidence on the usefulness of cash flow statements to investors, analysts and bankers is ambiguous in its findings.

FURTHER READING

Davies, M., Paterson, R. and Wilson, A. (1992) *UK GAAP*, Macmillan, Chapter 23.

FRS 1 (1991) *Cash Flow Statements*, Accounting Standards Board.

Heath, L.C. (1977) *Financial Reporting and the Evaluation of Solvency*, Accounting Research Monograph No. 3, American Institute of Certified Public Accountants, New York.

Neill, J.D., Schaefer, T.F., Bahnson, P.R. and Bradbury, M.E. (1991) The usefulness of cash flow data: a review and synthesis, *Journal of Accounting Literature*, Vol 10, pp. 117–150.

Olusegun Wallace, R.S. and Collier, P.A. (1991) The cash in cash flow statements: a multi-country comparison, *Accounting Horizons*, December, pp. 44–52.

Part C:

Other Issues in Group Accounting

10

OTHER GROUP RELATIONSHIPS

Previous chapters have examined the consolidation of each primary financial statement under acquisition accounting mainly for a group with a single UK subsidiary. This and later chapters deal with greater group complexities; this chapter with piecemeal acquisitions and interconnected group shareholdings, later chapters with foreign subsidiaries and segmental reporting. Consolidation can also be complex in a computational sense because of the sheer size of groups, most major groups using computer consolidation packages (see for example, Taylor, 1987, pp. 230–234).

PIECEMEAL ACQUISITIONS AND DISPOSALS

Techniques

In previous chapters goodwill is the difference between the fair value of the consideration given and the fair value of the parent's share of the identifiable assets and liabilities acquired, both measured at the date of acquisition. When parents acquire their holdings in a *series* of transactions, issues arise as to how goodwill and thus post-acquisition profits should be measured. Consider where a parent acquires a 25 per cent voting stake at one date, then later a 35 per cent stake. The most common accounting alternatives are the following approaches.

Single step approach

Fair values of both investments are aggregated, and goodwill is the difference between this and the fair value of the identifiable assets and liabilities acquired *at the date* control was gained – here the date the 35 per cent stake was purchased. Of the subsidiary's post-acquisition profits 60 per cent are included in consolidated profits from this date. However, under this alternative, goodwill is not homogeneously measured at the date control passes, since part of the fair value of the consideration given is measured at a different date.

Slice-by-slice approach

Under this alternative, goodwill is measured as the sum of a series of 'slices'. When the 25 per cent stake is purchased, goodwill is computed on the 25 per cent holding at that date by comparing the fair value of the investment with 25 per cent of the fair value of the identifiable assets and liabilities acquired. Another goodwill computation is made for the 35 per cent holding at the second date using fair values at that date. Goodwill is the sum of these two 'slices' computed at different dates. Post-acquisition profits consequently are also in 'slices' – 25 per cent of the subsidiary's profits from the date of the initial holding plus in addition, a *further* 35 per cent (making 60 per cent in total) from the date of the second investment.

Example 10.1 – Piecemeal acquisition

Consider the following balance sheets at 31 December 1995

	Hangover £m	Shady £m
Miscellaneous net assets	2,400	1,000
Investment in Shady	600	—
Share capital	(700)	(200)
Share premium	(800)	(200)
Retained profits	(1,500)	(600)

Hangover had acquired its 60% stake in Shady in two separate transactions:

Transaction date	% acquired	Consideration	Shady retained profits
31 March 1994	25	200	300
30 September 1994	35	400	400 – control attained
Total	60	600	

Required

(a) Calculate goodwill, consolidated profits and minority interests under both the single step and slice-by-slice approaches at 31 December 1995.

(b) Analyse Shady's equity at 31 December 1995 between the group's share of pre- and post-acquisition equity, and minority interests.

(c) Prepare a consolidation cancellation table for the Hangover Group at 31 December 1995 under the slice-by-slice approach.

Single step approach

Goodwill	=	Total consideration	–	60% of Shady's equity at control (September 1994)		
	=	(200 + 400)	–	60% × (200 + 200 + *400*)	=	120

Consolidated retained profits = Hangover's retained + 60% × Shady's post-acquisition reserves (from Sept 94)

$$= 1,500 \qquad + 60\% \times (600 - 400) \qquad = 1,620$$

Minority = 40% × Shady's current equity = 40% × (200 + 200 + *600*) = 400

Slice-by-slice approach

Goodwill	=	Goodwill at 31 March 94	+	goodwill at 30 September 1994		
	=	(200 – 25% × (200+200+*300*))	+	(400 – 35% × (200+200+*400*))		
	=	25	+	120	=	145

Consolidated retained profits = Hangover's + 25% Shady from 31 March + 35% extra from Shady from 30 September

$$= 1,500 \qquad + 25\% \times (600 - 300) + 35\% \times (600 - 400)$$
$$= 1,645$$

Minority = 40% × Shady's current equity = 40% × (200 + 200 + *600*) = 400

Comparison

The basic difference between the two approaches is in the treatment of Shady's retained profits

$$£100m = 400 - 300$$

between the first purchase and the second. Under the single step approach it is treated as *pre*-acquisition, and under the slice-by-slice approach it is treated as *post*-acquisition. Thus goodwill is 25% × £100m *less* under the former because the group's share of pre-acquisition equity over that period is *greater*. Also consolidated reserves are 25% × £100m *less* because this amount is treated as pre-acquisition equity under the single step approach. Minority interest is the *same* under both approaches as any change in the pre-post acquisition boundary is irrelevant to them as their stake is ongoing.

Cancellation table single step approach
The cancellation table for the single step approach, *as if* a 60% subsidiary had been acquired at the second purchase date, contains no new issues of principle and is the same as discussed in Chapter 4.

Cancellation table for slice-by-slice approach
The aim is to produce a consolidated balance sheet at 31 December 1995. At that date Shady is a 60% *subsidiary*. Therefore minority interest is 40%, and the issue is how to determine what is pre- and what post-acquisition profits for the *subsidiary*. Figure 10.1 analyses Shady's equity under the slice-by-slice approach, from the *current perspective* as a 60% subsidiary.

Vertically it analyses the equity over time at first purchase, up to second purchase and since second purchase. Horizontally it analyses these slices according to the components of the *current* holding, the 25% stake, the 35% stake and the remaining 40% (100 − 25 − 35) minority interest.

Time period	Subsidiary equity relating to time period		1st purch 25%	2nd purch 35%	Mino-rity 40%
		Analysis of equity slices			
Prior to 31/3/95	200 + 200 + 300	= 700	175	245	280
Retained earnings 1/4/95 to 30/9/95	400 - 300	= 100	25	35	40
Retained earnings 1/10/95 to 31/12/96	600 - 400	= 200	50	70	80
Total equity at 31/12/95	200 + 200 + 600	= 1,000	250	350	400

Figure 10.1 – Piecemeal acquisition; analysis of subsidiary's equity

Pre-acquisition equity for the 60% owned subsidiary is shaded. Shady's equity at 31 March is pre *both* purchases, so the shaded area represents 60% of Shady's equity at that date. The £100m change between 31 March and 30 September is *post* the first purchase (25%), and *pre* the second (35%), so the shaded area for that period represents 35%. The £200m change after 30 September is post *both* purchases, so none is shaded. Figure 10.2 is a cancellation table which uses the analyses of Figure 10.1, and produces the same results as the intuitive calculations earlier.

Description	Percentage stakes pre/post/min o	Invest-ment	Share capital	Share premium	Good-will	Consol retained profits	Minority interests
Hangover balances		600	(700)	(800)		(1,500)	
Shady equity analysis:							
Pre- March 1994	60 / zero / 40				(420) [1]		(280)
March - Sept 1994	35 / 25 / 40				(35)	(25)	(40)
Post- September 1994	zero/ 60 / 40					(120) [2]	(80)
Cancellation		(600)			600		
Consolidated		-	(700)	(800)	145	(1,645)	(400)

1.   420 = 175 + 245

2.   120 = 50 + 70

Figure 10.2 – Slice-by-slice approach cancellation table

FRS 2 – Piecemeal acquisitions and disposals

FRS 2 adopts a pragmatic approach to piecemeal acquisitions. Following the requirements of the Companies Act 1985 (Sch 4A para. 9), it requires that the single step
approach should be applied at the date control passes, and regardless of whether or not
the controlling stake has been acquired in stages, the fair values of identifiable assets and
liabilities are to be determined at that (*single*) date (para. 50).

However it recognizes that

> in special circumstances . . . not using the fair values at the dates of earlier purchases,
> whilst using an acquisition cost part of which relates to earlier purchases, may result in
> accounting that is inconsistent with the way that the investment has been treated pre-
> viously and, for that reason, fail to give a true and fair view.   (para. 89)

A subsidiary which had previously been an associate would have used the equity
method and at the date of the second purchase consolidated retained profits would
already include the group's share of post-acquisition profits of the then associate (in the
above example 25 per cent). Also goodwill at acquisition of the 25 per cent stake would
have been calculated and used in SSAP 1's note disclosure for associated companies (see
Chapter 4). Under such circumstances FRS 2 allows the slice-by-slice approach to be used,
deriving support from the 'true and fair' override provisions in the Companies Act 1985.
It further comments that 'the difference between the goodwill calculated on this method
and that [which would be calculated under the single step approach] . . . is shown in
reserves' (para. 89).

In practice, the parent is often not in a position to demand fair value information from
the then associate. Therefore 'goodwill' on the first purchase would have had to be computed on 'book values'. The stage-by-stage fair values necessary to compute the slice-by-
slice approach would not then be available, and it is not clear what groups do in practice
in such circumstances. The ASB Discussion Paper, *Associates and Joint Ventures*, issued in
1994, proposes that if such fair value information or other information for consolidated
adjustments is not provided by the affiliate, there is no ability to exert 'significant influence' and equity accounting should not have been used (para. 5.8).

Changes in the holding status of the acquired company

In the above example, the situation where a former 25 per cent associate became a 60 per
cent subsidiary was discussed. Figure 10.3 shows how piecemeal acquisitions in other circumstances may be handled.

Status after first purchase	Status after subsequent purchase	Accounting treatment
Cost	Cost	No change
Cost	Equity	Post-acquisition profit usually determined from date company becomes associate. Goodwill for SSAP 1 note disclosure determined at that date (based on fair valued net assets).
Cost	Consolidation	Single step approach at the date the company becomes a subsidiary
Equity	Equity	Post-acquisition profits (and goodwill for SSAP 1 note disclosure) determined on slice by slice approach (based on slice-by-slice fair values of net assets).
Equity	Consolidation	Slice-by-slice approach for determining post-acquisition profits and goodwill, as in earlier example.
Consolidation	Consolidation	Slice-by-slice approach to determine goodwill and post-acquisition profits, *and also*, the subsidiary's identifiable assets must be revalued at the subsequent purchase date.

Figure 10.3 – Piecemeal acquisitions and disclosures and measurement boundaries

Increasing stake in existing subsidiary

The last case in Figure 10.3 is dealt with in FRS 2. It requires that when a group increases its stake in an existing subsidiary, a full fair value exercise should be carried out to determine goodwill on the incremental slice if the change from previous carrying values is material (para. 51). FRS 2 argues that unless incremental goodwill is computed using new fair values, it will be confounded with changes in fair values since the time of previous purchase(s) (para. 90).

Suppose a 60 per cent holding were increased to an 80 per cent holding. The net assets of the subsidiary would be restated to fair values. The (imputed) *credit* to the subsidiary's revaluation reserve would be analysed 20 per cent pre-acquisition (the *incremental* goodwill 'slice'), 60 per cent to consolidated *revaluation reserves* (the fair value change is after the 60 per cent purchase), and 20 per cent to minority interests. Though not explicitly considered by FRS 2, the following example applies this principle to where a 25 per cent associate becomes a 60 per cent subsidiary.

Example 10.2 – Fair value adjustments in piecemeal acquisitions

Suppose in the Hangover-Shady example earlier that at the date the first slice was purchased, land held by Shady included in its 'Miscellaneous net assets' with a carrying amount of £500m had a fair value at that date of £550m. At the date the second slice was purchased, its fair value had increased to £630m. Assume that the land is still held. The adjustments have not been 'pushed down' into the records of Shady plc.

Required

Show the adjustments to the cancellation table in Figure 10.2 to effect the above fair value adjustments, assuming that the slice-by-slice approach is used.

Land has been chosen to illustrate the effects of fair value adjustments in piecemeal acquisitions because complications of 'extra depreciation' can be avoided! If the adjustments had been 'pushed down' land would have been debited and the subsidiary's revaluation reserve credited with £130m. How much is pre- and post-acquisition to the group? The first £50m revaluation is pre *both* share purchases. The £80m revaluation is pre- the 35% purchase, but post the 25% purchase, and so in the cancellation table 25% × 80 = £20m would be disclosed as a consolidated *revaluation* reserve. This is shown in the cancellation table in Figure 10.4. The distinction between pre- and post- is not made for minority interests, so their 'stake' in the revaluations is 40% × £130 = £52m.

Description	Percentage stakes pre/post/mino	Misc net assets	Invest- ment	Share capital	Share premiu m	Good- will	Consol reserve s	Minority interests
Consolidated per Figure 10.2		3,400	-	(700)	(800)	145	(1,645)	(400)
Fair value adjustments:								
At 31 March 1994	60 / zero / 40	50				(30)		(20)
At 30 Sept 1994	35 / 25 / 40	80				(28)	(20)	(32)
Consol with adj		3,530	-	(700)	(800)	87	(1,665)	(452)

Figure 10.4 – Effects of fair value adjustments on slice-by slice approach

Piecemeal disposals

The following subsections on piecemeal disposals and deemed disposals can be omitted without loss of continuity. FRS 2's provisions require that if say an 80 per cent holding were reduced to a 60 per cent holding, 20 per cent of the consolidated carrying values of the subsidiary's net assets and goodwill in the subsidiary at the date of disposal would be deducted from the consideration received by the group. The difference would be profit or loss on disposal. Minority interests would increase by this 20 per cent of this *carrying* value, reflecting the transfer of the 20 per cent from controlling interests. The partial disposal can be conceptualized as if a set of journal entries:

Description of 'journal' entry	DR	CR
Purchase consideration	Cash or shares	Profit & loss ('Sales')
Carrying value at date of disposal of 20% slice	Profit and loss ('Cost of sales')	Minority interests

Similar considerations would apply in measuring profit or loss on disposal if, say, a 60 per cent subsidiary became a 25 per cent associate. In this case the consolidated profit and loss account treatment would reflect that the affiliate was a subsidiary up to the date of disposal (its revenues and expenses would be included up to that date), would show the gain or loss on disposal of the 35 per cent stake, and finally would reflect the fact that it was an associate after disposal (i.e. only include its share of attributable profits from the disposal date to the end of the parent's accounting period). The consolidated balance sheet at the end of the period will be calculated based on the status of the group companies at that date and no special procedures are necessary to reflect disposals.

Deemed disposals

FRS 2 actual requirements on disposals are expressed in rather a convoluted fashion (para. 52) specifically to cover the case of *deemed* disposals – if the *subsidiary* issues shares or makes a rights issue to third parties, this too reduces the group stake and increases minority interests. In such cases, not only the group's proportionate stake changes, but also the amount of identifiable assets and liabilities it controls is increased simultaneously as a result of the new share issues by the subsidiary. FRS 2 requires the profit or loss to be calculated as the 'difference between the carrying amount of the net assets of that subsidiary undertaking attributable to the group's interest before the reduction and the carrying amount attributable to the group's interest after the reduction together with any proceeds received [by the group]' (para. 52). This is better illustrated by the example below. The slightly more complex case of a subsidiary rights issue is discussed by Patient, Faris and Holgate (1992, p. 102).

Example 10.3 – Applying FRS 2's piecemeal acquisition requirements

Required

In the Hangover-Shady example above, ignoring fair value adjustments and subsequent goodwill write-offs, prepare consolidated financial statements for the Hangover-Shady Group at 31 December 1995 under FRS 2's requirements, assuming:

(a) at the date of the first purchase Hangover plc could *not* exercise significant influence over Shady plc.
(b) at the date of the first purchase Hangover plc *could* exercise significant influence over Shady plc.

(a) The investment would have been recorded at cost after the first transaction even though the stake is 25% (see Chapter 4) and Shady would not have been an associate. At the second transaction, the single step approach would be applied.
(b) Because significant influence was exercisable, Shady would have been equity accounted from the first transaction date as an associate – 25% of its post-acquisition profits would have been included and so the slice-by-slice approach is to be used as in the cancellation table in Figure 10.2.

Hangover-Shady Group – consolidated balance sheet at 31 December 1995

	Transition as a result of series of purchases	
	a) Cost to consolidation	b) Equity to consolidation
Miscellaneous net assets	3,400	3,400
Goodwill	120	145
Share capital	(700)	(700)
Share premium	(800)	(800)
Retained profits	(1,620)	(1,645)
Minority interests	(400)	(400)

Example 10.4 – Actual piecemeal disposals

Water plc held a 60% interest in Ducksback plc. On 31 December 1995, (conveniently) the year end of Water plc, it sold 20% of its interest to another company for £20m. At the date of disposal the consolidated carrying values of the net assets of Ducksback plc including relevant goodwill were £40m.

Required

Calculate the consolidated profit or loss on disposal, and explain how Ducksback will be treated in the consolidated statements at 31 December 1995.

Profit on disposal will be measured as £20m – 20% × £40m = £12m. In the consolidated profit and loss account, Ducksback will be accounted for as a 60% subsidiary to the date of partial disposal. As it took place on the last day of the year, when it (probably) became an associate, no associated company results will be reported. In the consolidated balance sheet at 31 December 1995, it will be reported as a 40% associate.

Example 10.5 – Deemed disposal by subsidiary share issue

Water plc held a 60% interest in Ducksback plc. On 31 December 1995 the subsidiary made a share issue of 10m shares at £2.50 per share to third party shareholders. Assume (conveniently) cash was received that day. Prior to the issue the subsidiary had 20m shares in issue. At the date of the share issue, the consolidated carrying values of the net assets of Ducksback plc including relevant goodwill were £40m.

Required

Calculate the consolidated profit or loss on deemed disposal, and explain how Ducksback will be treated in the consolidated statements at 31 December 1995.

The amount raised by the subsidiary in the share issue would be 10m × £2.50 = £25m, therefore the carrying value of the *whole* of the subsidiary's net assets immediately *after* the issue would be £65m (= £40m + £25m).

Group's net assets pre-share issue = 60% × £40m = £24m

The group held 12m shares, i.e. 60% × 20m prior to the issue. After the issue, the group held $\frac{12m}{30m}$ shares = 40% × 30m

Group's net assets post-share issue = 40% × £65m = £26m

No proceeds were received by parent shareholders from the issue, but the group's stake in the subsidiary has become more valuable, i.e.

Gain on deemed disposal = £26m – £24m = £2m

Ducksback plc would be accounted for as a subsidiary in the consolidated profit and loss account to the date of disposal, and the gain on disposal would be shown. There would be no time for associated undertaking income. In the consolidated balance sheet at 31 December 1995, Ducksback would be accounted for as a 40% associate.

Conceptual issues

Slice-by-slice approach

Different variants of the slice-by-slice approach exist in the UK and USA, distinguished by how they determine fair values at the purchase of each slice. In the USA a *pure* slice-by-slice approach is adopted (termed by the FASB Discussion Memorandum, *Consolidation Policy and Procedures* (1991), the 'parent approach'). As each slice is purchased, goodwill for that slice is the difference between the consideration and the parent's portion of the fair values of identifiable assets and liabilities for that slice – but *only* for that slice. The consequence is that the value of say for land in the earlier Hangover-Shady example, would be a *composite* value, the sum of slices of differently dated fair values.

Implicitly in the UK, per FRS 2's requirements on the increase in a stake in an existing subsidiary, a *modified* slice-by-slice approach is adopted, in which goodwill is determined on a slice-by-slice basis, but at each stage the *whole* of the identifiable assets and liabilities of the subsidiary are homogeneously revalued to the fair value *at that date*. As discussed above, the credit for the proportion of the revaluation reserves on stakes *already held* will be to consolidated revaluation reserves. For these stakes already held the revaluation increment is *post*-acquisition. The subsidiary's net assets in the consolidation are, under this approach, always on a homogenous basis, at fair values at the date of the last purchase. This is consistent with the parent extension approach described in Chapter 6, and in the author's view aids comprehensibility. The situation when an associate becomes a subsidiary is outside FRS 2's scope, though by analogy a similar treatment would be adopted.

Single step approach

The problem with the single step approach is that the fair value of the investment is the sum of fair values at different dates, but is compared with the fair value of the identifiable assets and liabilities of the subsidiary at a single date, the date control is gained. Proposals to 'improve' this situation focus on how to modify measurement of the 'fair value' of the purchase consideration. These include

(a) the standard approach of just adding all slices at *cost*.
(b) *equity accounting* for previous slices from their date of purchase to the date control passes, crediting attributable retained profits to consolidated retained earnings. This is none other than the slice-by-slice approach under a different guise.
(c) the total investment reassessed at its *fair value at the date control passes*. The credit for the revaluation proportion relating to previous stakes will be to consolidated revaluation reserves. (the FASB Discussion Memorandum terms this the 'entity' approach).

FRS 2, constrained by the Companies Act 1985, requires alternative (a), unless it does not give a true and fair view, e.g. because the equity accounting approach has *already* been used for previous slices, in which case alternative (b) is to be used. The last two try to match the date of measurement of the investment with that of the fair values acquired, though the 'equity' approach is strictly an updating rather than a 'valuing'. According to the FASB Discussion Memorandum, if its 'entity' approach were adopted (alternative (c), not presently used in the US or UK), fair value restatements should not take place after the point control is gained, nor gains or losses on piecemeal disposals be computed where control is still retained, because under this approach, both sets of transactions would then be merely transactions between different classes of shareholders (controlling and non-controlling) and transactions between shareholders are not usually reflected in published accounts. See also 'Consolidation Concepts: A Framework for Alignment Adjustments?' in Chapter 6.

Exercises

10.1 Gradualist plc has acquired its 75% stake in Prey Ltd in two stages, 25% on 30 November 1992 for £3m when the reserves of Prey were £4m, and a further 50% on 30 November 1994 for £9m, when Prey's reserves were £8m. Ignore subsequent write-off of goodwill. The balance sheets of both companies at 30 November 1995 were:

	Gradualist £m	Prey £m
Miscellaneous net assets	103	15
Investment in Prey	12	—
Share capital	(15)	(2)
Share premium	(30)	(4)
Retained profits	(70)	(9)

Required

(a) Calculate intuitively goodwill, consolidated retained profits and minority interests at 30 November 1995 under the single step and the slice-by-slice approaches.

(b) Analyse the equity of Prey plc at 30 November 1995 as in Figure 10.1, and prepare a consolidated cancellation table under the slice-by-slice approach as in Figure 10.2.

(c) Applying FRS 2's provisions, prepare consolidated balance sheets at 30 November 1995 for the Gradualist Group, both assuming that (i) Gradualist was *not* able to exercise significant influence over Shady at 30 November 1992, and (ii) Gradualist *was* able to exercise significant influence at that date.

10.2 In Exercise 10.1, assume that at 30 November 1992 Prey's land, included in its miscellaneous net assets, had a fair value of £16m (carrying value £10m), and at 30 November 1994, the same land a fair value of £24m. Assume that the land is still held and that the adjustments have not been 'pushed down' into the records of Shady plc.

Required

Show the adjustments to the slice-by-slice cancellation table in Exercise 10.1 to effect the above fair value adjustments.

10.3 Oasis plc held a 75% interest in Thirsty plc. On 30 November 1995, the year end of Thirsty plc, it sold 50% of its interest to another company for £45m. At the date of disposal the consolidated carrying values of the net assets of Thirsty plc including relevant goodwill were £40m.

Required

Calculate the consolidated profit or loss on disposal, and explain how Ducksback will be treated in the consolidated statements at 31 December 1995.

10.4 Magnet plc held a 75% interest in Filings plc. On 31 December 1995 the subsidiary made a share issue of 30m shares at £3 per share to new non-group shareholders. Assume the cash (conveniently) was received that day. Prior to the issue the subsidiary had 40m shares in issue. At the date of the share issue, the consolidated carrying values of the net assets of Filings plc including relevant goodwill were £80m.

Required

Calculate the consolidated profit or loss on disposal, and explain how Filings plc will be treated in the consolidated statements at 31 December 1995.

COMPLEX SHAREHOLDING STRUCTURES

Now more complex group shareholding structures are considered: for example where the parent has subsidiaries which themselves own subsidiaries (*vertical* groups); secondly where in addition to subsidiaries themselves owning subsidiaries, the parent itself also has a direct stake in the sub-subsidiaries (*mixed* groups); and finally where group companies have bilateral shareholdings in each other (*cross holdings*).

Vertical Groups

Consider the following group shareholding structure (assuming voting rights are proportional to shareholding proportional stakes) where Top Dog holds a 70 per cent stake in Upper Cruft, which itself holds a 60 per cent stake in Underdog:

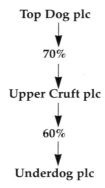

Top Dog plc

70%

Upper Cruft plc

60%

Underdog plc

Top Dog holds a 42 per cent (i.e. 70% × 60%) indirect stake in Underdog. The group minority is made up of two components, 30 per cent (i.e. 100–70 per cent) in Upper Cruft and 58 per cent (i.e. 100–42 per cent) in Underdog. Figure 10.5 shows how the 58 per cent is made up.

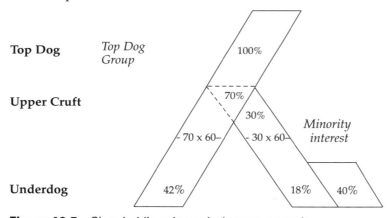

Figure 10.5 – Shareholdings in vertical group example

The main group comprises 100 per cent Top Dog plus a 70 per cent holding in Upper Cruft, and a 42 per cent indirect holding in Underdog, represented by the left-hand diagonal area. The minority interest has three components

(a) a 30 per cent minority in Upper Cruft held by non-controlling interests in that company, and
(b a 58 per cent minority in Underdog – a direct minority holding of 40 per cent held by its own non-controlling interests and an 18 per cent (30% × 60%) indirect stake held by the non-controlling shareholders of Upper Cruft.

Under the Companies Act 1985 (see Chapter 2) Underdog is a subsidiary undertaking of Top Dog as the subsidiary of a subsidiary, even though the group's multiplicative interest is only 42 per cent.

In such vertical groups the term 'minority interests' is a misnomer – here the 'majority' holding in Underdog is 48 per cent. The 'minority' stake could be even larger – where one company holds 51 per cent of another, which holds 51 per cent of another, which holds 51 per cent of the third, the first has an indirect $51\% \times 51\% \times 51\% = 13\%$ holding in the third with a 'minority' of 87 per cent! FRS 2 comments that 'despite the title "minority interests", there is in principle no upper limit to the proportion of shares in an undertaking which may be held as minority interests . . .' (para. 80). A more useful term, 'non-controlling interests', is used by the FASB Discussion Memorandum, *Consolidation Policy and Procedures* (1991), in the USA. However, 'minority interests' is enshrined in the Companies Act 1985, which fossilizes it in UK pronouncements.

Preparing consolidated accounts for the vertical group

Both the Upper Cruft *subgroup* and the Top Dog group (the *main* group) could be required to produce consolidated financial statements. However, as discussed in Chapter 2, a UK company which is the parent of a subgroup is exempted from producing consolidated accounts for the subgroup if

(a) it is unlisted; and
(b) has an immediate parent established in an EC member state which owns more than 50 per cent of its shares; and
(c) a minority veto is not exercised (S 228(1a)).

Two alternative methods of getting to the same consolidated balance sheet for the main group are used in practice by groups:

(a) *The sequential approach* – consolidated accounts for the Underdog subgroup are prepared and are themselves consolidated with the individual accounts of the parent.
(b) *The simultaneous approach* – consolidated accounts for the whole group are produced directly by using *multiplicative* ownership proportions attributable to the ultimate parent (Top Dog).

The decision often depends on whether it is necessary for subgroup consolidations to be prepared on their own right to satisfy legal requirements. Also in large groups, head office is sometimes supplied with subconsolidated information to help minimize the quantity of data processed centrally.

Example 10.6 – Vertical groups

The balance sheets of the three companies at 31 December 1995 were:

	Top Dog £m	Upper Cruft £m	Underdog £m
Miscellaneous net assets	250	230	100
Investment in Upper Cruft	250		
Investment in Underdog		70	
Share capital	(100)	(70)	(15)
Share premium	(150)	(80)	(25)
Retained profits	(250)	(150)	(60)

Top Dog acquired a 70% interest in Upper Cruft on 31 December 1993 when the latter's reserves were £100m. Upper Cruft acquired a 60% interest in Underdog on 31 December 1994 when the latter's reserves were £40m.

Required

Calculate consolidated balances for share capital, share premium, goodwill, retained earnings and minority interests for the Top Dog Group at 31 December 1995 using

(a) the simultaneous approach; and
(b) the sequential approach;
(c) analyse intuitively the meaning of the consolidated goodwill, retained earnings and minority interest balances you have calculated.

Simultaneous approach

The *main group* consolidation is done in one step using multiplicative ownership proportions (e.g. 70% × 60% = 42%). It is quicker than the sequential approach and simple enough for very small groups, though in practice may cause data management problems in large groups as discussed earlier. Figure 10.6 shows the simultaneous cancellation table for the main Top Dog group.

Description	Invest-ment	Share capital	Share premium	Good-will	Consol retained profits	Minority interests
Top Dog balances	250	(100)	(150)		(250)	
Upper Cruft (70/30):						
Subgroup investment in sub-subsidiary	49					21
- pre-acquisition (70 + 80 + 100)				(175)		(75)
- post-acquisition (150 - 100)					(35)	(15)
Underdog [42 (i.e. 70x60) / 58]:						
- pre-acquisition (15 + 25 + 40)				(33.6)		(46.4)
- post-acquisition (60 - 40)					(8.4)	(11.6)
Cancellation:						
Main group investment	(250)			250		
70% of subgroup investment	(49)			49		
Consolidated	-	(100)	(150)	90.4	(293.4)	(127.0)

Figure 10.6 – Simultaneous approach to vertical groups consolidation

Pre- and post-acquisition equity is calculated for both subsidiaries using the above acquisition dates and the multiplicative ownership proportions for Underdog. The only new technical procedure is that Upper Cruft's investment in the sub-subsidiary (Underdog) is apportioned between the investment and minority interest according to the parent's 70% stake in Upper Cruft. Intuitive analyses of main group goodwill and consolidated retained profits figures in the cancellation table are shown below. Minority interests will be discussed after the sequential approach:

Analysis of consolidated balances:

Goodwill	=	Upper Cruft goodwill	+		70% × Underdog goodwill
	=	[250 – 70% × (70+80+100)]	+	70% ×	[70 – 60%(15+25+40)]
	=	75	+		70% × 22 = 90.4

Consolidated retained profits = Top Dog + 70% Upper Cruft post-acq + 70% × 60% × Underdog post-acq

= 250 + 70% × (150 – 100) + 70% × [60% × (60 – 40)] = 293.4

Sequential approach

This provides another route to the same consolidated figures which may be preferred by many groups in practice for reasons discussed above. Figure 10.7 shows the subgroup consolidation cancellation table for the Underdog group, followed by the Top Dog main group cancellation table derived from it. The main group table has the following features:

(a) Upper Cruft's balances in the subgroup table are subsequently treated as a normal subsidiary's in the main group table.
(b) Only Underdog's post-acquisition profits belong to the main group (split 70/30), as its pre-acquisition profits were used in computing subgroup goodwill.
(c) The subgroup goodwill has been apportioned between ultimate parent shareholders (70%) and subgroup parent shareholders (30%).

Analysis of consolidated balances:

Upper Cruft subgroup consolidation	Invest-ment	Share capital	Share premium	Good-will	Consol retained profits	Minority interests
Upper Cruft balances	70	(70)	(80)		(150)	
Underdog equity analysis (60/40):						
Pre-acquisition (15 + 25 + 40)				(48)		(32)
Post-acquisition (60 - 40)					(12)	(8)
Cancellation	(70)			70		
Consolidated	-	(70)	(80)	22	(162)	(40)

Top Dog main group consolidation	Invest-ment	Share capital	Share premium	Good-will	Consol retained profits	Minority interests
Top Dog balances	250	(100)	(150)		(250)	
From subgroup table above (70/30):						
Upper Cruft:						
- pre-acquisition (70 + 80 + 100)				(175)		(75)
- post-acquisition (150 - 100)					(35)	(15)
Underdog:						
- post-acquisition main group (12)					(8.4)	(3.6)
Subgroup goodwill (22)				15.4		6.6
Underdog direct minority (40%)						(40)
Cancellation	(250)			250		
Consolidated	-	(100)	(150)	90.4	(293.4)	(127.0)

Figure 10.7 – Sequential approach to vertical groups consolidation

Goodwill and consolidated retained profits are as above. Main group minority interests can easily be interpreted as

---

Minority interests = 30% net assets of Upper Cruft (excluding the investment) + 58% net assets of Underdog

$$= \quad 30\% \times 230 \quad + \quad 58\% \times 100 \quad = \quad £127m$$

Derivation – if the above relationship is accepted on trust, the following derivation can be omitted without loss in continuity. Consider the basic balance sheet relationships for Upper Cruft and Underdog:

$$EQ_{UD} \quad = \quad NA_{UD} \qquad \qquad \text{(i.e. } 15 + 25 + \ 60 \ = \ 100\text{), and}$$
$$EQ_{UC} \quad = \quad NA_{UC} + \quad INV_{UC} \quad \text{(i.e. } 70 + 80 + 150 \ = \ 230 \ + \ 70\text{)}$$

The Equity of both Underdog and Upper Cruft comprise their net assets, plus in the latter case, the investment of Upper Cruft in Underdog. Consider the equity accounting identity from Chapter 4 for the 60% investment of Upper Cruft in Underdog:

$$INV_{uc} + 60\% \, \Delta \, RE_{UD} \quad = \quad GW_{UD} + 60\% \ NA_{UD}$$
$$70 \quad + 60\% \times 20 \quad = \quad 22 \quad + 60\% \times 100$$

Armed with these we can now examine the breakdown of the *main group* minority interest figure in Underdog. First we write down the composition of the main group minority components in the main group cancellation table in Figure 10.7 in terms of the symbols above:

$$\text{Minority interests} \quad = \quad (75 + 15) \quad + \quad 3.6 \qquad \qquad + \quad 40 \qquad - \quad 6.6 \quad = \quad 127.0$$
$$= \quad 30\% \, EQ_{UC} + 30\% \times 60\% \, \Delta \, RE_{UD} \quad + \quad 40\% \, EQ_{UD} \quad - \quad 30\% \, GW_{UD} \quad = \quad 127.0$$

Substituting for the Equity figures in terms of net assets and rearranging, we get

$$= \quad 30\% \, (NA_{UC} + INV_{UC}) + 30\% \times 60\% \, \Delta \, RE_{UD} \ + 40\% \, NA_{UD} - 30\% \, GW_{UD}$$
$$= \quad 30\% \, NA_{UC} \ + \ 30\% [INV_{UC} + 60\% \, \Delta \, RE_{UD}] \ + 40\% \, NA_{UD} - 30\% \, GW_{UD}$$

The second term is the left-hand side of the equity accounting relationship above, so substituting its right-hand side equivalent, we get

$$= \quad 30\% \ NA_{UC} \ + \ 30\%[GW_{UD} + 60\% \ NA_{UD}] + 40\% \ NA_{UD} - 30\% \ GW_{UD}$$
$$= \quad 30\% \ NA_{UC} \ + \ 58\% \ NA_{UD}$$

and verifying this much simpler expression, remembering for Upper Cruft that the net assets figure *excludes* the investment:

$$= \quad 30\% \times 230 \ + \ 58\% \times 100 \quad = \quad £127.0m$$

Measurement of goodwill in multi-tiered groups

Should the main consolidated financial statements include *all purchased* goodwill arising in the group, or just goodwill attributable to main group shareholders as in the examples above? Many writers (e.g. Shaw, 1976, pp. 69–70) recommend the latter, i.e. including as above only $70\% \times 22 = £15.4m$ of the total goodwill of the sub-subsidiary in the total of £90.4m. If *total* purchased goodwill were included, it would be stated at £97m (i.e. £75m (Upper Cruft) + £22m (Underdog)), and (gross) minority interests would be increased by the same £6.6m, so

Gross Minority = 30% net assets of Upper Cruft + 58% net assets + 30% goodwill
 interests   (excluding investment)   of Underdog   in Underdog
         = $30\% \times 230$ $+ \ 58\% \times 100$ $+ \ 30\% \times 22$
         =   £133.6m

At first sight, including minority goodwill seems to have more in common with the entity than the parent approach to consolidation. However, here only *purchased* minority goodwill would be included and *not imputed*, unlike the entity approach in Chapter 4. In vertical groups, there are at least three classes of owners: the ultimate group; intermediate subgroup(s); and of ultimate companies (sub-subsidiaries). The issue here is whether all classes of non-controlling interests should be treated the same, or even under the parent approach, different measurement treatments allowed for more 'influential' non-controlling holdings.

A glance at professional texts suggests that most include only the *main group* element of purchased group goodwill; there seems no pronouncement which prevents *total* purchased group goodwill being included. Including only main group goodwill states *all* classes of non-controlling interests at their share of *net assets* (only) in the subsidiaries they own, and so does *not* coincide with their proportionate share in the consolidated equity of the subgroup in which they have their stake, unless the immediate write-down of goodwill is adopted. The fact that immediate write-off has been the most widely adopted UK practice for goodwill probably explains why this issue has not been discussed further.

Sub-subsidiary acquired before the subsidiary joined the group

In the Top Dog example above, the sub-subsidiary was acquired after the subsidiary joined the group, hence the date for determining its main group post-acquisition profits is identical to the date which it entered the subgroup. Suppose the subgroup purchases its holding in the sub-subsidiary *before* the parent acquires the subgroup. Now some post-acquisition profits of the subgroup are pre-acquisition profits of the main group.

Example 10.7 – Sub-subsidiary acquired first

Suppose Upper Cruft had acquired its interest in Underdog on 31st December 1991 when the retained earnings of Underdog were £20m. Assume that on 31 December 1993 when Top Dog acquired its interest in Upper Cruft, retained earnings in Underdog were £30m.

Required

Show the effects of the change in assumptions of the change in date of acquisition of Underdog by Upper Cruft on the consolidated retained profits of the Top Dog Group.

A shortcut approach usually recommended is to treat the date of acquisition of the sub-subsidiary as 31 December 1993, the date the *main* group acquires the subsidiary. In this example, reserves of the sub-subsidiary at acquisition for main group purposes would be taken as £30m. This approach is pragmatic and adopted later in this section. Strictly however, sub-subsidiary profits between the date of acquisition by the subgroup and the main group should be treated as a capital reserve. In Figure 10.6 the following entry would be made :

	Consolidated profits	Capital reserve	Goodwill
Transfer of *group* pre-acquisition profits to capital reserve – 42% × (30 – 20)	4.2	(4.2)	

The reason why the shortcut approach is not strictly correct is because the investment market value is measured at 31 December 1991, whereas the sub-subsidiary joined the main group on 31 December 1993, hence they are measured at two different dates and so should not be compared. The shortcut approach aggregates this capital reserve with main group goodwill at acquisition.

Exercise

10.5 Consider the balance sheets (£m) of Bourgeoisie plc, Prole Ltd and Outcaste Ltd at 30 June 1996:

	Bourgeoisie	Prole	Outcaste
Miscellaneous net assets	2,600	120	200
Investment in Prole	200		
Investment in Outcaste		160	
Share capital	(400)	(60)	(50)
Share premium	(900)	(100)	(80)
Retained profits	(1,500)	(120)	(70)

Bourgeoisie acquired a 75% interest in Prole on 31 October 1993, when the retained earnings of Prole were £40m. Prole acquired its 80% interest in Outcaste on 31 March 1995, when Outcaste's retained earnings were £50m.

Required

(a) Produce cancellation tables for Bourgeoisie group under both the simultaneous and sequential approaches at 30 June 1996.
(b) Interpret the composition of the balances for consolidated reserves, goodwill and minority interests.
(c) Explain how the cancellation table in (a) above would be changed if Prole had acquired its stake in Outcaste on 31 March 1991, and if Outcaste's retained profits at that date had been £50m. At 31 October 1993 assume for this part that Outcaste's retained profits had been £60m.

Mixed Groups

Consider now where main group parent, Top Dog, has both a direct and an indirect holding in Underdog as follows:

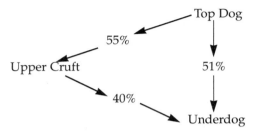

Figure 10.8 shows group and minority interest holdings. Underdog is now a direct subsidiary of Top Dog. However, as it is not now a subsidiary of Upper Cruft, no sub-group consolidation would be prepared, and the simultaneous method would have to be used. The group now has a direct *and* an indirect stake in Underdog, i.e. 73% = 51% + 55% × 40%.

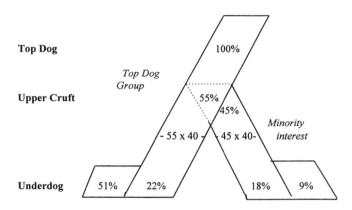

Figure 10.8 – Shareholdings in mixed group example

Example 10.8 – All holdings acquired at the same date

Assume the same balance sheets as in the previous example with the mixed group structure just discussed and given the following extra information. On 31 December 1993, Top Dog acquired a 55% interest in Upper Cruft for £160m and a 51% interest in Underdog for £90m, when their retained profits were respectively £100m and £30m. On the same date Upper Cruft acquired a 40% interest in Underdog for £70m.

Required
Calculate consolidated retained profits, goodwill and minority interests for the Top Dog Group at 31 December 1995. Ignore the effects of goodwill write-off.

Solution

All holdings now were acquired on the same date. For Top Dog:

Stake in Upper Cruft		=	55%
Stake in Underdog	= $51\% + (55\% \times 40\%)$	=	73%

and the simultaneous approach cancellation table is shown in Figure 10.9. As in the vertical group cancellation table, Upper Cruft's investment is split between investment and minority (now 55%/45%). The minority interest calculation can be checked as 45% of the net assets of Upper Cruft excluding its investment plus 27% of Underdog's net assets, i.e.

Main group minority   = $45\% \times (730 - 500) + 27\% \times (200 - 100)$ = 130.5m

Description	Invest-ment	Share capital	Share premium	Good-will	Consol retained profits	Minority interests
Top Dog balances	160		(150)		(250)	
	90	(100)				
Upper Cruft (55/45):						
Subgroup investment in sub-subsidiary	38.5					31.5
- pre-acquisition (70 + 80 + 100)				(137.5)		(112.5)
- post-acquisition (150 - 100)					(27.5)	(22.5)
Underdog [73 (i.e.51 + 55x40)/27]:						
- pre-acquisition (15 + 25 + 30)				(51.1)		(18.9)
- post-acquisition (60 - 30)					(21.9)	(8.1)
Cancellation:						
Main group investment	(250)			250.0		
55% of subgroup investment	(38.5)			38.5		
Consolidated	-	(100)	(150)	99.9	(299.4)	(130.5)

Figure 10.9 – Simultaneous approach to mixed groups consolidation

Example 10.9 – Subsidiary holding in sub-subsidiary acquired later

The piecemeal acquisition section at the start of this chapter should be reviewed again before this example. Suppose now on 31 December 1993, Top Dog acquired a 55% interest in Upper Cruft for £160m and a 51% interest in Underdog for £90m, when their retained profits were respectively £100m and £30m. Upper Cruft acquired its 40% interest in Underdog on 31 December 1994 for £70m, when Underdog's reserves were £40m (in the previous example the date was 31 December 1993, and reserves £30m).

Required

Calculate consolidated retained profits, goodwill and minority interests for the Top Dog Group at 31 December 1995. Ignore the effects of goodwill write-off.

Now the sub-subsidiary was acquired *piecemeal*, 51% on 31 December 1993, and a further 55% × 40% = 22% on 31 December 1994. The multiplicative approach of previous examples is combined with the piecemeal technique studied earlier in the discussion of FRS. 2. Figure 10.10 gives a 'piece-meal' analysis of the sub-subsidiary's equity (similar to Figure 10.1).

The shaded area represents pre-acquisition equity as before, and the Figure 10.10's interpretation is exactly as in Figure 10.1. Figure 10.11 is the simultaneous cancellation table derived from it. Minority interests are the same as in the previous example as the only change is in acquisition dates, which whilst they affect the pre-/post-acquisition split, do not affect their ongoing interest.

Subsidiary stake in sub-subsidiary acquired prior to joining group

The principle is no different from the previous section – the date of acquisition is usually

Time period	Subsidiary equity relating to time period		Analysis of equity slices		
			direct stake 51%	indirect stake 22%	Mino-rity 27%
Prior to 31/12/94	15 + 25 + 30	= 70	35.7	15.4	18.9
Retained earnings 1/1/95 to 31/12/95	40 - 30	= 10	5.1	2.2	2.7
Retained earnings 1/1/96 to 31/12/96	60 - 40	= 20	10.2	4.4	5.4
Total equity at 31/12/96	20 + 20 + 60	= 100	51.0	22.0	27.0

Figure 10.10 – Mixed groups piecemeal acquisition: analysis of subsidiary's equity

Description	Percentage stakes pre/post/min o	Invest-ment	Share capital	Share premium	Good-will	Consol retained profits	Minority interests
Top Dog balances		160 90	(100)	(150)		(250)	
Upper Cruft (55/45):							
Subgroup investment		38.5					31.5
- pre-acq to 12/93 (70 + 80 + 100)					(137.5)		(112.5)
- post-acq to 12/95 (150 - 100)						(27.5)	(22.5)
Underdog [73 (51+ 55x40) / 27]:							
- pre-both, to 12/93 (15 + 25 + 30)	73 / zero / 27				(51.1) [1]		(18.9)
- post first, to 12/94 (40 - 30)	22 / 51 / 27				(2.2)	(5.1)	(2.7)
- post-both, to 12/96 (60 - 40)	zero/ 73 / 27					(14.6) [2]	(5.4)
Cancellation:							
Main group		(250)			250.0		
55% of subgroup		(38.5)			38.5		
Consolidated		-	(100)	(150)	97.7	(297.2)	(130.5)

Notes
1.   51.1   =   35.7 + 15.4
2.   14.6   =   10.2 + 4.4

Figure 10.11 – Mixed groups and piecemeal acquisition example

taken as when the main group comes into being. Similar comments apply. The analysis of shareholdings chronologically can become complex if the parent and subsidiary are both acquiring piecemeal holdings, but similar principles apply, and percentage holdings are recalculated after each equity slice is acquired..

Exercise

10.6 Consider the balance sheets in Exercise 10.5, except the group structure is as follows. Bourgeoisie acquired a 60% interest in Prole for £162m, and a 25% interest in Outcaste for £38m on 31 October 1993, when the reserves of the latter two companies were respectively, £40m and £20m. Prole acquired a 70% interest in Outcaste on the same date for £160m.

Required

(a) Produce a simultaneous cancellation table for the main group at 30 June 1996.
(b) Interpret the composition of the balances thus computed. Ignore the subsequent write-off of goodwill.

10.7 Consider the balance sheets in Exercise 10.5, except that Bourgeoisie acquired a 60% interest in Prole for £162m, and a 25% interest in Outcaste for £38m on 31 October 1993, when the reserves of the latter two companies were respectively, £40m and £20m. Prole acquired its 70% interest at 31 March 1995, when Outcaste's reserves were £50m (unlike in the previous example when the interest was acquired on the same date).

Required

As for Exercise 10.5.

10.8 Consider the balance sheets in Exercise 10.5, except that Bourgeoisie acquired a 60% interest in Prole for £162m on 31 October 1993, and a 25% interest in Outcaste for £38m on 31 October 1995, when the reserves of the latter two companies were respectively, £40m and £55m. Prole acquired its 70% interest at 31 October 1992, when Outcaste's reserves were £15m. At 31 October 1993, Outcaste's reserves were £20m.

Required

As for Exercise 10.5.

Cross-Holdings

This section can be omitted without loss of continuity. Sometimes one group company acquires shareholdings in another which already holds its shares, creating *reciprocal* or *cross*-holdings, or such holdings are deliberately created for other strategic reasons. There is no restrictions on cross-holdings between subsidiaries where neither is the holding company of the other. In the author's experience such holdings are rare in the UK, though extremely common in certain other countries (see McKinnon (1984) on Japan). A simultaneous equations approach based on Brault (1979) is used below to deal with such situations.

Section 23 (1) of the Companies Act 1985 prohibits a company being a member of its holding company except where it is a trustee, a moneylender holding security in its ordinary course of business, or an authorized market-maker. However, as this restriction is based on the legal term 'holding company' rather than 'parent undertaking' (see Chapter 2), it would not seem illegal for a 'subsidiary undertaking' or 'quasi-subsidiary' which is not legally a 'subsidiary', to hold shares in its 'parent undertaking', which under these circumstances would not be its 'holding company', and the same simultaneous equations approach could be used under such circumstances.

The prohibition also does not apply if the subsidiary's shareholding in its holding company was acquired prior to the holder becoming a subsidiary, under which circumstances the subsidiary can remain a member, but cannot vote (Section 23 (5)). Accounting for this specialized case is more complex. Wilkins (1979, p. 187) suggests that such prior holdings should either be treated as a repurchase of shares by the group, or disclosed as a trade investment (disclosed under 'own shares' as a part of 'investments' in the consolidated balance sheet). Further discussion of this specialized case is beyond the scope of the current text – see Taylor (1995, Section VI.1.7.4).

Example 10.10 – Cross-holdings

Suppose the mixed group case is modified slightly so that, at its acquisition, Underdog already held a 10% interest in Upper Cruft. Apart from this cross-holding, the group structure is the same:

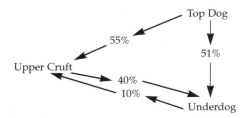

Required
Calculate consolidated retained profits, goodwill and minority interests for the Top Dog Group at 31 December 1995. Ignore the effects of goodwill write-off.

Expressing group relationships using linear equations
Using simple multiplication to calculate main group proportionate holdings does not work – a simultaneous linear equations approach must be used.

Mixed group example without cross-holdings
The approach is first illustrated for the previous mixed group example without the 10% cross-holding. In this case simple multiplication does work, but equations are used to demonstrate their use prior to looking at the cross-holdings case. The following equations express group proportional holdings (TD, UC, and UD are Top Dog, Upper Cruft, and Underdog respectively):

TD	=	1.0		
UC	=	0.55 TD		
UD	=	0.51 TD	+	0.40 UC

Taking for example the third equation, Top Dog has a 51% stake in Underdog, and Upper Cruft a 40% stake. Solving these we get the proportions used in the cancellation table, i.e.

TD	=	1.0
UC	=	0.55
UD	=	0.73

Mixed group example with cross-holdings
In this case the overall holdings cannot adequately be calculated without a simultaneous equations or analogous approach. The group relationships are:

TD	=	1.0		
UC	=	0.55 TD	+	0.10 UD
UD	=	0.51 TD	+	0.40 UC

Upper Cruft is now owned 55% 'downwards' by Top Dog and 10% 'upwards' by Underdog. Solving these equations by substitution, we get,

TD	=	1.0
UC	=	0.626
UD	=	0.760

So in the cancellation table the proportions used for Upper Cruft would be 62.6% for majority and (100 – 62.6) = 37.4% for the minority, and for Underdog 76.0% and 24.0% respectively.

Minority interests – complementary equations
The parent proportions can be checked using complementary equations to calculate minority interests. Consider the mixed group example without cross-holdings. Minority holdings in the Top Dog group are expressed by:

TD	=	0.00				
UC	=	0.45	+	0.55 TD		
UD	=	0.09	+	0.51 TD	+	0.40 UC

There is no minority interest in Top Dog. The minority in Upper Cruft is 45% plus any arising from Top Dog (which in this case is zero). The minority in Underdog is 9% direct plus any arising from holdings by other group companies. Solving these equations, we get,

TD	=	0.00			
UC	=	0.45			
UD	=	0.09	+	0.40×0.55 =	0.27

These equations show clearly the direct minority in Underdog (9%) and the indirect minority (22%) arising from subgroup holdings. In the cross-holdings case, the minority structure is expressed:

TD	=	0.00				
UC	=	0.35	+	0.55 TD	+	0.10 UD
UD	=	0.09	+	0.51 TD	+	0.40 UC

The minority in Upper Cruft is 35% (100% − 55% − 10%) held directly, and indirectly via Top Dog (55%) and Underdog (10%). Solutions are:

TD	=	0.000
UC	=	0.374
UD	=	0.240

consistent with the original solutions for the parent's holdings above. There are other ways of setting up cross-holding equations (see for example Shaw, 1973, Chapter 13), but Brault's approach has been used here as the simplest way of representing the group holding structure. In larger and more complex groups, such equation systems can be handled by matrix inversion computer routines (see for example Griffin, Williams and Larsen, 1980, pp. 455–458).

Piecemeal acquisitions
As each new shareholding is purchased a new set of simultaneous equations is formulated and solved at each ownership change to evaluate the new proportions to be used for the cancellation table. When these proportions have been calculated, the methods used in the mixed group with piecemeal acquisitions can be directly applied.

Exercise

10.9 For Exercise 10.6
 (a) Formulate a set of simultaneous linear equations for holdings in the Bourgeoisie group. Solve them and compare solutions with Exercise 10.6.
 (b) Formulate complementary equations for minority interests and verify that the solutions are consistent with part (a).

10.10 Formulate a set of simultaneous equations for following structure. Bourgeoisie holds a 60% interest in Prole and a 65% interest in Outcaste. Prole holds a 30% interest in Outcaste. Outcaste holds a 25% interest in Prole. Also formulate and solve the complementary equations for minority interests, verifying they are consistent with the parent shareholdings equations.

10.11 At 31 December 1995, the shareholdings in the Upper Echelon Group were as follows:

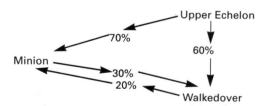

 (i) Upper Echelon plc had acquired both its 70% holding in Minion plc and its 60% holding in Walkedover plc on 31 December 1993 when the retained profits of both companies were £100m and £200m respectively.
 (ii) The 20% holding of Walkedover plc in Minion plc had been acquired some years prior to 31 December 1993.
 (iii) On 31 December 1994, Minion plc acquired a 30% stake in Walkedover plc when Minion's retained profits were £120m and Walkedover's were £240m.
 (iv) The retained profits of the three companies at 31 December 1995 were, Upper Echelon £500m, Minion £150m and Walkedover £290m.

Required

Calculate the balance sheet figure for consolidated retained profits for the Upper Echelon Group at 31 December 1995. Assume all holdings are in voting ordinary shares.

Acquisition of other classes of equity

Sometimes the subsidiary has different classes of equity and their acquisition affects the computation of goodwill and minority interests. FRS 4, *Capital Instruments*, issued in 1993, requires that resulting minority interests must be analysed into *equity* and *non-equity* components (para. 50). The latter are defined as shares restricted in rights in distributions and winding up surpluses to a limited amount which is not calculated with respect to the subsidiary's assets, profits or equity dividends, or redeemable other than at the option of the issuer, such as at the holder's option (para. 12).

They are accounted for as for non-equity instruments of individual companies (per FRS 4), recorded at their net issue proceeds, then the carrying amount is increased by the finance costs for the period (analogous to an interest charge), and reduced by dividend or other payments during the period (analogous to loan repayments) (para. 41). Similar to debt, the consolidated profit and loss is charged with the finance costs allocated over the debt term at a constant rate on the carrying amount (para. 28), and minority share computed accordingly. Though the calculation is as for 'liability-type' instruments, the charges are located with 'other dividends'.

Certain shares issued by subsidiaries should be classified as *liabilities* and *not* minority interests 'if the group taken as a whole has an *obligation* to transfer economic benefits in connection with the shares', such as where the payments are guaranteed by another group member (para. 49, emphasis added). Thus for shares issued by subsidiaries there are three possible classifications under FRS 4: equity, non-equity or liabilities, depending on their substance.

Example 10.11 – Different classes of debt/equity consideration

Consider the following balance sheets at 31 March 1996:

	Daddy £m	Sonny £m
Miscellaneous net assets	200	280
Investment in Sonny	190	
10% debentures in Sonny	30	(60)
Ordinary share capital (£1)	(80)	(40)
Preference share capital (£1)	—	(25)
Share premium	(150)	(60)
Retained profits	(190)	(95)

On 31 March 1994, Daddy acquired 80% of the ordinary share capital of Sonny and 60% of its preference share capital for £190m, and in addition, 50% of its debentures for £30m, when Sonny's retained earnings were £80m. The ordinary shares carry voting rights at general meetings of the companies, but the preference shares carry voting rights only if their dividends are in arrears, which is not currently the case.

Required

Prepare a consolidated cancellation table at 31 March 1996 showing goodwill, consolidated retained earnings, debentures and minority interests. Ignore goodwill write-off.

Solution

Given that preference dividends are not in arrears, retained profits here are all attributable to the ordinary shares. Thus, the investment is cancelled against 80% of the ordinary share capital, share premium and retained earnings at acquisition, and against 60% of the preference share capital. Note Sonny is a subsidiary of Daddy since Daddy has the majority of voting rights (see Chapter 2):

Debenture component – the debenture in the parent company balance sheet is an inter-company balance to be cancelled on consolidation. The debentures owned by outsiders are liabilities in the consolidated balance sheet and *not* a part of minority interests. The parent's portion of interest paid by the subsidiary would be cancelled against interest received by the parent, and the remainder, to outsiders, included as a part of consolidated interest payable and not minority interests. The effects of these entries are shown in Figure 10.12.

In this example it has been assumed for simplicity that the market value of debentures was equal

Description	Invest-ment	Share capital	Share premium	Good-will	Consol retained profits	Minority interests	Deben tures
Daddy balances	190	(80)	(150)		(190)		30
Sonny balances:							
Pre-acquisition ordinary (80/20)				(144)		(36)	
Pre-acquisition preference (60/40)				(15)		(10)	
Post-acquisition (80/20)					(12)	(3)	
Debentures							(60)
Cancellation	(190)			190			
Consolidated	-	(80)	(150)	31	(202)	(49)	(30)

Figure 10.12 – Cancellation with different equity and debt classes

to their face value at acquisition. Fair value adjustments should ensure that the liability is restated to fair value at acquisition (see Chapter 5), i.e. the present value at the market rate of interest at the *date of acquisition* for a similar loan with the same contracted interest payments and repayment of principal. Consolidated interest charges would then include the contracted interest payments plus an annual adjustment to charge part of the 'revaluation excess' over the life of the loan so that the effective overall rate is constant over its life.

Share component – if the preference dividends were in arrears, part of pre-acquisition retained earnings would relate to the preference shares and be split 60/40, the balance being split 80/20. See also Shaw (1973, Chapter 6) for further discussion of the complexities arising from more complex financial instruments (e.g. convertible debentures or participating preference shares). In the consolidated profit and loss account, preference dividends are dealt with in a similar manner to ordinary dividends. Similar considerations apply as in individual companies in deciding whether instruments are liabilities, equity and non-equity shares and in accounting for them under FRS 4, *Capital Instruments*. Probably the preference shares would be classified as non-equity minority interests in the notes to the accounts, though we are not given much detail as to their rights.

Exercise

10.12 Consider the following balance sheets of Geared plc and Cog plc at 31 December 1995:

	Geared £m	Cog £m
Miscellaneous net assets	1,140	530
Investment in Cog	210	
8% debentures in Cog	50	(100)
Ordinary share capital (£1)	(200)	(75)
Preference share capital (£1)	(100)	(40)
Share premium	(150)	(90)
Retained profits	(950)	(225)

On 28 February 1992, Geared acquired 70% of the voting ordinary share capital of Cog and 90% of its preference share capital, for £210m, and in addition, 50% of its debentures for £50m, when the Cog's retained earnings were £55m. The equity shares carry voting rights at general meetings of

the companies, and the preference shares only if dividends are in arrears, which is not currently the case.

Required

Prepare a consolidated cancellation table at 31 December 1995 showing goodwill, consolidated retained earnings, debentures and minority interests. Ignore goodwill write-off.

SUMMARY

*Technical problems arise where group shareholdings arise from a series of transactions (**piecemeal** acquisitions and disposals), whether the date of acquisition should be taken as a single date or a series of dates. UK pronouncements stipulate the former, but allow the second to be used in certain cases (e.g. where the subsidiary was formerly an associate). Care must be taken when a share transaction causes the holding to change treatment from trade investment to associate or say associate to subsidiary, or disposals cause the reverse to happen.*

*More complex group structures arise where subsidiaries hold shares in sub-subsidiaries (**vertical** groups), where in addition the parent holds shares in sub-subsidiaries (**mixed** groups), or where subsidiaries hold bilateral holdings in each other (**cross**-holdings). Controversy arises over whether consolidated accounts for the ultimate group should include all goodwill arising within the group, or just that attributable to ultimate parent shareholders. Acquisition of different classes of equity is also discussed.*

FURTHER READING

FRS 2 (1992) *Accounting for Subsidiary Undertakings*, Accounting Standards Board.

Brault, R. (1979) 'A simple approach to complex consolidations', *CA Magazine*, April pp. 52–54.

Topple, B. (1979) 'Goodwill on consolidation', *Accountancy*, February pp. 114–120.

11

FOREIGN CURRENCY TRANSLATION

This chapter focuses on the translation and consolidation of foreign currency financial statements. The translation of foreign currency transactions is dealt with as necessary to develop the concepts used in statement translation. The topic has assumed great economic importance with the vigorous expansion of multinationals and the decision of the major trading nations since 1971 to let their exchange rates 'float' freely. Both the number of companies affected and the size and variability of reported exchange gains and losses have mushroomed. It has generated vigorous debate – the conditions under one of the two contending approaches shows a gain, usually leads to the other showing a loss. It exposes contradictory assumptions underlying consolidation and the historical cost basis, and has been the subject of numerous empirical studies.

BASIC CONCEPTS

Foreign currency exposure

Economic and accounting exposure are distinguished. *Conversion* of foreign currency balances means physically changing one currency into another. *Translation* means restating a balance in one currency into another, with no actual currency swap taking place.

Economic exposure

In economics, assets are usually valued in terms of the net present value of *future* cash flows. If these are denominated in a foreign currency, their sterling amount will be affected by exchange movements. They are exposed to changes in current and future exchange rates, unless there are compensating changes in interest rates or risk. Such exposure is termed economic exposure.

Accounting exposure

This is concerned with exchange gains or losses arising from translation of balances or flows resulting from past transactions, or from the translation of foreign currency financial statements. Whether or not an item is exposed in an accounting sense is a matter of definition. Accounting exposure may or may not be correlated with economic exposure, since they measure different things. For each balance sheet item, there are two accepted translation alternatives, the *current* rate, the rate at the financial statements date, or the *historical* rate, the rate at the original transaction date. Items are subject to accounting exposure if they are translated at the current rate, but not if translated at the historical rate.

Example 11.1 – Accounting exposure

	Exchange rate (TM per £)
1 January 1995	4.1
31 December 1995	3.7

Suppose 100 Teutonic marks (TM) worth of stock are purchased on 1 January 1995 and held throughout the year.

Required
Calculate the transaction gain or loss on exposure in the financial statements at 31 December 1995 if the stock were translated (a) at current rate of exchange at 31 December 1995, and (b) at the historical rate.

Solution

Date	Current rate	Historical rate
1 Jan	100/4.1 = £24.39	100/4.1 = £24.39
31 Dec	100/3.7 = £27.03	100/4.1 = £24.39
Exchange gain/(loss)	£ 2.64	Nil

Under the historical rate, the rate remains unchanged at 4.1 at the year end and so there is no change in the translated balance. However, the *current* rate changes over the year as does the current rate translated balance, so there is a 'gain' of £2.64 because the Teutonic mark has *strengthened* against the pound.

Accounting exposure arises from past transactions. Figure 11.1 shows how such exposure results in accounting gains and losses when *individual* assets and liabilities are translated at the *current* rate.

	Type of balance	
	Asset	*Liability*
	(+)	(-)
Overseas *currency* :		
Strengthening (+)	+	–
Weakening (–)	–	+

Key
+ = Exchange gain – = Exchange loss

Figure 11.1 – Accounting exposure of individual assets and liabilities to exchange rate fluctuations

When the *overseas* currency weakens (i.e. more marks to the pound at the year end than at the beginning) liabilities translated at current rate will show an exchange gain. The amount to be repaid at the year end in sterling will be less than at the beginning, so the debtor (i.e. liability) firm will show a gain. This can be deduced by the algebra of signs: a liability (–) when the *overseas* currency weakens (–) gives – × – = +, hence an exchange gain (+). These basic principles apply to all statement translation approaches. Always reason in terms of the *overseas* currency.

Foreign currency transactions
In accounting for foreign currency transactions, assets and liabilities are first recorded by translating the foreign currency amount at the exchange rate ruling at the *transaction* date. Two main approaches are suggested for accounting for exchange rate changes between this date and the *settlement* date – *the one transaction approach*, which adjusts the cost of the asset to reflect the settlement date exchange rate, i.e. the cash actually paid, or *the two transaction approach*, which leaves the asset recorded at the transaction date amount, and

the difference on settlement is shown in the profit and loss account as an exchange gain or loss, a financing matter.

One objection to the one transaction approach is that it includes events *subsequent* to the original transaction. It could be suggested that the true cost should be the amount *expected* to be paid at settlement, but *estimated* at the original transaction date, e.g. using the three months forward rate, not affected by subsequent events. However, this raises other conceptual problems, e.g. whether discounting should be used, and both UK and US accounting standards require the more straightforward two transaction approach for transactions described above, the basis of the temporal approach for financial statements discussed later.

For transactions *not yet settled*, the rate at the current financial statements date is used as the best estimate of the settlement rate. A further adjustment is then made at settlement. This chapter does not consider the treatment of foreign currency hedging transactions in general, which are an individual company accounting matter, except in so far as net investments in subsidiaries are 'hedged' in the consolidated financial statements.

Example 11.2 – Translating foreign currency transactions

A fixed asset is purchased on credit by a UK company for 2,000 Teutonic marks when the exchange rate is 4.1 marks to the £. Three months later, the creditor is paid when the exchange rate is 3.9 marks to the £.

Required
(a) Show how to account for the transaction using the 'one transaction' and 'two transaction' approaches.
(b) Assume that the reporting date of the company is between transaction and settlement date. Show how the asset would be accounted for under the two transaction approach, given that the exchange rate at the reporting date is 4 marks to the £.

Solution
(a) *At the date of purchase* – the journal entry would be :

	DR.	CR.
Fixed asset	£488	
Creditors		£488

Subsequent to the date of purchase – relevant calculations are:

£ cost of fixed asset at date of purchase	=	2,000/4.1 =	488
£ payment for asset three months later	=	2,000/3.9 =	513
Exchange difference			25

The settlement of the balance would be:

	DR.	CR.
Creditors	£513	
Cash		£513

but the approaches differ on how to deal with the £25 difference on creditors between the transaction and settlement dates.

One transaction approach

	DR.	CR.
Fixed asset	£25	
Creditors		£25

Two transaction approach

	DR.	CR.
Profit and loss – exchange loss	**£25**	
Creditors		**£25**

The first shows the fixed asset cost as £513; the second as £488 and separately an exchange loss of £25.

(b) *Transactions not yet settled* – the *estimated* payment would be 2,000/4.0 = £500. The two transaction approach would result in the following :

	DR.	CR.
Profit and loss – exchange loss	**£12**	
Creditors		**£12**

The remaining £13 (i.e. £513 – £500) would be adjusted next period if 3.9 were the rate at settlement.

Exercises

11.1 How would the following be disclosed under (a) the one transaction approach, and (b) the two transaction approach? A fixed asset was purchased on 1 January 1994 for 5,000 Teutonic marks, the account being settled on 28 February. The exchange rate at 1 January was 2.3 marks to the pound and at 28 February, 2.0 marks to the pound. The asset has a ten year life with no scrap value and is to be depreciated using the straight–line method.

11.2 In what ways is the information reported by the two transaction approach more useful than the one transaction approach?

11.3 Compare and contrast accounting exposure and economic exposure.

FOREIGN CURRENCY FINANCIAL STATEMENTS – PRINCIPLES

In consolidated financial statements, foreign exchange gains and losses arise both from the translation of transactions of the parent and subsidiaries, and from translating the foreign currency statements of overseas subsidiaries. The translation of statements can be viewed as a three-stage process as shown in Figure 11.2.

Stage 1	**Completion** of *local* currency financial statements of each group company. Foreign currency **transactions** of each company are translated using the two transaction approach.
Stage 2	**Translation** of each foreign subsidiary's local currency financial **statements** into the reporting currency of the parent.
Stage 3	**Consolidation** of the group financial statements, all of which are now expressed in sterling.

Figure 11.2 – Three stages for consolidating foreign subsidiaries

Balance sheets

Many translation controversies arise because of the use of historical cost accounting. Since it is the main focus of external financial reporting in the UK for the foreseeable future, the approaches are studied in this context. Under current cost accounting the two main translation approaches described later give the same solution, and many of the problems disappear. Under historical cost, the statement translation approaches can be viewed as different *definitions* of which assets and liabilities should be translated at the current rate, and which at the historical rate. These are shown in Figure 11.3. 'C' means the individual balance described is translated at the current rate, and 'H' at the historical rate. The amount below the double lines in the Figure shows which balances in *aggregate* are exposed in an accounting sense (i.e. translated at the current rate). For example under the closing rate approach this is net assets (= total assets – total liabilities).

Balance sheet heading	Closing rate	Temporal	Current Non-current	Monetary Non-monetary
Cash, debtors and creditors	C	C	C	C
Stocks & short term investments:				
- at cost	C	H	C	H
- at NRV	C	C	C	H
Fixed assets	C	H	H	H
Long-term debt	C	C	H	C
Net aggregate balance exposed	**Total assets - total liabilities** **Asset-total (+)**	**Current *dated* assets - current *dated* liabilities** **Liability-total (-)**	Current assets - current liabilities Asset-total (+)	Monetary assets - monetary liabilities Liability-total (-)
Overseas currency:				
Stronger (+)	+	-	+	-
Weaker (-)	-	+	-	+

KEY: + = exchange gain   - = exchange loss

Figure 11.3 – Exchange rates for translating balance sheets/Accounting exposure under each approach

Long-term debt is a monetary, non-current asset, stated under historical cost at the amount to be repaid (i.e. it is 'current-dated'). The current/non-current approach (C-NC) translates it at the historical rate, monetary/non-monetary (M-NM) and temporal approach at the current rate, and the closing rate approach (CR) at the current rate. Stocks at cost are current non-monetary assets, stated at historical acquisition cost. However, stocks at NRV are stated at current market price and under the temporal approach are deemed 'current dated' and thus translated at the current rate, even though non-monetary. The 'shaded' approaches, the temporal and closing rate are the most important in practice.

The bottom part of Figure 11.3 is the direct analogue of Figure 11.1, showing how gains and losses are determined, but now *net aggregate* balances are exposed, not individual ones. In most firms, current assets exceed current liabilities and total assets exceed total liabilities, so the net *aggregate* exposed under the closing rate and current/non-current approaches tend to be asset balances. The converse applies under the temporal and monetary/non-monetary approaches. The inclusion of long-term loans in the exposed aggregate, means that such loans usually exceed short-term net monetary assets and other net current dated assets, resulting in a net *liability* aggregate balance.

The net aggregate exposed under the temporal approach (current dated assets minus current dated liabilities) is termed here 'net current dated liabilities' (NCDL). The term 'current-dated' refers to the 'datedness' of balances and is not the same as 'current' in 'current assets'. Consider how to apply the above information: if the net *aggregate* exposed is an asset (+) balance and the *overseas* currency is strengthening (+), the end-of-year translated sterling amount will be greater than at the start and an exchange gain (+) from accounting exposure will result. For a net liability (−) balance under the same circumstances, a loss (−) will be shown. Again, gains and losses can be deduced by the algebra of signs.

Exercises

11.4 The exchange rates for the mark and the franc against the pound at the beginning and end of the first three months of 1999 were as follows:

Date	Marks	Francs
1 January 1999	2.5	1.8
31 December 1999	2.7	1.7

Evaluate which of the four translation approaches discussed above will show a gain and which a loss if (a) the balance sheets are denominated in marks, and (b) if they are denominated in francs. Give an intuitive explanation why.

11.5 The gobbledegook/non-gobbledegook (G-NG) approach translates fixed assets and current liabilities at the current rate and all other asset and liabilities at the historical rate. Would you expect it to show a gain or loss if the overseas currency weakened?

11.6 A non-depreciable fixed asset was purchased by a foreign branch on 31 January 1991 for 70m krope. On 31 January 1993 it was written down by the branch to a recoverable amount of 60m krope. Exchange rates (krope to the £) were:

31 December 1991	7.0
31 December 1993	5.0
31 December 1995	4.0

Calculate the translated amount for the fixed asset at 31 December 1995 under (a) the temporal and (b) the closing rate approach.

The historical context

According to Nobes (1980), the closing rate was the first method to be widely adopted. Earlier in the century, exchange rates were fixed between major trading nations, and the dollar and pound tended to strengthen against the currencies of less developed countries. Thus the conservative closing rate approach was in keeping with the spirit of the period. Between the world wars, exchange rates tended to fluctuate gently around 'norms'. It was argued that non-current items should be translated at the historical rate as exchange rate changes were likely to reverse and average out over the life of the long-term asset or liability. Such reversals did not necessarily take place in the short term. Hence the current/non-current method became more common.

However, this approach was overtaken both by economic events and by conceptual shortcomings. Many countries decided to allow exchange rates to track more closely underlying economic changes, which meant that long-term reversals were less probable. Objections too, were raised to the somewhat arbitrary and ill-defined nature of the term 'working capital'. The literature gradually started to explore the monetary/non-monetary approach. At the same time a similar classification of monetary/non-monetary items was made in general price level accounting (CPP), vigorously debated at the same time in the 1950s.

The basic difference between the C-NC approach and the M-NM approach is in the treatment of stocks (a current but non-monetary asset) and long-term liabilities (non-current but monetary). The C-NC and closing rate approaches show a net asset aggregate as 'exposed', whereas the M-NM approach shows a net liability aggregate. Often then, the M-NM approach showed a gain when the C-NC and closing rate showed a loss, and vice versa if the exchange rate reversed. For the first time it was possible to show more 'favourable' results by choosing the 'right' translation approach. As the dollar weakened in the 1970s, US proponents of the M-NM approach were forced to seek justification of their method. The definition of a 'monetary' asset was as ambiguous as for a 'current' asset. For example, how were short-term marketable investments or stocks at NRV to be classified? The temporal approach can be seen as an attempt to provide theoretical respectability for a variant of the monetary/non-monetary approach.

The closing rate has been an ongoing contender for acceptance, mainly because of its simplicity. Whilst the US adopted the temporal approach in the 1970s followed by Canada, UK practice stuck to the closing rate. However, this approach did not have a respectable theoretical framework until the end of the 1970s. Then it swept aside the temporal approach, relegating its use to limited circumstances. Demirag (1987, pp. 84–5) provides a useful chronology of the development internationally of political pronouncements in the area.

The temporal approach

First discussed by Lorensen (1972) in an AICPA research study, it proposes an ingenious solution to the translation problem, providing a convincing theoretical rationale which can be extended to valuation bases other than historical cost. Assets and liabilities are translated according to their *datedness*. Balances at historical acquisition prices are translated at historical rates (e.g. fixed assets). Balances at 'current' prices (e.g. debtors and creditors) are translated at current rates. Under current cost accounting, all balances are 'current' dated and thus would be translated at the current rate.

Transactions of foreign subsidiaries are treated *as if* they were direct transactions of the parent, using the familiar two transaction approach described earlier. The parent's currency is taken as the unit of measurement (hence SFAS 52 in the USA terms it 'remeasurement'). When a foreign subsidiary purchases a fixed asset in its local currency, financed by a local currency loan, then *if* it were a direct transaction of the parent, the fixed asset would be recorded at the *historical* rate and not subsequently adjusted; the loan (an unsettled currency amount) would be translated at the current rate in any financial statements until settlement. Any gain or loss on translation would be taken to *profit and loss*. The temporal approach treatment for translating financial statements is consistent with this.

The temporal approach thus adds the extra assumption, '*as if* transactions of the parent' to the previously discussed two transaction approach. Key ideas are single *functional currency* (the parent's) and the group as a *single unified entity* for transaction purposes, with subsidiaries a *direct extension* of the parent (see Revsine, 1984).

The closing rate approach

This approach has had many different justifications. Under the *net investment* rationale, the group is viewed as a series of net investments in *autonomous* subsidiaries transacting in *local* currencies, not a unified entity transacting in the parent's currency. The US standard SFAS 52 characterizes such a group as having *multiple functional currencies*. The temporal approach assumes a single functional currency, the parent's. From this perspective, to treat each subsidiary's transactions as if transactions of the parent is misleading. The *net investment*, the net aggregate of assets and liabilities, is deemed to be exposed. Since assets and liabilities are purchased, financed and used in the same environment, gains and losses on each will tend to offset (hedge) each other, and so all of a subsidiary's assets and liabilities should be translated at the current rate. Supporters argue that it is nonsense to show gains or losses arising on say liabilities, whilst not showing similar effects on corresponding fixed assets; that gains and losses under the closing rate approach correlate better with economic exposure than the temporal approach. Also, since all balances are translated at the same rate, subsidiaries' local currency financial statement relationships are better preserved in the consolidated statements.

FOREIGN CURRENCY STATEMENTS –TECHNIQUE

This section gives a detailed example illustrating the three steps of the translation process discussed in Figure 11.2.

Example 11.3 – Translation of financial statements

Aufwiedersehen AG is the 75% owned subsidiary of Goodbuy plc, acquired on 31 August 1994 for £70,000m when its retained profits were TM 225,000m. Recent financial statements in millions of pounds (Goodbuy) and Teutonic marks (Aufwiedersehen) are:

Balance sheets at 31 December

	Goodbuy (£'m)		Aufwiedersehen (TM'm)	
	1995	1994	1995	1994
Fixed assets	371,000	300,000	600,000	500,000
Loan to subsidiary	20,000	—	—	—
Stocks	170,000	150,000	250,000	200,000
Debtors	150,000	140,000	125,000	100,000
Cash	81,000	60,000	200,000	100,000
	792,000	650,000	1,175,000	900,000
Long-term loans	120,000	80,000	300,000	300,000
Loan from parent	—	—	75,000	—
Creditors	140,000	119,000	350,000	250,000
Interest payable	7,000	6,000	—	—
Dividends payable	6,000	5,000	—	—
Share capital	105,000	105,000	75,000	75,000
Share premium	115,000	115,000	25,000	25,000
Retained profits	299,000	220,000	350,000	250,000
	792,000	650,000	1,175,000	900,000

Profit and loss account – year ended 31 December 1995

	Goodbuy £'m	Aufwiedersehen TM'm
Sales	525,000	1,000,000
COGS	(300,000)	(700,000)
Depreciation	(15,000)	(100,000)
Loss on fixed asset	(6,000)	—
Other expenses	(112,000)	(80,000)
Operating profit	92,000	120,000
Interest expense	(7,000)	(20,000)
Net profit	85,000	100,000
Dividends payable	(6,000)	—
Retained profit	79,000	100,000

Further information about Aufwiedersehen
1. All sales were on credit.
2. Fixed assets are at historical cost less depreciation. Aufwiedersehen's opening fixed assets were purchased when the subsidiary was acquired in 1984, and it purchased fixed assets totalling 200,000 million marks on 31 August 1995. No depreciation is provided in year of purchase.
3. An interest-free loan of 75,000 million marks was raised during the year from the parent, when the exchange rate was 3.75. The existing long-term loan was raised in Marks in 1984, repayable at par in 2004. It also carries no interest, being an investment incentive from the local government. Aufwiedersehen AG has made no share issues since acquisition.
4. Stocks are valued on a FIFO basis, representing at 31 December 1994 and 1995 about 4 months' purchases. All purchases are on credit. All other expenses were for cash.
5. Any goodwill on consolidation is to be amortized straight-line over a five year period,

6. Exchange rates – Marks to the £

1 January 1984	4.6	Average rate for 1995	4.0
31 August 1994	4.3	31 August 1995	3.9
31 October 1994	4.2	31 October 1995	3.8
31 December 1994	4.1	31 December 1995	3.7

Required

(a) Translate opening and closing balance sheets and the profit and loss account into £ sterling under both the temporal and closing rate approaches. Compute the gain or loss on exposure. Assume the average rate is used to translate Aufwiedersehen's profit and loss account under the closing rate approach.

(b) Calculate consolidated retained profits, minority interests and goodwill at 31 December 1995 under the closing rate approach assuming the historical rate is used to translate goodwill.

(c) Prepare a consolidated profit and loss account for the year ended 31 December 1995 for the Goodbuy Group under the closing rate approach.

Solution

Stage 1 – Foreign currency transactions
The loan from Goodbuy to Aufwiedersehen AG of TM 75,000m must be translated at the year end exchange rate under the two transaction approach. The year end amount translated at a rate of 3.7 is 75,000/3.7 = 20,270, giving a *transaction* exchange gain of £270m (= 75,000 [$\frac{1}{3.7} - \frac{1}{3.75}$]).

i.e. a change from when the rate was 3.75. The loan is restated to £20,270m, and in the closing balance sheet, Goodbuy's retained profits to £299,270.

Stage 2 – Foreign currency financial statements

Opening balance sheet

Description	Closing rate		Temporal	
	Rate	£m balance	Rate	£m balance
Fixed assets	4.1	121,952	4.6	108,696
Stocks	4.1	48,780	4.2	47,619
Debtors	4.1	24,390	4.1	24,390
Cash	4.1	24,390	4.1	24,390
Long-term liabilities	4.1	(73,171)	4.1	(73,171)
Creditors	4.1	(60,975)	4.1	(60,975)
Share capital & reserves	*diff*	(85,366)	*diff*	(70,949)

Closing balance sheet

Description	Closing rate		Temporal	
	Rate	£ balance	Rate	£ balance
Fixed assets	3.7	162,162	400 @ 4.6 200 @ 3.9	138,239
Stocks	3.7	67,568	3.8	65,789
Debtors	3.7	33,784	3.7	33,784
Cash	3.7	54,054	3.7	54,054
Loan from parent	3.7	(20,270)	3.7	(20,270)
Long-term liabilities	3.7	(81,081)	3.7	(81,081)
Creditors	3.7	(94,595)	3.7	(94,595)
Share capital & reserves	*diff*	(121,622)	*diff*	(95,920)

Under the closing rate approach, all *opening* balance sheet balances are translated at 4.1, the then *current* rate at 31 December 1994, and closing balance sheet ones at 3.7, the *current* rate one year later. Under the temporal approach, all *current dated* items are translated at 4.1 opening, and 3.7 closing (the current rate) whereas stocks and fixed assets are translated at their acquisition rates. Here stocks represent four months purchases, so their *average* purchase date could be taken either as two months prior to the balance sheet date or the average of rates over the four month period. In this example both give the same result. Share capital and reserves is a residual figure by *differencing*.

Under the temporal approach, opening fixed assets of TM 500,000m were translated at 4.6, the historical rate. In the closing balance sheet, TM 200,000m of fixed assets were purchased when the rate was 3.9 and the *net book amount* of the opening fixed assets remaining (TM 500,000m less TM 100,000m depreciation) is translated at the original acquisition rate of 4.6. This illustrates the greater record-keeping complexity and compliance costs necessitated by the temporal approach in keeping track of original datedness of historical dated assets bought and sold.

Translation approach	Rate (s)
Closing rate	All items at closing rate, i.e. current rate at the end of the period, 3.7 **OR** All items at average rate for period, 4.0
Temporal	Most items at transaction rate giving rise to them, approximated by average rate. Historical rates to be used where expenses and revenues relate to assets & liabilities translated themselves at historical rates

Figure 11.4 – Profit and loss translation rates under SSAP 20

Profit and loss

Current UK practice, based on SSAP 20, is shown in Figure 11.4.

Closing rate approach – SSAP 20 allows either the average rate or the year end rate, reflecting conflicting rationales for this approach discussed later. However, both SFAS 52 in the USA, and the revised IAS 21, *The Effects of Changes in Exchange Rates*, require the use of exchange rates at actual transaction dates. They allow the use of averages as an approximation. Neither allow the period end rate. *Company Reporting* reports UK survey results showing a dramatic movement towards the use of the average rate in translating profit and loss accounts under the closing rate approach from 25% in 1984–5 to 57% in 1990–1 (June 1991, p. 3).

Temporal approach – this requires *historical* rates for cost of sales and depreciation, consistent with their balance sheet asset counterparts, and *transaction* date rates for the rest, taken here as the average rate for the period, 4.0. The historical rate for cost of goods sold is approximated by using historical rates for opening (4.2) and closing (3.8) stocks and the average rate (4.0) for purchases.

Profit and loss translation

Description	Closing rate Rate	Closing rate £ balance	Temporal Rate	Temporal £ balance
Sales	4.0	250,000	4.0	250,000
Cost of sales:				
Opening stock			200 @ 4.2	
Purchases	4.0	(175,000)	750 @ 4.0	(169,330)
Closing stock			(250)@ 3.8	
Depreciation	4.0	(25,000)	4.6	(21,739)
Other expenses	4.0	(20,000)	4.0	(20,000)
Interest	4.0	(5,000)	4.0	(5,000)
Translated P&L amounts		25,000		33,931
Difference	*Gain*	*11,256*	**Loss**	*(8,960)*
Translated change in equity	per balance sheet (below)	36,256	per balance sheet (below)	24,971

Change in equity per balance sheet

Closing rate	=	121,622 − 85,366 = 36,256
Temporal	=	95,920 − 70,949 = 24,971

For an individual entity, retained profits for the year equals its change in equity if there are no share issues, etc. However, for foreign currency financial statements translated into sterling this relationship no longer holds. Translated revenues and expenses under the closing rate method above add to £25,000. However, the change in equity from the translated balance sheets is

   £121,622 − £85,366   =   £36,256,

the difference being the *gain on exposure*. A *loss* results from the temporal approach. This illustrates the tendency of one method to show a gain when the other shows a loss. The treatment of gains and losses under each approach is examined later. The 'sign' of the gains (+) and losses (−) can be intuited from Figure 11.3 since the *overseas* currency is *strengthening*.

Exercises

11.7   Pizza Cayka is an 80% owned Latin subsidiary of Gobbledegook plc, a fast-food chain, acquired at 31 December 1993, when its retained earnings were 3,000 maracas. Draft financial statements are shown below:

Balance sheets at 31 December

	Gobbledegook (£)		Pizza Cayka (maracas)	
	1995	1994	1995	1994
Fixed assets (net)	120,000	100,000	10,000	8,000
Investment in Pizza Cayka	3,000	3,000	—	—
Loan to Pizza Cayka	475	—	—	—
Stocks (cost)	36,000	31,000	4,800	3,800
Debtors	25,000	20,000	3,000	1,800
Cash	5,000	10,000	1,000	600
	189,475	164,000	18,800	14,200
Creditors	14,000	13,000	3,000	2,400
Interest payable	6,000	4,000	—	—
Dividends payable	5,000	3,000	—	—
Long-term loan	65,000	50,000	2,100	2,100
Loan from Gobbledegook	—	—	1,900	—
Share capital	30,000	30,000	2,000	2,000
Other reserves	20,000	20,000	3,000	3,000
Retained profits	49,475	44,000	6,800	4,700
	189,475	164,000	18,800	14,200

Profit and loss accounts – year ended 31 December 1995

	Gobbledegook £	£	Pizza Cayka maracas	maracas
Sales		160,000		112,000
Opening stock	31,000		3,800	
Purchases	105,000		108,000	
Closing stock	(36,000)		(4,800)	
Cost of sales		(100,000)		(107,000)
Gross profit		60,000		5,000
Depreciation	10,000		1,000	
Loss on fixed asset sale	5,000		-	
Other expenses	29,000		1,900	
		(44,000)		(2,900)
Operating profit		16,000		2,100
Interest payable		(6,000)		—
Profit for the financial year		10,000		2,100
Dividends		(5,000)		
Retained profit		5,000		2,100

Further information about Pizza Cayka:
1. There were no fixed asset disposals during the year. Depreciation is calculated on opening fixed assets.
2. Goodwill at acquisition is to be amortized straight-line over a five year period.
3. An interest-free maracas-denominated loan of 1,900 maracas was made by Gobbledegook to Pizza Cayka during the year when the exchange rate was 4.0 maracas to the £ sterling.
4. *Exchange rates to the £:*

Opening fixed assets and subsidiary acquisition	5.0 maracas
Opening stock	4.9 maracas
31 December 1994	4.8 maracas
Closing stock and average rate for 1995	4.7 maracas
31 December 1995	4.6 maracas

Required
(a) Translate the opening and closing balance sheets and the profit and loss account into £ sterling under both the temporal and closing rate approach. Compute the gain or loss on exposure. Assume the average rate is used to translate Pizza Cayka's profit and loss account under the closing rate approach.
(b) Using concepts already discussed, explain why a gain or loss has arisen under each approach.

11.8 Consider the following financial statements of Sniff plc, and its 70% owned Roman subsidiary Aroma Spa, acquired on 1 January 1990 when the retained profits of Aroma Spa were 80m denarii:

Balance sheets at 31 December (Denarii'm)

	Sniff (£m)		Aroma (denarii'm)	
	1995	1994	1995	1994
Fixed assets (net)	3,500	3,000	610	600
Investment in Aroma	165	165		
Loan to Aroma	36	—	—	—
Stocks (cost)	800	900	400	200
Debtors	700	750	400	150
Cash	450	200	50	70
	5,651	5,015	1,460	1,020
Creditors within one year	400	420	320	120
Interest payable	60	55	—	—
Dividends payable	40	40	—	—
Long-term loan	1,000	950	400	400
Loan from Sniff	—	—	90	—
Share capital	750	700	100	100
Share premium	1,250	1,200	120	120
Retained profits	2,151	1,650	430	280
	5,651	5,015	1,460	1,020

Profit and loss accounts – year ended 31 December 1995

	Sniff £m	£m	Aroma den'm	den'm
Sales		10,233		2,000
Cost of sales		8,700		1,100
Gross profit		1,533		900
Depreciation	200		130	
Gain on fixed asset sale	(8)		—	
Other expenses	700		600	
		(892)		(730)
Operating profit		641		170
Interest payable		(80)		(20)
Profit for the financial year		561		150
Dividends		(60)		—
Retained profit		501		150

Notes on Aroma Spa

(a) *Movement on fixed assets:*   **Dn'm**

Opening net book amount	600
Purchases (all on 30 April)	140
Depreciation	(130)
Closing net book amount	610

(b) Transactions are assumed to have taken place at an even rate throughout the year, except that 'other expenses' were incurred at 500 million denarii in the six months to 30 June and 100 million denarii in the last six months of the year, and fixed asset purchases are as in note (a) above.

(c) Depreciation is calculated on the opening fixed assets for the year. Goodwill is amortized over 10 years straight-line.

(d) On 31 March Sniff plc made an interest free denarii denominated loan to Aroma plc which is still outstanding at the year end. No exchange adjustments have yet been made on this loan. Aroma's other loans are from third parties.

(e) Exchange rates were as follows:

Date of transaction	Rate	Date of transaction	Rate
Opening fixed assets (1/1/90)	2.0	30 June 1995	2.6
Opening stock (1/10/94)	2.3	30 September 1995	2.7
31 December 1994	2.4	Closing stock (1/10/95)	2.8
31 March 1995	2.5	31 December 1995	3.0
30 April 1995	2.7		

Required

(a) Translate the opening and closing balance sheets and profit and loss account of Aroma SpA into £ sterling under both closing rate and temporal approach and calculate the gain or loss on translation. Assume the average rate is used to translate the profit and loss account.

(b) Explain why the 'sign' of the translation difference is a gain or loss.

11.9 How do the rationales for the temporal and closing rate approaches differ in how they conceptualize the group structure? Explain how their differing translation proposals are deduced from these different conceptions.

Stage 3– Consolidating the translated statements

As outlined in Figure 11.2, consolidation of the *translated* statements is Stage 3 of the process. Stages 1 and 2 being translation of *transactions* by the parent and individual subsidiaries within their own financial statements, and translation of the *statements* themselves into the reporting currency. A key issue here is how to analyse the translated equity of the subsidiary between pre-acquisition, post-acquisition and minority interests. Aufwiedersehen's analysed equity in Teutonic marks is

Description	Majority (75%)	Minority (25%)	Total
Share capital & premium	75,000	25,000	100,000
Reserves to acquisition	168,750	56,250	225,000
Pre-acquisition equity	243,750	81,250	325,000
Post-acq retained profits	93,750	31,250	125,000
Total current equity	337,500	112,500	450,000

Closing rate approach

The total translated *current* equity taken from the closing balance sheet, translated at current rate, i.e. TM 450,000m/3.7 = £121,622, must now be analysed in sterling between pre-acquisition equity, post-acquisition equity and minority interests. This necessitates deciding how the acquisition cost of goodwill is to be translated in financial statements subsequent to acquisition. This affects the capitalization and gradual amortization approach, but also arises under immediate write-off, in providing the SSAP 22's note disclosure of cumulative goodwill written off (Chapter 5).

Two alternatives are usually suggested, but SSAP 20 does not specify which is to be used:

(a) *historical rate goodwill cost:* pre-acquisition equity is to be translated in all subsequent financial statements at the exchange rate ruling at the *date of acquisition*, cancelled against the sterling cost of the investment – the cost of goodwill is *frozen* for future periods; or

(b) *current rate goodwill cost:* goodwill itself is retranslated at the closing rate each period – i.e. pre-acquisition equity is retranslated at the *current closing rate each year* (here 3.7), and the sterling investment is itself treated *as if* a foreign currency balance and also updated each period. Exchange differences on changes in goodwill cost and any amortization, are taken direct to reserves. This is the US position in SFAS 52 (para. 101).

Davies, Paterson and Wilson suggest (1992, p. 381), based on a painstaking analysis of the wording of SSAP 20 and its press release, that SSAP 20 might require historical rate goodwill cost. However, they prefer the current rate alternative since (p. 382) 'the value of the foreign company as a whole is likely to be based on the expected future earnings stream expressed in the foreign currency and the goodwill relates to a business which operates in the economic environment of that currency'. A case might be made for the translation of pre-acquisition equity at the current rate, but treating the sterling investment *as if* it were a foreign currency balance is questionable conceptually. See Taylor (1995, section V.4.5.1) for further discussion.

Chopping and Skerratt (1993) argue for historical rate goodwill cost so that goodwill 'reflects the value of the business over that of its separable assets as assessed at a *particular moment in time* and recorded in the reporting currency . . . [Retranslation] seems to take account of subsequent changes in a way that is inconsistent with the logic of SSAP 22' (p. 247 emphasis added). However other historical balances translated at current rates under the closing rate approach also reflect 'subsequent changes' and are also neither historical costs nor current values, so this line of argument is also not conclusive. *Historical rate goodwill cost* is used in this example, the subsidiary being acquired at 31 August 1994 when the rate was 4.3, viz.

	Rate	Majority	Minority	Total
Share capital & premium	4.3	17,442	5,814	23,256
Reserves to acquisition	4.3	39,244	13,081	52,325
Pre acquisition equity	4.3	56,686	18,895	75,581
Reserves since acq	*diff*	34,531	11,510	46,041
Total current equity	3.7	91,217	30,405	121,622

The consolidation cancellation table for the Goodbuy group is in Figure 11.5, and all other consolidated balances are simply the sum of the parent and subsidiary balances. Goodbuy's retained earnings is *after* Stage I.

The consolidated profit and loss account is shown in Figure 11.6. Note that annual goodwill amortization is £13,314/5 = £2,662, and minority interest in profit *after* tax in the consolidated profit and loss account is 25% × £25,000 = £6,250. Minority interests in the exchange gain on the net investment calculated earlier of £11,256 is calculated separately, and the net figure is taken *direct to (retained profit) reserves* under the closing rate approach. This net figure would be reported in the statement of total recognized gains and losses (see Chapter 8). The exchange gain on the *parent's* loan transaction has been dealt with in the profit and loss account as a *transaction* gain. Had it been a loss, it might have been subject to SSAP 20's 'cover' provisions discussed later.

Details	Invest-ment	Goodwill (75%)	Consol reserves	Minority interests (25%)	Intra-group loans
Goodbuy:					
Balances	70,000	-	(299,270)	-	20,270
Aufwiedersehen:					
Share capital and premium		(17,442)		(5,814)	
Pre-acq reserves		(39,244)		(13,081)	
Post-acq reserves			(34,531)	(11,510)	
Loan from Goodbuy					(20,270)
Cancellation:	(70,000)	70,000			
Subtotal	-	13,314	(333,801)	(30,405)	-
Goodwill amortisation (2/5)		(5,326)	5,326		
Consolidated balances	-	7,988	(328,475)	(30,405)	-

Figure 11.5 – Cancellation table – closing rate approach

Profit and loss account	Goodbuy	Aufwiedersehen	Minority interest	Goodwill	Consol-idated
Sales	525,000	250,000			775,000
COGS	(300,000)	(175,000)			(475,000)
Depreciation	(15,000)	(25,000)			(40,000)
Loss on fixed asset	(6,000)	-			(6,000)
Exchange gain on loan	270				270
Goodwill amortisation		-		(2,662)	(2,662)
Other expenses	(112,000)	(20,000)			(132,000)
Interest expense	(7,000)	(5,000)			(12,000)
Net profit	92,270	25,000		(2,662)	114,608
Minority interest	-	-	(6,250)		(6,250)
Profit for the financial year	85,270	25,000	(6,250)	(2,662)	101,358
Dividends payable	(6,000)	-			(6,000)
Retained profit	79,270	25,000	(6,250)	(2,662)	95,358
Retained profit reserve movements					
Exchange gain on net investments	-	11,256	(2,814)		8,442

Figure 11.6 – Profit and loss consolidation – closing rate approach

Current rate goodwill cost – If this had been used, the year's goodwill charge would have been

$$£13,314 \times \frac{4.3}{3.7} \times \frac{1}{5} \ = £3,095$$

i.e. the historical rate goodwill charge updated from a rate of 4.3 to equivalent cost at the *current* rate of 3.7. The opening net book amount would also be updated similarly and the adjustment would be part of the gain or loss on statement translation taken to reserves.

The closing net book amount for goodwill would become, from Figure 11.5

$$£7,988 \text{ (above)} \times \frac{4.3}{3.7} = £9,283.$$

Temporal approach

Pre-acquisition equity can *only* be determined by translating the subsidiary's balance sheet at acquisition, and cannot be determined as under the closing rate approach, by applying a single rate at a later date. The principles are otherwise similar to the closing rate example discussed above, except that the exchange loss on translation of Aufwiedersehen's financial statements would be reported in the *profit and loss account* and not taken direct to reserves.

Exercises

11.10 Using the information from the Exercise 11.7, the Gobbledegook Group,

    (a) Calculate consolidated retained profits, minority interests and goodwill at 31 December 1995 under the closing rate approach. Assume the historical rate is used to translate goodwill.

    (b) Prepare a consolidated profit and loss account for the year ended 31 December 1995 for the Gobbledegook Group under the closing rate approach, assuming the average rate has been used to translate profit and loss.

11.11 Using the information from the Exercise 11.8, the Sniff Group,

    (a) Calculate consolidated retained profits, minority interests and goodwill at 31 December 1995 under the closing rate approach. Assume the historical rate is used to translate goodwill.

    (b) Prepare a consolidated profit and loss account for the year ended 31 December 1995 for the Sniff Group under the closing rate approach, assuming the average rate has been used to translate profit and loss.

UNDERSTANDING THE STATEMENT GAIN OR LOSS ON TRANSLATION

This section can be omitted without loss in continuity by those only wishing to master the basic computations.

The problem with the above technical routines is that they 'mysteriously' pluck the exchange gain or loss 'out of the air' by taking the difference between the change in retained earnings in the balance sheet and the translated profit figure. A type of *cash flow matrix* is now used to provide a linking structure for the financial statement translation process discussed above, and to relate the gain or loss to the intuitive ideas of accounting exposure discussed earlier. Figure 11.7 is a cash flow matrix for Aufwiedersehen in *local* currency (Teutonic marks). The transactions for Aufwiedersehen are summarized for the year. Each column in the matrix is a 'T' account in vertical form; all debits are represented as positive and all credits as negative. The rule that debits equals credits becomes that each line of the matrix adds to zero (check that the opening balances in the top line add across to zero). The top line is the opening balance sheet and the bottom line is the closing balance sheet. Profit and loss items are entered first (sales is a credit (−ve) to the retained earnings column and a debit (+ve) to the debtors column); secondly, investing and financing transactions are gleaned from the notes to the accounts in Example 11.3. Finally, any remaining items are determined by taking the difference between the account totals so far and the closing balances. So for example in the debtors column (account) the difference between the opening balance plus credit sales, and the closing balance is receipts, and in the stock column (account) the missing figure is purchases – the double

private Description	Cash	Operating debtors	Stock	Fixed assets	Operating creditors	Loans	Share cap and prem	Retained profits
Opening balances	100,000	100,000	200,000	500,000	(250,000)	(300,000)	(100,000)	(250,000)
Reconstruct P & L:								
Sales		1,000,000						(1,000,000)
Cost of sales			(700,000)					700,000
Depreciation				(100,000)				100,000
Other expenses	(80,000)							80,000
Interest expense	(20,000)							20,000
Notes:								
Loan Issue	75,000					(75,000)		
Fixed asset purchases	(200,000)			200,000				
Differencing:								
Rec'd from customers	975,000	(975,000)						
Purchases			750,000		(750,000)			
Payments to suppliers	(650,000)				650,000			
Closing balances	200,000	125,000	250,000	600,000	(350,000)	(375,000)	(100,000)	(350,000)

Figure 11.7 – Cash flow matrix for AAufwiedersehen in Teutonic Marks (TM'm)

entry being completed to creditors *etc.*

Condensed matrix and exposed items flow statement

Temporal approach

Under the temporal approach, all 'current dated' balances are exposed. In the Aufwiedersehen example these are cash, debtors, creditors and loans. If we wish to see how *in aggregate* these (net current dated liabilities) have changed, we combine the corresponding four columns of the cash flow matrix to obtain Figure 11.8, termed a 'condensed' matrix, which has four sets of column (net current-dated liabilities, stock, fixed assets and equity) as against the eight of Figure 11.7. The last three shaded columns in Figure 11.8 correspond to the stock, fixed asset and share capital/retained profits columns in Figure 11.7. The first shaded column is obtained by adding the cash, debtors, creditors and loan columns of Figure 11.7. Each set of three columns has the first column in local currency, the third in reporting currency, and the second is the exchange rate to translate local to reporting currency. An asterisk denotes that the figure is obtained by differencing.

At the top of the left-hand column, opening net current dated liabilities (in TM'm) is calculated as

Cash 100,000 + Debtors 100,000 + Creditors (250,000) + Loans (300,000) = (350,000m) Cr.

Closing net current dated liabilities, a negative (credit) balance of (400,000m), is similarly derived from closing cash, debtors etc. *Purchases* is deduced by differencing. *Payments* to creditors does *not* appear, unlike in Figure 11.7, as the decrease in cash and the decrease in creditors cancel out when the four columns comprising NCDL are added together. The exchange rates are as used earlier. Purchases are translated at the *average* rate (4.0).

The condensed matrix integrates the four financial statements central to the translation process:

(a) Translated opening balance sheet (top line) and
(b) Translated closing balance sheet (bottom line).
(c) The translated profit and loss account and movements on retained profits showing gain or loss on translation (right-hand set of columns).
(d) *A translated exposed items flow statement* (left-hand set). Whilst not normally reported in published accounts this statement (left-hand columns) shows *why* the gain or loss on exposure arose. The reported loss (£8,960) comes only from this column, 'exposed items', showing that the *only* items exposed under the temporal approach are net current dated liabilities.

Closing rate approach

Figure 11.9 shows the *condensed* matrix for the closing rate approach. Since all items are exposed, it only has two sets of columns. The right-hand shaded column corresponds to the share capital/retained profits columns in Figure 11.7. The left-hand shaded column comprises all the other columns in Figure 11.7, added together. The *average* rate is used to translate profit and loss. The *exposed items flow statement* is in this case the mirror-image of the profit and loss account/movement on retained profit reserves.

Exercises

11.12 Prepare condensed matrices under both the temporal and closing rate approaches for the Pizza Cayka example (Exercise 11.7) showing both local currency and translated amounts, and identify the translated exposed items flow statement in each case.

11.13 Prepare condensed matrices under both the temporal and closing rate approaches for the Aroma example (Example 11.8) showing both local currency and translated amounts, and identify the translated flow statement of exposed items in each case.

11.14 (Further practice only) Prepare a condensed matrix under the current/non-current approach for the Aufwiedersehen case and identify the flow statement of exposed items. Compare the statement with the two exposed items flow statements under temporal and closing rate earlier in the chapter.

Description	Exposed items:						Non-exposed items						Residual	
	Net current dated liabilities			Stock			Fixed assets			Share cap & ret profits				
	marks'm	rate	£m	marks'm	rate	£m	marks'm	rate	£m	marks'm	rate	£m	rate	£m
Opening bals	(350,000)	4.1	(85,366)	200,000	4.2	47,619	500,000	4.6	108,696	(350,000)			*	(70,949)
Reconstruct P&L														
Sales	1,000,000	4.0	250,000							(1,000,000)			4.0	(250,000)
COGS				(700,000)	*	(169,330)				700,000			*	169,330
Depreciation							(100,000)	4.6	(21,739)	100,000			4.6	21,739
Other exp	(80,000)	4.0	(20,000)							80,000			4.0	20,000
Interest exp	(20,000)	4.0	(5,000)							20,000			4.0	5,000
From notes:														
F A purchase	(200,000)	3.9	(51,282)				200,000	3.9	51,282					
Differencing:														
Purchases	(750,000)	4.0	(187,500)	750,000	4.0	187,500								
Subtotal at translated rates	(400,000)		(99,148)	250,000		65,789	600,000		138,239	(450,000)				(104,880)
Exchange loss (difference)	-		(8,960)	-		-	-		-	-				8,960
Closing bals	(400,000)	3.7	(108,108)	250,000	3.8	65,789	600,000	*	138,239	(450,000)			*	(95,920)

Figure 11.8 – Temporal condensed matrix

Description	Exposed items: Net assets			Residual Share cap & ret profits		
	marks'm	rate	£m	marks'm	rate	£m
Opening bals	350,000	4.1	85,366	(350,000)	4.1	(85,366)
Reconstruct P&L						
Sales	1,000,000	4.0	250,000	(1,000,000)	4.0	(250,000)
COGS	(700,000)	4.0	(175,000)	700,000	4.0	175,000
Depreciation	(100,000)	4.0	(25,000)	100,000	4.0	25,000
Other exp	(80,000)	4.0	(20,000)	80,000	4.0	20,000
Interest exp	(20,000)	4.0	(5,000)	20,000	4.0	5,000
Differencing:						
-						
Subtotal at translated rates	450,000		110,366	(450,000)		(110,366)
Exchange gain (difference)	-		11,256	-		(11,256)
Closing bals	450,000	3.7	121,622	(450,000)	3.7	(121,622)

Figure 11.9 – Closing rate condensed matrix

Time pattern of exposure and statement exchange gain or loss
Under the temporal approach, the amount exposed (in TM) increases from a *credit* balance of (350,000m) to (400,000m), and under closing rate, the *debit* of 350,000m increases to 450,000m. The exposed items flow statement under each approach shows why. The temporal approach is discussed first since it gives a clearer illustration of the principles discussed.

Temporal approach – The exposed items flow statement, the left-hand column of Figure 11.8 is used to deduce the pattern of accounting exposure. Assume to simplify matters that the transactions for which the average rate is used, i.e.other than the fixed asset purchase, occur half way through the year. The initial net liability balance of (350,000m) is exposed from the start of the year until average rate) transactions affecting *net current-dated liabilities* occur half way through the year, in aggregate an inflow of 100,000m = 250,000 (sales) – 187,500 (operating purchases) – 20,000m (other) – 5,000 (interest), reducing the net current-dated liability balance exposed to (250,000m). We are told in the original example data that the fixed asset purchase, a (200,000m) outflow, occurs in August. The mid-year net *liability* balance of (£250,000m) is thus increased to (450,000m) and this residual balance is exposed for the final 4 months.

Figure 11.10 uses the above information to calculate the exchange difference in a way that links with the intuitive concept of accounting exposure. The top part for the temporal approach shows how relevant exchange rates applied to the above periods of exposure produce the exchange loss calculated earlier. It can also be cast into incremental form – the opening net liability of (350,000m) is treated as exposed for the whole year, the effects of mid-year transactions, a *reduction* of 100,000m as exposed for six months, and the incremental *increase* in net liability of (200,000m) because of purchasing the fixed asset as exposed for four months. This gives the same solution.

Temporal approach	Period of exposure	Amount		Exchange rate change				Exposure effect
Total	1 Jan 94 to 30 June 94	- 350,000	x	1/4.0	-	1/4.1	=	(2,134)
amounts	30 Jun 94 to 31 Aug 94	- 200,000	x	1/3.9	-	1/4.0	=	(1,282)
exposed	31 Aug 94 to 31 Dec 94	- 400,000	x	1/3.7	-	1/3.9	=	(5,544)
								(8,960)
Incremental	1 Jan 94 to 31 Dec 94	- 350,000	x	1/3.7	-	1/4.1	=	(9,229)
amounts	30 Jun 94 to 31 Dec 94	+ 150,000	x	1/3.7	-	1/4.0	=	3,041
exposed	31 Aug 94 to 31 Dec 94	- 200,000	x	1/3.7	-	1/3.9	=	(2,772)
								(8,960)

Closing rate approach	Period of exposure	Amount		Exchange rate change				Exposure effect
Incremental	1 Jan 94 to 31 Dec 94	+ 350,000	x	1/3.7	-	1/4.1	=	9,229
amounts	30 Jun 94 to 31 Dec 94	+ 100,000	x	1/3.7	-	1/4.0	=	2,027
exposed								11,256

Figure 11.10 – Calculating the exchange gain or loss given the exposure pattern

Closing rate approach – the exposed items flow statement in the first column of Figure 11.9 is used to deduce the pattern of exposure – a *net asset* balance of 350,000m is exposed until the operating transactions take place at the *average rate*, assumed mid-way through the year, increasing the net asset balance for the remainder of the year by 100,000m (1,000 (sales) – 700,000m (COGS) – 100,000m (depreciation) – 80,000m (other) – 20,000m (interest)) to 450,000m. In incremental terms the 350,000m is treated as exposed for the whole year, and the increment of 100,000m for six months. The bottom part of Figure 11.10 shows the incremental exposure for the closing rate approach agreeing with the earlier example's exchange gain of £11,256m.

If the *average* rate is used for profit and loss under the closing rate approach, statement translation gains and losses derive from two sources:

(i)   retranslation of opening equity from this period's opening rate to its closing rate (i.e. 9,229).
(ii) retranslation of profit and loss flows from the average rate to this period's closing rate (i.e. 2,027).

If the *closing rate* option under SSAP 20 is chosen to translate profit and loss, the gain on exposure would become £9,229 – implicitly all transactions would be treated as if they took place at the end of the period!

Using averages to approximate exchange rates

Groups using the average rate for translating the profit and loss account receive little guidance from SSAP 20: 'the average rate should be calculated by the method considered most appropriate for the circumstances of the foreign enterprise' (para. 54); 'factors ... include the company's internal accounting procedures and the extent of seasonal trade variations; the use of a weighting procedure will in most cases be desirable' (para. 18).

Under the temporal approach and under the *net investment* rationale for the closing rate, averages are approximations for using transaction date exchange rates. The use of the mid-year exchange rate in this example is unlikely to be acceptable in practice. An arithmetic average of monthly exchange rates would usually be better for evenly occurring transactions. With more complex or seasonal transaction patterns or if exchange rates move in irregular ways, quarterly or monthly transaction totals with quarterly or monthly average exchange rates for example, or some other kind of weighted average would probably be used. The approximation is good enough when it produces translated results not materially different from using actual transaction date rates – a matter of judgement. Cost and ease of calculation would be balanced against accuracy. The exposed items flow statement can be used to decide which flows are to be translated using such approximate rates.

Exercises

11.15 Calculate total and incremental exposure patterns
    (a) For the Pizza Cayka example (Exercise 11.12), temporal approach.
    (b) Repeat (Exercise 11.12), for the closing rate approach and compare the patterns of exposure.
11.16 Calculate exposure patterns as in 11.15 for the Aroma plc example (Exercise 11.13).
11.17 (Further practice only) Repeat for the Aufwiedersehen example (Exercise 11.14), current/non-current approach.
11.18 For any of the above, calculate the gain or loss on exposure and show how it relates to the intuitive notions of accounting exposure and the exposure patterns you have calculated.
11.19 Plastic Teeth plc acquired a 60% stake in an eastern European subsidiary, Fangen plc on 31 March 1987 for £50m, when the latter's retained profits were £150 TMU's (Transylvanian Monetary Units). At 31 March 1995, Fangen's financial statements were as follows:

Balance sheets at 31 March (TMU's millions)

	1995	1995	1994	1994
Fixed assets:				
– cost	900		600	
– accumulated depreciation	(350)		(250)	
		550		350
Net current assets:				
Stock	150		100	
Other	80		70	
		230		170
Creditors over one year:				
Loans		(300)		(100)
		480		420
Capital and reserves:				
Share capital & premium		100		100
Retained profits		380		320
		480		420

Profit and loss accounts for the year ended 31 March (TMU's millions)

	1995	1995
Sales		1,000
Cost of sales		(550)
Gross profit		450
Depreciation	100	
Other expenses	270	
		(370)
Operating profit		80
Interest		(20)
Profit retained for year		60

The following information is also available:

(i)   Opening fixed assets were all purchased when the subsidiary was set up except for the purchase of some machinery at 31 December 1994. There were no fixed asset disposals during the year.
(ii) Stocks on average represent about six months' purchases at each year end.
(iii) Exchange rates were as follows (TMU's to the £):

31 March 1987	10
30 June 1993	12
30 Sept 1993	14
31 Dec 1993	15
31 March 1994	16
30 June 1994	17
30 Sept 1994	18
31 Dec 1994	19
31 Mar 1995	20

(iv) Assume other expenses were all for cash.
(v)   Consolidated goodwill is to be gradually amortized on a straight-line basis over 10 years.

Required

(a) By demonstrating how the exposed amount changes over the year, calculate the exchange gain or loss arising in Fangen plc over the year to 31 March 1995 under the temporal approach; AND the closing rate approach using the closing rate for translating profit and loss. You do not need to translate fully all the financial statements for this.
(b) Comment on your results in (a). and explain how the relevant gains or losses would be dealt with under each approach, giving an intuitive rationale for the treatment.
(c) Calculate goodwill and consolidated reserves for the Plastic Teeth Group as they would appear in the consolidated financial statements at 31 March 1995 under the closing rate approach. Plastic Teeth's balance sheet retained profits at that date were £100m. Assume the historical rate is used to translate goodwill.
(d) Suppose in addition to the above, Fangen has recently purchased a fixed asset from a company in its eastern European neighbour state Slobodnia, and that included in Fangen's 1995 balance sheet 'Net current assets' 'other' balance above is a corresponding creditor of 15 TMUs, a balance of 600 Slobodnian roubles translated at the original transaction rate of 40 roubles to the TMU. The Slobodnian rouble – TMU exchange rate at 31 March 1994 is 30 roubles to the TMU. Explain how this would affect your calculations under the closing rate approach in (a) above.

SSAP 20, *FOREIGN CURRENCY TRANSLATION*

SSAP 20, supporting the closing rate approach but allowing the temporal approach in limited circumstances, was issued in 1983 after three exposure drafts. The ICAEW *Survey of Published Accounts* showed over 80 per cent of UK companies used the closing rate method in the three years *prior to* SSAP 20. In the USA the FASB had issued SFAS 8 in 1975, which required the temporal method. This was subject to heavy criticism that temporal gains or losses did not correlate with economic exposure and that it caused management to make hedging contracts, dysfunctional from an economic perspective, to obtain 'acceptable' accounting results. SFAS 52, issued in 1981, favoured the closing rate approach in most circumstances, and SSAP 20 in 1983 aligned most UK and US requirements.

Foreign currency transactions

SSAP 20 requires that at the 'individual company stage' the 'two transactions' perspective should be used by subsidiaries before submitting their local currency financial statements for translation, unless the rate is to be settled at a contracted rate, in which case that rate should be used – companies often use forward contracts to hedge trading transactions. In the USA, SFAS 52 has detailed provisions relating to the use of forward contracts and currency swaps. Required treatments there differ according to whether the contacts are, for example, for speculative or hedging purposes. As these are not specifically group accounting matters, they are not dealt with further here, except for the group 'cover' concept in SSAP 20 examined below – see Davies, Paterson and Wilson (1992), section 3.3 for further discussion.

Foreign currency financial statements

The closing rate/net investment method is required unless 'the trade of the foreign enterprise is more dependent on the economic environment of the investing company's currency than its own reporting currency' when the temporal method should be used (para. 55). Once the environmental conditions are decided, only one treatment is allowed; under a single currency structure use the temporal method, under a multi-currency, multi-environment structure use the closing rate. SSAP 20 illustrates conditions for the temporal method, e.g. for selling agencies, parts of vertically integrated operations, tax haven operations, etc. The usual currency of operations, the currency to which the operation is exposed, the extent of dependence and the extent of remittability of cash flows are all relevant. However, it is clear that the closing rate approach will predominate.

SFAS 52 makes similar recommendations in the USA using its *functional currency* concept, defined as the currency of the primary economic environment within which the entity operates, 'normally that is, the currency of the environment in which the entity generates and expends cash'. The temporal approach is allowed only where the functional currency of the foreign enterprise is the parent's, and the closing rate where the functional currency is that of the place of location, called in SSAP 20 the 'local currency'. SFAS 52 terms the temporal approach 'remeasurement' and the closing rate approach, 'translation'. The temporal approach implies a single functional currency for the group, the parent's, the closing rate multiple functional currencies. Finding the extent of dependence under SSAP 20 is analogous to identifying the functional currency under SFAS 52.

Accounting treatment of gains and losses

The destinations for exchange gains and losses required by SSAP 20 are as follows:

Description	Translation approach	Destination of gains and losses
Transactions	Two transaction	Profit & loss
Financial statements	Temporal	Profit & Loss
	Closing rate	Reserves

Temporal supporters advocate gains and losses on statement translation to be taken to profit and loss *as if* (the parent's) *transaction* gains and losses, whereas net investment supporters advocate that they be taken direct to reserves akin to *revaluations* of the net investment, similar to fixed asset revaluations. These reflect the differing underlying rationales. FRS 3's illustrative example accompanying its Statement of Total Recognized Gains and Losses (see Chapter 8) includes both revaluations and *closing rate* foreign currency exchange differences as 'recognized gains and losses'.

To preserve a local currency perspective, some argue that closing rate approach gains and losses should be 'excluded' from the sterling statements, since they do not appear in the local currency ones. Carsberg (1992, p. 104), on the other hand, supports a more 'all inclusive' income measure, concluding that closing rate statement gains and losses and revaluations are *genuine* gains and losses and if included in income would reflect total *economic* gains *gross* of inflation.

Disposals of foreign subsidiaries – FRS 3 further requires that (closing rate exchange) gains and losses once reported in this statement cannot be reported again in the consolidated profit and loss account. Gains and losses on disposals of fixed assets and foreign subsidiaries are thus based on carrying values *including* the effects of revaluations and closing rate translation gains. Therefore closing rate statement gains and losses, analogous to revaluation gains and losses will *never* go through the profit and loss account. This differs from US and much international practice, where cumulative (closing rate) translation gains and losses 'dealt with as equity', i.e. taken direct to reserves, have to be transferred back to the profit and loss account (effectively adjusting carrying values to *exclude* their effects) to determine the gain or loss on disposal. For further discussion see Taylor (1995, Section VI.1.5).

International alternatives – other treatments proposed internationally include the deferral and gradual amortization of statement gains and losses to profit and loss, or non-symmetrical treatment, e.g. immediate write-off of losses, deferral and amortization of gains. The first is not allowed in the UK and US, though the Canadian standard allows it for gains and losses on loans – arguments for are that companies forecast currency movements in transacting loans and so foreseen movements should be viewed as interest adjustments over the life of the loan. How accurate such forecasting can be is debateable. SSAP 20's accompanying technical release argued for a symmetrical treatment of gains and losses, and that gains on long-term monetary items dealt with in the profit and loss account should be regarded as unrealized for distribution purposes.

The cover concept: hedging net investments

The fact that *transaction* gains and losses are dealt with in the profit and loss account, whereas closing rate *statement* gains and losses are taken direct to reserves can cause problems for 'hedged' transactions, where foreign assets and liabilities are 'matched' so that gains and losses offset. Suppose a parent finances a 'net investment' in an overseas subsidiary by raising a foreign currency long-term loan in the same currency. If say the overseas currency is strengthening, statement gains from the net investment, i.e. translating the subsidiary's financial statements under the closing rate approach, would be taken to reserves. However, the parent's *transaction* losses on *its* loan under the two-transaction approach would be taken to the parent's (and hence the consolidated) profit and loss account. The linked decision would disclose gains and losses of approximately the same size in *different* locations, when it is argued that the *net position* is what is really exposed.

To counteract this, SSAP 20 allows gains or losses on *loans* used to finance overseas subsidiaries translated under the closing rate approach to be offset as reserve movements against gains or losses on linked 'net investments' to the extent of exchange differences arising on the latter. The currency of the loan does *not* have to be the same as for the net investment (unlike SFAS 52 in the USA which requires an effective hedge to be in the same currency or one that moves in tandem, and allows such hedges to include financial instruments other than loans). Little guidance is given in SSAP 20 as to what constitutes a hedge – even historically highly correlated 'hedges' offset for period after period can move in opposite directions in particular periods, resulting in large non-offsettable figures. The chapter example in Figure 11.6 reveals this situation – where a loan to a 'closing' rate subsidiary and the statement exchange difference both result in 'gains' and cannot be offset.

SSAP 20 requires that the aggregate of foreign currency borrowings available for offset should not exceed the total cash expected to be generated by the relevant net investments. What this means is not clear. Davies, Paterson and Wilson (1992, pp. 402) interpret this as meaning that the total cash generated is represented by the value of the (net) investment in immediate sale (a present value based concept). However, a literal interpretation might be the undiscounted sum of future cash flows. Harris (1991, p. 16–23) comments 'if a net investment is of an indefinite term, then any hedge is a matching obligation of the same duration . . . [and] it is hard to conceive of many companies having such hedges.'

The Polly Peck case reveals a different aspect of the hedging problem. Gwilliam and Russell (1991) argue that its 1989 earnings, prior to its collapse were greatly overstated and that SSAP 20's requirements contributed to this. Polly Peck borrowed in 'hard' low-interest rate currencies, and within its *foreign subsidiaries* lent in high-interest depreciating currencies. Large losses caused by translating the subsidiary's rapidly depreciating loans under the closing rate approach, were thus excluded from consolidated profit and loss and taken direct to reserves as part of the overall statement translation difference – these were much greater than smaller exchange differences on the parent's 'hard' currency loans. In the profit and loss account itself, high translated interest receivable (on the subsidiary's loans) was offset against low interest payable (on the parent's loans). In the 1989 accounts, interest receivable exceeded interest payable at a time when opening 1989 net monetary liabilities of £250m increased to £700m by the end of the year (Gwilliam and Russell, p. 25). Later, arguments will be examined (page 325) that the 'true' cost of a loan is its interest charge *net* of exchange differences.

Disclosure

Quantitative disclosures

SSAP 20's disclosure requirements are selective. It requires the method(s) of translation to be disclosed and two main quantitative areas: the *net* movement on reserves arising from exchange differences and the treatment of foreign currency net borrowings (para. 60). For foreign currency borrowings net of deposits, SSAP 20 requires the separate disclosure of amounts offset to reserves under its various 'cover' provisions, and the net charge relating to borrowings only to profit and loss. A notable omission is the profit and loss disclosure of total net exchange differences (a) on transactions and (b) on using the temporal approach for translating financial statements. The technical release with SSAP 20 argued such total disclosure is not necessarily helpful because exchange differences cannot be viewed separately from a company's total pricing policy (prices possibly including an element for foreseen exchange movements), and that a small net amount may disguise large offsetting movements. However, such arguments seem to support greater disclosure rather than none(!).

Qualitative information

The ASB Statement, *Operating and Financial Review*, issued in July 1993, recommends as best practice in its Financial Review, that management should discuss the management of exchange rate risk, and the currencies in which borrowings are made and in which cash and cash equivalents are held, the use of financial instruments for hedging, and the extent to which foreign currency net investments are hedged by currency borrowings and other hedging instruments. In addition the review should discuss any restrictions on the ability to transfer funds to meet the obligations of another part of the group where they are or might become a significant constraint on the group. *Company Reporting*, in its June 1991 issue found that in its sample of 700 companies or groups with evidence of foreign operations, 10 per cent gave details of exchange rates, and 14 per cent analysed indebtedness by currency, though virtually no information was given about foreign currency assets and accounting exposure (Company Reporting Limited, 1991, p. 7).

International comparisons

IAS 21, *The Effects of Changes in Foreign Exchange Rates*, revised in 1993, covers a number of SSAP 20's omissions and requires disclosure of the amount of exchange differences dealt with in the net profit or loss, a *reconciliation* of beginning and ending balances of cumulative exchange differences classified as equity (i.e. under closing rate approach), that such differences be *classified separately* rather than just taken to 'reserves' as under SSAP 20, and specifies details relating to any *changes in classification* of any significant foreign operations, including the impact of the restatement of shareholders' equity and prior periods profit and loss figures (paras 42–44). SFAS 52 in the USA requires details of the *total* net exchange gain taken to the profit and loss account and a detailed analysis of reserve movements caused by exchange differences (e.g. showing effects of hedges, intercompany balances, taxation and sales or disposals). The revised IAS 21 also encourages 'disclosure . . . of an enterprise's foreign currency risk management policy' (para. 47).

Hyperinflation

Problems arise with the closing rate approach under historical cost accounting when overseas economies are subject to hyperinflation, with consequent high interest charges and currency depreciation. Rapidly declining current exchange rates reflecting the inflationary spiral are applied to historical costs which do not, leading to the 'disappearing assets' syndrome. If current values were used, the increase in asset prices would counteract exchange rate depreciation. Under historical cost accounting, two alternative solutions have been proposed:

(a) SSAP 20 requires that 'local currency financial statements should be adjusted to current price levels before the translation process is undertaken'. No guidance is given as to whether this adjustment should be for general price levels (CPP) or specific price levels (current values).
(b) SFAS 52 in the USA requires the use of the temporal approach in hyperinflationary economies, which uses the parent currency as a 'store of value', but is inconsistent with the autonomous local subsidiary rationale for the closing rate.

Defining a hyperinflationary economy

UITF Abstract 9, *Accounting for Operations in Hyper-inflationary Economies*, issued in June 1993, defines more rigorously when an economy is deemed hyperinflationary: 'where the *cumulative* exchange rate over *three* years is approaching, or exceeds, 100% and the operations in the hyper-inflationary economies are material' (para. 5, emphases added). The annual average inflation rate consistent with this is 26 per cent – in the calculation below 200 per cent is doubling, hence the factor '2':

$$(2)^{1/3} - 1 \quad = \quad 0.26$$

Reconciling the approaches

UITF Abstract 9 tries to 'reconcile' the two alternatives above by interpreting SSAP 20 as allowing either

(a) *adjustment to current price levels before translation*: the Abstract interprets this in a general price level sense, requiring the gain or loss on net monetary items to be taken to the profit and loss account; or
(b) *re-measurement of the subsidiary's balances and flows into a relatively stable currency* before translation into the reporting currency. This 'pseudo' temporal approach is similar to the US solution above. The stable currency is allowed to be different from the parent's.

By 'sleight of hand' it links the two approaches, rationalizing 'the movement between the original currency of record and the stable currency . . . as a proxy for an inflation index' (para. 6). The method used must be disclosed. Other approaches can be used but the reasons for using them must be stated.

UITF Abstract 9 does not discuss the index to be used under (a) above. IAS 29 requires a CPP adjustment using the *local* inflation index, with the gain or loss on monetary items being included in profit and loss. This again derives from treating the foreign subsidiary as autonomous, and preserving *local* currency purchasing power. Balances restated for local general inflation are difficult to interpret other than as *approximations* to current values. Flower (1991) argues for a *home* country's inflation index to preserve the parent's shareholder's purchasing power, but this seems closer to the 'unified group' rationale for the temporal approach.

Exercises

11.20 What are the main criteria under SSAP 20 for determining when the closing rate approach should be used? Explain why its gains and losses do not go through the profit and loss account whereas those under the temporal approach do.

11.21 Why has SSAP 20 found it necessary to include a 'cover concept' in conjunction with the closing rate approach? Have its requirements in this area proved successful?

11.22 Why do hyperinflationary economies cause problems when the closing rate financial statement translation approach is used? How are such difficulties to be resolved?

FOREIGN CURRENCY TRANSLATION AND THE CASH FLOW STATEMENT

This section presumes knowledge of Chapter 9 on Consolidated Cash Flow Statements. It can be omitted without loss of continuity.

Foreign currency gains and losses can arise in the consolidated cash flow statement from foreign currency cash transactions or from the translation and consolidation of foreign currency cash flow statements. Since recent surveys have indicated net basis cash flow statements are prepared by 95 per cent of groups, discussions below are framed in this context.

Gains or losses on foreign currency transactions are normally dealt with in the consolidated profit and loss account as part of operating profit. In the reconciliation of 'operating profit' to 'net cash flow from operating activities' in the net basis cash flow statement, foreign exchange gains or losses on transactions classified within investing, financing, returns and taxation activities need to be adjusted for, but not gains or losses relating to operating activity transactions.

Suppose a parent transacts in foreign currency loans. The movement on the loan account will include loan transactions translated at their transaction dates and gains or losses on the changing exposed currency loan balance. Adjusting operating profit for exchange gains and losses arising from such financing-type transactions allows the cash flow matrix to reconstruct foreign currency loan transactions translated at the exchange rates ruling at their transaction dates. No further adjustment is necessary for exchange gains and losses on operating activity-type transactions because the adjustment in the reconciliation of operating profit to net cash flow from operating activities for stocks, operating debtors and operating creditors ensures the operating activities cash flow total is correctly stated (see Wild and Goodhead (1994, pp. 239–240)). A demonstration of this is beyond the scope of the current book.

Cash flow statement translation

FRS 1 states that 'the cash flows of [a foreign entity] . . . are to be included . . . on the basis used for translating the results of those activities in the profit and loss account of the reporting entity' (para. 36). Thus under the closing rate approach the average or year end rate might be used to translate cash flow statements of subsidiaries. This is unlike SFAS 95, *Statement of Cash Flows*, in the USA and internationally, the revised IAS 7, *Cash Flow Statements*, which both require all cash transactions to be translated at actual transaction rates. The decision by FRS 1 not to use actual rates causes problems for cancellation of intra-group cash flows as will be seen below. Since exchange gains or losses on subsidiaries' cash and cash equivalents balances resulting from financial statement translation are not actual cash flows, FRS 1 requires them to be reported in the note disclosure reconciling opening and closing cash and cash equivalents rather than in the consolidated cash flow statement itself.

Example 11.6 – Consolidating net format cash flow statements

The following are cash flow statements for Goodbuy plc and its 75% owned Teutonic subsidiary Aufwiedersehen AG in thousands of millions of pounds and of Teutonic Marks (TM):

Cash flow statements for the year ended 31 December 1995

	Goodbuy		Aufwiedersehen	
	£'000m	£'000m	TM'000m	M'000m
Operating activities				
Net cash inflow from operating activities		110		245
Returns on investments & servicing of financing				
Interest paid	(6)		(20)	
Dividends paid	(5)		—	
Net cash outflow on inv & serv. of financing		(11)		(20)
Investing activities				
Payments for fixed assets	(128)		(200)	
Sales proceeds from fixed assets	30		—	
Net cash outflow on investing activities		(98)		(200)
Financing activities				
Loan issue	40		—	
Loans proceeds received from parent	—		75	
Loans made to subsidiary	(20)		—	
Net cash inflow from financing activities		20		75
Increase in cash and cash equivalents		21		100

Reconciliation of operating profit to cash inflow from operating activities

	Goodbuy	Aufwiedersehen
	£'000m	TM'000m
Operating profit	92	120
Depreciation	15	100
Loss on fixed asset disposal	5	—
Exchange loss on investing items	9	—
Decrease/(increase) in (operating) debtors	8	(25)
(Increase) in stocks	(18)	(50)
(Decrease)/increase in operating creditors	(1)	100
Net cash inflow from operating activities	110	245

Reconcilations of opening and closing cash and cash equivalents

Reconciliation	Goodbuy	Aufwiedersehen
	(£'000m)	(TM'000m)
Opening	70	100
Net cash inflow	21	100
Closing	91	200

Further information

1. Intra-group cash flows were as follows:

	£'000m
Interest-free loan from Goodbuy to Aufwiedersehen on 31 March 1995	20

There were no other intra-group transactions. The exchange rate at 31 March was 3.75 Teutonic Marks to the £ sterling. All interest paid by Aufwiedersehen AG was to external parties.

2.   Exchange rates – Marks to the £

		31 March 1995	3.75
1 January 1984	4.6	Average rate for 1995	4.0
31 August 1994	4.3	31 August 1995	3.9
31 October 1994	4.2	31 October 1995	3.8
31 December 1994	4.1	31 December 1995	3.7

Required

(a) Prepare a sterling translated cash flow statement for Aufwiedersehen AG using a cash flow matrix. Assume the closing rate approach has been used to translate its financial statements with the average rate for translating the profit and loss account.

(b) Prepare a consolidated cash flow statement for the Goodbuy Group for the year ended 31 December 1995. Comment on the treatment of intra-group loans.

Solution

Stage 1 – translating the individual company foreign currency cash flow statement

Figure 11.11 is a net basis cash flow matrix for Aufwiedersehen AG, based on the example used throughout the chapter, prepared using the derivation approach discussed in Chapter 9. The reader is invited to take it as given, but can check it if they wish. In each cell the Teutonic mark amount has been translated into sterling using the opening balance sheet rate (4.1) for the top line, the average rate to translate transactions (according to FRS 1, as it (4.0) is used for profit and loss) (4.0), and the closing balance sheet rate (3.7) for the closing balance sheet on the bottom line. The line 'Cash flow from ops' subtotals the sterling amounts in the top shaded lines. The translated cash flow statement is the left-hand column:

Exchange differences: The bottom but one line of the matrix, 'Exchange gain/loss by differencing' shows a breakdown of the £11,256m exchange gain per the translated profit and loss account earlier in the chapter:

£11,256m = **gains on individual assets:** 4,664m (cash) + 3,144m (debtors) + 6,288m (stock) + 15,250m (fixed assets)
less losses on individual liabilities: – 8,620m (creditors) – 9,430m (loans)

The cash column exchange difference of £4,664m is used for FRS 1's note disclosure below, reconciling movements of cash and cash equivalents with opening and closing balances. Other exchange differences are also needed for note disclosures in the consolidated statements, such as in the statutory fixed asset movements note, a gain of £15,210m, and in FRS 1's required note on changes in financing, foreign exchange currency differences must be separately disclosed (para. 44) (e.g. loans (£9,430m)). The consolidated profit and loss account shows the net gain on net assets as a whole, so the cash flow matrix is needed to obtain a breakdown of this to determine gains or losses on individual assets and liabilities.

The exchange gain on cash – Using the average rate to translate the cash flow statement treats all cash transactions *as if* they took place at the average rate. The £4,664m exchange gain on cash comprises exposure of the opening balance (i.e. TM 100,000m) for the year, plus the net increment for transactions for the year (i.e TM200,000m – TM100,000m) from the 'date' corresponding to the average rate, viz.

$$\text{TM100,000m} \times [\frac{1}{3.7} - \frac{1}{4.1}] \quad + \quad (\text{TM200,000m} - \text{TM100,000m}) \times [\frac{1}{3.7} - \frac{1}{4.0}] = \text{£4,664m gain}$$

If the closing rate had been used to translate the cash flow statement, the gain on cash and cash equivalents would only have been the first term, i.e. £2,637m, as 'cash' transactions would have been treated *as if* they had taken place on the last day of the year, an imposed artificial rate rather than the actual transaction rates required in the USA or by IAS 7.

Stage 2 – consolidating the translated cash flow statements

The aggregation approach (see Chapter 9) is used in Figure 11.12 to consolidate the parent's cash flow statement with the translated subsidiary's statement (taken from the left-hand column of the cash flow matrix in Figure 11.11). The consolidated cash flow statement is shown below. Normally there would be minority dividends under the 'returns' heading, but here no subsidiary dividends have been paid.

Description	Cash	Operating debtors	Stock	Fixed assets	Operating creditors	Loans	Share cap and retained profits
Opening balances	100,000 / 4.1 = £24,390m	100,000 / 4.1 = £24,390m	200,000 / 4.1 = £48,780m	500,000 / 4.1 = £121,952m	(250,000) / 4.1 = (£60,975m)	(300,000) / 4.1 = (£73,171m)	(350,000) / 4.1 = (£85,366m)
Reconciliation:							
Operating profit	120,000 / 4.0 = £30,000m						(120,000) / 4.0 = (£30,000m)
Remove non-operating items							
Depreciation	100,000 / 4.0 = £25,000m			(100,000) / 4.0 = (£25,000m)			
Adjust for operating accruals							
Increase in operating debtors	(25,000) / 4.0 = (£6,250m)	25,000 / 4.0 = £6,250m					
Increase in stocks	(50,000) / 4.0 = (£12,500m)		50,000 / 4.0 = £12,500m				
Increase in operating creditors	100,000 / 4.0 = £25,000m				(100,000) / 4.0 = (£25,000m)		
Cash flow from operations	£61,250m	£6,250m	£12,500m	(£25,000m)	(£25,000m)		(£30,000m)
Below operating profit items							
Interest expenditure	(20,000) / 4.0 = (£5,000m)						20,000 / 4.0 = £5,000m
Notes:							
Loan Issue	75,000 / 4.0 = £18,750m					(75,000) / 4.0 = £18,750m	
Fixed asset payments	(200,000) / 4.0 = (£50,000m)			200,000 / 4.0 = £50,000m			
Differencing:							
Subtotal 'input' rates	£49,390m	£30,640m	£61,280m	£146,952m	(£85,975m)	(£91,921m)	(£110,366m)
Exchange gain / (loss) by differencing	£4,664m	£3,144m	£6,288m	£15,210m	(£8,620m)	(£9,430m)	(£11,256m)
Closing balances	200,000 / 3.7 = £54,054m	125,000 / 3.7 = £33,784m	250,000 / 3.7 = £67,568m	600,000 / 3.7 = £162,162m	(350,000) / 3.7 = (£94,595m)	(375,000) / 3.7 = (£101,351m)	(450,000) / 3.7 = (£121,622m)

Figure 11.11 – Translating the net basis cash flow matrix for Aufwiedersehen in Teutonic marks (TM'm)

Description	Goodbuy	Aufwieder-sehen	Adjustments	Consolidated
Operating profit	92,000	30,000	-	122,000
Depreciation	15,000	25,000	-	40,000
Loss on fixed asset disposal	5,000	-		5,000
Exchange difference on investing transactions	9,000			9,000
Increase in (op) debtors	8,000	(6,250)	-	1,750
Increase in stocks	(18,000)	(12,500)	-	(30,500)
Increase in (op) creditors	(1,000)	25,000	-	24,000
Cash flow from operating activities	110,000	61,250	-	171,250
Interest paid	(6,000)	(5,000)	-	(11,000)
Dividends paid - parent	(5,000)	-	-	(5,000)
Fixed asset payments	(128,000)	(50,000)	-	(178,000)
Fixed asset sale proceeds	30,000	-	-	30,000
Loans issued	40,000	-	-	40,000
Loan from parent		18,750	(18,750)	-
Loans advanced to subsidiary	(20,000)		20,000	-
Increase in cash before exchange differences	21,000	25,000	1,250	47,250
Exchange differences	-	4,664	(1,250)	3,414
Increase in cash & cash equivalents	21	29,664	-	50,664

Figure 11.12 – Goodbuy Group – Consolidating cash flow statements by direct aggregation (£'m)

Intra-group cash flows – Using the profit and loss rate to translate the subsidiary's cash flow statement rather than the actual rate has unfortunate consequences for intra-group transactions. Here a £20,000m loan was made by the parent to the subsidiary when the rate was 3.75 TM to the £. The subsidiary will have received at that date 20,000 × 3.75 = TM 75,000m. Using the actual rate to translate the loan (per SFAS 95 and IAS 7) would lead to perfect cancellation of intra-group balances since 75,000/3.75 = £20,000m. However, Goodbuy is constrained by FRS 1 to use the rate of 4.0, giving a translated balance of £18,750m, which leads to a spurious exchange difference of £1,250m. FRS gives no guidance on this. Davies, Paterson and Wilson (1992, p. 1,240) suggest netting it off against the net movement in debtors or creditors in reconciling operating profit to net cash inflow from operating activities. However, Wild and Goodhead (1994, p. 86) prefer placing it in the note reconciling opening and closing cash and cash equivalents for the year and this treatment is adopted here. What meaning the revised gain on cash and cash equivalents of £3,414m (= 4,664 – 1,250) has is unclear.

Consolidated cash flow statement for the year ended 31 December 1995 – Goodbuy Group

	£m	£m
Operating activities		
Net cash inflow from operating activities		171,250
Returns on investments & servicing of financing		
Interest paid	(11,000)	
Dividends paid	(5,000)	
Net cash outflow on inv & serv. of financing		(16,000)
Investing activities		
Payments for fixed assets	(178,000)	
Sales proceeds from fixed assets	30,000	
Net cash outflow on investing activities		(148,000)
Net cash inflow before financing activities		7,250
Financing Activities		
Loan issue	40,000	
Net cash inflow from financing activities		40,000
Increase/ decrease in cash and cash equivalents		47,250

Notes   **Reconciliation of operating profit to cash inflow from operating activities**

	£m
Operating profit	122,000
Depreciation	40,000
Loss on fixed asset disposal	5,000
Exchange loss on investing items	9,000
Decrease in (operating) debtors	1,750
(Increase) in stocks	(30,500)
Increase in operating creditors	24,000
Net cash inflow from operating activities	171,250

Reconciliation of cash flow changes with opening and closing balances

Cash and cash equivalents	Goodbuy (£'000)
Opening (70,000 + 24,390)	94,390
Net cash inflow (above)	47,250
Exchange gain (above)	3,414
Closing (91,000 + 54,054)	145,054

The exchange loss in the 'operating profit' reconciliation note is a transaction loss of the *parent* of the type discussed earlier. The adjustments for changes in operating debtors, operating creditors and stocks above will not be the same as differences between opening and closing consolidated balance sheets as they exclude the effects of foreign exchange differences, whereas balance sheet changes include them. FRS 1's required note on changes in financing is not shown here.

Consolidated cash flow statement preparation methods

Closing rate approach

If the average rate is used to translate profit and loss and hence cash flows under FRS 1's requirements, it will probably be necessary to use the aggregation rather than the derivation consolidation approach, and therefore for subsidiaries to send their local currency cash flow statements to be translated by the parent (Georgiou, 1993, pp. 235–6). Georgiou deduces preparation is simpler if the year-end rate is used for translating profit and loss account and hence the cash flow statement. Translated payments for fixed assets will be the same as translated amounts in the consolidated balance sheet. The derivation consolidation approach (i.e. deduced from the other consolidated statements) may then be fesible. However, he is unhappy that ease of preparation should influence the choice of rate. Using the year end rate to translate cash flows 'will indiscriminately distort the actual cash flows of a subsidiary' (p. 230) unlike SFAS 95 and IAS 7 with their insistence on *actual* rates. However, those who consider that translation should preserve local currency financial statement relationships in the translated figures will probably not see any great problem in this.

Temporal approach

It is not really clear what using the same rate as for translating the profit and loss account to translate cash flows means where the temporal approach is used. According to SSAP 20, 'the mechanics of the [temporal] method are identical with those used in preparing the accounts of an individual company' (para. 22). This would suggest using the actual rate when the cash flows occurred. However, FRS 1's requirements seem to imply using rates for purchases and sales dates instead. The aggregation consolidation approach would probably be used.

Exercises

11.23   The following are cash flow statements for Gobbledegook plc and its Latin subsidiary Pizza Cayka

Cash flow statements for the year ended 31 December 1995

	Gobbledegook plc £m	£m	Pizza Cayka plc Maracas (millions)	Maracas (millions)
Operating activities				
Net cash inflow from operating activities		25,000		1,500
Returns on inv & servicing of financing				
Interest paid	(4,000)		—	
Dividends paid	(3,000)		—	
Net cash outflow on inv & serv. of financing				
		(7,000)		—
Investing activities				
Payments for fixed assets	(45,000)		(3,000)	
Sales proceeds from fixed assets	7,000		—	
Net cash outflow on investing activities		(38,000)		(3,000)
Financing Activities				
Loan issue	25,000			
Loans repaid	(9,525)			
Loans proceeds received from parent			1,900	
Loans made to subsidiary	(475)		—	
Net cash inflow from financing activities		15,000		1,900
Increase/ (decrease) in cash and cash equivalents		(5,000)		400

Note – reconciliation of operating profit to cash inflow from operating activities

	Gobbledegook £m	Pizza Cayka Maracas (millions)
Operating profit	16,000	2,100
Depreciation	10,000	1,000
Loss on fixed asset sale	5,000	—
Exchange loss on investing items	3,000	
(Increase) in (operating) debtors	(5,000)	(1,200)
(Increase) in stocks	(5,000)	(1,000)
Increase in operating creditors	1,000	600
Net cash inflow from operating activities	25,000	1,500

Note – reconciliation of cash flow changes with opening and closing balances

Reconciliation	Gobbledegook £m	Pizza Cayka maracas (millions)
Opening	10,000	600
Net cash inflow/(outflow)	(5,000)	400
Closing	5,000	1,000

Further information
1. Intra-group cash flows were as follows: £m
        Loan from Gobbledegook to Pizza Cayka   475
    There were no other intra-group transactions.
2. Exchange rates – Maracas to the £

31 December 1994	4.8	Average rate for 1995	4.7
31 December 1995	4.6	At loan date	4.0

Gobbledegook made an interest free sterling loan to Pizza Cayka for £475m during the year when the exchange rate was 4.0 Maracas to the £ sterling.
3. An indirect cash flow matrix for the subsidiary in millions of maracas is shown in Figure 11.13 based on the information in the earlier example.

Required
(a) Prepare a translated indirect format cash flow matrix for Pizza Cayka Plc under the closing rate approach assuming the average rate has been used to translate the profit and loss account.
(b) Prepare a table to show how the exchange gain on cash is calculated.
(c) Prepare a consolidated cash flow statement for the Goodbuy Group for the year ended 31 December 1995 using the aggregation approach, together with a note reconciliation of 'operating profit' to 'net cash flow from operating activities' and a reconciliation of movements of cash and cash equivalents.
(d) In what ways would your statements change if the closing rate had been used to translate the profit and loss account instead of the average rate?

Description	Cash	Operating debtors	Stock	Fixed assets	Operating creditors	Loans	Share cap and prem	Retained profits
Opening balances	600	1,800	3,800	8,000	(2,400)	(2,100)	(5,000)	(4,700)
Reconcilation:								
Operating profit	**2,100**							**(2,100)**
Remove non-operating items								
Depreciation	**1,000**			**(1,000)**				
Adjust for operating accruals								
Increase in operating debtors	**(1,200)**	**1,200**						
Increase in stocks	**(1,000)**		**1,000**					
Increase in operating creditors	**600**				**(600)**			
[Cash flow from operations (O)	1,500	1,200	1,000	(1,000)	(600)			(2,100)]
Notes:								
Loan issue (F)	1,900					(1,900)		
Fixed asset payments (I)	(3,000)			3,000				
Differencing:								
-								
Closing balances	1,000	3,000	4,800	10,000	(3,000)	(4,000)	(5,000)	(6,800)

Figure 11.13 – Indirect approach cash flow matrix for Pizza Cayka in maracas

THE TRANSLATION DEBATE

SSAP 20 claims to relate the choice of approach to economic 'reality', dependent subsidiaries being translated under the temporal approach and autonomous subsidiaries under the closing rate. This claim is examined further below, as is an alternative claim, that the debate is better characterized as a political rather than conceptual one.

Objectives of accounting for foreign subsidiaries
SSAP 20's objectives are stated thus

> The translation of foreign currency transactions and financial statements should produce results which are generally compatible with the effects of rate changes on a company's cash flows and its equity and should ensure that the financial statements present a true and fair view of the results of management actions. Consolidated statements should reflect the financial results and relationships as measured in the foreign currency financial statements prior to translation. (para. 2)

consistent with the closing rate approach. However, according to SFAS 8, an earlier US standard

> For the purpose of preparing an enterprise's financial statements, the objective of translation is to measure and express (a) in dollars and (b) in conformity with US generally accepted accounting principles (GAAP) the assets, liabilities, revenues, or expenses that are measured or denominated in foreign currency.

consistent with the temporal approach! Which is correct? Different proposed objectives for the function of translation are outlined below and the consistency of each approach with them is examined.

To preserve the integrity of the historical cost accounting basis

The temporal approach scores highly. It 'remeasures' foreign currency balances into the reporting currency so as to preserve their 'datedness'. But, for example, should debtors be stated at a current or a future amount, in which case a forward exchange rate might be more appropriate? Lorensen (1972) concluded the former. Fortunately, Henning *et al.* (1978), in their empirical research, found current exchange rates can be used in both cases since the present rate of exchange is an unbiased estimate of future rates (Nobes, 1980, p. 425). Quoted forward rates are unsuitable as they include an interest element.

Many argue that under the closing rate approach, multiplying a historical dated balance by a current exchange rate produces a meaningless figure, neither a historical cost nor a good approximation to current values. Since the temporal approach was largely developed to preserve the integrity of differing valuation systems, it is not surprising that it ensures no changes in underlying measurement principles take place – indeed under *current* cost accounting it would translate all balances at the current rate when the two approaches would give the same solution. Temporal supporters argue price level adjustments are best dealt with directly, rather than being approximated by the translation process. Demirag (1987, p. 83) concludes that it will take the adoption of current value accounting to resolve the translation debate and to enable useful information to be produced.

Flower (1991, pp. 336–8) argues that a widely cited economic theory, the 'Fisher' effect, supports the temporal approach to the translation of foreign currency loans. The theory proposes if financial assets are held in two different countries, the change in exchange rate would be exactly counterbalanced by the interest rate differential between the countries. The 'true' cost of a foreign currency loan is therefore the interest charge *net* of currency appreciation or depreciation. Under the temporal approach both elements pass through profit and loss, and their offset will ensure a 'net' interest charge. As the Polly Peck case illustrated earlier, this is not the case under the closing rate approach. Empirical research by Aliber and Stickney (1985) showed that the Fisher effect seems to hold in the long run but not in the short. Flower does not consider this bars its usefulness in constructing accounting theories.

To be consistent with various consolidation objectives

One commonly stated consolidation objective is to present the statements of a group as if they are of a single economic entity. This is arguably more consistent with the temporal approach. However, there are other cited objectives including the amplification of parent financial statements (Chapter 2). The net investment rationale implicitly challenges the single entity argument. Some argue if its assumptions hold, line-by-line consolidation is not appropriate and the equity approach should be used, which could be viewed as consistent with the amplification objective.

To provide information compatible with economic exposure

It has been argued that closing rate gains and losses correlate much more closely with economic exposure, because when the foreign currency strengthens, the temporal approach shows a loss, but future currency flows have increased in value. However, Nobes (1980) and Flower (1991) question whether the main purpose of historical cost accounts is to aid prediction. Also, such correlations may not be high if exchange rate movements between countries are offset by countervailing price and interest rate movements. Carsberg (1991) deduces that the temporal approach would be closer to current (economic) values where under that approach 'an unrecorded increase in the current cost of fixed assets [under historical cost accounting] may be offset by the failure to recognise the effect on the value of the assets of a fall in the value of the foreign currency' (p. 103), whereas under other plausible assumptions the closing rate approach will be closer. Elitzur's (1991) mathematical analysis shows that if inflation exceeds the devaluation of a foreign currency, the temporal approach gives less distortion than the closing rate, whereas if the reverse is true, the closing rate provides less distortion. Therefore the opening argument is too simplistic.

To preserve relationships from the original currency statements

This relationship preserving rationale for the closing rate approach is *different* from the net investment one. It requires that local currency relationships, for example current ratios, remain unchanged in the translated figures. It is used to justify the use of the *year end* rate to translate the profit and loss account. Paterson (1986) terms it the 'removal of distortion' in translating statements. Rigorously followed, it would necessitate all financial statements, including comparatives and goodwill, being translated at or retranslated to a *single* common rate. Whether aggregating such relationship-preserving balances produces a meaningful consolidated total in historical or current cost terms is doubtful. Patz (1977) notes that on translation the place and time dimensions of balances can easily be *confounded* so that consolidated statements become meaningless.

The *net investment rationale* for the closing rate approach does not lead to retranslation of comparatives. It also leads to an average rate being used for translating the profit and loss account, as an approximation to actual transaction rates. This reflects the changing exposure of the 'net investment' throughout the period. SSAP 20 ambiguously states both rationales and allows either average rate or year end rate for translating the profit and loss account. Both SFAS 52 in the USA and the revised IAS 7 *only* allow average rates as approximations to actual rates.

To choose a measurement unit with desirable properties

None of the rationales for the different translation approaches is detailed enough to deduce from them which of multiple exchange rates to use, e.g. buying or selling rates, dividend remittance rates, official versus free market rates, or concessionary rates for foreign investment. SFAS 8 in the US (temporal approach) recommended the dividend rate. This seems inconsistent with translating the subsidiary's transactions as if those of the parent, which would seem to require the historical buying rate for stocks and fixed assets, but the current selling rate for debtors (to reflect the currency received to be converted into sterling). SSAP 20 recommends the mean of buying and selling spot rates under the closing rate. SFAS 52, the current US standard, requires the dividend remittance rate for the closing rate approach if there are no unusual circumstances.

Patz (1977) argues that actual exchange rates are not suitable for translating foreign currency balances and that *purchasing power ratios* should be used instead. He considers that such ratios reflect relative prices for goods within the two economies as a whole. Exchange rates reflect short-term volatility and only import–export trading. Under *idealized* assumptions, the 'purchasing power parity theorem' holds. This states that exchange rate changes over time between countries are proportionately related to their relative price level changes. Aliber and Stickney (1975) found US evidence that this held in the long run, but there were significant short-term departures. Proposals for purchasing power ratios are closely linked with the choice of measurement unit in the price level accounting debate. They have not been influential in practice and so are not examined further here (see Nobes, 1980, pp. 427–8). One application of their use, however, could be to address the problem of hyperinflationary economies.

The context of the debate

The political/economic consequences dimension

SSAP 20 thus is a compromise rationalizable from many angles but not completely consistent with any, suggesting that selection of approach and objectives may be based not only on theoretical criteria. Watts and Zimmerman (1979) argue that, in a regulated economy, accounting theories are primarily produced in response to vested interests' demands. Theories justify practice rather than leading it. From this perspective, it is likely that a consistent strengthening or weakening of home currencies over the period might have affected the debate. Sceptics argue that the choice of approach was dictated by the desire to show gains, or at very least to keep losses out of the profit and loss account. This is difficult to evaluate because of the long lead times in generating accounting standards, further complicated by the fact that the temporal approach affects the profit and loss account, whereas the closing rate differences bypass it. Certainly in the UK, a generally declining pound since the start of the 1970s is consistent with its allowing the closing rate when the US favoured the temporal method.

In the USA, the debate has proved a major arena for empirical research. This tends to focus on the periods immediately prior to SFAS 8 and 52, when voluntary accounting choice was allowed in the transitional periods. Griffin (1982) found that companies which made submissions to the FASB over SFAS 8 (temporal) tended to be large, and experienced greater swings in pre-tax earnings due to foreign currency accounting rules than non-respondents. Kelly (1985) found them to have a greater proportion of foreign sales. She also found those making submissions were likely to have high implementation costs. Griffin (1983) examined whether factors relating to managers' and firms' self-interest caused them to make submissions to standard-setters relating to the later SFAS 52 (closing rate) but his results were little better than those from more naive models.

Gray (1984) in a survey analysis of firms during the period of free choice between SFAS 8 and 52, found strong evidence that firms chose income increasing methods or ones which did not reduce their earnings per share. Ayres (1986), assuming the change to SFAS 52 (closing rate) was income increasing for most firms, hypothesized that more management-controlled firms (which she hypothesized were more likely to have management compensation contracts based on reported profits) would have an incentive to voluntarily adopt the closing rate approach early. Also firms with poorer prior performance and closer to contractual debt and dividend constraints would also tend to be early adopters to increase earnings (thus to improve their reported gearing, interest and dividend cover), but larger firms which were potentially more vulnerable to regulatory interference for too-high profits would wish to stick with the (income reducing) temporal approach. Using multivariate statistical techniques, her evidence supported her hypotheses. The basis for such 'contracting cost' research is explored in Chapter 12. Replication of such studies in the UK is needed.

Efficient markets research

What does the stock market think of the currency translation debate – is it viewed as merely a cosmetic change? Much of the evidence is US-based, but it is still instructive to examine it. At the time of the first US (temporal) standard US experience (e.g. Cooper, Fraser and Richards, 1978) was that management acted as though the changed accounting numbers had economic significance. If management did engage in *spurious* hedging of what were in reality only 'cosmetic' changes, this could impose needless economic costs on companies, increasing their riskiness. Early researchers hypothesized no reaction to 'cosmetic' changes and, e.g., Dukes (1978) found no significant market reaction to SFAS 8 in 479 multinationals. Later researchers looked for a negative market reaction to the effects of spurious hedging around the time of SFAS 8 (temporal), and positive reactions to the later SFAS 52 as 'spurious' hedging positions were unwound!

Ziebart and Kim (1987) looked for market reactions in response to each event affecting the likelihood that SFAS 8 would be overturned by a 'closing rate' standard (ultimately SFAS 52) including the early announcement by the standard-setting body of research sponsorship into translation methods, probably taken by the US stock-market as a sign that SFAS 8 would be replaced. Their results were mixed, but they argued that overall their tests showed a negative response to SFAS 8 and a positive one to SFAS 52 as hypothesized. However, tests by Garlicki, Fabozzi and Fonfeder (1987) using a different methodology found no such positive market reaction to events signalling SFAS 52 indicating events. The contradictions illustrate difficulties in specifying the *exact* date that reaction should be expected and also the exact direction in which the market *should* react. For example, although at the date when the exposure draft was published surveys show that managers and the market feel positive towards the change, the market will probably already have impounded the knowledge that the method will be changed, and if the exposure draft were less radical than previously expected, a negative reaction would be observed! It is also extremely difficult for investors or analysts to distinguish between cosmetic and real economic changes, which would require estimates of what would have happened if methods had not been changed. It is questionable whether current disclosure levels permit such estimation. The results are therefore ambiguous as to whether the market did react to changes in approach and precisely what they reacted to.

Analysts' forecast dispersion

A further series of tests in the US examined whether the change from the temporal to the closing rate approach affected investment analysts' published earnings forecasts – it was predicted that SFAS 52 would reduce their variability since closing rate exchange differences bypassed the income statement. Castanias and Griffin (1986) found that during SFAS No. 52's adoption and implementation, the dispersion of such forecasts *increased* and they were revised more often. Chen, Comisky and Mulford (1990) used a control group to eliminate confounding factors and investigated over a longer period. They suggested the earlier result might just have been a 'learning' effect, but their statistical results were not conclusive. Even if there were a reduction in the dispersion of analysts' earnings forecasts, it is not clear the extent to which the market would regard it as substantive or cosmetic, i.e. caused by a mere repositioning of exchange differences outside the profit and loss accounts.

See Chapter 12 for an overall assessment of the importance of such context-based research.

Exercises

11.24 'The foreign currency translation debate raises a number of fundamental conceptual issues including the very nature of a group for reporting purposes and the objectives for which group accounts are prepared. However, any resolution seems to depend as much on political and economic consequences as theoretical analysis.'   Discuss.

11.25 Assess the argument that the closing rate approach to the translation of foreign currency financial statements has supplanted the temporal approach owing to its conceptual superiority.

SUMMARY

*Accounting exposure to currency fluctuations arises from the translation of results of past transactions. SSAP 20 normally requires the translation of **transactions** using the **two transaction** approach, where the transaction is broken down into both purchasing and financing elements.*

*The consolidation of foreign subsidiaries involves three stages; **transaction** translation within individual company statements; **statement** translation into the parent's reporting currency; and **consolidation** of the translated statements. The temporal, closing rate, current/non-current and monetary/non-monetary approaches were discussed for **statement** translation; the closing rate approach and to a lesser extent the temporal approach form the basis of SSAP 20. Under the closing rate approach, either average or year end rates can be used to translate the profit and loss account. The cash flow matrix approach provides an integrating framework for the translation process deducing the **flow statement of exposed items** as a way of showing intuitively how the gain or loss arose and linking it to accounting exposure concepts. The consolidation of cash flow statements was also examined, including FRS 1's rather strange injunction to use the profit and loss rate for its translation.*

SSAP 20's criteria for deciding whether to use closing rate or temporal approaches, the treatment of gains or losses, their disposition to profit and loss or reserves, requirements relating to its cover (hedging) concept for net investments, hyperinflationary economies, and disclosure requirements were discussed and contrasted with international positions. The translation debate was considered: in terms of the conceptual objectives of translation, also in terms of the wider economic and political context.

FURTHER READING

ASC (1983) SSAP 20 – *Foreign Currency Translation*.

ASB (1993) UITF Abstract No 9, *Accounting for Operations in Hyper-inflationary Economies*.

Carsberg, B. (1991) FAS#52 – measuring the performance of foreign operations, in J.H. Stern and D.H. Chew (eds.) *New Developments in International Finance*, Blackwell.

Davies, M., Paterson, R. and Wilson, A. (1992) *UK GAAP* (3rd edn), Chapter 5, Macmillan.

Demirag, I.S. (1987) A Review of the Objectives of Foreign Currency Translation, *The International Journal of Accounting*, Spring 1987, pp. 69–85.

Flower, J. (1991) Foreign currency translation, in C.W. Nobes, and R.H. Parker, (eds.), *Comparative International Accounting* (3rd edn), Chapter 14, Philip Alan, Oxford.

IASC (revised 1993) IAS 21, *The Effects of Changes in Foreign Exchange Rates* .

IASC (1989) IAS 29, *Financial Reporting in Hyperinflationary Economies*.

Nobes, C.W. (1980) A review of the translation debate, *Accounting and Business Research*, Autumn, pp. 421–31.

12

SEGMENTAL REPORTING/UNRESOLVED ISSUES IN CONSOLIDATION

This chapter firstly examines segmental reporting. It then considers the extent of progress in group accounting in the last ten years, unresolved issues and possible future developments. Segmental reporting has become important because of greatly increasing corporate diversification across business sectors and continents in the last quarter of the twentieth century. In business finance, *portfolio theory* has shown how diversification reduces total risk, particularly where combining firms exhibit different but complementary risk characteristics. However, this theory implies that investors can carry out such diversification themselves and that it is unnecessary for companies to do so. Yet in an increasingly complex world with transaction costs, imperfect information and managers eyeing job security, diversification and conglomerate mergers are common. The amount of information available to users decreases as formerly separate results are consumed within consolidated aggregates. Thus it is argued that such groups should provide *dis*-aggregated information to assist prediction and assessment.

Consolidation aggregates the accounts of *legal* entities. Segment reporting *dis*-aggregates consolidated information over *economic* sub-units, called segments. Segments often are not the same as legal entities since, for example, one subsidiary may be involved in a number of lines of business, or a single geographical location may include a number of legally separate subsidiaries. Segmental information is disclosed in addition to consolidated information. In the UK, US, Canada and other developed countries there has been a movement towards requiring the consolidation of *all* controlled undertakings; mandatory segmental reporting has been viewed as *complementary* to this. Indeed the *total* consolidation stance has been based on the existence of segmental reporting standards.

The first requirement for segmental information in the UK came from the Stock Exchange listing agreement in 1965, requiring turnover and profits by line of business, and turnover by geographic segment (Roberts and Gray, 1991, p. 343). Geographical profit rate was required only if it differed from the group average. The 1967 Companies Act extended line of business disclosures to all companies. In the USA, the SEC had required 'line of business' information as early as 1970 – the FASB issued SFAS 14, *Financial Reporting for Segments of a Business Enterprise*, in 1976 considerably expanding US segmental disclosures and even today, exceeding most later pronouncements internationally. IAS 14, *Reporting Financial Information by Segment*, was published by the IASC in 1981.

The UK curiously lagged these developments. SSAP 25, *Segmental Reporting*, was issued in June 1990, finally bringing the UK up to international standards. Prior to this, the only statutory change resulted from the adoption of the EEC 4th Directive, introducing geographical segment turnover disclosure and requiring the audit of minimal segmental disclosures. FRS 3, *Reporting Financial Performance* (1992), requires disclosure and explanation of acquisitions, sales or terminations which have a material impact on each major business segment.

OBJECTIVES OF SEGMENT REPORTING

If consolidation is viewed as analogous to *averaging* (Chapter 4), then segmental reporting can be seen as providing information about *variability* or *risk*, or more precisely about the *heterogeneity* in the consolidated data. Boersema and Van Weelden (1992, p. 13), conclude that the main objectives of segment reporting are to assist in the assessment of *rewards* (profitability, returns and growth rates) and *risks* of component parts of an enterprise. They identify analysts/investors as the main user of segmental information, primarily for *predictive* purposes.

The ASB's draft *Statement of Principles* (ASB 1991) uses the term 'faithful representation' as an aspect of *reliability*. Though it is described in terms of 'transactions and other events' (para. 28), it also would seem to apply to the *entity* reported on, and if this is diverse, *valid description* should recognise such diversity. Solomons, in his *Guidelines of Financial Reporting Standards* (1989, pp. 39–40), in his discussion of faithful representation, identifies four kinds of risk: credit, market, foreign exchange and political – which suggests the need for both line of business and geographical segment information. Gray (1981) has argued that employees may also be interested in segmental information, but on a more detailed level than usually published – however they and creditors will also be interested in how their company/plant fits into overall group strategy.

SSAP 25, *SEGMENTAL REPORTING*

SSAP 25, issued in 1990, followed a consultative paper and an exposure draft, ED 45. The lateness of the UK standard probably indicates preparer resistance, since the ASC mooted segmental reporting as a topic in 1984. Rennie and Emmanuel (1992) examining the change in segmental disclosure over the thirteen years prior to SSAP 25, found no significant change in the level of disclosure for line of business data, though greater consistency with other parts of the annual report. Surprisingly they found some deterioration in geographical segment disclosure, many companies in 1988–9 ceasing to disclose profits, and combining country and continents in defining segments – this 'provides. . . perhaps, an indication of how burdensom SSAP 25 may be perceived to be by British companies'.

SSAP 25 is embedded within the Companies Act 1985 requirements for note disclosures of turnover and profit by classes of business, and for turnover by geographical location. Both allow managerial discretion in segment identification. The Stock Exchange requires a segmental analysis of sales by continent if foreign operations in total exceed 10 per cent of consolidated revenues; if 50 per cent or more of total foreign operations relate to a single continent, a further analysis by country is required; geographical profit disclosure is only required if the ratio of profit to turnover is substantially out of line with the rest of the group.

Scope
The requirements in SSAP 25 *additional* to the Companies Act *only* apply to plc's, parents of plc's, banking and insurance companies or groups, and other 'very large' private companies. The last category do not need to provide the additional disclosures if their parents provide their own disclosures. 'Very large' is defined as more than ten times the size criteria for a medium-sized company discussed in Chapter 2. Smaller entities are encouraged to comply voluntarily.

Following the Act and the EC 4th Directive, SSAP 25 allows *exemption* from providing segmental information, 'where in the opinion of the directors, the disclosure of any information required by this accounting standard would be seriously prejudicial to the interests of the reporting entity. . . The fact that such information has not been disclosed must be stated' (para. 43). Neither SFAS 14 nor IAS 14 allow such an exemption – another example of divergence of EEC law from other international pronouncements. However, information signalling theory (Prodhan and Harris, 1989, p. 468) may suggest firms will be under pressure *not* to use the exemption, to differentiate themselves from poorer performers.

Segment identification

Analyses by classes of business ('a distinguishable component of an entity that provides a separate product or service or a separate group of related products or services') and geographical segments ('a geographical area comprising an individual country or group of countries in which an entity operates, or to which it supplies products or services') is required. Both are to be defined according to the directors' judgement, 'hav[ing] regard to the overall purpose of presenting segmental information and the need of readers of financial statements to be informed if a company carries on operations in different classes of business or in different geographical areas' (para. 8). Directors should review the identification annually, redefining where appropriate. The nature of any changes in basis, with reasons and effects must be disclosed and comparatives restated (para. 39).

Qualitative and quantitative guidance for determining segments are provided in the 'explanatory note' to SSAP 25. They are 'to be taken into account' by directors, as 'no single set of factors is universally applicable, nor any single factor is determinative in all cases'. Therefore all segments meeting the quantitative criteria below may not *necessarily* be separately disclosed, though segments which are both *separate* and *of reportable size* would normally be disclosed.

Qualitative guidance

General criteria – potentially, separate segments exist

> where an entity carries on operations in different classes of business or different geographical areas that:

> (a) earn a return on investment that is out of line with the remainder of the business; or
> (b) are subject to different degrees of risk; or
> (c) have experienced different rates of growth; or
> (d) have different potentials for future development.' (para. 8)

SSAP 25 shies away from mechanical rules, but provides further guidelines for each classification.

Classes of business – directors should take into account the nature of the products or services, their market, their distribution channels, the nature of the production process, the organization structure, and any separate legislative framework relating to a part of the business (para. 12).

Geographical segments – factors relevant include expansionist or restrictive economic climates, stable or unstable political regimes, exchange control regulations and exchange rate fluctuations (para. 15).

Quantitative guidance – 'reportable' segments

Once segments are identified, those 'significant to the entity as a whole' are to be reported. These are normally those which have

> (a) *third party turnover* [of] ten percent or more of the total *third party* turnover of the entity as a whole; or
> (b) segment result, whether *profit* or *loss,* [of] ten percent or more of the combined result of all segments in profit or of all segments in loss, whichever combined result is greater; or
> (c) *net assets* [of] ten percent or more of the total net assets of the entity.

Comparison with the USA and IASC

SFAS 14 and IAS 14 also presume managerially determined segments and suggest that an entity's profit centres are a useful starting point. SFAS 14 contains similar quantitative criteria which refer to *total* not third party turnover. Identified segments meeting the US '10 per cent' criteria *must* be reported unless the only reason a segment *meets* the criteria is because of abnormal conditions, when exclusion *must* be disclosed, and also if a segment *fails to meet* the criteria in a year only because of abnormal conditions it must be included. Unlike SSAP 25, SFAS 14 contains a second test forcing disclosure, requiring that the combined sales of all reportable *industry* segments must amount to at least 75 per cent of total external group sales, otherwise more segments must be identified, up to a maximum of ten for normal purposes. Materiality criteria for geographical segments are different, but similarly comprehensive. Surprisingly Gray and Radebaugh (1984) found that UK multinationals disclosed significantly more geographical segments than their US counterparts, although the amount of information disclosed was less. IAS 14 like SSAP 25, provides only suggestive guidelines, noting that 'some consider it appropriate to provide guidelines on [segment materiality]. . . Such guidelines may be 10% of consolidated revenue, or operating profit or total assets. . . [These] are not the sole factors in identifying segments' (para. 15).

Segment disclosure and measurement

Companies subject to SSAP 25 must disclose turnover, segment result and net assets *both* by class of business and by geographical segment. Significant *associated companies* must also be analysed by segment. If necessary the total of segmental amounts must be *reconciled* to consolidated totals (para. 37) and comparatives given (para. 38).

Turnover

External and inter-segment turnover must be shown separately, analysed by segment (para. 34). Geographical turnover must be analysed by *origin* ('the segment from which the products or services are supplied') and third party turnover by *destination* ('the . . . segment to which the products or services are supplied'), unless there is no material difference, when only the former is required with a note disclosing that fact (para. 18). Intersegment sales are not normally disclosed by destination as this 'normally has little or no value' (para. 19). General statutory exemptions for certain activities from disclosing turnover (e.g. banking) also apply here. The dual analysis of geographical turnover by origin and destination is peculiar to the UK.

Segment result

Profit or loss before tax, minority interests and extraordinary items must be disclosed by segment. Normally the segment result is to be measured *before interest*. However, if interest earning is part of the business (e.g. a bank) or interest income or expense is central to the business (travel or contracting businesses are given as examples) the segmental result is to be measured after interest (para. 36) – in the USA under SFAS 14, segment result *must* always be before interest on the grounds that financing is usually carried out on a group basis.

Latitude is given by SSAP 25 in the treatment of common costs, i.e. costs relating to more than one segment. They are to be 'treated in the way that directors deem most appropriate in pursuance of the objectives of segmental reporting' (para. 23), either allocated to segments or if this is considered misleading, deducted from the total of segmental results. SFAS 14 in the USA specifically excludes the allocation of general corporate expenses and gain or loss on discontinued operations. Davies, Paterson and Wilson (1992, p. 900) give the examples of Standard Chartered Bank plc and Cookson Group plc in the UK which have both interpreted SSAP 25 as allowing directors to include allocated central expenses in the segmental result. There is no requirement in SSAP 25 unlike in its US counterpart to separately disclose unusual or infrequently occurring items.

The allocation problem – it is usually not possible to provide meaningful reported information at a greater level of disaggregation than used internally by the group, otherwise the quality of segmental profits becomes suspect because of *arbitrary allocations* (see Thomas, 1975). Gray (1981, p. 33) comments that such problems particularly arise in vertically integrated firms where there are no intermediate markets for the transferred product (e.g. semi-assembled car chassis) or in horizontally integrated firms where segments exhibit great interdependencies. Published accounts segmental reporting criteria implicitly treat all segments *as if* profit centres, which may not be how management evaluates segments internally, and it could be relatively easy for management to choose 'fair and reasonable' bases for allocation to enhance or mask underlying segment profit information!

One might conclude that for highly *interdependent* groups, segmental reporting is not very useful and the only meaningful information is consolidated information – the aggregate cannot meaningfully be broken down. On the contrary, for groups with heterogeneous activities but with low interdependence, e.g. financial conglomerates, the consolidated 'average' may itself be pretty meaningless and segmental information is essential. This illustrates problems in producing and interpreting general purpose financial statements, illustrating how the complexity of enterprises may not always be adequately represented in such statements.

Example 12.1 – Segment identification and measurement

Consider the following information for The Fudge Group plc for the year ended 31 March 1996 (£m):

	Cutting	Assembly	Retail
Turnover	500	5,000	2,000
Profit before common costs	150	200	600
Net assets	120	120	1,200

Management is concerned that the above results could show the group as too dependent on the Retail segment. In the published segmental report, common costs of £450m are to be allocated to determine segmental profit figures. Possible allocation bases proposed include (i) equally between segments, (ii) by turnover, (iii) by net assets.

Required
(a) Calculate the effects of each of these allocation bases on segmental *profits*,
(b) Assess which segments would be reportable under turnover, net assets and profit bases under SSAP 25's quantitative guidelines. Assume no intersegment trading.

Solution

(a)   **Segmental profit under different common cost allocation bases**

Description	Allocated equally			By turnover			By net assets		
Proportions	$\frac{1}{3}$	$\frac{1}{3}$	$\frac{1}{3}$	$\frac{500}{7,500}$	$\frac{5,000}{7,500}$	$\frac{2,000}{7,500}$	$\frac{120}{1,440}$	$\frac{120}{1,440}$	$\frac{1,200}{1,440}$
Allocated costs	150	150	150	30	300	120	37.5	37.5	375
Reported profits* —		50	450	120	(100)	480	113	162	225

*Reported profits = profit before common costs – allocated costs.

(b) The first thing to note is that the quantitative guidelines are not necessarily conclusive in determining reportable segments. Turnover and net asset criteria are as follows:

Turnover	=	10% × (500 + 5,000 + 2,000)	=	£750
Net assets	=	10% × (120 + 120 + 1,200)	=	£144

Under the *turnover* criterion assembly and retail would be potentially reportable. Under the *net assets* criterion only retail would be reportable.

Consider now the *profit* criterion. Which segments would be reportable depends on the cost allocation basis. The criterion is whether the absolute size of the segment result is 10% or more of the larger of the aggregated result of all segments in profit, or all in loss. If the equal weighting or net assets employed bases are used, all segments are in profit so the criterion becomes

Profit criterion under equal weighting	=	10% × (0 + 50 + 450)	=	£50
Profit criterion under net assets basis	=	10% × (113 + 162 + 225)	=	£50

Assembly (barely) and retail would be reported under profit under equal weighting, but all would be reportable under profit on the net assets cost allocation basis.

Under profit on the turnover cost allocation basis there is a loss-making segment, so it is necessary to calculate the results separately of profit and loss making segments:

Profit making segments (turnover basis)	= 10% × (120 + 480)	= £60m
Loss making segments (turnover basis)	= 10% × (100)	= £10m

The *greater* of these in absolute value is £60m. Therefore all three would be candidates for disclosure. Directors would choose equal weighting if they wanted no further disclosure. However, they are also allowed to take into account other (mysterious or apparent!) factors to determine what is actually reportable.

Net assets

SSAP 25 defines these as normally being *non-interest bearing* operating assets less *non-interest bearing* operating liabilities. If the alternative 'after interest' definition of segment result were used above, net assets must be defined consistently and corresponding interest bearing operating assets and liabilities included (para. 24). *Joint* operating assets are to be allocated, but not assets and liabilities which are not used in the operations of any segment. Intersegment balances should not be included unless the interest on them is included in the segment result (para. 26).

SSAP 25's segmental net assets are *net* of non-interest bearing liabilities (e.g. trade creditors) whereas SFAS 14 in the USA, and IAS 14 internationally, define segmental assets in a gross sense without deducting liabilities. SSAP 25 can be viewed either as a refinement or an increase in flexibility!

Associated company disclosures

SSAP 25 requires the inclusion of 'significant' associated companies if *in total* they comprise at least 20 per cent of the total result or of total net assets of the reporting entity (para. 27). They are to be analysed segmentally, showing (para. 26);

(a) share of profits or losses before tax, minority interests and extraordinary items.
(b) share of net assets (including goodwill not written off), stated where possible using fair values at acquisition of each associate.

The standard recognizes such information might not be obtainable since one cannot force an associate to carry out a fair value exercise.

Areas omitted from SSAP 25

SFAS 14 in the USA requires disclosure of *unusual items* and *depreciation* in segmental income statements, and also *capital expenditure*. SFAS 14 and IAS 14 also require, for example, the *basis of inter-segment pricing*, which was present in the exposure draft preceding SSAP 25, but dropped from the standard – a serious omission. *Financial Reporting 1992/3* (p. 269) shows that 9 per cent of large listed companies disclose capital investment by class of business and 5 per cent by geographical segment, and about half of large listed companies disclose employees by class of business and geographical segment. OECD and UN recommendations are not discussed here – see Radebaugh (1987).

Acquisitions and disposals
FRS 3, *Reporting Financial Performance*, issued in October 1992, extends SSAP 25 commenting

> It is important . . . that the effects of changes on material components of the business should be highlighted. To assist in this objective, if an acquisition, a sale or a termination has a material impact on a major business segment the FRS requires that this impact should be disclosed and explained

(para. 53)

Example 12.2 – SSAP 25's reporting requirements

Assume in Example 12.1 that common costs are allocated on a *net assets* basis for the profit quantitative criterion. Now included in the above figures are £500m sales from assembly to retail segments with an intra-group profit of £50m. The goods are still held in stock by retail segment at the year end. Not included in the above costs are general corporate expenses of £250m and general corporate assets of £200m, which the group directors decide are not to be allocated to segments, together with group interest of £25m.

Required

Recalculate which segments would be potentially reportable under the turnover, net assets and profit quantitative guidelines of SSAP 25 (using the net asset cost allocation basis). Draft a class of business segmental report complying with SSAP 25, based on the information given. Ignore tax.

Solution

The turnover and net asset quantitative guidelines need to be adjusted for the additional information, the former to remove inter-segment sales, as the criterion is based on *third party* turnover, and the latter by adding corporate assets to determine 'total net assets of the entity', but after reducing them to group costs. Turnover and net asset guidelines are:

$$\text{Turnover} = 10\% \times (500 + 5{,}000 + 2{,}000 - 500) = £700$$
$$\text{Net assets} = 10\% \times (120 + 120 + 1{,}200 + 200 - 50) = £159$$

Segmental profits under the net asset cost allocation approach (above) were £113m (cutting), £162 (assembly), and £225m (retail). Adjusting assembly for unrealized intragroup profits on stocks, it becomes £112 (= 162 – 50). SSAP 25 does *not* seem to require corporate expenses to be included in the profit materiality criterion since it refers to 'all *segments* in profit or . . . loss' and such expenses are not part of any segment, but it *does* seem to require general corporate assets to be included in the net assets criterion since it refers to 'total net assets of the entity'. All segments are in profit so the criterion is as follows, and all segments are reportable under the *profits* basis.

$$\text{Profits on net asset basis} = 10\% \times (113 + 112 + 225) = £45$$

Segment Report – Fudge Group, Year ended 31 March 1996

Classes of business	Cutting	Assembly	Retail	Group
Turnover				
Total sales	500	5,000	2,000	7,500
Inter-segment sales	—	(500)	—	(500)
External sales	500	4,500	2,000	7,000
Profit before tax				
Segment profit	113	112 *	225	450
General corporate expenses				(250)
Net interest				(25)
Group profit before tax				175
Net assets				
Segment net assets	120	120	1,150**	1,390
General corporate assets				200
Group net assets				1,590

Note   * 162 – 50   ** 1,200 – 50

ISSUES IN SEGMENTAL REPORTING

Costs and benefits

Efficient markets research suggests investors are sophisticated and that greater breakdowns of data can reduce risk and aid accurate pricing (see Dyckman and Morse, 1986), however, if the quantity of information is too great, preparation costs, potential information overload and loss of competitive confidentiality will exceed benefits. This trade-off is difficult to evaluate since beneficiaries may include prospective investors and governmental agencies, whereas the costs may be borne largely by the company and current shareholders. Benston (1984) found that regulators tended to underestimate preparation costs. Gray and Roberts (1989) in a survey of 116 UK multinationals, found that by far the main 'cost' factor in inhibiting further voluntary disclosure was loss of competitive advantage. This caused strong preparer resistance to narrowing the segment definition, particularly for line of business, and in reporting voluntarily, quantitative segmental forecasts. Others comment that competitors already know more than is disclosed in published segmental reports (Backer and McFarland, 1968). Contracting cost theory explains voluntary segmental disclosure to be part of an effective *monitoring package* which enables parties to the firm to benefit from the economic synergy caused by increased trust (see for example Watts, 1992).

Segment identification

Should segment identification be managerially determined or determined according to externally verifiable criteria? The former may be consistent with actual structures and strategy but obscures comparability *between* firms. The latter, e.g. by using the Standard Industrial Classification (SIC), facilitates such cross-sectional comparisons and may be less manipulable, yet bear no relationship to organizational structure. Also, the SIC is not designed for this purpose. Emmanuel and Gray (1980) suggested that the firm's organizational structure could first be matched to a SIC classification and management should only be able to depart from this if they can demonstrate it is inappropriate or to disaggregate further. This proposal tries to ensure greater cross-sectional comparability whilst allowing disclosures to be reasonably consistent with actual organizational structures. An initial UK consultative paper suggested SIC codes as a starting point.

Emmanuel and Garrod (1987, 1992, p. 34) consider cross-sectional comparability a quest for the 'Holy Grail' – that a management structure based segment report is probably the most useful that can be hoped for. Hussain and Skerratt (1992) point out that *monitoring of management* and the *prediction of enterprise performance* do not necessarily result in identical segment definition. They note that analyst firms are often organized on an industry basis of expertise. If segments are reported on, e.g., a management structure basis, this may conflict with analyst expertise, and could reduce the accuracy of analysts' forecasts. Boersma and Van Weelden (1992) suggest setting up analyst or industry groups to develop an agreed preparer/user stance on the standardization of line of business segment definition. They and Emmanuel and Garrod (1992, p. 32) both criticize the ineffectiveness of quantitative segment identification criteria in preventing the combining of non-homogeneous segments into less informative larger segments.

Segmental disclosure and measurement

Cash flow information

The ASB Statement, *Operating and Financial Review*, issued in 1993, recommends that 'where segmental cash flows are significantly out of line with segmental profits, this should be indicated and explained' (para. 31). This is a voluntary disclosure and the disclosure of segmental cash flow statements has not been widely suggested presumably because group financing is often planned centrally. Bagby and Kintzele (1987, p. 52) note proposed SEC regulations in the USA requiring management to discuss cash flow, liquidity and results of operations by identifiable business segment 'met with significant resistance'.

Examples

Thorn EMI plc's segmental information note illustrates SSAP25's features (comparatives are omitted here but shown in the original accounts) – Figure 12.1. It is possible to analyse segmental returns on net assets, into profit margin ratios and segment asset turnovers either for lines-of-business or geographically. It may be difficult to compare these with other multinational groups' segments since there is no guarantee their managerial defined segments will be defined in the same way.

A few companies integrate class of business and geographical disclosures into a *matrix* format, suggested but not carried forward from ASC's early consultative paper. Fig. 12.2 shows a 1994 matrix disclosure of turnover by The BOC Group plc (comparatives are also not shown here). This makes it possible to assess line-of-business turnover *within* each geographical segment, e.g. the Health Care segment across the different continents, or vice versa. Emmanuel and Garrod (1992, pp. 34–5) suggest that what determines the usefulness of the matrix approach is whether or not an enterprise is actually organized in that way.

1. Segmental analyses — 1994

	Turnover	Operating profit	Operating assets	Average employees
	£m	£m	£m	
By class of business				
Music	1,760.5	246.1	338.4	8,234
Rental	1,511.6	130.2	752.3	20,347
HMV	403.9	6.1	58.9	2,712
Principal businesses	3,676.0	382.4	1,149.6	31,293
TSE	407.7	(11.6)	128.2	7,858
Corporate	–	–	–	135
Continuing operations	4,083.7	370.8	1,277.8	39,286
Discontinued operations	208.4	11.7	(3.1)	2,137
	4,292.1	382.5	1,274.7	41,423
By origin:				
United Kingdom	1,562.2	97.6	455.0	21,238
Rest of Europe	1,153.0	138.9	106.1	6,186
North America	1,237.3	96.8	575.9	11,250
Asia Pacific	252.8	41.5	122.3	2,067
Other	86.8	7.7	15.4	682
	4,292.1	382.5	1,274.7	41,423
By destination:				
United Kingdom	**1,436.3**			
Rest of Europe	**1,182.8**			
North America	**1,257.8**			
Asia Pacific	**302.2**			
Other	113.0			
	4,292.1			

The reconciliation of operating assets to net assets is as follows:

	1994
	£m
Operating assets	**1,274.7**
Tax and dividends payable	**(134.1)**
Capital employed	**1,140.6**
Net borrowings	**(403.4)**
Net assets	**737.2**

Figure 12.1 – Segmental analysis – Thorn EMI

1. **Segmental information** 1) Turnover analysis	Gases and Related Products £ million	Health Care £ million	Vacuum Technology and Distribution Services £ million	Total by origin £ million	Total by destination £ million
1994					
Europe[1]	546.3	174.9	282.9	1 004.1	956.7
Africa	301.6	–	–	301.6	309.7
Americas[2]	691.9	332.3	115.2	1139.4	1 106.5
Asia/Pacific	940.1	60.7	37.2	1 038.0	1 110.2
Turnover[3]	2 479.9	567.9	435.3	3 483.1	3 483.1

[1] The UK turnover and operating profit were £759.4 million (1993: £692.1 million) and £95.3 million (1993: £125.0 million) respectively.

[2] The US turnover and operating profit were £1 053.3 million (1993: £1 016.0 million) and £33.5 million (1993: £89.5 million) respectively.

[3] Gases and Related Products includes Group share of related undertakings' turnover of £190.8 million (1993: 168.0 million).

Figure 12.2 – Matrix information – The BOC Group

USEFULNESS OF SEGMENTAL INFORMATION

What follows is illustrative rather than exhaustive – a more detailed discussion of empirical research of all types in this area is found in Chapter 5 of Emmanuel and Garrod (1992).

Survey based research

Attitude surveys generally support segmental disclosure, but highlight management's concern about increased disclosure (e.g. Backer and Macfarland, 1968) though a 1974 survey by the FASB in the USA found over 80 per cent of executives questioned recognised that such disclosures were useful to sophisticated users. Emmanuel and Garrod (1987) conducted interviews with investment analysts and senior preparers of financial statements in 1985. Analysts found segmental information useful, but expressed concerns over proper segment identification, citing inconsistencies with the rest of the annual report and wishing more segments to be identified, whilst recognizing cost constraints on preparers. Preparers used diverse but sensible identification methods but classifications were not reappraised regularly. Formal materiality criteria were not regularly used. Again the majority believed further disaggregation could place their companies at a competitive disadvantage. A minority objected to the matrix approach since it gave a misleading impression of how they were organized.

Gray and Roberts (1989) extended these findings in a postal survey in 1984–5 of 212 British multinationals with follow-up interviews. This confirmed the perceived highest cost factor of additional disclosure was loss of competitive advantage – greater than costs of data collection, processing and auditing. Quantitative forecasts and narrowing of segment definition were perceived as highest 'cost'. Public relations considerations were found to be the major factor influencing voluntary disclosure, above proposals by the UK accounting profession. Proposals by academics ranked 11th!

Laboratory studies

Emmanuel, Garrod and Frost (1989) (see Emmanuel and Garrod, 1992) gave disguised financial statements of a UK multinational to 15 analysts who were asked to forecast the following year's profit. Starting with merely consolidated data, analysts were given segmental information in five stages, concluding with matrix disclosure. For a significant minority, forecasts improved, mainly when the legal minimum disclosures were given and later with matrix information. The authors recognized the tentative nature of their conclusions.

Predictive ability studies

Profits

A number of studies, e.g. Kinney (1971) and Collins (1976) in the USA, and Emmanuel and Pick (1980) used simple prediction models to predict consolidated profits from line-of-business segmental information, finding that whilst segmental sales were useful, incremental information about segmental earnings did not appreciably increase predictive performance. Only simple models were used.

Balakrishnan, Harris and Sen (1990) examined the usefulness of US *geographical* segmental disclosures to predict next period's consolidated sales and income, compared with predictions based on consolidated data. Both sets of forecasts were adjusted for expected exchange rate changes and in some predictions for expected economic growth. The results for forecasting *sales* were ambiguous. The improvement in predicting profits was not significant unless they adjusted for (future) *actual* exchange rates and growth rather than *estimated* rates and growth. The study did not examine the *incremental* forecasting improvement of segmental profit over segmental sales.

Because of the ambiguity of these empirical findings, much research effort has been devoted to isolating the *particular* conditions under which segmental information may be useful. Silhan (1982,1983) computer-simulated notional conglomerates from independent single product firm data to overcome the allocation problem in segmental reported income. He also found that incremental segmental *profit* data did not improve forecasts. In a later study, Silhan (1984) found some forecast improvement in smaller simulated conglomerates. Garrod and Emmanuel (1988) tried to isolate conceptually certain profiles of companies for which segmental analysis would improve predictions, but their results are inconclusive.

Another strand is the use of mathematical analysis to determine conditions under which disaggregation is helpful. For example, Barnea and Lakonishok (1980) demonstrated that correlations within segmental data affect forecasting accuracy, and the use of allocation procedures reduce accuracy. Hopwood, Newbold and Silhan (1982) confirmed the intuition that disaggregated data only possessed incremental information content if each segment's profit series were generated by a different process, or when some segments led or lagged others, similar to seasonal effects – conditions lacking in Silhan's simulated data. Ang (1979) also isolated conditions where segmental forecasts may not outperform aggregate ones. See also the earlier discussion of Hussain and Skerratt (1992) who also deduce that segmental information is more useful the less each segment reflects the industry norm.

Analysts' forecasts

Baldwin (1984) assessed whether there was an increase in the accuracy in actual investment analysts' published forecasts when line-of-business disclosures were first mandated in the USA in 1970. He found that whilst analysts' forecasting improved generally over the period, the most significant improvement was for firms which *newly* produced segmental reports, indicating mandatory segmental reporting did help analysts – see also Emmanuel and Garrod (1992), Chapter 5.

Market reaction studies

Line of business disclosures

The main hypothesis tested has been that the publication of segmental information reduces the market's perception of risk. Kochanek (1974) found that voluntary disclosures reduced firms' total share price variability. However, Horowitz and Kolodny (1977) found no reduction in market (systematic) risk nor of any price reaction to firms disclosing *mandatory* segmental information for the first time in 1971. However, Collins and Simmonds (1979) using different methodology concluded that market risk *was* reduced by such disclosures. Dhaliwal, Spicer and Vickrey (1979) found a reduction in the cost of equity capital for new disclosers. Swaminathan (1991), with more sophisticated methodology than earlier studies, re-examined the market effects of mandatory disclosures in 1971, finding incremental market effects in new disclosers compared with a control group which already disclosed segmental information voluntarily; these effects were positively correlated with the numbers of segments disclosed.

Tse (1989) examined *why* class of business data is helpful. Adding a segmentally determined 'growth' variable to an established pricing model which linked share price, earnings and risk, he found that class of business data possessed incremental information content over primary industry data alone. Horowitz (1989) pointed out that the study did not examine the more interesting question of whether earnings had information content over sales.

Geographical disclosures

Prodhan (1986) examined the effects in 1977 in the UK of the voluntary first reporting of *geographical* segment information on firms' stock market *betas*. He found that first disclosure caused a significant change in beta compared to the control group of ongoing disclosers, though the sample he used was very small. Prodhan and Harris (1989) carried out a similar but larger study on 82 US companies around the exhaustively mined 'golden date' in 1971. They found betas reduced for first disclosers but not for the control group, suggesting segmental reporting effects.

Exercises

12.1 The following segmental information (in millions of pounds) is available for the Coverup Group plc for the year ended 31 March 1996 (£m):

	Toys	Chemicals	Bookshops
Turnover	3,200	800	8,000
Profit before common costs	400	200	1,000
Net assets	400	2,000	3,600

Management wishes to minimize segmental disclosure, and in order to do this, is examining the effects of allocating common costs of £750m in different ways.

Required
(a) Calculate the effects of allocating common costs (i) equally between segments, (ii) by turnover, and (iii) by net assets, on reported segmental profits.
(b) Assess which segments underturnover, net assets and profits bases would be reportable under SSAP 25's quantitative guidelines. Assume no inter-segment trading.

12.2 Assume in 12.1 that common costs are allocated on a *turnover* basis when considering the profit criterion. In addition, there are headquarters costs of £100m and headquarters assets of £1,100m which are to be included but not allocated between segments. Included in the above figures is £1,000m of sales of toy-books from the Bookshop segment to the Toy segment. The profit to Bookshops of such a sale was £100m. The goods are still held in stock by Toys at the year end. Group interest expense for the period was £150m.

Required
Draft a class of business segmental report as far as possible complying with SSAP 25, based on the information given. Ignore tax.

12.3 Assess the extent to which segmental reports increase the information content of the consolidated financial reporting package. Use the examples in Figures 12.1 and 12.2 for illustrative purposes.

12.4 What are the likely economic consequences of segmental reporting (a) on individual groups of companies, (b) from a market or societal point of view? Are there likely to be conflicts between these perspectives?

12.5 Compare and contrast the nature of information disclosed by
   (a) consolidated financial statements
   (b) parent company financial statements
   (c) segmental reporting

12.6 The Automotive Group has the following structure across industries and countries :

	GERMANY	FRANCE	AUSTRALIA
Heavy engineering – car bodies	X		X
Car assembly	X	X	
Motoring retail discount shops	X		X

In Germany, transfers from 'heavy engineering' to 'car assembly' are at cost plus 10%, whereas transfers to the rest of the group are at cost plus 25%. There is no external market for unassembled car chassis. German subsidiaries are heavily loan financed and have significant short-term financing. Australian subsidiaries are 51% owned and equity financed. In France, the discount shops also do car repair work. Group directors are proposing to disclose two segments geographically, Europe and the Rest of the World, and three 'line of business' segments.

Required
Discuss with the directors of the group the implications of SSAP 25 for the reported segmental disclosures of the Automotive Group. Also discuss with them the pros and cons of using matrix disclosures for the group and their shareholders.

OPERATING AND FINANCIAL REVIEW

The ASB Statement, *Operating and Financial Review* (1993), prompted by issues raised by the Cadbury Committee on corporate governance, is a statement of best practice. Its main contribution is to recommend *narrative commentary* on reported figures and strategy – specifically group accounting aspects include commentary on the operating performance of the various business units (para. 19), segmental cash flows which are significantly out of line with segmental profits (para. 31), the principal risks and uncertainties in the main lines of business (para. 12), the overall level of capital expenditure of the major business segments and geographical areas (para. 14), the management of exchange rate risk (para. 26), restrictions on the ability to transfer funds from one part of the group to meet another's obligations, where these form or forseeaably could form a significant restraint on the group, e.g. exchange controls (para. 34), strengths and resources of the business *not* included in the balance sheet, e.g. brands and intangibles (para. 37), and in the case of material acquisitions, the extent to which the expectations at the time of acquisition have been realized, including any unusual effects of seasonal businesses acquired (para. 10). How far companies will be 'shamed' or 'encouraged' by the market into following 'best practice' is presently unknown.

IMPACT OF CONCEPTUAL FRAMEWORKS

The impact of professional conceptual frameworks/statements of principles has started to really affect UK group accounting pronouncements since about 1989 when the IASC issued its *Framework for the Preparation of Financial Statements*, though in the USA sections of a conceptual framework were published by the FASB between 1978 and 1985. Between 1991 and 1994 the ASB has issued discussion drafts of its own *Statement of Principles* ('*Statement*'). Their impact on the ASB's group accounting pronouncements is now examined.

Potentially the most directly relevant conceptual framework area for group accounting is the definition of the reporting entity, but it is here that internationally most conceptual frameworks are weak. The ASB's Discussion Draft *Statement of Principles Chapter 7 – The Reporting Entity* (1994) is the most advanced in addressing group accounting issues *per se* – the nature of a group, criteria for consolidation, the status, purpose and limitations of consolidated financial statements and the definition and application of 'control' and 'significant influence' within such statements. Many of these aspects have been discussed in earlier chapters. The ambiguity of its discussion of the nature of the reporting entity under acquisition and merger accounting was discussed in Chapter 3.

Particularly controversial is the draft *Statement's* discussion of associates and joint ventures, in which there is a certain equating of the relationships in terms of 'significant influence' and 'participation as a partner in the business', and the deducing of the equity approach for both. For joint ventures the *Statement* distinguishes what it sees as the correct characterization, joint control over the investee as a whole, from an incorrect one, individual control over a proportion of the investee's net assets. This is an interesting conceptual distinction and the ball is now in IASC's court to further justify its preferred option of proportional consolidation for jointly controlled entities (Chapter 4). However, other factors may be relevant, and the empirical study by Whittred and Zimmer (1994) discussed in Chapter 4 claims, in the absence of regulation, the optimal choice between the use of the equity approach or proportional consolidation would depend on the nature of a group's borrowing agreements.

Other 'conceptual framework' influences on the ASB's group accounting standards can be seen in the centrality of substance over form, where considerable advances in group accounting have been made – in the definition of a merger (FRS 6), quasi-subsidiaries (FRS 5), distinctions between equity and non-equity elements of minority interests, and liabilities (FRS 4), and in proposed definitions of strategic alliances (in the Discussion Draft, *Associates and Joint Ventures*). There has been a clear change in emphasis, basing definitions on 'substance' criteria, backed up by clear anti-avoidance criteria and an increasing use of 'rebuttable presumptions'. This can be observed when comparing UK standards say with earlier UK and US standards in the same area. How effective this will be in terms of enforceability is still not clear.

The definition of 'liabilities' (para. 24) in the draft *Statement of Principles* is noticeably used by the ASB to restrict the making of provisions to situations where there is obligation, or demonstrable or irrevocable commitment, prohibiting provisions being made purely on the basis of management intention (consistent also with the IASC's *Framework*). Examples include reorganization provisions at acquisition (FRS 7) and provisions for sale and terminations (FRS 3). This has been criticized by those who dislike the ASB's 'narrow' focus on a balance sheet based approach, and prefer a more matching-based approach (e.g. Paterson, 1990).

The increased prominence given to reporting total recognized gains and losses in the draft *Statement of Principles* has upgraded the reporting of closing rate exchange differences, obtaining a similar status in FRS 3's illustrative example to fixed asset revaluation gains. It also highlights the anomaly of the immediate write-off of goodwill which is specifically *not* seen as a recognized 'loss'. Highly significant also is the ASB's decision that gains and losses once reported in this statement cannot be reported again in the consolidated profit and loss account. Gains and losses on disposals of fixed assets and foreign subsidiaries are thus based on carrying values *including* the effects of revaluations and closing rate translation gains and losses unlike US and much international practice (see Chapter 11).

However, there are clear gaps and omissions. The accounting implications of relationships between majority and minority interests are not discussed at all – there is no discussion of consolidation concepts in any conceptual frameworks worldwide, nor of the extent to which such concepts should influence the treatment of consolidation adjustments (Chapters 4 and 6). Some aspects are implicitly dealt with only piecemeal in other standards (e.g. FRS 2). Issues raised by the conflicting characterizations of the group as a reporting entity in the foreign currency translation debate also are not explored, nor any basis for resolution given (Chapter 11). The reporting of consolidated equity and its relationship to potentially distributable profits, discussed below, is also not examined. Further, consistency with 'conceptual frameworks' is not always sufficient – the ASB Discussion Paper, *Goodwill and Other Intangibles*, deduces that the immediate write-off of goodwill is contrary to its draft *Statement of Principles*, but it is interesting that this does not *per se* rule it out as a possible future requirement (Chapter 5).

CONSOLIDATED EQUITY AND DISTRIBUTABLE PROFITS

Extremely large discretionary write-offs such as those resulting from the immediate write-off of goodwill, exchange differences under the closing rate approach, and progressive cancellation under merger accounting affect consolidated reserves but not individual company reserves. Because management has discretion over which reserve to use, interpretation of consolidated reserves and comparisons between groups become almost meaningless. Statutory restrictions on uses of specific consolidated reserves like the prohibition for using consolidated revaluation reserves for the immediate write-off of goodwill, pale into insignificance in comparison. Given that consolidated reserves do not show distributable reserves, it is difficult to see why the revaluation reserve should be singled out. It is straightforward to use the share premium account with the court's permission. Are creditors really protected by this restriction?

The ASB has focused on greater disclosure of movements in reserves as a whole – the statement of total recognized gains and losses, and the reconciliation of movements in shareholders funds. The statutory requirement to show movements on individual reserves is merely a note disclosure. Using a separate write-off reserve for the immediate write-off of goodwill (Chapter 5), and a separate reserve for closing rate exchange differences as in the USA could minimize the 'damage' caused by the arbitrary choice of reserves used for such matters, discussed above. Hendricksen's (1982, pp. 464–468) conceptual difficulties in finding an unambiguous meaning for the elements of an individual company's equity are almost trivial in comparison to the issues discussed above. Rosenfield (Rosenfield and Rubin, 1986) proposes that consolidated equity including minority interests should be disclosed as a single total with distribution rights and restrictions disclosed as notes.

Morris (1991, p. 19) makes clear that in the UK 'the statutory definition of distributable profits only applies to individual companies and not to groups. . . [and] the distinction between realised and unrealised profits [does] not apply to consolidated accounts'. However, a common assumption is made that consolidated reserves could or should show *potential* distributability of the parent's funds. For example Campbell and Patient (1985, p. 36) suggest that 'the consolidated realised reserve [could] give an approximate indication of the potential distribution . . . if all the subsidiaries were to pay up their realised profits by way of dividends to the holding company'. To what extent is such a viewpoint tenable?

Consolidated reserves or income may not necessarily be a good predictor of parent distributable profits since, for example, constraints on remittances particularly between group companies such as from foreign subsidiaries only have to be voluntarily disclosed in the UK (see *Operating and Financial Review*), criteria for recognizing income by the parent, e.g. on intra-group distributions, are different from those used in consolidated statements (Chapter 6), and certain group charges such as for goodwill and foreign financial statement translation gains do not directly affect the parent's income.

No empirical evidence is available on whether investors or creditors base estimates of potential or minimum distributable profits on consolidated reserves, or whether they would do if changes made them more useful. It is likely that users estimate the parent's distributable profits or minimum distributable profits from other sources. Indeed FRS 3's 'information set' philosophy and its emphasis on total reserve movement disclosures suggests this might well be so. Finance theory demonstrates no link between distribution policy and consolidated profits and reserves, though it is possible that legal restrictions on 'distributable profits' might provide some lower end creditor protection – see Morris (1991).

PRICE-LEVEL ACCOUNTING AND CONSOLIDATION

This book focuses on historical cost accounting. In two areas current cost accounting may reduce the 'heat' generated by differences between group accounting alternatives. Ketz (1984) argues that the main problem in accounting for business combinations is asset valuation. He shows that under price-level accounting alternatives for acquisition and merger accounting, differences caused by fair values at acquisition would disappear. The effects of the different cancellation approaches would remain. The elimination of unrealized intra-group profits would be based on current costs, and in a current cost system the current operating profit element of the selling company and the holding gains of the receiving company would be eliminated, the latter to be adjusted to holding gains to the *group* on those goods. Minority interests would include operating profits and holding gains.

The foreign currency translation debate would be greatly simplified because the temporal approach would give the same result as the closing rate approach. Indeed it has been suggested that use of the closing rate approach under historical cost is a crude attempt to 'adjust' for price-level changes. Under current purchasing power accounting, the choice is whether to restate for the subsidiary's local inflation and then translate at the closing rate (restate–translate), or to translate balances at the historical rate and then restate for the parent's home country inflation (translate–restate). Nobes (1986b, pp. 34–35) comments that supporters of the former argue it is better for comparisons of performance, whereas he argues the latter is backed by sounder arguments from an accounting theory point of view, since as generally used, CPP is a historical cost based system. The debate is somewhat analogous to the temporal/closing rate debate and is not examined further here.

IMPACT OF EMPIRICAL RESEARCH

The ASB has recently been criticized on the grounds that there is now too much regulation – that the detailed prescriptive nature of accounting standards overrides the use of judgement and limits legitimate accounting choice. A powerful general critique of a too introspective development of accounting theory and of over-regulation, has come from developments in neoclassical economics. Their main impact has been in efficient markets research and in research into the impact of contracting costs on accounting.

Solomons (1986, pp. 202–203) provides a good summary of empirical conclusions of *efficient markets research*, such as its findings of non-reaction to 'cosmetic' changes, and the fact that the 'market' can disentangle alternatives provided enough information is disclosed. Efficient markets research in a number of group accounting areas has been examined in this book, the impact of pooling (merger) versus purchase (acquisition) accounting (Chapter 3), choice of foreign currency translation approach (Chapter 11), the information content of cash flows (Chapter 9), segmental reporting (Chapter 12) and the full consolidation of all subsidiaries (Chapter 4). Generally the evidence has been consistent with Solomons' summary, but in some cases interpretation is less clear. Solomons also summarises clearly important arguments showing why market reaction in itself is not a sufficient basis for setting accounting standards.

Contracting cost research examines the way accounting numbers are widely used through their being written into contracts – e.g. management compensation contracts based on, say, profits, between shareholders and management, or debt covenant restrictions based on, for example, gearing or interest cover, written into debt contracts between creditors and the group. Specific accounting methods are not prescribed down to the last detail since this would be too expensive, and often Generally Accepted Accounting Principles are used as the basis.

The theory suggests that this allows firms to choose particular accounting methods which are optimal in reducing contracting costs and hence maximising firm value, *ex ante* contracting – empirical studies of *ex ante* contracting reviewed earlier include whether the first introduction of consolidation was a way of minimizing debt contracting costs (Chapter 2), and whether the choice of equity accounting or proportional consolidation for joint ventures and the choice to exclude subsidiaries from consolidation have a similar cost-reducing rationale (Chapter 4).

The downside of the contracting use of accounting is that, if given the opportunity, management can change accounting methods to their own advantage after the contracts are in place (*ex-post* opportunism) – examined earlier in this regard were the choice between acquisition and merger accounting (Chapter 3), the decision whether or not to put brand valuations on the balance sheet (Chapter 5, though this also has *ex ante* contracting elements, e.g. the minimizing of Stock Market transaction costs) and the choice of foreign currency translation approach (Chapter 11). Also the theory deduces that managements are likely to make submissions to (or 'lobby') standard-setting bodies on exposure drafts and discussion papers to represent their own interests if benefits to them exceed the costs (e.g. over foreign currency translation alternatives (Chapter 11)). Watts and Zimmerman (1990) and Watts (1992) are good sources for this area.

The theory goes on to examine the role of the market in determining the optimal use of accounting methods. Standard-setting bodies potentially restrict the choice of alternatives and so may prevent a necessary variety in accounting methods to allow market completeness. In addition, standard-setting bodies may impose additional methods that the market itself would regard as too costly, since regulators do not have to bear the 'costs'. Empirical studies looking for positive or negative market reactions to the introduction of *mandatory* segment reporting could be viewed in this light (Chapter 12). However, even within such a market-driven framework, some regulation may have a role to play – for example, in devising and enforcing centralized 'quality standards' as a 'cheap cost' way of reducing overall contracting costs, rather than firms having to invent methods from scratch each time.

Others argue that this view of the role of regulation is too limited and that, on the contrary, regulation is needed to police and regulate market failures, and also to restrain the untrammelled operation of the market within wider social structures and objectives. There are conceptual difficulties in demonstrating that such intervention can result in unambiguous improvements to social welfare, but there are equally conceptual difficulties in demonstrating how far an idealized market solution can be expected to 'work' under real-life assumptions (see for example Wolk, Francis and Tierney (1989, pp. 80–90). At the other extreme, Gerboth (1973) suggests a 'muddling through' approach for standard-setting – of step-by-step experimentation, making small changes at the margin, observing their impact, then taking the next small step and seeing how the dust settles. He suggests this approach overcomes the need for such comprehensive and all-inclusive theories.

The main positive impact of the contracting cost framework is to enrich our understanding of how the diversity of accounting methods may have a sophisticated economic rationale, and also to provide an explanation of possible underlying factors. Also it is an antidote to the unquestioning assumption that all regulation and all accounting 'developments' are automatically a good thing. However, its assumptions about self-interest, the extreme faith of some of its supporters in the benign operation of the market, and the extent to which empirical findings 'prove' the theory, are strongly challenged by others, who also point to the role of accounting research in educating the market, and generally reflect more aspirational dimensions of accounting (e.g. Solomons, 1986; Whittington, 1987; Sterling, 1990).

What *is* certain is that the ASB has made financial accounting *exciting* once again. It is difficult to determine unambiguously whether the ASB's response to demands for greater coherence, by limiting alternatives through trying to ground its standards within fundamental principles, is consistent with free market functioning. It could be viewed as a response to the increasing complexity of the economic environment with its financial engineering of, for example, 'designer' financial instruments and entities. An alternative view is that such limitation of alternatives in its 'long' standards is preventing the free operation of the market. Yet another view is that the increasingly prescriptive nature of the standards is the result of market failure to 'self-police' itself and of social constraints on untrammelled market operations; the ASB needed to 'crack down' on the poor track record of accountants and auditors in following 'judgement' against expediency. Case interesting but unproven. (Privately, the author thinks that the ASB is doing a good job.)

INTERNATIONAL HARMONIZATION AND DEVELOPMENTS

The UK finds itself at the confluence of continental European and Anglo-Saxon accounting traditions. This causes some interesting twists and turns in UK standards. For example, the potential conflict over consolidation criteria between the US position of the consolidation of all subsidiaries and the mandatory European exclusion of too dissimilar activities has been resolved by embracing the mandatory exclusion and then emasculating it effectively by making *nothing* 'too dissimilar'. This creates potential differences with other European countries. The inclusion of unified management (with participating influence) in its subsidiary undertaking definition means the UK has embraced one aspect of the European (German) tradition and in this differs from the USA, Canada and Australia.

The UK differs from international practice (IAS 22 – capitalization and gradual amortization) in its dominant practice of immediate write-off of goodwill, and is presently conducting an innovative debate in the area (Chapter 5). The ASB also challenges international and European practice with its strongly argued proposals for the mandatory use of equity accounting for all joint ventures (Chapter 4), with the prominence given to unrealized gains and losses in its statement of total recognized gains and losses together with its decision that particularly revaluation and closing rate foreign currency translation gains and losses are not to be returned to profit and loss on disposal (Chapter 8), and its much stricter criteria for setting up, for example, reorganization provisions at acquisition and discontinuation/sale provisions to be based on obligations not management intentions (Chapter 5). In many cases (e.g. see Chapter 3) the UK seems to be a world leader in accounting standards based on 'substance over form'. Another major difference is the UK's different measurement basis for consolidation adjustments and minority interests (Chapters 5 and 6). This points to a major international need to review this area.

More ambiguous is the effective abolition of extraordinary items in the UK, even though counterbalanced by increased disclosures of, for example, provisions and discontinued items in the profit and loss account (Chapter 8). In the foreign currency area, the ASB needs to address its anomalous choice of the profit and loss exchange rate to translate foreign currency cash flow statements and to prevent reporting anomalies of the type represented by Polly Peck (Chapter 11). Longer-term areas of examination include the purpose of consolidated reserves and the relevance or irrelevance of consolidation concepts to measurement and disclosure issues. Better reporting internationally of group borrowing and hedging arrangements, e.g. in the reporting of group borrowing restrictions and the existence and extent of debt cross-guarantees, is necessary. Otherwise it is almost impossible to determine the extent to which groups are exposed to risk.

Exercises

12.7   To what extent are the ASB's proposals on group accounting consistent with its Draft Statements of Principles?

12.8   How far should the ASB modify its standards to be consistent with international harmonization?

12.9 Discuss the implications of empirical research based on efficient markets research and contracting cost theory to standard setting bodies in their deliberations on group accounting matters?

12.10 'Consolidated financial statements at present show no useful information for determining distributable profits, and consolidated equity has no information content at all for any purpose.' Discuss.

SUMMARY

*Consolidation aggregates financial statements of **legal entities**. Segmental reporting disaggregates into **economic units**. World-wide, standards require managerially determined segment **identification** by class of business and geographically. Quantitative materiality criteria are supposed to guide such discretion, but are potentially easy to override in the UK. Segmental **disclosure** requirements for **all** companies require turnover and profits by class of business, but only turnover for geographical segments. For plc's, and 'very' large private companies, SSAP 25 mandates disclosure by class of business and geographically, turnover, segment result (normally before interest) and net assets. Geographical turnover must be analysed by origin and destination if materially different. Other disclosures include inter-segmental transactions, significant associates by segment and a reconciliation to consolidated amounts. The basis for inter-segment pricing, depreciation and capital expenditure are not disclosed. The **allocation** problem haunts segmental profit measurement. Directors are allowed not to disclose segmental information if they consider it seriously prejudicial, but potential adverse market reaction must be a deterrent to using such an exemption in practice.*

Theoretical analysis supports the usefulness of segmental reporting. Empirical studies include surveys, laboratory-style studies, predictive ability studies and market reaction testing. They indicate that segmental reporting is asked for and used, but there is conflict over the amount needed. Segmental sales is useful for forecasting consolidated earnings, but there is dispute over the incremental usefulness of segmental profit. Both class of business and geographical data seem to affect the market's perception of risk.

*The ASB's pronouncements on group accounting are coherent in many respects with its Draft **Statement of Principles**. However, unresolved areas include the conceptualization of the reporting entity under merger accounting, the status of goodwill, the disclosure and measurement of minority interests and their relationship to consolidation concepts, and the reporting of consolidated equity and its usefulness in assessing potentially distributable profits of the parent.*

The impact of empirical research, particularly efficient markets and contracting cost-based research was reviewed. It was found to make a major potential contribution in understanding why and how accounting approaches may be used to optimize contracting costs. However, its general critique of regulation was found to be less convincing. The UK was found to be 'out of step' with much international practice, leading in many areas, but lagging in the areas of deferred tax and the translation of foreign currency cash flows. It embraces European and Anglo-Saxon accounting traditions and this throws up interesting differences and compromises. Possible future developments were reviewed.

FURTHER READING

Segmental reporting

SSAP 25 (1990) *Segmental Reporting*, Accounting Standards Committee.

Davies, M., Patterson, R. and Wilson, A. (1992), *UK GAAP – Generally Accepted Accounting Practice in the United Kingdom*, Chapter 16 Ernst & Young/Macmillan.

Emmanuel, C. and Garrod, N. (1992), *Segment Reporting – International Issues and Evidence*, Prentice-Hall.

Hodgson, E. (1990) *Segmental Reporting*, Coopers & Lybrand. @R:Roberts, C and Gray, S. (1991) Segmental reporting, in Nobes, C and Parker, R. (eds.) *International Accounting*, (3rd edn), Chapter 15 Prentice-Hall International.

Overviews and future developments

Gray, S.J., Coenenberg, A.G. and Gordon, P.D. (1993) *International Group Accounting: Issues in European Harmonisation*, (2nd edn.), Routledge.

Morris, R.D. (1991) Distributable profit in Britain since 1980: a critical appraisal, *Abacus*, Vol. 27, no. 2, pp 15–31.

Nobes, C. (1986) *Some Practical and Theoretical Problems of Group Accounting*, Deloitte, Haskins & Sells, London

APPENDIX

ABBREVIATED SOLUTION NOTES

These are intended to provide check figures to help you with your attempts at certain core numerical problems in the chapters. They are not complete solutions, which are provided in the Solutions Manual, available to teachers of courses using the text.

CHAPTER 1

1.1 'T' Account extracts

Profit and loss

T2 COGS	30	T2 Sales	80
T2 COGS (int)	10	T2 Sales (int)	20
T3 Depn	5	T5 Mgt fee	12.5
T4 Admin	40	*Spoke profits*	27.5

Profit and loss

T2 COGS	40	T2 Sales	80
T5 Mgt fee	12.5		
To H/O profits	27.5		

Branch account

Balance b/f	70		
T2 Sales (int)	20	T3 Remittance	42.5
T5 Mgt fee	12.5		
Spoke profits	27.5		

Head office account

T3 Remittance	42.5	Balance b/f	70
		T1 Purchases (int)	20
		T5 Mgt fee	12.5
		To H/O profits	27.5

The interlocking branch and head-office accounts cancel when divisional balances are aggregated

1.2 'T'Account extracts

Profit and loss

T2 COGS	30	T2 Sales	80
T2 COGS (int)	10	T2 Sales (int)	20
T3 Depn	5	T5 Mgt fee	12.5
T4 Admin	40	*Dividends*	20

Profit and loss

T2 COGS	40	T2 Sales	80
T5 Mgt fee	12.5		
Dividends	20		

Debtors – Spoke plc

Balance b/f	1		
T2 Sales (int)	20	T3 Remittance	42.5
T5 Mgt fee	12.5		
Dividends	20		

Creditors – Hub plc

T3 Remittance	42.5	Balance b/f	10
		T1 Purchases (int)	20
		T5 Mgt fee	12.5
		Dividends	20

The intra-group debtors and creditors cancel on aggregation. Group reserves are £190m

CHAPTER 2

2.5 (a) In group 1 'yes' as A controls 55% of the votes – subsidiary votes are included. In group 2 'no' on the basis of voting rights alone. As A holds a 'participating interest', there may be other evidence not given here to suggest A can exercise a dominant influence. This is likely unless B's holding is held 50/50 with another company.

(b) not necessarily unless there is evidence of *unified management*, which requires *integrated operations*, or otherwise *dominant influence*.

2.8 Not at June 19X1 because the option is exercisable at a *future* date. There is *benefit* but not power to *deploy*. Yes at December 19X2 even though the option is worthless as shares covered by the option are treated as shares held; only 40 per cent of the *shareholders'* votes are controlled [(10% × 10m + 100% x 5m) / (10m + 5m)], but 73 per cent of the directors votes [(10% × 10m + 100% × 2 x 5m) / (10m + 5m)] and it is a *member*. It is a subsidiary undertaking at 30 June 19X2.

CHAPTER 3

3.2 (a) Nominal value of shares issued = £50m, fair value = £150m, under the former (merger) Wholla's share capital, and share premium/merger reserve are £110m and £20m, and under the latter £110m and £120m.

(b) On merger cancellation in the *consolidated* balance sheet, share capital = (£110m), share premium (£20m), other consolidated reserves (subsidiary share premium) is (£10m) and retained profits (£190m).

Under acquisition accounting share capital = (£110m), share premium/merger reserve (£120m) and retained profits (£100m).

3.3 In both consolidated balance sheet assets are £630m, liabilities (£240m), share capital (£110m). Then in the merger balance sheet: share premium (£20m), other consolidated reserves (£10m) and retained profits (£250m), and the acquisition balance sheet share premium/merger reserve (£120m) and retained profits (£160m).

3.5 Nominal value investment = £75m, fair value £225m. Under merger accounting, if the investment is cancelled against Bitta's balances only, the consolidated share capital is (£135m), share premium (£20m), other consolidated reserves (subsidiary share premium) nil, and consolidated retained profits (£235m). Under acquisition accounting share capital is the same (the parent's), share premium/merger reserve (£170m), retained profits (£160m) and goodwill £75m.

3.6 Offer terms £4.5m cash plus £67.5m nominal (= £72m), or plus £202.5m fair value (= £207m). So adjusted Wholla share capital is £127.5m; share premium/merger reserve is £155m under acquisition accounting and retained profits £158m. Under merger accounting if progressive cancellation is done against the subsidiary's balances – consolidated retained profits is £221m; under acquisition accounting they are £158m, goodwill is £72m. Under both minority interests is (£17m).

CHAPTER 4

4.3 Goodwill = £12m, retained profits = (£300.4m), minority = (£45.6m).

4.6 Investment in associate = £26m (goodwill = £5m, net assets = £21m), retained profits = (£306.4m).

4.7 20 (cost) + 25% [55–31] (25% net profits since acq.) = 5 (goodwill) + 25% × 84 (net assets now).

4.8 72 (cost) + 60% × [64 – 50] (60% ret profits since acq) = 12 (goodwill) + 60% × 114 (net assets now). Under the entity approach goodwill = £20m (i.e. 12 + 8), minority = £53.6m (i.e. 45.6 + 8). Consolidated retained profits under all approaches = £300.4m.

4.13 (a) Investment in Tinyfry = £21m, retained profits = (£289.4m), goodwill = zero.

(b) Investment in Tinyfry = £25m, retained profits = (£304.8m), goodwill = £11.4m.

CHAPTER 5

5.2 Consequent extra depreciation is (£90m – £80m)/4 = £2.5m per annum, split pro-rata parent/minority.

Description	Consolidated retained profits	Goodwill (pre-acquisition)	Minority interests	Fixed assets
Fair values at acquisition		(6)	(4)	10
Extra depreciation – year 1	1.5		1.0	(2.5)
Extra depreciation – year 2	1.5		1.0	(2.5)
Extra depreciation – year 3	1.5		1.0	(2.5)
Extra depreciation – year 4	1.5		1.0	(2.5)
Net effect of fixed asset	6	(6)	—	—

5.5 Entries in the following columns of the balance sheet cancellation table are:
Goodwill = 72 – 60 – 1.2 (stock) – 3 – 6 + 6 (reorg) = 7.8 at acq – 20% × 0.5 × 7.8 (amortization) = 6.5
Minority = –40 – 5.6 – 2 (land) – 4 + 0.5 (extra depn) + 4 (reorg) – 2.4 (set-off) = – 49.5
Profits   = – 292 – 8.4 + 1.2 (stock) + 0.75 (depn) – 3.6 (set-off) + 1.3 (goodwill) = –300.75

5.12 Cost of investment   = 2m × £2.30 + £25m/1.12 + £1m (only incremental costs) = £69.32m.

5.21   **Bigfry Group – Balance Sheet under goodwill assumptions at 31 March 1995**

Description	W/off vs retained profits	W/off vs separate reserve	Gradual amortis-ation	Annual systematic review
Intangible fixed assets	—	—	11.7	11
Retained profits	(288.4)	(300.4)	(300.1)	(299.4)
Goodwill write-off reserve		12		
Minority interests	(45.6)	(45.6)	(45.6)	(45.6)

CHAPTER 6

6.2 Creditor Clinton's records (Yeltsin) – corrected company balance = (£24m) CR, aligned creditor = (£45m).
Debtor in Yeltsin's records – company balance 65 – goods in transit 20 = aligned debtor = £45m.

6.5 Opening stock profit = £2m, closing stock profit = £4m.

6.8 Full elimination against stock of £4m – all against consolidated retained profits if downstream, £2.4m against retained profits and £1.6m against minority if upstream.

6.15 Entries in the following columns of the balance sheet cancellation table are:
Goodwill = 120 – 90 – 9 (FA reval) – 4 (pre-acq div) = 17 at acq – 10% × 2 × 17 (amortization) = 13.6
Minority = –10 – 3 – 1 (FA reval) + 0.2 (extra depn) = –13.8
Profits   = – 195 – 27 + 1.2(stock in transit) + 1.8 (depn) + 4 (pre-acq div) + 3.2 (stock) + 3.4 (goodwill) = –208.4
Creditors = – 50 – 60 + 30 (intra-group)   = – 80
Stock   = 80 + 40 + 4.8 (in transit) – 3.2 (unrealized profits) = 121.6

CHAPTER 7

7.1 Goodwill at acquisition   =   £50m,   annual amortization =   £10m,
    Consolidated sales   =   1,255   retained profits   =   £73m.
7.2 Goodwill at acquisition   =   £30m   annual amortization =   £6m,
    Equitized profit *after* tax   =   60% × 65 – 6m (goodwill)   =   £33m
    Minority interest in profit *after* tax = 40% × 65   =   £26m
    SSAP 1 associate = Sales 835, COGS (300), Distribution (250), Admin (150), Divs rec
    10, Assoc profit *before* tax 48, Tax (60), divs parent (80) = Retained £53m.
    Conventional   = Sales 1,255, COGS (510), Distribution (300), Admin (220),
    Goodwill (6), Divs rec 10, Tax (70), Minority interests in profit *after* tax (26), Divs
    parent (80)   = Retained £53m.

Exercise 7.2 (d) – Overbearing Inadequate: with minority (60 per cent owned)

Details	Overbearing	Inadequate	Intra-group transfers	Intra-group dividends	Goodwill	Minority interests	Consolidated
Sales	835	460	(40)				1,255
COGS	(300)	(250)	40				(510)
Distribution costs	(250)	(50)					(300)
Administration expenses	(150)	(70)					(220)
Dividends receivable	40	—		(30)			10
Goodwill amortisation					(6)		(6)
Taxation	(45)	(25)					(70)
Minority Interests						(26)	(26)
Dividends payable	(80)	(50)		30		(20)	(80)
Retained profits	50	15	—	—	(6)	(6)	53

7.5 Opening intra-group stocks = + 3, closing intra-group stocks = –3.5
    Sales   =   835 + 460 – 40   = 1,255
    COGS   = – 300 – 250 + 40 + 3 – 3.5 (stocks)   = – 510.5
    Goodwill   =   – 3.6
    Minority interests   =   – 40% × [65 – 1 (extra depreciation)] = – 25.6
    No minority stock adjustment since *downstream* sale.
    Consolidated retained profit = £54.3m
7.8 In consolidated balance sheet cancellation table:
    Goodwill   =   150 – 120 – 12 (FA reval) = 18 (at acq) – 3 / 5 × 18 = £7.2m
    Retained profits =   – 200 – 45 + 1.8 (depn) + 3.5 (stock profit) + 10.8 (3 yrs goodwill)
    = – £228.9m
    Minority interest = – 80 – 30 – 8 (FA reval) + 1.2 (depn) = – £116.8m

    In consolidated profit and loss cancellation table:

Items for current year profit and loss are as above.

Opening retained profit = 150 + 140 − 3 (stock profit) − 7.2 (g/w) − 55.2 (mino) −
48 (pre-acq) − 2 (depn) = £174.6m
Closing retained profit = 200 + 155 − 3.5 (stock profit) − 10.8 (g/w) − 60.8 (mino)
− 48 (pre-acq) − 3(depn) = £228.9m

7.10 Dividend receivable of £10m = 40% × £25m is *removed* and replaced by assoc prof-
it before tax less goodwill, and associate share of tax. Workings:
Goodwill at acquisition = 20 − 40% × (5 + 5 + 20) = £8m, annual charge = £8m/5
= £1.6m
Assoc profit before tax = 40% × 55 − 1.6 (goodwill)= £20.4m
Associate tax = 40% × 15 = − £6m
Consolidated profit will be £58.71m = 54.3 (above) − 10m (dividend) + 20.4 (assoc
PBT) − 6 (assoc tax).

CHAPTER 8

8.5 Revenues and expenses of Inadequate are included for 6 months on a *pro-rata* basis
except for dividends − Overbearing is only entitled to receive the final dividend. Also
6 months goodwill amortization is charged.

Goodwill amortization
Equity at acquisition = Opening + Pro rata profit after tax − divs prior to acq
= (50 + 70 + 80) + 6/12 × £65 − 20 = £212.5m
Goodwill at acquisition = £150 - 60% × £212.5 = £22.5m, **amortization = 6/12 × 1/5
× £22.5 = £2.25m**
Minority interests in profit after tax = 40% × 65 × 1/2 year = £13m
Consolidated retained profits (bottom row of table) = 50 + 2.5 − 2.25 (g/w) − 1 (mino)
= £49.25m

8.6 Revenues and expenses of Grovel are included for 9 months on a *pro-rata* basis except
for dividends − Overbearing is only entitled to receive the interim. Also 9 months
goodwill amortization is charged, as is the *consolidated* profit on disposal.

Goodwill at acquisition =28 − 80% × (5+5+16) = £7.2m, **amortization = 9/12 × 1/5
× 7.2 = £1.08m**
Minority interests in profit *after* tax = 20% × 9/12 × 16 = £2.4m

---

***Consolidated profit on disposal* = Proceeds − [Inv + 0.8 Δ Ret Profit) − 2.75 yrs × goodwill]**
Retained profits since acq = 30 (opening) + 9/12 × 16 (9 months profits) − 5 (interim dividend) − 16m
= 21m
***Consolidated* profit on disposal =** 47 − [28 + 0.8 × 21 − 2.75 × 7.2 / 5] = **£6.16m**
Consolidated sales = 835 + 230 − 30 + 75 = 1,110
Consolidated retained profit (bottom row of table) = 49.25 (above) + 7 − 12.84 − 1.08 (g/w) − 1.4 (mino)
=£40.93m

CHAPTER 9

9.5
Rundown plc – Cash Flow Statement – year ended 31 March 1995

	£m	£m
Operating activities		
Cash received from customers	985	
Cash payments to suppliers and others	(920)	
Net cash inflow from operating activities		65
Returns on investments and servicing of finance		
Interest paid	(6)	
Dividends paid	(14)	
Net cash outflow from returns on investment and servicing of finance		(20)
Taxation		
Corporation tax paid	(10)	
Tax paid		(10)
Investing activities		
Payments for fixed assets	(160)	
Sale proceeds for fixed assets[3]	10	
Net cash outflow from investing activities		(150)
Net cash outflow before financing		(115)
Financing		
Issue of ordinary share capital	70	
Issue of loans	45	
Repayment of loans	(40)	
Net cash outflow from financing activities		75
Decrease in cash and cash equivalents		(40)

9.7 **Reconciliation of operating profit to net cash inflow from operating activities:**

	£m
Operating profit	78
Depreciation charges	15
Loss on fixed asset sale	2
Increase in (operating) debtors	(15)
Increase in (operating) creditors	25
Increase in stocks	(40)
Net cash inflow from operating activities	65

9.9 Includes: Operating receipts = £572m, interest paid (£6m), dividends paid (£23m) parent, (£6m) minority, loan issues £19m.

Reconciliation: Operating profit = £167m, depreciation 25m, loss on fixed asset £6m, debtors decrease £10m, stock increase (£30m), creditors decrease (£1m).

9.13   **Gruppe Group – Consolidated cash flow statement – for the year**
ended 31 December 1995

	£m	£m
Net cash inflow from operating activities (Note 1)		44
Returns on investments and servicing of finance		
Interest paid	(1)	
Dividends paid – parent	(5)	
Dividends paid to minority interests	(6)	
Dividends received from associate	2	
Net cash outflow from returns on investments and servicing of finance		(10)
Taxation		
Corporation tax paid	(11)	
Tax paid		(11)
Investing activities		
Payments for fixed assets (note 2)	(54)	
Sale proceeds for fixed assets	8	
Acquisition of subsidiary (note 3)	(4)	
Proceeds from sale of associate	4	
Reorganization payments	(—)	
Net cash outflow from investing activities		(46)
Net cash outflow before financing		(23)
Financing		
Issue of ordinary share capital (note 2)	—	
Loan issues	26	
Repayment of loans	(11)	
Net cash outflow from financing activities		15
Decrease in cash and cash equivalents		(8)

Reconciliation of operating profit to cash inflow from operating activities:

	£m
Operating profit	30
Depreciation charges	15
Increase in (operating) debtors	(5)
Increase in (operating) creditors	—
Decrease in stocks	2
Goodwill amortized	2
Net cash inflow from operating activities	**44**

Cash equivalents = cash + deposits – overdrafts
Subsidiary acquired: fixed assets 8, stocks 9, debtors 4, cash 2, creditors (5), tax (2), minority (4), goodwill 8.
Consideration: shares 14, cash 6.

CHAPTER 10

10.1   In cancellation table under slice-by-slice approach, goodwill = £2.5m, consolidated retained earnings = £71.75, and minority interests = £3.75.

10.5   In cancellation table under simultaneous approach, goodwill = £62m, consolidated retained earnings = £1,572m, and minority interests = £110m.

10.6   In cancellation table under simultaneous approach, goodwill = £75.5m, consolidated retained earnings = £1581.5m, and minority interests = £114m.

10.10 Majority holdings, B = 1.0, P = 0.6B + 0.25O, O = 0.65B + 0.3P
       Minority holdings, B = 0.0, P = 0.15 + 0.6B + 0.25O, O = 0.05 + 0.65B + 0.3P

CHAPTER 11

11.1   Journal entry at purchase date DR Fixed asset £2,174, CR Creditors £2,174.
       One transaction approach DR Creditors £2,500, CR Cash 2,500. DR Fixed asset £326, CR Creditors 326.
       Two transaction approach DR Creditors £2,500, CR Cash 2,500. DR Exchange loss £326, CR Creditors 326.

11.4   Marks are weakening against the £, temporal gain, closing rate loss, current/non-current loss, monetary/non-monetary gain. Francs are strengthening against the £, therefore gains and losses are exactly reversed.

11.7   Opening balance sheet – Share capital and reserves (by differencing), closing rate £2,021, temporal £1,937.
       Closing balance sheet – Share capital and reserves (by differencing), closing rate £2,565, temporal £2,406.
       Profit and loss account – Closing rate (average rate) exchange gain by differencing £97, temporal exchange loss by differencing £24.

11.10 (a) Using 'historical' rate to translate goodwill, 80 per cent of subsidiary's translated pre-acq equity = £1,280. Goodwill = £1,720.
       Parent's retained profits after adjusting for *transaction* loss on loan = £49,475 – (475 – 413)= £49,413.
       Consolidated retained profits = £49,497 (don't forget goodwill amortization).
       (b) Goodwill amortization is £344m p.a., minority interests = 25% × 447 = £89.4m, net reserve movement (gain) = £77.6m. Consolidated retained profit for year = £5,074m.

11.12 Flow statement of exposed items in *maracas*:
       Temporal – Sales 112,000, *Purchases* (108,000), Other expenses (1,900), Fixed asset purchases (3,000).
       Closing rate – Sales 112,000, COGS (107,000), Other expenses (1,900), Depreciation (1,000).

11.15	Calculating the exchange gain or loss given the exposure pattern				
Temporal	*Period of exposure*	*Amount*		*Exchange rate change*	*Gain/(loss)*
Incremental amounts _exposed	1 Jan 95 to 31 Dec 95	(2,100)	×	1/4.6 – 1/4.8 =	(19)
	30 Jun 95 to 31 Dec 95	(900)	×	1/4.6 – 1/4.7 =	(5)
					(24)

Closing rate	*Period of exposure*	*Amount*		*Exchange rate change*	*Gain/(loss)*
Incremental amounts exposed	1 Jan 95 to 31 Dec 95	9,700	×	1/4.6 – 1/4.8 =	88
	30 Jun 95 to 31 Dec 95	2,100	×	1/4.6 – 1/4.7 =	9
					97

CHAPTER 12

12.1 The 10 per cent quantitative criteria are based on turnover £1,200, net assets = £600, profits = £85.

Reported profits	Toys	Chemicals	Bookshops
Equal allocation	150	(50)	750
Turnover allocation	200	150	500
Net asset allocation	350	(50)	550

Turnover = Toys and Bookshops reportable, net assets = Chemicals and Bookshops reportable,
Profit equal = Toys and Bookshops, Profit turnover = all, Profit net assets = Toys and Bookshops.

12.2 Materiality becomes turnover £1,100, net assets £700 [10% × (400 + 2,000 + 3,600 + 1,100 – 100)], profits £75 [10% × (200 + 150 + 500 – 100)].
External sales = 3,200 Toys, 800 Chemicals, 7,000 Bookshops.
Segment profits = 200 + 150 + 400 (Bkshops – 100 stock profits) = 750.
Reported profits = 750 – 100 (corp costs) – 150 (int) = £500m.
Segment net assets = 300 (Toys – 100 stock profits) + 2,000 + 3,600 + 1,100 (corp assets) = £7,000.

BIBLIOGRAPHY

AASB, Accounting Standards/Statements of Concepts.
  AASB 24 – *Consolidated Accounts* (1991).
  AAS – *Consolidated Financial Reports* (1991).
  SAC 1 – *Definition of the Reporting Entity* (1990).
AICPA, *Accounting Research Bulletins*, American Institute of Certified Public Accountants, New York.
  ARB No. 51 – *Consolidated Financial Statements* (1959).
  APB Statement No. 4 – *Basic Concepts and Accounting Principles Underlying Financial Statements of Business Enterprises* (1970).
AICPA, *Accounting Principles Board Opinions*, American Institute of Certified Public Accountants, New York .
  APB Opinion No. 16 – *Business Combinations* (1970).
  APB Opinion No. 17 – *Intangible Assets* (1970).
  APB Opinion No. 18 – *The Equity Method of Accounting for Investments in Common Stock* (1971).
  APB Opinion No. 19 – *Reporting Changes in Financial Position* (1971).
ASB, *Financial Reporting Standards*, Accounting Standards Board, London.
  FRS 1 – *Cash Flow Statements* (1991).
  FRS 2 – *Accounting for Subsidiary Undertakings* (1992).
  FRS 3 – *Reporting Financial Performance* (1992).
  FRS 4 – *Capital Instruments* (1994).
  FRS 5 – *Reporting the Substance of Transactions* (1994).
  FRS 6 – *Acquisitions and Mergers* (1994).
  FRS 7 – *Fair Values in Acquisition Accounting* (1994).
  Interim Statement – *Consolidated Accounts* (1991).
ASB, *Urgent Issue Task Force Abstracts*, Accounting Standards Board, London.
  UITF 2 – *Restructuring Costs* (1991).
  UITF 3 – *Treatment of Goodwill on Disposal of a Business* (1991).
  UITF 9 – *Accounting for Operations in Hyper-inflationary Economies* (1993).
ASB, *Discussion Papers*, Accounting Standards Board, London.
  Fair Values in Acquisition Accounting (1993).
  Goodwill and Intangible Assets (1993).
  Associates and Joint Ventures (1994).
ASB, *Discussion Draft: Statement of Principles.*
  Chapter 1 – *The objectives of financial statements* (1991).
  Chapter 2 – *The qualitative characteristics of financial information* (1991).
  Chapter 3 – *The elements of financial statements* (1991).
  Chapter 4 – *The recognition of items in financial statements* (1992).
  Chapter 5 – *Measurement in financial statements* (1993).
  Chapter 6 – *Presentation of financial information* (1991).
  Chapter 7 – *The reporting entity* (1994).
ASC, *Statements of Standard Accounting Practice*, Accounting Standards Committee, London.
  SSAP 1 – *Accounting for Associated Companies* (1971), revised (1982).
  SSAP 14 – *Group Accounts* (1978).
  SSAP 20 – *Foreign Currency Translation* (1983).
  SSAP 22 – *Accounting for Goodwill* (1984).
  SSAP 23 – *Accounting for Acquisitions and Mergers* (1985).
  SSAP 25 – *Segmental Reporting* (1990).
ASC, *Exposure Drafts*, Accounting Standards Committee, London.
  ED 31 – *Accounting for Acquisitions and Mergers* (1971).
  ED 42 – *Accounting for Special Purpose Transactions* (1988).
  ED 46 – *Disclosure of Related Party Transactions* (1989).
  ED 47 – *Accounting for Goodwill* (1990).
  ED 48 – *Accounting for Acquisitions and Mergers* (1990).
  ED 49 – *Reflecting the Substance of Transactions in Assets and Liabilities* (1990).
  ED 50 – *Consolidated Accounts* (1990).
  ED 52 – *Accounting for Intangible Fixed Assets* (1990).

ED 53 – *Fair Values in the Context of Acquisition Accounting* (1990).

ASSC (1975) *The Corporate Report*, Accounting Standards Steering Committee, London.

Aliber, R.Z. and Stickney, C.P. (1975) Measures of foreign exchange exposure, *The Accounting Review*, January, pp. 44–57.

Anderson, J.C. and Louderbeck III, J.G. (1975) Income manipulation and purchase pooling: some additional results, *Journal of Accounting Research*, Autumn, pp. 338–343.

Ang, J.S. (1979) Aggregate versus component forecasts of financial statement items, *Review of Business and Economic Research*, Fall 1979, pp. 30–42.

Archer, G.H.S. (1994a) ASB Discussion paper on goodwill and intangibles: comments, Unpublished paper presented at the Financial Reporting and Auditing Research Conference, London Business School, July.

Archer, G. (1994b) A risk to auditors in related party disclosures, *Accountancy*, July 1994, p. 88.

Arnold, J., Egginton, D., Kirkham, L., Macve, R. and Peasnell, K. (1992) *Goodwill and Other Intangibles: Theoretical Considerations and Policy Issues*, Institute of Chartered Accountants in England and Wales.

Australian Accounting Research Foundation (1990) AAS 24, *Consolidated Financial Statements*.

Australian Accounting Standards Review Board (1990) ASRB 1024, *Consolidated Financial Statements*.

Ayres, F.L. (1986) Characteristics of firms electing early adoption of FAS No. 52, *Journal of Accounting and Economics*, Vol. 8, pp. 143–158.

Backer, M. and Mcfarland, W.B. (1968) *External Reporting for Segments of a Business*, National Association of Accountants.

Bagby, J.W. and Kinzele, P.L. (1987) Management discussion and analysis, *Accounting Horizons*, March, pp. 51–60.

Balakrishnan, R., Harris, T.E. and Sen, P.K (1990) The predictive ability of geographic segment disclosures, *Journal of Accounting Research*, Autumn, pp. 305–325.

Baldwin, B.A. (1984) Segment earnings disclosure and the ability of security analysts to forecast earnings per share, *The Accounting Review*, Vol. LIX, no. 3, pp. 376–389.

Barnea, A. and Lakinshok, J. (1980) An analysis of the usefulness of disaggregated accounting data for forecasts of corporate performance, *Decision Sciences*, Vol. 11, January, pp. 17–26.

Barton, A. (1974) Expectations and achievements in income theory, *The Accounting Review*, Vol. XLIX, no. 4, pp. 664–681.

Barwise ,P., Higson, C., Likierman, A. and Marsh, P. (1989) *Accounting For Brands*, Institute of Chartered Accountants in England and Wales.

Baxter, G.C. and Spinney, J.C. (1975) A closer look at consolidated financial theory, *CA Magazine*, Part 1, Vol. 106, no. 1, pp. 31–36; Part 2, Vol. 106, no. 2, pp. 31–35.

Benston, G.J. (1984) The costs of complying with a government data collection program: the FTC's line of business report, *Journal of Accounting and Public Policy*, Vol. 3, no. 2, pp. 123–37.

Bernard, V.L. and Stober, T.L. (1989) The nature and amount of information in cash flows and accruals, *The Accounting Review*, October, pp. 624–652.

Bircher, P. (1988), The adoption of consolidated accounting in Great Britain, *Accounting and Business Research*, Winter, pp. 3–13.

Bird, P. (1982) After Argyll Foods what is a 'true and fair view', *Accountancy*, Vol. 93, no. 1066, pp. 80–81.

Birkin, M. (1991) Brand valuation, Chapter 8 in D. Cowley (ed.) *Understanding Brands*, Kogan Page, London.

Boersma, J.M. and Van Weelden, S.J. (1992) *Financial Reporting for Segments*, Canadian Institute of Chartered Accountants.

Bowen, R.M., Burgstahler, D. and Daley, L.A. (1987) The incremental information content of accrual versus cash flows, *The Accounting Review*, October, pp. 723–747.

Brault, R. (1979) A simple approach to complex consolidations, *CA Magazine*, Vol. 112, no. 4, pp. 52–54.

Briloff, A. (1980) Leveraged Leasco, *Barron's*, October 20, pp. 4–5 & 22.

Campbell, L.G. and Patient, M.L. (1985) *Accounting for Goodwill*, Deloitte, Haskins & Sells, London.

Carsberg, B. (1991) FAS#52 – Measuring the performance of foreign operations, in J.H. Stern and D.H. Chew (eds.) *New Developments in International Finance*, Blackwell.

Casey, C.J. and Bartczak, N.J. (1985) Using operating cash flow data to predict financial distress: some extensions, *Journal of Accounting Research*, Spring, pp. 388–401.

Castanias, R.P. and Griffin, P.A. (1986) The effects of foreign currency translation accounting on security analysts' forecasts, *Managerial and Decision Economics*, Vol. 7, pp. 3–10.

Catlett, G.R. and Olsen, N.O. (1968) *Accounting for Goodwill*, ARS No 10, American Institute of Certified Public Accountants, New York.

Chalmers, J. (1992) *Accounting Guides – Accounting for Subsidiary Undertakings*, Coopers & Lybrand/Gee, Chapters 1–5.

Charitou, A. and Ketz, E .(1991) An empirical examination of cash flow measures, *Abacus*, Vol. 27, no. 1, pp. 51–64.

Chen, A.Y.S., Comisky, E.E. and Mulford, C.W. (1990) Foreign currency translation and analyst forecast dispersion: examining the effects of SFAS No. 52, *Journal of Accounting and Public Policy*, Winter, pp. 239–256.

Chopping, D. (1993) The comparability of financial statements: a review of FRS 3, in L. Skerratt and D. Tonkin, *Financial Reporting 1993/4*, Institute of Chartered Accountants in England and Wales.

Chopping, D. and Skerratt, L. (1993) *Applying GAAP 1993/4*, Institute of Chartered Accountants in England and Wales.

Colley, J.R. and Volkan, A.G. (1988) Accounting for goodwill, *Accounting Horizons*, March, pp. 35–42.

Collins, D.W. (1976) Predicting earnings with subentity data: further evidence, *Journal of Accounting Research*, Vol.

14, no. 1, pp. 163–177.

Collins, D.W. and Simmonds, R.R. (1979) SEC line-of–business disclosure and market risk adjustments, *Journal of Accounting Research*, Vol. 14, no. 2, pp. 352 – 383.

Conine Jr., T.E. (1990) A note on the theoretical irrelevance of FASB 94 on equity systematic risk, *Journal Business Finance and Accounting*, Autumn, pp. 575–577.

Cooke, T.E. (1985) SSAP 22 and 23: Do they lack clear objectives? *Accountancy*, Vol. 96, no. 1104, pp. 101–104.

Cooke, T.E. (1986) *Mergers and Acquisitions*, Basil Blackwell, Oxford.

Cooper, K., Fraser, D.R. and Richards, R.M. (1978) The impact of SFAS No. 8 on financial management practices, *Financial Executive*, Vol. XLVI, no. 6.

Copeland, R.M. and Wojdack, J.F. (1969) Income manipulation and purchase–pooling choice? *Journal of Accounting Research*, Vol. 7, no. 2, pp. 188–195.

Crichton, J. (1991) Consolidation – a deceptive simplicity, *Accountancy*, February, p. 26.

Davies, M., Paterson, R. and Wilson, A. (1992), *UK GAAP – Generally Accepted Accounting Practice in the United Kingdom* (3rd edn), Ernst & Young/Macmillan.

Davis, M. (1991) APB 16: time to reconsider, *Journal of Accountancy*, October, pp. 99–107.

Dealy, N. (1993) Chance for more meaningful reporting (cash flows), *Accountancy*, June, p. 98.

Deloitte, Haskins & Sells (1983) *Corporate Structure – Subsidiaries or Divisions?*, Deloitte, Haskins & Sells, London.

Demirag, R.S. (1987) A Review of the Objectives of Foreign Currency Translation, *The International Journal of Accounting*, Spring 1987, pp. 69–85.

Dhaliwal, D.S., Spicer, B.H. and Vickrey, D. (1979) The quality of disclosure and the cost of capital, *Journal of Business Finance & Accounting*, Vol. 6, no. 2, pp. 245–266.

Dukes, R.E. (1978) *An Empirical Investigation of the Effects of [SFAS No. 8] on Security Return Behaviour*, Financial Accounting Standards Board, Connecticut.

Dunne, K. (1990) An empirical analysis of management's choice of accounting treatment for business combinations, *Journal of Accounting and Public Policy*, Vol. 9, pp. 111–133.

Dyckman, T.R. and Morse, D. (1986) *Efficient Capital Markets and Accounting: A Critical Analysis* (2nd edn), Prentice-Hall, New Jersey.

Edey, H. (1985) SSAP 23 is about recognising business needs, *Accountancy*, Vol. 96, no. 1101, May, pp. 13–14.

Edwards, J.R. and Webb, K.M. (1984) The development of group accounting in the United Kingdom to 1933, *The Accounting Historians Journal*, Vol. 11, no. 1, pp. 31–61.

Egginton, D. (1965) Unrealised profits and consolidated accounts, *Accountancy*, Vol. 76, no. 861, pp. 410–415.

Egginton, D. (1990) Towards some principles for intangible asset accounting, *Accounting and Business Research*, Summer, pp. 193–205.

Elitzur, R.R. (1991) A model of translation of foreign financial statements under inflation in the United States and Canada, *Contemporary Accounting Research*, Vol. 7, no. 2, pp. 466–484.

Emmanuel, C.R. (1978) Segmental disclosures by multibusiness multinational.

companies: a proposal, *Accounting & Business Research*, Vol. 8, no. 31, pp. 169–177.

Emmanuel, C. and Garrod, N.(1987) On the segment identification issue, *Accounting and Business Research*, Winter, pp. 235–240.

Emmanuel, C. and Garrod, N. (1992), *Segment Reporting – International Issues and Evidence*, Prentice–Hall.

Emmanuel, C., Garrod, N. and Frost, C. (1989) An experimental test of analysts' forecasting behaviour, *British Accounting Review*, Vol. 21, no. 3, pp. 119–126.

Emmanuel, C.R. and Pick, R.H. (1980) The predictive ability of UK segment reports, *Journal of Business Finance & Accounting*, Vol. 7, no. 2, pp. 201–218.

Financial Accounting Standards Board, Connecticut.

Statements of FinancialAccounting Concepts:

   SFAC 1 – *The Objectives of Financial Reporting* (1978).

Statements of Financial Accounting Standards:

SFAS No. 8 – *Accounting for the Translation of Foreign Currency Transactions & Foreign Currency Financial Statements* (1975).

SFAS No. 14 – *Financial Reporting for Segments of a Business Enterprise 1976).

SFAS No. 52 – *Foreign Currency Translation* (1981).

SFAS No. 94 – *Consolidation of All Majority-owned Subsidiaries* (1987).

SFAS No. 95 – *Statement of Cash Flows* (1987).

   Discussion Memoranda:

Consolidation Policy and Procedures (1991) Chapters 1 and 3.

New Basis Accounting (1991).

   Preliminary Views:

Consolidation Policy (1994).

Flint, D. (1993) A true and fair view in consolidated accounts, in S.J. Gray, A.G. Coenenberg and P.D. Gordon (eds.) *International Group. Accounting – Issues in European Harmonisation* (2nd edn), Routledge, pp. 11–32.

Flower, J. (1991) Foreign currency translation, Chapter 14, in C. Nobes and R. Parker (eds.) *Comparative International Accounting*, 3rd edn, Prentice-Hall.

Foster, W.C. (1974) Illogic of pooling, *Financial Executive*, Vol. XLII, no. 12, December, pp. 16–21.

Gagnon, J.M. (1971) Purchase/pooling: empirical evidence, *Journal of Accounting Research*,Vol. 9, no. 1, pp. 52–72.

Garlicki, T.D., Fabozzi, F. J. and Fonfeder, R. (1987) *Financial Management*, Autumn, pp. 36–44.

Garrod, N. and Emmanuel, C. (1988) The impact of company profile on the predictive ability of disaggregated data, *Journal of Business Finance and Accounting*, Summer, pp. 135–154.

Gentry, J.A., Newbold, P. and Whitford, D.T. (1985a) Classifying bankrupt firms with funds flow components, *Journal of Accounting Research*, Spring, pp. 146–60.

Gentry, J.A., Newbold, P. and Whitford, D.T. (1985b) Predicting bankruptcy: if cash flow's not the bottom line, what is? *Financial Analysts' Journal*, September/October, pp. 47–56.

Gentry, J.A., Newbold, P. and Whitford, D.T. (1987) Funds flow components, financial ratios, and bankruptcy, *Journal of Business Finance and Accounting*, Winter, pp. 595–606.

Georgiou, G. (1993) Foreign currency translation and FRS 1, *Accounting and Business Research*, Summer, pp. 228–236.

Gerboth, D.L. (1972) 'Muddling through' with the APB, *Journal of Accountancy*, Vol. 133, May, pp. 42–49.

Ghosh, J. (1991) *Cash Flow Statements*, Coopers & Lybrand.

Gombola, M.J., Haskins, M.E. Ketz, J.E. and Williams, D.D. (1987) Cash flow in bankruptcy prediction, *Financial Management*, Winter, pp. 55–65.

Gray, D. (1984) Corporate preferences for foreign currency accounting standards, *Journal of Accounting Research*, Vol. 22, no. 2 (Autumn), pp. 760–764.

Gray, S.J. (1981) Segmental or disaggregated financial statements, Chapter 2, in T.A. Lee (ed.) *Developments in Financial Reporting*, Philip Alan.

Gray, S.J. and Radebaugh, L.H. (1984) International segment disclosures by US and UK multinational enterprises: a descriptive study, *Journal of Accounting Research*, Vol. 22, no. 1, pp. 351–60.

Gray, S.J. and Roberts, C.B. (1989) Voluntary information disclosure and the British multinationals: corporate perceptions of costs and benefits, in A.G. Hopwood (ed.) *International Pressures for Change in Accounting*, Prentice-Hall International.

Gray, S.J., Coenenberg, A.G. and Gordon, P.D. (eds.) (1993) *International Group Accounting – Issues in European Harmonisation* (2nd edn), Routledge.

Greenberg, R.R., Johnson, G.L. and Ramesh, K. (1986) Earnings versus cash flow as a predictor of future cash flow measures, *Journal of Accounting, Auditing and Finance*, Fall, pp. 266–277.

Greene, R. (1980) Equity accounting isn't equitable, *Forbes*, March 31, pp. 104–105.

Griffin, C.H., Williams, T.H. and Larsen, K.D. (1980) *Advanced Accounting* (4th edn), Irwin, Homewood, Ill.

Griffin, P. (1982) Foreign exchange gains and losses: impact on reported earnings, *Abacus*, Vol. 18, no. 1, pp. 50–69.

Griffin, P. (1983) Managerial preferences for FAS No. 52, *Abacus*, Vol. 19, no. 2, pp. 130–138.

Grinyer, J.R., Russell, A. and Walker, M. (1990, The rationale for accounting for goodwill, *British Accounting Review*, September, pp. 223–235.

Grinyer, J.R., Russell, A. and Walker, M.(1991) Managerial choices in the valuation of acquired goodwill in the UK, *Accounting and Business Research*, pp. 51–55.

Grinyer, J.R. and Russell, A. (1992) Goodwill – an example of puzzle solving in accounting – a comment, *Abacus*, Vol. 28, no. 1, pp. 107–112.

Gwilliam, D. and Russell, T. (1991) Polly Peck – where were the analysts? *Accountancy*, January, p. 25.

Gynther, R. (1969) Some conceptualising on goodwill, *The Accounting Review*, Vol. XLIV, no. 2, pp. 247–255.

Harris, T.S. (1991) Foreign currency transactions and translation, Ch 16, in F.D.S. Choi (ed.) *Handbook of International Accounting*, Wiley, New York.

Hendricksen, E.S. (1982) *Accounting Theory* (4th edn), Irwin, Homewood, Illinois.

Heath, L.C. (1977) *Financial Reporting & the Evaluation of Solvency*, Accounting Research Monograph No 3, American Institute of Certified Public Accountants.

Henning, C. N., Piggott, W. and Scott, R. H. (1978) *International Financial Management*, McGraw-Hill, New York.

Higson, C. (1990) *The Choice of Accounting Method in UK Mergers and Acquisitions*, Institute of Chartered Accountants in England and Wales.

Hodgson, A., Okunev, J. and Willett, R. (1993) Accounting for intangibles: a theoretical perspective, *Accounting and Business Research*, Spring, pp. 138–150.

Hodgson, E. (1990) *Segmental Reporting*, Coopers & Lybrand.

Hodgson, E. (1992) *Reporting Financial Performance*, Coopers & Lybrand/Gee.

Holgate, P.A. (1986) *A Guide to Accounting Standards – Accounting for Goodwill*, Accountants Digest No. 178, Institute of Chartered Accountants in England and Wales, London.

Holgate, P.A. (1993) *Reporting Financial Performance – 1993 Survey Results*, Coopers & Lybrand.

Holmes, G. and Sugden, A. (1993) Tweedie: the story so far, *Accountancy*, May, pp. 120–122.

Hong, H., Kaplan, R.S. and Mandelker, G. (1978) Purchase vs pooling: effects on stock prices, *The Accounting Review*, Vol. LIII, no. 1, pp. 31–47.

Hopwood, A.G. (ed.) *International Pressures for Change in Accounting*, Prentice-Hall International.

Hopwood, W.S., Newbold, P. and Silhan, P.A. (1982) The potential for gains in predictive ability through disagregation: segmented annual earnings, *Journal of Accounting Research*, Vol. 20, no. 2, pp. 724–732.

Horowitz, B. and Kolodny, R. (1977) Line of business reporting and security prices: an analysis of an SEC disclosure rule, *Bell Journal of Economics*, Vol. 8, no. 1, pp. 234–249.

Horowitz, B. (1989) Attributes of industry, industry segment and firm-specific information in security valuation, *Contemporary Accounting Research*, Spring, pp. 615–619.

Hughes, H.P. (1982) *Goodwill in Accounting: A History of the Issues & Problems*, Georgia State University, Georgia, USA.

Hussain, S. and Skerratt, L.C.L. (1992) Gains from disaggregation and the definition of a segment: a note on SSAP 25 'Segmental Reporting', *Working Paper 92/2*, Manchester University.

IASC, *International Accounting Standards*, International Accounting Standards Committee, London.
    IAS 7 – *Cash Flow Statements* (revised 1992).

IAS 8 – *Net Profit for the Period, Fundamental Errors and Changes in Accounting Policies* (1993).

IAS 14 – *Reporting Financial Information by Segment* (1981).

IAS 21 – *The Effects of Changes in Foreign Exchange Rates* (revised 1993).

IAS 22 – *Business Combinations* (revised 1993).

IAS 27 – *Consolidated Financial Statements and Accounting for Investments in Subsidiaries* (1990).

IAS 28 – *Accounting for Investments in Associates* (1990).

IAS 29 – *Financial Reporting in Hyperinflationary Economies* (1990).

IAS 31 – *Financial Reporting of Interests in Joint Ventures* (1992).

Framework for the Preparation and Presentation of Financial Statements (1993).

Institute of Chartered Accountants in Scotland (1988) *Making Corporate Reports Valuable*, Kogan Page.

Jordan, C.E., Pate, G.R. and Clark, S.J. (1992) SFAS 94: did it produce its desired effect? *CPA Journal*, March, pp. 56–59.

Kelly, L. (1985) Corporate management lobbying on FAS No. 8: some further evidence, *Journal of Accounting Research*, Vol . 23, no. 2, pp. 619–31.

Ketz, J. E. (1984) Accounting for business combinations in an age of changing prices, *Accounting and Business Research*, Vol. 14, no. 55, pp. 209–16.

Kinney, W. (1971) Predicting earnings: entity versus sub-entity data, *Journal of Accounting Research*, Vol. 9, no. 1, pp. 127–136.

Klammer, T.P. and Reed, S.A. (1990) Operating cash flow formats: does format influence decisions, *Journal of Accounting and Public Policy*, Vol. 9, pp. 217–235.

Kochanek, R.F. (1974) Segmental financial disclosures by diversified firms and security prices, *The Accounting Review*, Vol. XLIX, no. 2, pp. 245–258.

Kochanek, R.F. and Norgaard, C.T. (1988) Analysing the components of operating cash flow – the charter company, *Accounting Horizons*, March, pp. 58–66.

Lee, T.A. (1984), *Cash Flow Accounting*, Van Nostrand Reinhold (UK).

Lee, T.A. (1993) Goodwill – further attempts to capture the will-o'-the-wisp: a review of an ICAEW research report, *Accounting and Business Research*, Winter, pp. 79–81.

Lee, T.A. and Tweedie, D. (1977) *The Institutional Investor and the Corporate Report*, Institute of Chartered Accountants in England and Wales.

Lev, B. (1988) Towards a theory of equitable and efficient accounting policy, *The Accounting Review,* January, pp. 1–22.

Livnat, J. and Zarowin, P. (1990) The incremental information content of cash flow components, *Journal of Accounting and Economics*, May, pp. 25–46.

Lorensen, L (1972) *Reporting Foreign Operations of US Companies in US Dollars*, Accounting Research Study No. 12, American Institute of Certified Public Accountants, New York.

Ma, R. and Parker, R.H. (1983) *Consolidation Accounting in Australia: Concepts and Practice,* Longmans, Melbourne.

Ma, R. and Hopkins, R. (1988) Goodwill – an example of puzzle-solving in accounting, *Abacus*, Vol. 24, no. 1, pp. 75–85.

Ma, R. and Hopkins, R. (1992) Goodwill – an example of puzzle-solving in accounting – a reply, *Abacus*, Vol. 28, no. 1, pp. 113–115.

Mather, P.R. and Peasnell, K.V. (1991) An examination of the economic circumstances surrounding decisions to capitalize brands, *British Journal of Management*, Vol. 2, pp. 151–164.

McKinnon, J., Martin, C.A. and Partington, G.H. (1983) Clarifying funds statements – the two entity test, *Accounting and Finance*, May, pp. 79–87.

McKinnon, J.L. (1984) Application of Anglo-American accounting principles to corporate financial disclosure in Japan, *Abacus*, June, pp. 16–33.

McLean, A.T. (1972) *Accounting For Business Combinations and Goodwill*, The Institute of Chartered Accountants in Scotland.

Mian, S.L. and Smith, C.W. (1990a) Incentives for unconsolidated financial reporting, *Journal of Accounting and Economics*, Vol. 12, pp. 141–171.

Mian, S.L. and Smith, C.W. (1990b) Incentives associated with changes in consolidated reporting requirements, *Journal of Accounting and Economics*, Vol. 13, pp. 249–266.

Mohr, R.M. (1988) Illustrating the economic consequences of FASB Statement No. 94, 'Consolidation of All Majority-owned Subsidiaries', *Journal of Accounting Education*, Vol. 9, pp. 123–136.

Moonitz, M. (1951) *The Entity Theory of Consolidated Statements*, The Foundation Press, New York.

Morris, R.D. (1991) Distributable profit in Britain since 1980: a critical appraisal, *Abacus*, Vol. 27, no. 4, pp. 15–31.

Moses, O.D. (1991) Cash flow signals and analysts' earnings forecast revisions, *Journal of Business Finance and Accounting*, November, pp. 807–832.

De Moville, W. and Petrie, A.G. (1989) Accounting for a bargain purchase in a business connection, *Accounting Horizons*, September, pp. 38–43.

Nathan, K. (1988) Do firms pay to pool?: some empirical evidence, *Journal of Accounting and Public Policy*, Fall, pp. 185–200.

Nathan, K. and Dunne, K. (1991) The purchase-pooling choice: some explanatory variables, *Journal of Accounting and Public Policy*, Vol. 10, pp. 309–323.

Neill, J.D., Schaefer, T.F., Bahnson, P.R. and Bradbury, M.E. (1991) The usefulness of cash flow data: a review and synthesis, *Journal of Accounting Literature*, Vol. 10, pp. 117 – 150.

Nobes, C.W. (1980) A review of the translation debate, *Accounting and Business Research* Vol. 10, no. 39, pp. 421–31.

Nobes, C. (1986) *Some Practical and Theoretical Problems of Group Accounting*, Deloitte, Haskins and Sells, London.

Nobes, C. (1990) EC group accounting – two million ways to do it, *Accountancy*, December, pp. 84–85.

Nobes, C. (1992) 'A political history of goodwill in the UK: an illustration of cyclical standard setting', *Abacus*, Vol. 28, no. 2, pp. 142–161.

Nobes, C. (1993) Group accounting in the United Kingdom, in S.J. Gray, A.G. Coenenberg and P.D. Gordon (eds.) *International Group Accounting – Issues in European Harmonisation*, (2nd edn), Routledge, pp. 229–239.

Nobes, C. and Parker, R. (1991) *Comparative International Accounting*, (3rd edn), Prentice-Hall International.

Olusegun Wallace, R.S. and Collier, P.A. (1991) The cash in cash flow statements: a multi-country comparison, *Accounting Horizons*, December, pp. 44–52.

Pahler, A.J. and Mori, J.E. (1994) *Advanced Accounting: Concepts and Practice* (5th edn), The Dryden Press.

Parker, W. M. (1966) Business combinations and accounting valuation, *Journal of   Accounting Research*, Vol. 4, no. 2, pp. 149–S4.

Patient, M., Faris, J. and Holgatem P. (1992) Accounting solutions – goodwill, *Accountancy*, September, p. 102.

Paterson, R. (1986) Foreign currency translation, in L. Skerratt and D. Tonkin (eds.) *Financial Reporting 1985/6*, pp. 53–72, Institute of Chartered Accountants in England and Wales, London.

Paterson, R. (1990) Primacy for the P & L account, *Accountancy*, August, pp. 80–82.

Patz, D. (1977) A price parity theory of translation, *Accounting and Business Research*, Vol. 8, no. 29, pp. 14–24.

Peasnell, K.V. (1977) A note on the discounted present value concept, *The Accounting Review*, Vol. LII, no. 1, pp. 186–9.

Peasnell, K.V. and Yaansah, R.A. (1988) *Off-balance Sheet Financing*, Research Report No. 10, Certified Accountant Publications Ltd.

Pimm, D.(1990) Off-balance sheet vehicles survive redefinition, *Accountancy*, June, pp. 88–91.

Power, M. (1992) The politics of brand accounting in the United Kingdom, *The European Accounting Review*, Vol. 1, no. 1, pp. 39–68.

Prodhan, B.K. (1986) Geographical segment disclosure and multinational risk profile, *Journal of Business Finance and Accounting*, Spring, pp. 15–37.

Prodhan, B.K. and Harris, M.C. (1989) Systematic risk and the discretionary disclosure of geographical segments: an empirical investigation of US multinationals, *Journal of Business Finance and Accounting*, Autumn, pp. 467–492.

Radebaugh, L.H. (1987) *International Aspects of Segment Disclosures: A Conceptual Approach*, Research Monograph No 2, University of Glasgow.

Rayburn, J. (1986) The association of operating cash flow and accruals with security returns, *Journal of Accounting Research*, Vol. 24 Supplement, pp. 112–133.

Rennie, E.D. and Emmanuel, C. (1992) Segmental disclosure practice: thirteen years on, *Accounting & Business Research*, Spring, pp. 151–159.

Revsine, L. (1984) The rationale underlying the functional; currency choice, *The Accounting Review*, Vol. LIX, no. 3, pp. 505–14.

Robb, A.J. (1985) Funds statements and the two-entity test, *Abacus*, Vol. 21, no. 1, pp. 101–108.

Roberts, C. and Gray, S. (1991) Segmental reporting, Chapter 15, in C. Nobes and R. Parker *International Accounting*, (3rd edn), Prentice-Hall International.

Robinson, J.R. and Shane, P.B. (1990) Acquisition accounting method and bid premia for target firms, *The Accounting Review*, January, pp. 25–48.

Ronen, J. and Livnat, J. (1981) Incentives for segment reporting, *Journal of Accounting Research*, Autumn, pp. 459–481.

Rosenfield, P. and Rubin, S. (1986) Minority interests: opposing views, *Journal of Accountancy*, Vol. 161, March, pp. 78–88.

Salami, A.R. and Sudarsanam, P.S. (1994) An empirical analysis of the determinants of the method of payment and accounting policy choice in United Kingdom corporate acquisitions, unpublished paper, City University Business School.

Shaw, J. (1973) *Bogie on Group Accounts*, Jordans, Bristol.

Shaw, J. (1976) Criteria for consolidation, *Accounting & Business Research*, Vol. 6, no. 25, pp. 71–78.

Silhan, P.A. (1982) Simulated mergers of existent autonomous firms: a new approach to segmentation research, *Journal of Accounting Research*, Vol. 20, no. 1, pp. 255–262.

Silhan, P.A. (1983) The effects of segmenting quarterly sales and margins on extrapolative forecasts of conglomerate earnings extension and replication, *Journal of Accounting Research*, Vol. 21, no. 1, pp. 341–7.

Silhan, P.A. (1984) Company size and the issue of quarterly segment reporting, *Journal of Accounting and Public Policy*, Vol. 3, no. 3, pp. 185–197.

Skerratt, L. and Tonkin, D. (1993) *Financial Reporting 1993/4*, Institute of Chartered Accountants in England and Wales.

Skerratt, L. and Tonkin, D. (1994) *Financial Reporting 1994/5*, Institute of Chartered Accountants in England and Wales.

Smith, T. (1992) *Accounting for Growth*, Century Business.

Snavely, H.J. (1975) Pooling should be mandatory, *CPA Journal*, Vol. XLV, no. 12, pp. 23–6.

Solomons, D. (1986) *Making Accounting Policy: A Quest for Credibility in Financial Reporting*, Oxford University Press.

Solomons, D. (1989) *Guidelines for Financial Reporting Standards*, Institute of Chartered Accountants in England and Wales.

Sterling, R.R. (1990) Positive accounting: an assessment, *Abacus*, Vol. 26, no. 2, pp. 97–135.

Swaminathan, S. (1991) The impact of SEC mandated segment data on price variability and divergence of beliefs, *The Accounting Review*, Vol. 66, no. 1, pp. 23–41.

Swinson, C. (1993) *Group.Accounting*, Butterworths.

Taylor, P.A. (1979) What are funds flow statements? *Accountancy*, September, pp. 89–92.

Taylor, P.A. (1987) *Consolidated Financial Statements*, Paul Chapman Publishing.

Taylor, P.A. (1995) Group accounting in the United Kingdom, in D. Ordelheide (ed.) *Transnational Accounting*, Macmillan.

Thomas, A. (1975) The FASB and the allocation fallacy, *Journal of Accountancy*, November, pp. 65–68.

Thomas, P.B. and Hagler, J.L. (1988) Push-down accounting: a descriptive assessment, *Accounting Horizons*, September, pp. 26–31.

Tonkin, D. and Skerratt, L. (1992) *Financial Reporting 1992/3 – A Survey of UK Reporting Practice*, Institute of Charetered Accountants in England and Wales.

Tse, S. (1989) Attributes of industry, industry segment and firm-specific information in security valuation, *Contemporary Accounting Research*, Spring, pp. 592–614.

Walker, R.G. (1968) Disclosure by diversified companies, *Abacus*, Vol. 4, no. 1, pp. 27–38.

Walker, R.G. (1976) An evaluation of the information conveyed by consolidated financial statements, *Abacus*, Vol. 12, no. 2, pp. 77–115.

Walker, R.G. (1978a) *Consolidated Financial Statements: A History and Analysis*, Arno Press, New York.

Walker, R. G. (1978b) International accounting compromises: the case of consolidation accounting, *Abacus*, Vol. 14, no. 2, pp. 97–117.

Watts, R. L. and Zimmerman, J. L. (1979) The demand for and supply of accounting theories: the market for excuses, *The Accounting Review*, Vol. LIV, no. 2, pp. 273–305.

Watts, R.L. and Zimmerman, J.L. (1990) Positive accounting theory: a ten year perspective, *The Accounting Review*, January, pp. 131–137.

Watts, R. (1992) Accounting choice theory and market-based research in accounting, *British Accounting Review*, September, pp. 235–268.

Whittaker, J. and Cooke, T.E. (1983) Accounting for goodwill and business combinations: has the ASC got it right?, *Accountants' Magazine*, Vol. LXXXVII, no. 919, pp. 18–21.

Whittington, G. (1987) Positive accounting: a review article, *Accounting and Business Research*, Autumn, pp. 327–336.

Whittred, G. (1987) The derived demand for consolidated financial reporting, *Journal of Accounting and Economics*, Vol. 9, pp. 259–285.

Whittred, G. and Zimmer, I. (1994) Contracting cost determinants of GAAP for joint ventures in an unregulated environment, *Journal of Accounting and Economics*, Vol. 17, pp. 95–111.

Wild, K. and Goodhead, C. (1993a) Between the lines of FRS 3, *Accountancy*, July, pp. 92–93.

Wild, K. and Goodhead, C. (1993b) The spirit of a standard, *Accountancy*, August, pp. 68–69.

Wild, K. and Goodhead, C. (1994) *Financial Reporting and Accounting Manual – Getting Corporate Reports Right* (4th edn), Butterworths.

Willott, R. (1993) Why the abolitionists have a case, *Accountancy*, November, p. 99.

Wilkins, R. (1979) *Group Accounts* (2nd edn), Institute of Chartered Accountants in England and Wales.

Wilson, G.P. (1987) The incremental information content of the accrual and funds components of earnings after controlling for earnings, *The Accounting Review*, April, pp. 293–322.

Wolk, H.I., Francis, J.R. and Tearney, M.E. (1989) *Accounting Theory: A Conceptual and Institutional Approach*, (2nd edn), PWS-Kent.

Wyatt, A.R. (1963) *A Critical Study of Accounting for Business Combinations*, Accounting Research Study No. 5, Accounting Principles Board, New York.

Ziebart, D.A. and Kim, D.H. (1987) An examination of the market reactions associated with SFAS No. 8 and SFAS No. 52, *The Accounting Review*, Vol. 62, no. 2, pp. 343–357.

AUTHOR INDEX

GENERAL INDEX